**Eighth Edition**

# The REGIONAL GEOGRAPHY of CANADA

## Robert M. Bone

**OXFORD**

UNIVERSITY PRESS

# OXFORD
## UNIVERSITY PRESS

Oxford University Press is a department of the University of Oxford.
It furthers the University's objective of excellence in research, scholarship,
and education by publishing worldwide. Oxford is a registered trade mark of
Oxford University Press in the UK and in certain other countries.

Published in Canada by
Oxford University Press
8 Sampson Mews, Suite 204,
Don Mills, Ontario M3C 0H5 Canada

www.oupcanada.com

**Library and Archives Canada Cataloguing in Publication**

Title: The regional geography of Canada / Robert M. Bone.
Other titles: Geography of Canada
Names: Bone, Robert M., author.
Description: Eighth edition. | Includes bibliographical references and index.
Identifiers: Canadiana (print) 20210117699 | Canadiana (ebook) 20210117788 | ISBN 9780199037766
(softcover) | ISBN 9780199037834 (EPUB)
Subjects: LCSH: Canada—Geography—Textbooks. | LCGFT: Textbooks.
Classification: LCC FC76 .B66 2021 | DDC 917.1—dc23

Cover image: Dean Pictures/Getty Images

Cover and interior design: Sherill Chapman

Oxford University Press is committed to our environment.
This book is printed on Forest Stewardship Council® certified paper and comes from responsible sources.

Printed and bound in the United States of America
1 2 3 4 — 24 23 22 21

# Brief Contents

# Contents

## 1   Regions of Canada    3

## 2   Canada's Physical Base    19

## 3   Canada's Historical Geography    59

## 4   Canada's Human Face    113

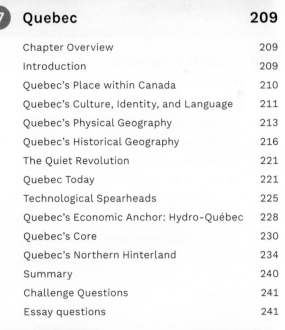

## 12 Canada: A Country of Regions Within a Global Economy 399

# List of Figures and Tables

## Figures

## Tables

# Boxes

## Contested Terrain

# Preface

The purpose of this book is to introduce university students to Canada's regional geography. In studying the regional geography of Canada, the student gains an appreciation of the country's amazing diversity, learns how its regions interact with one another, and grasps how regions change over time. By developing the central theme that Canada is a country of regions, this text presents a number of images of Canada, revealing its physical, cultural, and economic diversity, as well as its regional complexity. The COVID-19 pandemic that arrived in 2020 has had a devastating effect on Canada and its regions, and we are now in uncharted waters. Yet, Canada's geography remains anchored in its regional nature. Just what the future holds is considered in this text, but Canada's recovery is far from clear at this juncture.

Nevertheless, one fact is clear. The very nature of Canada lies in its regional composition. A second fact is that since Confederation this country has evolved. One measure of this evolution is reflected in its economic character. With an economy once heavily focused on resource development and then on manufacturing, Canada now finds high technology to be the wave of the future. Another measure of change lies in its population. At the time of Confederation, those of British and French origin comprised the vast majority of Canadians. Canada's population is now more diverse than ever before. The explanation for this diversity lies in a much more liberal immigration policy. Most significantly, these newcomers play a key role in Canada's economic and population growth. A third significant change comes from the Indigenous community, where court rulings and reconciliation have won the day, allowing the original inhabitants of Canada to find a place of their choosing within Canada. One example is the 1999 *Marshall* decision of the Supreme Court of Canada that opened the door to Indigenous commercial fishing in the Maritimes. While the Indian Act remains an impediment to self-determination, its abolishment requires First Nations to take action and for the federal government to facilitate such a historic move.

With its small population and vast resource base, Canada has always been a trading nation. Its agricultural and energy products have dominated global exports, while manufacturing, especially from the automobile industry, flows freely into the United States. Trade agreements facilitate such trade, with the newly minted US–Mexico–Canada Agreement (USMCA) leading the way. Each region plays a particular role: Ontario, for example, with automobile exports to the United States, and Western Canada, particularly Alberta, supplying oil to our neighbour to the south. As a trading nation, Canada is not immune to harsh global winds, notably the volatility in world commodity prices associated with the business cycle. These winds impact each region differently. Low oil prices, for example, have devastated the provincial economies of oil-rich Alberta, Saskatchewan, and Newfoundland and Labrador.

*The Regional Geography of Canada* divides Canada into six geographic regions: Ontario, Quebec, Western Canada, British Columbia, Atlantic Canada, and the Territorial North. Each region has a particular regional geography, story, population, and unique location. These factors have determined each region's character, set the direction for its development, and created a sense of place. In examining these themes, this book underscores the dynamic nature of Canada's regional geography, which is marked by a shift in power relations among Canada's regions. World trade opened Canada to global influences, which, in turn, transformed each region and the relationships between the regions. This text employs a core/periphery framework. Such an approach allows the reader to comprehend more easily the economic relations between regions, as well as modifications in these relations that occur over time. A simplified version of the core/periphery framework takes the form of "have" and "have-not" provinces.

At the same time, social cracks within Canadian society provide a different insight into the nature of Canada and its regions. Each faultline has deep historic roots in Canadian society. While they may rest dormant for some time, these raw tensions can erupt into national crises. Four such stress points exist between Indigenous and non-Indigenous Canadians, French and English Canadians, centralist (Ottawa and/or Central Canada) and decentralist (the other, less powerful regions) forces, and recent immigrants and those born in Canada. This book explores the nature of these faultlines, the need to reach compromises, and the fact that reaching compromises provides the country with its greatest strength—diversity. While more progress in resolving differences is required, these faultlines are shown to be not divisive forces but forces of change that ensure Canada's existence as an open society within the context of a country of regions.

## Organization of the Text

This book consists of 12 chapters. Chapters 1 through 5 deal with general topics related to Canada's national and regional geographies—Canada's physical, historical, and human geography—thereby setting the stage for a discussion of the six main geographic regions of Canada. Chapters 6 through 11 focus on these six geographic regions. The core/periphery model provides a guide for the ordering of these regions. The regional discussion begins with Ontario and Quebec, which represent the traditional demographic, economic, and political core of Canada. The two chapters on the core regions are followed by our exploration of fast-growing, slow-growing, and resource hinterland regions: Western Canada, British Columbia, Atlantic Canada, and the Territorial North. Chapter 12 provides a conclusion.

Chapter 1 discusses the nature of regions and regional geography, including the core/periphery model and its applications. Chapter 2 introduces the major physiographic regions of Canada and other elements of physical geography that affect Canada and its regions. Chapter 3 is devoted to Canada's historical geography, such as its territorial evolution and the emergence of regional tensions and regionalism. This discussion is followed, in Chapter 4, by an examination of the basic demographic and social factors that influence Canada and its regions as well as its population. Chapter 5 explores the national and global economic forces that have shaped Canada's regions. To sharpen our awareness of how economic forces affect

local and regional developments, four major themes running throughout this text are introduced in these first five chapters. The primary theme is that Canada is a country of regions. Two secondary themes—the integration of the North American economy and the changing world economy—reflect the recent shift in economic circumstances and its effects on regional geography. These two economic forces, described as continentalism and globalization, exert both positive and negative impacts on Canada and its regions, and are explored through the core/periphery model—a model introduced in the first edition back in 2000 that has had its basic premises shaken by the uneven effects of global trade on Canada's regions.

The regional chapters explore the physical and human characteristics that distinguish each region from the others and that give each region its special sense of place. To emphasize the uniqueness of each region, the concept of an advanced economy, discussed in Chapter 5, is examined in two ways: first by identifying leading or spearhead industries and second by a more in-depth discussion of the region's predominant or historic economic anchor. From this presentation, the unique character of each region emerges. In the concluding chapter, we discuss the future of Canada and its regions within the rapidly changing global economy.

## Eighth Edition

For Canada's regions, the consequences of recent global events—notably the remarkable industrialization of Asian countries, especially China, the geopolitical impact of trade conflicts with China, and the unexpected but profound effect of the COVID-19 pandemic—are threefold. First, fluctuations in the global economy result in sharp swings in commodity prices that are associated with "boom-and-bust cycles" in Canada's resource sector. Regions such as Western Canada, which depend heavily on their resource sector, are affected—either by stronger or weaker economies. Western Canada (led by Alberta and Saskatchewan) plus three other resource-dependent regions—Atlantic Canada, British Columbia, and the Territorial North—are currently suffering from low prices for their resources. During the last boom, the opposite happened. Then the economies of Alberta, Saskatchewan, and British Columbia attracted record numbers of newcomers: migrants from other parts of Canada and immigrants from abroad. High oil prices benefited Newfoundland and Labrador, though its population continued to decline. Since then, oil-dependent Alberta and Newfoundland and Labrador have fallen into an economic slump.

Second, while Ontario and Quebec remain the economic and population pillars of Canada, a shift of regional power is in the wind. The pace of economic and population gains in BC and Western Canada is tipping this shift westward. At the same time, Central Canada (Ontario and Quebec) has seen a shift to more knowledge-based economies, and the former heart of their economies, manufacturing, no longer remains central to their economic future, largely because the preferred location of many firms is offshore, where labour costs are significantly lower than in Canada.

Lastly, a decoupling of the world economy due to COVID-19 occurred in 2020. Just as the pandemic spread across the globe, the text for the eighth edition was completed. But since this global event is dramatically reshaping world trade, national economies, and Canada's place in the global economy, an effort has been made to address the initial impact of COVID-19. Efforts to contain the spread of this virus led to a lockdown of Canada's economy. On the world scene, a shift to protectionism seems in the cards, led by the United States, although with a new Joe Biden presidency in the US eager to re-engage with the world following the shambolic Trump years, even the extent of widespread or deep protectionism remains unknown. How Canada will react is also unknown, but a greater emphasis on national security is expected. Such security has already involved the manufacturing of health products and perhaps other products within Canada.

Reviews play an important role in crafting a new edition. How to recast Canada's regions within the global economic crisis and the unexpected arrival of the novel coronavirus were two challenges. Revisions had the goal of focusing on who we are, where we have been, and where we are headed—individually, collectively, and as a country of regions—all from a regional perspective.

The spatial concept provided by a Canadian version of the core/periphery model remains valid, with Ontario and Quebec forming the long-established core. Outside of the core, BC and Western Canada

continue to see their economies and populations expand, Atlantic Canada struggles to gain its footing, and the Territorial North lies on the northern fringe as a resource frontier where Indigenous peoples are gaining ground in both share of population and in emerging forms of government. Tellingly, this region to date also has borne the brunt of climate change in Canada.

Consequently, this new edition has experienced a major overhaul in content to account for changes both globally and within Canada. As well as features from the previous edition that helped students make connections and understand historical and contemporary processes, "Contested Terrain" boxes highlight controversial issues that make the regional geography of Canada dynamic and at times difficult for the major political actors to navigate. Many new photos, maps, vignettes, tables, graphs, websites, and glossary terms aim to facilitate and enrich student learning, and new essay questions have been added to each chapter.

## Acknowledgements

With each edition, I have benefited from the constructive comments of anonymous reviewers selected by Oxford University Press. As Canada has changed, so has each edition of this book. When I look back at the first edition, I see a much different Canada from today.

I have called on the resources of *The National Atlas of Canada* and Statistics Canada to provide maps and statistics. As well, both organizations have created important websites for geography students. These websites provide access to a wide range of geographic data and maps that, because they are constantly updated, allow the student to access the most recently available information on Canada and its regions.

The staff at Oxford University Press, but particularly Lauren Wing, made the preparation of the eighth edition a pleasant and rewarding task. Richard Tallman, who diligently and skillfully has edited my manuscript into polished finished products, deserves special mention. As copy editor, Richard has guided me through eight editions and, in doing so, has become an old friend who often pushes me to clarify my ideas.

Finally, a special note of appreciation to my wife, Karen, is in order, as well as to our four wonderful grandchildren, Casey, Davis, Austyn, and Bodhi.

# Important Features of this Edition

As in previous editions, the eighth edition of *The Regional Geography of Canada* incorporates a wide range of pedagogy for students that complement and enhance the text. Features appearing throughout the text include:

- New and revised content that addresses current and relevant events continuing to shape Canada and its regions, including the impact of COVID-19, climate change, and Indigenous issues.
- New and revised "Contested Terrain" boxes that draw attention to specific issues in the regional geography of Canada.
- New and revised "Vignette" boxes that focus on issues specific to each chapter.
- New and revised "Think About It" questions that prompt students to analyze the material both in and out of the classroom.
- New and revised cross-chapter "Connect" references that highlight the interconnectedness of content across chapters to ensure a comprehensive study of the material.
- Numerous new figures and tables that help to delineate the changing social and cultural face of Canada and its regions.
- New and updated maps that highlight the characteristics of various regions across Canada.
- New and updated colour photographs that engage the reader and provide strong visual references tied to the material.
- New and revised "Challenge" questions at the end of each chapter that test students' knowledge and comprehension of the material they have just read.
- New and revised essay questions at the end of each chapter that ask students to undertake research and think critically about important issues that have been introduced.

The result is a new edition that retains the strengths that have made *The Regional Geography of Canada* a best-selling text while introducing new concepts and exploring topics of interest to today's student.

## Oxford Learning Link ⊙ OXFORD. learning link

Oxford Learning Link is your central hub for a wealth of engaging digital learning tools and resources designed to help you get the most out of your Oxford University Press course materials. OUP Canada offers these resources free to all instructors using the textbook.

### For Instructors

- An instructor's manual includes chapter overviews, learning objectives, key concepts, concepts for discussion or debate, and teaching resources related to each chapter.
- A test bank provides a comprehensive set of multiple choice, true-or-false, short-answer, and essay questions to assess students' skills.
- PowerPoint slides summarize key points from each chapter.
- An image bank includes all photos, tables, figures, and maps from the text. **NEW!**

### For Students

- Self-graded quizzes help students test how well they understand each chapter's material. **NEW!**
- Videos with critical thinking exercises invite students to contemplate the broader themes of each chapter. **NEW!**
- Flashcards include key terms from each chapter, helping students test their knowledge of important concepts. **NEW!**

Talk to your sales representative, or visit www.oup.com/he/Bone8e for access to these materials.

# The REGIONAL
# GEOGRAPHY
## of CANADA

# 1 Regions of Canada

## Chapter Overview

The study of Canada's geography provides an intuitive grasp of the country's identity, regional nature, and tensions between regions and the central government. The following topics are examined in greater detail in Chapter 1:

- Geographic regions in Canada.
- Faultlines within Canada.
- Canada's place in the world.
- Core/periphery theory.

## Introduction

Geography[1] helps us understand our country. Since Canada is such a huge and diverse country, its geography is best examined from a regional perspective. In fact, the image of Canada as "a country of regions" runs deep in Canadian history, literature, and song. These images are embedded in our national psyche and **regional consciousness**. Together they are a reflection of the complex and varied set of regions set within a federal political framework. Keeping the country together is a challenge for Ottawa, while defending provincial/territorial interests falls to those governments. Each **region** has its own political agenda and economic objectives that sometimes collide with those of the federal government (Figure 1.1). Take, for instance, the fact that the land-locked Prairie provinces are trapped within the interior of North America, resulting in an age-old struggle on their part to gain access to ocean ports so necessary for their economic growth. Political solutions have ranged from the building of the Hudson Bay Railway over a hundred years ago to accommodate grain farmers to the current efforts to construct the Trans Mountain pipeline to increase the flow of bitumen to the west coast.

← The Grotto, a natural sea cave on Georgian Bay near Tobermory, Ontario, and only a few hours by car from Canada's largest city, Toronto. The contrast between the two areas—not just physically but culturally—is striking. By closely examining the reasons for such differences in places across Canada, we can better understand the country's geographic diversity.

123RF/Chris Gardiner

The search for a balanced solution to these national/regional disputes forces compromises on both sides to assure national unity and to keep the economies of the nation and its regions working smoothly.

A taste of geopolitics runs through this book and it often surfaces as trade issues. Canadians are aware that trade is an essential element to our economic well-being. The intense—some would say bitter—USMCA negotiations have soured our relations with Washington, leaving some parts of Canada and its economy winners and other parts losers. The big losers were dairy farmers, who will soon feel a squeeze from concessions to open the Canadian market more to US dairy products. Automobile workers in Ontario, while still facing pressure from firms moving to Mexico, supposedly came out winners. As for China, the 2018 arrest of Huawei CFO Meng Wanzhou in Vancouver has created a China–Canada crisis like no other. On 1 March 2019 China halted imports of Canadian canola. With China importing around 20 per cent of Canada's canola exports, Western Canadian farmers shied away from planting canola for the 2019 crop year, even though canola generates much greater profits than grain crops. The combination of trade, regions, and geopolitics turns our understanding of Canada's geographical regions into an intellectually challenging journey. In addition, the year 2020 brought a new and unexpected challenge—the COVID-19 pandemic.

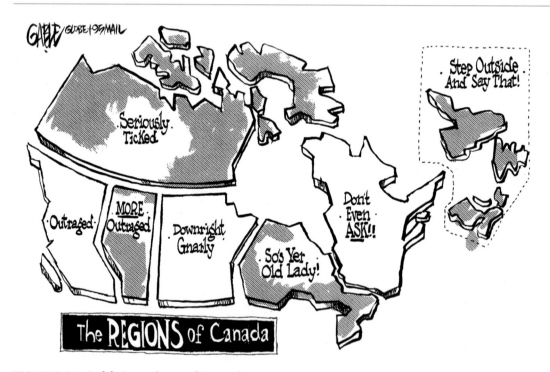

**FIGURE 1.1 Gable's regions of Canada**

Political cartoonist Brian Gable aptly captured the occasionally fractured relationships between Ottawa and the provinces and territories with his map of Canada. In 1985, regional tensions reached the boiling point over the threat of Quebec separating from Canada. The results of the 1995 referendum were almost a tie, but afterwards the heated political scene cooled somewhat and political separation lost its appeal—at least for now. Fast-forward to 2020, and the stresses between regions have taken on a more economic tone: the energy industry of Alberta still lacks access to tidewater; the carbon tax reveals the cost of reducing greenhouse gases; and the equalization payments are under fire from the "have" provinces.

Brian Gable/The Globe and Mail/Canadian Press Images

## Canada's Geographic Regions

The geographer's challenge is dividing a large spatial unit like Canada into a series of "like places." To do so, a regional geographer is forced to make a number of subjective decisions, including the selection of "core" physical and human characteristics that logically identify each region and, in doing so, create a series of distinct regions. Towards the margins of a region, its core characteristics become less distinct and merge with those characteristics of a neighbouring region. In that sense, boundaries separating regions are best considered transition zones rather than finite limits while the inhabitants' regional consciousness reflects their experiences.

**Regional identity** might best be understood in the following terms:

> A multitude of profound and often repeated extreme experiences mark people in a particular region, requiring them to respond. In turn, their responses help create a common sense of regional belonging, consciousness, and common identity.

In this book, we examine Canada as composed of six geographic regions (Figure 1.2):

- Atlantic Canada
- Quebec

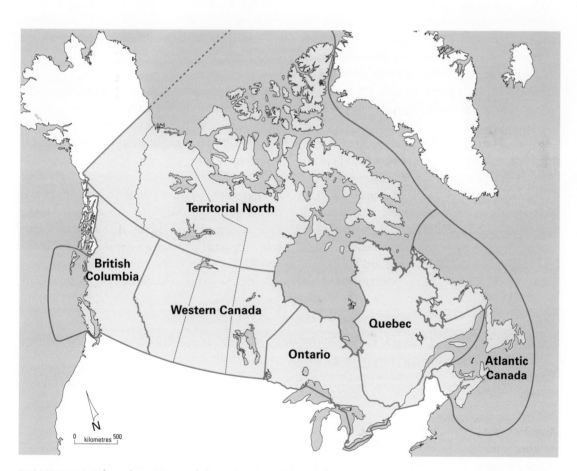

**FIGURE 1.2 The six geographic regions of Canada**

Five of Canada's six regions touch the border with the United States. This fact reflects the concentration of the nation's population close to the US border. As for Canada's ocean boundaries, they are recognized by other nations with the exception of the "sector" boundary in arctic waters north of Alaska/Yukon.

**THINK ABOUT IT**

Each region has had its struggles with Ottawa. What event(s) affected relations between your region and Ottawa?

- Ontario
- Western Canada
- British Columbia
- Territorial North

The six regions were selected for several reasons. First, a huge Canada needs to be divided into a set of manageable segments. Too many regions would distract the reader from the goal of easily grasping the basic nature of Canada's regional geography. Six regions allow us to readily comprehend Canada's **regional geography** and to place these regions within a conceptual framework based on the **core/periphery model**, discussed later in this chapter. This is not to say that there are not internal sub-regions. In Chapter 5, Ontario provides such an example. Ontario is subdivided into southern Ontario (the economic **core** of Canada) and northern Ontario (a resource **hinterland**). Southern Ontario is Canada's fastest-growing and most densely populated area in the country. As well, it contains the bulk of the nation's manufacturing industries, and houses the greatest number of technology hubs and employees. Northern Ontario, on the other hand, is sparsely populated and is losing population because of the decline of its mining and forestry activities.

Second, an effort has been made to balance these regions by their geographic size, economic importance, and population size, thus allowing for comparisons (see Table 1.1). For this reason, Alberta is combined with Saskatchewan and Manitoba to form Western Canada, while Newfoundland and

For discussion of Canada's claim to the Arctic seabed, see **Chapter 11**, especially the section titled "Arctic Sovereignty and the Northwest Passage," page 380.

Labrador along with Prince Edward Island, New Brunswick, and Nova Scotia comprise Atlantic Canada. The Territorial North, consisting of three territories, makes up a single region. Three provinces—Ontario, Quebec, and British Columbia—have the geographic size, economic importance, and population size to form separate geographic regions.

Canadians understand these as a set of regions because of the following features:

- They are associated with distinctive physical features, natural resources, and economic activities.
- They reflect the political structure of Canada.
- They facilitate the use of statistical data.
- They are linked to regional identity.
- They are associated with reoccurring regional disputes.
- They replicate regional economic strengths and cultural presence.

The critical question is: What distinguishes each of Canada's six regions? Certainly the emergence of regional consciousness in each region plays a key role. Within that consciousness, variations in population size (Figure 1.3), economic strength, and the number of French-speaking residents and **Indigenous peoples** in each region form another essential part of the puzzle (Tables 1.1, 1.2, and 1.3). Further understanding is provided by analysis of an important economic activity—an "economic anchor"—found in each region. By examining these economic activities, we gain an understanding of the nature,

### TABLE 1.1 General Characteristics of the Six Canadian Regions, 2016

| Geographic Region | Area* (000 km2) | Area (% of Canada) | Population | Population (% of Canadian total) | GDP (%) |
|---|---|---|---|---|---|
| **Ontario** | 1,076.4 | 10.8 | 13,850,000 | 38.5 | 37.8 |
| **Quebec** | 1,542.1 | 15.4 | 8,284,656 | 23.0 | 18.8 |
| **Western Canada** | 1,960.7 | 19.6 | 6,654,345 | 18.5 | 24.7 |
| **British Columbia** | 944.7 | 9.5 | 4,703,939 | 13.1 | 12.7 |
| **Atlantic Canada** | 539.1 | 5.4 | 2,374,154 | 6.6 | 5.6 |
| **Territorial North** | 3,909.8 | 39.3 | 111,867 | 0.3 | 0.4 |
| **Canada** | 9,972.8 | 100.0 | 35,985,751 | 100.0 | 100.0 |

*Includes freshwater bodies such as the Canadian portion of the Great Lakes.

Source: Statistics Canada (2017, 2019a).

strengths, and weaknesses of each region and are better able to identify the challenges they face. Traditional economic anchors are:

- Ontario: automobile manufacturing
- Quebec: hydroelectric power
- British Columbia: forest industry
- Western Canada: agriculture
- Atlantic Canada: fisheries
- The Territorial North: megaprojects

The task of interpreting Canada and its six regions poses a challenge. A spatial conceptual framework based on the core/periphery model helps us to understand the nature of this regional diversity within the national and global economies. Within this regional framework, cities play a key role. At the same time, the social frictions are captured in the concept of **faultlines** that identify and address deep-rooted tensions in Canadian society that sometimes stir negative feelings towards Ottawa and even other provinces. Such tensions present an obstacle to Canadian unity and often result in necessary adjustments to the regional nature of Canada. These faultlines require a reaction—a kind of challenge and response paradigm—that results in a continuous reshaping of Canada, its regions, and its society.

## Faultlines within Canada

Canada, like the earth's crust, has its weak points, making regional harmony elusive. In 1993, *Globe and Mail* columnist Jeffrey Simpson applied the term "**faultlines**"—the geological phenomenon of cracks in the earth's crust caused by tectonic forces—to the economic, social, and political cracks that divide regions and people in Canada and threaten to destabilize Canada's integrity as a **nation**. In this text, "faultlines" refers to four fractious tensions in Canada's collective psyche. For long periods of time, these cracks can remain dormant, but they can widen suddenly at any time, dividing the country into wrangling factions.

While many divisions in Canadian society emanate from the plight of the disabled, the homeless, the rural/urban divide, the treatment of people of colour reflected by the Black Lives Matter movement,

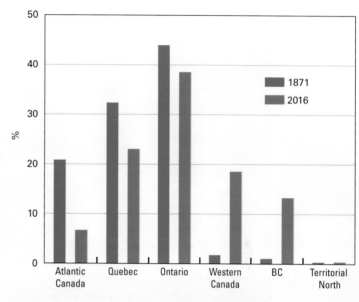

**FIGURE 1.3 Regional populations by percentage, 1871 and 2016**

In 1867, all Canadians lived in the four provinces that first joined Confederation: Nova Scotia, New Brunswick, Quebec, and Ontario. As Canada spread to the west, treaties were signed, opening the lands to settlers. Slowly but surely, the centre of population gravity for Canada has shifted westward, a trend that is likely to continue for the foreseeable future. By 2021, nearly one-third of Canada's population is expected to live in Western Canada and British Columbia, but, like the rest of Canada, most live close to the US border.

Sources: Adapted from Table 3.3 and Statistics Canada (1871, 2016).

and the seemingly relentless growing gap between the very rich and the rest of Canada's people, our discussion is confined to four principal faultlines that have had profound regional consequences and that have, from time to time, challenged our national unity. In our consideration of these faultlines, social and economic injustices are discussed. The four overarching faultlines begin with regional divides that often represent disagreements between provinces and the federal government. Other rifts within Canadian society are represented by English and French visions of Canada; the challenge of immigrants to adapt to Canadian society; and the reconciliation with Indigenous peoples in Canada from a colonial past.

Each faultline has played a fundamental role in Canada's historic evolution, and they remain critical elements of Canada's character in the twenty-first century. In extreme cases, these weak spots or cracks

**THINK ABOUT IT**

Why are "visible minority" Canadians subjected to racial profiling by police?

ti1993/iStockphoto

For more information on the nationalist movement in Quebec, see **Chapter 3**, "Quebec's Place in Confederation," page 103.

**PHOTO 1.1** Yellowknife, Northwest Territories, is no longer a rough-and-tumble mining town located in the Canadian Shield. This capital city also serves as a regional service centre, providing goods and services to surrounding villages and towns as well as to the mines and tourist camps. The public sector dominates the economy, with most workers employed by the territorial and federal governments. Expensive housing exists along its waterfront where, in the warm summer months, pleasure craft, sailboats, and floatplanes are moored along its sheltered coves on the north shore of Great Slave Lake.

Kyle Bedell/iStockphoto

**PHOTO 1.2** Cityscape of St John's, Newfoundland and Labrador, as seen from Signal Hill. St John's is one of the oldest cities in North America. For centuries the economy was based on the rich cod stocks, but now the province's economic focus is on offshore oil and on the mineral and hydroelectric resources of Labrador. Unfortunately, both hit rock bottom in 2020, dragging the province's economy ever downward and causing increased outmigration. St John's is home to Memorial University. It is also the home for the Canadian Coast Guard Atlantic Region.

have threatened the cohesiveness of Canada and, by doing so, have shaken the very pillars of federalism. Under these circumstances, compromise was essential to Canada's survival. From these traumatic experiences, Canada, over time, has become what John Ralston Saul (1997, pp. 8–9) describes as a **"soft" country**, meaning a society where conflicts, more often than not, are resolved through discussion and negotiations. The United States, on the other hand, would be considered a **"hard" country** where conflicts affecting minorities, for example, are more likely resolved by forceful means, as happened recently with the Trump administration threatening to deport millions of illegal Mexican and Central American immigrants now living in the United States and to build a wall along the Mexican border to prevent more Mexicans and other refugees and asylum seekers from entering the country, or, for that matter, by threatening to jail one's political opponents.

The earliest faultline emerged with the conquest of New France by the British. Since then,

Quebec has struggled to maintain its French language and its unique but distinct culture. In recent years, this disagreement came to a head twice with the sovereignty-association and independence referendums in Quebec in 1980 and 1995, the latter of which was won by the federalist side by a mere percentage point. At the height of the referendum campaigns, uneasy relationships tore at the very fabric of Canada. But the ensuing dialogue and goodwill between Quebec and the rest of the country have led to an unspoken and uneasy compromise that cements the country together. Still, tensions do arise, such as the appointment by the federal government in 2011 of two non-French-speaking Supreme Court judges, causing Quebecers to ask: how can the Supreme Court properly evaluate cases that involve documents written in French if judges are not bilingual?

## Regional Faultline

Of all the faultlines, the regional one leans the most heavily on Canada's political system and, in turn, its geography. The reason is simple: Canada's size determines regional differences. In this text, six geographic regions constitute the spatial form of regionalism. Each region has its own interests that provide the stage for bitter federal–provincial feuds. These heated disagreements encourage the balkanization of the country. To counter these decentralizing tendencies, Ottawa's primary responsibility must be the unity of the country. This task is not made easier by the sharing of powers between Ottawa and the provinces, but the search for compromise is a product Canadian federalism (Vignette 1.1).

Federalism involves the division of powers between the federal and provincial governments, and that division is often the root of jurisdictional disagreements. Natural resources, for example, fall under the jurisdiction of provinces. Provinces, especially oil-rich Alberta, complain that Ottawa is encroaching on its jurisdiction over natural resources. Much of this tension goes back to the 1980s, when the Liberal government introduced its National Energy Program (NEP). One of the goals of this federal legislation was to redistribute oil wealth from Alberta to the federal government. One unexpected outcome was a deepening of western alienation and mistrust of Ottawa's intentions (for more on this subject, see Contested Terrain 1.1). Rightly or wrongly, Ottawa is perceived as indifferent to the issues facing the oil sands, especially the need for access to tidewater. The federal rejection of the Northern Gateway project, in Alberta's eyes, was an indication that Ottawa was not supporting its economy (Contested Terrain 1.1). While the Trans Mountain pipeline expansion faces the same challenges, Ottawa is seeking a compromise that will satisfy Alberta's need for access to tidewater as well as gain approval from Indigenous peoples and environmentalists. This seemingly impossible task is made more difficult by Ottawa's

For discussion of the cultural divide between French- and English-speaking Canada, see **Chapter 3**, page 107, under the heading, "One Country, Two Visions."

## Vignette 1.1

### Canadian Unity: A Powerful Force

The unity of Canada was a struggle from the beginning. But the federal government, through such national institutions as the Supreme Court of Canada, legislation, and a series of national programs, has provided the political glue to keep the country united. The first example took place in the late nineteenth century when Ottawa's financial and political support for building the Canadian Pacific Railway provided a much-needed physical link across the vast wilderness of the Canadian Shield, the Interior Plains, and the Cordillera to bind the western lands to Central Canada as well as ensure that British Columbia joined Confederation (see Figure 2.1). More recent instances of nation-building have focused on ensuring a measure of equality among provinces through federal initiatives such as equalization payments to "have-not" provinces, multiculturalism legislation that supports a pluralistic society, and universal health care for all Canadians paid for through the tax system.

## Contested Terrain 1.1

### The Northern Gateway Pipeline: Centripetal or Centrifugal Effect?

The Northern Gateway pipeline project would provide access to Asian markets for Alberta's oil sands. The National Energy Board recommended its construction and the Harper government agreed. Yet, this project generated fierce opposition from Indigenous and environmental organizations. They feared that a bitumen spill, by either a pipeline rupture or a calamity at sea, could cause irreparable damage. In 2015, the Trudeau government banned crude oil tanker traffic along British Columbia's north coast, thus killing the Northern Gateway pipeline proposal.

commitment to reduce greenhouse gas emissions. Yet, Ottawa knows full well that the construction of the Trans Mountain pipeline will lead to an expansion of production in the oil sands and thereby increase greenhouse gas emissions (for more on this subject, see Vignette 2.12). Added to this mix, the premier of Quebec declared his opposition to new pipelines crossing Quebec territory, thus adding the final nail in the coffin of the failed Energy East pipeline proposal.

Underlying regional tensions lies the perception that the federal government favours Central Canada over the rest of the country. Two examples illustrate this point. Ottawa has supported both the automobile industry in Ontario and the aerospace industry in Quebec. Ottawa considers such support as in the national interest (see Contested Terrain 6.2 and 7.1). Stated differently, the federal government believes that economic success in Central Canada benefits the nation as a whole—a belief that has its roots in the National Policy of Canada's first prime minister, Sir John A. Macdonald (see Chapter 5). Those outside of Central Canada, however, would like to see similar support for their economic development.

## The Quebec Faultline

Quebec has a distinct culture that reflects its deep historic roots going back to New France. Quebec was a reluctant member of Confederation back in 1867. Unlike most of Canada, Quebec has considered separating from Canada. While this desire for independence has eased since the last referendum, the province's francophone residents often prefer to describe themselves as Québécois rather than Canadian.

Language has always been a contentious issue in Quebec and to a lesser degree in New Brunswick, where a large French-speaking Acadian population resides. While Canada is officially a bilingual country, the French language is not widely spoken in most parts of the country. For Quebec, protection of its French language remains paramount. This concern for the well-being of its language caused the Quebec government to pass its Official Language Act in 1974, making French the sole official language in the province. The rationale for this action was the desire to ensure and foster the French language and therefore the Québécois culture. In fact, only one province, New Brunswick, officially recognizes both official languages. As shown in Table 1.2, relatively few French-speaking Canadians live outside of New Brunswick and Quebec. But those francophones in other provinces still value their language and culture. Except for Newfoundland and Labrador and British Columbia, French-language schools exist in all provinces.

Language remains a sensitive issue and, because the proportion of French-speaking Canadians has declined over time, it forms a faultline. Quebec remains the heartland of the French-speaking people. In the last census (2016), nearly 86 per cent of Quebec residents spoke French as their first language. Back in 1867, the population of Canada consisted of two main groups: British, comprising 61 per cent, and French, making up 31 per cent, formed nearly 92 per cent of the population (*Atlas of Canada*, 2009). Today, though the total number of French-speaking

**TABLE 1.2 Populations of French-speaking Canadians in the Six Canadian Regions, 2016**

| Geographic Region | French-Speaking Population | % in Canada | % by Region |
|---|---|---|---|
| Ontario | 550,600 | 7.0 | 4.1 |
| Quebec | 6,890,300 | 87.1 | 85.5 |
| British Columbia | 64,325 | 0.8 | 1.4 |
| Western Canada | 127,025 | 1.6 | 2.0 |
| Atlantic Canada | 273,115 | 3.5 | 11.6 |
| Territorial North | 3,500 | 0.0 | 3.1 |
| Canada | 7,914,495 | 100.0 | 23.0 |

Source: Statistics Canada (2019b).

Canadians has increased, reaching nearly 8 million in 2016, their proportion of the total population has declined to 23 per cent. This drop represents a serious dilemma for that community and signals an erosion of their political power within Canada.

While language is less of a hot-button issue in Quebec today, some francophone leaders fear that the traditional Québécois way of life is slipping away, not because of any increased use of the English language but because of immigrants whose behaviour is not rooted in the cultural, historic, and linguistic factors that provide a **sense of place** for the majority of Quebecers. To that end, in 2019 the Quebec government passed Bill 21, which bans public workers from wearing religious symbols when at work.

Quebec has taken a strong position on the climate crisis. In fact, Quebec places a high priority on eliminating carbon emissions and introduced carbon pricing in 2013. Given its vast hydroelectric resources, the province is well positioned to support the reduction of greenhouse gases. It may also explain why Quebec has taken such a strong stand against pipeline construction in the province.

## Indigenous Minority

As the first people to occupy the territory now called Canada, many Indigenous peoples—legally referred to as "the Indian, Inuit, and Métis peoples of Canada"—still find themselves on the margins of Canadian society. While Canada prides itself on its open society, upward social mobility, and economic opportunities, Indigenous peoples were (and

remain) trapped in another world governed by the Indian Act. From their perspective, Canada is a **settler state** that has stripped them of their lands and resources, asserted absolute jurisdictional authority, and, by ignoring Indigenous customs and laws, diminished their place in Canada.

Yet, Canada's relationship with its diverse Indigenous population has evolved from the White Paper of the 1969 to the 2015 "Calls to Action" published by the Truth and Reconciliation Commission. Reconciliation efforts indicate that Indigenous peoples are breaking out of a tightly controlled world constrained by the Indian Act. For example, a number of First Nations have developed an economic base and individuals have risen to leadership positions in the corporate and public worlds. More and more Indigenous people are experiencing upward economic and social mobility, especially those who have completed university programs. From 2006 to 2016, Statistics Canada (2018, Chart 7) reported that the percentages of both Indigenous high school and university graduates had increased. More First Nations have successfully turned the corner and are pursuing their vision of economically self-sustaining communities on their reserves that respect Indigenous cultures and protect the environment. The success pattern depends on a mix of factors, but one is a connection to resource development (Vignette 1.2) and another depends on proximity to a city, where they can partake in urban economic growth.

Many other Indigenous people and groups, however, are geographically isolated and marginalized with seemingly little opportunity. There is

## Vignette 1.2

### Resource-Sharing with Indigenous Peoples

Impact benefit agreements (IBAs) emerged in the late 1990s as resource extraction companies realized that settling traditional land claims was a necessary component of their mining operations. An IBA is a legal and confidential contract between the company and the impacted Indigenous community for revenue-sharing.

While IBAs affect individual First Nations, the sharing of provincial and territorial royalties collected from mining companies varies, and goes to all First Nations in that jurisdiction. For instance, 25 per cent of NWT royalties go to First Nations that have completed land claim agreements (Coates, 2015, p. 20). As of 2015, resource-sharing of provincial royalties existed in only six jurisdictions: three provinces (British Columbia, Quebec, and Newfoundland and Labrador) and the three territories. In 2019, Ontario created resource revenue-sharing agreements that provide First Nations a share in the economic benefits of forestry and mining operations near their communities. At present, 31 northern Ontario First Nation communities stand to benefit (Ontario, 2020). Other provinces employ various ad hoc resource revenue-sharing agreements.

no simple answer to this complex question, but for many people, post-secondary education remains a key to open the door to full participation in Canadian society while retaining Indigenous identity within a pluralistic society.

Pivotal events in the mid- to late twentieth century saw changes to the Indian Act, the end to residential schools, and the rise of political activism. First and foremost, only in the mid-twentieth century did the doors to the economic and social opportunities available to other Canadians begin to open. Until then, the Indian Act served as the federal government's means to control, dominate, and manage First Nations peoples and their lands, as well as to keep them restricted to reserves. The treaty land selection process in earlier centuries and the relocation of northern Indigenous peoples to settlements in the 1950s brought mixed blessings. Access to public services and secure food supplies was a plus, but these villages had no economic foundation and therefore left the adults in no man's land—they were no longer self-sufficient hunters and trappers with a self-sustaining culture and way of life, nor could they become employed workers because few jobs existed in these settlements—except for the few local government and federal public service jobs that

| TABLE 1.3 | Populations of Indigenous Canadians in the Six Canadian Regions, 2016 | | |
|---|---|---|---|
| Geographic Region | Indigenous Peoples by Identity | % of Regional Population | % of Canadian Indigenous Population |
| Ontario | 361,125 | 2.7 | 22.2 |
| Quebec | 175,960 | 2.2 | 10.8 |
| British Columbia | 263,540 | 5.8 | 16.2 |
| Western Canada | 574,335 | 9.1 | 39.7 |
| Atlantic Canada | 129,340 | 5.4 | 7.5 |
| Territorial North | 56,225 | 50.3 | 3.6 |
| Canada | 1,629,800 | 4.7 | 100.0 |

Source: Statistics Canada (2019a).

**PHOTO 1.3** In July 2019, the Honourable Russell Mirasty became the first Indigenous person to serve as the lieutenant-governor of Saskatchewan. He is a member of the Lac La Ronge Indian Band. Before retirement in 2010, he served as the commanding officer of Saskatchewan's RCMPR "F" Division. The decision by the Saskatchewan government to nominate a person of Indigenous background marks a turning point that has had great meaning for both the Indigenous and non-Indigenous people of Saskatchewan.

were created. Consequently, dependency on social assistance became the foundation of their new economic system.

Second, the first crack in the door took place in 1960 when First Nations men and women were allowed to vote in federal elections. Since then, civil and human rights common to Canadians have been extended to Indigenous peoples, especially through numerous landmark court cases. Nonetheless, the Indian Act still leaves a role for the federal government in the affairs of Indigenous peoples. While the Métis and Inuit were not included in the Indian Act, they were, for the most part, treated equally badly and also suffered from this quasi-apartheid policy. For instance, all three groups were subjected to the long period of the residential schools from the late nineteenth century to the late twentieth century. These schools were designed to equip young Indigenous students to find and accept a place on the bottom rungs of the larger society, and resulted in the loss of their language and culture, as well as their connection to the land and their communities and parents, many of whom continued a traditional life of hunting and trapping. In fact, the residential schools created "lost generations" who fitted into neither world.

By the twenty-first century, a push towards reconciliation, rather than assimilation, began. Reconciliation provides a new start in relations between Indigenous peoples and other Canadians. It presents an opportunity to widen the concept of nation-building and to create a more inclusive society. Acts of reconciliation will help close the gap between Indigenous peoples and the rest of Canadian society.

## Immigration

While Canada is a land of immigrants, tensions are most visible in Quebec where the government passed Bill 21 to prevent civil servants from wearing symbolic markers of religious belief at work. The federal government determines the annual number of immigrants, and provinces and territories are responsible for their settlement in Canada, including housing, job training, and language education.

Many Canadians support immigration because the addition of more people to Canada not only increases our population size, but also stimulates economic growth. Recognizing this support, the Liberal government has raised the number of immigrants allowed into the country each year. For example, the number of new immigrants is planned to increase from less than 300,000 in 2018 to a goal of 350,000 by 2021 (Immigration, Refugees and Citizenship Canada, 2020). In 2020, however, the number of new immigrants fell dramatically when the COVID-19 pandemic caused Ottawa to restrict the movement of people into Canada.

Most immigrants have tended to settle in the major cities in Ontario, followed by Quebec, Western Canada, and British Columbia. However, more recent newcomers are establishing themselves in other cities and towns across Canada. These immigrants add to our population size, increase our cultural diversity, and keep the economy moving forward. Equally important, the steady flow of immigrants keeps Canadian society young and vibrant.

Yet, there are some rumblings along this faultline. The division of powers over immigration has raised warning signs. While Ottawa assists with the cost of settlement, provinces argue that this federal assistance falls far short of the actual costs. The disagreement reached its peak with the unexpected arrival of irregular asylum seekers at the border whose immediate need was and is housing. The burden for accommodating these would-be refugees falls most heavily on Quebec, Ontario, and Manitoba. This dispute represents the most recent eruption along the immigration faultline.

The political challenge is straightforward: balance the number of newcomers with the capacity of the nation to absorb them. The political reality is a different matter. A June 2019 Leger poll revealed that the majority of Canadians had second thoughts about the proposed increased level of immigrants (Wright, 2019). This issue has come to a head with an increase in the number of border crossers outside of the official entry points into Canada, beginning in 2017.

The history of immigration is a long one. The first European immigrants, the British and the French, shaped the early ethnic composition of the country by adding newcomers to the Indigenous population. After the fall of New France, the dominant source of immigrants came from Great Britain, while others came from Europe and the Russian Empire. In the 1960s, the federal government changed its immigration rules to focus on selecting skilled immigrants over their country of origin. Fast forward to the twenty-first century: the consequences of these reforms have had a profound impact on the population size of the country and its ethnic composition. The continuous waves of newcomers, each bringing their own cultures, languages, and religions, are both a benefit and challenge—but, for better or worse, this influx has changed Canada. The cultural rubbing and bumping between those whose cultural roots are in distant overseas homelands and those whose roots developed in Canada has created

a place where adjustments and compromises are required to allow everyone to feel at home. The capacity of Canada to absorb newcomers from different cultures, religions, and ethnic backgrounds is not perfect, but it is heading in the right direction where acceptance of differences is becoming commonplace, especially in major cities.

## The Core/Periphery Theory and Beyond

The core/periphery theory offers an important framework for the study of Canada and its regions. To understand our complex country and its regional nature, a modified **core/periphery model** helps us grasp the broad economic/political relationships within the country. This Canadian version has its roots in the dependency theory first articulated in 1949 but is based on John Friedmann's 1966 adaptation of the core/periphery model to the market economy found in Venezuela. One innovation was Friedmann's expansion of the number of **periphery** regions from one to three; another was a geographic shift from an abstract global model to a more realistic one based on the regional nature of a real country, Venezuela. These four regions—a core and three peripheries—are easily adaptable to Canada's six geographic regions:

- Core region centred on manufacturing (Ontario and Quebec);
- Rapidly growing region based on an expanding resource base (British Columbia and Western Canada);
- An older slow-growing region based on a declining resource base (Atlantic Canada);
- Resource frontier region where many resources exist but few are viable for extraction and shipment to market (the Territorial North).

The core/periphery model provides only a broad-brush interpretation of the spatial nature of Canada's economy. However, this spatial concept remains valid with Ontario and Quebec forming the long-established core. Outside of the core, BC and Western Canada continue to see their economies and populations expand; Atlantic Canada struggles to gain its footing; and the Territorial North lies on the northern fringe as a resource frontier but where the Indigenous peoples are gaining ground in both share of population and in emerging forms of governance. The model does have weaknesses; it falls short by only touching very lightly on political and societal matters; and it ignores social injustices, such as homelessness and racism.

Without a doubt, theoretical models, including the Canadian version of the core/periphery model, provide only a partial representation of geographic reality. The addition of city-regions and fault-lines brings issues of social justice, integration of immigrants, and economic competitiveness to the fore. By the beginning of the twenty-first century, globalization had strengthened the role of metropolitan centres while Canadian cities became the leading edge of regional prosperity and population growth within its emerging knowledge-based economy. Three metropolitan centres—Toronto, Montreal, and Vancouver—have reached the stage of a global city, while smaller cities take on a regional leadership. Scott (2001, 2019) was one of the early proponents of the city-region. He recognized that city-regions were a new element in the evolving concept of earlier versions of the core/periphery system of spatial organization.

In spite of the odd blemish, spatial theory has a place in geographic literature.[2] As Nobel laureate Paul Samuelson observed (1976):

> Every theory, whether in the physical or biological or social sciences, distorts reality in that it oversimplifies. But if it is a good theory, what is omitted is outweighed by the beam of illumination and understanding thrown over the diverse empirical data.

## Canada's Place in the World

Canada, by its very nature, is a trading nation. Its relatively small domestic market forces the country to seek foreign markets. The United States has always been its major trading partner. Diversification of trade has advantages and disadvantages. Canada's attempt to expand trade with the second most powerful country, China, has met with some successes but also failures. Following the detainment at the request of the United States of Meng Wanzhou, the chief financial officer of cell phone giant Huawei, China reduced its imports of Canadian products, arrested two Canadian citizens, and undertook coercive diplomacy to force the release of Meng.

The United States remains our primary trading partner. Our trading relationship opens up access to the richest market in the world. On the other side, such dependency leads to vulnerability. Yet, trade with the largest market in the world has kept Canada's economy strong. In addition, US markets are close at hand, thus keeping transportation costs low and profits high. Equally important, exports allow Canadian firms to achieve volume of production for economies of scale to set in and thus lower per-unit costs of production. The integration of the automobile industry permits the principle of just-in-time deliveries of parts to manufacturing plants—just one example of the integrated nature of trade between the two countries. On the negative side, Canada's dependency on one market leaves it vulnerable. Protectionism is a fact of life in the United States. Pressure from the US forest industry to ban Canadian lumber imports has put a squeeze on Canadian producers, especially in British Columbia. Past efforts by Ottawa to diversify Canada's trade has had little success. In a North American context, the term "continentalism" describes Canada's close trade relationship with the United States, resulting from the natural advantages of our geographical location in North America and from agreements between Canada and the United States. From a political scientist's perspective, continentalism is the opposite of nationalism, meaning that continentalism supports free trade while nationalism calls for tariffs to protect the domestic economy. Canada embraced a continental strategy back in the 1960s and has never looked back. The Auto Pact, signed in 1965, integrated this industry, and it had a profound impact on automobile manufacturing in Ontario. Since the Auto Pact, three North American agreements have come into force: in 1989, the Canada–US Free Trade Agreement; in 1994, the North American Free Trade Agreement; in 2020 the United States, Mexico, and Canada Agreement. As well, Ottawa has pursued other trade agreements with countries around the world, but the most

The core/periphery and city-regions are discussed more fully in **Chapter 5** under "Canadian Economic Landscape," page 164.

important agreement is the USMCA (United States, Mexico, and Canada). In 2017, most Canadian exports went to the United States (74.5 per cent), followed by the European Union (5.9 per cent), China (4.5 per cent), Mexico (1.7 per cent), and South Korea (1 per cent) (Statistics Canada, 2018). While the Canadian automobile industry has lost its luster, good news appeared in 2020 from Ford and GM. Ford, with massive investments by Ontario and the federal government, is creating an electric car assembly plant at Oakville for North America market, while GM is reopening its assembly plant in Oshawa.

## Summary

Canada's six regions provide a means to explore the geographic essence of Canada. To simplify the complexities of space is a tall order but a necessary one because Canada is a country of regions. Shaped by its history and physical geography, Canada is distinguished by six geographic regions: Ontario, Quebec, British Columbia, Western Canada, Atlantic Canada, and the Territorial North. Each has developed a sense of regional consciousness and this regional commitment by its residents distinguishes each region from the next. Within Canada and its regions, four key tensions exist that, through their interaction, demonstrate the very essence of Canada as a "soft" nation where conflicts are usually resolved or ameliorated through compromise rather than by political or military power.

The core/periphery model and the city-region concept provide an abstract spatial framework for understanding the general workings of the modern capitalist system in Canada. It consists of an interlocking set of industrial cores and resource peripheries within which cities are driving the shift to a new economic model known as the knowledge-based economy. This model can function at different geographic scales and serves as an economic framework for interpreting Canada's regional nature. In addition to the core region, three types of regions devised by Friedmann extend our appreciation of the diversity of the Canadian periphery. They are: (1) a rapidly growing region, (2) a slow-growing region, and (3) a resource frontier.

What does the future hold for Canada and its regions? Will the resource economy make a comeback or will Canada find its economic footing in the knowledge-based economy? Then, too, how will Canada deal with COVID-19 and foretold future pandemics? Social tensions within Canada involve social justice, integration of immigrants, and economic disparities, and COVID-19 has made solutions to these tensions more urgent than ever. Could a universal basic income provide one solution?

Geography, in the form of the vast size of Canada and its diverse population, feeds both regionalism and factionalism. Yet, the country remains whole because Canada, through its system of governance and national institutions, offers its citizens freedom and dignity as well as opportunities and the prospects of well-being. More than that, a powerful current flowing through Canadian society expresses a willingness to seek compromises, consensus, and accommodation. These values are the hallmark of unifying forces that hold Canada together. Beneath the surface, however, inequalities exist. Homelessness is one sign of the existence of income inequalities; racism serves as a barrier to upward mobility; and access to health is more difficult for rural folks than urban ones.

The central question for Canada and its regions is how best to respond to this rapidly evolving world. Opportunities and responses vary from one region to another. This critical topic is broached in each regional chapter and discussed further in the concluding chapter.

The next four chapters focus on Canada and, at the same time, set the stage for our discussion of Canada's six regions. These four chapters, respectively, examine Canada's physical geography, the country's historical geography, the human face of our country, and Canada's economy.

## Challenge Questions

1. Explain why boundaries separating regions are best considered transition zones rather than finite limits.
2. Why is the division of power between Ottawa and the provinces so critical for the emergence of political tensions? Does it explain, for example, why some provinces are so upset with Ottawa over its insistence that provinces impose a carbon tax?
3. How is resource-sharing with Indigenous peoples encouraged and how does it work?
4. Do you agree or disagree with Professor Samuelson's views of theoretic models? More importantly, do you think the core/periphery model does or does not provide a helpful interpretation of economic relations among Canada's six regions?
5. Over time, each of the four faultlines has posed a serious threat to Canada's unity. In your opinion, which one is most likely to create the biggest strain on national unity in the next five years? Explain your choice.

## Essay Questions

1. Canada is a country of regions. But how many regions make up Canada? This text organizes the country into six geographic regions. Discuss the author's reasoning for six regions and make a case for more regions.
2. Faultlines play a critical role by focusing our attention on key social issues troubling this country. For example, consider the lobster dispute between Indigenous and commercial fishers in Nova Scotia. Do you think that this dispute represents a challenge-and-response paradigm that will reach an acceptable solution?

# 2 Canada's Physical Base

## Chapter Overview

This chapter provides a basic introduction to Canada's physical geography, emphasizing how it has shaped the regional nature of Canada. It also addresses two key issues related to physical geography in the twenty-first century: climate change and pollution. Until this century, physical geography changed very slowly. However, climate change has thrust the world into a much different place. Added to the warming of the earth, world population is ever increasing, resulting in waste from human beings overwhelming landfills and polluting our oceans and lakes. In fact, plastic ocean pollution injures and kills marine life, spreads toxins, and poses a threat to human health. In Canada, the marine life—particularly the small whale population in the St Lawrence River—is affected by ocean pollution.

Chapter 2 lays the foundation for our discussion of the six regional chapters. In Chapter 2 we will examine the following topics:

- The geological structure, origins, and characteristics of Canada's physical base and its seven physiographic regions.
- The nature of Canada's climate, its seven climatic zones, and climate change.
- The concept of extreme weather events and how these events shape regional consciousness.
- Canada's cold environment as illustrated by the presence of permafrost in two-thirds of Canada's land mass.
- The five drainage basins that empty vast quantities of fresh water into Canada's three oceans—the Arctic, Atlantic, and Pacific.
- Environmental challenges caused by industrial pollution and climate change.

## Introduction

The earth provides a wide variety of natural settings for human beings. For that reason, physical geography helps us understand the regional nature of our world. The basic question posed in this chapter is: *Why is Canada's physical geography so essential to an understanding of its regional geography?* Physical geography, but especially our physiography and climatic regions,

← Spirit Island, located in Jasper National Park, Alberta, provides a breathtaking view of the Rocky Mountains within the Cordillera physiographic region.

benedek/iStockphoto

## Vignette 2.1

### Two Different Geographies

Canada and the United States occupy the northern and central parts of North America, yet the two countries have strikingly different physical geographies. Canada, while larger in geographic area, has a much smaller area suitable for agriculture and settlement. A significant portion of Canada lies in high latitudes where polar climates and permafrost place these lands far beyond the limits of commercial agriculture and settlement. Consequently, most Canadians live in a narrow zone close to the border with the United States (see Figure 4.5). Here, more temperate climates prevail. Geography, therefore, has been kinder to the United States, if this is to be judged by carrying capacity—how many people the land can sustain. The US simply has more suitable physical space for development, which has allowed its population to reach 330 million by 2020, compared to 38 million for Canada. Thus, Canada has a population density of 4 people per $km^2$ compared to 30 in the United States. This physical reality, best described as Canada's northern handicap, limits the areas suitable for settlement and development. Immigrants to Canada have recognized this geographic fact and most have taken up residence in one of Canada's three largest cities (Toronto, Montreal, and Vancouver), though more and more are now settling in smaller cities that lie close to the US border.

presents a variety of natural systems that demonstrate Canada's regional character.[1] For instance, physical geography provides a fundamental explanation for Canada's **ecumene**, which hugs a narrow zone just north of the border with the United States, leaving the less hospitable area of the country sparsely populated. Extending this argument, one can see that population differences between Canada and the United States can be attributed, in part, to their very different physical geographies (Vignette 2.1).

In this text, physical geography provides the raison d'être for the four types of economic regions found in the core/periphery model. The argument is a simple one: regions with a more favourable physical base are more likely to develop into core regions that contain large populations and diverse economies. Regions with less favourable physical conditions have fewer opportunities to encourage settlement and economic development. The growing influence of cities that account for the much-prized technological transformation sweeping across Canada adds a human dimension to regional dynamics. As pointed out in Chapter 1, natural and economic circumstances define a favourable physical base that, prodded by technology, can change over time, and such changes have the power to alter the prospects for regional expansion and contraction. Within this spatial construct, urban Canada provides the milieu for innovation and growth.

## Physical Geography across Canada

Physical geography varies across Canada. Seven physiographic regions illustrate the spatial distinctiveness of Canada's physical geography. For instance, the flat to gently rolling **topography** of the Prairies is totally different from that found in the Canadian Shield, which consists of rugged, rocky, hilly terrain.

Climate adds another element to these physiographic regions as the types of climate vary from region to region. Both BC and Atlantic Canada, for instance, have mild, wet climates, while Western Canada has a dry climate, but warm in the summer and cold in the winter. Climate also affects the shape of landforms (mountains, plateaus, and lowlands) through a variety of weathering and erosional processes. Millions of years of weathering and erosion have produced the Appalachian Uplands, which in distant geological times was a young, rugged mountain range similar in many ways to the Rocky Mountains.

Geographers perceive an interaction between human and physical worlds. This interactive two-way relationship is a fundamental component of regional geography. Favourable physical conditions can make a region more attractive for human settlement. The combination of a mild climate and fertile soils in the Great Lakes–St Lawrence Lowlands encouraged agricultural settlement followed by urban growth. The St Lawrence River and the Great Lakes provide low-cost water transportation to local, American, and world markets. The favourable physical features of this region have allowed it to become Canada's industrial heartland.

As scientists who study the spatial aspects of nature and the processes that shape nature, physical geographers are concerned with all aspects of the physical world: **physiography** (landforms), bodies of water, climate, soils, and natural vegetation. Regional geographers, however, are more interested in how physical geography varies and subsequently influences human settlement of the land. The Rocky Mountains, for instance, offer few opportunities for agricultural settlement, but the spectacular scenery has led to the emergence of an economy based on tourism. Nature tends to work slowly and change may take centuries; but nature can also work quickly. Floods and storms have had sudden and dramatic impacts on human occupation of the land. Climate warming, a product of industrialization, adds another dimension to a more rapid shift in nature.

In this century, climate change presents a challenge to our world. Climate change has added a dynamic element to physical geography, and has resulted in an increase in wildfires, floods, and storms. While some changes associated with climate change are positive, most fall into the negative category. Many see climate change as threatening our existence on earth. Climate activist Greta Thunberg argues that burning fossil fuels poses an immediate threat to our planet and should be halted immediately. Have we reached the tipping point when huge industrial projects that emit greenhouse gases into the atmosphere will no longer receive approval from governments or financial support?

By the end of this century, Canada will be a much warmer place. Already our warming world is triggering glaciers and ice sheets to melt, which in turn causes sea levels to rise, perhaps by half a metre by the year 2050 and a full metre by 2120 (Englander, 2012; Hunter, 2020; McClearn, 2018). While flooding of coastal areas and cities is expected, a warmer climate could allow agriculture to take place in higher latitudes in Canada. Hannah et al. (2020) predict about 4.2 million square kilometres of Canada that are currently too cold for crops like wheat will be warm enough by 2080 if greenhouse gas emissions continue to climb. While warm enough, the area may not have suitable soil for agriculture. For instance, much of the warmer land falls into the rocky Canadian Shield where soil is a rare commodity. Needless to say, as the agricultural frontier shifts to higher latitudes, the crops and pests at lower latitudes can be expected to change as well.

Prior to the emergence of climate change, urban sprawl was identified as an encroachment into farmland. The driving force was the difference in value between farm and urban/industrial land use. As the value placed on farmland is low, urban and industrial land developers have had relatively little trouble convincing farmers to sell their land. Unfortunately, urban sprawl has already gobbled up some of Canada's best farmland in the Niagara Peninsula, the Fraser Valley, and the Okanagan Valley.

A less pressing issue but still one altering nature is another version of urban sprawl. In this case, recreational land use is replacing natural land use. A critical example is found in the Bow Valley of the Rocky Mountains, where extensive recreational developments have reduced the size of the natural habitat of wild animals such as bears and elk. Ironically, if more land is converted into golf courses, resort facilities, and housing developments, the animals that make this wilderness region so unique and attractive to tourists may no longer be able to survive.

The discussion of physical geography in this chapter and in the six regional chapters is designed to provide basic information about the natural

**THINK ABOUT IT**

The Cordillera, particularly its many mountain ranges, acted as a barrier to a united Canada in the nineteenth century. Does it still pose as a barrier?

environment, while the negative impacts of human activities on the environment and climate are a warning sign for our future. This dynamic aspect of geography plays a critical role in each of the regions of Canada. To that end, the following points are emphasized:

- Physical geography varies across Canada, thus enriching natural diversity and varying the presence of natural resources.
- Physiographic regions provide the basis for Canada's six regions.
- Climate, soils, and natural vegetation vary across Canada, favouring settlement in a few physiographic regions.
- Human activity has created an urban industrial landscape and, in doing so, has caused air, soil, and water pollution for which there are long-term negative implications for all life forms.
- Climate change represents a major challenge to our physical world with rising ocean levels likely to flood coastal areas; but it also warms Canada's cold environment.

We begin our discussion of physical geography by examining the nature of landforms.

**THINK ABOUT IT**
Geomorphic processes work steadily but slowly. The Appalachian Mountains extending into Nova Scotia represent ancient, worn-down mountains. Some 500 million years ago, these mountains looked more like the Rocky Mountains.

## The Nature of Landforms

The earth's surface features a variety of landforms. A simple classification of landforms results in three principal types: mountains, plateaus, and lowlands. These landforms are subject to change by various physical processes. Some processes create new landforms while others reduce them. From a geological perspective, the earth, then, is a dynamic planet, and its surface is actively shaped and reshaped over thousands and millions of years (see Vignette 2.2 for more on the earth's origin and types of rocks). From a human perspective, however, the earth is relatively stable with few changes observable over a person's lifetime. For instance, the Appalachian Uplands in Atlantic Canada and Quebec are undergoing the very slow process known as **denudation**, which is the gradual wearing down of mountains by erosion and weathering over millions of years. How did this happen? First, **weathering** broke down the solid rock of these ancient mountains into smaller particles. Second, **erosion** transported these smaller particles by means of air, ice, and water to lower locations where they were deposited. The result is a much subdued mountain chain from what once resembled the Rocky Mountains. Denudation and

## Vignette 2.2

### The Earth's Crust and Major Types of Rocks

The earth's crust, which forms less than 0.01 per cent of the earth and is its thin solidified shell, consists of three types of rocks: igneous, sedimentary, and metamorphic. When the earth's crust cooled about 4.6 billion years ago, **igneous rocks** were formed from molten rock known as magma. Some 3 billion years later, **sedimentary rocks** were formed from particles derived from previously existing rock. Through denudation (weathering and erosion), rocks are broken down and transported by water, wind, or ice and then deposited in a lake or sea. At the bottom of a water body, these sediments form a soft substance or mud. In geological time, they harden into rock. Hardening occurs because of the pressure exerted by the weight of additional layers of sediments and because of chemical action that cements the particles together. Since only sedimentary rocks are formed in layers (called **strata**), this feature is unique to this type of rock. **Metamorphic rocks** are distinguished from the other two types of rock by their origin: they are igneous or sedimentary rocks that have been transformed into metamorphic rocks by the tremendous pressures and high temperatures beneath the earth's surface. Metamorphic rocks are often produced when the earth's crust is subjected to folding and faulting. Lava from volcanoes constitutes a metamorphic rock and basalt is a product of the cooling of a thick lava flow.

deposition, then, are constantly at work and, over long periods of time, dramatically reshape the earth's surface.

## Physiographic Regions

The earth's surface can be classified into a series of physiographic regions. A **physiographic region** is a large area of the earth's crust that has three key characteristics:

- It extends over a large, contiguous area with similar relief features.
- Its landform has been shaped by a common set of geomorphic processes.
- It possesses a common geological structure and history.

Canada has seven physiographic regions (Figure 2.1):

1. Canadian Shield
2. Cordillera
3. Interior Plains
4. Hudson Bay Lowlands
5. Arctic Lands
6. Appalachian Uplands
7. Great Lakes–St Lawrence Lowlands

The Canadian Shield is by far the largest region, while the Great Lakes–St Lawrence Lowlands is the smallest. Perhaps the most spectacular and varied **topography** occurs in the Cordillera, while the Hudson Bay Lowlands has the most uniform **relief**. The remaining three regions are the Interior Plains, Arctic Lands, and Appalachian Uplands. Most significantly,

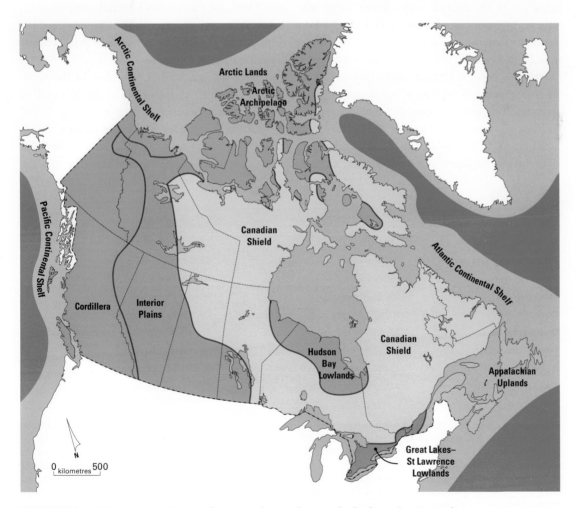

**FIGURE 2.1 Physiographic regions and continental shelves in Canada**

three of these physiographic regions—the Cordillera, Interior Plains, and Appalachian Uplands—display a strong north–south orientation to the topography of North America.

Each physiographic region has a different geological age and structure. Some 4.5 billion years ago, the Canadian Shield emerged from the sea to form the core of North America. Much of the Canadian Shield lies under other physiographic regions, including the Interior Plains and Hudson Bay Lowlands. At the surface, the Canadian Shield remains the largest exposure of Precambrian-aged rock in the world. Its geological structure has produced a particular set of mineral resources that contain deposits of copper, diamonds, gold, nickel, iron, and uranium. Other physiographic regions were formed much later, as shown in the geological time chart (Table 2.1). The formation of the Interior Plains began about 500 million years ago when ancient rivers deposited sediment in a shallow sea that existed in this area. Over a period of about 300 million years, more and more material was deposited into this inland sea, including massive amounts of vegetation and the remains of dinosaurs and other creatures. Eventually, these deposits were solidified into layers of sedimentary rock 1 to 3 km thick. As a result, the Interior Plains have a sedimentary structure that contains vast oil and gas deposits plus the Alberta oil sands, which have propelled Canada into the leading ranks of global oil producers, and, at the same time, added greatly to Canada's greenhouse gas emissions. Furthermore, as these regions developed their energy and mineral resources, differences in regional economies began to take shape and these differences were magnified by the global economy, which greatly increased demand for these subterranean resources.

The seven physiographic regions are all different. The Arctic Lands region is the most complex, consisting of a dozen large islands and numerous small islands that have been subjected to various geological events resulting in a mix of lowlands, uplands, and mountains. Together, these islands are known as the Arctic Archipelago. The Canadian Shield is the largest physiographic region and it extends beneath the Interior Plains, the Hudson Bay Lowlands, and the Great Lakes–St Lawrence Lowlands. The Cordillera and the Appalachian Uplands are products of plate tectonic activities—in the former case, less than 200 million years ago. The much older mountains of the Appalachian Uplands, which formed nearly 500 million years ago, show the effect of erosion.

Each physiographic region has its own topography. The most dramatic difference is between the mountainous Cordillera and the relatively flat

## TABLE 2.1   Geological Time Chart

| Geological Chart* | Geological Time | Physiographic Region(s) Formed |
| --- | --- | --- |
| Precambrian super eon | 4,500 to 600 million years ago | Canadian Shield |
| Paleozoic eon | 600 to 250 million years ago | Appalachian Uplands, Arctic Lands |
| Mesozoic era | 250 to 70 million years ago | Interior Plains |
| Cenozoic era | 70 million years ago to present | Cordillera |
| Quaternary period | 2.6 million years ago to present | The Great Lakes–St Lawrence Lowlands |
| Pleistocene epoch | 2.6 million to 12,000 years ago | Hudson Bay Lowlands |
| Holocene epoch | 12,000 years ago to AD 2000 | Stable climatic world |
| Anthropocene age | AD 2000 and beyond | Climate warms beyond temperatures experienced in Holocene |

*Geological Chart has the following terms, beginning with the oldest one: super eon; eon; era; period; epoch; and age. Our attention is focused on the most recent geological events. For instance, the Quaternary period consists two natural components—the cold Pleistocene epoch and the much shorter and warm Holocene epoch—and one human component—the Anthropocene age. The Anthropocene age is a product of human activities that are causing global warming. While the Anthropocene is linked to the Industrial Revolution that began in Europe in the later eighteenth century and first half of the nineteenth century, the accumulation of greenhouse gases in the atmosphere reached a tipping point approximately a century or so later. At that time, rising global temperatures were causing our climate to warm rapidly, marking the start of the Anthropocene age.

Hudson Bay Lowlands and, to a less degree, the Interior Plains. The surface material found in each region varies in hardness and thus resistance to erosional forces. Other factors affecting the rate of erosion are wind, water, and ice, which are more active in some regions than others, and, of course, gravity has a greater erosional impact in mountainous regions than on flatter landforms. In addition, the Arctic Lands are frozen for most of the year, thus limiting the activities of all erosional agents. Yet, melting of ice in permafrost, for instance, means that subsidence and collapse of ice-rich shoreline have become major geomorphic threats.

The series of advances and retreats of the Wisconsin ice sheets, but particularly the last one, shaped virtually all of the topography of Canada. These huge ice sheets spread out from their centre, which may have extended 4 km above the ground. Glacial movement is slow, behaving like a "stiff" liquid as it flows, oozes, and slides over the land. The last ice advance of the Holocene epoch is known as the Late Wisconsin. This ice advance began some 30,000 years ago and ended around 12,000 years ago, marking the end of the **Pleistocene epoch** (Figure 2.2 and Table 2.1). The Late Wisconsin ice advance consisted of two major ice sheets,

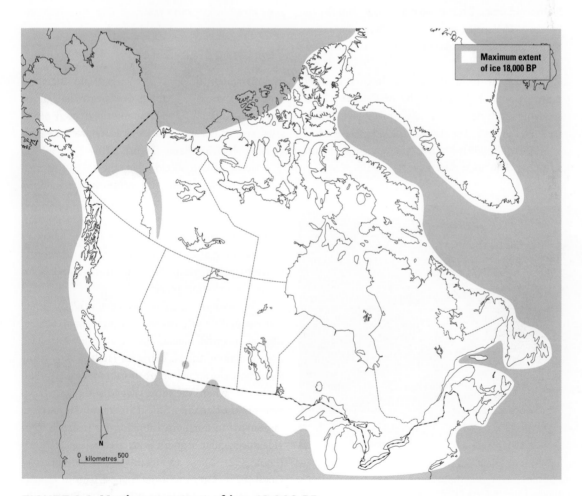

**FIGURE 2.2 Maximum extent of ice, 18,000 BP**

The Pleistocene era began some 2.5 million years ago and ended around 12,000 years ago when the climate warmed. The last ice advance, known as the Late Wisconsin Ice Age (the combined Laurentide and Cordillera ice sheets), covered almost all of Canada and extended into the northern part of the United States around 18,000 years ago. As the climate warmed around 12,000 years ago, the Holocene epoch began and massive ice sheets began to melt. During this Great Melt, vast amounts of fresh water surged to the oceans while some formed huge glacial lakes such as Lake Agassiz.

the Laurentide and the Cordillera. The Laurentide Ice Sheet was centred in the Hudson Bay area. As its mass increased, the sheer weight of the ice sheet caused it to move, eventually covering much of Canada east of the Rocky Mountains. In the Cordillera, a series of alpine glaciers coalesced into the Cordillera Ice Sheet, which spread westward into the continental shelf off the Pacific coast and eastward, eventually merging with the Laurentide Ice Sheet, which reached its maximum southern extent about 18,000 years ago (Figure 2.2). Gradually, the global climate began to warm, marking the start of the Holocene epoch, at which time the grip of colossal ice sheets weakened. Ice sheets retreated first in the Interior Plains and much later in what are now Ontario and Quebec. The major remnants of these massive ice sheets are found as glaciers in the Cordillera and Arctic Lands.

Glaciation from these two huge ice sheets radically altered the geography of Canada. Glacial scouring and deposition took place everywhere (see Photo 2.1). The Laurentide Ice Sheet slowly pushed southward across the Canadian Shield, stripping away its surface material and depositing it

much further south. When the ice sheet began to melt, it deposited material in situ, resulting in hummocky terrain. Meltwaters from the retreating ice sheet formed glacial lakes, including Lake Agassiz. As the world's greatest glacial lake, it created the nearly flat topography of the Manitoba Lowland in Western Canada. The Great Lakes provide a different example of the impact of glaciation. These lakes were formed by glacial scouring and then filled with meltwater from the receding ice sheet. Little remains of these huge ice sheets, with the largest glaciers and ice fields found in the mountains of Ellesmere Island and in the mountains of Kluane National Park, Yukon. Even here, glaciers and ice fields are disappearing almost before our eyes.

## The Canadian Shield

The Canadian Shield is the largest physiographic region in Canada. It extends over nearly half of the country's land mass and separates the densely populated area of the Great Lakes–St Lawrence Lowlands from the Interior Plains (Figure 2.1).

The Canadian Shield forms the ancient geological core of North America. More than 4.5 billion years ago, molten rock solidified into the Canadian Shield (Table 2.1). Today, these ancient Precambrian rocks not only are exposed at the surface of the Shield but also underlie many of Canada's other physiographic regions. Beneath this core rock is the molten heart of our planet.

The rock-like surface of the Canadian Shield consists mainly of a rugged, rolling upland. Shaped like an inverted saucer, the region's lowest elevations are along the shoreline of Hudson Bay, while its highest elevations occur in Labrador and on Baffin Island, where the most rugged and scenic landforms of the Canadian Shield are found. The Torngat Mountains in northern Labrador, for instance, provide spectacular scenery with a coastline of fjords (Photo 2.2). These mountains reach elevations of 1,600 m, making them the highest land in Canada east of the Rocky Mountains. The water divide of the Torngat Mountains serves as the political boundary between northern Quebec and Labrador.

Lynda Dredge—Natural Resources Canada

**PHOTO 2.1** Beyond the treeline, the rugged nature of the Canadian Shield, stripped of most overlying material, exposes bare bedrock on Melville Peninsula, Nunavut. As observed in the photograph, the Laurentide Ice Sheet altered the surface by scouring, scratching, and polishing. Only a few rocks and boulders were deposited when the ice sheet melted. These boulders are called erratics.

During the last ice advance, the surfaces of the Canadian Shield and those of other physiographic regions were subjected to **glacial erosion** and deposition (Vignette 2.3). Slowly grinding giant ice sheets changed the earth's surface by glacial erosion and then glacial deposition (see Photo 2.1). As the ice sheet moved over the Canadian Shield, the ice scraped, scoured, and scratched the massive rock surface. During the movement of the ice sheet, huge quantities of various loose materials such as sand, gravel, and boulders were trapped within the ice sheet. As the ice sheet reached its maximum extent, its edge melted, depositing rocks, soil, and other debris. This debris is called **till**. Towards the end of the **ice age**, these ice sheets melted in situ, depositing whatever debris they contained. Sometimes the huge amount of water from the melting ice was blocked from reaching the sea by the retreating ice sheet. These waters then formed temporary lakes. Then, as the ice sheet receded further, these waters surged towards the sea.

Evidence of the impact of these processes on the surface of the Canadian Shield is widespread. Drumlins and eskers, both depositional landforms, are common to this region. **Drumlins** are low, elliptical hills (also called whalebacks or hogbacks) composed of till (material deposited and shaped by the movement of an ice sheet and subglacial megafloods), while **eskers** are long, narrow mounds of sand and gravel deposited by meltwater streams found under a glacier. There are also **glacial striations**, which are scratches in the rock surface caused by large rocks embedded in the slowly moving ice sheet.

The wealth of the Canadian Shield lies in its vast and varied mineral resources. Along its southern fringe, huge deposits were sufficiently close to markets to permit exploitation. As an example, the rich nickel deposit near Sudbury has sustained that city for over 100 years and counting. In more remote areas, single-industry mining towns, such as the iron-mining town of Labrador City in Newfoundland and Labrador, were connected to global markets by rail and

John Sylvester/All Canada Photos

**PHOTO 2.2** Arctic landscape with tundra vegetation in the foreground, Saglek Fjord, Torngat National Park Reserve, Labrador.

then sea transportation. While these towns flourished, those deposits beyond modern transportation networks employ a fly-in and fly-out labour force. For mines with a highly valued per-unit product, such as diamonds, air transportation delivers the mineral to the marketplace. In the case of low-value-per-unit product, such as iron ore, the mine must have access to ocean transportation. The Raglan nickel mine in Arctic Quebec falls into that category while development of huge mineral deposits in the "Ring of Fire" zone in Precambrian rocks in remote northern Ontario are stalled due to the high cost of providing of rail and/or road access. The exception to that rule lies in high-value mineral deposits, such as diamonds and gold, which can be transported by air. The now defunct Victor Diamond Mine in northern Ontario serves as an example.

Like most of the Canadian Shield, the Laurentides, located just north of Montreal, contain many lakes and hills within a forested environment. Because of its close proximity to major cities in Quebec, Ontario, and New England, the landscape, like that of the Muskoka region in Ontario, is principally exploited for recreation and tourism, with local residents and tourists enjoying these surroundings in both summer and winter.

As shown in **Chapter 10** (Photo 10.3, page 328), the Torngat Mountains form an impressive mountain chain extending in a north–south direction in Labrador and the adjacent area of Quebec. The British Privy Council in 1927 used the Torngat water divide between Hudson Bay and the Atlantic Ocean to establish the Quebec and Newfoundland and Labrador boundary. Nearly a century later, Quebec still does not recognize this contentious decision (see **Chapter 7**, "From Confederation to the Quiet Revolution," page 220).

**THINK ABOUT IT**

In 500,000 years, the St Elias mountain range shown in **Photo 2.4** might look like the Appalachian Uplands shown in **Photo 2.8**.

For earthquake risk in British Columbia, see **Figure 9.8**, "Simplified seismic hazard map for British Columbia, 2015." Discussion of earthquake danger in British Columbia is found in **Chapter 9**, page 292, "Waiting for the 'Big One'?"

## The Cordillera

The Cordillera, a complex region of mountains, plateaus, and valleys, occupies over 16 per cent of Canada's territory. With its north–south alignment, the Cordillera extends from southern British Columbia to Yukon; its western border is the Pacific Ocean (Photo 2.3). The rugged nature of the Cordillera is illustrated in Figure 9.4, showing north–south aligned mountain ranges from the Vancouver Island Mountains on the Pacific coast to the Alberta border marked by the Rocky Mountains.

**Plate tectonics** played a critical role in the formation of the Cordillera. Beginning some 175 million years ago and ending around 85 million years ago, the Pacific and North American plates collided, uplifting the horizontal sedimentary rocks into a series of mountain ranges. During this time, tectonic movement was extremely slow, resulting in severe **folding** and **faulting** of the North American Plate that resulted in the series of mountains found in the Cordillera.

Along the **fault line** separating the Pacific and North American plates, tectonic movement continues, making the coast of British Columbia vulnerable to both earthquakes and volcanic activity. With the vast majority of the population and human-built environment of this region clustered along the coast in the cities of Vancouver, Victoria, New Westminster, and Nanaimo, the damage and loss of life from a major earthquake (measuring 7.0 or greater on the Richter scale) would be the worst natural disaster to strike Canada. The strongest earthquake ever recorded in Canada shook the sparsely populated Haida Gwaii (formerly called the Queen Charlotte Islands) in August 1949. This earthquake measured 8.1 on the Richter scale. Located along the Pacific Ring of Fire—a volatile expanse around the Pacific Ocean perimeter from New Zealand to southern South America, which is characterized by active volcanoes, fault lines, and shifting tectonic plates—the densely populated Lower Mainland of BC faces the threat of a powerful earthquake and possible tsunami sometime in the twenty-first century. The unknown question facing British Columbians is, when will the "Big One" strike?

In more recent geological times, the Cordillera Ice Sheet altered the landforms of the region. Over the last 20,000 years, alpine glaciation has sharpened the features of the mountain ranges in the Cordillera and broadened its many river valleys (Vignette 2.3). The Rocky Mountains are the best known of these mountain ranges. Most have elevations between 3,000 and 4,000 m. Their sharp, jagged peaks create some of the most striking landscapes in North America. The highest mountain in Canada—at nearly 6,000 m—is Mount Logan, part of the St Elias mountain range in southwest Yukon (Photo 2.4).

## The Interior Plains

The Interior Plains region is a vast and geologically stable sedimentary plain that covers nearly 20 per cent of Canada's land mass. This physiographic region lies between the Canadian Shield and the Cordillera, extending from the Canada–US border to the Arctic Ocean. Within the Interior Plains, most of the population lives in the southern area where a longer growing season permits grain farming and cattle ranching but low rainfall can affect yields and pastures. To those who are not native to this region, its topography often seems featureless, and bright sunshine does not offset the frigid winter months.

Millions of years ago, a huge shallow inland sea occupied the Interior Plains. Over the course of

knapjames/iStockphoto

**PHOTO 2.3** Located along the Continental Divide between British Columbia and Alberta, the Athabasca Glacier forms part of the massive Columbia Icefield. Known as the "mother of rivers," the meltwaters from the Columbia Icefield nourish the Saskatchewan, Columbia, Athabasca, and Fraser river systems, the waters of which empty into three oceans—the Atlantic, Arctic, and Pacific oceans.

## Vignette 2.3

### Alpine Glaciation, Glaciers, and Water for the Prairies

While glaciers still exist in the Rocky Mountains, they are melting and retreating. During the Late Wisconsin ice advance about 18,000 years ago, these glaciers grew in size and eventually covered the entire Cordillera. At that time, alpine glaciers advanced down slopes, carving out hollows called **cirques**. As the glaciers increased in size, they spread downward into the main valleys, creating **arêtes**, steep-sided ridges formed between two cirques. As these glaciers advanced, they eroded the sides of the river valleys, creating distinctive U-shaped glacial valleys known as **glacial troughs**. The Bow Valley is one of Canada's most famous glacial troughs. Cutting through the Rocky Mountains, the Bow Valley now serves as a major transportation corridor. It has also developed into an international tourist area. The centre of this tourist trade is the world-famous resort town of Banff and its surrounding national park. While many rivers, especially the South Saskatchewan River, rely on these melting glaciers for fresh water that eventually flows to the cities and towns of the Canadian Prairies, as well as to irrigation works and industrial/mining operations, the concern is that, at some future time—perhaps in the last half of the twenty-first century—these glaciers will disappear, thus greatly reducing the water supply for the Interior Plains.

time, sediments were deposited into this sea. Eventually, the sheer weight of these deposits produced sufficient heat and pressure to transform these sediments into sedimentary rocks. The oldest sedimentary rocks were formed during the Paleozoic era, about 500 million years ago (Table 2.1). Since then, other sedimentary deposits have settled on top of them, including those associated with the Mesozoic era when dinosaurs roamed the earth. Unlike the Cordillera, the Interior Plains occupies a stable zone of the North American Plate where tectonic forces are not at play.

Tectonic forces associated with the collision of huge plates have had little effect on the geology of this region. For that reason, the Interior Plains is described as a stable geological region. For example, sedimentary rocks formed millions of years ago remain as a series of flat rock layers within the earth's crust. Geologists have used such sedimentary structures as geological time charts. In Alberta and Saskatchewan, rivers have cut deeply into these soft rocks, exposing Cretaceous rock strata. The Alberta Badlands provide an example of this rough and arid terrain (Photo 2.5). Archaeologists have discovered many dinosaur fossils within these Mesozoic rocks in southern Alberta and Saskatchewan.

Beneath the surface of the Interior Plains, valuable deposits of oil and gas are found in sedimentary structures called **basins**. Known as fossil fuels, oil and gas deposits are the result of the capture of the

John Zada/Alamy Stock Photo

**PHOTO 2.4** Kluane National Park Reserve in southwest Yukon is the home of Canada's spectacular St Elias mountain range and the highest mountain in Canada, Mount Logan (5,959 m). Ice covers more than 80 per cent of the park. Glaciers were formed because of abundant snowfall from Pacific air masses plus cold temperatures through the year due to extremely high elevation and latitudes above 60°N. UNESCO in 1979 declared this park a World Heritage Site.

**PHOTO 2.5** The sedimentary strata dating back to the late Cretaceous period remain virtually undisturbed in the Alberta Badlands, but these horizontal strata have been exposed by stream erosion when vast meltwaters associated with the melting of the two ice sheets flowed through the Red Deer River and its tributaries. These quick-moving waters easily cut through soft sedimentary rocks of the Interior Plains to reach rock layers that date back to the days of dinosaurs, some 70 million years ago. The Dinosaur Trail that explores these badlands and the Royal Tyrrell Museum of Paleontology are located near Drumheller, Alberta.

sun's energy by plants and animals in earlier geologic time. The storage of this energy in the form of hydrocarbon compounds takes place in sedimentary basins. The Western Sedimentary Basin is the largest such basin. Most oil and gas production in Alberta comes from this basin, with the oil sands playing an increasingly important role. Fossil fuels are non-renewable resources, meaning that they cannot regenerate themselves. Renewable resources, such as trees, can reproduce themselves.

As the climate warmed some 15,000 years ago, the Laurentide Ice Sheet began to melt, releasing vast quantities of water that eroded the landscape and also deposited material held within the ice sheet. The Interior Plains, for example, was covered with as much as 300 m of debris deposited by the melting ice sheet. Huge glacial lakes were formed in a few places. Later, the meltwater from these lakes drained to the sea, leaving behind an exposed lakebed. Lake Agassiz, for example, was once the largest glacial lake in North America and covered much of Manitoba, northwestern Ontario, and eastern Saskatchewan— its lakebed is now flat and fertile land that provides some of the best farmland in Manitoba, but as part of the Red River flood plain it is subject to frequent spring floods. Glacial waters from the melting ice sheet greatly increased the flow of water in existing rivers, creating huge river valleys known as glacial spillways.

Just north of Edmonton, the Interior Plains slopes towards the Arctic Ocean while east of Edmonton, the land tilts towards Hudson Bay and the Atlantic Ocean. Across this west–east cross-section of the Interior Plains, elevations decline from 1,600 m at Kicking Horse Pass of the Rocky Mountains to about 200 m near Lake Winnipeg and then to sea level at the mouth of the Nelson River. A south–north cross-section has a much smaller elevation drop—from 1,100 m at Yellowhead Pass to sea level at the mouth of the Mackenzie River. The principal rivers draining the Interior Plains are the northward-flowing Athabasca and Peace rivers, whose waters eventually enter the Mackenzie River and proceed to the Arctic Ocean; the eastward-flowing Churchill River that begins in the Canadian Shield of Alberta and Saskatchewan and empties into Hudson Bay; and the North and South Saskatchewan rivers, which rise in the Rocky Mountains, join in central Saskatchewan, and empty into Lake Winnipeg. Then, by the Nelson River, these waters drain into Hudson Bay.

Three sub-regions based on sharp changes in elevations take place within the Canadian Prairies: the Manitoba Lowland, the Saskatchewan Plain, and the Alberta Plateau. Typical elevations are 250 m in

## Vignette 2.4

### Cypress Hills

The Cypress Hills, a sub-region of the Interior Plains, consist of a rolling plateau-like upland deeply incised by fast-flowing streams. Situated in southern Alberta and Saskatchewan, this area is the highest point in Canada between the Rocky Mountains and Labrador. The hills are an erosion-produced remnant of an ancient higher-level plain formed in the Cenozoic era (see Table 2.1). With a maximum elevation close to 1,500 m, these hills rise 600 m above the surrounding plain. During the maximum extent of the Laurentide Ice Sheet about 18,000 years ago, the Cypress Hills were enclosed by the ice sheet but the higher parts remained above the ice sheet. Known as nunataks, these areas served as refuge for animals and plants. As the alpine glacier melted, streams flowing from the Rocky Mountains deposited a layer of gravel up to 100 m thick on these hills.

Today, the Cypress Hills area is a humid "island" surrounded by a semi-arid environment and has entirely different natural vegetation compared to the area surrounding it. Unlike the grasslands, the Cypress Hills have a mixed forest of lodgepole pine, white spruce, balsam poplar, and aspen. The Cypress Hills also contain many varieties of plants and animals found in the Rocky Mountains. For the Plains Indigenous peoples, these hills were and are a sacred place.

the Manitoba Lowland, 550 m on the Saskatchewan Plain, and 900 m on the Alberta Plateau. The Cypress Hills, which reach elevations of nearly 1,500 m, provide a sharp contrast to the surrounding flat to rolling terrain of the Alberta Plateau (Vignette 2.4).

## The Hudson Bay Lowlands

The Hudson Bay Lowlands comprises about 3.5 per cent of the area of Canada. It is by far the youngest physiographic unit. Underlain by the Canadian Shield, this physiographic region consists of a thin cover of marine sediments deposited by the Atlantic Ocean some 10,000 to 12,000 years ago. The Hudson Bay Lowlands lies mainly in northern Ontario, though small portions stretch into Manitoba and Quebec. This region extends from James Bay along the west coast of Hudson Bay to just north of the Churchill River. Permafrost is widespread and the northern half lies beyond the treeline.

Surface water is everywhere in the short summer but a frozen landscape exists in the long winter months. **Muskeg**, a type of peat, is the dominant ground cover, beneath which lies permafrost (Photo 2.6). Low ridges of sand and gravel—remnants of former beaches of the **Tyrrell Sea**—separate these extensive areas of muskeg. Because of

its almost level surface, the presence of permafrost, and its immature drainage system, the Hudson Bay Lowlands is poorly drained. Underneath the muskeg are recently deposited marine sediments mixed with glacial till.

PHOTO 2.6 The Hudson Bay Lowlands is a vast wetland where the lack of slope and the presence of permafrost restrict the development of a drainage system. Consequently, this lowland is dotted with myriad ponds and lakes. Muskeg prevails while black spruce occupies the higher, better-drained land made up of terraces (old sea beaches) and drumlins found in Ontario. The northern half of the Hudson Bay Lowlands lies in Manitoba where tundra is the predominant natural vegetation.

*Lynda Dredge—Natural Resources Canada*

The Hudson Bay Lowlands, by far the youngest physiographic region, was formed around 10,000 years ago by three events. First, the huge Laurentide Ice Sheet covered the Hudson Bay Lowlands some 20,000 years ago and its weight depressed the land. Second, some 15,000 years ago, the climate warmed, causing the ice sheet to melt. By 12,000 years ago, the Hudson Bay Lowlands was covered by waters from Hudson Bay known as the Tyrrell Sea. Third, with the tremendous weight of the ice gone from this submerged land, the Hudson Bay Lowlands slowly rose above sea level as the earth's crust began to rise. This process is called isostatic rebound (Vignette 2.5). Slowly, the isostatic rebound caused the seabed of the Tyrrell Sea to rise above sea level, thus exposing a low, poorly drained coastal plain (most of which is called the Hudson Bay Lowlands). This process of isostatic rebound began some 12,000 years ago and continues today, but at a slower pace. Some 12,000 years ago the rebound was around 600 cm per century, but this has gradually slowed—to around 100 cm in the twentieth century. This relatively recent geomorphic process makes the Hudson Bay Lowlands the youngest of the physiographic regions in Canada (Table 2.1).

With few resources to support human activities, the region has only a handful of tiny settlements. From this perspective, the Hudson Bay Lowlands is one of the least favourably endowed physiographic regions of Canada. Moosonee (at the mouth of the Moose River in northern Ontario) and Churchill (at the mouth of the Churchill River in northern Manitoba) are the largest settlements in the region, each with a population of just over 1,000 people. These two settlements, formerly fur-trading posts, have an economic function as the termini of two northern railways (the Ontario Northland Railway and the Hudson Bay Railway, respectively). Regrettably, First Nation reserves have no similar economic functions and are a product of Ottawa's relocation policy of the 1960s.

## Arctic Lands

The Arctic Lands region stretches over nearly 10 per cent of the area of Canada. Centred in the Canadian Arctic Archipelago, this region lies north of the Arctic Circle. It is a complex composite of coastal plains, plateaus, and mountains. The Arctic Platform, the Arctic Coastal Plain, and the Innuitian Mountain Complex are the three principal physiographic sub-regions. The Arctic Platform consists of a series of plateaus composed of sedimentary rocks. This sub-region is in the western half of the Arctic Archipelago around Victoria Island. The Arctic Coastal Plain extends from the Yukon coast and the adjacent area of the Northwest Territories into the islands located in the western part of the Beaufort Sea. The third sub-region, the Innuitian Mountain Complex, is located in the eastern half of the Arctic Archipelago. It is composed of ancient sedimentary rocks. Like the Rocky Mountains, its sedimentary rocks were folded and faulted. However, unlike the Rocky Mountains, the plateaus and mountains in the Innuitian sub-region were formed in the early Paleozoic era (Table 2.1). During this geological time, volcanic activity took place, leaving behind vast areas

## Vignette 2.5

### Isostatic Rebound

At its maximum extent about 18,000 years ago, the weight of the huge Laurentide Ice Sheet caused a depression in the earth's crust. When the ice sheet covering northern Canada melted, this enormous weight was removed, and the elastic nature of the earth's crust has allowed it to slowly return to its original shape. This process, known as isostatic rebound or uplift, follows a specific cycle. As the ice mass slowly diminishes, the isostatic recovery begins. This phase is called a restrained rebound. Once the ice mass is gone, the rate of uplift reaches a maximum. This phase is called a postglacial uplift. It is followed by a period of final adjustment called the residual uplift. Eventually the earth's crust reaches an equilibrium point and the isostatic process ceases. In the Canadian North, this process began about 12,000 years ago and has not yet completed its cycle.

of basaltic rocks exposed at the surface, as found on Axel Heiberg Island (Photo 2.7). At 2,616 m, Mount Barbeau on Ellesmere Island is the highest point in the Arctic Lands region.

Across these lands, the ground is permanently frozen to great depths, never thawing, except at the surface during the short summer season. This cold thermal condition is called **permafrost**. Physical weathering, consisting mainly of differential heating and frost action, shatters bedrock and produces various forms of **patterned ground**. Patterned ground consists of rocks arranged in polygonal forms by minute movements of the ground caused by repeated freezing and thawing. Patterned ground and **pingos** (ice-cored mounds or hills) give the Arctic Lands a unique landscape.

The climate in this region is cold and dry. In the mountainous zone of Ellesmere Island, glaciers are still active. That is, as these alpine glaciers advance from the land into the sea, the ice is "calved" or broken from the glacier, forming icebergs. On the plains and plateaus, it is a polar desert environment. The term "polar desert" describes barren areas of bare rock, shattered bedrock, and sterile gravel. Except for primitive plants known as lichens, no vegetation grows. Aside from frost action, there are no other geomorphic processes, such as water erosion, to disturb the patterned ground.

Most people live on the coastal plain in the western part of this physiographic region. The three largest settlements are situated at the mouth of the Mackenzie River. Inuvik has a population of around 3,500, while Aklavik and Tuktoyaktuk are smaller communities.

David Nunuk/Science Photo Library

**PHOTO 2.7** Basalt on Axel Heiberg Island, Nunavut. Basalt is a hard, black volcanic rock that, when cooled, can form various shapes, including tabular columns. Because they are resistant to erosion, basalt columns often form prominent cliffs. These weathered basalt columns date to the Paleozoic era (Table 2.1).

## The Appalachian Uplands

The Appalachian Uplands region represents only about 2 per cent of Canada's land mass. Sometimes known as Appalachia, this physiographic region consists of the northern section of the Appalachian Mountains, though few mountains are found in the Canadian section. The Appalachians extend south in the eastern United States to northern Georgia and Alabama. With the exception of Prince Edward Island (Vignette 2.6), its terrain in Canada is a mosaic of rounded uplands and narrow river valleys. Typical Appalachian Uplands terrain is found in Cape Breton, Nova Scotia (Photo 2.8). These weathered uplands

## Vignette 2.6

### Prince Edward Island

Unlike other areas of the Appalachian Uplands, Prince Edward Island has a flat to rolling landscape. Sedimentary strata that underlie its surface consist of relatively soft, red-coloured sandstone that is quickly broken down by weathering and erosional processes. Occasionally, outcrops of this sandstone are exposed, but for the most part the surface is covered by reddish soil that contains a large amount of sand and clay. The heavy concentrations of iron oxides in the rock and soil give the island its distinctive reddish-brown hue. Prince Edward Island, unlike the other provinces in this region, has an abundance of arable land.

are either rounded or flat-topped. They are the remnants of ancient mountains that underwent a variety of weathering and erosional processes over a period of almost 500 million years. Together, weathering and erosion (including transportation of loose material by water, wind, and ice to lower elevations) have worn down these mountains, creating a much subdued mountain landscape with peneplain features. The highest elevations are on the Gaspé Peninsula in Quebec, where Mount Jacques Cartier rises to an elevation of 1,268 m. The coastal area has been slightly submerged; consequently, ocean waters have invaded the lower valleys, creating bays or estuaries, with a number of excellent small harbours and a few large ones, such as Halifax harbour. The island of Newfoundland consists of a rocky upland with only pockets of soil found in valleys. Like the Maritimes, it has an indented coastline where small harbours abound. The nature of this physiographic region favoured early European settlement along the heavily indented

PHOTO 2.8 The Appalachian Uplands have sustained much erosion and the resulting landscape represents "worn-down" mountains. In rugged Cape Breton Highlands National Park, a table-like surface or peneplain lies between steep valleys carved by streams.

coastline where there was easy access to the vast cod stocks. With the demise of the cod stocks, these tiny settlements are declining or, like Great Harbour Deep, have been abandoned (see Chapter 10).

## The Great Lakes–St Lawrence Lowlands

The Great Lakes–St Lawrence Lowlands physiographic region is small but extremely important in contemporary Canada, both economically and demographically. Extending from the St Lawrence River near Quebec City to Windsor, this narrow strip of land rests between the Appalachian Uplands, the Canadian Shield, and the Great Lakes.[2] Near the eastern end of Lake Ontario, the Canadian Shield extends across this region into the United States, where it forms the Adirondack Mountains in New York State. Known as the Frontenac Axis, this part of the Canadian Shield divides the Great Lakes–St Lawrence Lowlands into two distinct sub-regions.

As the smallest physiographic region in Canada, the Great Lakes–St Lawrence Lowlands comprises less than 2 per cent of the area of Canada. Yet this region is the most favoured of the seven regions. As its name suggests, the landscape is flat to rolling. This topography reflects the underlying sedimentary strata and its thin cover of glacial deposits. In the Great Lakes sub-region, flat sedimentary rocks are found just below the surface. This slightly tilted sedimentary rock, which consists of limestone, is exposed at the surface in southern Ontario, forming the Niagara Escarpment. A thin layer of glacial and lacustrine (i.e., lake) material, deposited after the melting of the Laurentide Ice Sheet in this area about 12,000 years ago, forms the surface, covering the sedimentary rocks (Vignette 2.7).

In the St Lawrence sub-region, the landscape was shaped by the Champlain Sea, which occupied this area for about 2,000 years. It retreated about 10,000 years ago and left broad terraces that slope gently towards the St Lawrence River (Vignette 2.7). The sandy to clay surface materials are a mixture of recently deposited sea, river, or glacial materials. For the most part, this sub-region's soils are fertile, which, when combined with a long growing season, allows agricultural activities to flourish.

## Vignette 2.7

### Champlain Sea

By 12,000 years ago, vast quantities of glacial water from the melting ice sheets around the world had drained into the world's oceans. Over the course of several thousand years, ice sheets were melting and sea levels were rising. Some 12,000 years ago, the sea level of the Atlantic Ocean reached the point where sea water surged into the St Lawrence and Ottawa valleys, perhaps as far west as the edge of Lake Ontario. Known as the Champlain Sea, this body of water occupied the depressed land between Quebec City and Cornwall, Ontario, and extended up the Ottawa River Valley to Pembroke, Ontario. These lands had been depressed earlier by the weight of the Laurentide Ice Sheet. About 10,000 years ago, as the earth's crust rebounded, the Champlain Sea retreated. However, the sea left behind marine deposits, which today form the basis of the fertile soils in the St Lawrence Lowlands.

**THINK ABOUT IT**

Sea levels are slowly rising due to melting glaciers and warming oceans. Oceans absorb most solar radiation; the warming of these waters is known as **thermal expansion**. With continuing climate change, the Champlain Sea could reach its former levels— some 150 feet above the current level of the Ottawa and St Lawrence rivers— perhaps as early as the twenty-second century. For such a rise in sea levels, the ice sheets in Greenland and the Antarctic would have to have melted.

The physiographic region lies well south of the forty-ninth parallel, which forms the US–Canada border from west of Ontario to Vancouver Island and then dips southward to allow Vancouver Island to remain in Canada. The Great Lakes sub-region extends from 42°N to 45°N, while the St Lawrence sub-region lies somewhat further north, reaching towards 47°N. As a result of its southerly location, its proximity to the industrial heartland of the United States, and its favourable physical setting, the Great

PHOTO 2.9 Rising sea levels following the last glaciation created the Champlain Sea, which extended up the Ottawa Valley, pictured here. Silt left behind by the receding waters formed the base for rich farmlands in the St Lawrence Lowlands. The gently rolling landscape is underlain by limestone.

Ian Cook/All Canada Photos

Lakes–St Lawrence region is home to Canada's main ecumene and manufacturing core.

## Geographic Location

Geographic location has two meanings. Absolute location refers to the exact location on the earth's surface as indicated by latitude and longitude. On the other hand, relative location focuses on relationships between two places or regions.

Because of the size of Canada, latitude and longitude vary enormously. Taking longitude as an example, the longitudinal distance between the westernmost area of Canada (as represented by Whitehorse, Yukon, at 135° 08' west of the prime meridian in Greenwich, England) and the easternmost point (as represented by St John's at 52° 43'W) is nearly 83 degrees. In kilometres, the distance between the two cities is about 5,200 km. From a standard time perspective, five and a half time zones stretch across the country, from the Newfoundland Time Zone in the east to the Pacific Time Zone in the west (Figure 2.3).

How did the concept of standard time emerge? In fact, we have Sir Sanford Fleming, a Scottish-born Canadian civil engineer working on the construction of the Canadian Pacific Railway, to thank for inventing a system of standard time (as against individual time for each place as calculated from the sun). Fleming, in 1878, proposed the system of worldwide time zones based on the premise that since the earth rotates once every 24 hours and there are 360 degrees of longitude in a sphere, each hour the earth rotates one-twenty-fourth of a circle or 15 degrees of longitude.

Because the earth is a spherical body, this measure is given in degrees (°) and minutes (') for both latitude and longitude. By longitude, we mean the distance east or west of the prime meridian. As the equator represents zero latitude, the prime meridian represents zero longitude. It is an imaginary line that runs from the North Pole to the South Pole and passes through the Royal Observatory at Greenwich, England. Canada lies entirely in the area of west longitude. Ottawa, for example, is 75° 28' west of the prime meridian. The distance between longitudes varies, being greatest at the equator and reaching zero at the North Pole.[3] Latitudes and longitudes for some other Canadian cities are found in Table 2.2.

By latitude, we mean the measure of distance north and south of the equator. For example, Ottawa is 42° 24' minutes north of the equator. How do we translate these latitudes into an understanding of Canada's northern location and its cold environment? One way is to examine the southernmost latitude near Windsor, Ontario, which is close to 42°N. Another way is to realize that over half of Canada

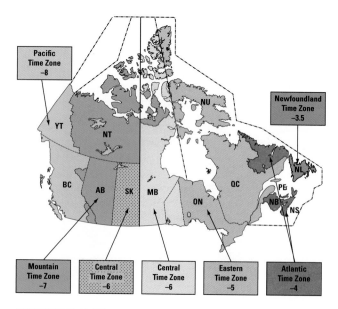

### FIGURE 2.3  Time zones

Most of Saskatchewan observes Central Standard Time year-round. Lloydminster, a border town situated in both Alberta and Saskatchewan, uses Mountain Standard Time and observes daylight saving time. Some communities in Canada may choose not to observe official time zones and this map does not reflect all such variances.

**TABLE 2.2  Latitude and Longitude of Selected Centres**

| Centre | Latitude | Longitude |
|---|---|---|
| **Windsor, Ontario** | 42° 19'N | 83°W |
| **Montreal, Quebec** | 45° 32'N | 73° 36'W |
| **St John's, Newfoundland and Labrador** | 47° 35'N | 52° 43'W |
| **Victoria, British Columbia** | 48° 27'N | 123° 20'W |
| **Winnipeg, Manitoba** | 49° 53'N | 97° 10'W |
| **Saskatoon, Saskatchewan** | 52° 10'N | 106° 40'W |
| **Edmonton, Alberta** | 53° 34'N | 113° 25'W |
| **Whitehorse, Yukon** | 60° 42'N | 135° 08'W |
| **Inuvik, Northwest Territories** | 68° 16'N | 133° 40'W |
| **Alert, Nunavut** | 82° 31'N | 62° 20'W |

lies north of the sixtieth parallel. Finally, we can look at the latitude of our capital. Ottawa is nearly 5,000 km north of the equator. Since the distance between each degree of latitude is about 111 km, the middle to high latitudes in Canada have considerable implications for the amount of solar energy received at the surface of the earth, and, hence, Canada's climate with short summers and long, dark winters.

## Climate

**Climate** is a central aspect of our physical world. Yet, it is changing. Climate describes average weather conditions for a specific place or region based on past weather over a very long period of time, perhaps thousands of years. On the other hand, weather refers to the current state of the atmosphere with a focus on weather conditions that affect people living in a particular place for a relatively short period of time.

Climate trends describe average weather changes over long periods of time (Figure 2.4). Often the focus for such trends takes place at the global scale where weather records demonstrate that our climate is warming. But what about Canada? According to the Prairie Climate Centre (2019), "Weather records from across Canada show that every year since 1998—that's 20 years ago now—has been warmer than the 20th century average. This means that a whole generation of Canadians has never

experienced what most of modern history considered a 'normal' Canadian climate."

In sum, climate is what we can expect while weather is what we get. Geography students can gain first-hand knowledge of current and historic patterns in climate and weather by referring to *Climate Atlas of Canada* (https://climateatlas.ca) produced by the Prairie Climate Centre at the University of Winnipeg.

Even though our world is warming, Canada has long been considered a "cold" country, with its long winters. "Coldness," wrote French and Slaymaker (1993, p. i), "is a pervasive Canadian characteristic, part of the nation's culture and history." They note that winter's effects include not only low absolute temperatures but also exposure to wind chill, snow, ice, and permafrost. As Canadians well know from personal experience, Canada has a cold environment. As seen on the map of climatic zones (Figure 2.5), the bulk of Canada's territory is associated with two northern climatic types, the Arctic and Subarctic zones. Both have extremely long, cold winters. Although the two maritime climatic types—along the coast of BC and in Atlantic Canada—have mild climates with relatively short periods of cold weather, winter is a fact of life for Canadians. Artists, musicians, and novelists have found this northern theme appealing. In "Mon pays," Gilles Vigneault, one of Quebec's best-known chansonniers, refers to Quebec, his country, in the

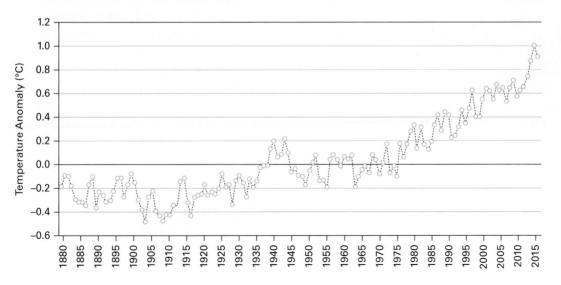

**FIGURE 2.4  Global Temperature, 1880 to 2017**

Source: Prairie Climate Centre (2019).

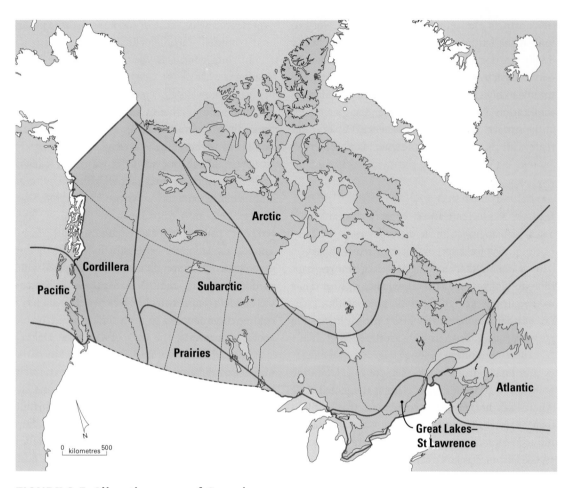

**FIGURE 2.5 Climatic zones of Canada**
Each climatic zone represents average climatic conditions in that area. Canada's most extensive climatic zone, the Subarctic, is associated with the boreal forest and podzolic soils.

**THINK ABOUT IT**

Figure 2.5 is based on the 1961 to 1990 Climate Normal calculated by Environment Canada. If this map were prepared using the next version of climatic records, namely the 1991–2020 Climate Normal, how might the boundaries change?

opening line: *Mon pays ce n'est pas un pays, c'est l'hiver* (My country is not a country, it is winter). Stan Rogers's heroic song "Northwest Passage" has become one of Canada's unofficial anthems.

## Climate Change and Global Warming

Canada, like other parts of the world, is caught in a warming trend referred to as global warming (Vignette 2.8). Until the mid-1970s, the increase in average annual temperature since the Industrial Revolution was modest—less than 1 per cent higher to the middle of the twentieth century. Over the last 50 years, the average annual temperature has increased much more rapidly—by 1.5°C (Warren &

Lemmen, 2014, p. 6). In turn, this warming trend has led to climate change—a term that includes global warming and the impact of higher temperatures on other components of weather as well as on the rest of the natural world (see Vignette 2.9). For instance, the Northwest Passage is no longer an impassible frozen body of water, and wildfires are now more common in the boreal forest. Another example is that those living beyond the conventional transportation network are dependent on ice roads that can only exist in very cold conditions. With the length of winters becoming shorter and shorter, delivering food and building supplies to remote communities and mine sites using ice roads is becoming more and more problematic.

While annual temperature increases are relatively simple to measure and interpret, precipitation is

## Vignette 2.8

### Global Warming, Climate Change, and the Consequences

The definitions of both *global warming* and *climate change* are centred on the premise that temperatures are increasing, which, in turn, contributes to changes in global climate patterns and an increase in extreme weather events.

The principal difference between the two terms is that global warming focuses on temperature change that results from increased emissions of **greenhouse gases** from human activities, notably the burning of fossil fuels and the release of carbon dioxide. Known as the **greenhouse effect**, this anthropogenic-caused warming trend began with the Industrial Revolution when great quantities of coal first began to be consumed to supply the energy necessary for industry. Carbon dioxide, the principal greenhouse gas, is the key driver of global warming. Originally, European countries were the major consumers of coal, but now China leads the world in consumption of coal with India not far behind. Both countries plan to expand their coal consumption in the next decade in order to fuel their industrialization.

Climate change, on the other hand, is not restricted to human-caused warming but considers natural forces, too. As well, climate change places more emphasis on other elements of climate, such as precipitation, wind patterns, and more frequent and violent weather events.

Photo by Scott Zolkos

**PHOTO 2.10** This lake, near Fort McPherson, NWT, is poised to disappear—as it mostly did in July 2015 when a permafrost slump encroached on its edges. Repeated many times, this phenomenon represents one of many giant-sized permafrost slumps that are changing the North's landscape on a scale not seen since the last ice age.

## Vignette 2.9

### Global Warming, the Paris Accord, and Greta Thunberg

The physics of global warming in the greenhouse model are elementary, but the actual process of climate change is extremely complex and remains unclear as it impacts our planet. For instance, a thermokarst landscape is the likely outcome when the ice-rich permafrost thaws, but the future of the boreal forest is less clear. Certainly, worldwide concern for our planet is growing; indeed, the potential effects of global warming and climate change are seen by the broad scientific community as an existential threat to communities, nations, economies, and human life as we have understood it. In 2015, the Paris Climate Change Conference declared a global warming goal for the twenty-first century of 1.5°C above pre-industrial levels (UN, 2015). The Paris Accord represents a global effort to contain rising temperatures from exceeding 1.5°C above pre-industrial levels. While pressure is mounting to move in that direction, all indications suggest fossil fuel production will increase by 2050, led by the expansion of coal-burning plants in China and India. Onto the world stage came Swedish high school student Greta Thunberg, frustrated by political inaction, who has succeeded in turning vague anxieties about the planet into a worldwide movement, calling for concrete action to prevent a climate catastrophe. Her solution is a fossil-free world now, meaning immediate halt to the fossil fuel industry.

**THINK ABOUT IT**

Laurence Smith predicts winners and losers in our warmer world. By 2050, the eight nations of the Arctic Rim (including Canada, Russia, and the United States) are forecast as winners and predicted to become increasingly powerful as a consequence of a warmer climate, while the nations near the equator, like Australia, Brazil, and India, are predicted to be losers as their climates become warmer, causing problems for agriculture.

more complicated. Evidence shows that annual precipitation is increasing and even the drought-prone Canadian Prairies may be benefiting from greater precipitation (Cutforth et al., 2000; Zhang et al., 2000; Bonsal et al., 2013). The basis of greater annual precipitation is the premise that air masses formed over warming oceans have a greater capacity to hold moisture and produce precipitation and violent storms over land areas. On top of the interplay of global temperatures and precipitation, different parts of the world are affected differently. In Canada's Arctic, for instance, an indisputable indicator of warmer summers is the summer retreat of Arctic sea ice. In another part of Canada, the Canadian Prairies, the jury is still out on how these two climatic elements of temperature and precipitation will play out. The semi-arid Prairies have long been subject to a cycle of wet and dry years. Now the question is whether, with longer and warmer summers, this region will turn into an arid environment or a more humid one.

As our planet warms, just how this increase will alter Canada is slowly unfolding before our eyes. Laurence Smith argues in his book *The World in 2050* that Canada's ecumene will be one of the main beneficiaries of climatic warming and associated economic events. The Arctic, on the other hand, sees its temperatures rising more rapidly than other areas of Canada,

largely because of the albedo effect. Albedo, a measure of the reflection of solar radiation from the earth's surface, is greatest in snow-covered areas. As the snow cover retreats, the darker surface absorbs more solar radiation, causing the surface to warm. So far, this warming effect has had negative impacts on Inuit accessing marine animals because of reduced shore ice. A 2019 climate report from the government of the Northwest Territories discusses the climatic changes further but is silent on the human impact:

> The Arctic is experiencing a rapid and intense warming trend, which is apparent when temperature increases in Northwest Territories (NWT), Yukon, and Nunavut are compared against temperature trends throughout the rest of North America. The Mackenzie Valley is considered a global hotspot in terms of climate change and warming temperatures. The 2005 Arctic Climate Impact Assessment (ACIA) describes annual temperature increases of 2–3°C in the Mackenzie Valley area and as much as 4°C in the winter during the past 50 years. Along with the rise in temperature, precipitation patterns are also expected to change as a result of climate change.

## Climate Factors

While the addition of greenhouse gases into the atmosphere is causing global warming, the four traditional climatic factors require our attention. First, the energy from the sun sets the parameters for climate. The amount of this energy received at the earth's surface varies by latitude. Low latitudes around the equator have a net surplus of energy (and therefore high temperatures), but in high latitudes around the North and South poles, more energy is lost through re-radiation than is received, and therefore annual average temperatures are extremely low. Canada, lying in middle to high latitudes, is subject to great variation in the amount of solar energy. In turn, this variation results in wide differences in temperatures, climatic types, and zones (see Figures 2.6 and 2.7).

**PHOTO 2.11** This NASA image shows Canada in the grip of winter, 28 February 2009. Canada is a northern nation with winter its dominant season.

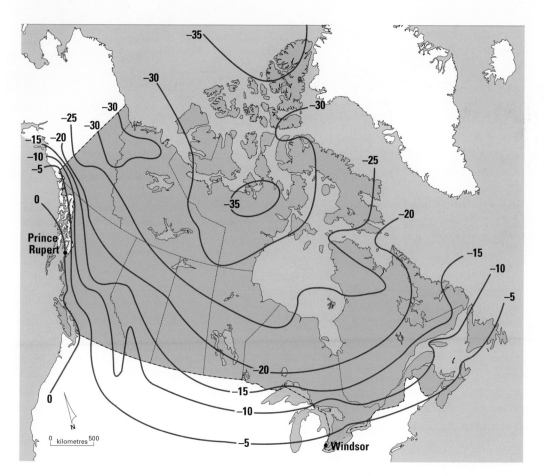

**FIGURE 2.6 Seasonal temperatures in Celsius, January**

The moderating influence of the Pacific Ocean and its warm air masses are readily apparent in the 0 to −5°C January isotherm. For example, Prince Rupert, located near 55°N, has a warmer January average temperature (0°C) than Windsor (−2°C), which is located near 42°N.

**THINK ABOUT IT**

Melt ice in permafrost causes massive ground subsidence, a form of irregular topography referred to by physical geographers as "thermokarst topography." With the on-going increase in global warming, how might such subsidence affect housing and other infrastructure built on permafrost?

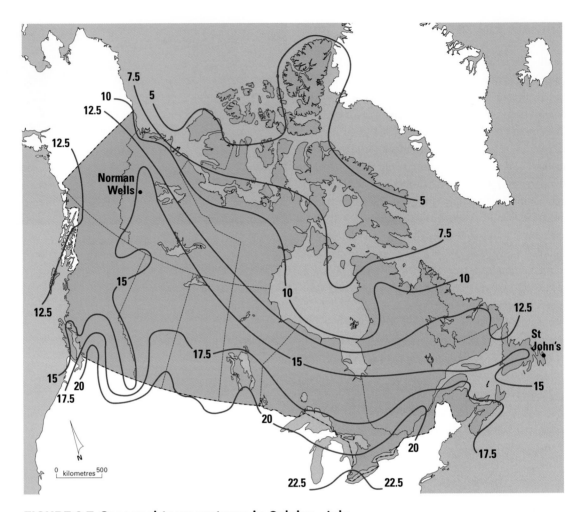

**FIGURE 2.7 Seasonal temperatures in Celsius, July**

The continental effect results in very warm summer temperatures that extend into high latitudes, as illustrated by the 15°C July isotherm. For example, Norman Wells, located near the Arctic Circle, has warmer July temperatures than St John's.

**Think About It**

Which air mass dominates the summer climate where you live?

Second, the global circulation system redistributes this energy (i.e., energy transfers) from low latitudes to high latitudes through circulation in the atmosphere (system of winds and air masses) and the oceans (system of ocean currents). For example, the Japan Current warms the Pacific Ocean, bringing milder weather to British Columbia. On Canada's east coast, the opposite process occurs as the Labrador Current brings Arctic waters to Atlantic Canada. While Halifax, at 44° 39'N, lies about 500 km closer to the equator than Victoria, at 48° 27'N, Halifax's winter temperatures, on average, are much lower than those experienced in Victoria.

Third, the global circulation system travels in a west-to-east direction in the higher latitudes of the northern hemisphere, causing air masses (Vignette 2.10) that develop over large water bodies to bring mild and moist weather to adjacent land masses. For Canada, air masses from the Pacific Ocean cross the Cordillera into the interior of Canada. Such air masses are known as marine air masses. In this way, energy transfers ultimately determine regional patterns of global weather and climate (see Tables 2.3 and 2.4). Air masses originating over large land masses are known as continental air masses. These air masses are normally very dry and vary in temperature depending on the season. In the winter continental air masses are cold, while in the summer they are associated with hot weather.

## Vignette 2.10

### Air Masses

Air masses are large sections of the atmosphere with similar temperature and humidity characteristics. They form over large areas with uniform surface features and relatively consistent temperatures where they take on these temperature and humidity characteristics. Such areas are known as source regions. The Pacific Ocean is a marine source region, while the interior of North America is a continental source region. During a period of about a week or so, an air mass may form over a source region. Canada's weather is affected by five air masses (Table 2.4).

### TABLE 2.3   Climatic Types

| Köppen Classification | Canadian Climatic Zone | General Characteristics |
| --- | --- | --- |
| **Marine West Coast** | Pacific | Warm to cool summers, mild winters<br>Precipitation throughout the year with a maximum in winter |
| **Highland** | Cordillera | Cooler temperature at similar latitudes because of higher elevations |
| **Steppe** | Prairies | Hot dry summers and long cold winters<br>Low annual precipitation |
| **Humid continental** | Great Lakes–St Lawrence Lowlands | Hot humid summers and short cold winters<br>Moderate annual precipitation with little seasonal variation |
| **Humid continental, cool** | Atlantic Canada | Cool to warm humid summers and short cool winters |
| **Subarctic** | Subarctic | Short cool summers and long cold winters<br>Low annual precipitation |
| **Tundra** | Arctic | Extremely cool and very short summers; long cold winters<br>Very low annual precipitation |

Source: Adapted from Christopherson (1998); Hare & Thomas (1974).

### TABLE 2.4   Air Masses Affecting Canada

| Air Mass | Type | Characteristics | Season |
| --- | --- | --- | --- |
| **Pacific** | Marine | Mild and wet | All |
| **Atlantic** | Marine | Cool and wet | All |
| **Gulf of Mexico** | Marine | Hot and wet | Summer |
| **Southwest US** | Continental | Hot and dry | Summer |
| **Arctic** | Continental | Cold and dry | Winter |

The fourth factor is the so-called "continental effect." Continental effect refers to the fact that land masses heat up and cool more quickly than oceans. In turn, greater distance from an ocean affects temperature and precipitation; that is, as distance from an ocean increases, the daily and seasonal temperature ranges increase and the annual precipitation decreases. For example, Winnipeg experiences a much greater daily and annual range in temperature than does Vancouver, even though both lie near 49°N. The principal reason is the "continental effect."

## Types of Precipitation

**THINK ABOUT IT**

Why did Köppen design his climate classification system based on the global pattern of natural vegetation rather than climatic data?

As an air mass rises, its temperature drops. This cooling process triggers condensation of water vapour within the air mass. With sufficient cooling, water droplets are formed. When these droplets reach a sufficient size, precipitation begins. Precipitation refers to rainfall, snow, and hail. There are three types of precipitation. Convectional precipitation results when moist air is forced to rise because the ground has become particularly warm. Often this form of precipitation is associated with thunderstorms. Frontal precipitation occurs when a warm air mass is forced to rise over a colder (and denser) air mass. Orographic precipitation results when an air mass is forced to rise over high mountains. However, as the same air mass descends along the leeward slopes of those mountains (that is, the slopes that lie on the east side of the mountains), the temperature rises and precipitation is less likely to occur. This phenomenon is known as the rain shadow effect (Figure 2.8).

A climatic zone is an area of the earth's surface where similar weather conditions occur. Long-term data describing annual, seasonal, and daily temperatures and precipitation are used to define the extent of a climatic zone (Vignette 2.11).

Canada has seven climatic zones (Figure 2.5): Pacific, Cordillera, Prairies, Great Lakes–St Lawrence, Atlantic, Subarctic, and Arctic. The Arctic climate

**THINK ABOUT IT**

Global warming has begun, but so far the boundaries of the Canadian climate zones shown in Figure 2.5 have not been altered. Does this mean that global warming has not yet had sufficient impact on our climate or is there a lag in updating these boundaries?

**THINK ABOUT IT**

As climate change continues in the twenty-first century, explain why more annual precipitation is likely in the Arctic.

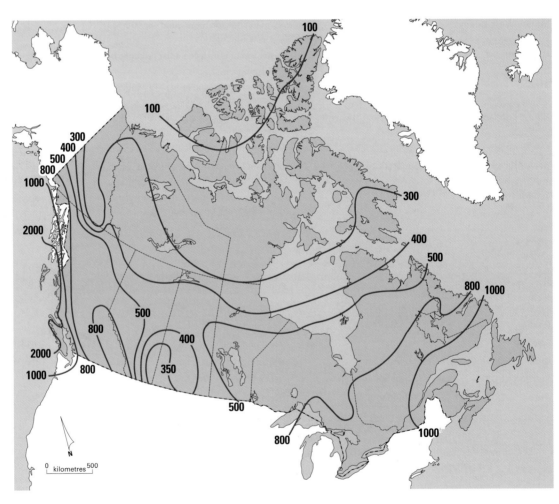

**FIGURE 2.8  Annual precipitation in millimetres**

The lowest average annual precipitation occurs in the Territorial North, indicating the dry nature of the Arctic air masses that originate over the Arctic Ocean. The highest average annual precipitation occurs along the coast of British Columbia due to the moist marine air masses and the coastal mountains.

## Vignette 2.11

### Köppen Climate Classification

Since climate was relatively stable over thousands of years, the earth developed a series of climatic types and zones. But how many types and zones exist? It all depends on the criteria. In the nineteenth century, well before global climatic stations existed, Wladimir Köppen, a Russian-German scientist, developed a climatic classification scheme for the world based on natural vegetation zones that, with later modifications by Köppen and more recent researchers, remains in use today. He correctly assumed that these natural vegetation zones required certain temperatures and precipitation to thrive and therefore these zones were a surrogate for climatic types and zones. Based on world patterns of natural vegetation, Köppen created 25 climate types, each of which was assigned particular temperature regimes and seasonal precipitation patterns. Seven of Köppen's climatic types are found in Canada (Table 2.3).

extends from the coast of Yukon to the Labrador coast. It dominates in Nunavut and Nunavik (far northern Quebec) and is found along the Hudson Bay coastlines of Ontario and Manitoba. The Subarctic climatic zone, Canada's largest, extends over much of the interior of Canada and is found in each geographic region. The Subarctic climate prevails in northern areas of Atlantic Canada, Quebec, Ontario, and Western Canada, and is present in northeast British Columbia. As well, the Subarctic climate is found in the Territorial North and is the principal climate in the Northwest Territories. The Subarctic reaches much higher latitudes in northwest Canada than in northeast Canada because of warmer temperatures in the northwest. In northwest Canada, the average July temperature often reaches or exceeds 10°C, thus permitting the growth of trees. In similar latitudes of northeast Canada, summer temperatures are much lower. In the extreme north of Quebec, for example, the average July temperature is below 10°C, thus resulting in tundra rather than a tree vegetation cover. The Subarctic climatic zone therefore has a southeast to northwest alignment (Figure 2.5). This alignment is somewhat modified in Quebec because of its proximity to the marine influences of the Atlantic Ocean.

Since environmental issues are the result of human actions, solutions are possible (Dearden & Mitchell, 2012, ch. 1). One solution involves establishing more protected areas and parks (Slocombe & Dearden, 2009). Another calls for more stringent regulations that will reduce damage to the

imageBROKER/Alamy Stock Photo

**PHOTO 2.12** Glacial retreat of the Athabasca Glacier since 2000 can be attributed to warmer annual temperatures. Part of the Columbia Icefield in Jasper National Park, Alberta, the glacier is retreating at a rate of about 5 m per year (see Vignette 2.12).

environment caused by both new and existing projects. But perhaps the most significant solution lies in "going green," which includes recycling waste products, moving towards electric automobiles, limiting discretionary air travel, and increasing the production of electricity from natural sources such as solar and wind rather than coal.

### Extreme Weather Events

Extreme weather events—such as blizzards, droughts, ice storms, and wildfires—are also part of climate and often have very powerful impacts on humans. In fact,

The section "Technological Gamble: Carbon Capture and Storage," in **Chapter 8**, page 260, discusses the efforts in Alberta and Saskatchewan to reduce greenhouse emissions from oil sands upgraders and coal-fired energy plants through carbon sequestration.

## Vignette 2.12

### Fluctuations in World Temperatures

Our climate seems relatively constant, but geological history reveals otherwise. The last 10,000 years—the **Holocene epoch**—represents a relatively warm period in the earth's history. For the most part, ocean levels remained fairly stable in this geological epoch, but ocean levels are expected to rise sharply in the late twenty-first century. One reason is the melting of glaciers and the Greenland and Antarctic ice sheets, and the other is warmer ocean waters.

However, within that epoch, a series of shorter cycles of warm and then colder periods have occurred. Often, these short cycles have lasted for around 500 to 1,000 years, and all were associated with natural causes. During these short cycles, the global average temperature either increased or decreased by one or two degrees Celsius. From roughly 1450 to 1850, a cooling of the climate occurred, known as the Little Ice Age. We are currently in a very rapid warming period caused by the ever-increasing use of coal and other fossil fuels that began with the Industrial Revolution, and now face the prospect of an increase in average global temperature of two or more degrees by 2100. The implications for countries in high latitudes may be less devastating than for those in lower latitudes.

NASA/Goddard Space Flight Center Scientific Visualization Studio

**PHOTO 2.13** Warm summer temperatures have caused the extent of Arctic sea ice to shrink, thus exposing more open water. In September 2007, for example, Arctic sea ice coverage had reached its lowest extent until 2012. Since then, this pattern of open water in the late summer has continued, with two routes through the Northwest Passage ice-free, but only for a short time. Differences do exist: the portion of the Arctic Ocean from the Beaufort Sea to the Bering Strait is ice-free for a longer time and its ice-free zone is much larger than in the central and eastern Arctic. Commercial ocean-going vessels are now plying these Arctic waters. In 2014 the first unescorted bulk carrier transported nickel concentrate from a Chinese-owned mine in Arctic Quebec through the Northwest Passage on a direct passage to China.

extreme weather events constitute the most serious of natural hazards, whether they take the form of droughts, floods, ice storms, hurricanes, or tornados.

The Intergovernmental Panel on Climate Change, which assesses and synthesizes the research of more than 2,000 climate scientists throughout the world, foresees an increase in extreme weather events because of rising world temperatures: a warmer atmosphere would have the capacity to hold increased moisture, thus supplying the fuel for heavier rainfalls, snowfalls, and other extreme weather events. Canada is seeing the effects of widespread warming already, and higher temperatures and more precipitation are projected to increase in all regions of Canada, thus increasing the potential for urban flooding and wildfires.

Often, extreme weather events occur with little warning and result in heavy losses of property and sometimes lives. Hurricanes are such extreme weather events. Atlantic Canada has been the site of many of these destructive tropical cyclones (Conrad, 2009, pp. 163–5). Conrad places such weather in a broader context:

> Canada's climate is typified by extremes, and thus Canadians are interested in the weather out of necessity and concern. With the inevitable changes in our global climate, scientists as well as the general public are concerned with the impact such change will have on extreme weather events in Canada. (Conrad, 2009, p. 1)

Not surprisingly, extreme weather events often have a cultural impact by providing a common threat and, as people struggle against this threat, creating a common bond. As indicated in Chapter 1, natural disasters have contributed to people's sense of belonging to a region, and often they are recurring phenomena, such as floods in a flood-prone area. As de Loë (2000, p. 357) explains, "Floods are considered hazards only in cases where human beings occupy floodplains and shoreland." Heavy rainfall combined with rapid snowmelt often triggers catastrophic floods. An excellent example is found in the flat Manitoba Lowland where the normally benign Red River winds its way from North Dakota in the

United States northward to Lake Winnipeg. Since 1950, residents of Winnipeg and other communities along the Red River have suffered through nine major spring floods—in 1950, 1979, 1996, 1997, 2001, 2006, 2009, 2011, and 2013—and the frequency of these floods appears to be increasing, giving credence to the fears of the Intergovernmental Panel on Climate Change. In 1950, the Red River flood drove over 100,000 people from their homes. Following that disaster, the Red River Floodway, a wide channel nearly 50 km long, was constructed. Its purpose was to divert the flood waters around the city of Winnipeg. However, small communities in the Red River Basin remained vulnerable to flooding. In 1997, the largest flood in the twentieth century occurred (Rasid et al., 2000). While the Red River Floodway saved Winnipeg, the towns of Emerson, Morris, Ste Agathe, and St Adolphe and the surrounding farm buildings and lands were less fortunate. From 2006 to 2020 waters overflowed the banks of the Red River nine out of 15 years (Photo 2.14).

## Permafrost

Permafrost is a relic from a very cold Pleistocene climate (Table 2.1). This distinctive feature of Canada's physical geography is permanently frozen ground with temperatures at or below zero for at least two years. For the past several decades, annual temperatures have increased, causing permafrost to retreat as ice contained in this frozen ground melts.

PHOTO 2.14 The town of St Jean Baptiste, 40 km north of the Canada–US border, is surrounded by a ring dike to protect it from the flooding Red River, 20 April 2011.

Joe Bryksa/Winnipeg Free Press

**THINK ABOUT IT**

If our climate is warming, what are the consequences for the landscape if ice in the ground known as permafrost melts?

Even so, the vast extent of permafrost in Canada and, in places, its great depth provide a measure of the country's cold environment (Figure 2.9). Permafrost exists in the Arctic and Subarctic climatic zones and occurs at higher elevations in the Cordillera zone. Overall, permafrost is found in just over two-thirds of Canada's land mass.

In more northerly regions, permafrost extends far into the ground. North of the Arctic Circle, the permafrost may be several hundred metres deep. Further south, permafrost is less frequent, and where it occurs it rarely penetrates more than 10 m into the ground. Permafrost is found in all six of Canada's geographic regions and reaches its most southerly position along 50°N in Ontario and Quebec. Along the southern edge of permafrost,

there is a transition zone where small pockets of frozen ground have a depth of less than 1 m. In the warming environment, these pockets of permafrost have disappeared and the transition zone is slowly shifting northwards.

Permafrost, like glaciers, is undergoing a retreat due to global warming. The most vulnerable permafrost lies mainly in the northern reaches of provinces where the permanently frozen ground is relatively warm at temperatures of zero to −5°C; its thickness is less than 5 m; and less than 30 per cent of the area contains permafrost (Warren & Lemmen, 2014, p. 37). Known as sporadic permafrost, it may disappear well before the end of the twenty-first century (Figure 2.9). In sharp contrast, the temperature of the ground in the continuous permafrost

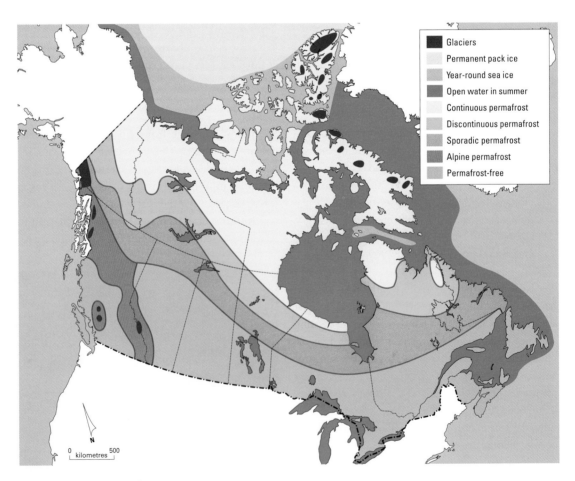

Glaciers
Permanent pack ice
Year-round sea ice
Open water in summer
Continuous permafrost
Discontinuous permafrost
Sporadic permafrost
Alpine permafrost
Permafrost-free

0    500
kilometres

**FIGURE 2.9  Permafrost zones**

Canada's cold environment is best demonstrated by permafrost. Permanently frozen ground extends over two-thirds of the country. The melting of permafrost reflects the impact of global warming.

zone is much lower (−15°C or colder) and its thickness exceeds 10 m. Continuous permafrost most likely will remain intact for this century, though its characteristics could degrade.

The warming of permafrost is changing the appearance of the northern landscape. One change involves the slumping of land and the disappearance of lakes (Kokelj et al., 2015). For example, on 15 July 2015, near Fort McPherson, NWT, the headwall that had kept the waters of a small, unnamed lake from plummeting into a valley below gave way (Photo 2.10). Reporter Bob Weber (2015) wrote:

> Within two hours, 30,000 cubic metres of water—the equivalent of a dozen Olympic-sized swimming pools—gushed over the edge in a waterfall up to five storeys high. Mud and debris filled more than a kilometre of the valley below and flowed for two days at the rate of 50 metres an hour.

Permafrost is divided into four types. **Alpine permafrost** is found in mountainous areas and takes on a vertical pattern as elevations of a mountain increase. Over most of Canada, however, permafrost follows a zonal pattern, which does not correspond to latitude but rather to the annual mean temperatures that fall below zero.[4] The zonal pattern has a northwest to southeast alignment, that is, from Yukon to central Quebec (see Figure 2.9).

As the mean annual temperature varies, the type of permafrost also changes. **Continuous permafrost** occurs in the higher latitudes of the Arctic climatic zone, where at least 80 per cent of the ground is permanently frozen, although it also extends into northern Quebec. Continuous permafrost is associated with very low mean annual air temperatures of −15°C or less. **Discontinuous permafrost** occurs when 30 to 80 per cent of the ground is permanently frozen. It is found in the Subarctic climatic zone where mean annual air temperature ranges from −5°C in the south to −15°C in the north. **Sporadic permafrost** is found mainly in the northern parts of the provinces, where less than 30 per cent of the area is permanently frozen. Sporadic permafrost is associated with mean annual temperatures of zero to −5°C.

## Sea and Lake Ice

Another measure of the impact of climate change is found in sea and lake ice. While sea ice varies in thickness and duration across the North, the most durable and thickest ice is found in the permanent **Arctic ice pack**. Seasonal melting of lake and sea ice follows a temporal pattern: lake ice disappears first in the Great Lakes and sea ice in Hudson Bay; next, sea ice melts in the offshore waters of Atlantic Canada; and last, the pack ice in the Arctic Ocean diminishes in extent. Over the last several decades, satellite imagery has indicated that the annual extent of open water in the Arctic Ocean has gradually but irregularly increased. An increase in open water does not occur each year. For example, open water reached its greatest extent in 2012, followed by an increase of 41 per cent in 2013, when the summer was 5 per cent cooler than the previous year (European Space Agency, 2015). This annual pattern continued to 2020 when the Arctic ice cap was both thinner and smaller than in the previous year. In 2020, the minimum extent was 2.48 million km², marking only the second time on record that the minimum extent has fallen below 4 million km² (Ramsayer, 2020).

## Major Drainage Basins

Canada, bounded by the Arctic, Atlantic, and Pacific oceans, is a maritime country (Figure 2.10). Canada has four major drainage basins: the Atlantic Basin, the Hudson Bay Basin, the Arctic Basin, and the Pacific Basin. The Atlantic and Hudson Bay basins both drain into the Atlantic Ocean (Figure 2.10 and Table 2.5).

**TABLE 2.5 Canada's Drainage Basins**

| Drainage Basin | Area (million km²) | Streamflow (m³/second) |
|---|---|---|
| **Hudson Bay** | 3.8 | 30,594 |
| **Arctic** | 3.6 | 20,491 |
| **Atlantic** | 1.6 | 29,087 |
| **Pacific** | 1.0 | 24,951 |
| **Gulf of Mexico** | <0.1 | 12 |
| **Total** | 10.0 | 105,135 |

Sources: Laycock (1987, p. 32); Dearden & Mitchell (2012, p. 136).

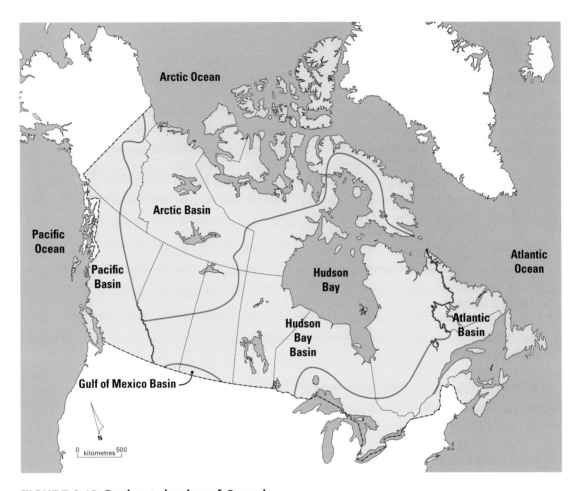

**FIGURE 2.10  Drainage basins of Canada**

The four divides determine Canada's drainage basins. They are the Continental or Great Divide, the Northern Divide, the Arctic Divide, and the St Lawrence Divide. The Hudson Bay Basin lies between three divides—the Continental Divide, the Arctic Divide, and the Northern Divide—and is by far the largest of the five basins in Canada. It also serves as a boundary between southern Alberta and British Columbia, and between northern Quebec and Labrador.

In addition, a small portion of southern Alberta and Saskatchewan drains southward to the Missouri River, which forms part of the Mississippi River system that empties its water into the Gulf of Mexico. A **drainage basin** slopes towards the sea and is separated from other lands by topographic ridges. These ridges form drainage divides. The Continental or Great Divide of the Rocky Mountains, for example, separates those streams flowing to the Pacific Ocean from those flowing to the Arctic and Atlantic oceans. On the east coast, the Northern Divide extends along the Labrador/Quebec boundary and separates waters flowing into the Atlantic Ocean and

Hudson Bay. Canada's five drainage basins are shown in Figure 2.10. Given its size and number of islands, Canada has the longest coastline in the world.

While the geographic extent of these drainage basins is fixed, the volume of water flowing through them varies by basin. As well, this volume is expected to increase due to climate warming and the resulting acceleration of the melting of glaciers and permafrost (Menounos et al., 2009; Clarke et al., 2015). Both glaciers and permafrost contribute meltwater containing organic and inorganic materials to freshwater systems and, with these additional waters added to the world's oceans, they play a role in the phenomenon of rising sea levels. In addition, the warmer climate is expected to produce more rainfall and less snowfall, especially in the Cordillera. In time, a tipping point will be reached when the volume of meltwater from glaciers and permafrost will decline, leading to a gradual stabilization of sea levels at much higher sea levels.

A few rivers cross the US–Canada border, and part of the Great Lakes lies in the United States. The Columbia River leaves British Columbia and continues its journey to the Pacific Ocean through the US states of Idaho, Washington, and Oregon. Two small rivers, the Milk and the Poplar, flow from southern Alberta and Saskatchewan into the Missouri River, which drains much of the northern half of the US Great Plains. The Red River flows from the US states of North Dakota and Minnesota into Manitoba and beyond to Lake Winnipeg and eventually to Hudson Bay by means of the Nelson River. The Richelieu River flows from Lake Champlain, which lies mainly in New York, and drains into the St Lawrence River near Sorel, Quebec. The headwaters of the Saint John River partially originate in Maine, and this river empties into the Bay of Fundy at the city of Saint John, New Brunswick.

Water is a scarce commodity, particularly in the dry Southwest of the United States. Arizona and California, for instance, depend on water diverted from the Colorado River to help meet their needs. Even so, these two states are facing severe water shortages. Under the North American Free Trade Agreement (NAFTA), water was classed as a commodity and therefore Canadian water could be exported to the United States. Since Canada has the world's largest supply of fresh water, large-scale transfer of water from Canada has appeal to water-short American states, but not only is the cost of such massive diversion too great at the moment, Ottawa is not in favour of such transfers.

Nevertheless, two huge continental diversions have been proposed. One—first put forth in 1959—was the Great Recycling and Northern Development Canal that called for diversion of water from James Bay to the Great Lakes and then, by pipelines, to the water-short American Southwest. Another continental scheme, the North American Water and Power Alliance, was conceived by the US Army Corps of Engineers in the 1950s and proposed diverting the Yukon River and the two major tributaries of the Mackenzie River, the Liard and the Peace, to the US along the Rocky Mountain Trench. Neither proposal has ever come to fruition.

## The Atlantic Basin

The Atlantic Basin is centred on the Great Lakes and the St Lawrence River and its tributaries, but the basin also includes Labrador. The Atlantic Basin has the third-largest drainage area and also the second-greatest streamflow. As seen in Figure 2.10, the Atlantic Basin receives considerable precipitation, making it second only to the Pacific Basin. The largest hydroelectric development in this drainage basin is located at Churchill Falls in Labrador while the second one is at Muskrat Falls on the Lower Churchill River. Earlier hydroelectric developments took place along the St Lawrence River in southern Quebec and along its tributary rivers that flow out of the Laurentide Upland of the Canadian Shield. Rivers such as the Manicouagan River originate in the higher elevation of the Laurentide Upland. Here, abundant precipitation, natural lakes, and a sharp increase in elevation provide ideal conditions for the generation of hydroelectric power. Because there is a large market for electrical power in the St Lawrence Lowlands, virtually all potential sites in the Laurentides have been developed.

## The Hudson Bay Basin

The Hudson Bay Basin is the largest drainage basin in Canada (Table 2.5), covering about 3.8 million km². Precipitation varies greatly across this basin. In the West, precipitation is low while it is greater in the East (Figure 2.8), where the headwaters of its rivers in the uplands of northern Quebec flow westward into James Bay. In northern Ontario and Manitoba, rivers drain into James and Hudson bays.

The large rivers and sudden drops in elevation that occur in the Canadian Shield make this part of the basin ideal for developing hydroelectric power stations. In fact, most of Canada's hydroelectric power is generated in the Canadian Shield area of the Hudson Bay Basin—the largest installations are

**THINK ABOUT IT** Examine **Figures 2.9** and **2.10**, which illustrate the extent of glaciers, permafrost, and drainage basins, to determine which drainage basin would benefit the least from the melting of glaciers and permafrost.

For further discussion of Quebec's hydroelectric developments, see **Chapter 7, "Quebec's Economic Anchor: Hydro-Québec,"** page 228.

on La Grande Rivière in northern Quebec and on the Nelson River in northern Manitoba. La Grande Rivière's hydroelectric developments are the first stage in the James Bay Project. The Great Whale River Project was to follow the completion of the hydroelectric projects on La Grande Rivière, but a variety of circumstances (low energy demand, low prices in New England, and strong opposition from environmental groups and the Cree of northern Quebec) stalled its development. Instead, Quebec focused its attention on the Eastmain Diversion Project and the Romaine Hydro Complex.

## The Arctic Basin

The Arctic Basin is Canada's second-largest drainage basin, but this basin has the largest coastline, thanks to the many islands in the Arctic Ocean. The Mackenzie River dominates the drainage system in this basin. Along with its major tributaries (the Athabasca, Liard, and Peace rivers), the Mackenzie River is the second-longest river in North America. However, because of low precipitation in the Arctic, this basin has only the fourth-largest streamflow. There are few hydroelectric projects in the Arctic Basin because of the long distance to markets, with the exception of the hydroelectric development on the Peace River that flows from the Rocky Mountains into the Interior Plains of northern British Columbia. Here, power from the Gordon M. Shrum and Peace Canyon dams is transmitted to the population centres in southern British Columbia and to the United States, primarily to the states of Washington, Oregon, and California. The construction of a third dam and hydroelectric generating station at Site C continues, though its estimated costs have more than doubled. As well, this project has come under heavy opposition from Indigenous peoples living in the area.

## The Pacific Basin

The Pacific Basin is the smallest basin. However, it has the third-highest volume of water draining into the sea. Heavy precipitation along the coastal mountains of British Columbia accounts for this unusually high streamflow. As a result, the Pacific Basin is the site of one of Canada's largest hydroelectric

**THINK ABOUT IT**

In Margaret Atwood's famous novel *The Handmaid's Tale*, the narrative is constructed on the decline of human fertility due to the pollution of our planet, which leads to the rise of an authoritarian government in the United States. While this is a fictional story, do you think Atwood and the young Swedish activist Greta Thunberg are on the same page with regard to the future of our world?

projects. Located at Kemano, this facility is owned and operated by Rio Tinto, which uses the electrical generating station to supply power to its aluminum smelter at Kitimat. The ice-free, deep-water harbour at Kitimat and low-cost electric power generated at Kemano make Kitimat an ideal location for an aluminum smelter. Kitimat at some point may become a terminal port for a natural gas pipeline. At one time, Kitimat was designated as a location for the Northern Gateway pipeline. However, in 2015 Prime Minister Justin Trudeau imposed a ban on oil tanker traffic along BC's north coast, thereby apparently ending the plans for the Northern Gateway pipeline (see Chapter 8). This was confirmed in November 2016 when the government definitively rejected the Northern Gateway pipeline proposal.

## Canada and Pollution

In our contemporary world, humans are the most active and dangerous agents of environmental change (Pacheco-Vega, 2015). All human activities affect the environment. Cultivation of the land, building of cities, burning of coal, exploitation of renewable and non-renewable resources, and processing of primary products have forever changed our natural environment into an industrial landscape. The mining industry is a major polluter of our lands and waters while the burning of fossils fuels by coal-burning thermal generating plants and by the operation of vehicles and planes pollutes our air and atmosphere.

Waste affects Canada's regions. Governing waste is a complex and risky activity involving all three levels of government. Their regulations extend over transportation, recycling, and ultimately, disposal. Nuclear waste disposal, for instance, tops the list in terms of dangerous waste products. Mining wastes stored in tailing ponds are less dangerous, but the risk of leakage or rupture in containment structure dams is always present.

## Mining and Pollution

Mining, before environmental regulations were in place, left behind toxic wastes. The Giant mine in Yellowknife left behind toxic waste that will cost the

## Contested Terrain 2.1

### The Oil Sands Tailing Ponds

Alberta's tailing ponds cover about 97 square miles and hold 340 billion gallons of waste (Orland, 2018). For decades, companies have pumped a goopy mix of sand and chemicals into ponds so the toxic solids could settle to the bottom and the treated water released into natural water bodies. But the water is taking longer than anticipated to reach acceptable levels for discharge, causing the size of the tailing ponds to increase. In an ideal situation, the toxic solids on the bottom of the pond would either be removed or covered to prevent seepage into natural water bodies. There are a few success stories of reclaiming smaller tailing ponds in the oil sands, but much remains in the years ahead, with industry costs perhaps reaching $27 billion (Orland, 2018). From the perspective of Suncor Energy Inc. and Canadian Natural Resources Ltd, the release of treated water into the Athabasca River is critical. Since the waters of the Athabasca River flow into the Northwest Territories and First Nations traditional lands in Alberta, the treated water must reach acceptable levels, and such levels have not yet been reached. Still, the oil companies have only one option, namely, to release treated waters into the Athabasca River. The first release may occur in 2023 (French, 2020).

public millions of dollars to neutralize. Even now, mining operations remain major polluters. Tailing ponds, for example, while an economic solution to toxic waste disposal, remain a threat to the environment. Two examples drive this point home. First, toxic chemicals from Alberta's vast oil sands are stored in tailing ponds (Contested Terrain 2.1). These contaminants have been leaching from the ponds into groundwater and seeping into the Athabasca River for years (Kurek et al., 2013). Second, the spectacular breach of the Mount Polley tailing pond at a gold/copper mine in central British Columbia in 2014 is cause for concern (Photo 2.15). Mining operations across Canada have hundreds of tailing ponds, all containing toxic solutions. Minor breaches are not that uncommon, but the Mount Polley disaster spewed out tonnes of polluted water and toxic sludge. The scope of this disaster is revealed in the report of the Mount Polley Review Panel (2015) and in videos and reports from Global News (2015).

### The Alberta Oil Sands

Canada's greenhouse gas emissions peaked in 2007 (Figures 2.11 and 2.12). The Alberta oil sands are a major contributor. In fact, oil sands extraction is the primary reason why Alberta is the leading province in greenhouse gas emissions and why Alberta's emissions keep increasing. Extraction of bitumen also poses risks both to the local environment and to global warming. Open-pit mining is the worst offender and such mining takes place at several sites, including the Suncor mine (Photo 2.16). Environmental organizations, ranging from international ones such as Greenpeace and the Sierra Club to local ones such as the Pembina Institute, have long targeted the oil sands as a major source of greenhouse gas emissions and therefore one of the industrial culprits affecting global warming.

Although steps such as reclamation have been taken to reduce the severity of these impacts, greenhouse gas emissions from oil and gas production went up 23 per cent between 2000 and 2018, largely from increased oil sands production (Natural Resources Canada, 2020). Companies are under pressure to reduce their carbon footprint, and they are making progress by investing in technology. Natural Resources Canada (2020) reports a 30 per cent reduction per barrel of greenhouse gas emissions by bitumen production from 1990 to 2018. The main source of reductions came from co-generation, where oil sands companies used

THE CANADIAN PRESS/Jonathan Hayward

**PHOTO 2.15** An aerial view shows the damage caused by a tailing pond breach at the Mount Polley mine near the town of Likely, BC. The containment dam broke, discharging 25 million m³ of contaminated water and mining waste into nearby creeks and rivers. The BC government is now strengthening the rules for construction and maintenance of tailing ponds. Is this a case of closing the barn door after the horse has gone?

Cavan/Alamy Stock Photo

**PHOTO 2.16** Alberta's oil sands are a major source of greenhouse gases, both in the extraction and refining processes and in the ultimate burning of the oil produced. Decisions over economic growth or environmental sustainability usually favour economic growth. The oil sands and vast tailing ponds, such as those serving the Suncor oil sands operation near Fort McMurray, Alberta, are a consequence of production. While the oil sands produce the bulk of Canada's oil, the environmental cost is high, including huge greenhouse gas emissions from the upgrading of bitumen.

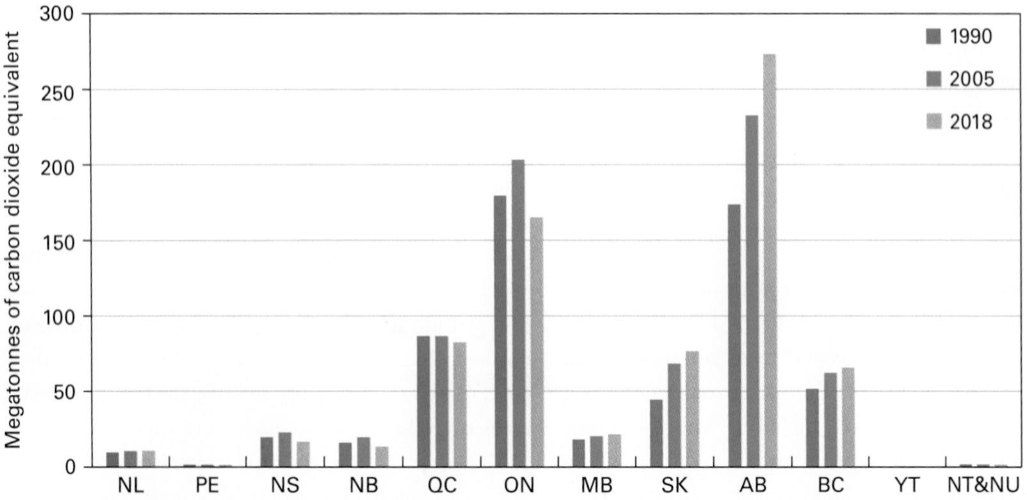

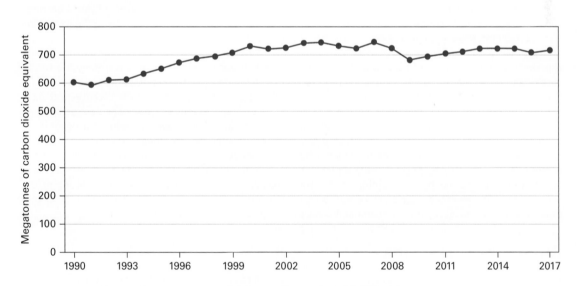

**FIGURE 2.11 Greenhouse gas emissions, by provinces and territories, Canada, 1990, 2005, and 2018.**

The largest contributors to Canada's greenhouse gas emissions are the energy and transportation sectors. Within the energy sector, oil and gas production and the production of electricity from coal-fired generators are the leading contributors. Oil sands development is singled out because it has much higher emissions than conventional oil production. Within the transportation sector, cars and trucks produce the greatest amount of these emissions.

Source: Environment Canada and Climate Change Canada 2020: https://www.canada.ca/en/environment-climate-change/services/environmental-indicators/green-house-gas-emissions.html

**FIGURE 2.12 Greenhouse gas emissions, Canada, 1990 to 2017**

Canada's annual emissions have increased slightly over the last few decades. On the other hand, global emissions increased at around 2 per cent annually over the same period. Despite long-standing warnings of a climate emergency, fossil fuel emissions—and with them global greenhouse gas emissions—continue to increase. In fact, global carbon emissions, though slowing, were expected to hit an all-time high in 2019 (Friedlingstein et al., 2019). China, followed by the United States, India, and the European Union, remain the major emitters with increases occurring in China and India.

Source: © Her Majesty the Queen in Right of Canada, as represented by the Minister of the Environment, 2020

co-generation to produce steam and electricity simultaneously. Still, increased oil sands production continues to see Alberta's total greenhouse gas emissions increasing (Figure 2.11).

## Air Pollution and Greenhouse Gas Emissions

Canadians are all too familiar with smog and other forms of **air pollution**. Most air pollution results from industrial emissions and from automobile and truck exhaust. Residents of Canada's major cities feel the effects of air pollution, including smog. Automobiles account for much of the urban pollution, while nationwide the main sources are coal-burning plants and oil sands production. These two sources also

account for most greenhouse gas emissions, followed by the internal combustion engines found in cars and trucks. All are under pressure to reduce greenhouse emissions. Many electric power stations are converting to natural gas, while the movement to electric cars is slow to develop. In total, Canada's effort to reduce greenhouse gas emissions has met with little success. Over the past decade, these emissions have remained around 700 megatonnes. The most recent data (2017) indicated that Canada's total GHG emissions reached 716 megatonnes of carbon dioxide equivalent (Mt $CO_2$ eq) (Figure 2.12). In 2017, the top three provinces by industrial emissions were Alberta, Ontario, and Quebec. Unlike the slow increase in emissions in Canada, global emissions have increased over the same time period (Friedlingstein et al., 2019).

## Summary

Physical geography varies across Canada. This spatial variation is critical in understanding Canada's regional character. Physiographic regions—large areas with similar landforms and geological structures—represent a basic measure of Canada's physical diversity and provide a broad and simple geomorphic framework for understanding Canada. Climate adds another dimension to physiography by creating a zonal arrangement of climate types, soils, natural vegetation, and wildlife across Canada. Physical and human worlds are linked, with some regions having a more favourable mix of physical characteristics for settlement and economic development. The Great Lakes–St Lawrence Lowlands region is the most favoured physical region in Canada and is also the most densely populated area. Physical barriers, such as the Rocky Mountains, slowed the expansion of Canada to the Pacific Ocean.

Canada has entered the Anthropocene epoch, in which our physical world is warming due to climate change. Global temperatures are predicted to continue to increase during the twenty-first century, perhaps reaching 3 per cent above the level recorded at the start of the Industrial Revolution. Dramatic changes no longer remain on the distant horizon. Scientists warn of a much different physical world by the end of this century, one that is much warmer and, with the melting of the Greenland Ice Sheet and those in Antarctica, that has much higher ocean levels.

## Challenge Questions

1. The warming of our world presents a major challenge, with those countries near the equator struggling in a much warmer climate. The albedo effect is causing the Canadian Arctic to warm more rapidly than other areas of Canada. What is the albedo effect and why is its impact much greater in the Arctic than in southern Canada?

2. What personal evidence do you have to suggest that climate change is affecting the area where you live? Such evidence could include warmer average temperatures, larger annual precipitation, more frequent flooding, and even higher home insurance rates.

3. Climatologists have determined that over the last 50 years the annual precipitation in

Canada has increased. How do they explain this phenomenon?

4.  Explain why Prince Rupert, at latitude 54°N, has a warmer January than Windsor, at 42°N (see Figure 2.5).

5.  The Mount Polley catastrophe was a classic example of the old idiom, "closing the barn door after the horse has gone." Discuss why the barn door is still open for the enormous tailing pond at the Suncor site in the Alberta oil sands.

6.  While many are calling for a swift shift to a fossil-free world, few governments have made much progress in this direction. Would you support a significant increase in the price of energy, such as doubling the price of gasoline? Why or why not?

## Essay Question

1.  Political decision often represents trade-offs. For example, curtailing the production of fossil fuels in Canada would not affect all regions equally. On the other hand, if Greta Thunberg is correct that the world is heading into a climate catastrophe, Ottawa and the provinces should increase their efforts to halt coal production and begin to apply the same policies to others forms of fossil fuels, starting with the worst polluters: bitumen from the oil sands. But since the regional impact would be felt chiefly in Alberta, should the federal government provide funding to transition to a fossil-free economy in that province?

# 3 Canada's Historical Geography

## Chapter Overview

In this chapter we will consider the following topics:

- The arrival of Canada's first people.
- The colonization of Canada by the French and the British.
- Treaties, the CPR, and settlement of Western Canada.
- The marginalization of Indigenous peoples.
- The spatial evolution of Canada.
- The unique place of Quebec in Canada.
- Federalism and regional tensions.

## Introduction

In one sense, Canada is a young country. Its formal history began in 1867 with the passing of the British North America (BNA) Act by the British Parliament. In another sense, Canada is an old country with a human history that goes back perhaps as far as 40,000 years. As an old country, its history has followed many twists and turns, but two events stand out because they continue to have a profound impact on the nature of Canadian society and its regions.

The arrival of the first people in North America marked the first event. The appearance of Europeans signalled the second event. The first clashes between European colonists and Indigenous peoples ended with Indigenous peoples losing their hunting lands and ways of life.

In the nineteenth century, the impact of colonization reached its peak with land surrenders through treaties, the passing of the **Indian Act**, and the establishment of residential boarding schools. While Indigenous populations declined, the capacity of their descendants to survive European assimilation efforts was remarkable. After 1867, the federal government illegally restricted the movement of Indigenous peoples through the **pass system**; outlawed traditional ceremonies, notably the sun dance and **potlatch**, by means of the Indian Act; and suppressed the Northwest Resistance. Treaties resulted in transferring title to the land from Indigenous peoples to the Crown—first the British government and later the Canadian government. The impact of

← Indigenous peoples have deeply influenced the historical geography in all regions of Canada. This inukshuk found in St-Michel de Bellechasse, Quebec, provides one example.

the colonization of North America by France and England and the establishment of British institutions, laws, and values, and, in the early twentieth century, the influx of people from Central Europe and czarist Russia, many of whom settled the prairie lands, have shaped Canada's historical geography. In later years, these newcomers provided the political push behind government-backed multicultural programs and policies and, at the same time, challenged the previous vision of a French/English Canada.

The search for solutions to these tensions between regions and groups is a dominant feature of modern Canadian society and, to a large degree, this process of seeking a middle ground accounts for many Canadians' high degree of acceptance of various religious and ethnic groups, as well as their desire to resolve regional disagreements. However, this tolerance did not magically appear, nor does it mean that Canadian society is free of intolerance. But a culture of tolerance has been "learned" over time—often after reconsidering past intolerant acts towards minority groups, especially towards Indigenous peoples and visible minorities, and these reconsiderations still continue today.

## The First People

The first people to set foot on North American soil were Old World hunters who, as early as 40,000 years ago, crossed a land bridge (known as Beringia) from Asia into Alaska and Yukon. Beringia was exposed with each ice advance when so much water was contained in the continental ice sheets that the sea level dropped by at least 100 m, thus exposing the ocean bottom between Siberia and Alaska. At the time of the Late Wisconsin ice advance some 18,000 years ago, these paleolithic hunter-gatherers had reached Alaska and Yukon but were blocked from proceeding south by an ice sheet that was perhaps 4 km thick (Figure 2.2).

Beginning around 15,000 years ago, the climate warmed and the Great Melt began. Why the climate warmed remains a puzzle, but the result was clear—the ice sheets began their retreat and eventually the Old World hunters migrated into the heart of North America (Dickason with McNab, 2009, p. 15). But just when these hunters arrived in the south and then evolved culturally into Paleo-Indian peoples poses one question. A second question involves which migration route they took.

Did paleolithic peoples from Asia travel beyond the ice sheets into the heart of North America as early as 30,000 years ago? What is the archaeological evidence? Solid evidence indicates that, some 13,500 years ago, the Paleo-Indians known as Clovis culture inhabited New Mexico. However, in 2016, archaeological finds in Florida and Mexico revealed that the Americas were occupied at least a thousand years earlier (Halligan et al., 2016; Ardelean et al., 2020). As a result, the question now becomes, how did these pre-Clovis peoples get to the heart of North America?

The first peopling of the Americas is a contested and evolving topic, with the exact timing of the earliest arrivals still unknown. At Chiquihuite Cave stone tools suggest Old World hunters may have reached Mexico and beyond well before 13,500 years ago. But just when and who they were remains a mystery. Ardelean et al. suggest Homo sapiens might have reach Mexico's Chiquihuite Cave well before the last ice age began—some 30,000 years ago—but they did not survive. Analysis of plant and animal DNA at the cave site supports this hypothesis by suggesting that the human occupation of the Chiquihuite Cave site took place some 30,000 years ago (Ardelean et al., 2020).

Until the evidence became clear that Old World hunters had reached the interior of North America before 13,500 years ago, the Corridor Route seemed to provide the answer. Accordingly, the Old World hunters who had been blocked from proceeding south by the ice sheet were now able to migrate south through the narrow ice-free route between the Cordillera and the Laurentide ice sheets (Figure 3.1). Archaeologists estimated that this ice-free corridor appeared about 14,000 years ago. However, Pedersen

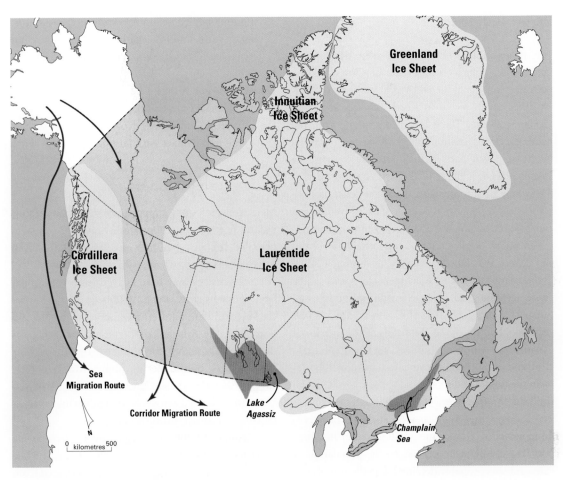

## FIGURE 3.1 Migration routes into North America

Archaeologists originally believed that the Corridor Route along the eastern edge of the Rocky Mountains was ice-free by 14,000 years ago, allowing the descendants of the Old World hunters to reach the heart of North America. More recently, the Sea Route has gained favour because it explains how human beings could have arrived south of the ice sheet before the Great Melt created the ice-free corridor between the two ice sheets (Pedersen et al., 2016; Hirst, 2019). The Sea Route is now the accepted path that historians believe Old World hunters used to reach the coast of British Columbia and beyond to the unglaciated lands of the United States, Mexico, and South America.

and colleagues (2016) demonstrate that natural vegetation and wildlife took another 1,000 years or so to make the Corridor biologically sustainable for human migration. As a result of this recent finding, the Corridor Route was clearly not the first passage taken by Old World hunters to the heart of North America. Nevertheless, this land route to the unglaciated lands of America remained an important natural route for more recent migrations from the Old World.

The Sea Route theory provides the most plausible explanation for the peopling of the Americas before 14,000 years ago (Hirst, 2019). The Old World hunters used an island-hopping system just off the sea edge of the Cordillera Ice Sheet. Once they reached the unglaciated US Pacific coast, these newcomers had access to the interior of North America and its rich flora and fauna well before 14,000 years ago. However, archaeological evidence of such a route is lacking because these ancient island campsites, if they existed, are now well below the current sea level, as is Beringia, where generations of Old World hunters likely lived before migrating further south into the North American continent. The Chiquihuite Cave supports this thesis (Ardelean et al., 2020).

## Paleo-Indians

The **Paleo-Indians**, the people who devised the fluted spear points characteristic of Clovis culture, were descendants of the Old World hunters. The oldest fluted points found in North America are about 13,500 years old. These spearheads, along with the bones of woolly mammoths, have been discovered in the southern part of the Canadian Prairies. By 11,000 years ago, many of the large species, such as the woolly mammoths and the mastodons, had become extinct, possibly as a result of excessive hunting and/or climatic change. Later Paleo-Indian cultures, which archaeologists refer to collectively as Folsom and Plano, developed a variety of unfluted stone points with stems for attachment to spear shafts. These technological changes made weapons more suitable for hunting buffalo and caribou. About 8,000 years ago, hunters in the grasslands of the interior of Canada used various techniques, such as the buffalo jump and the buffalo impound, to trap and kill buffalo. In the tundra and forest lands of northern Canada, similar techniques were employed to kill caribou.

Unlike larger prey species, such as the woolly mammoth, buffalo and caribou could not support large numbers of people, so the population of Paleo-Indians probably declined. Equally important, they had to develop new survival strategies. These strategies involved remaining in one area (and presumably keeping other peoples out of that area), developing effective hunting techniques for the local game, and making extensive use of fish and plants to supplement their principal diet of game. The time frame provided by Thomas (1999, p. 10) divides Paleo-Indians into three groups:

- Clovis culture from 13,500 to 12,500 years ago;
- Folsom culture from 11,000 to 10,200 years ago;
- Plano culture from 10,000 to 8,000 years ago.

This link between geographic territory and hunting societies marked the development of Paleo-Indian **culture areas** with the following two characteristics:

1. Each area had a common set of natural conditions that allowed a particular group of plants and animals to emerge.

2. Inhabitants, by using a common set of hunting, fishing, and food-gathering techniques and tools, harvested these plants and animals.

Under these conditions, Paleo-Indians formed more enduring social units that became the forerunners of the numerous Indigenous North American groups that came into contact with Europeans.

## Indigenous Peoples

Most archaeologists support the idea that Algonquians (e.g., Cree, Ojibwa) are direct descendants of Paleo-Indians, but they are less certain about Athapaskans (e.g., Dene, Chipewyan, Gwich'in), whose ancestors may have arrived from Asia much later, perhaps only some 10,000 years ago. Since the Paleo-Indian culture had emerged some 13,500 years ago, the Athapaskans represent a distinct Indigenous culture. But how did the early Athapaskans cross waters of the Bering Strait? Archaeologists suggest that the ancient ancestors of the Athapaskans either walked across the frozen Bering Strait or crossed it in small, primitive boats.

Around 12,000 years ago, the Laurentide Ice Sheet had retreated from the Interior Plains and the Great Lakes. At that time, climatic zones ranged from a tropical climate in Mexico to an Arctic climate just south of the Laurentide Ice Sheet that extended into the United States. The warmer climatic zones provided agricultural opportunities for early Indigenous groups in North America, marking a shift from the Paleolithic Age to the Neolithic Age. The most important differences between the two ages are:

- People were no longer nomadic but had permanent structures.
- People had a stable food supply.
- People had time to think about a variety of things, including art, governance, and religion.

About 5,000 years ago, Indigenous peoples living in the tropical climate of Mexico began to domesticate plants and animals. Corn, or maize, was a key crop (Ranere, 2009). This agricultural system and its people gradually spread northward into areas with more restrictive growing conditions. These climatic differences required Indigenous peoples to adapt their agricultural system accordingly. About 3,000 years ago, Indigenous peoples in what is today the eastern United States planted corn, beans, and squash (known as "the three sisters"), which supplemented their diet of game and fish. Table 3.1 outlines significant events in the peopling of what is today Canada to the time of contact with Europeans.

Geography controlled the spatial limits of agriculture. The growing season for corn and other crops was too short north of the Great Lakes–St Lawrence Lowlands. Algonquian-speaking Indigenous peoples who lived in the boreal forest north of the Great Lakes hunted big-game animals for sustenance. They also traded with those more sedentary Indigenous peoples, such as the Huron and Iroquois, who practised a form of slash-and-burn (swidden) agriculture in the Great Lakes–St Lawrence Lowlands and in the Ohio Valley. By the sixteenth century, the Huron controlled the agricultural lands between Lake Simcoe and the southeastern corner of Georgian Bay, where about 7,000 acres were under cultivation and where Indigenous villages with populations as large as 1,500 persons, and in some cases considerably larger, were commonplace (Dickason with McNab, 2009, pp. 46–7). In western North America, agriculture spread northward along the valleys of the Mississippi River and its major

## TABLE 3.1   Timeline: Old World Hunters to Contact with Europeans

| Date | Events: Possible and Actual |
| --- | --- |
| (BP = years before present) | |
| 40,000–35,000 BP | Old World hunters from Asia may have crossed the Beringia land bridge into the unglaciated areas of Alaska and southern Yukon but were blocked by the Cordillera Ice Sheet from moving into the rest of North America. Stone tools found in the Chiquihuite Cave support this thesis. |
| 35,000–32,000 BP | Corridor Route became ice-free in this interglacial period, and, in pursuing the woolly mammoth, Old World hunters may have found their way further south. |
| 24,000–18,000 BP | Late Wisconsin Ice Age: Old World hunters from Asia crossed the Beringia land bridge into the unglaciated areas of Alaska and southern Yukon, but were blocked by the ice sheet from moving into the rest of North America. |
| 20,000 BP | The Wisconsin ice sheets reach a maximum geographic extent, covering virtually all of Canada. |
| 15,000 BP | As the climate warmed, the ice sheets retreat rapidly in western Canada, exposing a narrow ice-free area along the foothills of the Rocky Mountains known as the Corridor Route. At the same time, the Cordillera Ice Sheet withdrew from the Pacific coast, making island-hopping along the Sea Route more amenable. |
| 13,500 BP | Carbon dating of stone points from the Clovis culture provides solid evidence of Paleo-Indian presence in New Mexico. |
| 11,000 BP | Mammoths and mastodons become extinct, forcing early inhabitants of North America to adjust their hunting practices to buffalo, caribou, and other animals. In doing so, they become more mobile and less numerous. |
| 5,000 BP | As the Arctic coast became ice-free, pre-Inuit hunters known as the Denbigh were the first people to cross the Bering Strait to the Arctic coast of Alaska. Within 2,000 years, they moved eastward along the Canadian section of the Arctic coast and eventually reached Greenland. |
| 3,000 BP | The Dorset people represented another wave of Arctic immigrants and, with a more advanced technology suited for an Arctic marine environment, they either absorbed or replaced the Denbigh hunters. What are believed by some scholars to have been the last Dorset people, known as Sadlermiut, lived in isolation principally on Southhampton Island in Hudson Bay and became extinct around 1902. |
| 1,000 CE (common era) | A third wave of Arctic hunters, known as the Thule, migrated across the Arctic, eventually reaching the coast of Labrador. Their primary source of food was the bowhead whale. At the same time Vikings reached Greenland and North America, where they established a settlement on the north coast of Newfoundland (L'Anse aux Meadows). |
| 1450 CE | Climate cooling marked the onset of the Little Ice Age. Both Thule and Vikings suffered in the colder environment with the Viking settlement disappearing and the Thule culture evolving from hunters of bowhead whales to the Inuit culture of small-game hunters (see Vignette 2.13). |
| 1497 CE | John Cabot lands on the east coast (Newfoundland or Nova Scotia). |
| 1534 CE | Jacques Cartier plants the flag of France near Baie de Chaleur. |
| 1576 CE | Martin Frobisher sails to Baffin Island and makes contact with Inuit. |

Source: Friedlingstein, Pierre, et al. 2019. Earth System Science Data, 11, 1783-1838, 2019, DOI: 10.5194/essd-11-1783-2019.

**THINK ABOUT IT**

In all societies, food security is a critical element. Which of the two groups—the Old World hunters or the Huron agriculturalists—would have better food security and thus be less likely to face starvation?

A discussion of the Little Ice Age is found in **Vignette 2.12**, "Fluctuations in World Temperatures," page 46.

tributary, the Missouri River. Tribes on the Canadian Prairies engaged in trade for agricultural products with tribes along the upper reaches of the Missouri River. In the Northwest, Athapaskan-speaking Indigenous peoples, whose ancestors probably came from Asia much later (perhaps between 7,000 and 10,000 years ago), continued to engage in a nomadic lifestyle of hunting and gathering. They moved about in the boreal forest stalking big-game animals and made summer hunting trips to the tundra where the caribou had their calving grounds.

## Arctic Migration

Arctic Canada became a human habitat much later than the forested lands of the Subarctic. Before humans could occupy the Arctic, two developments were necessary. The first was the melting of the ice sheets that covered this physiographic region. About 8,000 years ago, the western Arctic was ice-free and only small remnants of the great Laurentide Ice Sheet remained in mountains found in northeastern Canada. Equally critical, open water in the summer facilitated the dispersal of Arctic peoples across the northern tip of Canada. The second development

**PHOTO 3.1** A tent ring located near Igloolik, Nunavut. The stone ring indicates the edges of the tent's skin walls, which were weighted down with rocks. Tent rings similar to this one mark sites where Thule families located their tents.

was the emergence of a hunting technique that would enable people to live in an Arctic marine environment. About 5,000 years ago, the pre-Inuit had developed an Arctic sea-based hunting tradition. Shortly thereafter, they began to move eastward from coastal Siberia to the marine environment of Alaska and then into Arctic Canada. This pre-Inuit hunting culture is known as the Denbigh. Unlike previous marine hunting societies, these people invented a harpoon and other tools that enabled them to hunt seals and other marine mammals, though they also relied heavily on terrestrial game such as the caribou. About 3,000 years ago, a second migration from Alaska took place. Known as the Dorset culture, this culture replaced the Denbigh. The third and final Arctic migration took place roughly 1,000 years ago, when the Thule people, who had developed a sophisticated sea-hunting culture, spread eastward from Alaska and gradually succeeded their predecessors. The Thule, the ancestors of the Inuit, hunted the bowhead whale and the walrus. Like the woolly mammoth, bowhead whales provided a huge amount of meat, permitting a more sedentary lifestyle where clusters of Thule families lived together, forming a relatively large population for paleolithic peoples.

The climate, however, began to cool around 1450, marking the start of the Little Ice Age. The impact of a cooler climate had a dramatic impact on the Thule because their principal source of food, the bowhead whale, ceased to migrate to the now ice-covered Arctic Ocean (Vignette 2.12). The Thule were forced to become more nomadic and rely on smaller game such as seals and caribou. Around the time of Frobisher's visit to Baffin Island in 1576, the Thule culture was transforming into an Inuit one.

## Initial Contacts and Depopulation

Long before the time of European contact, the descendants of Old World hunters occupied all of North and South America. Yet, Europeans considered the New World **terra nullius** or empty lands. North American First Nations and Inuit tribes met the European explorers searching for a trade route to the Orient. While the total population of these tribes can only be estimated, many scholars now believe there may have been as many as 500,000 First Nations peoples and Inuit living in Canada at the time of first contact. Following contact, their numbers dropped sharply, perhaps declining to 100,000. Diseases introduced by Europeans were the principal reason for this remarkable decline. By 1871, the Census of Canada reported an Indigenous population of 122,700 (Romaniuc, 2000, p. 136). Besides the loss of life attributed to new diseases, Indigenous peoples in southern Canada were pushed aside to allow the occupation of fertile lands by settlers.

The geographic distribution of the Indigenous population was not evenly spread across Canada but heavily concentrated in more favourable areas—the very areas desired by European settlers. For example, the largest populations were found along the Pacific coast, where marine resources provided abundant food, and in the Great Lakes–St Lawrence Lowlands, where hunting combined with agriculture based primarily on corn supported relatively large sedentary populations.

## Huronia

In the early seventeenth century, the sudden collapse of Huronia, the most powerful Indigenous group in the region, took place shortly after contact with the French. Their numbers dropped from 21,000 to less than half this number within a decade. This demographic catastrophe was not unique to Huronia, but it does provide one example of the deadly impact of European diseases and the cost of colonial alliances on Indigenous groups. French missionaries unwittingly brought diseases to the Huron villages, while the Iroquois, who opposed the French–Huron alliance, attacked the weakened Huron in 1649, thus destroying the Huron Confederacy. From the peak of their power in the first years of the seventeenth century (Figure 3.2), the Huron Confederacy had collapsed in little more than a generation. Huron villages were abandoned, the cornfields of Huronia reverted to forest, and its people were greatly reduced in numbers and scattered across the land, some finding their way to the French fortress at Quebec City, where they eventually formed an urban reserve known as Wendake; others were

**PHOTO 3.2** Relationships between European explorers and Indigenous peoples were often tense. In this painting by John White, the artist, a member of Frobisher's second expedition in 1577, records a fight between Frobisher's crew and Baffin Island Inuit.

captured or assimilated by the Iroquois, and some joined related Indigenous groups in what are today Michigan and Ohio.

## Big Bear and Treaty 6

Centuries later, the Indigenous peoples of the Great Plains faced a similar challenge. With the demise of their principal source of food, the buffalo, and the arrival of European settlers, these Indigenous groups faced a bleak future. Disease and hunger reduced their numbers. The Cree had little choice but to sign treaties and surrender their claim to the vast Prairies, living instead on a series of small landholdings called reserves. Unlike other chiefs, **Big Bear** (Mistahimaskwa) refused to sign Treaty 6 of 1876, only relenting six years later when his people were starving.

**FIGURE 3.2 The land of the Hurons**

Cahiagué was a Huron village serving as an assembly place for warriors from the surrounding area. From here, the Huron warriors staged attacks on the Iroquois villages south of Lake Ontario. In 1615, Champlain joined the Huron in an attack on the village of Onondagas.

Source: Route Champlain (2017).

He sought to unite the Cree and negotiate with Ottawa for a single large Cree reserve on the northern Saskatchewan River. Following the North West Rebellion of 1885 (better known as the Northwest Resistance in Indigenous historiography), Big Bear was arrested, convicted of treason-felony, and sentenced to three years in prison. He died in 1888.

## Culture Regions

At the time of contact with Europeans, Indigenous peoples occupied specific territories (cultural regions). Within each cultural region, these first human inhabitants developed distinct techniques suitable for the local environment and wildlife. The seven culture regions in present-day Canada are the Eastern Woodlands, Eastern Subarctic, Western Subarctic, Arctic, Plains, Plateau, and Northwest Coast (Figure 3.3). The Inuit occupied the Arctic cultural region. In the Eastern Subarctic, the Cree were the principal Algonquian group, and further east the Innu (Naskapi and Montagnais) resided. The Cree in this region had developed a technology— snowshoes—to hunt moose in deep snow. In the Western Subarctic, the Dene tribes hunted caribou and other big-game animals. Indigenous peoples of the Northwest Coast harvested the rich marine life found along the Pacific coast. Tribes such as the Haida, Nootka (Nuu-chah-nulth), and Salish comprised the Northwest Coast cultural region. In the southern interior of British Columbia, the Plateau peoples—including the Carrier, Lillooet, Okanagan, and Shuswap—occupied the valleys of the Cordillera, forming the Plateau cultural region.

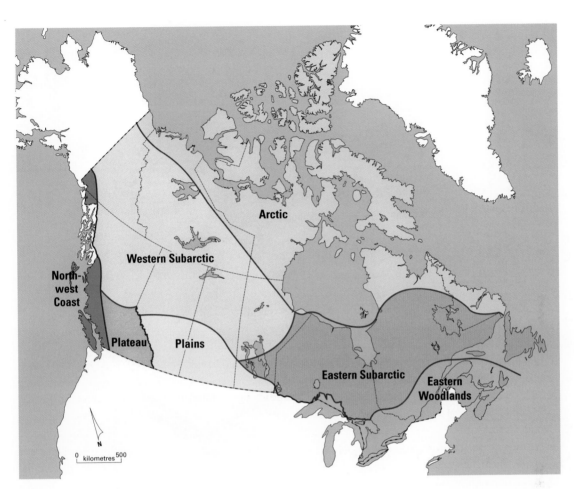

**FIGURE 3.3 Culture regions of Indigenous peoples**

Across the grasslands of the Canadian West, Plains peoples—such as the Assiniboine, Blackfoot, Sarcee, and Plains Cree—hunted bison. The Iroquois and Huron were among those living in the Eastern Woodlands of southern Ontario and Quebec, although the Iroquois were primarily based further south, in present-day New York State. Both groups combined agriculture with hunting. In the Maritimes, the Mi'kmaq and Maliseet also occupied the Eastern Woodlands, where they hunted and fished. The complexity and diversity of Indigenous peoples can be gleaned from the spatial arrangement of their languages (Figure 3.4).

## The Second People

The colonization of North America by the French and the British set the stage for Canada's early settler history. While France and England established colonies in North America in the seventeenth century, the original inhabitants were forced to retreat. Quebec City, founded in 1608 by Samuel de Champlain, was the first permanent settlement in Canada. By 1663, the French population in New France was about 3,000 compared to a population of about 10,000 Indigenous peoples (mainly Huron and Iroquois), who lived in the same area of the St Lawrence Valley, the Great Lakes, and the Ohio Basin. By 1750, the French Canadians numbered about 60,000, while the Indigenous population continued to drop because of disease and warfare. Following the British Conquest of New France in 1759, the flow of French colonists ceased and British immigrants began to move to what used to be New France. Meanwhile, the French-Canadian population depended entirely on natural population increase for its population growth.

**THINK ABOUT IT**

European countries claimed various parts of North America. What was the basis of their claim of sovereignty over lands they "discovered"?

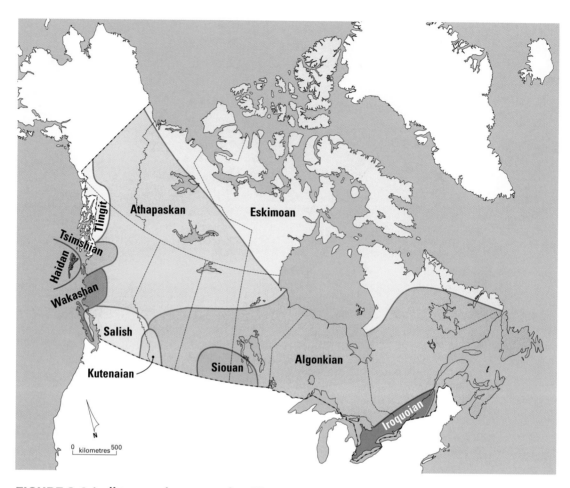

**FIGURE 3.4 Indigenous language families**

Indigenous peoples in Canada form a very diverse population. At the time of contact, there were over 50 distinct Indigenous languages spoken. These languages formed 11 language families, five of which were in one natural cultural region, the Northwest Coast. Following contact, language loss was swift. By the end of the twentieth century, only three Indigenous languages, Cree, Inuktitut, and Ojibwa, had over 20,000 speakers.

## The First Wave of British Immigrants

The first large contingent of British immigrants to Canada consisted of Loyalists who had supported Britain during the American War of Independence (1775–83). After the defeat of the British army, they sought refuge in other parts of the British Empire, including its North American possessions. In North America, most Loyalists settled in Nova Scotia, while a smaller number moved to the Eastern Townships of Quebec and to Montreal. Others settled in what is now southern Ontario. At the end of the American War of Independence, the forty-fifth parallel was established as the border between Lower Canada (Quebec) and New York State and Vermont. The St Lawrence River and the Great Lakes became the boundary between Upper Canada and the United States.

## The Second Wave of British Immigrants

The second wave of British immigrants occurred in the first half of the nineteenth century. Almost a million people migrated from Britain to British North America, most landing in Quebec and Ontario. In the 1840s, for example, the potato famines in Ireland caused terrible hardships. Thousands

© North Wind Picture Archives

**PHOTO 3.3** The American Revolution (1775–83) divided the residents of the Thirteen Colonies. With the defeat of British forces, those British subjects who did not support the revolutionary cause were forced to leave, losing their property and sometimes their lives. Considered traitors by Americans, Loyalists were often subjected to mob violence.

fled the countryside and many left for North America, settling in the towns and cities of British North America and the United States. The Highlanders in northern Scotland faced similar hardships. They became the Selkirk settlers and founded the Red River Colony. In 1812, they arrived in York Factory and proceeded by the Nelson and Red rivers to the point where Winnipeg now stands.

British immigrants greatly changed Canada, by turning the demographic balance of power from a French-Canadian majority to an English-speaking one. At the time of Confederation in 1867, the population of British North America had reached 3 million, with over 60 per cent of British descent. While the French Canadians were concentrated in Quebec and New Brunswick, most English speakers lived in Upper Canada, the major cities in Quebec, and the Maritimes. Across the rest of British North America, Indigenous peoples made up most of the population.

In the Red River Settlement, a new Indigenous people, the Métis, who were of Indigenous and European descent, had emerged. By 1869, the Métis, who were split between French- and English-speaking, greatly outnumbered European residents, some of whom were descendants of the Selkirk settlers. The Métis formed over 80 per cent of the 12,000 members of the Red River Settlement (Table 3.2).

The population of British North America began to change after the War of 1812–14. At that time, the population was almost entirely English or French. Now migration brought other members of Great Britain to the shores of Canada. The Irish were the largest group, followed by Scottish and Welsh migrants. Moreover, by the 1860s, Canada's ethnic character varied by region. In Atlantic Canada, the Scottish and Irish outnumbered the English. In Quebec, the English and Irish formed a sizable minority in the towns and cities, though rural Quebec

The Death of Brock at Queenston Heights, [ca.1908]. C. W. Jefferys. Watercolour on paper, 25.4 cm x 38.1 cm (10"x 15"). Government of Ontario Art Collection, 619,871. Archives of Ontario, Toronto.

**PHOTO 3.4** The death of General Brock at Queenston Heights. On 13 October 1812, the first major battle of the War of 1812 took place when American troops crossed the Niagara River with the objective of establishing a military base on Canadian soil before winter set in. British troops, Canadian militia, and Mohawk warriors repelled the invaders, forcing the Americans to retreat back into the United States. Early in the battle, General Isaac Brock was mortally shot while he led a charge on American forces who had taken a strategic position at the top of Queenston Heights. The War of 1812 was a stalemate, though both the British/Canadians and the Americans claimed victory. As Laxer (2012, p. 1) points out, however, the Indigenous forces led by Tecumseh lost, and Tecumseh lost his life in battle at Moraviantown in present-day southern Ontario. Inevitably, then, the war failed to halt the unyielding westward march of settlers, first in America and later in Canada. This C.W. Jefferys painting, *c*. 1908, romantically and heroically depicts Brock's death.

| TABLE 3.2 Population of the Red River Settlement, 1869 | | |
| --- | --- | --- |
| Ethnic Group | Population Size | Population Percentage |
| **Europeans born in Canada** | 294 | 2.5 |
| **Europeans born in Britain or a foreign country** | 524 | 4.4 |
| **Indigenous peoples** | 558 | 4.7 |
| **Europeans born in Red River** | 747 | 6.2 |
| **English-speaking Métis** | 4,083 | 34.1 |
| **French-speaking Métis** | 5,757 | 48.1 |
| **Total population** | 11,963 | 100.0 |

Source: Adapted from Lower (1983, p. 96).

remained solidly French-speaking except in the Eastern Townships. Ontario, like Atlantic Canada, was decidedly British.

Canada began as a collection of four small British colonies—Upper and Lower Canada, New Brunswick, and Nova Scotia—with a population under 4 million. Under the leadership of Prime Minister John A. Macdonald, Canada expanded territorially to become the second-largest country in the world. The building of a transcontinental railway was one of his accomplishments, but his treatment of the Indigenous population was harsh and, in today's light, racist. Under his reign, residential schools were established with the purpose of assimilating

Indigenous children. In 2018, as an act of reconciliation, the city of Victoria removed John A. Macdonald's statue from the front of City Hall.

## The Third People

In 1870, Ottawa obtained the vast land of the Hudson's Bay Company and was faced with the question of settling this territory. Few settlers arrived until after treaties were signed with various Indigenous Plains groups, the completion of a land survey, and the driving of the final spike in the Canadian Pacific Railway in November 1885.

### The Land Survey of Western Canada

The land survey system was crucial to the European settling of the Prairies and, in turn, this system organized the human landscape into townships and sections. In 1872, the federal government passed the Dominion Lands Act. This legislation established a survey system that divided the land into square townships made up of 36 sections, each measuring 1 mile by 1 mile, with allowances for roads. Each section was further subdivided into four quarters, each quarter section measuring one-half mile by one-half mile and comprising 160 acres. This survey system gave the Canadian Prairies a distinctive "checkerboard" pattern. This survey system also sparked a negative reaction in the Red River Settlement, where the Métis already had their own land ownership system. The clash between the Red River Settlement and Ottawa led to the Red River Rebellion or, from the Métis perspective, the Red River Resistance.

### Unity through the CPR

Prime Minister Macdonald envisioned a transcontinental railway that would bind the West to Canada. Without a railway, Macdonald realized that those living in the Red River Valley saw St Paul, Minnesota, as their natural market for trade and that this north–south linkage could cause the West to drift into the orbit of the United States. Macdonald feared that American settlers would turn to the fertile lands in the Red River Valley and then beyond into the Canadian Prairies—a repeat of the annexation of the Oregon Territory in 1846 (Vignette 3.3). He knew that British Columbia, isolated on the Pacific coast, felt the same north/south pull of the United States. In 1871, Macdonald made a daring decision by promising to build a railway across Canada to unite the country. By 1885, his promise came true, and the Canadian Pacific Railway (CPR) remains one of Macdonald's greatest legacies. Canada's first transcontinental railway has been the subject of numerous books and songs. These include Pierre Berton's books *The National Dream* (1970) and *The Last Spike* (1972), Gordon Lightfoot's well-known song "Canadian Railroad Trilogy," and Harold Innis's *A History of Canadian Pacific Railway* (1923). There is, however, a much darker side when it comes to Prime Minister Macdonald's relations with Indigenous peoples. Macdonald pursued an assimilation policy by way of the Indian Act of 1876 and residential schools. These measures were widely accepted by Canadian society of the day but are now considered repressive colonial efforts to subjugate the original peoples of the Prairies.

### Settling the Land

In the late nineteenth century, the last large area of arable lands in North America was opened to settlers. A free grant of one quarter section was available to persons 21 years or older with the payment of a $10 fee. Upon fulfilling cultivation and residency requirements within three years of acquiring the property, the **homesteader** would receive title to the land. Since Ottawa had made substantial land grants to the Canadian Pacific Railway and to the Hudson's Bay Company (HBC), not all the land was free. Both the CPR and the HBC sold their land at market prices, thus making a considerable profit.

For Canada, occupying the Prairies allowed the country to expand its population and to remove the threat of America annexing these lands. Also, the creation of a grain economy would provide freight for the Canadian Pacific Railway, thereby helping turn it into a viable operation. But where to find such people? Some came from Ontario, Quebec, and Atlantic Canada to claim their 160 acres as homesteaders; others came from Britain and the United States. But the bulk came from non-English-speaking

Further discussion of two visions of Canada is found later in this chapter in the section "One Country, Two Visions" page 107.

**THINK ABOUT IT** Homesteaders far from the railway had to use local resources for building materials. What resource was readily available in the prairie landscape for the construction of houses?

countries in Continental Europe and czarist Russia. As these settlers came west, the hegemony of the British and French was broken and Western Canada became a mixture of British, French, and non-English-speaking people. At the same time, the original Indigenous peoples of the Plains were left out of this hegemony and, instead, were swept aside from these nation-forming events, isolated on their reserves, and under pressure to assimilate.

By the end of the nineteenth century, much of Western Canada still was not occupied. Clifford Sifton, the minister of the interior, accepted the challenge to settle the West. By the beginning of the twentieth century, Sifton had launched an aggressive and innovative advertising campaign to lure people from Britain and the United States to "The Last Best West," but this effort failed to bring sufficient immigrants. At that point, he recognized the need to go beyond these two countries. In a break with past immigration policy, Sifton turned his attention to the people of Central Europe, Scandinavia, and czarist Russia. Land-hungry peasants from Ukraine formed the largest single group of immigrants but Doukhobors and German-speaking Mennonites also came from czarist Russia, giving Western Canada a distinct and different mix of ethnic groups and landholdings, with

communal rather than individual landholdings the norm among some groups. From 1901 to 1921, Western Canada's population increased from 400,000 to 2 million, and Saskatchewan became the third-most populous province by 1921 (Table 3.3). As these ethnic groups and individuals spread across the Prairies, their impact was enormous on a natural landscape that only recently had felt the hooves of vast herds of buffalo and of the horses of Indigenous hunting groups (see Kerr & Holdsworth, 1990, Plate 17).

By opening the door for immigration from European countries without a French or British background, Sifton's immigration policy changed the face of Canada. His goal of settling the West was accomplished, and a new dimension had been added to Canada's social fabric—people with neither a French nor a British background who eventually would press Ottawa for a multicultural, rather than a bicultural, interpretation of Canada. Shortly after the settling of Western Canada, this new region saw its self-interests in conflict with those of Central Canada. Signs of western alienation appeared, often centred on a sense of exploitation. One particular complaint was aimed at the CPR. According to farmers, the CPR charged them far too much to ship their grain to British and other European markets.

### TABLE 3.3    Canada's Population by Provinces and Territories, 1901 and 1921

| Political Unit | Population 1901 | % of Total Population | Population 1921 | % of Total Population |
|---|---|---|---|---|
| Ontario | 2,182,947 | 40.6 | 2,933,662 | 33.4 |
| Quebec | 1,648,898 | 30.7 | 2,360,510 | 26.9 |
| Nova Scotia | 459,574 | 8.6 | 523,837 | 6.0 |
| New Brunswick | 331,120 | 6.2 | 387,876 | 4.4 |
| Manitoba | 255,211 | 4.8 | 610,118 | 6.9 |
| Northwest Territories* | 20,129 | 0.4 | 8,143 | 0.1 |
| Prince Edward Island | 103,259 | 1.9 | 88,615 | 1.0 |
| British Columbia | 178,657 | 3.3 | 524,582 | 6.0 |
| Yukon | 27,219 | 0.5 | 4,147 | 0.1 |
| Saskatchewan | 91,279* | 1.7 | 757,510 | 8.6 |
| Alberta | 73,022* | 1.3 | 588,454 | 6.7 |
| Canada | 5,371,315 | 100.0 | 8,787,949** | 100.0 |

*Saskatchewan and Alberta did not become provinces until 1905. In 1901 they were officially included in the population of the Northwest Territories, but for ease of comparison over the two time periods I have identified their 1901 populations.
**Includes 485 members of the armed forces.
Source: Adapted from Statistics Canada (2003).

The farmers wanted to break the CPR's monopoly by building the Hudson Bay Railway to Churchill, Manitoba. As a result of this pressure on Ottawa, the government of Canada provided public funds for the railway prior to World War I. Construction ceased during the Great War but then recommenced until the railway was completed in 1929.

## The Territorial Evolution of Canada

Canada's formal history as a nation began with the proclamation of the British North America Act on 1 July 1867. This Act of the British Parliament united the colonies of New Brunswick, Nova Scotia, and the Province of Canada (formerly Upper Canada and Lower Canada) into the Dominion of Canada.[1] Canada soon acquired more territory. In 1870, the Deed of Surrender transferred Rupert's Land and the North-Western Territory to the federal government, at which time this large expanse that had been under HBC control was renamed the North-West Territories. In 1871, British Columbia joined Confederation, and Prince Edward Island followed two years later. In 1880, Ottawa acquired the Arctic Archipelago from Great Britain. Thus, while Canada began as a small country, consisting of what is now known as southern Ontario, southern Quebec, New Brunswick, and Nova Scotia, it quickly became one of the largest in the world (Figures 3.5 and 3.6).

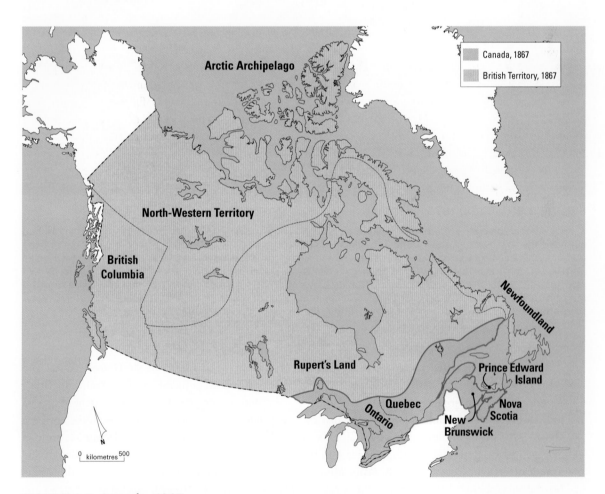

**FIGURE 3.5 Canada, 1867**

At Confederation, Canada, consisting of Ontario, Quebec, Nova Scotia, and New Brunswick, was only a fraction of its current territorial extent. The Hudson's Bay Company controlled most of British North America, including Rupert's Land and the North-Western Territory. With the transfer of these British lands to Canada, a transcontinental nation was born (Table 3.4).

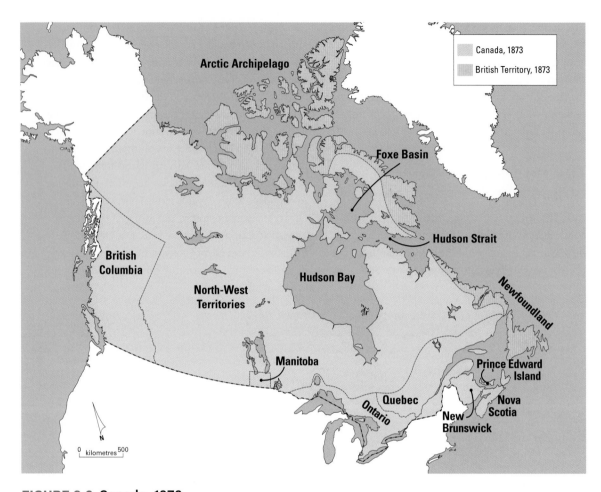

**FIGURE 3.6  Canada, 1873**

Canada's geographic extent increased between 1867 and 1873. During that short span of time, Canada had obtained the vast Hudson's Bay Company lands (including the Red River Settlement and a small part of the Arctic Archipelago whose streams flow into Hudson Bay and Foxe Basin) as well as two British colonies (British Columbia and Prince Edward Island). For the North-Western Territory and Rupert's Land, the Crown paid the HBC £300,000, granted the Company one-twentieth of the lands in the Canadian Prairies, and allowed it to keep its 120 trading posts and adjoining land. In 1870, these lands were renamed the North-West Territories. In 1880, Britain transferred the Arctic Archipelago to Canada (see Vignette 3.2).

At the time of Confederation, Ottawa was concerned about American designs on British North America. These concerns were caused by the American **Manifest Destiny** philosophy, a belief that the United States would eventually expand to all parts of North America, thus incorporating Canada into the American republic. Not surprisingly, Prime Minister Macdonald recognized that a trans-Canada railway could unite all British territories into one country and dampen American thoughts of grabbing more territory. Oddly enough, many Americans came

north to take advantage of the Homestead Act and became important members of the Prairie society.

Within a decade, the territorial extent of Canada expanded from four British colonies to the northern half of North America. The new Dominion grew in size with the addition of other British colonies and territories and the creation of new political jurisdictions (Figure 3.6). Negotiations between Ottawa and the British colonies in British Columbia and Prince Edward Island soon brought them into the fold of Confederation, in 1871 and 1873, respectively.

## Vignette 3.1

### Manitoba: Negotiating into Confederation

Immediately after Confederation, the federal government saw no need to involve the peoples of the newly acquired lands from the Hudson's Bay Company. The Métis of the Red River Colony thought otherwise. They formed a provisional government in order to negotiate the entry of the Red River Settlement into Confederation. In 1869, the Métis went to Ottawa to discuss their terms. They wanted assurances that their rights would be respected, their lands would be adopted into the Canadian land survey, and their way of life would be protected. While the government of John A. Macdonald agreed, a flood of newcomers from Ontario arrived and soon took over the newly formed province. While the Métis won concessions, circumstances drove many of them to Saskatchewan where they created another version of the Red River Colony.

The "numbered treaties" began the process of assimilation of Indigenous tribes in the West. The first treaty was achieved in 1871. No such negotiations took place with the Red River Métis. The result was the Red River uprising of 1869–70, the formation of the Métis Provisional Government, and then negotiations with Ottawa that led to the Manitoba Act of 1870 and entry into Confederation of a small part of what is today Manitoba (Vignette 3.1). In 1870, Manitoba consisted of the Red River Settlement and surrounding area. Sometimes referred to as the "Postage Stamp Province," Manitoba reached its present geographic size after gaining territory in 1881 and 1912.

By 1880, Canada stretched from the Atlantic to the Pacific and north to the Arctic. However, political control over its western lands was limited for two reasons—there were few people and no transportation link existed between the western regions and Central Canada. Still, Canada had begun the slow journey to independence and nationhood. By 1882, its political geography took on a new look with four districts in what is now Alberta and Saskatchewan. These administrative districts were Athabasca, Alberta, Saskatchewan, and Assiniboia (Figure 3.7). At the same time, Manitoba (then Assiniboia) and Ontario vied for the land known as the "disputed area." In 1899, this land was awarded to Ontario. In 1905 the provinces of Alberta and Saskatchewan were created, and much later, in 1949, Newfoundland joined Canada, completing the union of British North America into a single political entity.

(The territorial evolution of Canada is illustrated in Figures 3.5 to 3.10 and Table 3.4.)

## National Boundaries

Well before Confederation in 1867, wars and treaties between Britain and the United States shaped many of Canada's boundaries. The southern boundary of New Brunswick, Quebec, and Ontario was settled in 1783 when Britain and the United States signed the Treaty of Paris. Under this treaty, the United States gained control of the Indigenous lands of the Ohio Basin, with Britain controlling Quebec lands draining into the St Lawrence River. Earlier, in the Royal Proclamation of 1763, Britain had formally recognized the rights of "Indians" to the lands of the Ohio Basin, and to the north and west, which provided the constitutional framework for negotiating treaties with Indigenous peoples. This recognition was the basis of Indigenous rights in Canada (see "Indigenous Rights" in this chapter). Based on the fur trade route to the western interior, the boundary of 1783 passed through the Great Lakes to Lake of the Woods. In 1818, Canada's southern boundary was set at 49°N from Lake of the Woods to the Rocky Mountains. As for the northwestern boundary, Britain and Russia set the northern boundary at 141°W (the Treaty of St Petersburg, 1825). In Atlantic Canada, the boundary between Maine and New Brunswick had not been precisely defined in 1783, and in 1842 Britain and the United States finalized the boundary in the Webster-Ashburton Treaty.

For further discussion of the first Louis Riel-led resistance, see "The First Clash: The Red River Resistance of 1869–70," page 96.

See **Vignette 11.2**, "The Northwest Passage and the Franklin Search," for discussion of the lost Franklin expedition and the search that only ended in 2016.

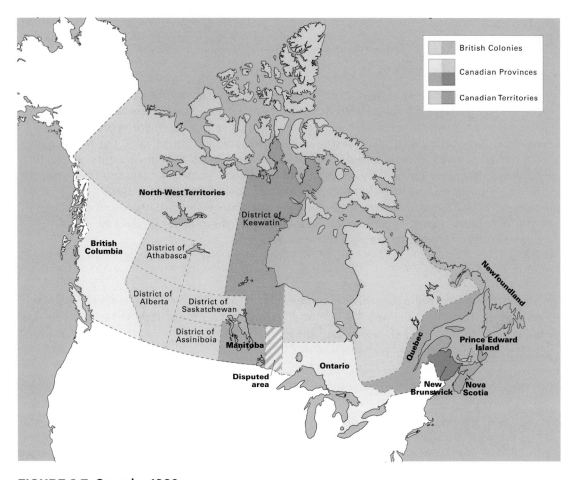

**FIGURE 3.7  Canada, 1882**

Governance west of Ontario consisted of two provinces, Manitoba and British Columbia, plus four districts designed to provide a minimum of administrative services to the yet-to-be settled Prairies. The key to settlement and later two more provinces would be the construction of the Canadian Pacific Railway. By the start of 1882, the prairie section of the CPR extended from Winnipeg to just west of Brandon. This and other railway building bound Canada together (see Morrison, 2003).

**TABLE 3.4  Timeline: Territorial Evolution of Canada**

| Date | Event |
|------|-------|
| 1867 | Ontario, Quebec, New Brunswick, and Nova Scotia unite to form the Dominion of Canada. |
| 1870 | The Hudson's Bay Company's lands are transferred by Britain to Canada. The Red River Colony enters Confederation as the province of Manitoba. |
| 1871 | British Columbia joins Canada. |
| 1873 | Prince Edward Island becomes the seventh province of Canada. |
| 1880 | Great Britain transfers its claim to the Arctic Archipelago to Canada. |
| 1949 | Newfoundland joins Canada to become the tenth province. |

In the early nineteenth century, the border separating Canada's western territories from the United States was not well defined. In fact, it depended on the natural boundary between Rupert's Land and the Louisiana Territory. Those lands whose waters flow into Hudson Bay were defined as Rupert's Land, while the rivers draining into the Mississippi River system defined the geographic extent of the Louisiana Territory. Some oddities resulted—Rupert's Land extended into Minnesota and North Dakota while the basin of the Missouri River reached into what is now Canada. In 1818, Britain and the United States decided on a compromise where the forty-ninth parallel west of Lake of the Woods made more sense. Following the Oregon Boundary

## Vignette 3.2

### The Transfer of the Arctic Archipelago to Canada

As with the transfer of Hudson's Bay lands in 1870, the territorial size of Canada was greatly increased when Great Britain transferred the Arctic Archipelago to Canada in 1880. Ten years earlier, Canada had acquired the small portion of these lands that drained into Hudson Bay, which included the western half of Baffin Island and several islands located in Hudson Strait, Hudson Bay, and Foxe Basin. Britain's claim to this vast archipelago was based on its naval exploration of the Arctic Ocean. The first venture by Britain into these waters took place in 1576 when Martin Frobisher and his crew sailed to southern Baffin Island. The most intensive exploration took place in the mid-nineteenth century with the search for the lost British naval expedition led by Sir John Franklin.

Treaty of 1846, the forty-ninth parallel boundary was extended to the Pacific coast (Vignette 3.3). With the establishment of the North American Boundary Commission in 1872, the boundary line across the Prairies was surveyed and marked (see Photo 3.5). At this time, the Indigenous peoples of the Prairies roamed the land while the Métis were based at the Red River Settlement.

### Internal Boundaries

Since Confederation, the internal boundaries of Canada have evolved (Figures 3.5–3.10). In 1898 Yukon Territory was created in reaction to the Yukon gold rush, and in 1905 Alberta and Saskatchewan were carved out of former Hudson's Bay lands. In 1949 the former British colony of Newfoundland (more recently renamed as Newfoundland and Labrador) joined Confederation, and in 1999 Nunavut was hived off from the Northwest Territories to become the third territory.

In 1870, the boundary of Manitoba formed a tiny rectangle comprising little more than the Red River Settlement. The province's western boundary, while extended in 1881 and 1884, did not reach its present limit until 1912, at the same time that Ontario and Quebec reached their present northern extents. (In all cases, these political changes took

## Vignette 3.3

### The Loss of the Oregon Territory

The last major territorial dispute between Britain and the United States took place over the **Oregon Territory**, which included present-day Oregon, Washington, Idaho, and small portions of Montana and Wyoming, as well coastal British Columbia and Vancouver Island. Britain's claim to the Oregon Territory hinged on exploration and the fur trade while the American claim was based on the large number of recent settlers who cultivated the fertile soils of the Willamette Valley. In the final outcome, there was no doubt that occupancy was a more powerful claim to disputed lands than that based on exploration and the presence of a fur-trading economy. Too late, the British urged the HBC to bring settlers from Fort Garry to the Oregon Territory (the **Red River migration**). With the Oregon Boundary Treaty of 1846, the boundary between British and American territory from the Rockies to the Pacific coast was set at 49°N with the exception of Vancouver Island, which extended south of this parallel.

**PHOTO 3.5** A crew from the North American Boundary Commission building a sod mound marking the border between Canada and the United States, August or September 1873. Without a natural feature dividing the two countries, sod mounds marked the boundary between the two countries. Until the completion of the CPR in 1885, these prairie lands remained largely empty of European settlers.

The **Chapter 10** section "Hydroelectricity: White Elephant or Megaproject of the Century?," page 343, discusses the hydroelectric relationship between Quebec and Newfoundland and Labrador.

**THINK ABOUT IT**

Examine **Figures 3.8** and **3.9**. Did the decision of King Charles II in 1670 that gave the Hudson's Bay Company control over lands draining into Hudson Bay affect the determination by the British Privy Council of the 1927 border between Quebec and Labrador?

land away from the Northwest Territories.) By this time, Manitoba spread north to the boundary with the Northwest Territories (now Nunavut) and east to Lake of the Woods.

Quebec, too, received northern territories. In 1898, its boundary was extended northward to the Eastmain River and then eastward to Labrador. In 1912, Ottawa assigned Quebec more territory that extended its lands to Hudson Strait. Canada also believed that the province of Quebec should extend to the narrow coastal strip along the Labrador coast, while the colony of Newfoundland contended that Newfoundland owned all the land draining into the Atlantic Ocean. In 1927, this dispute between two British dominions (Canada and Newfoundland) went to London. The British government ruled in favour of Newfoundland (Figure 3.9). The Quebec government has never formally accepted this ruling, and though Quebec has respected this ruling of nearly a century ago it still impacts relations between the two provinces, especially in regard to hydroelectric development and transmission.

In the years following Confederation, Ontario gained two large areas. In 1899, its western boundary was set at the Lake of the Woods (previously this area belonged to Manitoba); at the same time, its northern boundary was extended to the Albany River and James Bay. Then, in 1912, Ontario obtained its vast northern lands, which stretch to Hudson Bay.

The final adjustment to Canada's internal boundaries occurred in 1999 with the establishment of the territory of Nunavut (Figure 3.10 and Table 3.5), which was hived off from the Northwest Territories in the eastern Arctic.

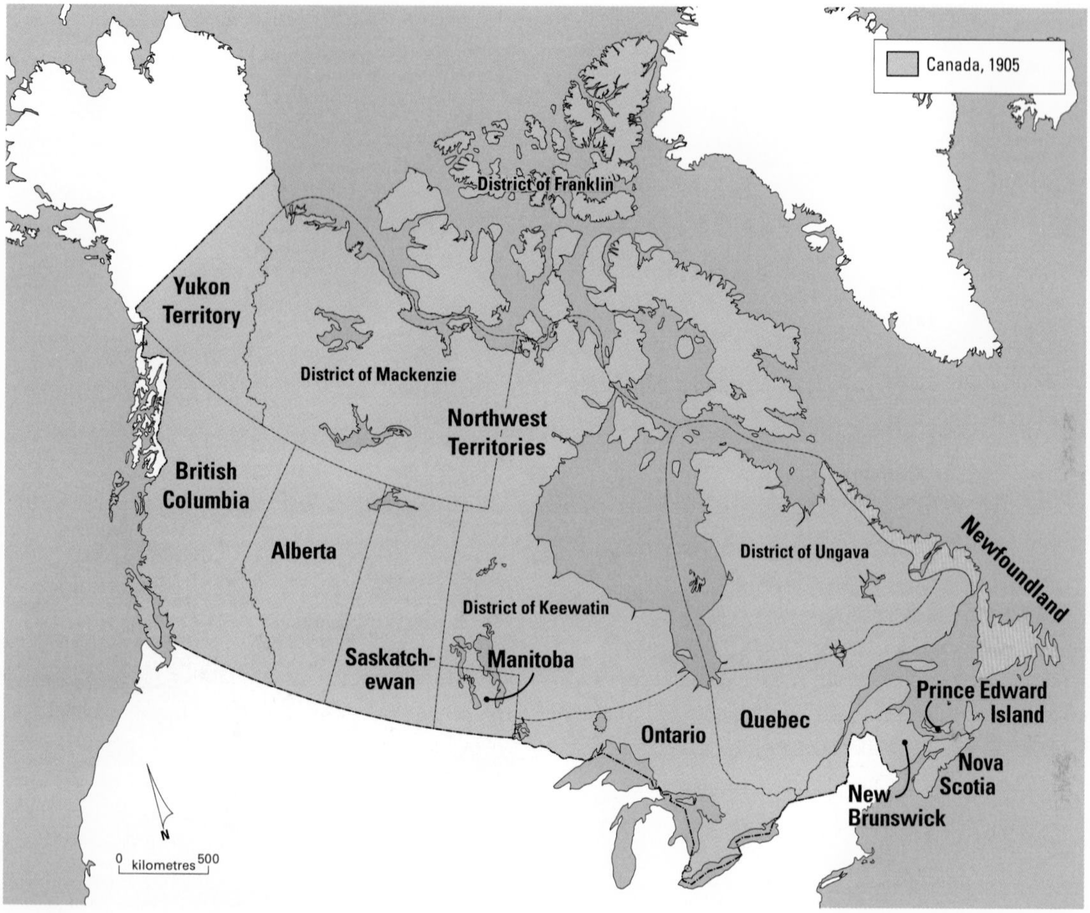

**FIGURE 3.8 Canada, 1905**

By 1905, two new provinces (Alberta and Saskatchewan) and two territories (Yukon and the Northwest Territories) were created out of the North-West Territories and the Arctic Archipelago, which was ceded to Canada in 1880 and later formed the District of Franklin. As well, the provinces of Ontario, Quebec, and Manitoba expanded their boundaries into the former North-West Territories. British Columbia lost a small strip of land along its north coast with the 1903 settlement of the Alaska Boundary Dispute.

## Faultlines in Canada's Early Years

Canada's geography has always been defined by its faultlines, a notion introduced in Chapter 1. For better or worse, this aspect of regionalism is a fact of life in Canada and it may well be the most telling characteristic of Canada's changing national character over the centuries. Four faultlines described in this text have their roots in Canada's historical geography. In all cases, these cracks in Canada's unity pose powerful challenges to the federal government. The federal government, because it is charged with establishing national policies and programs, tries to keep the country united—but what a task. Even so, the national political parties are most aware that the political power (the number of seats in the House of Commons) is concentrated in Central Canada. Despite whether it's true, federal policies have seemed to favour the two largest provinces, Quebec and Ontario, under the guise of policy decisions being "in the national interest."

In the nineteenth century, under the leadership of John A. Macdonald, the federal government launched three initiatives that determined the course of Canada's history. The first initiative,

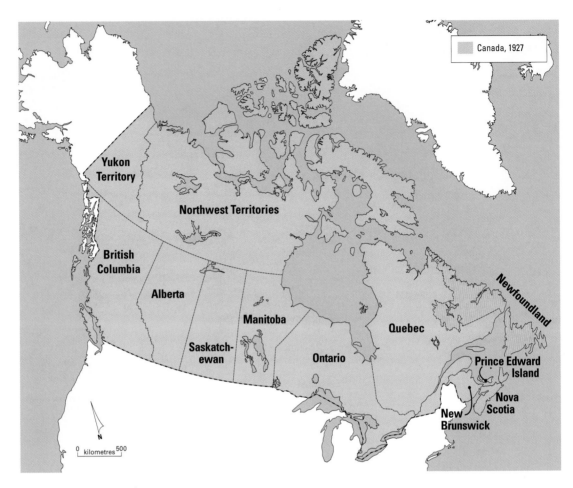

**FIGURE 3.9  Canada, 1927**

The complicated history of Lower Canada and Newfoundland provided ample justification for both parties to claim the land between the Northern Divide and the coastal strip associated with the fisheries. In 1927, the Privy Council of the British Parliament ruled in favour of Newfoundland by selecting the watershed boundary, a decision that dated back to 1670 when King Charles II created Rupert's Land. In 1912 Ontario, Quebec, and Manitoba gained additional northern lands to reach their current geographic size.

the CPR, linked the country from the Atlantic to the Pacific and thus sought to overcome Canada's vast space and link its regions together. The second initiative established an industrial core in Central Canada through the National Policy, which set high tariffs on imported goods and encouraged a home market for the manufactures of the core. The assimilation of Canada's Indigenous populations forms the third initiative.

Rightly or wrongly, Canadians living outside Central Canada believed that Ontario and Quebec had an unfair influence over national policies and therefore Ottawa would favour economic

development in Central Canada over that in the rest of the country.

Since most Canadians lived in Central Canada, it held most of the political power. In 1911, for example, 62.9 per cent of Canadians lived in Central Canada and they held 68.3 per cent of the seats in the House of Commons. By 2019, Central Canada still had a stranglehold on the democratic system with 61.6 per cent of the population and 58.9 per cent of the 338 seats in the Commons (see Table 3.6). Even though their political weight declined over this span of time, Central Canada and especially Ontario still held sway. Over this same time, Atlantic Canada's

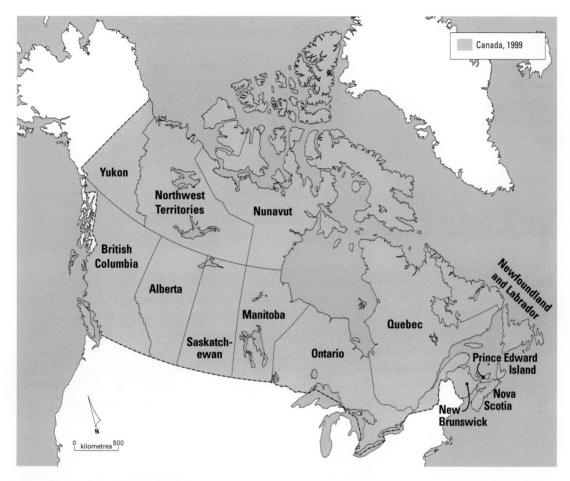

**FIGURE 3.10 Canada, 1999**

On 1 April 1999, Nunavut became a territory. Fifty years earlier, in 1949, Newfoundland had joined Confederation following two contentious referendums, and in 2001 Newfoundland officially added "and Labrador" to its provincial name.

**TABLE 3.5   Timeline: Evolution of Canada's Boundaries**

| Date | Event |
|------|-------|
| **1881** | Ottawa enlarges the boundaries of Manitoba. |
| **1898** | Ottawa approves extension of Quebec's northern limit to the Eastmain River. |
| **1899** | Ottawa decides to set Ontario's western boundary at Lake of the Woods and extend its northern boundary to the Albany River and James Bay. |
| **1905** | Ottawa announces the creation of two new provinces, Alberta and Saskatchewan. |
| **1912** | Ottawa redefines the boundaries of Manitoba, Ontario, and Quebec, extending them to their present position. |
| **1927** | Great Britain sets the boundary between Quebec and Labrador as the Northern Divide. Quebec has never accepted this decision. |
| **1949** | Newfoundland joins Canada following the second of two referendums held to determine its political future; in 2001 the province adds "and Labrador" to its official name. |
| **1999** | A new territory, Nunavut, is hived off from the Northwest Territories in the eastern Arctic. |

**TABLE 3.6    Members of the House of Commons by Geographic Region, 1911 and 2019**

| Geographic Region | 1911 | | 2019 | |
| --- | --- | --- | --- | --- |
| | Members (no.) | Population | Members (no.) | Population |
| Territorial North | 1 | 15,019 | 3 | 111,663 |
| British Columbia | 7 | 392,480 | 42 | 4,573,321 |
| Western Canada | 27 | 1,328,121 | 62 | 6,087,811 |
| Atlantic Canada* | 35 | 937,855 | 32 | 2,357,325 |
| Quebec | 65 | 2,005,776 | 78 | 7,979,663 |
| Ontario | 86 | 2,527,292 | 121 | 13,372,996 |
| Total | 221 | 7,206,543 | 338 | 34,482,779 |

*In 1911, the province of Newfoundland and Labrador had not yet joined Confederation.

Source: House of Commons, *Party Standings in the House of Commons*, 2019, at: https://www.ourcommons.ca/Members/en/party-standings.

place in Canada declined as it suffered both demographic and political losses—its share of Canada's population dropped from 10.4 per cent in 1911 to 6.5 per cent in 2019 while its political representation in the House of Commons declined from nearly 16 per cent to just under 10 per cent.

## The Indigenous Faultline

Without a doubt, the Indigenous divide represents the most complex and troubling one facing the nation. Past efforts to assimilate Indigenous peoples failed miserably. Reconciliation represents a positive way forward.

Canada's Indigenous peoples form an important part of our history and an essential part of our future. The diversity among Indigenous peoples is great and their relationships with Ottawa vary. For example, Indigenous peoples whose ancestors made treaty receive certain assistance, such as annual cash payments, that other Indigenous peoples do not. Most importantly, Indigenous peoples, as the original inhabitants of Canada, have rights to ancestral lands and resources. Ottawa's responsibility stems from the Royal Proclamation of 1763. While the original purpose of this Proclamation was to consolidate Britain's position in North America following the defeat of the French forces, Britain soon became embroiled in suppressing the American Revolution and the dream of an Indigenous land west of the Appalachian Mountains went up in smoke (Vignette 3.4).

In the nineteenth century, the belief that British culture was far superior to Indigenous cultures was reflected in British and later Canadian policies towards Indigenous peoples. For example, residential boarding schools operated by Christian churches were an attempt to isolate Indigenous children from their parents and then proceed to assimilate them into Canadian society by destroying their Indigenous cultures and languages. The social price of this failed assimilation program was extremely high. As pointed out by the report of the Truth and Reconciliation Commission (Sinclair, 2015), the damage caused to survivors and their descendants still haunts Indigenous communities, and, in the opinion of Justice Murray Sinclair, **residential schools** were an institutional form of cultural genocide.

The diversity of Indigenous peoples, the scattered nature of their reserves and settlements, the erosion of their cultures and languages, and, for many, their educational and geographic disadvantages on the margins of the larger society have produced different needs for different groups, as well as calls for a variety of responses by Ottawa. Two overarching points must first be understood:

- The federal government's responsibility for Indigenous peoples has been uneven. It began in 1867 with First Nations; in 1939, this responsibility was extended to Inuit; finally, in 2016, Métis and non-status Indians were recognized as a federal responsibility (Vignette 3.5).
- As Canadian society has changed over time the federal government has made some effort to shift its direction from advocating assimilation policies, such as residential schools, to a

## Vignette 3.4

### How the Royal Proclamation Was Trumped by the American Revolution

In the Royal Proclamation of 1763, Great Britain recognized that Indigenous peoples west of the Appalachian Mountains had an undefined right to these lands, but more importantly, those Indigenous peoples under the leadership of Pontiac, an Odawa war chief, controlled those lands by their military prowess. To ensure their alliance with Pontiac and therefore maintain control over the former French interior, Great Britain set the eastern boundary of its thirteen colonies as the Appalachian Mountains, thus designating the Ohio lands as Indigenous lands under British control. The British, anticipating that settlers from their Atlantic colonies would move across the Appalachian Mountains, set out guidelines for settlers to legally acquire land from Indigenous groups, namely that the extinguishing of Indigenous land rights must be approved by the Crown. After the American Revolution, the geopolitical reality of the late eighteenth century made it impossible to halt the movement of British settlers into the lands of the Ohio River Basin. This reality was driven by a rapidly increasing population in the former thirteen British colonies along the Atlantic seaboard, a shortage of agricultural land in those lands, and an awareness on the part of American settlers that land in the Ohio River Basin could solve their land crisis. To these New Englanders, lands west of the Appalachian Mountains were "unoccupied" forested lands that they wished to clear and farm. While the term "Manifest Destiny" was coined in 1845, the American settling of the Indigenous lands is an early example of American territorial expansion.

more accommodative approach as exemplified by modern treaties, the duty to consult over resource projects, and the Truth and Reconciliation Commission.

By the beginning of the twenty-first century, the federal question had become whether, in a sovereign state such as Canada, there is political room for Indigenous peoples *on their terms*. So far, two main examples exist for accommodating Canada's Indigenous peoples.

- *Reserves*. In the nineteenth and twentieth centuries, treaties created over 3,100 reserves that are governed by just over 600 band councils, in many cases under the control of the federal Indian Act.
- *Territory*. Nunavut is a territory within the existing Canadian political unit and with a largely Inuit population. Although an Inuit initiative, the result was a public government rather than an ethnic territory. Earlier, in 1975, the Dene Nation proposal for their own homeland called

Denendeh, within the Northwest Territories, was rejected by Ottawa (Bone, 2016, p. 226).

The current federal accommodation of Indigenous peoples, guided by rulings of the Supreme Court of Canada, has launched the redefining of the relationship between Indigenous peoples and the nation-state of Canada. For Indigenous peoples, the question has become whether any redefinition will provide the political control and territorial space sought by them. Some scholars think not (Nadasdy, 2003; White, 2006; Kulchyski, 2013; Willow, 2014). After all, any redefinition of the relationship could lead to a dead end for Indigenous peoples because the process is inevitably dominated by Canada. In other words, any resulting agreements could smother Indigenous cultures and values while slowly but quietly integrating the people into Canadian society.

A third path has been described by Manuel (1974) and Dyck (1985). In their view, Indigenous peoples must find their own path within a nation-state. In Canada, this path could take the form of a third level of government, sometimes described

## Vignette 3.5

### The Federal Government and Indigenous Peoples

Indigenous peoples do not comprise just one group but many diverse groups with different customs and cultures. In the Constitution Act of 1982, three Indigenous groups are recognized: First Nations, Métis, and Inuit. Yet, under the Indian Act of 1876, the federal government was only responsible for First Nations. One reason for Ottawa's reluctance to recognize the other two groups was the desire to keep the cost to the federal treasury at a minimum. Over the years, rulings by the Supreme Court of Canada forced Ottawa to expand its acceptance of responsibility to include the Métis and Inuit. In 1939, Inuit were considered "Indians" by the Court and therefore fell under the responsibility of the federal government. In 2016, the Supreme Court ruled that the federal government was responsible for Métis and non-status Indians, but the definition of this responsibility was not defined. As of August 2020, the negotiations with Ottawa to determine the exact nature of these obligations and benefits had not yet begun.

**THINK ABOUT IT**

In a modern, globalized world, it can be argued that the inevitable trajectory of democratic societies is towards social and cultural integration. How would you argue that such integration is not inevitable?

as "nested federalism" (Wilson, 2008, 2017). Such a path is possible but difficult to achieve. For example, Nunavik was on such a path but the Quebec Inuit rejected the proposition for self-government in a 2011 referendum; still, they may revisit this option (CBC News, 2011; Bone, 2016, p. 232).

Canada's Indigenous citizens are seeking a new place in Canada and a new relationship with the Canadian government. Some First Nations, such as the Onion Lake Cree First Nation and the Whitecap Dakota First Nation in Saskatchewan, have come a long way toward finding that place and relationship. Others, such as the Innu Nation in Labrador, the Attawapiskat First Nation in northern Ontario, and the Lubicon Cree in northern Alberta, have struggled because of government actions and inaction, remote and resource-poor geographic location, and, sometimes, weak or divided local leadership. Each Indigenous community and individual will define this new place and relationship, and those in remote areas have different needs and goals than those in urban Canada.

Two key events have laid the groundwork for post-colonial Indigenous relations in Canada. One is the recognition by the federal government of past wrongs, reflected in the formal residential schools apology by Prime Minister Stephen Harper in Parliament in 2008, along with Ottawa's ongoing promise to negotiate from a respectful appreciation of Indigenous peoples' place in Canada. The Truth and Reconciliation Commission, created in 2008 as part of the Residential Schools Settlement Agreement, represents the second key event. In 2015, this Commission presented its report after holding many meetings with survivors of the residential schools. The Commission's goal is to provide closure for these former students and, through this process, better educate the broader Canadian public of past wrongs.

A third significant change involved the rise of the Idle No More grassroots movement, founded in 2012 by three Indigenous women and one non-Indigenous woman in response to a Conservative government omnibus bill that, among other things, aimed to gut important environmental protections, as well as their concern for a lack of accountability among Indigenous leadership.

## Education and the Elusive Nature of the Indigenous Faultline

Many Canadians still remain ill-informed about Indigenous history in Canada. Much of that lack of awareness is due to the public education system, which, until recently, did not discuss Indigenous history. As a result, many non-Indigenous adults are still unclear about the relationship between Indigenous peoples and the Crown.

Education is a key element in social change. First Nations, by controlling education, are able to support their culture and language. One problem exists, however: the graduation gap remains large between reserve schools and their provincial counterparts. At the political level, the education shortfall at reserve-run schools has been discussed but not addressed. The gap in high school graduation between band-operated schools on Indigenous reserves and provincial schools is well documented. So far, attempts to narrow this gap have failed. Over the past decade, both federal Conservative and Liberal governments sought the support of the Assembly of First Nations to address this problem with the promise of an increase in federal funding for First Nation's education. While the Assembly approved federal education plans, the real power lies with the treaty chiefs. Some chiefs feared that the Conservatives' Bill C-33, which was designed to reform the First Nations elementary and secondary education system and release more funding for First Nations education, was merely a veiled attempt at assimilation—after all, education in the past was a tool used by the federal government to assimilate Indigenous youth. In 2014, Manitoba Chief Derek Nepinak (2014) accused the Conservative government of trying to make "Indigenous peoples more like them." This political dispute has had consequences: the federal government refuses to release funds that would strengthen reserve schools until the curriculum is strengthened, which would hopefully lead to higher graduation rates. As of 2020, this standoff continues. However, in the long run, a slow but steady devolution of control of education from Ottawa to reserves continues on its winding journey, not unlike the slow process of the First Nations University moving to the University of Regina (see below).

The legacy of assimilation still runs deep in Indigenous communities, but much of Canada seems unaware of its impact. In more recent years, a few high-profile attempts at reconciliation have caught the public's attention. One such reconciliation effort resulted in the removal of the statue of John A. Macdonald from the front of Victoria's City Hall. In the spirit of reconciliation, the removal of the statue of Canada's first prime minister made Canadians more aware of a different interpretation of history, one from the perspective of Indigenous peoples.

While such acts are important, even more significant is the growing number of Indigenous people finding socio-economic success. In that process, Indigenous identity need not be lost. An early step in that direction involved the First Nations University of Canada. Its roots go back to the Federation of Saskatchewan Indian Nations (FSIN), which created the Saskatchewan Indian Federated College (SIFC) to meet the educational needs of Indigenous youth in Saskatchewan. In 1976, the FSIN and the University of Regina arranged an agreement to place the SIFC within the University of Regina. As such, the SIFC would be eligible for provincial funding. Such an agreement was not easy because the FSIN wanted to maintain its control over the SIFC while the provincial funding normally went to the university. Direct governance of the SIFC by the FSIN was a sticking point, but it evolved into a board made up mainly of Indigenous graduates. This agreement continues and, while there were a few bumps along the way, the First Nations University of Canada is a unique post-secondary institution designed to support and enhance Indigenous culture and history. Unlike other universities, learning at this federated college takes place in an environment of Indigenous cultures and values "based on a foundation of Indigenous knowledge" (First Nations University of Canada, 2020).

As in all societies, education is a key for economic and social advancement. For Indigenous students, does education provide a platform to support Indigenous culture as well as to participate more fully in Canadian society? Success stories based on education are found in our Indigenous communities, while others are taking place in our cities. Looking at our universities, we can see structural advances in the increasing number of Indigenous departments, Indigenous professors, and Indigenous students. According to Universities Canada, in 2015, 233 undergraduate and 62 graduate programs on Indigenous issues or for Indigenous students were available. While this number is important, what is even more important is the increase in such programs. From 2013 to 2019, Universities Canada (2020) reported a 55 per cent increase in these Indigenous courses and programs.

## A Historical Overview

The tangled historical relations between Indigenous peoples and European settlers, first in New France, then in British North America, and finally in Canada, placed a cloud over the search for accommodated solutions in the twenty-first century. In the nineteenth century and for much of the twentieth century, the forced assimilation policies of the federal government solidified an Indigenous distrust of the Canadian state, and the Crown effectively made any accommodated solution impossible. These failed policies created an enormous divide between Indigenous peoples and the rest of Canadian society. The net result was a disaster for Indigenous peoples, who, pushed to the social and geographic margins of Canadian society, were caught in a dependency relationship with Ottawa. At that time, they faced unrelenting forms of racism and became the ignored members of Canadian society.

The recognition by the federal government of past wrongs and an increased (though far from complete) awareness by the general population of the circumstances facing Indigenous peoples marked a turnaround. An initial step in that direction was federal funding for post-secondary education for status Indians. First begun in a limited fashion in the 1960s, the Post-Secondary Student Support Program (PSSSP) now provides financial assistance to status First Nation and Inuit students who are enrolled in eligible post-secondary programs. By fostering a more educated Indigenous population, a new leadership class has emerged and greater upward mobility within Indigenous communities has become a possibility. In 2018, the federal government agreed that those of Métis descent should be included, but this progressive federal policy does not include non-status Indians.

## The Royal Proclamation and the Haldimand Grant

History sometimes makes strange allies. Shortly after Pontiac led a successful uprising against the British in 1763, Britain decided to form an alliance with him and other Indigenous leaders.[2] Pontiac's goal was to keep the Ohio Valley lands free of settlers from New England, and the British knew they could not hold these lands without the support of Pontiac. For strategic reasons, then, to keep colonists along the eastern seaboard from further encroaching on Indigenous territory and to maintain a peace with the Indigenous peoples, George III issued the Royal Proclamation of 1763, which identified British territory west of the Appalachian Mountains as Indigenous lands. The British also believed that Indigenous peoples had a "limited" ownership over the forested lands they inhabited, and that therefore such lands could not be occupied by settlers but must be purchased from the Indigenous "owners." This somewhat ambiguous concept remains the basis of land claims by Canadian Indigenous peoples.

With the colonists' victory in the American Revolution 20 years later, the concept of Indigenous lands in the Ohio Valley quickly disappeared as a flood of land-hungry settlers poured across the Appalachian Mountains. Indigenous forces that had been loyal to and fought for the King during the Revolutionary War retreated to Canada following the war, where they received the first major Indigenous land grant, the Haldimand Grant of 1784. The purpose was to reward the Iroquois who had served on the British side during the American Revolution. In his proclamation, the governor of Quebec, Lord Haldimand, prohibited the lease or sale of land to anyone but the government in the tract extending from the source of the Grand River in present-day southwestern Ontario to the point where the river feeds into Lake Erie.

However, Joseph Brant, the leader of the Iroquois, insisted that they had the same rights as the colony's Loyalist settlers, that is, freehold land tenure. And so the waters were muddied by the early sale and lease of plots of land in the original Haldimand Grant. This issue has been part of the contemporary conflict between local residents and Six Nations Iroquois at Caledonia, Ontario.

## Canada Takes Over with the Indian Act

In 1867, the British North America Act transferred government responsibility of Indigenous groups from Great Britain to Canada. Nine years later, in 1876, the government pulled together the various pieces of colonial legislation and regulations to create the repressive Indian Act. From Ottawa's perspective, the Act allowed the federal government to "manage" all these diverse groups. As part of this management scheme, Ottawa created a form of

For further discussion of the Iroquois Confederacy, see "The Six Nations of the Iroquois Confederacy," page 105.

For further discussion of the Haldimand Grant and a map illustrating the area of the original grant in 1784 and the current size of the reserve of the Six Nations of Grand River, see **Chapter 6**, "Ontario's Historical Geography," page 179, and **Figure 6.6**, "The Haldimand Tract."

See **Vignette 6.3**, "Timeline of the Caledonia Dispute," page 186.

governance known as band councils to administer federal programs and to receive federal funding.

The Indian Act had the effect of isolating Indigenous communities from the rest of Canada and stripping them of the power to govern themselves. Basing its action on the premise that Indigenous communities could not manage their own affairs, Ottawa, through the federal Department of Indian Affairs, served as their guardian until First Nations were fully integrated into Canadian society—as defined by Ottawa. As a result, the federal department intervened in band issues, including managing Indigenous lands, resources, and moneys, with the objective of assimilating Indigenous peoples into Canadian society. This Act promoted a dependency on Ottawa and left control of band affairs in the hands of local Indigenous agents, thus stifling Indigenous initiatives. Even though Indigenous peoples were living in Canada, they were isolated from other Canadians and did not have the rights of citizenship, including the right to vote. Perhaps the only positive outcome of the Act was, unlike the situation of the Métis, Indigenous land could not be sold to private individuals unless approved by Ottawa—though over the years the government frequently did downsize reserves by selling and leasing reserve lands. Oddly enough, the Métis and Inuit did not fall under this Act, but they too fell into this twilight zone of living in Canada but not being fully accepted. Today, Inuit have a homeland in the territory of Nunavut, as well as in the northern extremes of the Northwest Territories, Quebec, and Labrador. While politically independent, Nunavut lacks the funds to properly address a number of social issues, including a housing shortage. In 2013, the Manitoba Métis Federation (MMF) won a landmark case in the Supreme Court in regard to the government's failure—in 1870 and ever since—to provide the Métis a proper land base, and in September 2018 Ottawa announced a first payment of $154 million as part of the complicated resolution of this case.

## Residential Schools: An Assimilation Tool

From the beginning, Ottawa's objective was the assimilation of Indigenous peoples into Canadian society (Milloy, 1999). Education was an important tool in federal efforts to "civilize" Indigenous peoples. One such effort, residential schools, stands out. Spread across Canada but concentrated in the West, the residential schools were operated by the major religious groups, especially the Roman Catholic Church. Without a doubt, residential schools were the most painful experience for many Indigenous children and their parents, and this experience has had long-term effects (Vignette 3.6). After a detailed examination of Indigenous–white relations, J.R. Miller (2000: 269) concludes that:

> While some students of these residential schools were thoroughly converted by the experience, many more absorbed only enough schooling to resist still more effectively. It would be from the ranks of former residential school pupils that most of the leaders of [Indigenous] political movements would come in the twentieth century. By any reasonable standard of evaluation, the residential school program from the 1880s to the 1960s failed dismally.

Not only did this assimilation program fail, but many students were abused, some sexually, by their religious teachers. By the 1990s some residential school survivors began to seek reparation for harms through the courts, and the Canadian legal system demanded financial compensation. The churches claimed that they were unable to pay for these claims and Canada offered to pay 70 per cent of compensation in respect of joint government and church liabilities to victims of sexual and physical abuse at residential schools. The churches involved—Roman Catholic, United, Methodist, Presbyterian, and Anglican—negotiated separate financial agreements with Ottawa. The Anglican Church, in 2003, was the first to reach a settlement, for payment of up to $25 million. It had also been the first church to formally apologize, in 1993, for its part in the tragic residential schools history. On 23 November 2005, the Canadian government announced a $1.9 billion compensation package to benefit tens of thousands of survivors of the residential schools. The settlement provides for a lump-sum payment to former students: $10,000 for the first school year plus $3,000 for each additional year.

For further discussion of treaty making, see "The Second Clash: The Northwest Resistance of 1885," page 99.

## Vignette 3.6

### The Failure of Residential Schools

In 1892, the federal government entered a formal arrangement with several Christian churches—Roman Catholic, Anglican, Methodist, and Presbyterian—to provide a boarding school education for young Indigenous children. The churches ran the schools; Ottawa paid the bills. The plan was to quickly assimilate these young children into society by removing them from their families and home communities and by insisting that they not use their native languages. The effect was to destroy their culture and leave them between two worlds without roots in either one. From 1931 to 1996, about 150,000 First Nations, Inuit, and Métis children attended boarding schools. At least 3,000 students died at the schools, largely from diseases such as the 1918 flu pandemic (*CBC News*, 2013a). And, as we now know, many of the children were subjected to physical and sexual abuse.

The federal government (and society in general) believed that Indigenous children could be successful in modern society if they abandoned their culture and language and adopted Christianity, learned English or French, and had a basic education—though only enough to fit onto the lower rungs of the economy, as manual labourers, farm workers, seamstresses, and domestic workers. Attendance was mandatory and this rule was enforced by federal Indian agents, other federal officers, and missionaries. By the 1980s, the failure of this program was self-evident, although Indigenous families and communities had lived with the failure for generations. The last school was closed in 1996.

The average payout has been about $28,000. Those who suffered sexual or serious physical abuses, or other abuses that caused serious psychological effects, could apply for additional compensation or seek redress through the courts. Finally, on 11 June 2008 the Prime Minister made a formal apology in the House of Commons for the harm done to individuals, families, and cultures by the residential schools.

Since the 1970s, Ottawa has adopted a more enlightened policy towards resolving issues related to Canada's Indigenous peoples, stressing three elements: settling outstanding land claims, recognizing an Indigenous right to self-government, and accepting that the concerns and rights of each Indigenous group (First Nations, Métis, and Inuit) are different and that such concerns and rights require specific solutions.

## Defining Indigenous Peoples

The Indigenous peoples of Canada—First Nations, Métis, and Inuit—are those now living in Canada who trace their ancestry to the original **inhabitants** who were in North America before the arrival of Europeans in the fifteenth century and who identify with that ancestry. From a cultural perspective, the legal terms used to describe First Nations people as status, non-status, and treaty "Indians" have little meaning in regard to their traditional groups, such as Plains Cree. People legally defined as **status (registered) Indians** are recorded by the federal government as "Indians," according to the Indian Act as amended in June 1985, and have certain rights acknowledged by the federal government, such as tax exemption for income generated on a reserve. The Indian Register is the official record identifying persons registered as status Indians under the Indian Act who are therefore eligible to receive certain benefits and rights. According to data compiled by the federal department responsible for Indigenous affairs, the number of status Indians—from over 600 First Nations—had grown to 744,855 by 2016 (Statistic Canada, 2019). **Treaty Indians** are status or registered Indians who are members of (or can prove descent from) a First Nations band that signed a treaty. They have a legal right to live on a reserve and participate in band affairs. Less than half of treaty Indians live on reserves. **Non-status Indians** are those of Indigenous ancestry who are not registered as status Indians and therefore have no rights under the Indian Act. The **Métis** are people of European and North American Indigenous ancestry. The **Inuit** are the Indigenous people located mainly in the Arctic.

Statistics Canada records Indigenous peoples by their identity as declared by those individuals on census day. In 2016, the census recorded 1,673,785 Indigenous peoples: 977,230 First Nations, 587,545 Métis, and 65,025 Inuit (Statistics Canada, 2017). First Nations people includes both status and non-status Indians.

First Nations, Inuit, and Métis constitute a highly diverse population. One indication of their cultural diversity is linguistic classification. As noted earlier, there were approximately 55 distinct Indigenous languages (of 11 language families) spoken in Canada at the time of original contact (Figure 3.4). The largest language family is Algonkian. There are 15 distinct Algonkian-based languages, the most common of which are Cree and Ojibwa. Inuktitut, the Inuit language, has regional dialects and is spoken across the Canadian Arctic.

Another measure of Indigenous diversity is self-identification. Many people prefer to identify themselves using the name of their nation, while others prefer the name of their band, For example, the Cree nation occupies a vast territory that stretches from northern Quebec to Alberta. There are many Cree bands within that territory. A Cree living in northern Saskatchewan might identify her or himself as a member of a Cree band, such as the Lac La Ronge band.

The largest First Nations are southern Ontario's Six Nations of the Grand River (Iroquois) with a population in 2017 of 27,276, but only 12,848—or 47 per cent—live on reserve (Six Nations of the Grand River, 2019). While approximately half of status Indians live on reserves, the growing number of urban Indigenous people is sociologically and demographically significant.

Indigenous peoples are reclaiming their identity and place names. Some bands are relinquishing the names given to them by Europeans in favour of their original names, such as Anishinabe (instead of Ojibwa) and Gwich'in (instead of Kutchin). The landscape is also being reclaimed. For example, the Arctic community of Frobisher Bay, named after the English explorer Martin Frobisher, is now Iqaluit ("the place where the fish are"), the capital city of Nunavut ("our land"). On the west coast, the Queen Charlotte Islands have been renamed Haida Gwaii.

## Indigenous and Treaty Rights

Indigenous rights are group or collective rights that stem from Indigenous peoples' occupation of the land before contact. Such rights apply most readily to status Indigenous people and Inuit, while Métis have been less well protected in regard to rights. Recent court decisions and agreements may change this.

### Métis Rights

In 1870, Ottawa, in an effort to quell the resistance at the Red River Settlement, accepted that the Métis, by virtue of their Indigenous ancestry, had Indigenous rights. However, the government viewed these rights in the narrowest possible manner by offering individual land grants to the Métis. The agreement had three components. First, land occupied before 1870 became private property. Second, the children of the Métis were eligible for a land grant of 140 acres. Third, each head of a Métis family received 160 acres in **scrip**, which could be either claimed or sold. The federal government set aside 1.4 million acres for the Métis children, estimated in 1871 at around 10,000. Based on these figures, each Métis child, at adulthood, could claim 140 acres. Before the actual land allocation began, the government ordered a census of the Métis population and this 1872 census identified just over 5,000 eligible Métis children. Accordingly, their individual allocation was increased to 240 acres (Library and Archives of Canada, 2012). Unfortunately for the Métis, much of the land on offer was marginal for agriculture and it certainly did not provide the basis for a homeland; plus, the government was slow to act while settlers from the east continued to take up land in the region. Consequently, many adults sold their land scrip to speculators, sometimes at half its value, or accepted a one-time payment from the government (money scrip) for the value of the land they might have taken (Dickason & Newbigging, 2019, p. 243). By 1880, the outcome was clear—the dream

**THINK ABOUT IT**

Why did the Métis sell their scrip instead of converting it to farmland? When did the "responsibility" for Inuit fall to Ottawa?

For more on the subject of land allotments to the Métis, see page 96, "The First Clash: The Red River Resistance of 1869–70."

of a Métis land base was dead. In March 2013 the Supreme Court overturned a lower court decision, ruling in *Manitoba Métis Federation v. Canada (Attorney General)* that the Canadian government in 1870 and the ensuing years did not act in good faith in its dealings with the Métis. The focus of the dispute is the 1870 federal commitment to set aside 5,565 km$^2$ for 7,000 children of the Red River Métis. In 2013, the president of the Manitoba Métis Federation stated that some kind of compensation, not necessarily land, is most important to the Métis (*CBC News*, 2013b). In 2018, the Liberal government and the Manitoba Métis Federation signed an agreement that begins the process of resolving past failings back to the 1870 promise; the agreement also extends to Métis in Saskatchewan and Alberta (Haig, 2019).

### Treaty Rights

Treaty rights are the most generous of Indigenous rights. Treaties set aside reserve land, held collectively by and for the benefit of the band, and define other negotiated rights (benefits).

The reasons for signing treaties varied depending on the historical context. During the late nineteenth century, treaties were signed throughout the Prairies to remove Indigenous communities from the land and make way for European settlement; at the same time, this helped ensure that the Indian Wars, which were common south of the border between the US military and various Indigenous groups, would not erupt in Canada. For Indigenous peoples, treaties promised land (reserves) that would not be available to settlers, as well as support to shift from nomadic hunting to sedentary farming. The numbered treaties for the Plains peoples therefore offered protection from the anticipated flood of settlers and

some guarantee that the federal government would care for them now that their principal source of food, the buffalo, was gone (Figure 3.11). However, treaty assurances of federal assistance were often not met (see Brownlie, 2003; Carter, 2004).

The terms of each treaty varied, although they generally included cash gratuities and presents at the signing of the treaty, annual payments in perpetuity, the promise of educational and agricultural assistance, and the right to hunt and fish on Crown land until such land was required for other purposes, as well as land reserves to be held by the Crown in trust for the First Nations. In Treaty 6 of 1876, for example, which covered much of central Saskatchewan and Alberta, each tribe was assigned land based on the size of its population, i.e., each family of five received one square mile. Reserves represent land collectively owned by First Nation bands, though legally the Crown holds the land in trust.

Conflicting ideas as to the significance of treaties between the signing parties largely shaped Indigenous–Crown relations in Canada during the twentieth century. When treaties were signed, Crown authorities viewed them as vehicles for extinguishing Indigenous rights and titles to land and thus for opening the land to agricultural settlement. First Nations, however, understood them as agreements between "sovereign" powers to share land and resources. With such diverging perceptions, disagreements were inevitable.

Modern or comprehensive treaties came about in the latter part of the twentieth century, the first being the James Bay and Northern Quebec Agreement of 1975, and have continued to be negotiated into the twenty-first century (Figure 3.12). Comprehensive treaties or agreements extend rights to those

---

## Contested Terrain 3.1

### The Supreme Court and the Métis

The Supreme Court of Canada began hearing the case brought by the Manitoba Métis Federation in December 2011. With the Court ruling in favour of the Métis claim that the federal government of the day did not safeguard the interest of the Métis, Ottawa has moved forward and struck an agreement that paves the way to finding a solution not only in Manitoba but also in Alberta and Saskatchewan where Métis from Red River resettled in the late nineteenth century. See also Vignette 3.5.

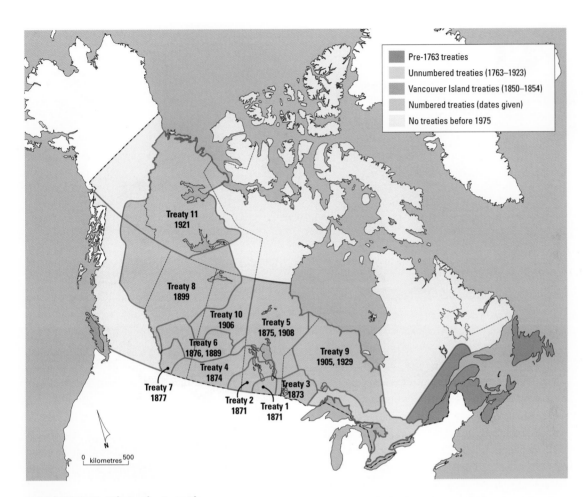

**FIGURE 3.11 Historic treaties**

The first treaties, made between the British government and Indigenous groups, were "friendship" agreements. In Upper Canada, the Robinson treaties of 1850 set aside reserve lands in exchange for the title to the remaining lands. With the settlement of lands in the Canadian West, Indigenous peoples became concerned about their future, so many of the 11 numbered treaties, which spanned a half-century from 1871 to 1921, included provisions for agricultural supplies. When the last numbered treaty was signed, many Indigenous peoples in Atlantic Canada, Quebec, and British Columbia were without treaties.

Indigenous groups, especially in northern Canada and British Columbia, that had never signed treaties, and generally include large cash settlements, a portion of the group's traditional lands, surrender of the larger portion of traditional lands, self-governance agreements, and environmental/natural resource co-management agreements.

### Modern Treaties

The legal meaning of **Indigenous title** to land has evolved over time. Until the 1970s, Ottawa recognized two forms of land rights. Reserve lands were one type of right or ownership, which the Canadian government held for First Nations peoples. The second type was a usufructuary right to use Crown land for hunting and trapping—in other words, to freely use and enjoy Crown lands without any claim to ownership of these lands. At that time, Crown lands (both provincial and federal) included most of Canada's unsettled areas. First Nations, Inuit, and Métis families lived on Crown lands, continuing to hunt, trap, and fish. However, federal and provincial governments could sell such lands to individuals and corporations or grant them a lease to use the land for a specific purpose, such as mineral exploration or logging, without compensating the

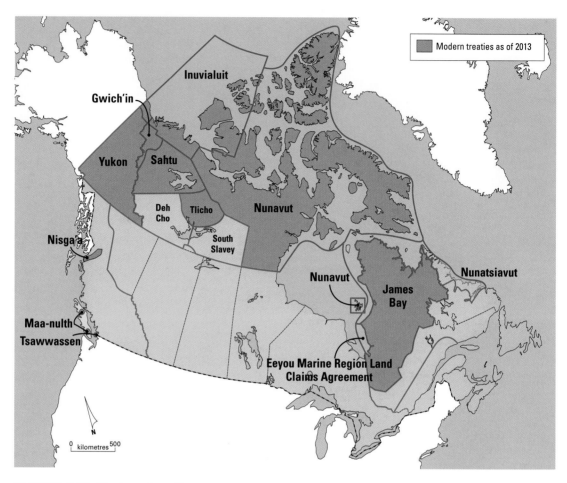

**FIGURE 3.12 Modern treaties**

The first modern treaty was the James Bay and Northern Quebec Agreement (JBNQA), signed in 1975. By 2020, the main areas without treaties were much of BC, parts of Labrador and the Northwest Territories, and lands in central and southern Quebec.

Indigenous users of those lands. By the 1960s, many Indigenous groups still did not have treaties with the Canadian government. Atlantic Canada, Quebec, the Territorial North, and British Columbia contained huge areas where treaties had not been concluded. As a consequence, Indigenous peoples had no control over developments on these lands.

A combination of events radically changed this situation. One factor was the emergence of Indigenous leaders who understood the political and legal systems. They used the courts to force the federal and provincial governments to address the issue of Indigenous rights and land claims. The first major event took place in 1969, when Ottawa proposed reforms to the Indian Act in its White Paper on Indian Policy.

This galvanized treaty First Nations into action. The White Paper proposed to treat all Canadians equally. For First Nations, it meant the abolition of their treaty rights and the reserve land system. At about the same time, the Nisga'a in northern British Columbia took their land claim, known as the *Calder* case, to court.

In 1973, the Supreme Court of Canada narrowly ruled (by a vote of four to three) against the Nisga'a argument that they still had a land claim to territory in northern British Columbia. However, in their ruling, six of the seven judges agreed that Indigenous title to the land had existed in British Columbia at the time of Confederation. Furthermore, three judges said that Indigenous title still existed in British Columbia because the British Columbia government had not extinguished Indigenous title, while three other judges stated that the various laws passed by the British Columbia government since 1871 served to abolish Indigenous title. The seventh judge ruled against the Nisga'a claim on a legal technicality. Even though the judgment went against the Nisga'a, the course of Indigenous land claims in Canada changed because three judges agreed that Indigenous title was not extinguished. In the same year, 1973, the federal government agreed that Indigenous peoples who had not signed a treaty may very well have a legal claim to Crown lands, and in 1974 an Office of Native Claims was first established to deal with both specific and comprehensive land claims.

In the early and mid-1970s the James Bay Project in northern Quebec and the proposed Mackenzie Valley Pipeline Project in the Northwest Territories added fuel to the political fire over Indigenous rights. The possible impact of these industrial projects on Indigenous peoples was made clear through the Mackenzie Valley Pipeline Inquiry of 1974–7 (the Berger Inquiry) into possible environmental and socio-economic impacts. Indigenous organizations obviously were prepared to take action to defend their land claims. Their position in the 1970s was "no development without land claims settlements." All these events changed both the public's views of Indigenous rights and the government's position. At first grudgingly and then more willingly, governments, corporations, and Canadian society recognized the validity of Indigenous land claims.

A **comprehensive land claim agreement** is sought when a group of Indigenous people who have not yet signed a treaty can demonstrate a claim to land through past occupancy. Such agreements are considered modern treaties (Table 3.7). The **James Bay and Northern Quebec Agreement** is regarded as the first modern treaty, although negotiations between the governments of Canada and Quebec and the James Bay Cree and the Inuit of northern Quebec had begun before the federal government policy was established. As well, the 1978 Northeastern Quebec Agreement, signed between the Innu (Naskapi) and governments, can be considered a part of the James Bay and Northern Quebec Agreement.

In 1984, the Inuvialuit of the Western Arctic became the first Indigenous group to settle a comprehensive land claim with the federal government under the comprehensive land claim process. Since then, 28 comprehensive claims have been finalized in Canada, involving well over 90 Indigenous communities. Negotiations can be extremely slow and complex, and approximately 60 comprehensive claims are in various stages of negotiation at present. Most of these

 For more on BC land claims, see page 300, **Vignette 9.3**, "Indigenous Title: Who Owns BC?"

### TABLE 3.7 Modern Land Claim Agreements, 1975–2019

| Name of Agreement | Year |
| --- | --- |
| James Bay and Northern Quebec Agreement | 1975 |
| Northeastern Quebec Agreement | 1978 |
| Inuvialuit Final Agreement | 1984 |
| Sechelt Act | 1986 |
| Gwich'in Comprehensive Land Claim Agreement | 1992 |
| Nunavut Land Claims Agreement | 1993 |
| Yukon First Nations Final Agreements: | |
|     Champagne and Aishihik First Nations | 1993 |
|     First Nation of Nacho Nyak Dun | 1993 |
|     Teslin Tlingit Council | 1993 |
|     Vuntut Gwitchin First Nation | 1993 |
|     Little Salmon/Carmacks First Nation | 1997 |
|     Selkirk First Nation | 1997 |
|     Tr'ondek Hwechin'in First Nation | 1998 |
|     Ta'an Kwach'an Council | 2002 |
|     Kluane First Nation | 2003 |
|     Kwanlin Dun First Nation | 2005 |
|     Carcross/Tagish First Nation | 2005 |
| Sahtu Dene and Métis Comprehensive Land Claim Agreement | 1993 |
| Nisga'a Final Agreement | 2000 |
| Tlicho Land Claims and Self-Government Agreement | 2003 |
| Labrador Inuit Land Claims Agreement | 2005 |
| Westbank First Nation Agreement | 2005 |
| Nunavik Inuit Land Claims Agreement | 2007 |
| Tsawwassen First Nation Final Agreement | 2009 |
| Eeyou Marine Region Land Claims Agreement | 2010 |
| Maa-nulth Final Agreement | 2011 |
| Yale First Nations Final Agreement | 2013 |
| Sioux Valley Dakota Agreement | 2014 |
| Tla'amin Final Agreement | 2015 |
| Déline Final Agreement | 2016 |
| Cree Nation Governance Agreement | 2018 |

Sources: Fact Sheet: Implementation of Final Agreements at: https://www.rcaanc-cirnac.gc.ca/eng/1100100030580/1542728997938; and Modern Treaties and Self-Government Agreements at: https://www.aadnc-aandc.gc.ca/eng/1290453474688/1290453673970#h6.

**THINK ABOUT IT**

Why have modern treaty agreements resulted in more benefits and powers than did the earlier numbered treaties?

claims involve First Nations in British Columbia. Virtually the entire province of British Columbia, except for parts of Vancouver Island (where 14 treaties—the Douglas treaties—were signed between First Nations and the Hudson's Bay Company in the early 1850s), is claimed by First Nations. In BC, progress has been extremely slow. Until 1992, the provincial government claimed that British occupancy had extinguished Indigenous title. However, in 1992 the British Columbia government accepted the principle of Indigenous land claims. The following year, Ottawa and Victoria agreed to a formula for settling outstanding claims. The federal government would pay 90 per cent of the money needed to settle outstanding claims and the province would provide the land. In 2000, the Nisga'a Agreement was finalized, followed by 12 other ratified agreements by 2019.

Those Indigenous groups that have concluded modern treaties are moving forward. They are better able to focus on economic and cultural developments rather than expending their energies on land claim negotiations. In 1993, the Nunavut agreement broke new ground by effectively establishing self-government over an entire territory. Since then, modern land claim agreements, such as the Nisga'a Agreement, have included arrangements for self-government. As a result, a gap is emerging within the Indigenous community between those with a modern treaty and those without, as well as between those on reserve and those who live in urban areas among Canada's increasingly pluralistic majority society. Also, as with countries and with regions, some Indigenous groups reside on lands rich in natural resources, resource developments, and development potential (e.g., oil and gas deposits, oil sands, pipelines, prime timber land) that provide a base for economic growth and considerable wealth, while many other groups live in areas with little resource potential where even subsistence from the land is marginal if not impossible.

## Bridging the Indigenous/ Non-Indigenous Faultline

Indigenous peoples are taking the control of their affairs away from Ottawa (Vignette 3.7). Some First Nations and Inuit have made substantial advances in economic development, while others have gained increasing control over their own affairs through self-government and sovereignty. Unfortunately, some Indigenous people, including the Métis, have just begun this self-government process.

In 1996, the Report of the Royal Commission on Aboriginal Peoples identified two major goals: Indigenous economic development and self-government. The gap between Indigenous and non-Indigenous societies will not be bridged until these goals are achieved. The principal factor is transferring power from Ottawa (the political power core) to the various Indigenous communities (the politically weak periphery). The economic and social well-being of Indigenous reserves varies widely. Some, such as the Whitecap Dakota First Nation near Saskatoon with its casino and top-tier golf course, have gained a high level of economic and social stability. The Labrador Inuit provide another example since they gained a share of the royalties from the Voisey's Bay nickel mine within their land claim agreement. Many others remain trapped in poverty and, without an economic base, breaking the dependency on the federal government seems an impossible task. Many individuals and families have made a choice, relocating to cities where a variety of opportunities and amenities are available.

While the total Indigenous population continues to increase, the percentage of Indigenous people living in cities continues its upward trend. According to the 2016 census, the number of Indigenous people residing in cities increased to nearly 870,000, forming 52 per cent of the total Indigenous population (Statistics Canada, 2017). Most significantly, this demographic movement is shifting the geographic location of First Nations people, Inuit, and Métis from their cultural homes on reserves and in small communities to major urban centres. The cities with the largest Indigenous populations in 2011 and 2016 were Winnipeg (78,420 and 92,810), Edmonton (61,765 and 76,205), Vancouver (52,375 and 61,460), and Toronto (36,995 and 46,315). The highest percentages of Indigenous people are in smaller cities, such as Thunder Bay, with 12.7 per cent of its population Indigenous, Winnipeg at 12.2 per cent, and Saskatoon at 10.9 per cent. These figures, however, mask a degree of "churn" or back and forth of individuals between

## Vignette 3.7

### A Final Attempt at Assimilation: The White Paper of 1969

Until 1969, Canada's Indigenous peoples were largely invisible to other Canadians. Most were geographically separated, as many status Indians lived on reserves, Métis were in isolated communities, and Inuit remained in the Arctic. By and large, all were outside the political process and thus denied access to political decision-making. In fact, status Indians did not receive the right to vote in federal elections until 1960. Shunned by Canadian society, these marginalized peoples had been subjected to assimilation policies for many years.

However, the political and social landscape began to change in 1969. Ottawa made one last attempt to assimilate the First Nations people of Canada through its "Statement of the Government of Canada on Indian Policy," more popularly known as the White Paper. The Liberals under Pierre Trudeau proposed to eliminate the legal distinction between First Nations people living in Canada and other citizens of Canada by repealing the Indian Act and amending the British North America Act to remove those parts that called for separate treatment for status Indians, and to abolish the Department of Indian Affairs. Some Indigenous leaders—soon labelled "Uncle Tomahawks" by their less conciliatory peers—supported this solution, but many others did not.

In the same year, Harold Cardinal published *The Unjust Society*, and the following year, under his leadership, the Alberta chiefs published a formal rebuttal to the White Paper, commonly known as the "Red Paper" and titled *Citizens Plus: A Presentation by the Indian Chiefs of Alberta to the Right Honourable P.E. Trudeau*. In brief, the vast majority of First Nations and their leaders were unwilling to be assimilated and to give up their status as "citizens plus," meaning that they might be Canadian citizens but they also had certain inalienable rights as Canada's First Peoples. In 1970 Trudeau reluctantly withdrew the White Paper, and by 1973, despite being a fierce believer in *individual rights*, he began to recognize that Canada had to begin to find a place within its polity for the *collective rights* of its Indigenous peoples. This was the start of Indigenous peoples regaining their power.

urban places and reserves. Nevertheless, urbanization is reshaping the contours of contemporary Inuit society.

But for those who remain within their cultural homes, developing an economic base on a reserve or in a remote community is not an easy task. Some have benefited from resource development through impact benefit agreements (IBAs), but most have not. One of the most successful IBA negotiations took place in Arctic Quebec, where Makivik Corporation obtained a 4.5 per cent share of the profits of the Raglan mine as well as the standard commitments to employment and business opportunities (Lewis & Brocklehurst, 2009, pp. 21–9). Yet, most Indigenous communities do not have the business experience and expertise of Makivik, which is a product of the James Bay and Northern Quebec Agreement of 1975. Leadership in remote communities and reserves,

while improving, is ill-equipped to negotiate impact benefit agreements with international mining companies.

Consider Attawapiskat First Nation, whose IBA negotiators focused on an annual cash payment of $2 million per year from De Beers for the development and operation of its Victor Diamond Mine in northern Ontario. While that is a substantial amount of money, it pales in comparison to a percentage of the annual revenue, estimated at $400 million in 2012 (Porter, 2013). However, annual cash payments usually begin upon the signing of the IBA, while a percentage of royalties starts after the mine turns a profit. The key is the length of the mining operations. As a rule, an annual payment works best for short-term mining operations (i.e., around 10 years or less). For long-term mining operations, a percentage of royalties provides the best return for

**THINK ABOUT IT**

The Métis of the Red River Settlement had established self-governance institutions before Rupert's Land was transferred to the Dominion of Canada. Since Canada did not recognize this government, the Métis under the leadership of Riel attempted to negotiate a solution. Why did they largely succeed in 1870 but not in the 1885 uprising?

involved First Nations. The Victor mine closed in 2019 after 11 years of operations.

## Indigenous Relations with Europeans

Over time, circumstances determining the relationship between Indigenous groups and Europeans changed. In broad terms, in the early days of the fur trade, each side depended on the other for goods. As the British took a firmer hold of these lands, the power relationship shifted and Indigenous groups became dependent on the Hudson's Bay Company and its rival, the North West Company.

Given this general observation of the changing relationship, how did the two peoples view each other at different historic times? Starting in the seventeenth century, the British and French colonial powers saw their colonies as an extension of their homelands but always asked the question, "How do the colonies benefit the imperial centre?" On the other hand, Indigenous groups asked different questions, such as "How do we gain access to European goods to enhance our way of life?" and "Will these two nations help us defeat our traditional enemies?" The relationship between New France and the Huron Confederacy illustrates this point. In 1609, the Huron chiefs met with Samuel de Champlain to discuss both trade and a military alliance. The Huron had three objectives: (1) to gain access to European goods, including firearms, by supplying the French with beaver pelts; (2) to improve their material well-being with the trade goods and, in turn, trade these goods to more distant Indigenous peoples for more beaver pelts; and (3) to strengthen their military position against their traditional enemy, the Iroquois, who were allied with the Dutch and later the English traders based in New York.

The French had different objectives. First and foremost, their goal was to secure a supply of furs for sale in Europe. A secondary goal—but related to the supply of furs—was a military alliance to prevent the British and Iroquois from gaining access to the highly valued fur pelts coming from the forest lands north of the Great Lakes. A third objective was to convert the Huron to Christianity. At the height of the fur trade in the seventeenth century, New France

greatly prospered and the Huron accounted for around half of the furs shipped to France (Dickason with McNab, 2009, p. 101). Trade was so important to the Huron tribes that when the French insisted that the Huron allow Jesuit missionaries to live among them as a condition for continued trade, the Huron reluctantly agreed. Unfortunately, the missionaries brought with them smallpox and other diseases that quickly swept through the Huron tribes, causing a sharp decline in their population.

The experiences of the original occupants of Western Canada—the Plains peoples and the Métis—ended badly. Even the **Manitoba Act of 1870**[3] did not protect the hard-fought gains of the **Provisional Government** of the Métis led by Louis Riel.

In all instances, the pressure to conform to the majority society was both overt and covert; and in each case, the outcome pushed these peoples to the margins of Western Canadian society. The leader of the Métis, Louis Riel, was forced into exile in the United States. Later, Riel returned to lead the second Métis uprising in 1885, which was suppressed, and he was convicted of treason and hanged on 16 November 1885. The final irony was that Riel's death came only nine days after the driving of the last spike on the Canadian Pacific rail line at Craigellachie, British Columbia. Of these two events, one drove a wedge between Ottawa and Quebec; the other, redolent in symbolism, united the new nation from sea to sea.

## The First Clash: The Red River Resistance of 1869–70

With the transfer of the vast lands administered by the Hudson's Bay Company, Canada changed from a small territory to a truly continental country. While the boundary between Western Canada and the United States had been determined earlier, the survey of lands for agricultural settlement took place in the 1880s. The land survey system, based on a township and range model, stamped a rectangular-shaped grid on the cultural landscape, thus determining the shape and placement of farms, roads, and towns. As Moffat (2002, p. 204) points out, this survey system "enabled the division of western lands among the HBC, the Canadian Pacific Railway (CPR),

Ron Garnett/AirScapes.ca

**PHOTO 3.6** The confluence of the Red and Assiniboine rivers is known as the Forks. Today, the Forks lies in the heart of Winnipeg. In times past, the strategic location of the Forks provided Plains peoples with ready access by canoe to the lands south of the forty-ninth parallel and to the vast western interior. In 1738, the French explorer La Vérendrye established Fort Rouge at the Forks. With the founding of the Red River Settlement in 1812, the Forks became its focal point.

and homesteaders, and set aside two sections in each township for the future of local education."

The land grant to the CPR was a way Ottawa was able to help finance its construction. However, when the federal surveyors set foot in the Red River Colony in 1869, Ottawa had failed to acknowledge the presence and rights of the Métis. As well, the federal government had not yet begun negotiations with the Indigenous peoples of the prairie. In fact, Ottawa did not inform the residents of the Red River Settlement of its plans for the Hudson's Bay lands, nor did the government signal that it recognized local landholdings and the 1817 Selkirk Treaty with the Peguis First Nation. With the clash between the surveyors and the Métis, events quickly spun out of control, resulting in the Red River Resistance.

The Red River Resistance pitted the tiny Métis settlement against Ottawa. In 1869, the Red River community was the only settled area of any size in the North-Western Territory, with a population of nearly 12,000 evenly divided between French- and English-speaking residents (Table 3.2). Most consisted of mixed-race peoples, born of French and British fur traders and their First Nations wives. Following their fur-trading days, these families settled in long lots along the banks of the two major rivers. Their economy was a blend of buffalo hunting and subsistence farming (Vignette 3.8).

By early 1869, news of the pending transfer of Hudson's Bay Company lands to Ottawa had reached the Red River Settlement, and the arrival of land surveyors resulted in open hostility. When Canadian surveyors began to survey Métis-occupied lands,

## Vignette 3.8

### The Origin of the Métis Nation

The fur trade and the Métis are part of the historical fabric of Western Canada. With their command of English/French and Indigenous languages, the Métis were logical intermediaries in the fur trade. In the early nineteenth century, the settlement near the confluence of the Red River and the Assiniboine River consisted mainly of French and Scottish Métis and Scottish settlers brought from Scotland to fulfill Lord Selkirk's dream of an agricultural community. By 1821, the French and British fur-trading empires—the North West Company and the HBC—had amalgamated, throwing many of the Métis out of work. Many Métis gathered in the Red River Settlement, which officially formed the Métis Nation. The Métis culture was neither European nor Indigenous, but a fusion of the two.

the Métis feared for their rights to those lands and even for their place in the new society. Matters came to a boil when, in October 1869, Louis Riel put his foot on a surveyor's chain and told them to leave. Thus, the Red River Resistance began, during which the Métis took control of Upper Fort Garry and the HBC headquarters. At the same time, William Mc-Dougall, the appointed lieutenant-governor of the HBC lands, was travelling west to the HBC headquarters to demonstrate Canadian sovereignty, but members of the recently formed Comité National des Métis blockaded the Pembina Trail and forced him back, effectively signalling to Ottawa that a Red River government existed (Dickason & Newbigging, 2019, pp. 198–201).

A month later, in early December 1869, the Métis under Riel formed their Provisional Government and soon began to negotiate with Canada over the terms of entry into Confederation. The three-man delegation sent to Ottawa by Riel's Provisional Government gained much of what they sought, including agreement to the establishment of a new province, but anti-Roman Catholic Orange Order elements from Ontario who had come to the Red River area were not pleased that Catholic and French-speaking Métis were in charge, and one man, Thomas Scott, who had been arrested by the Métis but persisted in being belligerent and unruly, was summarily executed after a brief trial. This inevitably led to further difficulties.

One advantage Riel had in his negotiations with the Canadian government was "remoteness." Without rail connection to the settlement, Ottawa could not rush troops to quell the resistance, which, with the execution of Scott, seemed on the verge of full-scale warfare. Although a rail line reached St Paul in Minnesota, the US government refused to allow Canadian troops to cross the border. In April 1870, Macdonald authorized a military force of 1,000 troops—the Wolseley Expedition—to advance on Red River and assert Canada's sovereignty over the settlement. The Canadian troops followed an old fur trade route and took four months to finally reach the

**PHOTO 3.7** By 1875, conditions were no longer friendly in Manitoba for Métis. Many moved west to Batoche in the District of Saskatchewan to regain their old lifestyle that was pushed aside by the flood of settlers that followed Manitoba joining Confederation.

Red River in August 1870. Fearing for their lives, Riel and his lieutenants fled to the United States. On 15 July 1870, Manitoba became a tiny province of Canada with an area of about 2,600 km² (1,000 square miles). The Métis had obtained most of their demands (the use of English and French languages within the government and a dual system of Protestant and Roman Catholic schools); at the same time, Prime Minister Macdonald ensured Canadian control over Western Canada.

## The Second Clash: The Northwest Resistance of 1885

Shortly after Manitoba came into Confederation, life in the former Red River Settlement changed so drastically that many Métis sought to regain a lifestyle of buffalo hunting and subsistence agriculture in present-day Saskatchewan. Far from the world of the settlers, Batoche and Duck Lake formed new centres where the Métis thrived. Within a decade, however, Ottawa again sought to incorporate these Métis lands into Canada. Another land survey was ordered by the federal government. Frustrated with Ottawa, a Métis delegation went to Montana in 1884 and convinced Louis Riel, in exile as a schoolteacher and an American citizen, to return to Canada to lead their quest for their rights. Late in 1884, Riel sent a petition to Ottawa with various demands for all the inhabitants of the North-West—First Nations people, Métis, and whites—effectively asking that they be treated with the dignity deserving of loyal British subjects. Eventually, when no remotely supportive government response was forthcoming, Métis soldiers, with a few warriors from local bands, ambushed a North West Mounted Police (NWMP) contingent at Duck Lake on 26 March 1885, killing 12 men and losing six of their own. Big Bear, a Plains Cree chief, was seeking a peaceful solution to the plight of his people, but a few of his warriors, too, went on the warpath. On 2 April 1885 Cree warriors led by Wandering Spirit rode to Frog Lake to demand food. When the local Indian agent refused them, the agent was shot, marking the beginning of the **Frog Lake Massacre**. The warriors then looted the settlement, shooting and killing eight other settlers, including two Catholic priests.

The Métis, under the leadership of Riel but led militarily by Gabriel Dumont, were prepared to fight the advancing Canadian army, which had arrived quickly from Ontario by means of the Canadian Pacific Railway. Attempts to unite with the Cree failed. Still, the Métis and a few warriors from nearby reserves were successful in surprising the Canadian troops, led by Major-General Frederick D. Middleton, at Fish Creek, but the larger and well-equipped Canadian army eventually wore down the smaller and less well-equipped Métis and First Nations forces at Batoche (see Figure 3.13). From Ottawa's perspective, the Northwest Resistance was crushed and Ottawa's sovereignty over these lands was confirmed. From the Métis perspective, they were defending their lands. The consequences were harsh: Louis Riel and eight First Nations leaders were hanged while **Big Bear** and **Poundmaker** were sent to prison. But the uprising had an enduring effect on the Cree and the Métis, and soured Ottawa's relations with Quebec.

## The Making of Canada

After the completion of the CPR, Canada became a country linked together by the "iron horse," which in turn brought thousands to its western territories. Not only was the migration to Western Canada one of the greatest world immigrations, it also placed a "British/Canadian" brand on the landscape, and, with Indigenous treaties and the dispersal of the Métis, Canada relegated the earlier occupants to the margins. The emerging cultural landscape of Western Canada took three forms—the rectangular appearance of its rural landholdings, the orientation of villages and cities to the railways, and the symbols of ethnic/religious diversity as expressed by farm buildings and churches. By 1895, Western Canada had a predominantly British population that had established its own land survey and ownership system, local governments and police to ensure "law and order," and a variety of social institutions.

As evident from the experience of the Métis pattern of landownership, elements of the landscape that did not conform ran into serious problems. During a 10-year span from 1870 to 1880, the Métis lost their majority due to an influx of immigrants

For more on the reasons for the spoiling of relations between Ottawa and Quebec, see this chapter, "Strained Relations," page 106.

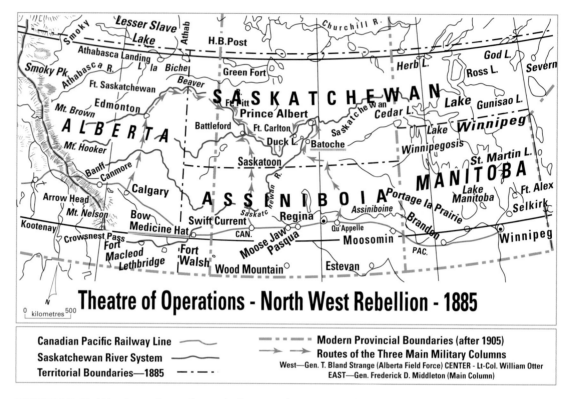

**FIGURE 3.13 Western Canada and the Northwest Resistance of 1885**

The Canadian Pacific Railway played a key role in the Northwest Resistance by transporting the Canadian forces quickly from Ontario to Qu'Appelle, Saskatchewan. In 1885, the political boundaries in Western Canada (except for Manitoba) still were part of the North-West Territories. The provinces of Alberta and Saskatchewan were formed in 1905 while Manitoba reached its current size in 1912.

Source: Based on Rattlesnake Jack's Old West Clip Art Parlour, Font Gallery, North West Rebellion Emporium and Rocky Mountain Ranger Patrol, at: members.mem-lane.com/gromboug/P5NWReb.htm

from Ontario, many of whom either belonged to or supported the views of the Orange Order. Some newcomers saw no place for the Métis and First Nations peoples in the emerging society, thus creating tensions between the existing population and the newcomers. From 1871 to 1881, Manitoba's population increased from 25,228 to 62,260, with most immigrants coming from Ontario, the British Isles, and the United States (Table 3.8). At this time, those of British ancestry formed 54 per cent of the population; other Europeans made up 17 per cent; Métis, 17 per cent; and First Nations, 11 per cent (Canada, 1882, Table III). The newly formed English-speaking majority focused their attention on the dual school system. By 1891, Manitoba's population exceeded 150,000 (Table 3.8). In an example of the tyranny of the majority, the English-speaking population argued that with so few French-speaking students,

funding for the Catholic school was not warranted. In 1890, the government of Manitoba abolished public funding for Catholic schools. This decision

**TABLE 3.8 Population\* in Western Canada by Province, 1871–1911**

| Year | Manitoba | Saskatchewan | Alberta |
|------|----------|--------------|---------|
| **1871** | 25,228 | | |
| **1881** | 62,260 | 21,652 | 9,875 |
| **1891** | 152,506 | 40,206 | 26,593 |
| **1901** | 255,211 | 91,279 | 73,022 |
| **1911** | 461,394 | 492,432 | 374,295 |

\*Indigenous Plains peoples were not recorded in the 1871 and 1881 censuses.

Note: The boundaries of Manitoba did not reach their present limits until 1912, and Saskatchewan and Alberta became provinces in 1905. Their populations for 1881, 1891, and 1901 have been calculated from the censuses of Canada for 1881 and 1891.

Sources: Canada (1882, pp. 93–6; 1892, pp. 112–13); Statistics Canada (2003).

took on national significance by becoming a critical issue between Quebec and the rest of the country.

What caused this initial influx of settlers? One reason was that Ontario no longer had a surplus of agricultural land and sons of farmers looked to the unsettled lands on the Great Plains of the United States and to Manitoba. A second reason was that the promise of a railway would make farming in Manitoba more viable. With completion of the CPR line from Fort William on Lake Superior to Selkirk, Manitoba, in 1882, grain could be transported by rail and ship to eastern Canada and Great Britain rather than by the more circuitous steamship route to St Paul and then by rail to New York. Wheat farming in Manitoba had become a profitable business because of advances in agricultural machinery and farming techniques, and rising prices for grain. Equally important, new strains of wheat, first Red Fife and then Marquis, both of which ripened more quickly than previous varieties, lessened the danger of crop loss due to frost. Marquis wheat, which matured seven days earlier than Red Fife, allowed wheat cultivation to take place in the parkland belt of Saskatchewan and Alberta where the frost-free period was shorter than in southern Manitoba.

## Sifton Widens the Net

By the end of the nineteenth century, the Canadian government was still looking for more settlers to migrate to Canada's West. Clifford Sifton of Manitoba, the federal minister responsible for finding settlers, realized that he had to expand his recruitment area beyond Great Britain into Central Europe and Russia. Even though this ran against the creation of a British-populated Western Canada, Sifton (1922) took a pragmatic approach, which he summed up in later years: "I think a stalwart peasant in a sheepskin coat, born on the soil, whose forefathers have been farmers for ten generations, with a stout wife and a half-dozen children is good quality." Under Sifton, the pattern of immigration took a sharp turn from the main sources of immigrants to the West, namely Canada, the British Isles, and the United States. Within two decades of entering Confederation, Manitoba's population had increased by just over 600 per cent (Table 3.8). Most were of British

stock, but substantial numbers of Mennonites and Icelanders had also come to Manitoba. At the same time, few settlers had reached Saskatchewan and Alberta, though many of the Métis had relocated in Saskatchewan, primarily around the settlement of Batoche on the South Saskatchewan River just north of Saskatoon. In the next decade, the volume of immigrants from Central Europe, Scandinavia, and Russia increased substantially. As peasants, they were prepared for the harsh physical conditions associated with breaking the virgin prairie land and were willing to deal with the psychological stress of living on isolated farmsteads in a foreign country where their native tongue was not accepted. As the numbers of these European immigrants grew, the anglophone majority became concerned about the newcomers and their possible effect on the existing social structure. The demographic impact of the non-British migration to Western Canada is shown in the 1916 census (Table 3.9).

This wave of Central Europeans had tremendous implications for Western Canada. While most newcomers assimilated into the English-speaking society, a few did not. Often these ethnic groups settled in one area where they were somewhat insulated from the larger society and where they attempted to maintain their traditional customs, language, and religion. The federal government, by providing land reserves for ethnic groups such as the Mennonites and Doukhobors, reinforced this tendency.

While they were successful farmers, the cultural differences between the more conservative Doukhobors and Canadian society were too great for the majority society to accept. Some Doukhobors were able to integrate into local society, but the Community Doukhobors simply were not prepared to adapt. They remained faithful to their religious beliefs that emphasized communal living. In choosing to settle in Canada, they were granted blocks of land and exemption from military service.

Through negotiations with the Canadian government, Doukhobor leaders had obtained four large blocks of land totalling 750,000 acres. In 1899, the Doukhobors—7,500 in total—arrived in Canada and took possession of pre-selected lands where they built 57 villages. The four colonies were located just west of Swan River, Manitoba (North Colony), and

**TABLE 3.9    Population of Western Canada by Ethnic Group, 1916**

| Ethnic Group | W. Canada Population | % of W. Canada Population | % of Manitoba Population | % of Sask. Population | % of Alberta Population |
|---|---|---|---|---|---|
| British | 971,830 | 57.2 | 57.7 | 54.5 | 60.2 |
| German | 136,968 | 8.1 | 4.7 | 11.9 | 6.8 |
| Austro-Hungarian | 136,250 | 8.0 | 8.2 | 9.1 | 6.4 |
| French | 89,987 | 5.3 | 6.1 | 4.9 | 4.9 |
| Russian | 63,735 | 3.7 | 2.9 | 4.5 | 3.8 |
| Norwegian | 47,449 | 2.8 | 0.6 | 4.2 | 3.4 |
| Indigenous | 39,147 | 2.3 | 2.5 | 1.7 | 2.9 |
| Ukrainian | 39,103 | 2.3 | 4.1 | 0.7 | 1.8 |
| Swedish | 37,220 | 2.2 | 1.4 | 2.5 | 2.7 |
| Polish | 27,790 | 1.6 | 3.0 | 1.0 | 0.9 |
| Jewish | 23,381 | 1.4 | 3.0 | 0.6 | 0.6 |
| Dutch | 22,353 | 1.3 | 1.3 | 1.4 | 1.3 |
| Icelandic | 15,800 | 0.9 | 2.2 | 0.5 | 0.1 |
| Danish | 9,556 | 0.6 | 0.3 | 0.5 | 0.9 |
| Belgian | 9,084 | 0.5 | 0.8 | 0.4 | 0.4 |
| Italian | 5,348 | 0.3 | 0.3 | 1.0 | 0.9 |
| Other | 26,219 | 1.5 | 0.9 | 1.5 | 2.3 |
| Total | 1,701,220 | 100.0 | 100.0 | 100.0 | 100.0 |

Source: Census of Prairie Provinces, 1916, Table 7. Data adapted from Statistics Canada: www12.statcan.ca/English/census01/products/analytic/companion/age/provpymds.cfm

**THINK ABOUT IT**
Discrimination against Indigenous peoples and Doukabours was common in the nineteenth century and early twentieth century. How has this changed over the past 100+ years? How has it not?

at Prince Albert (Saskatchewan Colony) and Yorkton, Saskatchewan (South Colony and Good Spirit Lake Annex).

Farming was not only an economic activity, it was also central to their religious beliefs, which emphasized the value of a simple, communal life. For example, Doukhobors shared in the returns from farming, and no one person owned the land or the tools. In a land of individual landholdings and the pursuit of profit, the Doukhobors were seen as "out of step" with the surrounding community. As public resentment increased, the federal government took action. In 1905, Frank Oliver succeeded Clifford Sifton as Minister of the Interior. Oliver decided to enforce the Dominion Lands Act, so when the Doukhobors refused to swear an oath of allegiance to the King, Oliver had his excuse to deny them homestead lands.

Failure to take such an oath had two implications. First, it suggested that these people were disloyal to the monarch. Second, it meant that the Doukhobors could not obtain title to their homestead lands. Under this pretext, Oliver used the Dominion Lands Act to cancel their right to land. Most of the Doukhobors who remained committed to the communal way of life eventually moved to British Columbia; others abandoned the village life and took title to homesteads. The villages gradually lost members and lands. The South Colony just north of Yorkton, Saskatchewan, was the last holdout, but by 1918 it ceased to exist.

One explanation for the ultimate failure of the Doukhobor experiment was that Canada's model of individual settlement was simply too rigid to accept a communal one. Primarily for that reason, the Community Doukhobors were unable to find a place in Western Canada. They represent a classic example of a people being too different from the majority to be allowed a comfortable space within the predominately British landscape. Ironically, the village model of settlement was perhaps the most effective way of settling the Prairies in the late nineteenth and early twentieth centuries. Carl Tracie (1996, p. xii) puts it this way:

> At the very time when the individual homesteader was struggling with the very real problems of isolation and loneliness, the Doukhobor settlements, whose compact form allayed these problems, were being dismantled by forces which could not accommodate the communal aspects of the group. Also, although the initial government concern was the survival of the Doukhobors, their very prosperity, based as it was on communal effort, may have worked against them since it illustrated the success of a system diametrically opposed to the individualistic system dictated by government policy and assumed by mainstream society.

## Quebec's Place in Confederation

Although Indigenous peoples were the first to occupy North America, the colonization of the continent pushed them to the margins, leaving the two European powers—the French and the British—to place their mark on the land. Following the British military victory at Quebec in 1759, the Treaty of Paris (1763) confirmed British hegemony over a French-Canadian majority and its control over the lands of New France. This historic fact underscores the dominant position of the British and their impact on later Canadian institutions and governments. The British way of life formed a new cultural landscape except in rural Quebec, where its French language, the seigneurial agricultural system, and the Roman Catholic religion remained dominant. Differences between these two cultures have come to represent a major faultline in Canadian society.

Nonetheless, the union of Lower Canada (a small version of present-day Quebec) and Upper Canada (a small version of present-day Ontario) in 1841 meant that French and English had to work together in a single parliament, which made each dependent on the other and was instrumental in the 1867 Confederation. Significantly, most of British North America remained under the Hudson's Bay Company, including what is now northern Ontario and Quebec.

This balance of political power between the French and English has done much to shape the political nature of Canada, particularly the need to find a middle ground. Over the years, they have accomplished much together. Yet, significant differences between the two communities exist, and from time to time these differences flare into serious misunderstandings. Without a doubt, Canadian unity depends on the continuation of this relationship and the need for compromise, which has become a feature of modern Canadian political life and is a basic aspect of Canadian tolerance between the two official language groups and towards newcomers.

The serious nature of the French/English rift has profound geopolitical consequences for Canada. While blowing hot and cold over the years since Confederation, the rift was boiling hot at the time of the 1995 referendum but has since cooled down.

## Origin of the French/ English Faultline

The British Conquest of the French on the Plains of Abraham in 1759 marks the origin of this faultline. An event that remains a dark page in French-Canadian history culminated in the battered remnants of the French army and the French colonial elite boarding ships to return to their mother country. The French Canadians had no thought of leaving, but what would happen to them under British military rule? Would they, like their Acadian brethren, be deported to other British colonies? Britain did not need to take such drastic action by this time—the Acadian deportations had occurred in the 1750s when there still was a French threat to Britain's North American possessions. In the Treaty of Paris, France ceded New France to Britain, which placed the French-Canadian majority under the British monarchy. While the English lived in cities in Quebec and dominated the Quebec economy and politics, French Canadians lived mostly in rural areas where they successfully maintained their culture within a British North America. This relationship between British rulers and the French Canadians would be strengthened with the Quebec Act of 1774.

## The Quebec Act, 1774

With the Quebec Act of 1774, the unique nature and separateness of Quebec were recognized, thus affirming its place in British North America. This Act is sometimes described as the Magna Carta for French Canada.[4] Its main provisions ensured the continuation of the aristocratic seigneurial land-holding system and guaranteed religious freedom for the colony's Roman Catholic majority and, by implication, their right to retain their native language.[5] This gave the most powerful people in New France a good reason to support the new rulers. The Roman Catholic Church was placed in a particularly strong position. Not only was the Church allowed to collect tithes and dues but its role as the protector of French culture went unchallenged. Therefore, the clergy played an extremely important role in directing and maintaining a rural French-Canadian society, a role further enhanced by the Church's control of the education system. The **habitants** (farmers) were at the bottom of French-Canadian society's hierarchy. They formed the vast majority of the population and continued to cultivate their land on seigneuries, paying their dues to their lord (seigneur) and faithfully obeying the local priest and bishop. The British granted another important concession, namely, that civil suits would be tried under French law. Criminal cases, however, fell under English law.

The seigneurial system formed the basis of rural life in New France and, later, in Quebec. In 1774, there were about 200 seigneuries in the St Lawrence Lowland. This type of land settlement left its mark on the landscape (the long, narrow landholdings extending to the river and the vast estate of the seigneur) and on the mentality of rural French Canadians—close family ties, a strong sense of togetherness with neighbouring rural families (the long-lot system of land tenure meant that rural neighbours were not so far away), and staunch support for the Church. A habitant's landholding, though small, was the key to his family's prosperity, and by bequeathing the farm to his eldest son the habitant ensured the continuation of this rural way of life. In 1854, the habitant was allowed to purchase his small plot of land from his seigneur, but the last vestiges of this seigneurial system did not disappear until a century later. Even today, the landscape along the St Lawrence shows many signs of this type of landholding.

While the heart of this new British territory was the settled land of the St Lawrence Lowland, its full geographic extent was immense. Essentially, the Quebec Act of 1774 recognized the geographic area of former French territories in North America. Quebec's territory in 1774 was extended from the Labrador coast to the St Lawrence Lowland and beyond to the sparsely settled Great Lakes Lowland and the Indigenous lands of the Ohio Basin. After the British defeat in the American Revolution, the geographic size of Quebec shrank with the southern part of the Great Lakes Lowland and the Indigenous lands of the Ohio Basin ceded to the Americans.

## The Loyalists

The American War of Independence changed the political landscape of North America. Within the newly formed United States, a number of Americans, known as the **Loyalists**, remained faithful to Britain. Like the French-speaking people in North America, most of these Loyalists were born and raised in the New World. For them, North America was their homeland. During the revolution, they had sided with the British. They were hounded by the American revolutionaries and many lost their homes and property. Most resettled in the remaining British colonies in North America, where Britain offered them land. The majority (about 40,000 Loyalists) settled in the Maritimes, particularly in Nova Scotia. About 5,000 relocated in the forested Appalachian Uplands of the Eastern Townships of Quebec. A few thousand, including Indigenous peoples led by Joseph Brant, took up land in the Great Lakes Lowland in present-day Ontario.

Within a few decades, more English-speaking settlers arrived in the Great Lakes region. As their numbers grew, they felt frustrated as a small part of the sprawling Quebec colony. Its capital city, Quebec, was too far away and these English-speaking settlers sought to control their own affairs so they could have a more "British" government with British civil law, British institutions, and an elected assembly. The solution took the form of the Constitutional Act of 1791, when Quebec was split into Upper and Lower Canada.

## The Six Nations of the Iroquois Confederacy

The Mohawk, Oneida, Onondaga, Cayuga, Seneca, and Tuscarora formed the Six Nations of the Iroquois Confederacy. In alliance with the French, the Confederacy blocked British settlers from entering the Ohio Valley. During the American Revolution the Confederation split, with the Oneida and Tuscarora joining the American cause, while the rest of the league, led by Chief Joseph Brant's Mohawk, sided with the British. After the end of the American Revolution in 1783, those loyal to the British moved from New York to Ontario and settled along the Grand River in southwestern Ontario on a vast tract—the Haldimand Grant—given to them in 1784 by the governor of Quebec, Lord Haldimand. In a sense, these lands were both a reward for serving with the British troops and a buffer from settlers who sought farmland.

## The Constitutional Act, 1791

The Constitutional Act of 1791 represented an attempt by the British Parliament to satisfy the political needs of the French- and English-speaking inhabitants of Quebec. These were the main provisions of the Act: (1) the British colony of Quebec was divided into the provinces of Upper and Lower Canada, with the Ottawa River as the dividing line, except for two seigneuries located just southwest of the Ottawa River; and (2) each province was governed by a British lieutenant-governor appointed by Britain. From time to time, the lieutenant-governor would consult with his executive council and acknowledge legislation passed by an elected legislative assembly.

In 1791, Lower Canada had a much larger population than Upper Canada. At that time, about 15,000 colonists lived in Upper Canada, most of whom were of Loyalist extraction, plus about 10,000 Indigenous people, some of whom had fled northward after the American Revolution. Lower Canada's population consisted of about 140,000 French Canadians, 10,000 English Canadians, and perhaps as many as 5,000 Indigenous people.

Following the Constitutional Act, Upper and Lower Canada each had an elected assembly, but the real power remained in the hands of the British-appointed lieutenant-governors. In Lower Canada the lieutenant-governor had the support of the Roman Catholic Church, the seigneurs, and the Château Clique. The Château Clique, a group consisting largely of anglophone merchants, controlled most business enterprises and, as they were favoured by the lieutenant-governor, wielded much political power. In Upper Canada the Family Compact—a small group of officials who dominated senior bureaucratic positions, the executive and legislative councils, and the judiciary—held similar positions in commercial and political circles. While these two elite groups promoted their own political and financial well-being, the rest of the population grew more and more dissatisfied with blatant political abuses, which included patronage and unpopular policies that favoured these two groups. Attempts to obtain political reforms leading to a more democratic political system failed. Under these circumstances, social unrest was widespread.

In 1837 and 1838, rebellions broke out. In Lower Canada Louis-Joseph Papineau led the rebels, while William Lyon Mackenzie headed the rebels in Upper Canada. Both uprisings were ruthlessly suppressed by British troops. The goal of both insurrections was to take control by wresting power from the colonial governments in Toronto and Quebec City and putting government in the hands of the popularly elected assemblies. In Lower Canada the rebellion was also an expression of Anglo–French animosity. While both uprisings were unsuccessful, the British government nevertheless sent Lord Durham to Canada as governor general to investigate the rebels' grievances. He recommended a form of responsible government and the union of the two Canadas. Once the two colonies were unified, the next step, according to Durham, would be the assimilation of the French Canadians into British culture.

## The Act of Union, 1841

In response to Durham's report, in 1841 the two largest colonies in British North America, Upper and Lower Canada, were united into the Province of Canada. This Act of Union gave substance to the geographic and political realities of British North America. The geographic reality was that a large French-speaking population existed in Lower Canada, while a smaller

See **Figure 6.6**, "The Haldimand Tract," page 183, for more details about the Haldimand Grant.

| TABLE 3.10 Canadian Population by Colony or Province, 1841–1871 (%) | | | | |
|---|---|---|---|---|
| Colony/Province | 1841 | 1851 | 1861 | 1871 |
| **Ontario** | 33.0 | 41.1 | 45.2 | 46.5 |
| **Quebec** | 45.0 | 38.5 | 36.0 | 34.2 |
| **Nova Scotia** | 13.0 | 12.0 | 10.7 | 11.1 |
| **New Brunswick** | 9.0 | 8.4 | 8.1 | 8.2 |
| **Manitoba** | | | | 0.1 |
| **British Columbia** | | | | 0.8 |

Source: McVey & Kalbach (1995, p. 38). © 1995 Nelson Education Ltd Reproduced by permission. www.cengage.com/permissions.

English-speaking population was concentrated in Upper Canada (Table 3.10). The political reality was two-fold. Both groups had to work together to accomplish their political goals and neither group could achieve all of its goals without some form of compromise. When the two cultures were forced to work together in a single legislative assembly, a new beginning to the French/English faultline surfaced.

## Demographic Shifts

In a democracy, political power is based on population numbers. During the early days of the Act of Union most people lived in Lower Canada, but by 1851 the reverse was true (Table 3.10). In this way, the balance of power shifted to Upper Canada and this shift continues. In 1841, Quebec's population stood at 45 per cent of British North America's population, but after Confederation, in 1871, Quebec represented 34 per cent of the total population.

## Strained Relations

During these formative years, several events seriously strained relations between the Dominion's two founding peoples:

- the Red River Resistance, 1869–70;
- the Northwest Resistance, 1885, and its aftermath, with the execution of Riel;
- the Manitoba Schools Question, 1890.

### The Red River Resistance, 1869–70

As we have seen, the Métis uprising, led by Louis Riel, soon became a national issue, reopening differences between English, Protestant Ontario, and

The background to the Red River Resistance is presented earlier in this chapter in "The First Clash: Red River Resistance of 1869–70," page 96.

The background to the Northwest Resistance is presented above in this chapter in "The Second Clash: The Northwest Resistance of 1885," page 99.

French, Roman Catholic Quebec. Quebec considered Riel a French-Canadian hero who was defending the Métis, a people of mixed Indigenous and French origin, who spoke French and followed the Catholic religion. Protestant Ontario, on the other hand, considered Riel a traitor and a murderer. For Canada, the larger issue was the place of French Canadians in the West. A compromise was achieved in the Manitoba Act of 1870. Accordingly, the District of Assiniboia became the province of Manitoba. Under this Act, land was set aside for the Métis, although a number of them sold their entitlements (scrip) to land allotments to incoming settlers and either moved to what is now Alberta and Saskatchewan or continue their hunting lifestyle in Manitoba. The elected legislative assembly of Manitoba provided a balance between the two ethnic groups with 12 English and 12 French electoral districts. Equally important, Manitoba had two official languages (French and English) and two religious school systems (Catholic and Protestant) financed by public funds.

### The Northwest Resistance, 1885

As settlers began to spread into Saskatchewan, the Métis who had gathered around Batoche, about 60 km northeast of present-day Saskatoon, again feared for their future. In 1884, when a party of Métis went to Montana to plead with Louis Riel to return to Batoche and lead them again, Riel, convinced of his destiny, accepted this challenge. As we have seen, this uprising ended in failure for the Métis and their First Nations allies. For Quebec, the defeat of the Métis and the subsequent hanging of their leader not only represented a defeat for a French presence in the West but also widened the gulf between French and English Canadians. Riel's link to Quebec and the Roman Catholic Church made him a powerful symbol of language, religious, and racial divisions for over 100 years. Indeed, to this day historians remain divided about Louis Riel's legacy, his place in the story of Canada, and even his sanity as the messianic leader of a doomed resistance.[6]

### The Manitoba Schools Question, 1890

The British North America Act of 1867 established English and French as legislative and judicial languages in federal and Quebec institutions. The remaining three provinces (New Brunswick, Nova Scotia, and

Ontario) had only English as the official language. The question of French-language and religious rights in acquired western territories first arose in Manitoba.

The French/English issue became the focal point for the entry of the Red River Settlement (now Manitoba) into Confederation. Local inhabitants—mostly French-speaking Roman Catholic Métis and the less numerous English-speaking Métis—were determined to have some influence over the terms that would include their community as part of Canada. One of their concerns was language rights, an issue ultimately resolved when a list of rights drafted by the Riel's Provisional Government became the basis of federal legislation. When the settlement and surrounding territory of Red River entered Confederation in 1870 as the province of Manitoba, it did so with the assurance that English- and French-language rights, as well as the right to be educated in Protestant or Roman Catholic schools, were protected by provincial legislation.

During the 1870s and 1880s, with the influx of a large number of Anglo-Protestant settlers from Ontario, the proportion of Anglo-Protestants in the Manitoba population increased and the proportion of French and Roman Catholic inhabitants decreased. This demographic change created a stronger Anglo-Protestant culture in Manitoba. In 1890, the provincial government ended public funding of Catholic schools. From Quebec's perspective, this legislation shook the very foundations of their version of Confederation—an equal place in Western Canada. Sir Wilfrid Laurier became prime minister in 1896 and, in the following year, Laurier negotiated a compromise agreement with the government of Manitoba. The compromise allowed for the teaching of Catholic religion in a public school when there were sufficient Catholic students. Similarly, if there were sufficient French-speaking students, classes could be taught in French.

## One Country, Two Visions

Apart from the Indigenous/non-Indigenous faultline, the greatest challenge to Canadian unity comes from the cultural divide that separates French- and English-speaking Canadians and their respective visions of the country. The two predominant visions are (1) a partnership between French and English Canada, and (2) equality of the 10 provinces.

In the early years of Confederation, events such as those outlined above widened the French/English faultline. For French Canadians these events demonstrated the "power" of the English-speaking majority and their unwillingness to accept a vision of Canada as a partnership between the two founding peoples. The root of each vision lies in the history of Canada and its division of powers.

## Partnership Vision

One vision of Canada is based on the principle of two founding peoples. This vision originated in French-Canadian historical experiences and compromises that were necessary for the sharing of political power between the two partners. This vision began with the Conquest of New France, but its true foundation lies in the formation of the Province of Canada in 1841. From 1841 onward, the experience of working together resulted in a Canadian version of cultural dualism.

Henri Bourassa, a French-Canadian politician and journalist (and Canadian nationalist) in the early twentieth century, was a strong advocate of cultural dualism. He wrote, "My native land is all of Canada, a federation of separate races and autonomous provinces. The nation I wish to see grow up is the Canadian nation, made up of French Canadians and English Canadians" (quoted in Bumsted, 2007, p. 307). Bourassa argued that a "double contract" existed within Confederation. Even today, Bourassa's "double contract" is an essential element in the concept of two founding peoples. He based the notion of a double contract on a liberal interpretation of section 93 of the BNA Act, which guarantees denominational schools. Bourassa expanded the interpretation of the religious rights to include cultural rights for French- and English-speaking Canadians. In more practical terms, Bourassa regarded Confederation as a moral contract that guaranteed French/English duality, the preservation of French-speaking Quebec, and the protection of the language and religious rights of French-speaking Canadians in other provinces.

From a geopolitical perspective, Canada is a bicultural country. In one part the majority of Canadians speak English, and in another part French is the majority language. Thus, French culture dominates in Quebec and has a strong position in New

Brunswick. In addition to provincial control over culture, two other geopolitical factors ensure the dynamism of French in those provinces. One factor is the large size of Quebec's population—the vitality of Québécois culture is one indication of its success. The second factor is the geographic concentration of French-speaking Canadians in Quebec and adjacent parts of Ontario and New Brunswick. In New Brunswick the French-speaking residents, known as Acadians, constitute over one-third of the population.

The Royal Commission on Bilingualism and Biculturalism was designed to bridge the gap between English and French Canadians. This Commission, set up in 1963, examined the issue of cultural dualism, that is, an equal partnership between the two cultural groups. But by the 1960s, Canada's demographics revealed a third ethnic force and the concept of duality no longer reflected reality. English-speaking Canada had changed. English-speaking Canada had evolved from a predominantly British population to a more diverse one with several large minority groups who also spoke other languages besides English, especially German and Ukrainian. This ethnic force became of special importance after 1967, when Canada revamped its immigration criteria to be based on merit (education, official language facility, work experience, etc.) rather than the formerly discriminatory country-of-origin policy. Consequently, in searching for a compromise to accommodate both the French and English and this newly recognized third force, Ottawa established two policies, bilingualism (1969) and multiculturalism (1971).

## The Vision of Equal Provinces

In the second vision, Canada consists of 10 equal provinces—yet this, too, is misleading. On the one hand, it represents the simple notion based on provincial powers granted under the British North America Act, which ensured that Canada consists of a union of equal provinces, all of which have the same powers of government. Nonetheless, by assigning provinces powers over education, language, and other cultural matters within their provincial jurisdictions, the BNA Act ensured that Quebec's French culture was secure from political tampering by the anglophone majority in the rest of Canada. Thus, Confederation provided a form of collective rights

for French culture within Quebec. Under Canada's federal system, the powers of government are shared between the federal government and 10 provincial governments. But are all provinces really equal? As noted earlier, population size, geographic extent, and financial strength vary considerably, which is reflected in the need for equalization payments.

The vision of 10 equal provinces, which has an analog in the long-held American political posture of states' rights, may reflect English-Canadian nationalism. For some time, English-speaking Canadians have been searching for their cultural identity and a sense of national belonging. Before World War I, English-speaking Canadians saw themselves as part of the British Empire, but with Canadian troops fighting as a unit in Europe the first signs of nationalism appeared. Canada's efforts during World War II pushed the sense of nationalism to new heights. In the years following, symbols of nation-building took the form of the Maple Leaf flag, adopted by Parliament in 1964, and "O Canada," the new national anthem approved by Parliament in 1967 and officially adopted in 1980. While the Québécois culture was flourishing, thanks in part to generous provincial funding for the arts, English-speaking Canadians continued to lean heavily on American culture. Some looked with envy at the cultural accomplishments of the Québécois and wondered aloud if similar achievements in English-speaking Canada were possible. The answer could be yes, providing the provincial governments offered similar financial support for the arts, and providing that English-speaking Canadians supported their artists at the same level as the Québécois public supported francophone artists and cultural producers.

## Compromise

Given the incompatibility of the two visions—two founding peoples versus 10 equal provinces—and the historical development of the country, Canadian politicians have had the unenviable task of trying to accommodate demands from different groups—especially French Canadians, new immigrants, and Indigenous peoples—and from different regions without offending other groups or regions. As in the past, politicians have continued to struggle with this Canadian dilemma, but in reality there is no perfect solution, only compromise. With this object in mind the federal government has made many efforts in search of the elusive middle ground. It seems the search for an acceptable compromise between the two opposing visions of Canada will never end, and perhaps that is a good thing because the process is more important than the end result. To understand the current struggle for compromise, it is important to understand the political, economic, and cultural developments that have taken place in Quebec over the past five decades.

## Resurgence of Quebec Nationalism

After World War II, Quebec broke with its past. A rise of Quebec nationalism had begun much earlier but gained political momentum during the **Quiet Revolution** of the early 1960s. This development was the result of four major events. The most important was the resurgence of ethnic nationalism, that is, a pride in being Québécois. The second was Quebec's joining the urban/industrial world of North America and the subsequent expansion in the size of its industrial labour force and business class. The third was the removal of the old elite. This reform movement was profoundly anticlerical in its opposition to the entrenched role of the Church in Quebec society, particularly the Church's control over education. In many ways, this reform was based on the aspirations of the working and middle classes in the new Quebec economy. The fourth was the state's aggressive role in the province's economic affairs.

With the election of Jean Lesage's Liberal government in 1960, which held power until 1966, the province moved forcefully in a new direction. It created a more powerful civil service that allowed francophones access to middle and senior positions often denied them in the private sector of the Quebec economy, which was controlled by English-speaking Quebecers and American companies. It nationalized the province's electricity system, thereby creating the industrial giant known as Hydro-Québec, now a powerful symbol of Quebec's revitalized economy and society. In turn, Hydro-Québec built a number of huge energy projects that demonstrated the province's industrial strength. By 1968, this Crown corporation had constructed one of the largest dams in the world on the Manicouagan River. Called Manic 5, this dam demonstrated Hydro-Québec's engineering and construction capabilities. To Québécois, Hydro-Québec was a symbol of Quebec's economic liberation from the years of suffocation associated with Maurice Duplessis and his Union Nationale government, which had been closely tied to big businesses owned by English-speaking Canadians and Americans. Clearly, Lesage's political goal of becoming "*maîtres chez nous*" (masters in our own house) had materialized. Within that political goal, the success of Hydro-Québec provided a concrete example of the role of the state and a symbol of Quebec nationalism. Quebec's desire for more autonomy in its own affairs intensified with increased confidence. In short, a new society had arisen in Quebec, a society that wanted to chart its destiny. Charles Taylor (1993, p. 4) summed up this new feeling as "a French Canada which, after a couple of centuries of enforced incubation [under London and then Ottawa], was ready to take control once more of its history." The political question Taylor raised is a simple one: Would this "control" take place within the framework of Canada's political system or outside it?

## Separatism

Separatism—the desire for an independent francophone nation in North America—grew out of the Quiet Revolution. The embers of nationalism were ignited in 1967 by French President Charles de Gaulle, who, when visiting the province for Expo '67, uttered the incendiary words "*Vive le Québec. Vive le Québec libre*" (Photo 3.8) during a speech from a balcony at Montreal City Hall. Soon, René Lévesque, who as a member of the Lesage government had been the architect of the nationalization of electricity generation in the province, had formed a new separatist political party, the Parti Québécois. By 1976, the PQ had won a stunning election victory, and since that time separatism, though waxing and waning in public support, has taken on a mainstream political form. By the time of the first referendum on independence in 1980, the separatists made up a substantial minority within Quebec's population, with perhaps 20 per cent dedicated separatists and another 40 per cent strongly dissatisfied with their place within Canada.

**THINK ABOUT IT**
Why is Quebec's emphasis on its culture so much stronger than in the other provinces of Canada, with the possible exception of Newfoundland and Labrador?

Archives de la Ville de Montréal

**PHOTO 3.8** French President Charles de Gaulle during his incendiary "*Vive le Québec libre*" speech in Montreal, 24 July 1967.

In the 1980 referendum, Quebec voters rejected the **sovereignty-association** option, with almost 60 per cent voting to remain in Canada, which suggests that just over half of the francophone voters stood with the "Non" side, along with almost all of the English-speaking residents. The rest of Canada responded with a collective sigh of relief, but separatism was far from dead.

The dream of an independent Quebec remained a strong political force. In fact, the 1995 referendum vote on independence almost succeeded. "No—by a Whisker!" screamed the headline of the *Globe and Mail* on the morning after the referendum of 30 October

1995 (Vignette 3.9). Quebec came within 40,000 votes of approving the separatist dream of becoming an independent state.

## Moving Forward

The 1995 referendum was a low point in French–English relations, and its after-effects were many and varied. English Canada was dazed by the outcome, but the separatists appeared to be a spent force. In 1996, provincial premiers added their voice to the discussion in the Calgary Declaration, stating: "the unique character of Quebec society with its French-speaking majority, its culture and its tradition of civil law is fundamental to the well-being of Canada." In the typical fashion of Canadian provincial leaders, the premiers remained clearly in the camp of 10 equal provinces by adding to their conciliatory Declaration that "any power conferred to one province in the future must be available to all." This Declaration was the third attempt at reconciliation with Quebec since the patriation of the Constitution in 1982. The next step was for each provincial government to pass the appropriate legislation, giving the Calgary Declaration legal status. By July 1998, all provinces (except Quebec) and territories had passed this resolution in their legislatures.

Since the 1995 referendum, separatism, while not gone, has lost its spark, in part because the threat of being absorbed by English-speaking North America has subsided for Quebecers, who are more

**THINK ABOUT IT**

Why does separatism remain an issue?

For historical background on the French/English faultline in Quebec, see Chapter 7, "British Colony, 1760–1867," page 219.

## Vignette 3.9

### The Results of the 30 October 1995 Referendum

The Question: "Do you agree that Quebec should become sovereign, after having made a formal offer to Canada for a new Economic and Political Partnership within the scope of the Bill respecting the future of Quebec and of the agreement signed on June 12, 1995?"
The Answer (at 10:30 p.m. Eastern Time, 21,907 of 22,427 polls):

|  | Number | Per cent |
|---|---|---|
| **No** | 2,294,162 | 49.5 |
| **Yes** | 2,254,496 | 48.7 |
| **Rejected** | 83,340 | 1.8 |
| **Total** | 4,631,998 | 100.0 |

Source: *Globe and Mail* (1995).

confident in the security of their language and culture than had been the case in the immediate post-World War II period. Equally important, Ottawa is more comfortable with the idea of Québécois being recognized as a "distinct cultural group" or nation within Canada. In November 2006, the House of Commons overwhelmingly passed a motion by Prime Minister Harper (*CBC News*, 2006) that stated, "Our position is clear. Do the Québécois form a nation within Canada? The answer is yes. Do the Québécois form an independent nation? The answer is no and the answer will always be no." But Québécois nationalism remains deep inside Québécois culture and language.

## Summary

History and geography explain the nature and complexity of contemporary Canada. Why is Canada both a young and an old country? Such complexities are reflected in the evolution of a country and its peoples. Yet, these historic events vary sharply from an Indigenous lens to a Canadian one, and from a Québécois perspective to the one prominent in the rest of Canada. While Quebec seems more comfortable within Confederation, it remains a region culturally different from the rest of Canada. This difference stems from its birth as New France. Then too, the Indigenous faultline has deep historic roots constructed on failed assimilation tactics that created a loss of trust, and this distrust continues to trouble federal–Indigenous relations. As well, survivors of Indigenous residential schools have begun to move forward, but the aftermath continues as the post-residential school generation exhibits intergenerational trauma.

In sum, geography teaches Canadians that our past is not a simple one and that tensions between regions and peoples will continue. Consequently, Canada's national unity, regional harmony, and social justice can only exist through compromises and by applying the rule of law. Going forward into the twenty-first century, the question is, are Canadians up to the task?

## Challenge Questions

1. Why did the doctrine of "terra nullius" allow Europeans to consider North America "unoccupied" and therefore open to their ownership and settlement? Did the Royal Proclamation of 1763 issued by King George III modify this perception?
2. World War I was a turning point in Canada's identity as an independent country from Britain while World War II cemented this identity. Discuss.
3. Do you believe that demographic reality forces federal governments to favour Ontario and Quebec over other parts of the country? Can you supply an example?
4. The building of the CPR and the settling of Western Canada a great achievement orchestrated by Prime Minister John A. Macdonald. Yet, particularly from the perspective of Indigenous peoples, Canada's first prime minister is not held in high regard. Explain.
5. What did Henri Bourassa mean by a "double contract"?

## Essay Questions

1. Since 1876, the Indian Act has determined the relationship between the federal government and status Indians. What was the purpose of this Act from the perspective of Ottawa and then from the perspective of First Nations?
2. World War I divided the nation into two parts: those English-speaking Canadians who jumped to support Britain's war effort and the French-speaking Canadians who felt less loyalty to Britain. The straw that broke the back of a united Canada was conscription. Conscription forced French-speaking Canadians of military age to join the army, and this political decision bolstered the French/English divide. Discuss this divide.

Parents please stand behind
white line

# 4 Canada's Human Face

## Chapter Overview

Issues examined in Chapter 4 are:

- Canada's population, including population increase, density, distribution, zones, and the impact of immigration on population.
- Urban population and census metropolitan areas.
- Canada's aging population.
- The growing Indigenous population.
- Canada's changing culture, ethnicity, and multiculturalism.
- The COVID-19 pandemic.

## Introduction

Human geography provides a broad framework for examining Canada's human face. In this chapter, two major elements of human geography are examined: population and culture. Population geography lays the foundation for this discussion while cultural geography provides a sense of its social character and a vision of the future. In both cases, the emphasis is divided between the national picture and the six geographical regions.

Canada is home to over 37 million people. Most live in large urban cities. For instance, Toronto, Montreal, and Vancouver are home to more than one-third of all Canadians, with a combined population of 12.5 million. While its rate of natural increase has fallen, Canada's population size continues to grow due to the arrival of large numbers of immigrants. Until 2019, most population increase took place in Ontario, British Columbia, and Western Canada. Looking to the future, if these demographic trends continue, Canada's population could reach 40 million by 2025 (Statistics Canada, 2015a), with BC and Western Canada experiencing the greatest rates of population increase, followed by Ontario. However, the COVID-19 pandemic, caused by a novel coronavirus identified in China in late 2019, significantly reduced the number of immigrants in 2020, meaning that Canada's population growth slowed. What the future brings is unknown as this time, but immigration may no longer drive Canada's population increase.

Canada has evolved into a **pluralistic society**. This transformation began in the 1960s. At that time, most immigrants came from Europe. Now,

← The COVID-19 pandemic has changed the way Canadians live. Here, students form a socially distanced line and wait to receive hand sanitizer on their first day of school.

**THINK ABOUT IT**

Has the COVID-19 pandemic caused the age of world migration to end?

a significant majority come from Asia, with the Philippines, India, China, Pakistan, and Iran providing Canada with almost 50 per cent of its newcomers in 2016, thus injecting fresh cultural, ethnic, and religious elements into Canadian society. Over the past 25 years, 200,000 or more immigrants have arrived each year. In the last five years, this figure was closer to 300,000. As a result, the character of Canada has evolved into a more diverse and, some would say, interesting society. Since most newcomers settle in large cities, this diversity is most visible in urban Canada. Our metropolitan areas have changed, and while hockey and Tim Hortons still resonate with Canadians, cricket and samosa are no longer strangers to the playgrounds and eateries of these cities.

Cultural change is not without its challenge as accommodation of newcomers remains near the top of the national political agenda. For the most part, however, such adjustment to a new way of life occurs relatively smoothly, though less smoothly for visible immigrants. The federal government's response to cultural diversity takes the form of its multicultural policy and programs. Yet, the troubled relationship between Indigenous peoples and Ottawa has made the accommodation of Canada's Indigenous peoples difficult. Past government policies, such as Indigenous residential schools, were so harsh that former chief justice Beverley McLachlin (2015) categorized them as "cultural genocide." It is little wonder, then, that trust between Indigenous peoples and the federal government was lost and has been difficult to regain. In 2018, The National Inquiry into Missing and Murdered Indigenous Women and Girls concluded that:

> violence against Indigenous people—including Indigenous women and girls—is rooted in colonization. For the violence against Indigenous women and girls to end, the ongoing colonial relationship that facilitates it must end. (National Inquiry into Missing and Murdered Indigenous Women and Girls, 2018)

## Canada's Population

Canada's population reached 37 million at the start of 2019. Such growth is not surprising. Since Confederation, the country's population has increased steadily (Figure 4.1). In the twenty-first century the nation continues to grow, thanks in large measure to the annual flow of newcomers. Yet, population growth may stall because of the restrictions on international travel related to COVID-19, and climate change could alter Canada's **population optimum** and thereby either increase or decrease the need for more immigrants.

At present, three key features mark Canada's population geography: (1) the concentration of Canadians near the US border, a zone known as the ecumene; (2) the shift of the centre of population gravity to the West; and (3) the "empty" northern lands. In terms of the six geographic regions, Ontario and Quebec remain the two most populous regions, though the fastest-growing region is now Western Canada, led by Alberta (Table 4.1). The Territorial North, with less than 1 per cent of Canada's population, has the smallest population of the six regions. The impact of climate change could expand Canada's ecumene by creating a more favourable climate for settlement in higher latitudes. In his book, *The World in 2050: Four Forces Shaping Civilization's Northern Future*, Laurence Smith implies such a development.

### Population Increase

Canada's population is driven by two components: natural increase and immigration. As Figure 4.2 illustrates, immigration now accounts for most of Canada's annual population increase. In 2019, the **crude birth rate** and **crude death rate** per 1,000 population were 10.1 and 7.7, respectively, giving a **rate of natural increase** of 2.4 per 1,000 persons or 0.24 per cent (Table 4.2).

Until 1986, most of Canada's population growth was due to natural increase (Figure 4.2). With the rate of natural increase declining and changes in Canada's immigration regulations, two key elements

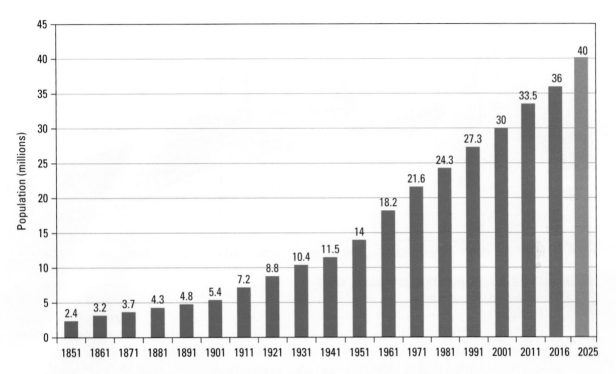

**FIGURE 4.1 Population of Canada, 1851–2016, with an estimate for 2025**

Sources: Statistics Canada (2012b, 2015b, 2016a).

emerged: immigration began to replace natural growth as the principal factor causing Canada's population growth; and immigrants from outside of Europe and the United States were forming the majority of newcomers.

How do we explain these shifts in Canada's demography? The **demographic transition theory** provides a general framework for all countries that pass from a pre-industrial economy to an industrial one. Most significantly, this theory calls for the death rate to decline well before the birth rate, resulting in a population explosion. In terms of application to Canada, this theory has one weakness—its failure to include the impact of immigration. Based on natural increase, demographic changes occur in five phases, each of which has a distinct set of vital rates that coincide with the phases in the process of industrialization and urbanization (Table 4.2).

Oddly enough, demographic statistics present a paradox. On the one hand, the number of births per year continues to increase, while a measure of fertility—the total **fertility rate**—is trending in the

**TABLE 4.1 Population Size, Increase, and % Change by Geographic Region, 2001–2016**

| Geographic Region | Population 2001 | Population 2016 | Population Increase 2001–2016 | % Change, 2001–2016 |
|---|---|---|---|---|
| Territorial North | 92,779 | 118,658 | 25,879 | 27.9 |
| Atlantic Canada | 2,285,729 | 2,375,828 | 90,099 | 3.9 |
| British Columbia | 3,907,738 | 4,707,021 | 799,283 | 20.5 |
| Western Canada | 5,073,323 | 6,678,425 | 1,605,102 | 31.6 |
| Quebec | 7,237,479 | 8,294,656 | 1,057,177 | 14.6 |
| Ontario | 11,410,046 | 13,873,933 | 2,463,887 | 21.6 |
| Canada | 30,007,094 | 36,048,521 | 6,041,427 | 20.1 |

Sources: Adapted from Statistics Canada (2002, 2016a).

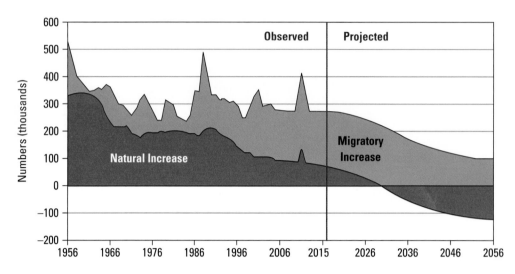

**FIGURE 4.2 Population increase, 1956–2056**
Sources: Statistics Canada (2009b, 2016a).

opposite direction. The explanation for the increase in births is simple: it is due to the rising number of women in the prime productive years for childbearing and not to an increase in the number of children per woman. On the other hand, the declining total fertility rate reflects the tendency for women to have fewer children.

A cursory examination of Canada's birth and death rates over the last 150 years reveals strong similarities to the early industrial, late industrial, and post-industrial phases of this theory. Assuming that Canada is now in the early post-industrial phase, the theory makes sense when applied to Canada's natural increase (i.e., the difference between births and deaths for a given year) (Table 4.3). Supporting that position, demographers argue that Canada's rate of natural increase has fallen below its replacement level (Vignette 4.1). Furthermore, Statistics Canada projects that natural increase will drop below zero by 2030 (Figure 4.2). As well, the proportion of

senior citizens will rise while the number of those in the so-called productive age group (15 to 64) is expected to decline.

Projections of Canada's natural increase are based on past vital statistics and therefore are not always accurate predictors of the future. The baby boom that took place after World War II presents a perfect example, while the COVID-19 pandemic may turn out to be another example. During the late 1940s and lasting to the early 1970s, birth rates ceased to decline and, instead, increased sharply. The result was a bulge in the age structure of Canadian society that continues to have both economic and social implications (Foot with Stoffman, 1996). As consumers of goods and services, baby boomers have had a decided impact on the economy as they move through their life cycle. Companies have geared their products to meet the strong demand created by baby boomers. In the early 1950s, the emphasis was on baby products and larger

| TABLE 4.2 | Phases in the Demographic Transition Theory | | |
|---|---|---|---|
| **Phase** | **Birth and Death Rates** | **Rate of Natural Increase** | **Percentage Urban** |
| **Late pre-industrial** | High birth and death rates | Little or no natural increase but possible fluctuations because of variations in the death rate | Extremely low |
| **Early industrial** | Falling death rates | Extremely high rates of natural increase | Low |
| **Late industrial** | Falling birth rates | High but declining rates of natural increase | Medium |
| **Early post-industrial** | Low birth and death rates | Little or no natural increase; stable population | High |
| **Late post-industrial** | Birth rate at or below zero | Declining population | Extremely High |

## Vignette 4.1

### The Concept of Replacement Fertility

Replacement fertility refers to the level of fertility at which women have enough daughters to replace themselves. If women have an average of 2.1 births in their lifetime, then each woman, on average, will have given birth to a daughter and a son. The number 2.1 was determined to represent the minimum level of replacement fertility because, on average, slightly more boys than girls are born. In 1961, the Canadian total fertility rate was 3.8 births per woman of child-bearing age (15–49). Since 2009, the total fertility rate began its sharp descent, reaching 1.47 in 2019 (Statistics Canada, 2020d).

houses. In the 1960s, a similar age-related pressure was exerted on school facilities, creating a demand for more schools and teachers. As the baby boomers enter old age, the demand for health-care services has and will continue to rise. Governments are facing rising health-care costs associated with the increase in senior citizens. In addition, the emergence of pandemic diseases in our global world has placed our health-care system under extreme pressure. While the 2003 SARS outbreak was contained to the Greater Toronto Area, the 2020 COVID-19 pandemic has spread across Canada.

**TABLE 4.3** Canada's Rate of Natural Increase, 1851–2019

| Year | Crude Birth Rate | Crude Death Rate | Natural Increase (%) | Natural Increase (000s) |
|------|------------------|------------------|----------------------|-------------------------|
| 1851 | 45.0 | 20.0 | 2.5 | 61 |
| 1871 | 42.0 | 20.0 | 2.2 | 81 |
| 1891 | 38.0 | 18.0 | 2.0 | 97 |
| 1911 | 32.0 | 14.0 | 1.8 | 129 |
| 1921 | 29.3 | 11.6 | 1.8 | 160 |
| 1941 | 22.4 | 10.1 | 1.2 | 145 |
| 1961 | 26.1 | 7.7 | 1.8 | 335 |
| 1981 | 15.2 | 7.0 | 0.8 | 200 |
| 2001 | 10.5 | 7.1 | 0.3 | 108 |
| 2011 | 11.3 | 7.2 | 0.4 | 134 |
| 2014 | 10.9 | 7.3 | 0.4 | 126 |
| 2019* | 9.9 | 7.8 | 0.2 | 85 |

*Author's estimates based on Statistics Canada (2016d, 2016a, Q4).

Sources: Adapted from Statistics Canada (1997, 2003a, 2006, 2007a, 2007b, 2012a, 2015a, 2019a, 2020a, 2020b); Provencher et al., 2018; Shumanty, 2018; McVey & Kalbach (1995, pp. 268, 270).

## Millennials and Generation Z

Within the global population, age groups (see Figure 4.3) form critical masses that represent generational change. Technology provides one measure of change. Generation Z, the youngest age group, makes the greatest use of the Internet and other social media devices, while the Silent Generation (those born between 1925 and 1945) has the lowest use. Since technology is the defining indicator of our society in the twenty-first century, Millennials and Generation Z are best situated to take advantage of the rapid advance in communications and transportation technology. For example, Generation Z may be more likely to use ride-sharing services and may more easily fit into the technology companies.

The Pew Research Institute (Dimock, 2019) focuses on technology as a defining generation marker:

> Technology, in particular the rapid evolution of how people communicate and interact, is another generation-shaping consideration. Baby Boomers grew up as television expanded dramatically, changing their lifestyles and connection to the world in fundamental ways. Generation X grew up as the computer revolution was taking hold, and Millennials came of age during the internet explosion.

> In this progression, what is unique for Generation Z is that all of the above have been part of their lives from the start. The iPhone launched in 2007, when the oldest Gen Zers were 10. By the time they were in

**THINK ABOUT IT**

Over the past 10 years or so, the annual number of deaths has increased. Two factors offer an explanation. First, population growth results in a larger population that in turn generates a higher number of deaths. What is the second factor?

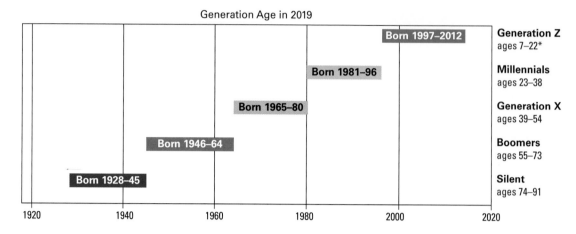

**Generation Age in 2019**

| Born 1997–2012 | **Generation Z** ages 7–22* |
| Born 1981–96 | **Millennials** ages 23–38 |
| Born 1965–80 | **Generation X** ages 39–54 |
| Born 1946–64 | **Boomers** ages 55–73 |
| Born 1928–45 | **Silent** ages 74–91 |

1920    1940    1960    1980    2000    2020

*No chronological endpoint has been set for this group. For this analysis, Generation Z is defined as those ages 7 to 22 in 2019.

**FIGURE 4.3 The generations defined**

The Pew Institute characterizes age groups with particular characteristics, such as adaptability to technology changes. At one end, Generation Z is born within the most recent technological age and readily absorbs new technology. The Silent age group comprises those over age 74; on average, they are least able to adapt to technological changes.

Source: Pew Research Centre.

their teens, the primary means by which young Americans [and Canadians] connected with the web was through mobile devices, WiFi, and high-bandwidth cellular service. Social media, constant connectivity, and on-demand entertainment and communication are innovations Millennials adapted to as they came of age. For those born after 1996, these are largely assumed.

The relationship between immigration and technology is considered in Vignette 4.2.

## Immigration and Population Increase

Immigration keeps Canada growing. As Figure 4.2 suggests, immigration accounts for two-thirds of Canada's annual population increase and its increasing

## Vignette 4.2

### Tech Immigrants

Technology is the wave of the future. In our knowledge-based economy, a shortage of technology workers exists in both Canada and the United States. In the past, Canadian technology workers were often lured to the United States by the attraction of higher wages and more innovative work. Since 2017, this "brain drain" has stopped and now a reverse flow is taking place. As a result, Canada has several technology hubs equivalent to the best in the United States. The explanation lies in a combination of the introduction of more stringent US immigration regulations and the opposite approach in Canada through its Global Skills Strategy program. This federal program expedites the immigration process for high-skilled workers to two weeks or less. In 2018, the Global Skills Strategy program brought in more than 12,000 highly skilled foreign workers. Canada's technology sector has benefited. One tech CEO, Yung Wu of MaRS Discovery District in Toronto, stated: "I was a serial entrepreneur and I spent most of my career watching a brain drain from Canada. This is the first time in my career I've seen a brain gain" (Emrich, 2019).

**TABLE 4.4** Foreign-Born Immigrants, by World Region, Canada, 1871 to 2036 (%)

| Year | Britain | USA | Europe | Central/ South America | Asia | Africa | Other |
|------|---------|-----|--------|------------------------|------|--------|-------|
| 1871 | 83.6 | 10.9 | 4.8 | – | – | – | – |
| 1971 | 29.5 | 9.4 | 50.2 | 3.2 | 5.0 | 1.4 | 1.3 |
| 2001 | 11.6 | 4.4 | 30.4 | 11.0 | 36.5 | 5.2 | 1.0 |
| 2016 | 7.0 | 3.4 | 20.7 | 11.6 | 48.1 | 8.5 | 0.8 |
| 2036* | 3.9 | 3.0 | 12.0 | 11.3 | 57.4 | 11.7 | 0.7 |

*Statistics Canada projections.

Source: Statistics Canada (2017).

diversity. Two events might reduce the number of immigrants in the coming years. One is COVID-19, and the other is deteriorating geopolitical relations, especially with China.

Immigration plays a key role in the federal policy of multiculturalism. This remarkable flow of people to Canada is central to understanding Canada's population increase and its changing identity. From 1971 to 2016, the proportion of immigrants born in Europe and Asia has reversed (Table 4.4). From 2011 to 2016, Statistics Canada (2017) reported that 1.2 million immigrants entered Canada. The five countries providing the most immigrants to Canada were the Philippines (188,805), India (147,190), People's Republic of China (129,020), Iran (42,070), and Pakistan (41,480). For those five years, these accounted for nearly half of the 1.2 million new immigrants to Canada. Figure 4.4 indicates

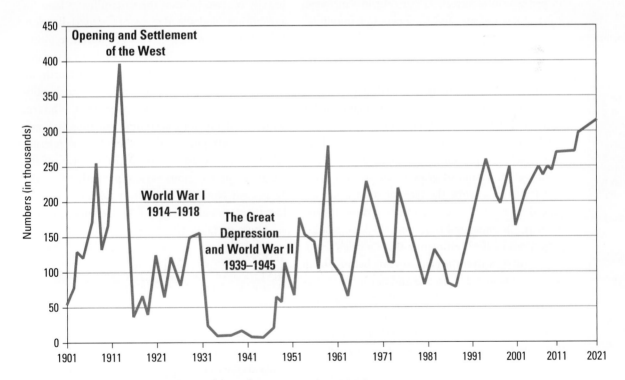

**FIGURE 4.4 Annual number of immigrants, 1901–2020**

Canada's natural increase has declined from around 200,000 per year to around 130,000 per year. Over the same time span, immigration numbers are now more than double the annual figure for natural increase. By 2016, the number of immigrants reached 300,000, with a projection for 2021 of about 320,000 (Statistics Canada, 2020c). However, restrictions on international travel due to COVID-19 dramatically reduced the number of immigrants in 2020, perhaps by more than half the 2016 figure.

Sources: Statistics Canada (2003a, p. 2; 2009a); Citizenship and Immigration Canada (2011, 2016); Statistics Canada. 2020c.

**THINK ABOUT IT**

Unlike most other developed countries, Canada has experienced a high rate of population growth. Could this demographic trend end?

**THINK ABOUT IT**

Laurence C. Smith's *The World in 2050: Four Forces Shaping Civilization's Northern Future* predicts that global migration will greatly increase due to global warming. Could the recent surge of migrants into Europe be a harbinger of an even more dramatic and uncontrolled global movement of people in the future?

**THINK ABOUT IT**

If COVID-19 infections remain lower in Canada than in the United States, could this work in Canada's favour regarding the recruitment of foreign tech workers?

how much Canada has relied on immigration since the beginning of the twentieth century. These newcomers to Canada often arrive with large families or form them after arriving. But large families tend not to translate into the next generation. As Bélanger and Gilbert (2006) observe, the next generation tends to have fertility rates closer to the national average, a sign of adjusting to Canadian culture norms. The implication is that immigration's impact on Canada's growth rate is short-lived (i.e., one generation).

The destination of these newcomers follows the economic strength of Canada's six geographic regions. According to Statistics Canada (2017), the 1.2 million **recent immigrants** settled mainly in Ontario (39 per cent), Western Canada (26 per cent), Quebec (18 per cent), and BC (15 per cent), leaving only 2 per cent for Atlantic Canada and less than 1 per cent for the Territorial North. Within those five regions, the major cities received the bulk of these newcomers. Nearly 30 per cent went to Toronto, 15 per cent to Montreal, 12 per cent to Vancouver, 8 per cent to Calgary, and 7 per cent to Edmonton.

## Population by 2063

Statistics Canada regularly undertakes population projections to provide insights into demographic changes that Canada probably will experience in the future. So far, the combination of natural increase and immigration have combined to produce a relatively high annual growth rate of over 1 per cent for Canada while the rate for most other advanced industrial countries is closer to zero. In 2014, Bohnert, Chagnon, and Dion undertook population projections to 2063, estimating that Canada's population will slow over the next 50 years because birth rates are anticipated to decline and death rates to increase; and because levels of immigration are not anticipated to increase beyond their current annual level of 300,000. However, the authors considered that if immigration annual levels more than double to 750,000, Canada could continue to have a positive growth rate. The authors made their projections before COVID-19 affected immigration and, therefore, population growth. If travel restrictions continue to slow immigration to Canada, our growth rate will decrease accordingly.

## Population Density

As the second-largest country in the world by land mass, Canada's **population density** is one of the lowest. The explanation is simple—relatively few people inhabit its vast northern lands of Arctic and Subarctic climates (Figure 2.5). Canada has a population density of 3.6 persons per km², which means the country has an extremely low population density (but not as low as Australia and Mongolia). The United States, by comparison, has 32 persons per km². But are population density figures more meaningful if they are expressed as the amount of arable land per person? This measure is called physiological density. By eliminating non-productive agricultural land, Canada's physiological density is similar to that of the United States.

The explanation for these variations between countries is that land varies greatly in its capacity to support human settlement. Capacity depends heavily on two factors: the suitability of land for agriculture, and the degree of industrialization. When we look at Canada's six geographic regions, the Territorial North falls short on both accounts. Not surprisingly, then, the Territorial North accounts for less than 1 per cent of Canada's population (Table 1.1). In sharp contrast, Ontario scores well on both accounts and thus is home to nearly 40 per cent of Canada's population (Table 1.1). The 2016 population densities of the six geographic regions varied, but only two—the Territorial North and Western Canada—fell below the national average of 3.6 persons per km², as shown in Table 4.5.

**TABLE 4.5   Population Density by Region, Canada, 2016**

| Geographic Region | Population Density (persons per km²) |
|---|---|
| **Territorial North** | 0.03 |
| **Western Canada** | 3.4 |
| **Atlantic Canada** | 4.4 |
| **British Columbia** | 4.9 |
| **Quebec** | 5.4 |
| **Ontario** | 12.9 |
| **Canada** | 3.6 |

Source: Adapted from Table 1.1.

## Population Distribution

Canada is a huge country, but almost all Canadians live in the national ecumene (Figure 4.5). Beyond that relatively dense population area, few live in the other parts of Canada. One interpretation describes Canadians as "huddling" near the border with the United States. This observation was made half a century ago in a well-known American geography text, which explained that Canada's population is "drawn by a magnet toward the giant neighbour on the south, for they [Canada's inhabitants] are strikingly concentrated along the United States border" (Trewartha et al., 1967, p. 542). Underlying this understanding are two key factors: Canadian agricultural lands are found near the US border, and trade with the United States dictates that Canada's industrial economy is closely linked with—and close to—that of the United States.

Canada's **population distribution** is reflected by six geographic regions (Table 1.1 and Table 4.1) and by population zones (Figure 4.5). A more geographic view involves classifying Canada's population into four zones.

Led by Vancouver, Calgary, and Edmonton, the two western regions of British Columbia and Western Canada grew more rapidly than the national average from 2001 to 2016 (Table 4.1).

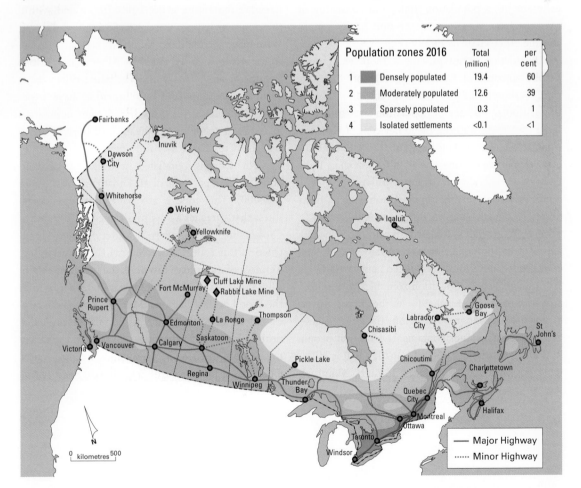

**FIGURE 4.5 Canada's population zones, ecumene, and highway system**

Canada's population is heavily concentrated in its national ecumene (zones 1 and 2). Within this ecumene, southern parts of Ontario and Quebec have the highest density of population, at nearly 80 persons/km². A secondary belt of population spans a southern strip of Western Canada and parts of Atlantic Canada with population densities close to 15 persons/km². Together, the densely and moderately populated zones account for 99 per cent of Canada's population. Population zones 3 and 4 contain only 1 per cent of Canada's population.

Ontario also outpaced Atlantic Canada and Quebec, the slowest-growing regions of the country. Paradoxically, the Territorial North, the largest geographic region, contains the smallest number of residents. Added to its distinctive demographic character, the Territorial North had the second-highest rate of **population increase** of the six geographic regions over the last 15 years (Table 4.1).

## Population Zones

Canada's population falls into four zones. Its two more densely populated zones are described as Canada's national **ecumene**. Beyond the Canadian ecumene lies a population hinterland consisting of two sparsely populated areas—one nearly empty and the other virtually empty (Figure 4.5).

Population zones provide a more exact geographic picture of Canada's population distribution. As shown in Figure 4.5 and Table 4.6, the four population zones vary in population size from very large (nearly 22 million, or 60 per cent of Canada's population, in zone 1) to very small (the fewer than 100,000 people in zone 4 account for less than 1 per cent of Canada's population). Similarly, the four zones vary considerably in population density, from about 80 persons/km$^2$ in zone 1 to 0.01 person in zone 4. The overall spatial pattern reinforces the image of a highly concentrated population core surrounded by more thinly populated zones.

Canada's core population zone lies in the Great Lakes–St Lawrence Lowlands. As the most naturally favoured physiographic region, the Great Lakes–St Lawrence Lowlands contains 21.6 million people and almost three-quarters of Canada's major cities. This population core includes Toronto, Montreal,

Ottawa–Gatineau, Quebec City, Hamilton, Oshawa, London, and Windsor, to name only some of the largest cities in the region. As Canada's most densely populated area, its economy is based on manufacturing and its agriculture lands are the most fertile in Canada.

The secondary core zone extends in a narrow band across southern Canada. In general, its northern boundary corresponds with the polar edge of arable land. As the second-most favoured zone, it occupies the more southerly portions of the Appalachian Uplands, the Canadian Shield, the Interior Plains, and the Cordillera. About 14 million Canadians, or nearly 40 per cent, live in this moderately populated zone. Canada's remaining major cities are located within this zone, including Vancouver, Edmonton, Calgary, Winnipeg, and Halifax. Within the secondary zone, some areas, such as southern Alberta and British Columbia, are growing quickly while other areas, such as Newfoundland and Labrador, have experienced much slower growth and even population losses. As a result, the population of the secondary zone is increasing slowly and unevenly.

The sparsely populated or tertiary zone contains about 1 per cent of all Canadians (just under 400,000). This zone is associated with the boreal forest that stretches across mid-Canada. Only one of Canada's major cities, Fort McMurray, Alberta, is situated in this zone. Fort McMurray is an outstanding example of a **resource town**. As the hub of northern Alberta's oil sands, Fort McMurray (which is within the Wood Buffalo Regional Municipality) is the largest city in the tertiary zone. Its population peaked at nearly 82,000 just before the oil crash and devastating wildfire in 2016 and now stands around 75,000. Other larger urban centres range in size from 10,000

**THINK ABOUT IT**

While Ontario has a population density of 15 persons per km², the figure for southern Ontario is much higher—nearly 100 persons per km²—while northern Ontario's figure is less than 1 person per km². Do the other five geographic regions contain similar internal population density variations?

**TABLE 4.6    Population Zones, 2016**

| Zone Description | Population (millions) | Percentage of Canada's population | Major City | Population of Major City (est. 2020) |
|---|---|---|---|---|
| 1. Core zone: densely populated | 21.6 | 60 | Toronto | 6,400,000 |
| 2. Secondary zone: moderately populated | 14.0 | 39 | Vancouver | 2,900,000 |
| 3. Tertiary zone: Sparsely populated | 0.3 | 1 | Fort McMurray* | 75,000 |
| 4. Empty zone: Isolated settlements | <0.1 | <1 | Labrador City | 9,000 |

*Wood Buffalo Regional Municipality.

Source: Statistics Canada (2016a, 2016b).

to 20,000. Whitehorse and Yellowknife, as the capital cities of Yukon and the Northwest Territories, are administrative centres and regional service centres, since they also provide most of the service functions for their areas. These two cities, with estimated populations of 25,000 and 21,000, respectively, in 2020, also mark the poleward edge of zone 3.

The last population zone has fewer than 100,000 inhabitants. Most reside in resource towns, Indigenous settlements, or regional centres. Most of its territory lies in the Arctic and the northern edge of the boreal forest. The challenging cold climate limits settlement possibilities. One exception is resource towns and administrative centres. The iron-mining town of Labrador City is the largest centre, with a population of just over 9,000. Iqaluit, the capital of Nunavut and the second-largest town, has a population approaching 7,000. The Indigenous settlements that dot zone 4 resulted from an initiative of the federal government back in the 1950s to relocate Indigenous hunters and their families to existing outposts, such as fur trading posts and missions. Unlike in the other zones in Canada, Indigenous peoples form the majority in this zone; however, the percentage of Indigenous people living in cities in zone 1 is increasing.

## Urban Population

Canada has evolved into an urban country. Before World War I, most Canadians lived in a rural setting and farming was the principal activity (Figure 4.6). The reverse is now true. In 2020, 7 in 10 Canadians—over 28 million people—were living in census metropolitan areas (CMAs) with populations over 100,000. Not only do large cities dominate the population landscape, but the bulk of Canada's population growth is in these cities. From 2006 to 2019, nearly 90 per cent of Canada's population increase of 4 million took place in CMAs. Furthermore, urban dwellers are concentrated in six CMAs, all with populations exceeding one million: Toronto, Montreal, Vancouver, Calgary, Edmonton, and Ottawa-Gatineau (Table 4.8). Not surprisingly,

espiegle/iStockphoto

**PHOTO 4.1** Founded in 1642, Montreal, Quebec, is one of Canada's oldest cities. Located on the St Lawrence River, Montreal is a transportation hub for international shipping. With a 2020 population of just over 4 million, the city has the largest francophone urban population in North America and is the second-largest French-speaking city in the world, behind only Paris, France.

Bufflerump/Shutterstock

**PHOTO 4.2** Toronto, Ontario, with a population of more than 6.4 million in 2020, is Canada's most populous city and serves as the economic engine for Ontario and as the financial capital for Canada. Toronto, in conjunction with the urban hierarchy theory, has the largest variety of urban amenities. Toronto has also become the nation's most culturally diverse city. Toronto is the major destination for recent immigrants.

David Nunuk/All Canada Photos

**PHOTO 4.3** Vancouver, British Columbia, is Canada's leading ocean port, with most goods coming and going to China and other Asian countries, and is the third-largest Canadian city, with a 2020 population of almost 3 million. Some Vancouverites are concerned about potential oil spills in Vancouver's harbour and consequently have opposed a twinning of the existing oil pipeline from Alberta's oil sands. In the foreground, the Cambie Street Bridge spans False Creek and leads to BC Place; to the west of the bridge, at the bottom of the photo, is Granville Island with its public market.

the highest percentage of urban population is found in Ontario, followed by Quebec and British Columbia, with the lowest percentage in Atlantic Canada.

Urban population has increased because of three primary factors:

1. The arrival of immigrants has greatly added to urban growth, especially in the larger cities, with Toronto leading the way.
2. Canadians in slow-growing areas are relocating to larger cities.
3. Indigenous peoples have more recently formed a small but growing percentage of the population in Canadian cities, especially in Western Canada.

## Census Metropolitan Areas

CMAs serve as the economic and cultural anchors of their hinterlands. Statistics Canada defines **census metropolitan area** (CMA) as an urban area (known as the urban core) together with adjacent urban and rural areas that have a high degree of social and economic integration with the urban core. The urban core population of a CMA must be at least 50,000 and total CMA population must be at least 100,000. On this basis, no city in the Territorial North qualifies as a CMA.

These large cities are a barometer for population increases in the six geographic regions. Toronto clearly dominates Canada's urban world. With a population of nearly 6.5 million, Toronto gained in population by 1.4 million residents from 2006 to 2019. To put that population increase in perspective, a new city of 1.4 million alone would rank seventh-largest in Canada, ahead of Winnipeg and just behind Ottawa-Gatineau. Over the same period (2006–19), Statistics Canada (2019) recorded that the two fastest-growing CMAs (Calgary and Edmonton) were located in Western Canada (Table 4.8).

What is the attraction of cities? First, most business and employment opportunities are found in cities, especially large cities. Second, Canadians prefer to live in an urban setting where a wide variety of amenities are readily available. Cities are also important for other reasons. Major urban centres are at the cutting edge of technological innovation and capital accumulation. In the new world of the knowledge economy, manufacturing does not

Vladone/iStockphoto

**PHOTO 4.4** With the Parliament Buildings (left) and the Château Laurier in the background, the Rideau Canal provides a winter skating experience in Ottawa, Canada's capital. The canal, completed in 1832, was originally built as a military supply route between Kingston and Ottawa. Metropolitan Ottawa in 2015 had more than 1.3 million residents.

determine a city's prosperity; rather, the determining factor lies in the creativity of its business and university communities.

Despite the remarkable growth of Canadian cities, all is not well. The cost of housing has risen sharply, making the dream of owning a home out of reach for many Millennials in Canada's six largest cities. Urban sprawl affects all cities, forcing them to spend heavily on infrastructure in these outlying areas while their downtowns lose their raison d'être. Competition from malls and big-box stores in the suburbs has hurt downtown retail areas. In the twenty-first century, city governments face the daunting task of finding solutions to the twin challenges of urban congestion and urban sprawl by making downtowns more pedestrian- and

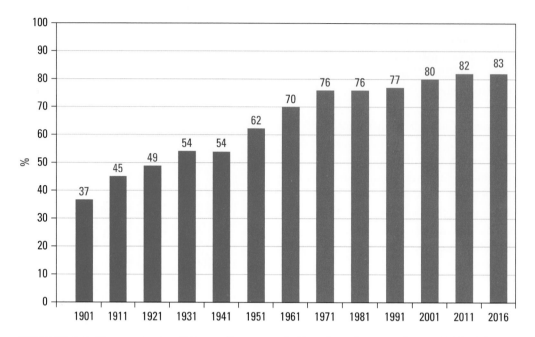

**FIGURE 4.6  Percentage of Canadian population in urban regions, 1901–2016**

Sources: Adapted from Statistics Canada (2007c, 2013a, 2016b).

bicycle-friendly, turning inner-city residential areas into a much denser form of residential housing, and adding more "urban parks." While not a perfect solution for even the very largest cities, rapid transit systems in conjunction with other innovations reduce downtown congestion, encourage people to move to condos in the heart of these cities, and moderate the urge to live in the suburbs in traditional single-family homes, duplexes, and townhouses. Without a doubt, rapid rail systems transform major metropolitan cities. Toronto, Montreal, and Vancouver have had such systems in play for some time, namely the Montreal Metro, the Toronto subway, and the Vancouver SkyTrain. All three of these cities have plans to expand their rapid rail systems.

For middle-sized cities, the volume of traffic necessary for expensive rapid rail systems remains out of reach. Light rail transit (LRT) systems are an option for smaller metropolitan centres: Edmonton has an LRT system, Calgary has its C-Train, and the O-train operates in Ottawa. Table 4.7 ranks the public transit of 15 major cities.

The sociological contrast between suburban and downtown living is sharp and carries implications

**TABLE 4.7   Ranking of Public Transit, 2019**

| Rank | City | Transit Score |
|---|---|---|
| 1 | Toronto | 78 |
| 2 | Vancouver | 74 |
| 3 | Montreal | 67 |
| 4 | Mississauga | 56 |
| 5 | Brampton | 53 |
| 6 | Winnipeg | 51 |
| 7 | Calgary | 50 |
| 8 | Ottawa | 50 |
| 9 | Edmonton | 49 |
| 10 | Markham | 49 |
| 11 | Quebec City | 47 |
| 12 | Surrey | 47 |
| 13 | Laval | 46 |
| 14 | Hamilton | 45 |
| 15 | London | 45 |

Note: Transit Score is calculated by Redfin. Its methodology is based on indicators showing that local public transit is both convenient and runs frequently. Toronto leads the way among Canadian cities. With a score of 78, Toronto's Transit Score holds an edge over several large US cities. It ranks higher than Boston's rating of 72 and falls just shy of San Francisco's score of 80, earning a comparable place among the largest cities in North America. Vancouver, at 74, ranks above Boston and Washington DC (71). Montreal and Philadelphia both earned a score of 67.

Source: Redfin (2019).

| TABLE 4.8 Population Change in Top 10 Census Metropolitan Areas, 2006 and 2019 | | | | |
|---|---|---|---|---|
| CMA | Rank* | Population 2006 (000s) | Population 2019 (000s) | Change (000s) | Change (%) |
| Toronto | 1 | 5,113 | 6,472 | 1,359 | 26.6 |
| Montreal | 2 | 3,636 | 4,319 | 683 | 18.8 |
| Vancouver | 3 | 2,117 | 2,691 | 574 | 27.1 |
| Calgary | 4 | 1,079 | 1,515 | 436 | 40.4 |
| Edmonton | 5 | 1,035 | 1,447 | 412 | 39.8 |
| Ottawa–Gatineau | 6 | 1,134 | 1,441 | 307 | 27.1 |
| Winnipeg | 7 | 695 | 845 | 150 | 21.6 |
| Quebec City | 8 | 719 | 824 | 105 | 14.6 |
| Hamilton | 9 | 693 | 795 | 102 | 14.7 |
| Kitchener–Cambridge–Waterloo | 10 | 451 | 584 | 133 | 29.5 |

*Ranking based on 2019 population figures.

Source: Statistics Canada (2019d).

for our ever-changing society. On one hand, the seemingly ever-expanding suburban nature of cities that accommodates our automobile-oriented society may be reaching its peak. First, the costs of providing urban services to new suburbs are taxing city budgets for new roads, schools, fire halls and trucks, parks, transit services, and water/sewer systems. Second, the viability of central business districts is threatened by the loss of business to suburban stores where parking spaces are readily available. On the

PHOTO 4.5 With a population increase of nearly 40 per cent from 2006 to 2020, Calgary is the fourth-largest and fastest-growing city in Canada (Table 4.8). Its downtown is dominated by skyscrapers, many of which are associated with the petroleum industry. Beyond the skyscrapers, Calgary, like other major cities, faces several challenges, including urban sprawl, homelessness, and inadequate revenue-sharing from provincial and federal governments. As the oil capital of Alberta, Calgary's economy is suffering from the much-weakened oil industry.

**PHOTO 4.6** The North Saskatchewan River frames Edmonton's downtown. Like Calgary, Edmonton is experiencing rapid population growth and this growth is pushing the residential areas further and further from the central city. For the downtown area, the challenge is to make its main street, Jasper Avenue, into a more people-friendly place. By 2020, Edmonton's population had surpassed 1.4 million, making it the fifth-largest city in Canada and the second-fastest growing city in Canada.

© Fallsview|Dreamstime.com

other hand, the attraction of living downtown appeals to more and more Canadians, especially Millennials. Reasons vary from practical concerns that condo prices are lower than housing in the suburbs and travelling to work is often quicker and simpler to more social concerns that downtown is "where the action is." The sociological implication is that condo living encourages smaller family units, thus adding another demographic factor driving the Canadian fertility rate lower and lower.

In Canada, city governments are handicapped by having little power to raise money. Taxation, with the exception of property taxes, remains a prerogative of the federal government and provincial/territorial governments. Lack of fiscal autonomy represents a major impediment for urban development and planning, forcing cities to turn to provincial and federal governments for funds to deal with major infrastructure, public housing, and a variety of social services, including a number of social ills such as drug addiction and shelters for abused women. Without that funding, necessary major infrastructure and social projects remain on the drawing board. Over 10 years ago, Calgary's mayor, Naheed Nenshi, stated, "I am the mayor of a city that has more people in it than five provinces, yet I have the exact same legislative authority as any village of 30 or 40 people. And that has to change" (Agrell, 2011, p. A6). Unfortunately, nothing has changed and urban governments are still chafing under what, for them, is an inequitable constitutional and taxation regime.

## Canada's Aging Population

A country where seniors outnumber children is uncharted territory for Canada. This scenario represents a serious demographic event with economic and health-related implications. Such implications mean that the working-age taxpayers will have to foot the bill for public pensions drawn by the increasing number of seniors plus soaring health costs due to seniors making greater use of Canada's health-care system. By 2021, seniors are projected to form over 18 per cent of the population (Figure 4.7). Since this aging process is linked to the Baby Boomers, aging will accelerate from now until 2031 when all Baby Boomers will have reached age 65 or older. At that time, over 20 per cent of the population could fall into the senior citizen category (Figure 4.7). The aging of populations of advanced industrial countries like Canada fits with the last stage of the demographic transition theory.

The predicted trend to an older population of 20 per cent or greater is driven by three factors:

• an increase in life expectancy;
• a decline in the fertility rate and a resulting decrease in the youthful population;
• the movement of the Baby Boom generation into retirement and old age.

What are the implications of an older Canada? First, Canada's population structure will change with a smaller proportion of children (under 15 years of age), a smaller proportion of the population in the workforce (ages 15–64), and a much larger percentage over 64 years of age.

Second, Canadians are living longer, which adds economic costs in the form of greater drug and health costs, creating a larger tax burden on those in the productive age group and rising costs to the federal treasury to pay for Canada's public pensions—Old Age Security and the Canada Pension Plan. The burden for the provinces and territories may be unsustainable because health costs for the growing number of senior Canadians are projected to turn sharply upward. The cost gap between health-care expenses for seniors and for the rest of the population is almost fivefold. In 2018, average health-care costs for seniors were around $12,000 per year compared to $2,700 for everyone else (Blatchford, 2018). Already, health costs make up the major component of provincial/territorial budgets, at around 40 per cent. Could these costs reach or exceed 50 per cent and thus squeeze federal transfer funds from post-secondary education and social services budgets to meet the growing health needs?

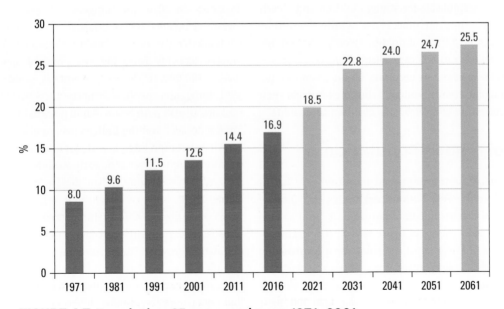

**FIGURE 4.7 Population 65 years and over, 1971–2061**

In 1960, 7.6 per cent of Canadians were aged 65 and over. By 2061, those in the senior age group are projected to represent 25.5 per cent of the population. The driving forces behind this increase are low fertility rates and increasing life expectancy.

Source: Human Resources and Development Canada (2015, 2019); Statistics Canada (2019a).

Third, the burden to pay for the growing number of seniors falls to a smaller and smaller group. The **age dependency ratio** provides another road marker to Canada's future demographic destination. Age dependency ratio is expressed as the number of persons in the "dependent" age groups (in the calculations of Statistics Canada, under 20 and over 64 years of age) per 100 persons in the "economically productive" age group (between 20 and 64 years). This rough measure offers an indication of the economic burden on those in the economically productive age group. According to Statistics Canada (2014a), this ratio, with some relatively minor ups and downs, has remained steady for the past several years, at about 60 persons in the combined youth and senior groups compared to 100 in the working-age population. But in the coming decades this ratio is expected to change. A Statistics Canada analysis projects that by 2056 the dependency ratio will have climbed to 84 dependants per 100 people of working age, with 50 seniors for every 100 in the "economically productive" age group (Statistics Canada, 2015c).

A social concern linked to this aging process is called the "sandwich generation" where many couples are responsible for young children and elderly parents at the same time. Placed within the broader social context of the unfolding twenty-first century, an intergenerational care relationship within family units appears as a necessary fallout from two demographic trends: seniors living well beyond their seventies and couples having children later in life.

## Indigenous Population

When Jacques Cartier sailed into Baie de Chaleur in 1541, the First Nations and Inuit population of what would become Canada may have been as high as 500,000. The exact figure will never be known. What we have are only estimates. By reconstructing the land's capacity to support wildlife and therefore also hunting societies, anthropologist James Mooney (1928, p. 7) estimated that about 220,000 **First Nations people** and Inuit lived in Canada at the time of contact. More recently, scholars have revised this figure upward. Dickason (2009, p. 40) and Denevan (1992, p. 370) estimate that the number of Indigenous peoples living in Canada was closer to half a

million. Whatever the exact figure, initial contact with Europeans resulted in a rapid depopulation. The principal factor was the introduction of new diseases among Indigenous peoples with devastating results. Communicable diseases, such as smallpox, caused great suffering and many deaths. Epidemics quickly reduced the size of Indigenous groups by half. Depopulation did not take place across British North America at once but in a series of regional depopulations associated with the arrival of British settlers, although European epidemic diseases spread through Indigenous trade networks often preceded the actual appearance of Europeans. In 1857, the first comprehensive counting of the Indigenous population for British North America, undertaken by the Hudson's Bay Company at the request of the British House of Commons, totalled 139,000 (Bone, 2016, p. 61). By 1881, the census of Canada recorded 108,000 Indigenous peoples by their **ethnic origin** (ancestry) (Canada, 1884, Table 3.1). As shown in Figure 4.8, the low point was reached in 1911 when the Indigenous population dropped to 105,611.

By the 1930s, the rebound in the Indigenous population had begun (Figure 4.8). From 1931 to 2016, the Indigenous population increased over 15 times. In 2016, the Indigenous population, as measured by ancestry, was just short of 2 million, a remarkable rate of population growth and demographic recovery from the low point of approximately 100,000 in the early twentieth century. In 1951, Indigenous peoples comprised less than 2 per cent of Canada's population. Rapid growth in the following decades saw the Indigenous population near 2 million, comprising close to 5 per cent of Canada's population. Clearly, the early twentieth-century myth of the "vanishing Indian" has been put to rest (Bone, 2020).

Since European contact, Indigenous populations have faced depopulation, recovery, and then rapid population growth. These demographic changes are classified into five phases in Table 4.9.

Early European contact was associated with Indigenous population decline, while Indigenous population stabilized in late European contact. By the mid-twentieth century, the last phase shows an extremely high rate of natural increase. While this rate remains well above the Canadian average, Indigenous birth rates have begun to decline. During the most

**THINK ABOUT IT**

Why are Indigenous residential schools considered a form of cultural genocide?

For a broader discussion of change affecting Indigenous peoples in their interaction with Canadian society, see "The Indigenous Faultline" in **Chapter 3**, page 82.

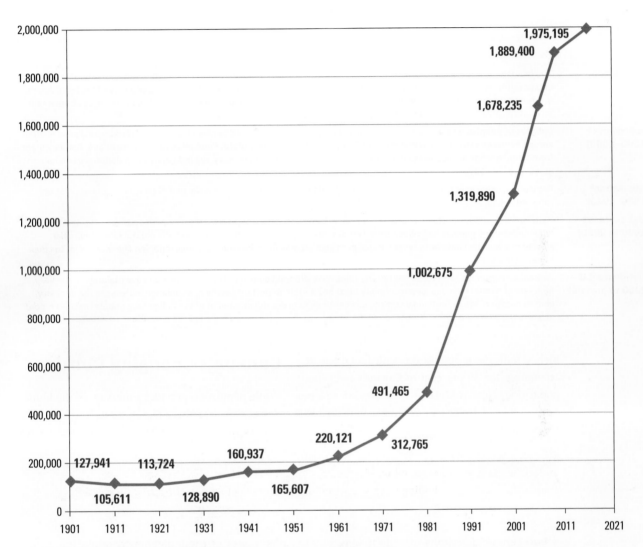

**FIGURE 4.8 Indigenous population by ancestry, 1901–2016**

*Total Indigenous ancestry responses are the sum of persons who identified themselves as of a single Indigenous ancestry or multiple Indigenous ancestry.

Sources: Adapted from Statistics Canada (2003b, 2013b, and 2019).

recent phase, the Indigenous population has increased at a higher rate than Canada's population, totalling 2 million by ancestry (ethnic origin), according to the 2016 census. However, the population measure was slightly smaller (1.7 million) by identity (see Vignette 4.3).

## Indigenous Populations by Identity

In 2016, the census recorded 1.7 million Indigenous people in a self-enumerating census question. The three groups of Indigenous peoples, who are represented nationally by a number of Indigenous

organizations (Vignette 4.4), made up the following proportions (Statistics Canada, 2020e):

- First Nations [status and non-status Indians] formed the largest group with nearly one million (977,230).
- Métis comprised nearly 600,000 (587,545).
- Inuit accounted for 65,025.

The distribution of Indigenous people across Canada varies widely (Table 4.10). Eighty per cent reside in three regions—Western Canada, Ontario, and British Columbia. Western Canada has the

| Phase | Characteristics |
|---|---|
| **TABLE 4.9** | **Major Phases for the Indigenous Population in Canada** |
| Pre-contact | The Indigenous population in Canada in the centuries preceding European contact and settlement was at least 200,000 and possibly as large as 500,000. This population may have varied in size due to the carrying capacity of the land, which, in a hunting society, is controlled by the availability of game (food). Groups residing in the Great Lakes area supplemented game with corn and other agricultural products. |
| Early contact (1500–1900) | Indigenous peoples who came into contact with Europeans were exposed to new diseases, and these new diseases often spread across the land prior to the arrival of Europeans in a particular place. Population losses were heavy. Displacement from hunting lands also added to their demise. By the early twentieth century, the Indigenous population was estimated at just over 100,000. |
| Late contact (1900–1940) | Population increase began slowly, but epidemics kept the number low. Towards the end of this phase, the population rebound began. |
| Post-contact I (1940 to 2000) | High fertility and low mortality accounted for remarkable population explosion. Most growth occurred after the 1960s when Indigenous peoples had relocated to settlements. Towards the end of this phase, the natural rate of increase slowed due to a declining fertility rate. Population kept increasing, sustained by ethnic mobility. The movement to cities began in this period. |
| Post-Contact II (2000 to present) | Population continues to increase but fertility rates have dropped considerably. Only the Inuit have maintained the very high rate of natural increase. Ethnic mobility becomes a more important source of population increase in the ancestry census question. While traditional settlements continue to grow, the number of urban Indigenous people reached record levels in the 2016 census. |

highest Indigenous population, with a total 656,965 accounting for 39 per cent of Canada's Indigenous population. Next is Ontario with 374,385 (22 per cent), followed by British Columbia with 270,585 (16 per cent).

## Canada's Changing Culture

While population provides a measure of the human size of Canada, culture represents its heart and soul. Historically speaking, **culture** is a product of the mix

**THINK ABOUT IT**

Canada's multicultural programs recognize the need for public support for newcomers to adjust to their new world. From this perspective, why shouldn't the same level of support and programs be extended to urban Indigenous people who, as new arrivals to cities, are struggling to adjust to this urban world?

## Vignette 4.3

### Census Recording of Indigenous Populations and Ethnic Mobility

Two census questions provide measurements of the size of the Indigenous population. One question calls for a person to record his or her ancestry or ethnicity. The second and more recent question attempts to narrow the definition to membership in Indigenous organizations. By the 1971 census, changes to Indigenous ancestry population counts became noticeable as more and more Canadians of mixed ancestry changed their ethnicity from non-Indigenous to Indigenous. The explanation for this change in interpretation of ancestry is simple: Canadians with one or more Indigenous ancestors began to feel comfortable declaring this association in response to the ancestry census question. Demographers (Caron-Malenfant et al., 2014) refer to this "switching ethnicity" from one census to the next as **ethnic mobility**. In 1986, the census introduced a second question based on Indigenous identity for two reasons. First, the federal government wanted a population figure more accurately reflecting membership in First Nations (both status and non-status Indians), Métis, and Inuit organizations. Second, this identity question was designed to deal with ethnic mobility. While Canadians still have the option to switch their ethnicity from one census to the next in the ancestry (ethnicity) census question, this option is not available in the identity census question. In post-1986 censuses, more and more non-Indigenous people have switched their self-identification from a non-Indigenous ethnicity to an Indigenous one, primarily to non-status Indian or Métis. As a result, Indigenous population figures from the two census questions vary. Measured by ancestry, the number is higher than that recorded by identity.

## Vignette 4.4

### Indigenous Organizations

The diversity of Indigenous peoples is reflected in their five national organizations. The largest and best known is the **Assembly of First Nations (AFN)**, which represents the more than 600 First Nations in Canada. Its members consist of the chiefs of these First Nations, who vote to select their National Chief for a three-year term. The present National Chief is Perry Bellegarde. The federal government recognizes the AFN as the official body with which Ottawa interacts on the business of First Nations. The federal government funds the operations of the AFN. Some First Nation band members fear that the AFN has been co-opted by the federal government while others feel that the AFN represents the interests of the chiefs rather than their band members. Grassroots organizations, such as the Idle No More movement, appear from time to time to take the lead in espousing Indigenous concerns, rather than the AFN.

Métis and Inuit have their own political organizations, the Métis National Council and the Inuit Tapiriit Kanatami (ITK). Two other organizations represent other Indigenous peoples and Indigenous women. One is the Congress of Aboriginal Peoples, which aspires to give voice to non-status Indians and Indigenous people living in southern cities. The Native Women's Association of Canada (NWAC) offers Indigenous women and girls a place to "enhance, promote, and foster the social, economic, cultural and political well-being of First Nations and Métis women within First Nation, Métis, and Canadian societies."

of those living in Canada. Of course, British, French, and Indigenous beliefs and traditions formed the early cultures of Canada. After the 1960s, the addition of immigrants and their cultures from around the world greatly enriched Canada. Multiculturalism, a product of international immigration, is now a key pillar of Canada's culture.

Language plays a key role in the shaping of culture. Officially, Canadian languages are English and French. While the English language is found in most parts of the country, Quebec is home to the Québécois culture, based on the French language and traditions that have a different root from English-speaking Canada. The only exception to this rule is found in New Brunswick, the cultural home of the Acadians, but elsewhere in Atlantic Canada the French fact largely disappears.

Through the process of incorporating elements of these world cultures into Canada's ever-expanding cultural mélange, the nation has become known as a country where cultural differences are readily accepted and respected. This diversification did not

**TABLE 4.10 Indigenous Population by Identity, Canada and Regions, 2001 and 2016**

| Region | Indigenous Population 2001 | Indigenous Population 2016 | Increase 2001–16 | Increase 2001–16(%) | % by Canada, 2016 |
|---|---|---|---|---|---|
| Territorial North | 47,990 | 59,605 | 11,615 | 24.2 | 3.5 |
| Atlantic Canada | 54,120 | 129,340 | 75,220 | 239.0 | 7.7 |
| Quebec | 79,400 | 182,890 | 103,490 | 130.3 | 10.9 |
| British Columbia | 170,025 | 270,585 | 100,560 | 59.1 | 16.2 |
| Ontario | 188,315 | 374,395 | 186,080 | 98.8 | 22.4 |
| Western Canada | 436,455 | 656,970 | 220,510 | 50.5 | 39.3 |
| Canada | 976,305 | 1,673,780 | 697,475 | 71.4 | 100.0 |

Note: Regional increases over the 10-year period that exceed the national increase of 71.4 per cent are due to ethnic mobility and, in the case of Atlantic Canada, the inclusion in the newly formed Qalipu First Nation of some 23,000 Newfoundlanders who could prove Mi'kmaw ancestry. The Qalipu First Nation, which has no reserve or land base, is now the second-largest band in Canada.

Sources: Statistics Canada (2013b, 2019b).

appear overnight, and unfortunately it is not always a reality. Over time, racism has taken different forms, but it has made lives particularly miserable for Indigenous people and visible minorities, and has served to keep the English/French divide festering. At the root of the racism that marked Canada for many years was the belief that British culture was superior to other cultures in the world. After Confederation, this superiority complex continued. Several extreme examples come to mind—the Chinese head tax of 1885, the **residential schools**, the "continuous passage" legislation intended to keep South Asians from coming to Canada's shores and which led to the racially charged *Komagata Maru* incident in 1914 when a ship loaded with immigrants from the Indian subcontinent was turned back at Vancouver, and the internment of Japanese Canadians during World War II. The denial of entry to Jewish refugees from Nazi Germany on the eve of World War II is another historical stain on the national fabric.

Prime ministers in recent years have made some (though long overdue) apologies. Nonetheless, minorities and newcomers still experience racism in Canada. The Quebec City mosque shooting in 2017 left six dead and 19 others injured, prompting widespread discussion about Islamophobia in Canada, and the rise of the **Black Lives Matter** movement to protest mainstream police culture and its racial profiling of and unjust violence towards those in urban Black communities attests to the fact that racism continues to be problem (Cole, 2020).

## Dynamic Nature of Culture

All cultures evolve over time. Canadian culture evolves at a very rapid rate due to the inflow of peoples from around the world. The ways of the newcomers, including their dress, languages, customs, and religions, represent both a challenge to existing Canadian culture and an opportunity for that culture to be enriched. Indeed, at times the simple enactment of a law can alter significantly the culture (or cultures) of the society (Vignette 4.5). The legalization of cannabis was a remarkable socio-cultural event with relatively few negative consequences. Still, one goal of this legislation has not been achieved, namely, the disappearance of the black market trade in cannabis. The Cannabis Act (C-45) became law on 17 October 2018. One reason for the survival of the black market involves the slow response by provinces to provide retail outlets. Another reason is the price differential: black market products have a lower price. A third fact is the convenience of home delivery by illegal cannabis sellers.

Canadian culture, flexible and porous as it is, includes core values that are defined by Canada's history and geography. Four core values are: (1) government is based on British parliamentary institutions and the rule of law; (2) two official languages ensure a place for French as well as English, which also means that other languages have no standing in the political and public affairs of Canadian society (except in Nunavut, where Inuktitut also is recognized as an

## Vignette 4.5

### Number of New Cannabis Users Increasing

More Canadians began to use cannabis in the first quarter of 2019. Some of these new cannabis consumers were first-time users, while others were former cannabis users who tried cannabis again post-legalization.

During the first quarter of 2019, 646,000 cannabis users reported trying cannabis for the first time in the past three months. This number of first-time users was nearly double the corresponding estimate of 327,000 people one year earlier, when non-medical cannabis use was not yet legal.

Results suggest that first-time users in the post-legalization period are older. Half of new users were aged 45 or older, while in the same period in 2018, this age group represented about one-third of new users.

Source: Statistics Canada (2019c).

official language); (3) Indigenous peoples, but especially status Indians, have special rights, which flow out of historic treaties, modern land claim agreements, recognition in Canada's Constitution, and numerous court cases, as we have seen in Chapter 3; and (4) tradition and law are encapsulated in the Canadian Constitution, which includes the Charter of Rights and Freedoms.

## Ethnicity

An **ethnic group** is made up of members of a population who share a culture that is distinct from that of other groups. Each group has a common identity, shared values, and cultural/linguistic/religious bonds and symbols. Within Canada, ethnicity does not indicate a separation from Canadian culture but is simply a measure of the diversity of those members of Canadian culture (Figure 4.9). Still, the 2016 census revealed that the leading so-called ethnic group at 32 per cent was "Canadian." Single responses revealed five ethnic

groups with over one million. They included Canadian (6.4 million), Chinese (1.4 million), English (1.1 million), East Indian (1.1 million), and French (1 million).

## Language

In spite of Canada's multicultural society, the two official languages, English and French, represent the key cultural element leading to a successful integration into Canadian society. Yet, English-language proficiency is most sought after by newcomers. While the status of the French language is guaranteed by the Constitution, outside Quebec and New Brunswick the use of French is limited. Canada's two official languages, but especially English, are crucial elements in unifying Canadian society. Employment without a command of English is virtually impossible except in Quebec, where proficiency in French is required.

In 2016, an overwhelming number of Canadians declared that they spoke either English or French.

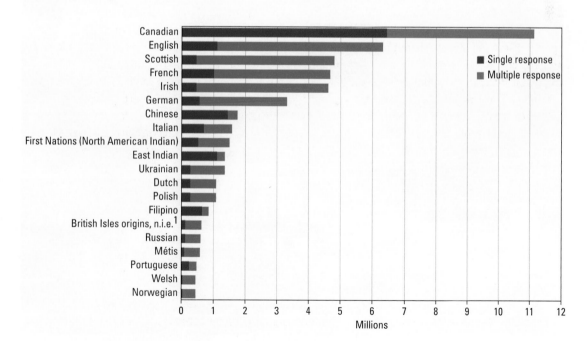

**FIGURE 4.9 The top 20 ethnic origins reported alone or in combination with other origins (single or multiple response), Canada, 2016**

1. "British Isles origins n.i.e." includes general responses indicating British Isles origins (e.g., "British," "United Kingdom") as well as more specific responses indicating British Isles origins that have not been included elsewhere (e.g., "Celtic").

Note: The sum of ethnic origins is greater than the total population because a person can report more than one ethnic origin in the census questionnaire.

Source: Statistics Canada, Census of Population, 2017.

Among the 2 per cent who did not speak one of the two official languages, most of those newcomers spoke Punjabi, Chinese, or Spanish. Most of them likely either had just arrived in Canada or were older parents of newcomers and had entered Canada as family class immigrants. The key point is that children of newcomers, by attending schools, quickly become fluent in one or both of Canada's official languages. Of the six geographic regions, Ontario contained over half of these newcomers who did not speak one of the official languages, followed by British Columbia and Western Canada at around 20 and 18 per cent, respectively; Atlantic Canada and the Territorial North each had less than 1 per cent of the non-English/French-speakers (Statistics Canada, 2011).

## Religion

Religion is another key element of culture. While religion remains an important cultural element, especially among non-Christian Canadians, Canada has moved more and more to a secular state. Quebec in particular has adopted a secular state more than other provinces by removing religious symbols from public places.

The 2016 census did not include a question on religion. However, this question will be included in the 2021 census. Based on the 2011 census, the two largest religious groups in Canada were Christians and those with no religious affiliation. Sixty-seven per cent or 23 million declared that Christianity was their faith while 24 per cent or 7.9 million had no religious affiliation (Statistics Canada, 2014b). Consistent with changing immigration patterns over the past several decades, four religions grew in numbers from the 2001 census: Islam (with 1.1 million members), Hinduism (498,000) Sikhism (454,965), and Buddhism (366,800). At the same time, the number of Canadians declaring no religious affiliation grew from 4.9 million to 7.9 million (Statistics Canada, 2005, 2016c).

**PHOTO 4.7** The Basilica of Notre Dame, opened in 1829, is the principal Roman Catholic Church in Montreal, and is a reminder of the Church's powerful role in the history of French-Canadian society. Today, however, the Church has lost not only its central role in Quebec society but also much of its active church membership.

Chrishowey/Dreamstime.GetStock.com

Canada is thought of as a Christian country. This image was certainly true until the twenty-first century. Now Canada is much more religiously diverse; plus, as noted above, a significant number claim no religious affiliation. As recently as 1971, nearly 90 per cent of Canadians declared themselves to be Christian (though some may not have been active church members). Fewer than 5 per cent declared no religious affiliation. The Jewish religion formed the second-largest religious group at that time. By 2011, the number of Christians had grown but their percentage had dropped to 67 per cent of the total population. Those following Judaism remained at just under 1 per cent. Other religions have grown in numbers and form 8 per cent of Canada's population, and their future place in Canada's religious landscape is anticipated to increase.

## Multiculturalism

Multiculturalism is the cornerstone of Canada's social policy towards newcomers. Over the past half-century, multiculturalism has taken root in Canadian society and it is a distinctively Canadian approach to social equality in nation-building. From the federal government's perspective, multicultural policies and funding encourage respect for cultural diversity. Ironically, this federal policy emerged as a direct result of the work of the Royal Commission on Bilingualism and Biculturalism (1970), which recommended that Ottawa recognize the multiplicity of Canada's population. The following year, in 1971, the federal Liberal government made multiculturalism official policy and in 1972 the cabinet position of Minister of State for Multiculturalism was created. Government funding to ethnic organizations soon followed. In 1988, the federal government passed the Canadian Multiculturalism Act, which is designed to encourage greater human understanding and stronger bonds among Canadians of different cultural backgrounds and ethnic origins.

For Charles Taylor (1994), a noted Canadian philosopher, multiculturalism is a way for the Canadian government and society to recognize the worth of newcomers' distinctive cultural traditions without compromising Canada's basic political principles. The outer boundary of multiculturalism is where it rubs against the edge of strongly held conventional values within mainstream society.

In many ways, multiculturalism is the opposite of **ethnocentricity**. While ethnocentricity aims to defend and keep an ethnic group united, multiculturalism attempts to broaden an ethnic group's perspectives and interactions with those outside its circle. Tolerance and respect of others are not an automatic outcome of life in pluralistic societies (Contested Terrain 4.1). Canadian tolerance and respect were learned the hard way, going back centuries to often bitter (and sometimes violent) conflicts between French- and English-speaking Canadians. For Canada to survive as a nation, the two antagonists had no choice but to become partners. One product of this

**THINK ABOUT IT**

Do you favour a strict separation of state and church? If so, where do you stand on public support for Roman Catholic schools and why?

## Contested Terrain 4.1

### Immigration and Multiculturalism

Immigration dictates that Canada will become an increasingly more pluralistic society and, therefore, that multiculturalism will continue to play a role not only as an adjustment mechanism for newcomers but also as a core Canadian value. On the other hand, has a rural/urban divide emerged because immigrants tend to settle in Canada's larger cities? For instance, the ethnic/racial/religious composition of Toronto's population is strikingly different from that of Timmins, where the population consists of English- and French-speaking residents and only very small numbers of Italian, Cree, and Finnish speakers (Statistics Canada, 2016e). As a consequence, socio-political events such as Pride parades and Black Lives Matter protests are commonplace in large cities but much less so or not at all in smaller centres, towns, and villages.

**PHOTO 4.8** Muslims comprised 2.7 per cent of Canada's population in 2016 and could reach 6.8 per cent by 2031 (Statistics Canada, 2016c, Table 5). The growing Muslim population in Western Canada is reflected in Canada's largest mosque, the Baitun Nur mosque in Calgary (pictured here), which serves the Ahmadiyya Muslim community. Another indicator of the rapidly growing Muslim population is the construction of the second-largest mosque, the Ahmadiyya Muslim Jama'at mosque in Saskatoon, opened in late 2016. The Madina Masjid is one of the oldest and largest Masjids in Canada, catering to the culturally diverse Muslim population of Toronto.

© Dunja Bond|Dreamstime.com

so-called partnership was biculturalism. The other path to nation-building—a classic European-style nation-state founded on a single common ethnicity and language—was not possible in the northern half of North America. Reaching an accord (not a solution) between the two founding peoples was not a simple task and disputes continue to emerge, as discussed in Chapter 3. Since dominance is not feasible in the long term, then compromise becomes a political necessity and eventually the search for compromise becomes ingrained as a national trait.[1]

Within a generation or two, the children and grandchildren of immigrants are more likely to find a place in mainstream Canada. Upward mobility is associated with education. But the question remains: "Might multiculturalism increase ethnic group identification at the expense of Canadian social cohesion?" Without doubt, tensions have arisen from time to time in Canada as people of different cultures, languages, and racial origins have chafed against what they perceive as barriers within Canadian society, but peaceful discord is not in itself a failure of multiculturalism but part of a process of social interplay necessary to expose and resolve differences (Vignette 4.6). While this process has not always been easy, the challenge for visible minorities and, we might add, Indigenous peoples is even greater since they are readily identifiable, and unfortunately their upward mobility is sometimes hampered by overt racism and covert racialization.[2]

## Key Cultural Issues

### French/English Language Imbalance

Canada is a bilingual country.[3] Yet, the weight of numbers is working against French-speaking Canadians.

## Vignette 4.6

### Social Inequality and Ethnic Neighbourhoods

Canada's regions and cities are constantly undergoing cultural adjustments resulting from new arrivals from around the world. Such adjustments are a product of an open immigration policy begun in the late 1960s. This policy has drawn people from a variety of world cultures, and the vast majority of these immigrants have relocated to major cities, with Toronto receiving the greatest number. Urban adjustment is a particularly sensitive matter in major cities where social inequalities and racism exist.

Why are social inequalities so prevalent in large urban cities? The first part of the answer lies in limited economic opportunities for many new arrivals (especially because foreign education credentials and work experience often have not been recognized by Canadian employers) and their desire to live near members of the same ethnic group. To be sure, racism and racialization contribute to these institutional and personal choices. The second part of the answer is founded on various factors. First, does the initial selection of a place of residence lead to entrapment and the solidification of that neighbourhood into a permanent ethnic ghetto? Walks and Bourne (2006) suggest that the forces of upward mobility and assimilation into Canadian society will, in time for the second generation to take root, see the dispersal of ethnic groups throughout the residential areas of Canadian cities. Stated slightly differently, some immigrants are trapped in poverty because their qualifications from their home country are not recognized, leaving them with limited and often dead-end economic opportunities. In the short term, recent immigrants prefer to live in the same neighbourhoods for the affordability, comfort, and security that this sense of place provides them. In addition, one magnet for new arrivals is religious institutions. Such institutions play a key role not only in maintaining the social cohesion of ethnic groups, but also in the selection of places to live. In the long term, however, the diffusion of ethnic groups normally takes place and the neighbourhood takes on another group of low-income people.

Since Confederation, even though their population size has increased, the percentage of French-speaking Canadians has declined, from 32 per cent in 1901 to 20 per cent in 2016 (Statistics Canada, 2019a). With this decline, the place of French-speaking Canadians within Canada has weakened. Only in Quebec has the French language remained strong and vibrant. In 2016, the percentage of Canadians whose mother tongue was French formed 79 per cent of Quebec's population while, in sharp contrast, less than 4 per cent of Canadians residing in other provinces and territories spoke French.

The language imbalance has increased over time for the simple reason that the English-speaking population benefits from the number of new Canadians arriving each year who adopt English. For all regions except Quebec, newcomers learn English.

French/English dualism is a fundamental aspect of Canada. As Jacques Bernier (1991, p. 79) of Université Laval stated: "Canada's duality is intrinsic, and as long as it is not clearly recognized and dealt with, the issue of Canadian unity will remain." This duality is a political concept embedded in the historical relationship between the two cultures. The main indicator of the stability of this dualism is language; in other words, the stability of this concept depends on a relatively constant number of Canadians speaking each language. But how should we measure duality? Should mother tongue or household language hold the key? Or is the number of bilingual Canadians the most important criterion? Outside of Quebec and New Brunswick, the French language is losing ground.[4] Anne Gilbert (2001, p. 173) points to the decision of the government of

Ontario to reject the concept of recognizing both English and French as official languages as a missed opportunity to showcase Canada's serious commitment to its dual languages.

## Cultural Damage and the Truth and Reconciliation Commission

Indigenous peoples are not a homogeneous group but rather a culturally diverse array of peoples. At the time(s) of initial European contact and settlement, more than 50 Indigenous languages thrived in what is today Canada. Contact with Europeans took various forms at different times, and through this contact the peoples' spirituality and harmonious relationship with the land lost some of its influence within Indigenous communities. Indigenous peoples were enlisted in the European fur-trading enterprise and in European wars in North America. Some European traders and missionaries learned Indigenous languages; many more Indigenous people, out of necessity, learned French or English. Indigenous language loss is but one measure of the impact of Europeans on the first inhabitants.

Later on, residential boarding schools attempted to assimilate Indigenous children by forcing them to speak English. Assimilation deeply scarred these children, and many carried those wounds with them into their adult lives. Without a doubt, this attempt at assimilation failed. The consequences were and are severe: this attempt to assimilate damaged Indigenous culture by severing children's cultural and language connection with their parents and their larger communities.

Indigenous language loss and residential schools are only two examples of the impact Europeans have had on Indigenous peoples. These and other examples, such as the Christian missionaries and the Indian Act of 1876, combine to show the extreme efforts undertaken to assimilate Indigenous peoples into a settler society. The toll of these efforts was recorded in the 2015 report of the Truth and Reconciliation Commission. The intention of the Truth and Reconciliation Commission was, according to the chair of the Commission, Justice Murray Sinclair, to strike a balance between revealing old wounds and providing the opportunity for healing. Most importantly, the Commission wished to:

> open the eyes of the Canadian public to the truth of the residential school experience,

not so much through the words of experts and the words of the commissioners, but through the stories and experiences of residential school survivors. And by showcasing them as we did in public hearings through the use of webcasts and video recordings, that raw emotion and feeling that they brought forward in the course of their stories was compelling. And I don't think anybody who watched survivors giving their testimonies at our hearings walked away not believing. (Sinclair, 2015)

In the twentieth century, unfettered resource development took its toll. Perhaps no single impact of this kind has been worse than the mercury poisoning, from an upstream pulp mill, of the members of the Grassy Narrows band living along the English-Wabigoon River system in northwestern Ontario (Shkilnyk, 1985), which was first identified in the late 1960s. Since then, regulations governing industrial pollution have toughened and Indigenous peoples have gained more power over resource development, largely through a series of Supreme Court of Canada decisions, including the duty to consult. Indigenous peoples still have a special relationship with the land, but that relationship often takes place within the parameters of the global industrial world. And mercury pollution takes years to dissipate. Not surprisingly, then, a half-century later, in September 2016, Japanese researchers determined that 90 per cent of the residents of the Grassy Narrows community suffered from mercury poisoning—notably brain damage resulting in sensory impairment and lack of co-ordination—including those born long after the dumping of mercury had ceased. The causes, apart from the original pollution of the river system from the mill in Dryden, Ontario: company and government failure to clean up the pollution, unsafe storage of toxic waste, indemnity provided by government to the successive owners of the mill and timber operations, and court rulings and government–business settlements that worked against the welfare of the First Nation people (McGrath, 2016).

As Canada has entered the third decade of the twenty-first century, vestiges of colonialism still exist. Among them, the Indian Act serves as a major detriment to the emergence of Indigenous governance. Nunavut is an early example of a post-colonial form of Indigenous governance, but within a public rather than ethnic context. To take the next step forward to more robust Indigenous governments, both sides—Indigenous communities and their leaders and the federal government—must come to an agreement on how to dismantle the Indian Act, and then provide the Indigenous peoples time and resources to shape their versions of governance.

## Summary

Up to 2020, Canada's population grew, thanks in large part to immigration. Along with this growth, Canadian society has become more culturally and ethnically diversified and yet more Canadian. COVID-19 has thrown a wrench into this population growth trend. By 2020, immigration slowed considerably and restrictions on international travel account for this decrease. At this moment, it is unclear if the number of immigrants will return to pre-2020 levels. If not, Canada's continued population growth is in doubt.

In the past, Canada has relied on immigration to fuel its population growth. Multiculturalism remains a central plank in Ottawa's effort to accommodate newcomers. Balance is key to successful cultural adaptation. The search for accommodation of the values associated with immigrants without jeopardizing Canada's traditional values remains an ongoing process, though the elastic nature of Canadian culture makes the task easier. Quebec faces a greater challenge as its cultural pliability is more rigid due to its historic defence against forces of anglicization. Its provincial government is concerned about its identity being swamped by immigrants and has passed legislation to ensure its francophone identity.

Tolerant as many Canadians are, blemishes occurred in the past and some are with us today. Inequalities within Canadian society do exist, most notably among visible minorities. Turning again to former Chief Justice Beverley McLachlin: "Living together in the ethic of tolerance is not easy. But it is worth the effort." It is the Canadian way.

## Challenge Questions

1. What are the consequences of Canada's population growth if the number of immigrants decreases?
2. From 2001 to 2016, Western Canada increased its share of Canada's population while other regions did not. Is this just a short-term blip on the demographic radar screen or are the fundamentals in place for this demographic shift to continue for the foreseeable future?
3. Why is the Indian Act an imposed form of colonialism?
4. What is the Black Lives Matter movement?

## Essay Questions

1. Canada's Indigenous communities are struggling to find a footing within Canadian society. This struggle lies along the Indigenous faultline. Has this struggle turned a corner with the Truth and Reconciliation Commission? More specifically, has the Commission's call to redress the legacy of residential schools and advance the process of Canadian reconciliation worked? Provide examples by referring to the Commission's 94 Calls to Action statement.
2. Like other advanced countries, Canada's fertility rate is below replacement level. According to the demographic transition theory, this event results in population stagnation or even decline. How, then, has Canada's population kept increasing at a robust rate?

# 5 Canada's Economic Face

## Introduction

In response to the twists and turns in the world economy, Canada has had to adjust its economy accordingly. The latest twist came in the form of a forced lockdown of the Canadian and global economies due to the rapid spread of COVID-19. This unexpected shutdown was an attempt to slow the spread of the virus. How long the global economy will remain in this state is uncertain, but the implications for Canada are extremely serious.

In the past, agriculture, resource development, and manufacturing were the chief generators of wealth in Canada. Canada still relies on these sectors, but, like other advanced economies, its economy has shifted more to a **knowledge-based economy** where highly developed technology is employed throughout society. Such technology depends on basic research often undertaken within a university environment to provide the scientific foundation for advanced "practical" technology. At the individual level, digital voice assistants and parking apps make everyday life more convenient. At a more sophisticated level, **artificial intelligence** (AI) machines have the capacity to analyze massive amounts of data quickly, but so far, none have passed the **Turing test**. Such data analysis has wide-ranging applications, such as in medicine where AI algorithms seek better diagnostics, more sophisticated patient care, and identification of diseases. In the long run, Canadian governments, both federal and provincial, believe that the future lies in a more vibrant knowledge-based economy. In the short run, unfortunately, the transition from a resource-based economy in some regions of Canada is extremely painful.

← Canada is well positioned as a global trade hub. Here, canola is grown and stored in Alberta, Canada.

How can we place the events that affect the Canadian economy into a global context? The economic process of globalization provides much of the explanation for the loss of manufacturing jobs in developed economies, including Canada and the United States; while Rostow's Stages of Economic Growth model offers a historic framework allowing for insights into a capitalist version of the nature and process of industrialization over time. In this chapter, our attention is focused on Canada's attempt to navigate through these turbulent global waters and, in doing so, chart a new direction to fossil resource extraction and processing by shifting towards a greener and more technically advanced economy. At the same time, a new challenge to globalization has emerged: the possibility of pandemic diseases spreading across the world carried by global travellers. In 2020, Canada and other nations faced such a challenge with the COVID-19 pandemic. Depending on how seriously this pandemic virus damages the global economy, individual countries may conclude that national security demands that manufacturing take place within their national state. Canada is already considering converting auto manufacturing firms to medical equipment firms, while funding for basic research for a vaccine is finally flowing (Vignette 5.1).

## Canada's Traditional Economies: Resources and Manufacturing

Traditionally, Canada has had two economies. One focused on manufacturing while the other concentrated on resource development. Geography offers an explanation for this situation. Since its founding, Canada has depended on the exploitation of its natural resources and the sale of those resources to foreign countries. The reason for this resource-based economy is simple. Geography has blessed Canada with abundant natural resources, but its relatively small population compels it to export these resources to foreign countries. At the same time, Canada's small and dispersed markets made the emergence of an industrial core difficult. Harold Innis, the first Canadian economist with a sense of geography, recognized these facts.

In his writings, Innis presented his interpretation of the historic development of Canada and its regions as the **staples thesis** (Innis, 1930). In this view, regional development took place as the resources of the region were exploited. The staples thesis provides the raison d'être for the National Policy of Canada's first prime minister, John A. Macdonald. This federal policy created a wall of tariffs that sheltered infant manufacturing operations in Central Canada. Much has transpired since 1879 when the National Policy was passed into law. The most striking event was the shift from a nationalist approach to a continental one. The first sign of this shift took place with the Auto Pact in 1965 and was cemented into place in 1988 with Canada–US Free Trade Agreement and then by the North America Free Trade Agreement (NAFTA) of 1994, which included Mexico. In 2018, the three countries agreed to renew NAFTA, renamed as the

## Vignette 5.1

### The Knowledge-Based Economy Has Many Faces and Places

In the global race to find a COVID-19 vaccine, the Vaccine and Infectious Disease Organization (VIDO) at the University of Saskatchewan is playing a leading role. Started as a modest veterinary lab in 1975, VIDO has evolved into a world-class facility that is one of only a few high-level facilities in the world able to conduct research on a vaccine for COVID-19. Funding for a pan-coronavirus vaccine for humans was not a priority for governments or pharmaceutical companies until COVID-19 turned such research into a high priority. In short, funding for basic research, such as discovering vaccines, takes place after society is faced with a serious crisis.

United States–Mexico–Canada Agreement (USMCA), which came into force on 1 July 2020.

In the next section, the future direction of Canada's economy is examined. Radical shifts in Canada's **industrial structure** are already underway and more changes are coming as the knowledge-based economy transforms our society. Students reading this book will have to make their way in a much different world than their parents knew. The key factor is not so much the type of change but the rate of change. The speed of change marks this generation from the previous one. Rapid advances in artificial intelligence set the stage for another round in our technological evolution.

## Canada's Future Economic Face

What will Canada's future economic face look like? Prime Minister Justin Trudeau provided his vision at the 2016 World Economic Forum in Davos, Switzerland: "My predecessor [Stephen Harper] wanted you to know Canada for its resources. I want you to know Canadians for our resourcefulness" (Wherry, 2016).

As the world enters what Klaus Schwab, the German founder of the World Economic Forum, has called the Fourth Industrial Revolution (Vignette 5.3), what do those words of Canada's prime minister mean? Most governments around the world embrace the idea of knowledge-based economies that are expected to provide robust economic growth. In applying this notion to Canada, Dan Breznitz of the University of Toronto's Munk School of Global Affairs suggests that "each region should focus on exploiting existing strengths, such as energy-related innovations in Alberta or agricultural technology in the grain belt, where strong knowledge bases already exist" (Milner, 2016, p. B8). But is the knowledge-based economy, with its innovative clusters, a magic elixir? Those with technological skills living in the clusters stand to benefit, but what about the rest of Canada's workforce? Certain sectors bore the brunt of the coronavirus lockdown, including airlines, shopping malls, the hospitality sector (hotels, restaurants, bars), and tourism. Already cracks have appeared, with low-wage workers facing exposure to COVID-19 in senior homes and grocery stores, and agricultural workers taking high risks in their workplaces. The

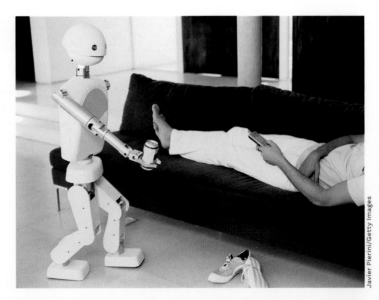

**PHOTO 5.1** Robot serving beer to a young man lying on a sofa with a remote control that connects with the robot. Can you imagine having a robot to bring you your textbook for this class? And will the next step be to have the robot read the book and give you a summary?

full impact of COVID-19 has yet to be seen, but it has already illustrated and exacerbated a widening of income between those at the top and those at the bottom. Many lost their jobs, turning to the Canada Emergency Response Benefit (CERB) as a temporary support for Canadians who had to stop working due to the pandemic. Could the next step be a guaranteed income?

As Canada hurtles down the economic development path, a quick look at the historic evolution of Canada's industrial structure provides a framework for interpreting the past and hints for the future. This evolution is similar to that experienced by other industrialized countries. Economic historians, including Walter Rostow in *Stages of Economic Growth* (1960) and Klaus Schwab in *The Fourth Industrial Revolution* (2016), have charted this course.

## Industrial Structure

An industrial structure, defined by the number of people employed in the three sectors of an economy, provides an insight into the nature of that particular economy; permits a historic view; and allows for comparisons with other economies. The growing role of women in industrial structure is one of the most remarkable social shifts in the last two centuries (Vignette 5.2).

## Contested Terrain 5.1

### Coal, the Industrial Revolution, and Climate Change

Coal remains the principal energy source used in industrialization, especially in the "take-off" stage described by Rostow. China and India are moving through this historic process by harnessing coal to drive their economies forward. The attraction of coal is its abundance and low-cost of production. However, because coal contributes heavily to climate change, world pressure is increasing for an end to coal production and to cease generating electricity from coal-burning thermal plants. Ontario has already closed its coal-generated electric plants and other provinces are moving in the same direction. Such political decisions result in cleaner air but higher electricity rates for Ontarians. If such a policy were extended to all countries, the opportunity for economic growth in developing countries, including China and India, would be reduced dramatically. The choice these countries are leaning towards is clear: economic growth trumps the call for a reduction in coal. Given this situation, is the goal of the Paris Agreement to reduce global greenhouse gases and thus keep global temperatures from increasing by more than 2°C by 2100 likely to be achieved?

## Vignette 5.2

### The History of Women in the Workforce

Three events in the last two centuries marked women's emergence into Canada's industrial workforce. The first event occurred during World War I, when women filled the work positions left by men who had joined the army. Most employed women during World War I worked in the service and manufacturing sectors and, despite proving their value as skilled employees, most were unjustly fired from their jobs when the men returned from the war. The second event took place during World War II, which provided a similar employment opportunity. The third event followed in the post-World War II era, when society relaxed its position on women entering the workforce. One factor promoting such change was the growing presence of women in post-secondary institutions. By 2019, women formed nearly half of the Canadian workforce: most are employed in the tertiary sector (88 per cent); fewer in the secondary sector (10 per cent); and fewest in the primary sector (2 per cent) (Statistics Canada, 2020e).

The three economic sectors, known as the primary, secondary, and tertiary sectors, divide the workforce by their types of employment:

- **Primary sector**: resource extraction, including minerals, farming, fishing, and logging.
- **Secondary sector**: construction and manufacturing, i.e., the processing of extracted resources for commercial sale.
- **Tertiary sector**: services, ranging from the Walmart cashier and the person who pours your first cup of the day at Tim Hortons to teachers, bankers, hairdressers, health-care workers, truckers, and computer programmers.

Advanced countries like Canada have most of their workers in the tertiary sector. Some analysts speak of a fourth sector, the **quaternary sector**, which essentially involves high-end knowledge-based workers and decision-makers, but Statistics Canada does not collect data to identify workers falling into this sector.

Over time, employment numbers have shifted from the primary sector to the secondary sector, and finally to the tertiary sector. This shift has occurred in all advanced industrial countries where the vast bulk of employees are now found in the tertiary sector. By the end of the twenty-first century, this shift to the tertiary is expected to continue and possibly reach 90 per cent for advanced countries like Canada.

**TABLE 5.1   Historic Shifts in Canada's Industrial Structure**

| Shifts | Year | Primary (%) | Secondary (%) | Tertiary (%) |
|---|---|---|---|---|
| Agricultural | 1881 | 51 | 29 | 19 |
| Early industrial | 1901 | 44 | 30 | 26 |
| Late industrial | 1961 | 14 | 32 | 54 |
| Post-industrial | 2011 | 4 | 19 | 77 |
| Current | 2019 | 5 | 17 | 78 |

Sources: Adapted from McVey & Kalbach (1995, Table 10.3); Statistics Canada (2006, 2012a, 2016b).

The historic shift in Canada's industrial structure as measured by employment is revealed in Table 5.1.

In this chapter, our primary interest lies in the evolution of the three industrial sectors. Our secondary interest focuses on the regional variations in these sectors. Canada's economic evolution provides a connection to the general theory presented in Rostow's *Stages of Economic Growth* and Schwab's *Fourth Industrial Revolution* (Vignette 5.3). For example, in 1881 just over half of Canada's workforce engaged in agriculture and other primary sector work (Table 5.1). This dominance of agriculture fits well with Rostow's second stage, *pre-conditions for take-off. By examining the broad historic changes* in the percentage of workers in each sector, insights into the nature of Canada's economy at various historic times are possible; and historic shifts in these sectors provide a means of observing and measuring changes in the labour force over time. For instance, the primary sector formed only 5 per cent of the national labour force in 2019 (Table 5.1).

Certain major forces caused this evolution in Canada's industrial structure over time: the settling of western lands in the late nineteenth and early twentieth centuries resulted in more farm labourers; the mechanization of agriculture through the development and use of tractors, harvesters, and combines led to the consolidation of small farms and drove farmhands and then small farmers into cities in search of factory work; automation and, more recently, the offshoring of manufacturing to developing countries pushed manufacturing employees into the service industries. Similar processes have occurred in the resource sector based on fossil fuels and minerals, but also renewable resources such as fishing. In these industries, new technologies have meant extracting more product and doing so more quickly, with the end result being that fewer workers are needed. At the same time, increased automation of processing

and manufacturing translated into fewer jobs in the secondary sector. The broad outlines of this evolution are revealed in Table 5.1. From 1881 to the present, the percentage of workers in these three sectors of the economy has moved to the tertiary/quaternary sector. By 2019, the tertiary/quaternary sector accounted for close to 80 per cent of the Canadian labour force.

The evolution of Canadian industry has its historic roots in the National Policy of Prime Minister John A. Macdonald in the late 1870s. His protectionist policy created the industrial core in Central Canada and set the tone for Canada's economy well into the twentieth century. At this juncture, Canada adopted more open trade policies, beginning with the Auto Pact in 1965, which ultimately led to the **Canada–US Free Trade Agreement** (FTA) signed by the two countries in 1988 and then to the **North American Free Trade Agreement** (NAFTA) of 1994, which included Mexico. The formalization in 1995 of the General Agreement on Tariffs and Trade as the World Trade Organization solidified the role of Canada—and the rest of the world—in a neo-liberal regime of freer trade. Since that time, Canada has signed and pursued bilateral and multilateral free trade agreements with other countries and blocs of countries throughout the world. Four topics—globalization, Rostow's Stages of Economic Growth model, the historic evolution of Canada's labour force, and the super cycle—offer insights into the global economic adventure and Canada's place in what Schwab has called the world's "Fourth Industrial Revolution" (Vignette 5.3).

## The National Policy and the Birth of an Industrial Core

As noted above, Canada's prime minister of the day, Sir John A. Macdonald, recognized the vulnerability of the newly formed state of Canada to the industrial

## Vignette 5.3

### The Fourth Industrial Revolution

Klaus Schwab argues that the world has experienced four phases to the Industrial Revolution (Table 5.2). Each phase denotes an abrupt and radical change to the world economy; each has been driven by fossil fuels; and each phase has required a shorter and shorter time to reach maturity. Concerns about climate change have given rise to green energy in Schwab's fourth phase. However, green energy remains a minor factor—and a more expensive one—in world energy production. Then along came COVID-19. To respond, Schwab called for a "great reset" of our economic and social systems. Economic disparities such as the ever-widening gap between low- and high-income earners are but one weakness in the global economy. What is the path forward? According to Schwab (2020):

> During the COVID-19 crisis, companies, universities and others have joined forces to develop diagnostics, therapeutics, and possible vaccines; establish testing centres; create mechanisms for tracing infections; and deliver telemedicine. Imagine what could be possible if similar concerted efforts were made in every sector.

Unfortunately, the competition between the leading nations to win the race for a COVID-19 vaccine reveals a basic weakness in Schwab's scenario. Instead of co-operating, national governments are focusing on the well-being of their citizens rather than the global good. One example was the collapse of the Canada/China agreement that involved the Chinese company CanSino Biologics. For geopolitical reasons, China's government blocked shipments of vaccine materials to Canada for testing (Cooper, 2020). During the height of the pandemic, trade in medical supplies collapsed, resulting in the decoupling of this economic segment from the global system and the emergence of production of these supplies in each country. Global trade depends on trust and that trust is gone.

Table 5.2 briefly summarizes Schwab's time frame for the four phases of the Industrial Revolution.

colossus south of the border. Macdonald also recognized the importance of a manufacturing economy in a modern country. He faced the choice of economic and possible political integration with the United States or protectionism. In 1879 Macdonald chose a form of protectionism based on the protection of infant industries, whereby tariffs raised the cost of otherwise low-cost imported products, such as shoes, clothing, and farm machinery, thus allowing local firms to produce these products and thrive in the local market until they could compete in the global market. The downside of this policy was the much higher cost of manufactured goods in Canada, especially in the places distant from the newly formed industrial core in Ontario and Quebec. Manufactured goods in Ontario and Quebec cost more than those produced in the United States largely because the much larger US market allowed for greater

**economies of scale** than in Canada, plus its road and railway system served a denser population than did the transportation system in Canada. While extremely popular in Central Canada, the rest of the country felt left out of the major benefits of the National Policy, despite their increased access to national markets with the completion of a transcontinental railway. Over time, resentment in Canada's periphery grew against what was perceived as the "entitlement" of Ottawa's catering to the interests of Ontario and Quebec. Not until the Auto Pact of 1965 and then the 1989 Free Trade Agreement with the US did this national core/periphery relationship undergo significant changes. One change was the integration of Canada's manufacturing sector into its much larger American counterpart; another was the emergence of a north–south transportation axis, i.e., the expansion of the CN railroad system into the United States (Figure 5.3).

**TABLE 5.2  Major Economic Revolutions over the Last 10,000 Years**

| Time | Event | Main Characteristic |
|---|---|---|
| **10,000 years ago** | Agrarian Revolution | Human/animal power: farming begins to replace hunting; village and urban life appears. |
| **1750–1870** | Industrial Revolution: Phase 1 | Water/steam power: steam engine and rail system begin the transformation of society from an agriculturally oriented one to an industrial one. |
| **1870–1950** | Industrial Revolution: Phase 2 | Coal power: industrialization accelerates with heavy industry driving the economy into a system of mass production and the division of labour. |
| **1950–2000** | Industrial Revolution: Phase 3 | Coal power: automation and computers become an integral part of the economy while global energy consumption increases dramatically as developing countries undergo industrialization and demand for electricity from coal-generated plants increases. |
| **2000–?** | Industrial Revolution: Phase 4, interrupted by the lockdown of the global economy | Green power: robotics make their presence felt, but the developing world continues to rely heavily on coal while the developed world shifts away from coal.<br>COVID-19 has disrupted the global economy, forcing major adjustments and restrictions in international trade. |

Source: Adapted from Schwab (2016).

## Globalization and the Stages of Economic Growth Model

In recent decades the world has entered a new epoch whereby globalization, by widening, intensifying, and accelerating worldwide interconnectedness, has created rapidly shifting economic terrain. In this unfolding world, the grip of any nation on its economic and political levers of power weakens, giving way to the rules found in international trade arrangements and allowing for the unprecedented role for transnational industrial and financial business interests in national affairs. The consequences for developed countries like Canada are considerable, and the most identifiable results are seen in the growing dominance of these transnational players in their economies. Imports of Asian manufactured goods have provided Canadians with an array of low-priced consumer products. At the same time, Asian state capital has reached deep into the Canadian oil and mining sectors and private Chinese capital has flowed into real estate. The question facing Canadians is whether this is an acceptable trade-off. The withdrawal of the United Kingdom from the European Union following a surprising 2016 referendum result and the emergence in the United States of a protectionist economic nationalism, which in some iterations verges on a populist xenophobia, are signs of discontent with globalization. For many workers, globalization has meant that their jobs have gone offshore, where workers receive much lower wages for the same work; and back home, high-paying manufacturing jobs have turned into low-wage service jobs.

In his book, Rostow (1960) presents a sweeping historical perspective on the process of industrialization as seen from America. By examining the European experience over time, Rostow identifies five stages that developed countries passed through to reach their degree of economic development. Since Rostow wrote his book, the world economy has moved on and developed countries have passed through his last stage of "the Age of Mass Consumption" into another stage. This most recent stage has been marked by the spread of industrialization to developing countries; the unprecedented pace of industrialization in countries like China; the record levels of international trade; and the unrelenting advance of technological innovations. This stage may well be called "Globalization."

Rostow's five stages of economic growth, plus the current globalization stage, are outlined below.

1. *Traditional society* involved an agricultural economy consisting mainly of subsistence farming on small plots of land. The bulk of the population, perhaps as high as 80 per cent, engaged in this agricultural economy. This period of time is often referred to as the pre-industrialization stage.
2. *Pre-condition for take-off* sees the first signs of industrialization. In this stage, agriculture turns into

**THINK ABOUT IT**

In advanced countries, globalization has had a negative effect on the working class. Canada is no exception in this "race to the bottom" that exacerbates the growing income gap between rich and poor. If the closure of the profitable Caterpillar plant in London, Ontario, in 2012 was a result of the seemingly relentless push by global companies to seek out countries with low wages and few benefits, what message does it send to Canada's manufacturing industry and its workers?

a more commercial endeavour with larger farms and the substitution of machinery for farm workers. Farm workers, in turn, are forced to move to the cities to seek jobs in the emerging factories. This period sees the start of a rural-to-urban migration along with the emergence of large cities.

3. *Take-off* occurs when industrialization clearly dominates the economy. Manufacturing surpasses agriculture in terms of economic importance, although as much as half of the population still resides in rural areas. In contrast to the highly productive factories, productivity in agriculture remains low. In this stage, the rural-to-urban migration reaches its peak and urban growth is rapid.

4. *Drive to maturity* is associated with a more diverse economy and the diffusion of economic growth to the hinterland. The vast majority of workers are engaged in the secondary and tertiary sectors of the economy. Agriculture is highly mechanized. Large farms are necessary to maximize the efficiency of agricultural machinery.

5. *An age of mass consumption* occurs when economic output reaches record levels and high wages permit increased consumer expenditure. Growth is sustained by the expansion of a middle class of consumers, not by exports. By now, the tertiary sector accounts for the vast majority of the labour force.

6. *Globalization* calls for the transformation of the world economy by reducing trade barriers and increasing the opportunity for industrialization in developing countries. Its defining characteristics are the emergence of an international industrial and financial business structure and a weakening of the role of nation-states in their domestic economies. Technology takes centre stage, and technological advances take on a relentless pace not seen before in human history. These advances are characterized by automation, digitization, and robotics, which have dramatically transformed economic life in developed countries where blue-collar and white-collar jobs are no longer secure.

Globalization is not a smooth linear process. Workers in developed countries have felt a few bumps in the road. One bump is the relocation of jobs offshore while another is workplace automation that reduces the need for workers. But perhaps the biggest bump is the realization that the average workers are not better off than they were 15 years ago. The political reaction is to turn against trade agreements and, in the case of the United States under President Trump, to renegotiate NAFTA into the USMCA.

As for the developing world, major countries like China are moving through this development process in record time. China, for instance, has passed through the take-off stage and is now entering the drive-to-maturity stage. Indeed, Heap (2005) even suggests that China's purchasing of resources has buoyed commodity prices, thus triggering the super cycle. A slowing or collapse of the super cycle (Vignette 5.4) would have detrimental implications for Canada's resource economy. Sure enough, by 2020 Canada's resource economy was reeling from a slowdown in the Chinese economy due to a trade war with the United States, trade skirmishes with Canada, and the outbreak of COVID-19.

## Shortcomings in Rostow's Model

Several shortcomings can be found in Rostow's Stages of Economic Growth model. First, Rostow's thesis is based on a US model of **modernization**. The question arises: can such a US-centric model bridge cultural differences found in non-Western countries? As well, does it apply to command economies? Without a doubt, most of the nearly 200 countries in the world have chosen the industrialization process, but not all have embraced the US model in which private capital plays a leading role in economic development. In fact, China poses a challenge to the US version. Clearly, for many emerging countries a different pathway from that posed by Rostow may take place.

Second, Rostow based his model on the historical experience of Western countries to the 1950s. Hence, his five stages do not take into consideration more recent economic events. For example, globalization as we know it had not yet occurred. The addition of a sixth stage, as suggested above, perhaps provides a solution to this issue.

Third, the notion of stages of economic growth may not apply equally well to all countries. Not all countries, for example, have the basic

## Vignette 5.4

### China: The Engine of a Commodities Super Cycle

When the People's Republic of China was admitted to the World Trade Organization in December 2001, global trade was radically changed as Chinese manufactured goods became able to penetrate markets around the globe. Canada and its main manufacturing provinces of Ontario and Quebec felt the brunt of low-cost Chinese goods displacing the products of local manufacturers, as these Chinese goods were readily available in big-box stores and Walmart outlets across the nation. In turn, China's rapidly expanding industrial capacity required more and more imports of coal and iron to fuel its steel industry. Prices for those and other commodities rose sharply, thus creating another commodity super cycle.

**THINK ABOUT IT**

Alan Heap and Klaus Schwab have identified variations in the global **business cycle**. Why is Schwab looking at long-term shifts in the global economy while Heap is more focused on short-term variations in the commodity cycle?

resources—coal and iron ore—for the take-off stage. Also, large countries with a diverse resource base stand a better chance of successfully completing the industrialization process than small countries. Japan and South Korea, of course, provide important exceptions to both points. While coal and iron ore are in short supply in both countries, imports of lower-priced coal and iron are the basis of their iron and steel industries and these industries form the heart of their industrialization process. The success of both countries lies not in geography but in culture and history. According to Sachs (2015), small countries now starting the industrialization process have less chance of mounting the development ladder. Many are in Africa, where the forces of colonialism divided the continent into numerous small yet ethnically diverse populations.

## The Super Cycle Theory

Economists consider **super cycles** to be extended periods of high global growth driven by the emergence of large, new economies that are undergoing the early stages of industrialization. One effect of this surge in demand is the unusual rise of prices for energy and raw materials within the global economy. In terms of Rostow's stages of economic growth, the demand for energy and raw materials peaked in the take-off stage. The most recent super cycle began with China's remarkable spurt of industrial growth that drove commodity and energy prices to new highs (Heap, 2005). Canada was one of the chief beneficiaries, and its resource exports to China and other Asian countries, led by coal and iron ore,

soared. But in 2014, economic growth in China and the rest of the world slowed, marking the end of this super cycle (La Caixa, 2015). Since then, global growth has languished. In a provocative report, the chief economist of the Organisation for Economic Co-operation and Development (OECD), Catherine Mann, claimed the global economy had fallen into a "low-growth trap" (Mann, 2016). If Mann is correct, then Canada and the rest of the world have to wait for India, the second-largest country by population, to rapidly industrialize and trigger a new super cycle (Vignette 5.5).

Oil provides one measure of the volatile nature of commodity prices. Annual oil prices (**Brent**) took a rollercoaster ride in the last 10 years (USEIA, 2019). From 2001 to 2020, demand caused the price to exceed US\$120/barrel and fall to as low as US\$30/barrel. In 2019, its average price was relatively stable at \$64/barrel, thus permitting higher-cost producers such those in Canada to operate at a profit. In 2020, the global economy crashed, causing demand and prices for oil to drop slightly below \$30/barrel. If that price is sustained over much of 2021, higher-cost producers would be squeezed out of the marketplace.

## Energy and the Environment

Canada has long harnessed its natural resources and exported these products to foreign markets, but especially to the United States. For coal—and possibly for oil—those days are coming to a close. Canada and coal-producing provinces are in an energy transition, shifting to forms of energy that

## Vignette 5.5

### The Third Super Cycle

Alan Heap declared that "There have been two super cycles in the last 150 years: late 1800s–early 1900s, driving economic growth in the USA; 1945–1975, prompted by post-war construction in Europe and by Japan's later, massive economic expansion" (Heap, 2005). The current one began with the rapid industrialization of China's economy. In all three cycles, rapid economic growth created a high demand for energy, minerals, and other commodities, thus pushing their prices higher. But like all economic cycles, what goes up, eventually comes down. Accordingly, Heap roughly estimated that the present super cycle would come to an end when China's economic expansion slows. Put in terms of Rostow's Stages of Economic Growth model, as China shifts from its take-off stage to the drive-to-maturity stage, its demand for foreign sources of energy and raw materials will ease and its exports of higher-end consumer and food products will increase.

emit fewer greenhouse gases, such as natural gas. Currently, the provinces of Alberta, Saskatchewan, New Brunswick, and Nova Scotia generate a significant portion of their electricity from coal. All are moving away from coal-burning plants, but more slowly than suggested by Ottawa. One reason is the impact this shift is having on workers and communities.

Without a doubt, concern about the warming of our planet is driving the shift away from oil and other fossil fuels. Environmentalists have warned for years that fossil fuel consumption must slow, and now their voices insist the burning of coal must halt now. Environmentalists have also targeted Alberta's oil sands, calling for a halt to production. The question confronting Canada is not a simple one, and it has deep and troubling regional complications. Should governments pursue policies to shut down coal production, restrict pipeline construction, and limit new developments in the Alberta oil sands? Federal policy, while mixed at times, is following those three strategies. First of all, the production of metallurgical coal, which comprises nearly half of Canada's coal output, is exported to steel-producing countries and can continue unabated. Second, coal used to generate electricity must stop. In 2018, Ottawa announced regulations to phase out traditional coal-fired electricity by 2030. Yet, these regulations are slow to take hold in the coal-burning provinces because the price of such electricity is low and because workers in such plants would be displaced. Looking to 2050, coal

for use in electric generation seems destined to end while oil output will increase, perhaps doubling by 2050 (Figure 5.1). However, oil production can only make such an increase by 2050 if the Trans Mountain pipeline is operating.

Pipelines are a highly controversial issue in Canada. The federal government will continue to face the important political question of whether to approve or reject oil pipeline projects. Pipelines are important for several reasons. First, pipelines represent the most economic method of transporting oil and gas. Second, pipelines to the Pacific and Atlantic coasts would diversify markets. At the moment, all gas exports and 99 per cent of oil exports flow to the United States. Third, the expansion of the Alberta oil sands depends on new pipelines, such as the Trans Mountain pipeline expansion.

The Trudeau government proposed to replace the National Energy Board (NEB) with the Canadian Energy Regulator (CER) in 2018. Previously, the NEB had recommended the construction of two oil pipelines, the Northern Gateway Project (2014) and the Trans Mountain pipeline expansion (2016), and was reviewing the Energy East pipeline proposal (2014). At the end of November 2016 the Trudeau government gave the go-ahead for Trans Mountain, put the final nail in the coffin of Enbridge's Northern Gateway (see *Canadian Press*, 2016), and saw TransCanada withdraw its Energy East pipeline proposal. These pipelines have polarized Canadians, with some supportive and others opposed.

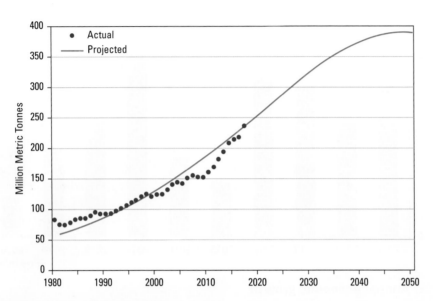

**FIGURE 5.1 Canada's oil production to 2050**

Source: Li (2018).

## Vignette 5.6

### GDP: A Measure of the Economy

**Gross domestic product** is a measure of the size of the economy. GDP represents the total dollar value of all goods and services produced over a year or some other period of time within a country or province. However, the most critical measure of an economy's performance is found in annual percentage changes in GDP, which can be positive or negative.

This polarization has regional consequences, with the BC government opposing the Trans Mountain pipeline much to the annoyance of Alberta, while the Quebec government has expressed its strong opposition to all pipelines.

## Canada's Economy

At this juncture, the discussion turns to Canada's economy, as recorded by GDP. This measure reflects the overall health of the Canadian economy (Vignette 5.6). GDP represents the total dollar value of all goods and services produced over a year within the country. In 2019, Canada's GDP totalled $2.5 trillion (Statistics Canada, 2020a). However, the annual growth rate of GDP provides a more meaningful measure.

As a rough interpretive guide, a buoyant Canadian economy occurs when annual GDP growth ranges between 2 and 3 per cent; a weak economy is marked by an annual GDP rate below 1 per cent; and GDP figures falling between those two extremes represent a stagnant one at the low end and a slow-growing economy at the high end. To place Canada's economic performance in context, annual GDP growth rate in Canada averaged 3.1 per cent from 1962 until 2009, when the economy, caught in the global collapse, fell by 4 per cent (Trading Economics, 2016). From 2011 to 2019, annual GDP has fluctuated from a high of 3.3 per cent in 2011 to a low of 0.9 per cent in 2015. Within two years, it had again reached the 3 per cent level but dropped to 1.5 per cent in 2019 (Figure 5.2). While the projected figure for 2020 was

**THINK ABOUT IT**

Which oil-producing provinces use Brent oil pricing and which use West Texas Intermediate oil pricing?

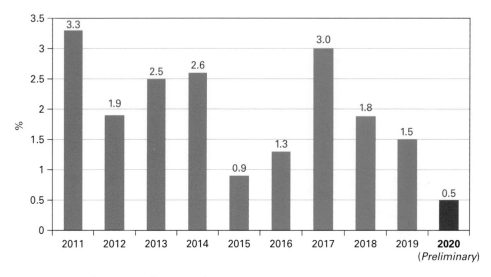

**FIGURE 5.2 Annual economic growth**

Source: Adapted from Evans (2016).

1.9 per cent growth, economic difficulties caused it to fall into negative territory.

Back in 2016, the chief economist at the Conference Board of Canada, Glen Hodgson, saw mixed economic signals ahead, i.e., unless oil and commodity prices were to regain their strength there was little chance of a significant upturn in the economy. So serious was the collapse in oil and commodity prices that the Bank of Canada governor, Stephen Poloz, "characterized the commodities price rout as a 'seismic shift' [in Canada's economy] that could last up to five years and drain $50-billion a year from the Canadian economy" (McKenna, 2016). While both oil and commodity prices remained low, the Canadian economy continued to grow, but this growth was halted in early 2020 when two events struck the economy. One was the arrival of the COVID-19 pandemic, and the other was the crash of the stock market. Later in the year the stock market would recover, but as fall turned to winter a deadly second wave of the coronavirus crept across the country.

## Unemployment Rates

Another measure of the economy takes the form of annual **unemployment** rates. In times of severe economic troubles, annual unemployment rates can exceed 8 per cent. At the peak of the 2009 recession, for example, the unemployment rate rose to 8.3 per cent (Table 5.3). On the other hand, when the economy is strong, the unemployment rate can drop below 6 per cent. Since 2014, the annual unemployment rate has stayed well below 7 per cent, reaching a low of 5.7 per cent in 2019. Unfortunately, the economic shock of the coronavirus pandemic delivered an unprecedented blow to Canada's workforce when, in late March 2020, nearly one million Canadians applied for unemployment benefits (Parkinson, 2020). The consequences of this may mean that unemployment rates exceed the 8 per cent level reached in 2009. By August 2020, Statistics Canada (2020d) revealed that Canada's unemployment rate had reached 10.2 per

**TABLE 5.3  Canada's Annual Unemployment Rate, 2006–2020**

| Year | Rate | Year | Rate |
|------|------|------|------|
| 2006 | 6.3 | 2013 | 7.3 |
| 2007 | 6.0 | 2014 | 6.9 |
| 2008 | 6.1 | 2015 | 6.9 |
| 2009 | 8.3 | 2016 | 7.0 |
| 2010 | 8.1 | 2017 | 6.3 |
| 2011 | 7.5 | 2018 | 5.8 |
| 2012 | 7.3 | 2019 | 5.7 |
|      |     | 2020 (August) | 10.2 |

Source: Statistics Canada (2016a, 2020b, 2020d).

cent, with rates much higher among Arab, Black, and Southeast Asian Canadians.

## Key to Canada's Prosperity: Trade

Canada depends heavily on trade. Exports are especially important to Canada's economic well-being for several reasons:

- *Resources.* Canada's vast resource base ranges from agriculture to oil and gas, forestry, and minerals.
- *Global market.* Canadian production far exceeds the capacity of its domestic market, making access to foreign markets critical.
- *Economies of scale.* Production for global markets allows producers to take advantage of economies of scale (and therefore lower per-unit costs of production) than would occur if they were restricted to the domestic market.
- *Prosperity.* Exports increase employment levels, draw foreign capital, and help balance international trade.

Trade with the United States dominates Canada's economic picture. In 2019, exports to the United States reached 75 per cent of total Canadian exports; imports from the United States were considerably less, at 51 per cent of Canada's total imports (Statistics Canada, 2020c). In comparison, exports and imports from China in 2019 were nearly 5 per cent and 8 per cent, respectively. These trade figures indicate the high degree of integration with the United States, as well as increasing trade with China. Yet, warning signs have appeared that may dampen trade with China. For instance, Ottawa is considering banning Huawei Technologies for security reasons (see Vignette 5.11) even though its **5G wireless technology** is the most advanced in the world and certainly at a lower price than competitors.

High levels of trade between Canada and the United States are due to a number of factors:

- North America is a natural economic trade zone, expressed by the term "continentalism."
- The economies of the two countries complement each other. The United States requires

large quantities of Canada's resources, especially oil, and Canada requires American technology.
- Several trade agreements, from the 1965 Auto Pact to the USMCA of 2020, have greatly accelerated trade between the two countries, leading to the integration of the North American automobile industry and—most importantly for the knowledge economy—technology industry.
- A north–south transportation system facilitates high volumes of trade (see Vignette 5.7).

## Trade Agreements

Trade agreements with the United States allow access to the world's largest and richest market. These agreements have (1) allowed Canadian firms to increase production to serve a larger market; (2) led to a more integrated North American economy; and (3) included trade conflict resolution mechanisms. In dealing with a superpower like the United States, a **dispute settlement mechanism** in trade agreements is essential to protect the smaller partners. Fortunately, the vast majority of trade in North America in recent decades has taken place in accordance with the rules of the **North American Free Trade Agreement**, the World Trade Organization (WTO), and, most recently, the 2020 USMCA. Disputes do occur between Canada and other countries, particularly with the United States. Canada has used the dispute settlement mechanism to seek compensation from US tariffs and quotas.[1]

Raw materials and energy have always formed a major portion of Canadian exports to the United States. The free flow of these products into the United States occurs when the US experiences a shortage. In other cases, US producers have called for tariffs and quotas on Canadian products. Lumber provides one example. In this case, Ottawa decided that a bilateral agreement would prove more beneficial to Canadian producers than applying to NAFTA's dispute settlement mechanism. The two countries reached the Softwood Lumber Agreement in 2006, thus setting the conditions for Canadian exports to the United States. From the American perspective, the heart of the dispute is that the Canadian

**THINK ABOUT IT**

China is closing the economic gap on the United States. Should Canada pay more attention to trade with China, including its 5G wireless technology?

## Vignette 5.7

### New Link in the North–South Transportation System

Canada is committed to building a new bridge over the Detroit River as the latest link in North America's transportation system. By 2024, the Gordie Howe International Trade Crossing is expected to provide a second bridge across the Detroit River, thus facilitating trade with the United States. An estimated one-quarter of the merchandise trade between the two countries travels over the privately owned Ambassador Bridge, which spans the river between Windsor and Detroit. With the increasing volume of trade, this bridge, built in 1930, has turned into a choke point.

AP Photo/Paul Sancya

**PHOTO 5.2** The Ambassador Bridge seen from the US side of the Detroit River. Construction on a new bridge began in 2019 with a completion date of 2024. The new bridge will be located roughly three kilometres downriver from the Ambassador Bridge.

lumber industry is unfairly subsidized by federal and provincial governments because, outside of the Maritimes, access to timber is managed by provincial governments and the price for that access is too low. The means of limiting Canadian shipments to the US takes the form of an export charge when the price of lumber is at or below US$355 per thousand board feet. In this way, the profit margin for Canadian producers disappears and exporting is no longer a viable transaction. The Softwood Lumber Agreement agreement ended in October 2016, and by November of that year the US Lumber Coalition, among the most powerful lobby groups in Washington, DC, had filed a lengthy petition with the US Department of Commerce asking it, once again, to investigate unfair trade practices (McGregor, 2016). As of the fall of 2020, no replacement agreement had emerged.

Trade with the United States reached its peak in the years following the signing of the Canada–US Free Trade Agreement in 1988. By 2020, Canada's trade with the United States had more than tripled

(Statistics Canada. 2020c). Access to the US market has allowed manufacturers in Canada, especially in Ontario and Quebec, to achieve **economies of scale** and thus lower per-unit costs of production. In this way, Canada's manufacturing industries have become more competitive, and that competitive edge has encouraged exports to the United States and, to a lesser degree, other countries.

Thomas Courchene (1998) argued that the Free Trade Agreement broke Central Canada's stranglehold on Canadian markets outside of Ontario, but opened the US market to Canadian manufactured products. Since most were produced in Ontario, the principal beneficiary was Ontario. In Courchene's

words, Ontario became a "North American Region State" rather than a Canadian province. The growth of Canadian National Railway (CN) from a national railway system to a North American one supports Courchene's argument (Figures 5.3 and 5.4).

In 1965, the political force behind the Auto Pact was founded in an economic philosophy known as **continentalism**, as have been the FTA and NAFTA. In Canada, continentalism has always lurked just below the surface of serious political thought among federal politicians and the wish of Canadian business people. The Canadian public, looking across the border at lower prices for similar goods, had no trouble understanding the advantages of that aspect

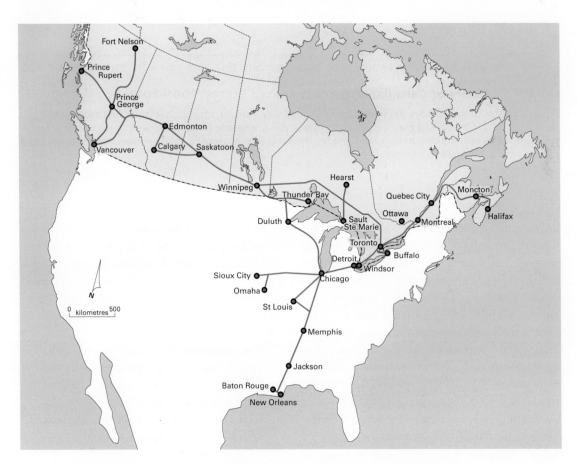

**FIGURE 5.3 CN: Symbol of the integrated North American economy**

With the Canada–US Free Trade Agreement, CN switched its emphasis from a predominantly Canadian east–west railway system to a North American continental system. CN now operates in eight Canadian provinces and 16 US states. Not surprisingly, the trend to expand from a Canadian base to a North American one has attracted other firms, including Canadian banks that now have substantial holdings in the US. By 2020, the Bank of Montreal's US operations were about one-third in size and value to those in Canada.

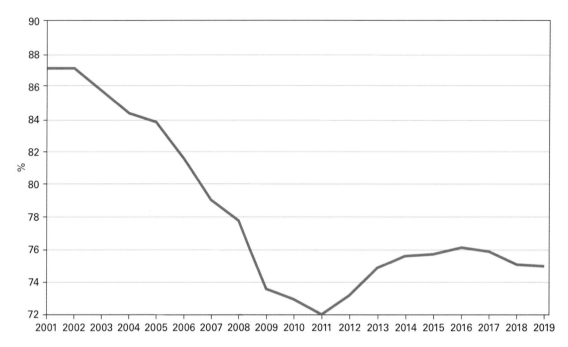

**FIGURE 5.4 Share of Canadian exports to United States, 2001–2019**

Exports to the United States declined from 2001 (87 per cent of total Canadian trade) to 2011 (72 per cent); by 2014, US trade had bounced back to 75 per cent, where it remains. While the US remains by far the most important trading nation for Canada, the increase in exports to other countries represents a diversification in Canada's exports.

Sources: Statistics Canada (2011, 2016c, 2020c).

of free trade but they did have concerns about the political and cultural implications of such close economic ties with the United States. Indeed, in the early 1970s, the government of Pierre Trudeau sought to move beyond Canada's reliance on trade with the US by pursuing a "Third Option" of expanding trade connections with Europe, but as political scientist Stephen Brooks remarks, this policy proved "about as effective as a statute repealing the law of gravity" (Brooks, 2012, p. 534). The close bilateral relationship and the geographical imperative of proximity were, and remain, too strong for major change in the direction of Canadian trade. Table 5.4 outlines some the shifts and events in Canadian trade policy from the Auto Pact to the present.

Good relationships also have played a role as Canada and the United States have been close allies for a long time. As President Kennedy remarked in his speech to Canada's Parliament in 1961: "Geography has made us neighbors. History has made us friends. Economics has made us partners. And necessity has made us allies." Derek Burney, former Canadian ambassador to the United States, and policy expert Fen Hampson (2012, p. A13) expressed the significance of the long-standing Canada–US relationship in more pragmatic terms:

> The cornerstone of Canada's foreign policy is the management of relations with the United States, not for reasons of sentiment but because that's how we preserve our most vital economic and security interests and our capacity for global influence.

## Manufacturing: Alive or Dead?

Manufacturing in Canada has suffered from a steady decline over the last two decades (Figure 5.5). Competition from countries where labour costs are

## TABLE 5.4 The Orientation of Canadian Trade: From North American to Global?

| Date | Continental Orientation |
|------|------------------------|
| 1965 early 1970s | The Auto Pact between Canada and the United States creates a continental market for automobiles. Failed "Third Option." |
| 1989 | The Canada–US Free Trade Agreement (FTA), designed to integrate the two economies, comes into effect. |
| 1994 | North American Free Trade Agreement (NAFTA) broadens the geographic area of the FTA to include Mexico, but to the disadvantage of Canada and the United States. |
| 2001 | Auto Pact ends because of a WTO ruling that it discriminated against foreign companies. |
| 2006 | Softwood Lumber Agreement sets the terms for lumber exports to the US for the next 10 years. |
| 2016 | Softwood Lumber Agreement ends in October amid growing protectionist and anti-free trade political climate in the US. |
| 2020 | USMCA (the new name for NAFTA) among Canada, the US, and Mexico comes into effect. |
| **Date** | **Global Orientation** |
| 1997 | Free trade agreements are reached with Israel and Chile; from then to 2016, bilateral agreements are made with Peru, Columbia, Panama, and South Korea. |
| 2002 | Kyoto Protocol commits Canada and 38 other countries to cut their emissions of greenhouse gases between 2008 and 2012 to levels 5.2 per cent below 1990 levels. |
| 2011 | Canada withdraws from the Kyoto Protocol. |
| 2016 | The Comprehensive Economic and Trade Agreement (CETA) with the European Union is completed and ratified. |
| 2020 | In 2015, a **Trans-Pacific Partnership** agreement is reached among 12 Pacific Rim countries—Canada, the US, Mexico, Peru, Chile, Brunei, Singapore, New Zealand, Australia, Japan, Vietnam, Malaysia—but full ratification, if accomplished, can take several years. In November 2016, President-elect Trump declared that, under his administration, the US would not sign the TPP. By 2020, seven countries had ratified this agreement (Canada, Australia, Japan, Mexico, New Zealand, Singapore, and Vietnam). |
| **Pending** | Negotiations for trade agreements with China and India are stalled. |

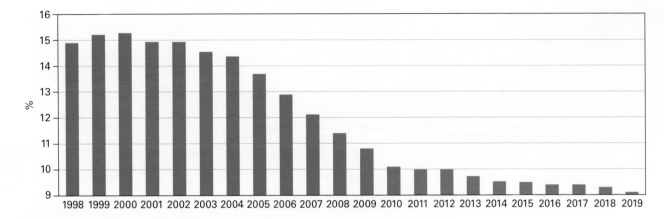

## FIGURE 5.5 Manufacturing's share of total employment, 1998–2019

While those employed in manufacturing declined from nearly 2 million in 2001 to 1.5 million in 2019, the percentage of those involved in manufacturing declined even more sharply—from 13.3 per cent to 7.9 per cent. One factor in this percentage decline is related to the increase in the total number employed, which increased from 15 million to 19 million.

Source: Statistics Canada (2012a, 2015c, 2016c, 2020e); OICA (2020).

much lower than in Canada is central to this demise, while automation, outsourcing, and offshore relocation also play a role. In spite of this decline, manufacturing continues to play an important role in Canada, especially in Ontario. Canada is not unique in the retreat of manufacturing; rather,

For discussion of the auto industry in Ontario, see the section "Ontario's Original Economic Anchor: The Automobile Industry" in Chapter 6, page 190.

this downhill trend is common to other advanced industrial countries. Keep in mind that manufacturing is now more efficient thanks to advanced systems of assembly and the integration of technology. Manufacturing now is leaner and more efficient than before. The reasons for the decline in manufacturing vary from country to country but the common factors for Canada are:

- Canada has higher wages than most other countries.
- Automation has displaced workers.
- Outsourcing sees jobs move overseas.
- Offshore relocation by firms moves jobs out of the country.

Glen Hodgson, chief economist at the Conference Board of Canada (2016), made the point that "the future of Canadian manufacturing is like running an endless marathon to stay ahead of the competition—but running in the marathon is far better than the alternative of dropping out."

The heart of Canadian manufacturing lies in the automobile and auto parts industries. The Auto Pact (1965) made Canada an important manufacturing country and provided the Big Three North American manufacturers (Ford, General Motors, and Chrysler) a decided advantage in the single market of Canada and the United States. Unfortunately for Canada, NAFTA (1994) brought Mexico into the North America market. Mexico, with its much lower wage rates, soon attracted automobile manufacturers. Under these circumstances, Canada's automobile industry lost ground to Mexico as most investment in new plants went there. In 2000, Canada's share of North American vehicle production was 17 per cent while Mexico's share was 11 per cent. Over the next 18 years, Canada's share dropped to 12 per cent while Mexico increased its share to 24 per cent (Figure 5.6).

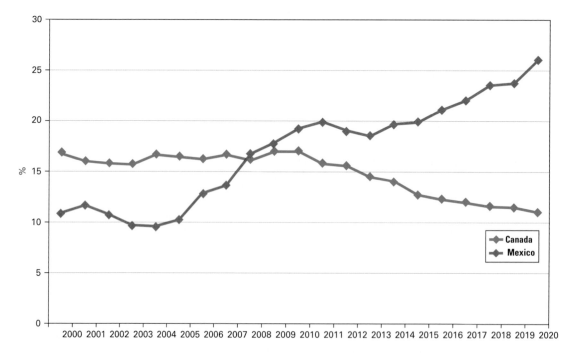

**FIGURE 5.6  Canadian and Mexican percentage shares of North American vehicle production, 2000–2020 (including heavy-duty trucks)**

Sources: Keenan (2015); OICA (2020a, 2020b).

## Vignette 5.8

### What Comes after Automobile Parts Production?

Could medical manufacturing take the place of auto parts production? Automobile parts manufacturers are extremely nimble in shifting from one product to another. They could fill the gap at a time of emergency, or some could switch production permanently if such manufacturing is declared in the national interest. The problem is cost: products made in Asia are less expensive, but in time of an epidemic, supply is more crucial than price. According to Flavio Volpe, president of the Automotive Parts Manufacturers' Association:

> The shift to medical supplies would be easy enough to do, and they could convert back to automotive manufacturing quickly. Right now, the country needs masks, gowns, goggles and ventilators, and Volpe is looking to assign some of the auto manufacturers' capacity to help with the cause. (Jamzer, 2020)

## The Wave of the Future: The Knowledge-Based Economy

Economists Peter Drucker (1969) and Daniel Bell (1976) and geographer David Harvey (1989) were among the first scholars to recognize a knowledge-based economy. Until then, production was centred on assembly line production; now information and knowledge to use that information have widened the scope of labour and created a digital world.

From Bell's perspective, the **knowledge-based economy** offers hope for advanced industrial countries like Canada to offset a decline in manufacturing activities caused by globalization of trade and thus keep the unemployment rate low. Yet Bell failed to recognize that workers in many manufacturing firms could not make the transition to a high-tech workplace. Many drifted into low-paying jobs in the service industry. For Bell, success in the knowledge-based economy depends on integrating scientific knowledge, in the form of technology and innovation, into new products and services that can successfully compete internationally.

Futurist and author Martin Ford, on the other hand, fears that this technology-driven economy and its robotic machines will not reduce but increase unemployment because human workers will be replaced by robots and androids (2015, p. xii). Already, robots are effectively completing repetitive tasks in the manufacturing sector (Photo 5.3). As Ford (2015, p. 7) explains, "we are, in all likelihood, at the leading edge of an explosive wave of innovations that will ultimately produce robots geared toward nearly every conceivable commercial, industrial and consumer task." Ford argues that Western society needs a *new economic paradigm* because, in the robotic age, extremely high rates of unemployment coupled with an unacceptably wide income inequality gap will be the norm; to meet this economic and social challenge, Ford calls for a guaranteed income (Ford, 2015, ch. 10; Vignette 5.9).

## Information Society and Innovative Clusters

An information society functions within a knowledge-based economy. Within such a society, a **creative class** places a high priority on innovative and scientific research. Such research creates new products that transform society: the potential impact of an electric car on city design and greenhouse emissions; biotechnical innovations that have led to higher-yielding grains; application of green technology (e.g., green roofs) to city buildings, thus making large cities more livable places (see Cleary & Grant, 2019).

Innovative clusters are not spread evenly across the country. Instead, they tend to locate in large cities near major universities. Toronto, Montreal, and Vancouver form key hubs of knowledge-based firms. Even so, these firms are found in the middle- and lower-sized cities. The reason is that this technical

Robotiq

**PHOTO 5.3** In this photo, automation engineers program a robot to tend a CNC (Computer Numerical Control) machine-tool that is used in manufacturing. Robotic machine tending frees floor workers from repetitive tasks and usually increases the productivity and safety of the workers.

**THINK ABOUT IT**

What are the implications of the shutdown of cultural and sporting events on the "interesting" aspects of Canada's metropolitan cities?

innovation has reached all sectors of the economy. Britton (1996, p. 266) stated that "Canadian urbanization is the key to understanding the location of technology-intensive activities." Marc Busch takes this idea further. His answer is "clusters" (Atkin, 2000, p. C1). A cluster is a place where institutions, companies, and individuals have a commitment and enthusiasm for innovative technological research along with the capital necessary to develop and market new products. Innovative clusters often are anchored around a university or a public research agency like the National Research Council.

Richard Florida (2002b, 2012) adds to this cluster idea by contending that members of the creative class want to live in "interesting" cities. He proposes that these creative people are the drivers of urban and regional growth and the concept of "clustering," namely, that the creative class is attracted to cities with a "liberal" cultural soul, where a wide variety of artistic and cultural events flourish and where

ethnic diversity and tolerance of non-mainstream lifestyles are well established (Florida, 2002a, 2002b, 2005, 2008, 2012). Florida further claims that innovative firms, public research centres, and universities situated in culturally rich cities have an advantage in recruiting and retaining a highly creative labour force (Florida & Jackson, 2010; Florida et al., 2010, Hracs et al., 2011).

As the centre of the Canada's music, film, and sports world, does Toronto provide such an "interesting" city? The concept of "interesting," according to Florida and his colleagues, involves world-class events such as the Toronto International Film Festival, which has rocketed Toronto onto the world stage. The Blue Jays, Raptors, Toronto FC, and Maple Leafs offer North American major league sports action, while the Toronto Caribbean Carnival and Pride Parade draw tourists and participants from across Canada, the United States, and other countries.

## Vignette 5.9

### Income Inequality

In his discussion of the Fourth Industrial Revolution, Klaus Schwab warns that this phase of the capitalist system is likely to generate greater income inequalities. Like regional inequalities, income inequalities can lead to social discontent and protests. While unlikely, the world revolution predicted by Marx lurks in the background. The flaw in the capitalist system lies in the unequal distribution of wealth generated by modern economies. Concentration of wealth in the hands of a few people, known as the "1 per cent," poses a problem. In economic terms, this phenomenon reflects income inequality. The expectation that economic development would, to use an aphorism, "lift all boats in a rising tide," seem logical, but in the twenty-first century, most gains from economic growth have flowed to a few at the top of the economic pyramid, leaving the majority with little to show for their efforts (Yalnizyan, 2010; OECD, 2019; Green et al., 2017). In its video "Opportunity and Equality for All," the OECD expressed its concern that social resentment leading to political instability is spreading in advanced countries and, if not checked, could have devastating impacts on these democratic countries, including Canada.

Martin Ford weighs in on this matter by concluding that the potential for such a disruption to society is highly likely. To avoid such a catastrophe, Ford calls for national governments to provide a basic income guarantee that, in his opinion, would alleviate poverty, mitigate income inequality, and maintain social order (2015, p. 261).

## Regional Economies

Canada's economic face has a different look in each of the six geographic regions. Industrial structure by employment type provides one measure of the spatial divide. At the national level, looking at the primary, secondary, and tertiary sectors provides an overall picture of Canada's industrial structure, with the tertiary sector accounting for 79 per cent of all workers, the secondary sector 17 per cent, and the primary sector only 4 per cent (Table 5.5).

The industrial structures for the six regions, on the other hand, reflect the core/periphery model with Canada's two core regions, Ontario and Quebec, having higher percentages of workers in the secondary sector than the national average but the lowest in the primary sector. Western Canada, on the other hand, with its strong agriculture and resource activities, scores highest, with 12.3 per cent in the primary sector. The dominance of the tertiary sector is found in all six regions, reflecting the evolution of Canada's economy into an advanced industrial one.

**TABLE 5.5** Industrial Structure of Canada and Regions, Percentage of Workers by Industrial Sector, 2019

| Economic Sector | Ontario | Quebec | Western Canada | British Columbia | Atlantic Canada | Territorial North[*] | Canada (%) |
|---|---|---|---|---|---|---|---|
| **Primary** | 1.9 | 3.2 | 12.3 | 4.4 | 7.6 | 5.0 | 4 |
| **Secondary** | 17.8 | 18.2 | 16.0 | 15.9 | 17.3 | 10.0 | 17 |
| **Tertiary** | 80.3 | 79.6 | 71.7 | 79.7 | 75.1 | 85.0 | 79 |
| **Total workers (000s)** | 7,453 | 4,340 | 3,750 | 2,603 | 1,199 | 46 | 19,388 |

*Estimate.

Source: Adapted from Statistics Canada (2020e).

As a frontier region, the Territorial North is a special case because of its lack of manufacturing jobs and its extremely high proportion of public employees, which pushes its percentage of tertiary workers to 85 per cent.

## Canadian Economic Landscape

From a geographic perspective, the core/periphery model is adaptable to Canada's economic landscape. In this spatial version, Canada's six geographic regions are placed within the four categories: the core, the rapidly growing, the slow-growing, and the resource frontier. Within this version, regions have the possibility—at least in theory—of shifting their position within these four categories. For example, with the rapid industrialization of economies of Pacific Rim countries, trade and investment with British Columbia could shift it from a rapidly growing region into a core region. With BC already leading the five provincial regions in terms of the percentage of labour force in the tertiary sector, perhaps this process is already underway.

The *core* represents the focus of economic, political, and social activity in the national economy. Most people live in the core, which is highly urbanized, diverse, and industrialized. Much of its population growth stems from in-migration rather than natural increase. Its capital city or cities have a high capacity for innovation and economic change. Innovations and economic advances are disseminated outward to other cities in the core and then through the national urban hierarchical system to places outside of the core. In applying this theoretical model to Canada, two geographic regions, Ontario and Quebec, best represent Canada's core.

Beyond the core, the hinterland portrayed in this theoretical spatial model contains three types of areal units. The three types differ by the level of their economic development. The *rapidly growing region* has a rich resource base that is well on the road to full economic development. Of the three hinterland types, only one has the potential to grow and diversify its resource base into a core. The reason is simple. Its rich resource base and thriving urban centres draw both capital and workers.

Initial development occurs in its resource base but spreads into its cities. In this diversification process, the *rapidly growing region* duplicates the features found in the core cities, including high-technology firms. In many ways, this rapidly growing region follows Innis's staples thesis, which sees such regions evolving into diversified economies. British Columbia and Western Canada already have core-like areas and, in time, could evolve into core regions outside of Central Canada.

The economy and population growth in a *slow-growing region* are trailing behind the performances of the core and the rapidly growing region. For the slow-growing region, economic growth is stalled, unemployment is high, and out-migration is common. Often, because it is an "older" region, resource development has passed its prime. Without sufficient diversification of its economy and with an aging population, the regional economy is treading water. Atlantic Canada is an example of a slow-growing region.

While the first two types of hinterland regions have undergone economic development, the *resource frontier* is still in the early process of such development. Far from the core, its resources are costly to develop and therefore often remain untouched. Mostly Indigenous peoples live in the remote areas of the Territorial North and resource companies are recognizing the necessity of including Indigenous communities in their development proposals. Even so, the process of regional diversification that took place in other regions of Canada has yet to take hold in the Territorial North, largely because of the leakage of economic benefits to cities in southern Canada.

## Provincial Unemployment Rates

From 2009 to 2019, the unemployment rate in Canada decreased, from a high of 8.3 per cent to 5.7 per cent (Table 5.6). In 2020, the unemployment rate jumped because of the economic lockdown caused by COVID-19.

During this time of prosperity, the economic performance of Canada's provinces varied from high unemployment rate in Newfoundland and Labrador of 15.5 per cent in 2009 to a low of 3.8 per

**TABLE 5.6 Provincial Unemployment Rates, 2009, 2014, and 2019 (%)**

| Province | 2009 | 2014 | 2019 | Difference 2009–19 |
|---|---|---|---|---|
| Saskatchewan | 4.8 | 3.8 | 5.4 | –0.6 |
| Ontario | 9.0 | 7.3 | 5.6 | 3.4 |
| Manitoba | 5.2 | 5.4 | 5.3 | 0.1 |
| Alberta | 6.6 | 4.7 | 6.9 | –0.3 |
| British Columbia | 7.6 | 6.1 | 4.7 | 2.9 |
| Quebec | 8.5 | 7.7 | 5.1 | 3.4 |
| New Brunswick | 8.9 | 9.9 | 7.9 | 1.0 |
| Nova Scotia | 9.2 | 9.0 | 7.2 | 2.0 |
| Prince Edward Island | 12.0 | 10.6 | 8.8 | 3.2 |
| Newfoundland and Labrador | 15.5 | 11.9 | 11.9 | 3.6 |
| Canada | 8.3 | 6.9 | 5.7 | 2.6 |

Sources: Statistics Canada (2009, 2010, 2015, 2016a, 2019; Duffin, 2020).

cent in Saskatchewan for 2014. By the end of this decade, the oil boom had ended, causing Alberta and Saskatchewan to record higher unemployment rates. British Columbia replaced Saskatchewan as having the lowest unemployment rate, at 4.7 per cent. At the same time, Newfoundland and Labrador continued its place at the bottom with an unemployment rate of 11.9 per cent. In terms of overall improvement, with a 3.4 per cent improvement in their unemployment rates, Ontario, Quebec and BC each achieved the greatest gains over this decade.

While several economic events affected these province rates, the crash of **oil prices** let the air out of the resource sector's balloon, resulting in an increase in unemployment figures for oil-rich provinces— Alberta's rate rose from 6.6 per cent in 2009 to 6.9 per cent in 2019; Saskatchewan went from 3.8 per cent to 5.4 per cent unemployment. With Alberta's economy facing stiff head winds in 2020, unemployment rates could rise significantly due to its strong dependency on oil. By the end of March 2020, the **Western Canadian Select** prices for oil had hit rock bottom at just under US$10/barrel. Of course, if oil prices rise sharply, Alberta's economy could regain its former status as the "engine of economic growth." However, such a scenario seems highly unlikely. With the arrival of COVID-19 and greater concern shown by governments and publics regarding climate change and green energy sources, Canada and the world economies could be heading in a different direction, away from the fossil fuels that drove economic growth in the past (Contested Terrain 5.2).

**THINK ABOUT IT**

Alberta is so determined to have the Trans Mountain pipeline to the Pacific coast completed because this pipeline would allow Alberta oil to receive much higher Brent prices compared to the much lower Western Canadian Select prices.

**THINK ABOUT IT**

Innovations take many forms. Canada's Arctic benefits from innovations, such as the multi-beam echo sounder technology that measures the depth of the ocean and creates a detailed image of the topography of the seafloor. Such collaborative technology is helping the Canadian Hydrographic Service prepare Canada's claim to the Arctic Ocean seabed. See Chapter 11 for a fuller discussion.

## Contested Terrain 5.2

### Is There a Place for Canada's Fossil Fuels Sector?

Canada is an exception to most advanced industrial nations because of the enormous size of its natural resource base, especially its energy sector. The paradox facing Canada is how to balance its long-standing advantage in fossil fuels with the need to reduce greenhouse gas emissions. The challenge lies in climate change. What are the facts?

- The energy sector is a huge emitter of greenhouse gases, with coal-burning plants the worst offender.
- Although the world energy demand for coal and oil are predicted to increase until 2050, pressure to end coal production used to generate electricity is intense.

The new right-wing government of Alberta moved quickly to rescind the former NDP government's efforts to end coal-burning electric generating plants. Under Premier Rachel Notley, coal plants were either closed or converted to burn natural gas by 2030. The new premier, Jason Kenney, has vowed to end the statutory shutdown of coal-burning plants. Yet, the marketplace trumps politics as TransAlta and Capital Power, the two biggest players, are converting their coal-fired power-generating facilities to lower-cost natural gas before 2030.

## Equalization Payments

The Canadian federal government has long recognized that economic opportunities vary across the country. Much of this regional variation stems from differences in population, natural resources, and economic activities. The net result is that some provinces have more revenue to meet their fiscal obligations than others. Equalization payments also divide the country into "have" and "have-not" regions. In this way, the equalization program should support the core/periphery model. The logical expectation would be that the two core regions, Ontario and Quebec, and the rapidly growing regions of British Columbia and Western Canada would qualify as "have" regions while the slow-growing region (Atlantic Canada) and the resource frontier (Territorial North) would qualify as "have-not" regions. Reality proves this hypothesis incorrect because Quebec, one of the core regions, has received equalization payments since the program began in 1957. Even more surprising, Quebec has consistently obtained the bulk of the annual payments, indicating that this province lags far behind "have" provinces, but especially Alberta and British Columbia.

Equalization payments are designed to ensure a reasonable level of economic equality across the country. Yet, regional tensions have often surfaced. The squabble between Alberta and Quebec is but one indication of such tensions. So how are equalization payments calculated? Ottawa uses a complex formula that provides federal support to those provinces whose per capita revenue falls below a national average. While Canadians generally support the principle of equalization payments to offset regional differences, they have trouble understanding how these payments are allocated. For example, even Ontario benefited from such payments for four fiscal years, ending in 2019–20, but while Alberta also hit a rough patch, it did not qualify for federal support.

Clearly, the equalization program does not follow the core/periphery path perfectly. Or does it? Let us examine the record. Oil revenues caused Newfoundland and Labrador to move from "have-not" status to "have" status in 2009–10 while Ontario, because of the global recession and economic slowdown in the US, saw its revenues fall below the national average and therefore qualified for equalization payments. For a variety of reasons, Quebec's economy has always performed just below the national average, but the province also has the advantage of low revenues from its Crown corporation, Hydro-Québec. Accordingly, Quebec's total revenues used to calculate its equalization payments are low. In short, Quebec's reliance on hydroelectric power affects its revenue and, in turn, its equalization payments. On the other hand, Alberta, with its main revenue stream coming from its fossil fuel energy sector, finds its total revenues too high to qualify for payments. Memorial University economics professor Jim Feehan (2014, p. 1) expressed it this way:

> A more fundamental and long-recognized problem [with the calculation of equalization payments] is the incentive for provinces receiving equalization payments to underprice the water-rental rates they charge for hydro production. Lowering water-rental rates has the effect of reducing provincial hydro revenues, which can entitle those provinces to larger equalization payments, while benefitting residents with cheaper hydro rates.

In 2019–20, the federal funds allocated for the equalization program totalled almost $20 billion (Department of Finance, 2019). Sixty-five per cent went to Quebec ($13.1 billion), followed by Manitoba ($2.2 billion), New Brunswick ($2 billion), Nova Scotia ($2 billion), and Prince Edward Island ($419 million). As well, the three territories received nearly $4 billion in Territorial Formula Financing as follows: Nunavut $1.6 billion, Northwest Territories $1.3 billion, and Yukon just under $1 billion (Department of Finance, 2019).

On a per capita basis, PEI received the highest allocation of equalization funds from Ottawa (Table 5.7). These payments formed around 20 per cent of PEI's total revenue, while the figure was lower for the other "have-not" provinces. Quebec, for instance, was at the low end with these payments, making up just under 10 per cent of its total revenue.

**TABLE 5.7  Federal Equalization Payments to Provinces, Fiscal Year 2019–2020**

| Province | Total Equalization Payment | Payment Per Capita |
|---|---|---|
| Prince Edward Island | $419 million | $2,793 |
| New Brunswick | $2,023 million | $2,627 |
| Nova Scotia | $2,015 million | $2,145 |
| Manitoba | $2,255 million | $1,735 |
| Quebec | $13,124 million | $1,581 |
| Total | $19,837 million | |

Note: Equalization payments to the three territories, called Territorial Formula Financing, are based on a different formula and, on a per capita basis, are much higher than those for the provinces.

Source: Calculated from Department of Finance (2019).

## Vignette 5.10

### No Place for Millennials?

Canada's economy has evolved over the past several generations. Those in the tech revolution have, in general, done well, while those in other employment sectors have done less well. In fact, the tech revolution has accelerated the income gap between the rich and poor.

Age is also a factor as young people are disadvantaged because of the high cost of housing and the financial burden of post-secondary education. Housing costs vary across Canada, but especially from small communities to major urban centres. Prices in Toronto and Vancouver are particularly high, raising the question, "Is the dream of home ownership slipping away for most Millennials?" Except for the very highest income earners, the answer is yes.

According to Robert Hogue of RBC Economic Research, housing demand isn't at risk of falling anytime soon. What could fall, however, is the rate of young households who own a home. Housing prices set an impossibly high bar to clear for many Millennials to become homeowners in a big city. It is expected that a greater proportion of the younger generations will rent in the future or turn to various types of shared home ownership.

Oddly enough, Toronto, Montreal, and Vancouver, in spite of high housing prices, have seen the biggest net inflow of Millennials over the last decade (Hogue, 2019). Many are from abroad, some were attracted to high-paying jobs in the tech sector, and others are attending post-secondary institutions. While the pull of these three metropolitan centres continues to outweigh the push factors, only those with extremely high incomes can manage home ownership.

## Vignette 5.11

### Meng Wanzhou

On 1 December 2018, Canadian authorities arrested Meng Wanzhou, a senior executive with Huawei Corporation, a giant Chinese telecommunications company, at Vancouver International Airport while she was en route from Hong Kong to Mexico. The US government, which has charged Wanzhou with circumventing American trade sanctions against Iran, along with theft and racketeering, has been seeking to extradite her to the US since she was taken into Canadian custody, but she remains under house arrest in Vancouver, where she maintains a permanent residence, on charges of conspiracy, bank fraud, and wire fraud. China demands Canada release Meng. Canada has not released her, and China has taken actions—for example, reducing trade with Canada, detaining Canadians in China, and preventing the Canada–China vaccine partnership—to place pressure on Ottawa. In late September 2020 Meng appeared in BC Supreme Court on a motion to throw out the extradition order, but no final resolution was expected until mid-2021 (Proctor, 2020).

## Summary

Canada is in the midst of a technological revolution, with its economic future depending on the success of its knowledge-based economy. All was well until the unexpected arrival of the COVID-19 pandemic in 2020 turned Canada's economy upside down. The discovery and eventual distribution of a vaccine would ease the negative impact of this disease and allow social interaction so necessary in many aspects of our economy to resume. Other elements affecting our economic future include a return of commodity prices associated with the super cycle. The United States holds the key for Canada to again enjoy a robust economy, but China offers a means of diversifying Canada's trade. Unfortunately, trade with China has stalled and even reversed over the Meng Wanzhou affair (Vignette 5.11).

Could globalization stall because of national security interests? Issues ranging from high-speed 5G technology for wireless devices to manufacturing of medical supplies to food exports could tip the balance away from trusting other countries to supply such goods and services.

In spite of the international turmoil over trade, Canada's economy remains strong, largely because Canada has embraced a knowledge-based economy. Already, several world-class technology hubs, led by Greater Toronto, have emerged. At the same time, Canada's oil sector might regain its footing if the Trans Mountain pipeline is ever completed. Coupled with partial ownership by an Indigenous group, such a development could go a long way in the reconciliation process.

In the coming chapters, our focus is on the six geographic regions of Canada. Each region is unique in terms of its geography, history, and challenges.

## Challenge Questions

1. What is the knowledge-based economy?
2. Why does trade define Canada's economy?
3. How have the arrest and intended extradition of Meng Wanzhou affected Canada's trade relations with China?
4. What is the difference between income inequality and regional inequality?
5. Would you support a guaranteed income for all adult Canadians even if it meant higher income taxes?
6. In what ways do Millennials and Generation Z face a harder time than their parents did?

## Essay Questions

1.  Over 40 years ago, Daniel Bell predicted a vastly different post-industrial society. Its dimensions would include the spread of a knowledge class, a shift in the economy from manufacturing to services, and an expanded role for women. While Bell's predictions came true, what are the downsides to this post-industrial society?

2.  "When America sneezes, Canada catches a cold" still holds true because Canada relies so heavily on trade with the US. Trade agreements with the United States facilitate access to the world's largest market, but trade disagreements do arise. Explain why Canada is more concerned than the United States about including a **dispute settlement mechanism** for resolving trade disagreements in the USMCA.

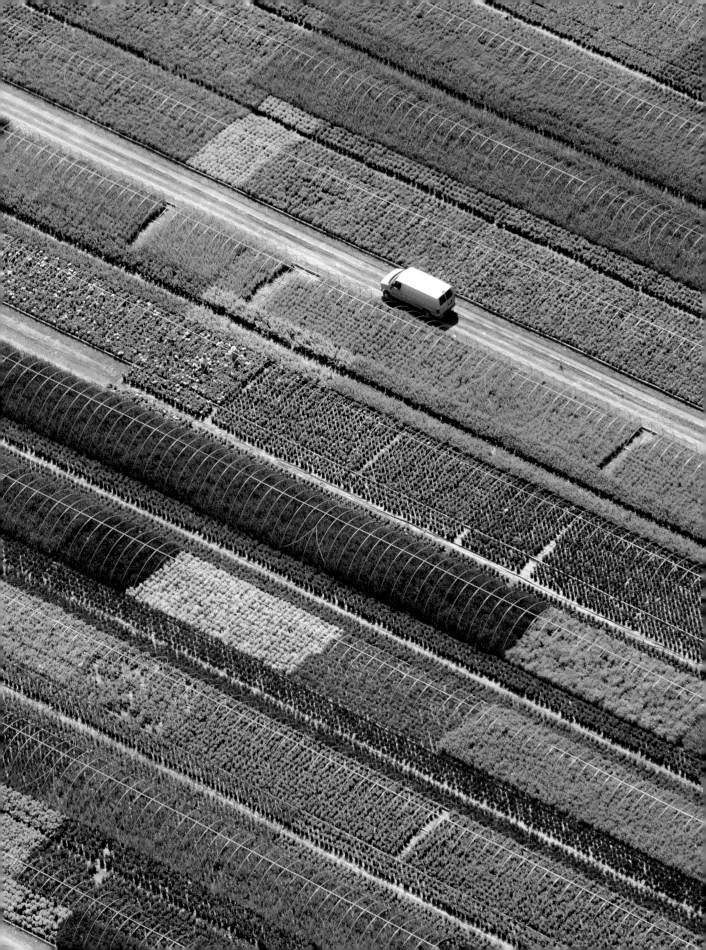

# 6 Ontario

## Chapter Overview

Ontario remains the dominant region of Canada. Its share of Canada's economy and population—nearly 40 per cent in each case—illustrates this point. More specifically, Ontario leads the emerging knowledge-based economy by accounting for almost half of Canada's employees in high technology, financial services, and other knowledge-intensive industries. Clearly, Canada's core region has momentum. Within this vast geographic region, these twin strengths—economy and population—are concentrated in southern Ontario. The rest of Ontario is, in truth, a northern hinterland where the economy, based on natural resources, is sputtering, its population growth is stalling, and regional disparities are widening. This chapter will examine the following topics:

- Ontario's physical geography and historical background.
- The basic characteristics of its population and economy.
- The emergence of a knowledge-based economy.
- Toronto as a world-class hub.
- The impact of COVID-19.

## Introduction

Ontario's prominent position within Canada and North America remains a central feature of Canada's geography. Over the past decade, Ontario has tried to reinvent itself. Its economy holds a central place in this transformation, driven in large part by the technology revolution that has led to the knowledge-based economy. While badly shaken by the global meltdown that began in late 2008, Ontario has recovered and, as a consequence, is no longer receiving equalization payments. Despite this recovery, manufacturing is struggling as it searches for a replacement to automobile manufacturing. Once the kingpin of Ontario's economy, automobile manufacturing is barely keeping its head above water. Mexico, with its low labour costs and direct access to US and Canadian markets, has already replaced Canada as the number two producer of vehicles in North America.

Still, the basic factors that propelled Ontario to the leading position within Canada have not changed. In spite of all, Ontario remains the dominant

← A plant nursery in southern Ontario. Although most Ontarians are employed in service industries such as finance, tourism, and culture, southern Ontario is the second-most important agriculture area in Canada.

dan_prat/Getty Imagesda.

region of Canada. It is, as before, the **heartland** of Canada's population, economy, and culture for English-speaking Canada. While the best days for Ontario's manufacturing industry are in the past, its technology-driven economy is quickly coming into focus. In 2020, the unexpected shutdown of Ontario's economy caused by COVID-19 had dire effects. For Ontario to prosper and progress into the next decade, as well as to retain its title as the economic engine of Canada, bold and innovative measures are necessary. Such measures include a strategy for the post-COVID-19 era and a strong flow of migrants to counterbalance a low birth rate and an aging population.

## Ontario within Canada

Ontario remains Canada's largest province by population and economic output (Figure 6.1). As the leading industrial region of Canada, Ontario is the dominant economic force in Canada and continues its role in the North American economy. Besides its manufacturing sector, Ontario plays a leading role in the technological revolution sweeping across Canada and serves as the cultural centre for English-speaking Canada.

At first, the twenty-first century was not kind to Ontario. In the fiercely competitive global economy, Ontario manufacturing firms had to compete with foreign imports. The consequences were not always favourable, as some were forced to close while others relocated offshore. This hollowing out of Ontario's economy was follow by the global recession that began in late 2008, sending shock waves through Ontario's economy and pushing Ontario

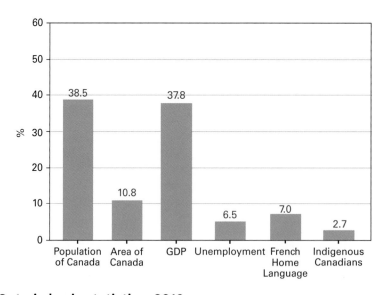

**FIGURE 6.1 Ontario basic statistics, 2016**

Ontario's share of the nation's GDP and population indicates the province's economic and political strength within Canada. With the lower Canadian dollar, the province's economy has regained considerable momentum. The good news is that its share of GDP rose from 36.7 in 2014 to 37.8 in 2019, while its unemployment rate dropped from 7.3 per cent to 5.6 per cent. The bad news results from the wreckage caused by the sudden stop in the economy due to the COVID-19 pandemic. For Ontario, the economic pain focused on supply chain disruptions and financial market weakness. GDP could drop significantly while unemployment could soar beyond 10 per cent—in August 2020, Statistics Canada reported a rate of 10.6 per cent. The depth of the economic damage all depends on the length of the economic stoppage and the quickness of the recovery. A vaccine is crucial to a recovery.

Sources: Tables 1.1, 1.2, 5.6.

into the "have-not" group of provinces that received equalization payments. A decade later, Ontario recovered and rejoined the "have" provinces. During this recovery, Ontario was leading the charge into an advanced economy employing cutting-edge technology in automation and robotics, with artificial intelligence playing an ever-increasing role. But what about the future? On the one hand, Toronto has much appeal for recruiting foreign tech workers. On the other hand, has COVID-19 cut short this recovery by limiting foreign tech workers and other immigrants from entering Ontario? Lastly, will a vaccine turn the tables and allow Toronto to regain its "interesting" status?

In the early twenty-first century, Ontario's woes sparked a debate over the future direction of the province's economy. In 2008, two of Canada's leading economists, Don Drummond and Derek Burleton (2008), declared that Ontario was at a fork in the road. In their opinion, Ontario faced two choices: it could remain committed to the manufacturing sector, or it could reinvent itself. The first option would likely result in a slow-growing economy; the second option could lead to an economy driven by high technology. Drummond and Burleton expected

the Liberal provincial government to take the lead: "With much of Ontario's economic success driven by advantages that no longer exist, a new direction is required. We look to the provincial government to take leadership on this front by developing a vision on where it plans to take the economy down the road."

Since Drummond and Burleton's 2008 report, Ontario has regained its footing and, according to actual and projected GDP per capita figures, the province is following the "Regain Dominance" curve rather than the downward projected "Wither" curve shown in Figure 6.2 (Ontario Ministry of Finance, 2015c). Statistics back up this upward-trending economy. Exports from Ontario in 2018—mainly manufacturing products to the United States—reached $244 billion, up significantly from $126 billion in 2009, thus providing additional evidence for the region's recovery (Ontario Ministry of Finance, 2020). With the arrival of COVID-19, all bets are off. Ontario, like other regions, faces a rebooting of its economy. Manufacturing may get an unexpected boost from the decoupling of the global economy on strategic "health" goods, but total exports are likely to decline below the $250 billion level.

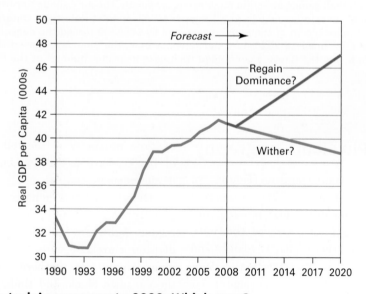

**FIGURE 6.2 Ontario's economy to 2020: Which way?**

Drummond and Burleton created this graph in 2008 to shock the provincial government into action. Fortunately, Ontario has followed the "Regain Dominance" curve. By 2018, Ontario's GDP/per capita was $55,000, up significantly from the $41,000 in 2009.

Sources: Adapted from Drummond & Burleton (2008, p. 1); Ontario Ministry of Finance (2015); RBC (2019).

maximimages.com/Alamy Stock Photo

**PHOTO 6.1** The Rogers Centre (originally named SkyDome) is the home of the Toronto Blue Jays. Such high-order cultural and sport facilities are found only in Canada's largest city. The Toronto Raptors, who play their basketball games at Scotia Bank Arena (originally, the Air Canada Centre), provide another example. Cultural landmarks include Roy Thompson Hall, the Art Gallery of Ontario, and the Royal Ontario Museum. The lockdown of the economy caused by COVID-19 forced the cancellation of cultural and sporting events for much of 2020. In a shortened season, the Blue Jays played their home games in Buffalo, New York, and the Raptors concluded their season in the "bubble" at the Disney complex in Orlando, Florida.

## Ontario's Physical Geography

Ontario is larger than most countries (Figure 6.3), encompassing over 1 million km². Extending over Ontario are three of Canada's physiographic regions (Great Lakes–St Lawrence Lowlands, Canadian Shield, and Hudson Bay Lowlands) and three of the country's climatic zones (Arctic, Subarctic, and Great Lakes–St Lawrence) (Figures 2.1 and 2.5). Manitoba lies to its west, Hudson and James bays to its north, while Quebec, on its eastern boundary, is bordered in part by the Ottawa River. This central location within Canada and

its close proximity to the industrial heartland of the US have facilitated Ontario's economic development.

Ontario is not a homogeneous natural region. For that reason, it is divided into two sub-regions (northern and southern Ontario). This division correlates with its physiographic regions. Accordingly, northern Ontario consists of the Canadian Shield and Hudson Bay Lowlands while southern Ontario matches the geographic extent of the Great Lakes–St Lawrence Lowlands that fall within Ontario (Figure 6.4). Each sub-region has a different economy. Northern

**FIGURE 6.3 Ontario**

Ontario has the largest economy and population of Canada's six regions, but this region represents a geographic paradox. The contrasts between southern Ontario and northern Ontario are extreme. The two sub-regions have very different physical conditions and resources. Over time, two distinct economies have emerged, each with its own spatial pattern of population distribution. While southern Ontario forms the industrial and population heartland, northern Ontario is an old resource hinterland. More evidence of this paradox is that northern Ontario occupies over 80 per cent of the land mass of Ontario but contains only 6 per cent of the province's population.

Source: *Atlas of Canada*, 2006, "Ontario," atlas.nrcan.gc.ca/site/english/maps/reference/provincesterritories/ontario

THINK
ABOUT IT

Northern Ontario relies on three economic activities: forestry, mining, and tourism. In what ways does this explain why northern Ontario is a slow-growing region?

Ontario has the characteristics of a resource hinterland, while southern Ontario is the epitome of an agricultural-industrial core.

Northern Ontario stretches across 10 degrees of latitude—from 46°N to nearly 57°N. Fort Severn First Nation is located on the shores of Hudson Bay at 56° 37'N while Sudbury is at 46° 30'N. The Subarctic climate of northern Ontario has longer and colder winters as well as shorter and cooler summers than those occurring in southern Ontario. Even along its southern edge at 46°N, short summers make crop agriculture vulnerable to frost damage. In addition

**FIGURE 6.4 Physiographic regions in Central Canada**

Central Canada consists of Ontario and Quebec. Three physiographic regions are found in Ontario and four in Quebec. Canada's most productive agricultural lands, its **manufacturing belt**, and its core population zone all are located in one physiographic region—the Great Lakes–St Lawrence Lowlands.

The section on "Physiographic Regions" in **Chapter 2**, page 23, especially the figures and tables, provides important background information for Ontario.

to a difficult climate for agriculture, the rocky Canadian Shield has very little soil suitable for crops while the Hudson Bay Lowlands has none. The rugged, rocky terrain of the Canadian Shield has only a few pockets of land where former lakebeds provide the basis for soil development. Climate, soils, and physiography combine to limit agriculture in northern Ontario.

Southern Ontario, located in the southernmost part of Canada, has Canada's longest growing season. Windsor, for example, is at latitude 42°N and Toronto is close to 44°N. Southern Ontario has a

moderate continental climate. This climate is noted for long, hot, and humid summers, warm autumns, short but cold winters, and cool springs. Annual precipitation is about 1,000 mm. The greatest amounts of precipitation occur in the lee of the Great Lakes (Figure 6.5), where winter snowfall is particularly heavy (see Vignette 6.1). The Great Lakes modify temperatures and funnel winter storms into this region. During the winter, this region experiences a great variety of weather conditions. The Niagara Escarpment represents the most significant relief feature.

## Vignette 6.1

### Ontario's Snowbelts

Ontario's snowbelts are legendary. On the upland slopes facing Lakes Huron and Superior and Georgian Bay, huge snowfalls totalling in the 300–400-cm range occur each winter from November to late March. The uplands on the northeast shores of Lake Superior receive the greatest total snowfall amounts of any area in Ontario, exceeding 400 cm annually. Much of the snowfall in snowbelt areas can be attributed to cold northwest to westerly winds blowing off the lakes and ascending the highlands. As the Arctic air travels across the relatively warmer Great Lakes, it is warmed and moistened. Snow clouds form over the lakes and, once onshore, intensify as the air is then forced to ascend the hills to the lee of the lakes, triggering heavy snowfalls. Areas on the downslope side of the higher ground to the lee of the lakes receive less than half the annual snow totals of the upslope snowbelt areas. For example, Toronto, Hamilton, and other places to the lee of the Niagara Escarpment are snow-shadow regions with winter amounts of 100 to 140 cm. In the snowbelt regions, snowfall accounts for about 32 per cent of the year's total precipitation; but in the snow-sparse area around Windsor and Chatham, the snow contribution is only about 13 per cent.

## Environmental Challenges

Ontario faces two major environmental challenges—air and water pollution. Solutions are costly and require lifestyle changes. Both types of pollution represent the hidden costs of our industrial world.

In Ontario, most air pollution comes from vehicle exhaust. While the number of vehicles continues to rise, the good news is that more efficient engines and the growing number of electric cars have limited the increase in exhaust fumes. While this is a step in the right direction, until Canadians' love affair with the automobile ends, relief from automobile and truck pollution will be slow in coming. After all, the country's vast physical geography and urban sprawl make it difficult for public transit to replace the need of many for individual transportation, and electric-powered vehicles have yet to reach a mass market. Still, the number of electric cars is slowly increasing each year, but Ontario is far behind BC and Quebec. Sales are not likely to increase since the Ontario government removed the consumer subsidy to purchase an electric car in 2018.

Another step in the right direction came in April 2014 when Ontario ceased to produce electricity from coal. A little over 10 years ago, Ontario's coal-fired generating stations produced 25 per cent of the province's electricity. In 2016, the Ontario government announced plans to subsidize the purchase of electric cars and to encourage homeowners to switch from natural gas heating to electrical and geothermal heating, but a change in government in 2018 slowed this shift. Nevertheless, the cost of electricity is now much higher and some Ontarians have fallen into **energy poverty** (Green et al., 2016). On the bright side, air quality has improved, especially in the densely populated Golden Horseshoe. **Smog**, for instance, is no longer a dominant feature of summer weather. In 2014, Toronto experienced a summer free of smog for the first time in 20 years, and few smog alerts have occurred since. Now the source of smog comes from automobile exhaust and from industrial air pollution emanating from Ohio, where a large number of coal-fired electric plants still exist.

The pollution of drinking water is a serious problem in Indigenous communities across Canada, nowhere more so than in Ontario. Boil-water orders are commonplace. Patrick (2017) describes drinking water on Indigenous reserves as "a geography of poor water" forcing band councils to seek water from off-reserve sources and to truck it to the individual homes where the water is

THINK ABOUT IT

Smog, so common in larger cities, is a product of the Industrial Revolution when the burning of fossils fuels began. Now the principal source of *smog* comes from exhaust fumes from cars and trucks. The word *smog* is a combination of "smoke" and "fog."

## Contested Terrain 6.1

### Urban and Industrial Needs versus Precious Farmland

Urban and industrial Ontario is expanding. In its search for more land for urbanites and industry, Ontario is eating into the limited stock of high-quality agricultural land. While such farmland is scarce, its market value is low compared to the same land used for housing and business. Consider the 2011 proposal by Highland Companies. Highland wanted to convert some of Ontario's most valuable farmland, with soil rated as Class I, into a quarry to extract Amabel dolostone. The farmland lies in the Township of Melancthon, just an hour northwest of Toronto. The potential value of the extracted Amabel dolostone exceeds $6 billion. Farmers in the area protested and, given the strong opposition, Highland sold its interest to Bonnefield Financial, a farmland investment and property management company. In turn, Bonnefield leased the land to local farmers who want the land to increase their economies of scale. In this case, potatoes won the day over a much more valuable mineral.

stored in a cistern in each house. Unfortunately, this approach, often due to contamination of the water stored in a cistern, too often fails to provide secure drinking water. An example from the Grassy Narrows First Nation[1] in northern Ontario provides one insight into this troubling situation, as described by Amanda Klasing (2016) of Human Rights Watch:

PHOTO 6.2 The Pickering Nuclear Generating Station, located in southern Ontario just east of Toronto, is one of the three active nuclear plants in the province. About 3,000 people work at the facility, which produces about 14 per cent of Ontario's power. In January 2016, the provincial government approved a plan to continue producing electricity at Pickering until 2024, and the facility now hopes to operate until the end of 2025, subject to approval from the Canadian Nuclear Safety Commission. Decommission begins in 2028 and could last for over 40 years.

The water in the well that supplies her home is contaminated with uranium; [instead,] water trucked in from a local treatment plant to fill a cistern at her house has dangerous levels of a cancer-causing by-product that comes from treating dirty source water.

Exposure to the contaminants found in this water can cause illnesses ranging from gastrointestinal disorders to increased risk of cancer. Knock-on effects—like bathing less when people can't trust their water—include the proliferation or worsening of skin infections, eczema, psoriasis, and other skin conditions.

While the reasons behind such poor performance are complicated, drinking water on reserves falls under the federal government. Ottawa provides 80 per cent of the funding, but the band council is responsible for raising the remaining 20 per cent as well as for building and maintaining the drinking water system on each reserve and training the operators. Band councils, however, often do not have the financial resources and technical expertise to provide safe and reliable water systems. The bands face an additional challenge in the scattered nature of housing on reserves, making the delivery of drinking water by a pipe network from a clean water source extremely expensive. As a result, boil-water orders are widespread.

Ontario Power Generation

## Ontario's Historical Geography

When the American Revolution began in 1775, Ontario—except for the French settlement around Detroit (established 1701)—was a densely forested wilderness inhabited by Indigenous peoples and a few fur traders. In 1760, British troops took control of Fort Detroit and the surrounding settled area. After losing the American colonies, Loyalists moved north to Nova Scotia and New Brunswick, while others resettled in the Eastern Townships of Quebec. A smaller number, perhaps as many as 10,000 Loyalists, including members of the Six Nations who had fought alongside British troops, settled on land in what is today southern Ontario, thus colonizing the wilderness area that later became known as Upper Canada. In 1784, Britain created the Haldimand Tract for its Indigenous allies, and this land followed the Grand River and totalled 385,000 hectares (Darling, 2007). Over the next several decades, American, British, and European newcomers came in search of land suitable for farming. By 1812, the wilderness forest landscape of southern Ontario had been transformed into a sparsely populated British agricultural colony. The War of 1812 effectively ended the influx of American settlers into Upper Canada, but the flow of settlers from the British Isles, especially Ireland and Scotland, continued. By 1851, Canada West (as Upper Canada had become with the Act of Union of 1841) had reached a population of 952,004, 86 per cent of whom lived in rural settings (Statistics Canada, 2007a). At the time of Confederation, the mixed forest found in the Great Lakes Lowland was gone, replaced by thousands of small farms. Some turned further north to try their luck in the few pockets of arable land within the Canadian Shield, but few were successful. Others migrated to Manitoba or to growing towns and cities in Ontario. The majority of the migrants from rural Ontario were lured to the last great American land rush, the open prairie lands west of the Mississippi River.

When Canada West joined Confederation in 1867, it was renamed Ontario (Figure 3.5). At that time, the geographic extent of Ontario was about 100,000 km² —a fraction of its present size—but as Canada acquired more territory from Great Britain, Ontario and Quebec obtained some of these new lands (Figures 3.6–3.8). They had little immediate value for economic development and settlement, however, because they were carved from two physiographic regions (the Canadian Shield and the Hudson Bay Lowlands) that were far from markets and had little or no agricultural potential. Since Confederation, the borders of Ontario have been extended three times, greatly increasing the geographic size of the province, but not its agricultural lands. The first expansion occurred in 1874 when Ontario's boundaries were pushed northward to about 51°N and westward towards Lake of the Woods. Ontario's second expansion, in 1889, ended the bitter contest between Manitoba and Ontario for the land around Lake of the Woods. At the same time, Ontario's northwest boundary was adjusted to the Albany River, which flows into James Bay, gaining Ontario access to James Bay. In 1912, the final boundary modification occurred when the District of Keewatin south of 60°N was assigned to Ontario and Manitoba. As a result, Ontario extended its political boundary to the northwest, stretching from Manitoba to Hudson Bay at the latitude of 56° 51'N. Through these boundary adjustments, Ontario reached its present geographic extent of 1 million km².

At the time of Confederation, the economic essence of Ontario was its fledgling industrial base. Transportation routes played a key role, especially the Welland Canal, which facilitated low-cost transportation (Vignette 6.2). At that time, most manufacturing activities depended on water power, so most industries were located near a stream or river. In 1879 the National Policy of Prime Minister Macdonald came into effect by imposing high tariffs on imported manufactured goods, which allowed manufacturing in southern Ontario to flourish.

## Indigenous Territory within Ontario

Ontario has 126 First Nations holding Indigenous territory, known as reserves, determined through treaty negotiations between government and individual First Nations. Most treaties were classified as "unnumbered" and took place before 1923.

**THINK ABOUT IT**

Does the Lake of the Woods decision by the federal government that favoured Ontario represent Ontario's political power within the federation?

The National Policy and its impact on Ontario and the rest of Canada is discussed in **Chapter 5** under the heading "The National Policy and the Birth of an Industrial Core," page 147.

**FIGURE 6.5 The Great Lakes Basin**

Created 10,000 years ago at the end of the last continental glaciation, the Great Lakes form the largest freshwater system on the planet. The Great Lakes are under pressure, with declining water levels and constant pollution from human sources. The water levels of the Great Lakes have declined over the last 50 years due primarily to the warming climate (International Great Lakes Study, 2012). This decline translates into stranded cottage docks, the loss of wetlands, and receding shorelines. The Great Lakes Water Quality Agreement expresses the commitment of Canada and the United States to restore and maintain the chemical, physical, and biological integrity of the Great Lakes Basin.

Source: Based on *Atlas of Canada*, 2004, "Great Lakes Basin," atlas.nrcan.gc.ca/site/english/maps/reference/provinceterritories/gr_lks/index.html

Figure 3.11, "Historic treaties," page 91, shows the location of the numbered and unnumbered treaties that blanket Ontario.

Three numbered treaties—3, 5, and 9—cover portions of northern Ontario. The first land grants to Indigenous peoples took place during the days of British North America, beginning with the Haldimand Proclamation of 1784, which assigned land along the Grand River to the Iroquois who fought alongside the British in the American Revolution (Figure 6.6). In 1850, the two **Robinson treaties** were completed; they covered large areas east and north of Lake Huron and north of Lake Superior.

In Ontario, First Nations were granted land hundreds of years ago. When disputes arise today, reaching an agreement is challenging because the "facts" are buried in time (see Vignette 6.3). The slow pace of resolution is frustrating to Indigenous Canadians, and two land disputes (Ipperwash and Caledonia) have led to protests by Indigenous groups from the Kettle and Stony Point and Six Nations reserves. In the Ipperwash dispute, the facts are relatively clear: land from Stony Point was taken

## Vignette 6.2

### The Welland Canal

The Welland Canal connects Lake Ontario and Lake Erie, allowing ocean-going ships to enter the heart of North America. To avoid the Niagara River and its huge falls, the first canal-builders faced the daunting task of constructing a canal across the Niagara Peninsula, a distance of some 44 km. The first canal, opened in 1829, was dug by hand. A series of locks made from hand-hewn timbers connected a series of creeks and lakes, and horses and oxen pulled the boats along the canal by a tow line. As the size of ships increased, the original canal proved inadequate and a new canal was built in 1845. Within 40 years, even larger ships required a third renovation, which was opened in 1887. The present canal was completed in 1932. In 1973, to bypass the city of Welland, a new channel was constructed, for which a series of lift locks were needed to overcome a difference in elevation of nearly 100 m between Lake Ontario and Lake Erie. The Welland Canal has been part of the St Lawrence Seaway since 1959 and is operated by the St Lawrence Seaway Management Corporation.

PHOTO 6.3 The Welland Canal is a strategic link between Lake Ontario and Lake Erie that provides a water route around Niagara Falls. To accommodate ever-increasing traffic, the lock system was divided into two at several places, as shown in this aerial photograph. In 2019, approximately 28 million tonnes of goods passed through these locks. The three leading products were grain, iron ore, and coal.

Designpics/All Canada Photos

in 1942 to serve as a military training camp, named Camp Ipperwash. After the war, the land was supposed to have been returned, but the Department of National Defence decided to keep the camp—adjoining Ipperwash Provincial Park, established in 1936—to train cadets. Promises from Ottawa to return the land were not fulfilled. By 1993, the Stony Point First Nations people were utterly frustrated with the repeated failure of Ottawa to act on its promises, and in September 1995, Indigenous protestors moved into Ipperwash Provincial Park, where a confrontation with the Ontario Provincial Police took place, ending in the shooting of an unarmed Kettle and Stony Point protestor, Dudley George, by an Ontario police sniper. In 2003, the Ontario government asked Justice Sidney Linden to conduct a public inquiry into the circumstances surrounding the 1995 death of Dudley George, including the role of Premier Mike Harris. In May 2007, Justice Linden issued the Ipperwash Inquiry Report, in which he concluded that Harris had not explicitly ordered the Ontario police into the Ipperwash Provincial Park to remove the Indigenous protestors. At the same time, Justice Linden called for the immediate return of Camp Ipperwash to the Kettle and Stony Point First Nation. Jim Prentice, the federal Minister for Indian Affairs and Northern Development, responded by stating that, "We'll do something immediately" (*National Post*, 2007). That didn't happen.

Library and Archives Canada/C-034334

**PHOTO 6.4** In 1794, York became the capital of Upper Canada. Despite its political status, this frontier village remained on the western edge of British settlement that stretched westward from Lower Canada along the north shore of Lake Ontario. By 1812, York had only 700 residents. This painting (dated 1804) illustrates a group of houses strung along the shore of Toronto Bay. Beyond this narrow strip of cleared land lies the original forest of southern Ontario.

Library and Archives Canada/C-001669

**PHOTO 6.5** "View of King Street [Toronto], Looking East" (1835) by Thomas Young. At the time of this painting, York had just been renamed "Toronto" and had a population of nearly 10,000.

The provincial park was returned to the Chippewas of Kettle and Stony Point by the Ontario government at the end of 2007 with the understanding that the province and the First Nation would jointly run the park, but the Chippewas closed the 56-hectare park. At that time, the Ontario government transferred the land to the federal government, which alone has the power to add it to the reserve. Finally, under a new federal government, negotiations to return the land to the First Nation were successfully completed in April 2016 with the signing of an agreement that returned all of the land and included $95 million in compensation. The agreement "specifies that work will be done to ensure that the land . . . is safe and environmentally sound." This has meant clearing the land of unexploded devices from more than 50 years of military use of First Nation land (Mehta, 2016).

**Specific land claims** by Indigenous groups are not usually as "straightforward" as the Ipperwash claim. The Caledonia dispute exemplifies the complexity of some claims. An outline of the historical evolution of the Six Nations claim to a 40-hectare parcel owned by a land developer at Caledonia, Ontario, near Hamilton, suggests why, in many instances, settlements have been achieved at such a slow rate (Vignette 6.3). The basis of the Six Nations claim goes back to the original Haldimand Grant of 1784 and land surrenders in the eighteenth and nineteenth centuries. History is not clear on these issues. While the protest finally ended, negotiations between the Six Nations and the federal government are at an impasse since the federal government, in 2009, rejected the $500 million claim of the Haudenosaunee/Six Nations, leaving its offer of $125 million on the table. More recently, another issue flared up where a sale of reserve land to a housing developer by the elected Six Nations council was opposed by members of the band (*Brantford Expositor*, 2020).

## Ontario Today

Canada's centre of gravity—as measured by economic performance and population size—remains in Ontario. For a while, Ontario fell into the "have-not" group of provinces, but recent data reveal that Ontario is once

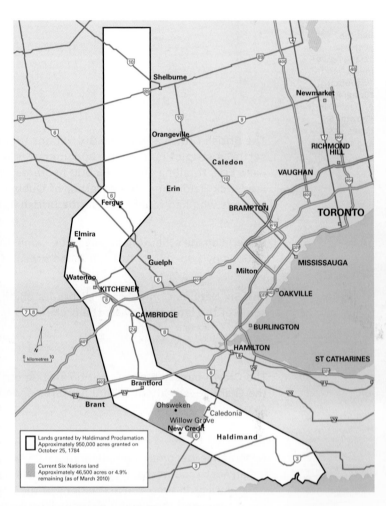

**FIGURE 6.6 The Haldimand Tract**

Source: Redrawn from Six Nations Land Resources. Based on a map at www.sixnations.ca/LandResources/HalfProc.htm

again a "have" province. Unexpectedly, the COVID-19 epidemic has thrown a monkey wrench into Ontario's 2020 economic performance. How quickly Ontario will rebound is unclear at this moment.

By 2019, Ontario turned the corner thanks to a combination of factors. The emergence of a strong technology-based economy was a crucial factor. As well, a low Canadian dollar was helpful in exporting goods to the United States, and an upswing in vehicle and parts exports to the United States was a big contributing factor.

By regaining its status as Canada's engine of economic growth, Ontario confronted the question posed by Drummond and Burleton in 2008: How can Ontario reinvent itself and move from an

**THINK ABOUT IT**

Why is land worth more than money to members of the Six Nations?

**THINK ABOUT IT**

Does the term "global decoupling" spell an end to globalization or an adjustment towards national security?

See the sections "Trade Agreements" and "Manufacturing: Alive or Dead?" in **Chapter 5**, pages 155 and 158.

## Vignette 6.3

### Timeline of the Caledonia Dispute

#### Eighteenth Century

#### 1784

The British Crown allows the Six Nations (Iroquois Confederacy) to "take possession of and settle" a strip of land nearly 20 kilometres wide along the Grand River, from its source to Lake Erie, totalling about 385,000 hectares; it is called the Haldimand Grant. The intent of Frederick Haldimand, the governor of Quebec, was to provide land for settlement to loyal Iroquois who had fought beside the British in the American Revolution.

#### 1792

Upper Canada's lieutenant-governor, John Graves Simcoe, reduces the grant to the Six Nations by two-thirds, to 111,000 hectares.

#### 1796

The Six Nations Confederacy grants its chief, Joseph Brant, the power of attorney to sell some of the land and invest the proceeds.

#### Nineteenth Century

#### 1850

The Crown passes a proclamation setting out the extent of reserve lands on both sides of the Grand River—about 19,000 hectares agreed to by the Six Nations chiefs.

#### Twentieth Century

#### 1924

Governance becomes complicated as Canada creates an elected band council under the Indian Act to counterbalance the traditional form of governance known as the Haudenosaunee Confederacy. In time, the Six Nations of the Grand River became the common name for both the reserve and the Haudenosaunee First Nation.

#### 1992

Henco Industries Ltd purchases 40 hectares of land near the town of Caledonia and names it the Douglas Creek Estates.

#### 1995

The ownership of this land was not clear—the Six Nations claimed the land was leased to Canada but Canada argues it was sold back in the nineteenth century.

emphasis on *basic* manufacturing to *advanced* manufacturing? This path lies in the application of technology to all economic activities and is made easier by what can be called the "Ontario advantage." More recently, so-called advanced manufacturing takes the form of manufacturing a variety of health products to ensure a supply of these products in times of medical crisis.

### The Ontario Advantage

Ontario, with the bulk of Canada's creative wealth, as reflected in its universities and provincial/federal research facilities, is well placed to succeed in the knowledge-based economy. Indeed, if Richard Florida (2002, 2012) is correct in thinking that the creative class (which includes knowledge-based

## Twenty-First Century

### 2005–6

Henco Industries begins its Douglas Creek Estates housing project. The following year, a group of Six Nations members occupies the housing project, erecting tents, a teepee, and a wooden building. In a search for a compromise, the Ontario government buys out Henco's interest in the disputed property for $15.7 million, thus maintaining Crown ownership of this disputed land.

### 2007

The federal government enters negotiations with the Six Nations to resolve the historic and current land claim disputes. Canada makes an offer of $125 million to compensate the Six Nations for four outstanding historic claims based on nineteenth-century land surrenders known as Grand River Navigation Company investment; Block 5 (Moulton Township); Welland Canal flooding; and the Burtch Tract. As well, Ottawa compensates Ontario for $26.4 million for the province's costs incurred as a result of the occupation near Caledonia and the province's purchase of the land.

### 2008–14

In 2008, Canada receives a formal counter-offer of $500 million from the Six Nations. The following year, Canada rejects the claim for $500 million and restates its offer of $125 million. As a result of the inability of the two parties to breach this gap, negotiations ceased. By mid-2014, the federal government continued to refuse to seek a negotiated settlement, merely calling on the Ontario government to make sure police protect the people of Caledonia.

### 2020

Matters continue over the surrender of lands. Some members outside of the elected council see such surrenders as a colonial trick to dispossess them of their lands and resources due to the issue of divided governance in Caledonia. On the other hand, the Six Nations elected council approves the housing project at 1535 McKenzie Road after the band was "accommodated" with 42.3 acres and $325,000, which will be used for future land purposes. Demonstrators, having renamed the location 1492 Land Back Lane, disagreed with the elected council's decision, stating, "We don't pretend to know what a collective voice of 20,000+ people from Six Nations will look like. What we do know is that our connection to the land is the thread that binds us all." By early October, 25 protestors had been arrested.

Sources: Adapted from *CBC News* (2006, 2020); INAC (2009); Leslie (2014); Moro (2016); Thomson (2020).

workers) wants to live in "interesting" cities, then that relationship reinforces the concentration of these firms in such urban places. As the centre of the Canada's music, film, and sports industries, Toronto provides such an interesting city (Florida & Jackson, 2010; Florida et al., 2010, Hracs et al., 2011). One of the best examples perhaps is the Toronto International Film Festival (TIFF), which has become one of a handful of truly major film festivals in the world.

The unbelievable response to the Toronto Raptors' 2019 NBA championship victory, complete with a downtown parade consisting of an estimated one to two million people, reveals how far Toronto has risen on the global popular culture stage, not least because of the Raptors' widely admired Nigerian-born president, Masai Ujiri, and the Toronto-born pop music superstar, Drake, who serves as the Raptors' "global ambassador." Marcus Gee (2019) of *The Globe*

For discussion of the primary, secondary, and tertiary sectors of the Canadian economy, see **Chapter 5**, "Industrial Structure," page 145.

Kevin Kerr

**PHOTO 6.6** Less than a week after the US presidential election in November 2016, racist, white supremacist, anti-immigration "alt-right" posters appeared in public parks and on street corners in Toronto. Many citizens quickly complained and in short order the Toronto police had removed all of the signs (Siekierska, 2016).

**THINK ABOUT IT**

While the future lies in the technological revolution, three questions remain unresolved. How will the advanced economy generate more jobs, or is it time for a universal basic payment? How will it lead to a more equitable distribution of the wealth generated from these gains? Has COVID-19 decoupled global supply chains, especially for medical products, leading to greater domestic production?

*and Mail* considered the victory parade an important reflection of Canada:

> Monday's parade in Toronto was more than just a joyous celebration of the Raptors' victory. It was a glimpse of today's Canada. The throngs that gathered to cheer their team were the image of the country's future: youthful, full of life, energy, and hope, stunningly diverse.

Adding to the cosmopolitan nature of urban Ontario, Canada's multicultural policy and immigration record have made those cities, but especially Toronto, special on the world scene. Urban Ontario is well on the road to creating open, pluralistic, and tolerant cities. Still, these cities have their shortcomings, usually expressed by various forms of racism and poverty. Overall, urban Ontario highlights the region's technological advantage as measured by the number of universities and provincial/federal research facilities found in these cities.

## Ontario's Industrial Structure

An industrial structure, defined by the percentages of the workforce employed in the three sectors

of an economy, provides insight into the nature of that particular economy and allows for comparisons with other economies.

Most Ontario workers are employed in the tertiary sector (Table 6.1), which accounted for 80.3 per cent of all employed persons in 2019. On the other hand, Ontario's secondary sector was just short of 18 per cent, leaving the primary sector with the tiny remainder. From 2005 to 2019, the tertiary sector gained nearly 6 per cent while the secondary sector lost almost 6 per cent (Table 6.1). These sector trends are expected to continue, with the tertiary sector perhaps reaching 85 per cent and the secondary and primary sectors dropping to 14 per cent and 1 per cent by 2021. This trend is not unique to Ontario; it is occurring in all developed countries and therefore can be interpreted as one measure of the evolving nature of national and regional economies.

In spite of the dismal future for labour-intense types of manufacturing in advanced countries, the distinguishing feature for Ontario remains in its secondary sector. The reason is simple: the size of Ontario's secondary sector, at 17.8 per cent of all employed persons in the province in 2019, forms a much larger proportion than that found in the other five geographic regions. Most of these workers are in manufacturing. On this basis, Ontario's industrial structure confirms the province as the manufacturing heartland of Canada as well as a core region within the Canadian version of the core/periphery model.

But all is not well in the manufacturing world. Ontario is caught in a global shift as manufacturing activities move to other countries with lower wages. Rostow and Schwab, as discussed in Chapter 5, provide a detailed account of the historic industrialization process and Canada's place within that process. An analysis of Ontario's current economic situation points to the need for a cutting-edge knowledge-based economy with a highly trained workforce, supported by innovative companies and the state, to produce more sophisticated products and export them to other countries.

While Ontario remains Canada's heartland of manufacturing, employment in the secondary sector has not kept pace, losing close to 200,000 jobs over the 2005–19 period. At the same time, the

**TABLE 6.1** Ontario Industrial Sectors by Number of Workers, 2005 and 2019

| Industrial Sector | Workers, 2005 | Workers, 2005 (%) | Workers, 2019 | Workers, 2019 (%) | Percentage Difference |
|---|---|---|---|---|---|
| Primary | 128,000 | 2.0 | 143,900 | 1.9 | –0.1 |
| Secondary | 1,509,000 | 23.6 | 1,323,900 | 17.8 | –5.8 |
| Tertiary | 4,761,000 | 74.4 | 5,984,800 | 80.3 | 5.9 |
| Total | 6,398,000 | 100.0 | 7,452,600 | 100.0 | |

Sources: Adapted from Statistics Canada (2006, 2020a).

percentage of secondary-sector workers as a part of Ontario's total employment has dropped from 23.6 per cent in 2005 to 17.8 per cent in 2019 (Statistics Canada, 2006, 2020a). In spite of the continued relative decline, the good news for assembly workers is that their wages continue to increase. This increase can be attributed to the adaptation of technology by manufacturing firms. Still, auto firms, while profitable in Canada, are much more profitable in Mexico. This downward trend in manufacturing employment, as noted above, is common to other advanced industrial countries. The reasons vary from country to country but globalization's dark side leads to job loss and dampens wages in the manufacturing industry. Factors common to Ontario are:

- automation and digitization replacing workers;
- outsourcing of work to low-wage countries; and
- offshore relocation of firms to low-wage countries.

Globalization brought a double whammy to Ontario's manufacturing companies. On the one hand, many left Ontario to set up their operations in countries with lower costs of doing business, leaving their highly paid Canadian workers out of work. One example was the 2012 closure of the Caterpillar assembly plant in London, Ontario. The closure of this plant was a result of the seemingly relentless "race to the bottom" by global companies to move manufacturing jobs to those countries with low wages, few benefits, weak labour laws, tax concessions, and weaker environmental protections.

While globalization and freer trade have hurt Ontario's manufacturing sector, technology has brought new life to Ontario's economy and, at the same time, increased the province's cultural diversity by attracting foreign tech immigrants. In fact,

Ontario has encouraged skilled workers to immigrate to its major technology hubs through its Ontario Immigrant Nominee Program. Many foreign workers in the United States have relocated to Canada and many have resettled in the Greater Toronto Area (GTA), where the demand for skilled tech workers is at a high point. All of these events have combined to make the technology industry in Ontario a recognized world-class hub, and, through high-tech immigrants, enriched its cultural diversity and life.

According to Immigration Canada (2019):

> The technology industry in the Greater Toronto Area, home to nearly half of Ontario's 14.8 million people, has grown by more than 50 per cent in the past five years. And according to a recent report from BMO Capital Markets, there's no sign of it slowing down anytime soon. Indeed, there are currently 241,000 tech workers in the GTA, making this the fourth-largest tech hub in North America.

## Technological Spearheads

Technology spearheads represent innovative economic thrusts that are transforming urban centres into knowledge-based hubs. By attracting highly qualified employees from across Canada and the rest of the world to southern Ontario, but especially to Toronto, Ottawa, and the Waterloo region, technology is not only boosting economic performance but also is diversifying their populations.

What are the principal reasons for this unprecedented surge in technology? One reason is that major urban centres have reached the critical mass necessary to nurture leading-edge technology firms. Much of that mass came from the expansion of the

**THINK ABOUT IT**
Is the theory valid that wages in developing countries, including Mexico, will eventually reach the level of those in developed countries, or is it more likely that wages in developed countries will fall in the "race-to-the-bottom" syndrome?

See **Chapter 5**, "Industrial Structure," page 1, for discussion of how technology has been central to each historic shift in Canada's industrial structure.

**THINK ABOUT IT**

Has COVID-19 changed the globalization game? Will Canada decide that domestic manufacturing of critical medical products is essential for national security, regardless of price?

## Vignette 6.4

### Consequences of High Housing Prices

According to the Toronto Housing Market Analysis (2019, p. 3), Toronto's population is projected to reach nearly 4 million by 2041. By then, a much higher percentage will live in rented accommodation. The explanation for this dramatic increase lies in the high price of single-family homes. Unlike their parents, Millennials face a daunting task in reaching the goal of home ownership. This dream, the cornerstone of middle-class Canada, comes with economic benefits and social status, such as the ability to accumulate wealth and access credit by building home equity. Unfortunately, slow-growing wages and rapidly rising house prices have placed this dream out of the financial reach of most Canadians looking for their first home. Those with high-paying jobs in technology firms are the main exception to this rule. Toronto, according to a 2019 CBRE Group report, was the world's fastest-growing market for tech jobs in 2018 and the fourth-largest tech hub in North America.

Housing affordability is most acute in metropolitan centres like Vancouver and Toronto. Ownership of houses in many cities across Canada, from Victoria on the Pacific coast to Halifax on the Atlantic coast, is beyond the reach of most young Canadians, forcing them to turn to smaller rental units. This housing trend shows no signs of relenting, and the next generation, Generation Z, may face an even more difficult time purchasing housing.

What are the consequences for society? One may be the demise of suburbia, while another could see a reduction in family size. Then too, the shortage of low-cost rental accommodation could force more people to live on the street. Could the extension of rapid rail transportation systems solve part of this problem? In Greater Toronto, the recent extension of its rapid transit rail system by **Metrolinx** to Niagara Falls has made this area much more attractive for home buyers. Still, the fear is that Canada is falling into the trap of a diminishing middle class, a widening of income inequality (Osberg, 2018), and a growing number living on the streets.

knowledge-based infrastructure led by universities and research institutes and from the emergence of a critical number of innovative researchers and the graduation of skilled tech-trained students, especially from computer sciences, engineering, and social sciences. Public support played a key role as governments recognized the significance of industry in shaping the future economy.

A second reason is the retention of Canadian graduates and an increased supply of foreign skilled workers in Canada. In the past, Canada's technology sector was weakened by the loss of many graduates to the United States. This migration of young, skilled Canadians to the US was often due to employment opportunities not found in Canada. With the growth of the Canadian industry, however, employment opportunities have expanded, resulting in

fewer workers leaving for the United States and even some returning home from the US. Marc Morin, the CEO of Auvik Networks in the Waterloo region, expressed it this way (CBC News, 2019):

> It feels like the attitude of Canadian tech talent working in the US is shifting— there's a changing tide. They're more open to moving back, and the Waterloo region is a big part of that. Reverse migration is a lot less risky when there are open opportunities at so many awesome, growing tech companies.

Foreign tech workers find Canada a more attractive workplace than before. One reason is that Canada's immigration system makes a concerted

## Vignette 6.5

### Timber Species Identifier Software

A system of automated software known as the Timber Species Identifier analyzes forest inventory data to determine the location and species of individual trees. This software and similar technologies are changing the way business is done in the forestry sector.

effort to attract skilled workers from overseas. Other factors may include the more restrictive US immigration rules, the anti-immigrant stance of the Trump administration, political and social upheaval in the United States over the past few years, and diminished US standing in the world. Consequently, some foreign tech workers in the United States have moved to Canada. As well, US tech companies are expanding their operations in Canada, where hiring foreign nationals is much easier.

## Technology Diffusion

Along the entire economic front, advances in technology are pushing firms into the knowledge-based world, making them more efficient but needing fewer workers. The diffusion of technology marks a turning point in modern business.

While tech hubs represent concentrations of tech innovation and service firms, the rest of the spatial landscape is undergoing technological change. In the primary sector, for instance, agriculture, forestry, and mining all have seized on the opportunities for greater efficiency derived from employing various forms of advanced technology. Consequently, the number of workers in these fields is reduced and the productivity of those remaining has increased. In a sense, the tech revolution is the latest version of modification of our market economy. Take, for example, the logging industry. Some 100 years ago, logging was a labour-intensive occupation based on hand-powered saws operated by one or two persons. With the introduction of the mechanical chainsaw, the cutting of trees by a single logger, and then cutting them into suitable lengths for transportation to sawmills, became easier and quicker, thus greatly improving productivity. Today, the logging industry benefits from various types of advanced technology solutions, from strategic timber supply designs to on-the-ground forest operations. The timber species identifier software (Vignette 6.5) is just one of many technology solutions for this industry.

## A Digital Future for Banks

When was the last time you stood in line at the bank to see a teller and do your banking business? Even before the recent coronavirus pandemic, visiting a bank in person had largely become a thing of the past. Canadian banks, after all, have chosen a digital future, and signs of that future are clear. For instance, the Bank of Montreal is experimenting with operating small branch banks without human tellers (Shecter, 2015). Brian Porter, the CEO of Scotiabank, described this paradigm shift in banking: "We're in the technology business. Our product happens to be banking, but largely that's delivered through technology" (Berman & Kiladze, 2016). Leading the charge into the digital world of banking in Canada, the CEO of Laurentian Bank, François Desjardins, called the traditional banking model "obsolete." In late September 2016, Laurentian Bank, based in Montreal, announced plans "to close dozens of branches and cut about 300 staff" (Berman, 2016b).

Two things are clear. First, banks are on the path to become more efficient and more profitable. Second, this path means fewer bank branches and employees.

Where does that digital banking system appear on the Canadian landscape? One place is Toronto. As the financial capital of Canada, Toronto is home to the five largest banks—Royal Bank of Canada, Toronto-Dominion, Canadian Imperial Bank of Commerce, Bank of Montreal, and Bank of Nova Scotia. (The sixth-largest bank, the National Bank

**THINK ABOUT IT**

If advanced technology displaces workers in the tertiary sector, where will they go? Note that McDonald's has automated its ordering system, thus reducing the number of its employees taking orders.

**THINK ABOUT IT**
Workers are also consumers, and they rely on their wages to purchase products and services. If workers are replaced by robots, how will unemployed workers pay for the goods and services? Does the solution involve some form of guaranteed income?

**Table 5.5,** "Industrial Structure of Canada and Regions, Percentage of Workers by Industrial Sector, 2019," page 163, provides an overview of each region's employment pattern.

of Canada, is headquartered in Montreal, where the Bank of Montreal [BMO] maintains its official legal headquarters although the BMO chair, its president, and many senior executives are located in Toronto.)

Automation has hit bank employees and branch banks hard. As more and more customers find online banking convenient, the need for branch banks and their tellers decreases. For example, Royal Bank of Canada reduced its workforce by an average of 1,200 employees a year from 2010 to 2017. Most cuts occurred with tellers, whose numbers fell from 11,000 to 5,000 (Berman, 2016a), but cuts of investment and management personnel are also occurring as banks adopt digital, data, and investment technology (Alexander, 2017).

### The Global Reach of Financial Institutions

Canadian banks ceased to serve just the Canadian market some 40 years ago. The Bank of Nova Scotia is the most international of the Big Five, with an extensive presence in the Caribbean and Latin America. By 2019, Scotiabank operated in over 50 countries. The Bank of Montreal and Toronto-Dominion have a strong foothold in the US. This international strategy parallels the move by CN back in the 1980s. At that time, CN jumped at the opportunity to become a North American railway system (Figure 5.3). Canadian banks move into the global economy for three reasons. First, the Canadian banks are strengthened by their presence in a larger market. Second, the rapid growth of the middle classes in developing countries provides an opportunity for banks to expand their customer base at a more rapid pace than in Canada. Third, the digital banking system, once fully defined in Canada, can be transferred to other countries at a very low cost. The shift to a digital banking system is compelling because it increases profits over the traditional banking model.

## Ontario's Original Economic Anchor: The Automobile Industry

For decades, the automobile industry was the heart and soul of manufacturing activity in developed countries (Dicken, 1992). This is no longer the case, as developing countries have taken over that role.

The manufacturing of automobiles is on life support: the number of employees has dropped below 40,000 while those engaged in auto parts manufacturing has slumped to 70,000. Consequently, Ontario faces the question: Does this industry have a future in Canada?

The answer is complicated and the future, while seeming to be heading in one direction, can change course. For instance, in November 2020 the federal and provincial governments announced they are providing a half-billion dollars to Ford for the production of electric vehicles and the batteries that power them at Ford's Oakville assembly plant (*Global News*, 2020). Next came General Motors' announcement that it would reopen its Oshawa assembly plant (Atkins, 2020). No doubt, General Motors is expecting similar public support. Could such investments save Ontario's automotive industry from its downward slide?

The answers remain in the future. However, we do know that:

- Robotics technology and government support have kept assembly and parts firms alive, though with a smaller workforce.
- Survival for now seems likely, but in a diminished way, because investment for new plants in North America gravitates to low-wage countries such as Mexico.
- Conversion of auto parts firms to produce medical products is underway, but is it a short- or long-term commitment?

One automobile analyst predicts a bleak future for Ontario's automobile industry:

> "The bad news is behind us but there's no good news in front of us," reckons Dennis DesRosiers, an industry analyst. He predicts that Canada will continue gradually to lose its production base until "somewhere between 2030 and 2040 we'll be Australia," where the last carmaker with a factory in [that] country is scheduled to close its gates by 2018. (*The Economist*, 2015)

Added to that gloomy prediction, GM shut its plant in Oshawa in 2020 and moved it to Mexico, where production costs are much lower. The loss of this manufacturing plant has had serious repercussions for its assembly workers and its auto parts suppliers.

While the auto industry has moved into robotic forms of manufacturing, it is feeling the cold chill generated by the dark side of globalization. Canada's automobile manufacturing industry matured into a major industry with the Auto Pact and, later, the Canada–US Free Trade Agreement. However, Canada lost its edge when Mexico joined NAFTA. Wages in Mexico remain a fraction of those in Canada. Then, a 2001 WTO ruling unravelled protection from foreign automobile producers in Japan and South Korea. The application of modern technology, such as robotic welding,[2] and substantial federal and Ontario grants and loans have slowed the auto industry's decline, but the huge wage difference between Canada and Mexico makes the odds of survival low.

Without a doubt, the automobile industry that once drove the Ontario economy has dwindled—from 3.1 million vehicles coming off the line in 1999 to 1.9 million in 2019 (Table 6.2). Consequently, nearly one-third of those employed in this industry were let go over the last decade, due partly to the relocation of plants to Mexico and partly to the replacement of workers by robotic machines (Figures 6.7 and 6.8). Even the electric car manufacturing plan for Ford's Oakville assembly plant and the anticipated reopening of GM's Oshawa assembly plant will slow but not reverse this trend (*Global News*, 2020; Atkins, 2020). The low Canadian dollar has offered a short-term ray of hope, but the long-term prognostication for Canada's automobile industry, as well as for the auto industries of the European Union and the United States, is grim. The global shift of this industry, like the textile industry in previous decades, is moving inevitably to low-wage industrializing countries. With GM's pull out and Toyota's 2015 decision to relocate its Corolla production to Mexico, Ontario's automobile industry was back on its heels, but, three years later, Toyota Canada announced an investment of $1.4 billion in its Cambridge and Woodstock manufacturing plants, making Ontario the manufacturing hub for the RAV4 in North America. In spite of this "good" investment news, the future of automobile manufacturing plants remains extremely precarious.

### Automobile Assembly Plants

Eight automobile assembly plants are concentrated in southern Ontario where transportation links to the major markets of Canada and the United States are readily available and driving distances are short between auto parts factories and assembly plants (Table 6.3). Since the addition of Mexico to the North American Free Trade Agreement (NAFTA), Canada's competitive advantage has slipped and three plants have closed: two GM plants, one at Sainte-Thérèse near Montreal, which closed in 2002, and the other in Oshawa, and one Ford plant in St Thomas, Ontario, which closed in 2011. Toyota's decision

See **Table 5.4**, "The Orientation of Canadian Trade: From North American to Global?" page 159, for more on the Auto Pact and the FTA.

**THINK ABOUT IT**

Without public support for the automobile industry, Dennis DesRosiers's prediction regarding the demise of the Canadian auto industry may well be true.

## Vignette 6.6

### Decoupling Globalization: Domestic Manufacturing of Medical Products

By April 2020, Canada was facing a severe shortage of ventilators, medical masks, and other key supplies needed to combat the spread of COVID-19. The federal government reacted by providing financial assistance. For example, Toronto-based Thornhill Medical Inc. and Ottawa's Spartan Bioscience Inc. both agreed to do their part to help. As well, auto parts firms have claimed they can mass-produce products, but need a long-term commitment because retooling their production lines from auto parts to surgical masks and other medical products is costly. It's unclear whether this political decision is a short-term reaction to cope with the pandemic crisis or a long-term commitment to ensure that domestic supplies are available when the next crisis occurs.

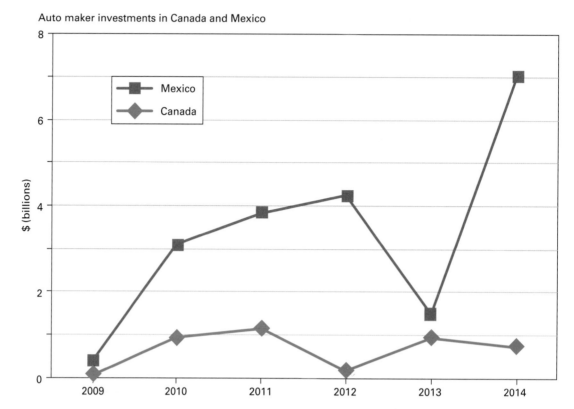

Auto maker investments in Canada and Mexico

**FIGURE 6.7 The heart of the problem: Mexico attracts more investment in new automobile assembly plants than Canada**

Source: Keenan (2015).

## Contested Terrain 6.2

### The Bailout of Chrysler and GM: Sound Public Policy?

At the time of the major recession of 2008–9, Canada and Ontario were loath to see the core of the Canadian manufacturing sector—motor vehicles—die. In 2009, Canada and Ontario intervened in the marketplace to provide financial assistance to Chrysler Canada (US$3.8 billion) and General Motors Canada (US$10.6 billion). In 2020, as noted above, Ontario and Ottawa continued this strategy by providing a half-billion dollars for Ford's plan to transform its Oakville plant for electric car production.

Is this sound public policy by the federal and Ontario governments, which are now calling for a knowledge-based economy? Public investments might have been better placed with the technology industry, such as Nortel (which filed for bankruptcy protection in January 2009 and subsequently was wound down) and BlackBerry (originally Research In Motion, which was unable to compete successfully against Apple's iPhone).

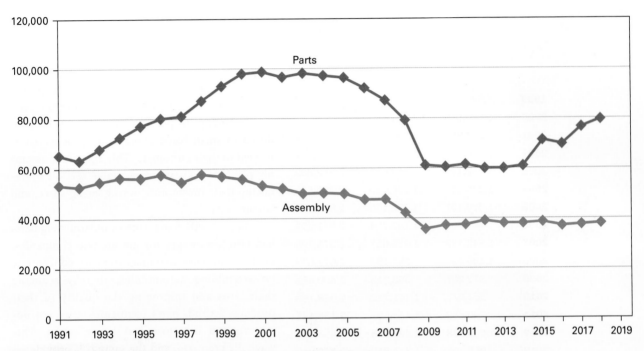

**FIGURE 6.8 Employment in Canada's automobile industry**

By 2019, employment in the automobile industry totalled over 100,000, with those in assembly production comprising nearly 40,000. At the turn of the twenty-first century, employment reached its peak at just below 150,000. The decline began in the recession of 2008–9 when automotive industries experienced significant job losses, reducing the size of the workforce from 152,600 in 2007 to 109,100 in 2009 (Bernard, 2015). Most job losses took place in the parts industry. Since then, Canada has been unable to complete with low-wage production in Mexico. Consequently, most automobile firms have invested in new Mexican assembly and parts plants rather than in Canada.

Sources: Canadian Auto Workers Union (2012, Figure 1), from Statistics Canada, CANSIM Table 281-0024, reprinted with permission from Canadian Auto Workers Union (CAS-Canada); Industry Canada (2015a, 2015b); Statistics Canada (2020b).

to move its Corolla production from Cambridge to Mexico in 2015 represents a similar corporate decision. These decisions follow a fundamental principle in economic geography: companies seek to manufacture products where cost of production is lowest.

Not surprisingly, employment dropped from nearly 60,000 in the 1990s to less than 40,000 by 2019. If this **hollowing-out** of Ontario's automobile manufacturing continues unabated, then perhaps DesRosiers's dire prediction of the end of such manufacturing in Ontario will take place within the next 20 years (*The Economist*, 2015).

### Automobile Parts Firms

The automobile industry (Figure 6.9) consists of two separate operations: the assembly of automobiles and trucks and the production of their parts. In addition, some manufacturing firms supply semi-processed materials. In southern Ontario, fabricating firms produce steel, rubber, plastics, aluminum, and glass parts for automobile assembly and parts plants in Canada and the United States. Finally, service firms, ranging from the advertisers and designers to the sales and service staff, manage the finished product. In short, the auto industry is a final-product type of manufacturing; as such, its added value reaches a maximum.

The automobile parts industry in Canada employed almost 100,000 workers in the first decade of the twenty-first century, but by 2009 this number fell to 60,000. For the next decade, employment

**TABLE 6.2    Ontario Motor Vehicle Production, 1999–2019**

| Year | Small Cars | Large Cars and Trucks* | Total |
|------|-----------|------------------------|-------|
| 1999 | 1,626,316 | 1,432,497 | 3,058,813 |
| 2000 | 1,550,500 | 1,411,136 | 2,961,636 |
| 2001 | 1,274,853 | 1,257,889 | 2,532,742 |
| 2002 | 1,369,042 | 1,260,395 | 2,629,437 |
| 2003 | 1,340,175 | 1,212,687 | 2,552,862 |
| 2004 | 1,335,516 | 1,376,020 | 2,711,536 |
| 2005 | 1,356,197 | 1,332,165 | 2,688,362 |
| 2006 | 1,389,536 | 1,182,756 | 2,572,292 |
| 2007 | 1,342,133 | 1,236,657 | 2,578,790 |
| 2008 | 1,195,426 | 882,153 | 2,077,579 |
| 2009 | 822,267 | 668,215 | 1,490,482 |
| 2010 | 967,077 | 1,101,112 | 2,068,189 |
| 2011 | 990,482 | 1,144,639 | 2,135,121 |
| 2012 | 1,040,298 | 1,423,066 | 2,463,364 |
| 2013 | 965,191 | 1,414,615 | 2,379,806 |
| 2014 | 913,533 | 1,480,357 | 2,393,890 |
| 2015 | 888,565 | 1,394,909 | 2,283,474 |
| 2016 | 802,057 | 1,568,219 | 2,370,276 |
| 2017 | 749,458 | 1,450,331 | 2,199,789 |
| 2018 | 655,896 | 1,364,944 | 2,020,840 |
| 2019 | 461,370 | 1,455,215 | 1,916,585 |

*This category consists of light-duty vehicles, including large sedans, mini-vans, and pickup trucks, and heavy-duty vehicles such as buses, cargo vans, and armoured vehicles.

Source: oica (2020).

in the parts industry stayed around 60,000 (Figure 6.8). However, the closure of the Oshawa assembly plant in 2020 may cause this number to edge downward.

By being highly efficient and strategically located, automobile parts firms can operate on a just-in-time principle—auto components are produced in small batches and quickly delivered as needed to their customers. This allows the assembly plants to achieve considerable savings by reducing their inventories, warehousing space, and labour costs.

As well, subcontracting or outsourcing parts had two advantages for automobile companies. First, it allowed manufacturers to concentrate on assembling automobiles, thereby reducing their costs and improving the quality of their product. Second, parts companies were not unionized and therefore had lower wages. This wage differential—and the savings it provides—is the main reason why General Motors, Ford, and DaimlerChrysler continue to divert work from assembly plants to parts firms. In Ontario, the Canadian-based Magna International has grown into the third-largest auto parts company in North America. The company will benefit from the USMCA because this agreement provides greater incentive for automobile manufacturers to source components from Canadian part firms despite their paying higher wages than parts firms in Mexico.

## Vignette 6.7

### USMCA Confronts the Mexican Wage Advantage

Under NAFTA, Mexico's automobile industry was growing by leaps and bounds. The reason was simple. Companies decided to place new investment in automobile plants in Mexico because of its lower costs of production. The problem was the wage differential between Mexico and its two NAFTA partners. Under NAFTA, Canadian and US wages were much higher than their Mexican counterparts—perhaps close to 10 times higher. To address this issue, the USMCA (the reworked United States–Mexico–Canada Agreement) contains a requirement that automobile manufacturers in Mexico must increase wages to $16 an hour or pay a tariff on vehicles entering the United States. With Mexican auto workers making just over US$3 an hour, this wage jump to US$16 represents an increase of five times. However, this wage requirement only applies to 30 per cent of automobile manufacturing in Mexico until 2023, when it increases to 40 per cent.

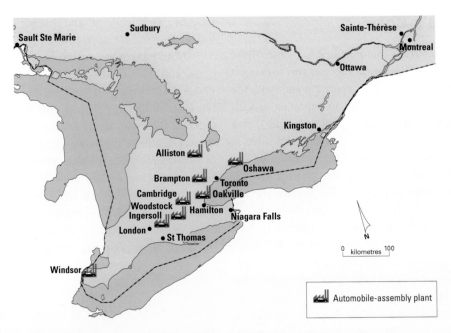

**FIGURE 6.9 Automobile assembly centres in Ontario**

Honda and Toyota expanded their Ontario manufacturing plants primarily because of strong demand for their automobiles in the US. Ontario is an attractive production and export site in North America for several reasons. One is easy access to the US market. Another is strong support from both the federal and provincial governments. The two Japanese companies also prefer non-unionized workforces that seem acceptable for their employees.

**TABLE 6.3    Ontario Automobile Assembly Plants, 2018**

| Location | Products |
| --- | --- |
| **Fiat Chrysler Canada Inc.** | |
| Brampton | Chrysler 300; Dodge Challenger; Dodge Charger |
| Windsor | Dodge Grand Caravan; Chrysler Pacifica; Pacifica Plug-in Hybrid |
| **Ford of Canada Ltd** | |
| Oakville | Ford Edge; Flex; GT; Lincoln MKT; Lincoln MKX |
| **General Motors of Canada Ltd** | |
| Oshawa (to close in 2020) | Chevrolet Impala; Cadillac XTS; Silverado; Sierra |
| Ingersoll | Chevrolet Equinox |
| **Honda Canada Inc.** | |
| Alliston | Honda Civic; Honda CR-V |
| **Toyota, Canada** | |
| Cambridge | Toyota Corolla; Lexus RX350; Lexus RX450h Hybrid |
| Woodstock | Toyota RAV4 |

Note: In 2018, Windsor's assembly plant ceased producing the Chrysler Town & Country sedan and replaced it with the Chrysler Pacifica. The Oshawa plant lost the Chevrolet Camaro to Lansing, Michigan, while Ingersoll saw the GMC Terrain move to Mexico; Cambridge had the Toyota Corolla moved to Mexico and replaced with the RAV4.

Source: Industry Canada (2019). Reproduced with the permission of the Minister of Public Works and Government Services Canada.

## Ontario's Core

Southern Ontario is the most highly industrialized area in Canada. The region also contains the largest concentration of Canada's population and, with the bulk of its Class I soils, is also an important agriculture area. By 2020, nearly 13 million people—over 93 per cent of the province's total population—resided in southern Ontario. The vast majority lived in 13 major cities known as census metropolitan areas (CMAs). Most importantly, the Greater Toronto Area (GTA) had a population of just over 6.4 million in 2016 and was expected to reach 7 million by 2020. Toronto is by far the largest city in Canada and, as a result of its size, contains many higher-order businesses, cultural attractions, and services not found in other cities.

Southern Ontario's urban geography delivers an enormous population cluster, signalling its significance within Ontario, Canada, and North America. In comparison with the other five geographic regions, Ontario has 15 CMAs (13 of which are located in southern Ontario); Quebec and Western Canada have five each while BC and Atlantic Canada have four each.

Urban growth has varied considerably for these CMAs, and this variation mimics economic growth (Table 6.4). From 2001 to 2016, the fastest-growing cities in Ontario were Guelph (29.6 per cent), Oshawa (28.2 per cent) Toronto (26.6 per cent), Ottawa–Gatineau (26.5 per cent) (although some of its residents live across the Ottawa River in Quebec), and Kitchener–Cambridge–Waterloo (26.5 per cent). In contrast, the only city to see its population decline over this 15-year period was Thunder Bay in northern Ontario. With the closure of the GM assembly plant, Oshawa's population growth will likely slow and perhaps even decline.

## The Golden Horseshoe

The Golden Horseshoe obtained its name because of its horseshoe-like shape around the western end of Lake Ontario and its outstanding economic performance over the years. This tiny area of the Great Lakes Lowland forms the most densely

### TABLE 6.4 Population of Census Metropolitan Areas in Southern Ontario, 2001 and 2016

| Census Metropolitan Area | Population 2001 (000s) | Population 2016 (000s) | Change (%) |
|---|---|---|---|
| Thunder Bay | 122.0 | 121.6 | −0.1 |
| Peterborough | 110.9 | 121.7 | 9.7 |
| Brantford | 118.1 | 134.2 | 13.6 |
| Guelph | 117.3 | 152.0 | 29.6 |
| Kingston | 146.8 | 161.2 | 9.8 |
| Sudbury | 155.6 | 164.7 | 5.9 |
| Windsor | 307.9 | 329.1 | 6.9 |
| Oshawa | 296.3 | 379.9 | 28.2 |
| St Catharines–Niagara | 377.9 | 406.1 | 7.5 |
| London | 432.5 | 494.1 | 14.2 |
| Kitchener–Cambridge–Waterloo | 414.3 | 523.9 | 26.5 |
| Hamilton | 662.4 | 747.6 | 12.9 |
| Ottawa–Gatineau* | 1,067.8 | 1,323.8 | 24.0 |
| Toronto | 4,682.9 | 5,928.0 | 26.6 |
| Total | 9,012.7 | 10,987.9 | 21.9 |

*Statistics Canada has combined Ottawa, Ontario, and Gatineau, Quebec, as a single CMA although these cities are in different provincial jurisdictions.

Sources: Adapted from Statistics Canada (2007b, 2019a).

populated area of Canada. The Golden Horseshoe is anchored by Toronto and it extends from the US border at Niagara Falls westward to Hamilton (Vignette 6.8), northward to Toronto, and then on to Oshawa to the east. Well over 8 million Canadians live, work, and play in Canada's largest population cluster, and many visitors come either as tourists or on business trips. Accounting for nearly one-quarter of Canada's population, the Golden Horseshoe contains numerous towns and cities, including Toronto, Hamilton, Oshawa, St Catharines, Niagara Falls, Burlington, Oakville, Pickering, Ajax, and Whitby. Toronto forms its urban anchor, while Hamilton has been the focus of heavy industry. Until 2020, Oshawa was Canada's leading automobile manufacturing city, but with the loss of its GM automobile plant, its future is uncertain. Outside of Toronto, three

## Vignette 6.8

### Hamilton: Steel City or Rust Town?

Hamilton, situated at the west end of Lake Ontario only 50 km from Toronto, is known as Steel City. Unfortunately, the North American steel industry fell on hard times and Hamilton was hurting. Journalist Trevor Coleen visioned a gloomy future for Hamilton: "As prosperity plumped nearby rivals such as Burlington, Oakville, Mississauga, Kitchener–Waterloo and—especially—Toronto, it skipped Hamilton completely, cruelly, until most of its big-name companies were gone, the stores along Barton Street deteriorated into dark and crumbling shells, downtown became a kind of forbidden zone, and even the Mafia couldn't make any money" (Cole, 2009). Fast-forward to 2019. What are the facts? According to the Conference Board of Canada, Hamilton took advantage of a weaker Canadian dollar and a strengthening US economy in 2015 to boost manufactured exports to the United States (Arcand et al., 2015). The spillover of demand for housing in the Greater Toronto Area (GTA) has also given a boost to Hamilton's housing market, while the removal of the US tariff on Canadian steel imports has rejuvenated its steel industry. In 2019, Stelco opened its new state-of-the-art steel processing plant (McNeil, 2019). Have these events saved Hamilton from turning into a Rust Belt town?

John Rennison/Hamilton Spectator

**PHOTO 6.7** The Stelco steel mill in Hamilton, Ontario.

**THINK ABOUT IT**

If you were a successful farmer on prime agricultural land and were offered millions of dollars by a developer to sell your farm, what would you do: Sell your farm and take an early retirement? Continue to farm because you enjoy it and believe this is the ethical thing to do? Look to sell the property at a lower price to someone who will continue to farm?

cities—Kitchener, Cambridge, and Waterloo—form Canada's "Technology Triangle," where innovative research benefits from exchanges between universities and technology firms.

Agriculture plays an important role. Ontario has over half of the highest-quality agricultural land (known as Class I) in Canada. Leading crops by value are corn and soybeans (Ontario Ministry of Agriculture, 2016). The Niagara Fruit Belt is a particularly rich farming area on the narrow Ontario Plain that extends from Hamilton to Niagara-on-the-Lake. This small agricultural zone contains the best grape and soft-fruit growing lands in Canada, and is home to vineyards that account for most of Canada's quality wines, including the unique ice wine, made from grapes left on the vine (Photo 6.8) and not harvested until sustained temperatures of −8°C or lower are reached, normally sometime from December to February (Wine Country Ontario, n.d.). While the Niagara Fruit Belt

occupies a northerly location for grapevines and soft-fruit trees, local factors have more than offset the threat of frost at 43°N latitude:

- Air drainage from the Niagara Escarpment to Lake Ontario reduces the danger of both spring and fall frosts.
- The water of Lake Ontario is warm in autumn and its proximity to the Niagara Fruit Belt helps to moderate advancing cold air masses.
- In early spring, the cool waters of Lake Ontario keep air temperatures low, thereby delaying the opening of the fruit blossoms until late spring when the risk of frost is much lower.

While natural factors can adversely affect fruit and grape harvests, urban sprawl is a much more dangerous threat to this unique corner of Ontario. The Greenbelt Act of 2004 protected about 1.8 million acres of forest and agricultural and wetlands

Barrett & Mackay/All Canada Photos

**PHOTO 6.8** The Niagara Fruit Belt extends about 65 km between Hamilton and Niagara-on-the-Lake. The fertile sub-region is one of the major soft-fruit and grape-producing areas in Canada. Most vineyards are located on the slopes of, or below, the Niagara Escarpment. For many years, hardy vines that produced low-quality grapes resulted in poor-quality, inexpensive wine. With the Free Trade Agreement, Canada had to remove its tariffs, making it difficult to compete with foreign wines. Since that time, farmers in the Niagara Fruit Belt have been successful in growing the finest varieties of grapes and have been able to make some of the finest wines in the world.

around the perimeter of the Golden Horseshoe, but municipal exceptions occur and the amount of productive farmland continues to dwindle.

### Toronto

Toronto is Canada's largest and most dynamic metropolis. What makes Toronto "interesting" are its wide variety of cultural and sporting events. Hopefully, these events, now curtailed because of COVID-19, will return once a vaccine is available. As defined as the Greater Toronto Area (GTA), Toronto includes the four regional municipalities that surround it: Durham, Halton, Peel, and York. Falling within Greater Toronto are 16 cities and towns: Pickering, Ajax, Whitby, Oshawa, Clarington, Markham, Richmond Hill, Vaughan, Aurora, Stouffville, Newmarket, Bradford, Brampton, Burlington, Mississauga, and Oakville.

Toronto is the focus of the province's cultural, demographic, and economic growth. It continues to draw many newcomers, who, in turn, enrich Toronto's culture. Located on the shore of Lake Ontario, Toronto has a spectacular skyline dominated by the CN Tower, the third-tallest tower in the world (Photo 6.9). A cluster of universities, including the University of Toronto, York University, and Ryerson University, plus a host of technical colleges, offers the widest variety of programs in Canada.

Within Canada, Toronto sits at the top of Canada's urban hierarchy. One sign of its dominance is the number of corporate headquarters, including the main offices of national and international banks

AndresGarciaM/Getty Images

**PHOTO 6.9** The CN Tower at 553 m high dominates Toronto's skyline on an early summer evening, as seen from Toronto Island. The illuminated structure on the left is the Rogers Centre (originally named SkyDome), home of the Blue Jays baseball team. The COVID-19 pandemic forced the team to play a shortened season with a home base in Buffalo, New York. Similar dislocations were faced by Toronto's Raptors and Maple Leafs in the major North American basketball and hockey leagues. What might happen going forward will depend largely on the widespread distribution of recently discovered COVID vaccines.

and investment firms. A more conventional sign is that the city offers a range of urban services to residents in the GTA, plus "high-end" ones to those within and beyond the GTA. High-end services include opera presented at the famous Roy Thomson Hall concert venue; a lively theatre and concert scene; financial transactions at Canada's primary stock exchange, the Toronto Stock Exchange; and top-level North American professional sport teams not found elsewhere in Canada. National and international events add another unique aspect to Toronto.

Toronto is known as a city of neighbourhoods, partly because immigrant groups have clustered in certain areas. Little Italy and Little Portugal are older, well-established ethnic neighbourhoods. More recently, Asian, African, and Caribbean neighbourhoods have emerged. Immigration has had an impact on Toronto's cityscape, including architecturally and in commercial activities designed to meet the demands of these new Canadians. Asian theme malls are common in Canada's largest cities where Asian populations congregate. Toronto's Pacific Mall is the largest Chinese mall in North America.

Toronto Island is a unique neighbourhood that has survived confrontation with city planners who had decided to transform the area, accessible by a short ferry ride from downtown, into public open space. Its geography—essentially a sandbar extending into Lake Ontario that at one time was attached to the mainland—consists of a series of islands, most of which now is dedicated to parkland. However, residential communities exist on two islands (Ward's Island and Algonquin Island).

## Ottawa Valley

The national capital is located in the Ottawa Valley and federal government operations are found on both sides of the Ottawa River. The major city in the valley, Ottawa–Gatineau, is not only a major population cluster in Canada, but this politically hybrid city lies on both sides of the Ottawa River in two different provinces. Taken together, Ottawa–Gatineau is the fourth-largest metropolitan area in Canada and an important technology hub. In 2016 its population totalled 1.3 million (Table 6.4). Its growth is driven by expanding job opportunities found in the federal government and in the technology sector. Shopify, a leading e-commerce company in North America, is one of several major high-tech companies based in this region.

Post-secondary education takes place through many institutions, but three play a key role: Carleton University, the University of Ottawa, and the Université du Québec en Outaouais.

In its early days, the Ottawa–Gatineau region along the Ottawa River was an important juncture for fur brigades—French traders and their Algonquin and Huron partners—that travelled between Montreal and Huronia in the first half of the seventeenth century, but by the mid-1640s Iroquois blockades of the river often stopped the passage of fur traders (Dickason with McNab, 2009, pp. 104–5). By the early nineteenth century, logging and sawmilling were important activities in the Ottawa Valley, but those days, too, are gone. Zibi, a bold urban project, is transforming the former derelict industrial land making up Chaudière and Albert Island (Photo 6.10). This mixed-use urban project entails residential, retail, recreational, and commercial components (Windmill Developments, 2015).

In today's Ottawa–Gatineau, the federal government is the major employer, followed by the high-technology sector. The federal government requires a wide variety of goods and services in its daily operations. This demand provides an opportunity for many small and medium-sized firms in the Ottawa Valley. By locating its departments and agencies in both Ottawa and Gatineau, the federal government has ensured that Ottawa's economic orbit extends to a number of small towns on both the Ontario and Quebec sides of the Ottawa River.

## Southwestern Ontario

Southwestern Ontario represents the southernmost territory in Canada. Windsor, for instance, lies just north of 42 degrees north. The geographic extent of this prosperous agriculture area reaches south to the Detroit River and Lake Erie, while Lake Huron forms its western and northern boundary. The Golden Horseshoe defines its eastern limits. Southwestern

zibi.ca

**PHOTO 6.10** This artist's rendition shows the bold plan of the Domtar Lands Redevelopment that would transform derelict and contaminated land in the Chaudière area into a world-class sustainable community. The project, called Zibi (meaning "river" in Algonkian) after the Kitigan Zibi First Nation in Quebec, straddles both Ottawa and Gatineau. While the two cities are separated only by the Ottawa River, different provincial jurisdictions have resulted in a historic cultural divide. The intent of the plan is to create a community that respects the unique history and culture of both sides of the river while providing a cohesive connection point that draws the two sides of the National Capital Region together.

Ontario contains the third major urban cluster in the province and a solid agricultural base. London (population 506,400) and Windsor (population 319,000) are the largest cities. With several major universities, including Waterloo, Wilfrid Laurier, Western, and the University of Windsor, southwestern Ontario has a strong knowledge-based economy. On the other hand, manufacturing, represented by automobile assembly plants in Ingersoll, Woodstock, and Windsor, are unlikely to expand. Agriculture continues to produce high-value crops, including sweet corn, soybeans, and tobacco. Its long growing season has made it an ideal place for vegetable crops, such as tomatoes and carrots.

London provides administrative, commercial, and cultural services for the larger region. It is also the headquarters of several insurance companies, including London Life. Among its economic activities, London is noted for manufacturing, including the production of armoured personnel carriers and diesel locomotives by General Dynamics Land Systems, and, in recent years, its controversial sale of armoured military vehicles to Saudi Arabia.[3] London is also a food-processing centre for Southwestern Ontario.

## Ontario's Hinterland: Northern Ontario

Ontario's hinterland is found in the north of Ontario. Many northern Ontarians are dissatisfied with their lot. Such grumbling is common in resource hinterlands. Claiming to be isolated and ignored by the provincial government based in Toronto,

**PHOTO 6.11** Thunder Bay was the centre for Flexity streetcars production. These are the latest model in the rolling stock of the Toronto streetcar system owned by the Toronto Transit Commission (TTC). Flexies have proven popular with the riding public because of their air conditioning, smooth ride, large windows, higher capacity, and ease of access for handicapped people. Most were produced in Thunder Bay, but numerous delays prevented the Bombardier order from its final delivery. For a variety of reasons, the Thunder Bay plant had trouble establishing an efficient assembly line (Spurr et al., 2017) and distance to its market added another disadvantage. Under new ownership, the question is, can Alstom SA overcome the manufacturing inefficiencies and its suboptimum location, or will it simply throw up its hands and close this marginal manufacturing plant?

some of its citizens have called for a new province called Mantario (Di Matteo, 2006). But would that solve this hinterland's problem of slow economic and population growth? Geographers will note that the resource potential of northern Ontario's physiographic region of the Canadian Shield pales in comparison to the St Lawrence and Great Lakes Lowlands, where the agricultural lands of southern Ontario are situated. Besides a currently limited resource economy, this northern hinterland has a small but aging population and is distant from major markets. Under these circumstances, manufacturing is particularly challenging. For example, the Bombardier manufacturing plant in Thunder Bay had trouble meeting deadlines for the Flexity streetcars in Toronto (Photo 6.11). With Bombardier selling its rail interest to French rail giant Alstom SA in February 2020, concerns about the future of the Thunder Bay facility remain cloudy.

In 2016, northern Ontario had a population of under 800,000—around 6 per cent of Ontario's total population. Looking to the future, northern Ontario's population may continue its slow decline, but its share of the total Ontario population could drop to 4 per cent or lower (Figure 6.10). Within its population, only the Indigenous people show signs of growth.

While the size of its land base is considerable, its two physiographic regions—the Hudson Bay Lowlands and the Canadian Shield—contain little

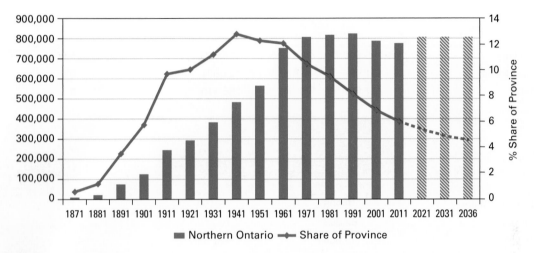

**FIGURE 6.10** **Historical and projected population in northern Ontario, 1871–2036**

Source: Cuddy (2015, p. 7).

or no agricultural land and offer few opportunities for the industrial development found in southern Ontario. Its people mostly reside in towns along the two major transportation routes:

- The southern route, defined by the CP rail line and the Trans-Canada Highway, connects North Bay with Sudbury, Sault Ste Marie, Nipigon, Thunder Bay, Dryden, and Kenora.
- The northern route, defined by the CN line and a major highway, connects North Bay, Timmins, Kirkland Lake, Cochrane, Kapuskasing, and Nipigon to Thunder Bay.

In addition, this resource hinterland has experienced business closures and population losses over the last decade. The problem is simple: the region is suffering from an economic decline and an aging population. Added to that dire situation, few immigrants settle in northern Ontario, while many of its young people leave for other regions.

Like other slow-growing regions, northern Ontario's resource base is losing its economic strength for two reasons:

1. The most accessible mineral and timber resources have been exploited, so new resource production is more costly. The rich and varied deposits in the remote Ring of Fire are a case in point. Its development is stalled for several reasons, including the absence of a transportation link.

2. Resource companies are under pressure to modernize by employing more advanced technology, and this process results in a reduced labour force. Those firms that cannot afford to modernize are often driven from the market by costs or by failing to meet higher environmental standards.

The urban population of northern Ontario reveals the demographic plight facing this hinterland. Since 2001, only two cities have shown strong growth: Sudbury and North Bay. Thunder Bay—northern Ontario's second-largest city after Sudbury—has a stalled population of around 122,000 (Tables 6.5 and 6.6). In 2019, it was announced that Thunder Bay's train manufacturing plant might close, which could push its population into negative numbers.

Northern Ontario's resource economy is based on forests and minerals. In 2018, the value of forest products reached $16.6 billion, while mining came in slightly lower at $10 billion (Ontario Forest, 2019; Natural Resources Canada, 2019a, 2019b). Ontario ranks first among provinces in the value of mineral production and third in forestry behind BC and

Figure 2.1, "Physiographic regions and continental shelves in Canada," page 23, and Figure 6.4, "Physiographic regions in Central Canada," page 176, delineate Ontario's physiographic regions. Also see "Physiographic Regions" in Chapter 2, page 23.

**TABLE 6.5    Population of Northern Ontario CMAs, 2001–2016**

| CMA | Population 2001 | Population 2016 | % Change 2001–16 |
|-----|-----------------|-----------------|------------------|
| Sudbury | 155,601 | 164,689 | 5.9 |
| Thunder Bay | 121,986 | 121,621 | 0.0 |
| Total | 277,587 | 286,310 | 3.1 |

Source: Statistics Canada (2012, 2017a).

**TABLE 6.6    Population of Cities and Towns in Northern Ontario, 2001–2016**

| Centre | Population 2001 | Population 2016 | % Change 2001–16 |
|--------|-----------------|-----------------|------------------|
| Sault Ste Marie | 78,908 | 78,159 | 0.0 |
| North Bay | 62,303 | 70,378 | 1.3 |
| Timmins | 43,686 | 41,788 | −4.5 |
| Kenora | 15,838 | 15,096 | −0.5 |
| Temiskaming Shores* | 12,904 | 9,920 | −23.1 |
| Elliot Lake | 11,956 | 10,741 | −10.2 |
| Kapuskasing | 9,238 | 8,292 | −10.2 |
| Kirkland Lake | 8,616 | 7,981 | −7.3 |
| Total | 243,449 | 242,355 | −0.1 |

\* Temiskaming Shores is the restructured area comprising the three former municipalities of New Liskeard, Haileybury, and Dymond Township.

Sources: Adapted from Statistics Canada (2007b, 2017a).

Quebec. Access to the US market remains the major hindrance for Ontario's forest industry. The US employs tariffs to increase the cost of Canadian exports and thus keep Canadian lumber from displacing US lumber.

From an economic perspective, the forestry industry remains by far the most important primary industry in northern Ontario. At least a dozen communities depend on the forest industry, including Kenora, Red Rock, Dryden, Thunder Bay, Terrace Bay, and Kapuskasing. Within Canada, Ontario ranks just behind British Columbia and Quebec in forestry employment and production. Ontario's mills produce pulp and paper, lumber, fence posts, and plywood. The pulp and paper industry in northern Ontario accounts for about 16 per cent of the national production, and Ontario, along with Quebec and BC, is a leading exporter of newsprint and pulpwood to the US.

The mining industry is northern Ontario's second economic anchor. In 2018, Ontario ranked first for metallic mineral production but the province slipped to second place in 2019, just behind Quebec (Natural Resources Canada, 2020). Yet, with the exception of the Sudbury nickel deposit, the lifespan of mines is short, often less than 20 years. A recent example is the former Victor Diamond Mine that began production in 2008 and closed in 2019.

The future of mining in northern Ontario depends on higher commodity prices and the development of the mineral belt in northern Ontario known as the "Ring of Fire." This belt contains an estimated $60 billion worth of minerals, including base metals, platinum, and palladium, along with North America's largest deposit of chromite (Figure 6.11). Development in the Ring of Fire has been delayed for several reasons, including the vast size of the required capital investment, lack of accessibility to the site, environmental concerns, and negotiations with Indigenous groups. However, the main stumbling block is low commodity prices.

**FIGURE 6.11 Northern Ontario's Ring of Fire, A Stalled Project**

The Ring of Fire mineral region in northern Ontario was reportedly named after one of Johnny Cash's best-known songs, "Ring of Fire." The exploitation of these remote resources depends on a strong global demand. Even so, their remote nature will require careful planning and co-operation among the major players: the provincial government, the mining companies, and more than a dozen First Nations whose traditional homelands are in this region of Ontario's North.

Source: Shufelt (2012).

## Indigenous Communities in Northern Ontario

Northern Ontario contains nearly 80 per cent of the Indigenous population of Ontario. Its percentage of the total population has increased over the years. In 1996, Moazzami (2003) reported an Indigenous population of nearly 78,000, forming 9.2 per cent of the total population. Twenty years later, Statistics Canada (2017b) reported that the figure for Indigenous peoples had risen to nearly 82,000, comprising

20.1 per cent of northern Ontario. The Indigenous population increase over this period is attributed to a high rate of natural increase and a surge in those reporting Indigenous ethnicity between censuses 1996 and 2016.

Most Indigenous people live in the cities and towns found in the more developed area close to the railway and highway routes. For example, Thunder Bay's population in 2016 included 15,075 Indigenous people, who formed 12.7 per cent of that city's population (Statistics Canada, 2019b).

**THINK ABOUT IT**

While the populations of Indigenous communities continue to increase, so does the growing number of Indigenous residents in northern Ontario's cities. In the next 10 years, which population in Canada do you think will increase the most, urban Indigenous people or reserve and settlement-based Indigenous people?

Beyond the gold belt near the CN rail line, resource development in Ontario's Far North depends on global demand. With the closing of the Victor mine in 2019, only one mining operation in Ontario's far north—at Red Lake—existed. The likelihood of more mining developments looks particularly dim at a time of global downturn. Low commodity prices and the high cost of development mean that the rich deposits in the highly mineralized Ring of Fire will remain "potential" mine sites for the foreseeable future. As well, mining companies must adhere to stronger environmental regulations and successfully complete negotiations with Indigenous communities, including the **duty to consult** and the signing of impact benefit agreements (IBAs).

## Summary

Once the pandemic threat is reduced, likely with the widespread availability of a vaccine, Ontario should regain its momentum. In any case, Ontario remains central to Canada's economic and social geography. Two signs of its strength are solid population growth and a buoyant economy, with GDP up and unemployment down, along with rising exports to the US. Equally important, Ontario is reinventing itself as it moves from manufacturing to a knowledge-based economy. From that perspective, Toronto is leading the charge as a rapidly growing North American technology hub.

Still, Ontario is not totally out of the woods. First, prospects for the immediate future look bleak because of the consequences of COVID-19 shutting down its economy in 2020 and possibly well into 2021. Added to that economic disaster, US exports are anticipated to drop dramatically. The net result is that GDP is predicted to fall sharply while unemployment rates rise to record levels. Another unknown is Canada's position in regard to the long-term manufacture of medical products—a sign of decoupling from the global economy in order to secure a greater level of national security.

Such a political decision could give a boost to Ontario's manufacturing sector. Second, northern Ontario, with its dependency on natural resources, faces a bleak future as a declining hinterland, while the former bellwether of southern Ontario's economy, its automobile industry, continues to lose ground. Yet, the signs are clear: for Ontario to prosper and progress throughout the new decade, technology must play a greater role. However, such drastic change, as revealed in the digitization model for banks, creates more profits for firms but fewer workers. The application of advanced technology to all sectors of the economy is a win-win situation for companies: increased production per worker and higher profits for the firm. The danger is that this path will lead to higher levels of income inequality and a greater division of well-being between its core, southern Ontario, and its hinterland, northern Ontario. Yet, in our global economy, Ontario and Canada's five other regions have no choice but to follow this path and rely on the public sector to soften these negative consequences of a market economy. Could that mean extending our safety network with a guaranteed income?

## Challenge Questions

1. For much of its history, Ontario has fashioned its prosperity on trade with the United States. Is this "all eggs in one basket" strategy still valid in a post-COVID-19 era?

2. Southern Ontario's rapid expansion into the high-tech industry is pushing the region into the knowledge-based economy. What are some of the factors causing the high-tech

industry to locate to southern Ontario, but particularly to Greater Toronto?

3. If the knowledge-based economy represents the future of Ontario, would you have "saved" Nortel rather than General Motors and Chrysler during the recession of 2008–9? Explain your answer.

4. Ontario is divided into two parts: southern and northern Ontario. Considering the physical and locational differences, would you consider this division an inevitable outcome? Explain your answer.

## Essay Questions

1. Has the COVID-19 pandemic signalled a new dimension to the manufacturing of health products, one based on natural security? Does this prove that security trumps cost? Why or why not?

2. Electricity prices are much higher in Ontario than in Quebec. Why doesn't Ontario import more low-cost Quebec power?

# 7  Quebec

## Chapter Overview

This chapter will examine the following topics:

- Quebec within Canada.
- Quebec's physical geography and historical roots.
- Quebec's population and economy.
- Industrial structure and economic spearheads.
- Quebec's advantage: abundant low-cost hydroelectric power.
- Quebec's northern economy and Indigenous peoples.

## Introduction

By virtue of its geography, language, and history, Quebec occupies a unique place in Canada and North America. As a French-speaking region making up 23 per cent of Canada's population and 2 per cent of the population in North America, the province considers the preservation of the French language and, therefore, the culture of the province as its fundamental political goal. Yet, Quebec faces a dilemma. Since immigration is the driving force for both economic and population growth, is Quebec prepared to slow this growth by reducing the number of immigrants to the province?

Geography has blessed Quebec in many ways. The St Lawrence Lowlands provides both an agricultural and industrial heartland, with the St Lawrence River facilitating its exports to the rest of the world and imports to North America. As an additional benefit, the Canadian Shield, located in the province's north, contains an exceptional combination of water and topography uniquely suitable for producing hydroelectric power.

Since Confederation, Quebec and Ontario served as the core of Canada's manufacturing industry. In more recent times, Canada's manufacturing industry has been in retreat. Quebec's grip on its share of the economy, as measured by GDP, had softened but now shows signs of revitalization. While the province retains its place as the second-ranked region in terms of population size, its economy trails the resource-based economy found in Western Canada. Yet Quebec has taken the first steps towards a knowledge-based economy with the rapid expansion of its

← Quebec City is one of the oldest European settlements in North America. The district of Old Quebec City captures the historic essence of the region and has been designated a UNESCO World Heritage Site.

digital industry. While two of its traditional spearheads—Bombardier and SNC-Lavalin—hit a rough patch, Hydro-Québec and digital firms, such as Stingray, Lightspeed POS Inc., and Stradigi AI have moved the economic yardsticks forward. Then too, the breakdown in supplies of medical equipment from China has caused the Canadian government to support domestic manufacturing of key medical products. Medicom, a manufacturer and distributor of medical-grade personal protection equipment, plans to manufacture such products in Canada. Most importantly, Hydro-Québec provides low-cost energy rates for homes, business, and industry, plus a sizable dividend to the province each year. As a legacy from the Quiet Revolution of the early 1960s, Hydro-Québec is a Québécois success story and a demonstration of engineering and business know-how by Quebecers.

## Quebec's Place within Canada

Quebec remains the second most important geographic region in Canada. However, its share of the national economy and population has slipped over the years. In 1961, Quebec's share of the national population was 29 per cent, but by 2020 it had slipped to 23 per cent (Figure 7.1). This downward trend is predicted to continue. By 2040, the Conference Board of Canada (2020) predicts that this share will fall to 21 per cent. In a similar fashion, Quebec's share of the national economy has fallen to third place, behind Ontario and Western Canada. On the other hand, the province's economy enjoyed a short-term economic boom from 2016 to 2019; but will that trend continue into the next decade? The boom was largely a product of its exploding digital economy. As Eric Boyko, chief executive of Montreal-based entertainment company Stingray Group Inc. (Carmichael, 2019), observed:

A decade ago, the very public shrinking of Bombardier Inc. and SNC-Lavalin Group Inc. would have caused considerable fear and loathing. Today, with the exception of the shareholders of those two companies, I'm not sure many people care. There are far more jobs on offer than there are qualified workers to fill them.

Yet, this growth based on technology may slow as Quebec plans to reduce the number of immigrants. Both economic and population growth are linked to immigration. This downward trend is due to relatively low immigration figures compared to other parts of Canada. For instance, the population gains taking place in Western Canada easily outstrip those in Quebec (Figure 7.3). In 1966, the population of Quebec was 5.8 million compared to 3.4 million in Western Canada, a gap of 2.4 million (Statistics Canada, 2009). By 2019, this gap had narrowed to 1.5 million (Statistics Canada, 2020b).

## Solving the Dilemma

Quebec wants rapid economic and population growth. Such growth flows from a vigorous immigration policy. At the same time, the preservation of the French language and its Québécois culture is foremost in the mind of the provincial government of François Legault. The solutions are to increase

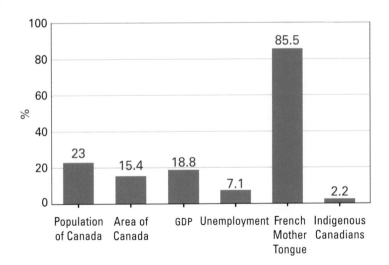

**FIGURE 7.1 Quebec basic statistics, 2016**

By population size, Quebec remains the second-ranking geographic region in Canada, though Western Canada and British Columbia are quickly narrowing this demographic gap. Its economy now ranks third behind those of Ontario and Western Canada. Quebec remains a French-speaking province.

Sources: Stastics Canada, 2019b.

immigration from French-speaking countries, select those who meet the needs of the labour market, and/or to encourage others to learn French. The premier's political answer in 2019 was **Bill 9**. This bill amends the Quebec Immigration Act by expressing three goals designed to integrate newcomers into Quebec:

- competence in French;
- familiarity with its democratic/secular values; and
- recognition of the Quebec Charter of Human Rights and Freedom.

In the short run, Quebec has reduced the number of economic immigrants. In 2018, the figure was 50,000; in 2019, it was 40,000 (Laforest, 2020). In the long run, such a policy could restrict economic growth and slow population increase. While the province has identified a short-term solution, will it be a sustainable policy over the long run?

## Quebec's Culture, Identity, and Language

Following the founding in 1608 of the first European settlement at Quebec City by Samuel de Champlain, settlers came from France to the St Lawrence Valley. Over the centuries, their ancestors made this corner of North America a homeland for the French-speaking people. La Fête nationale du Quebec (Saint-Jean Baptiste Day, the national holiday of Quebec) celebrates this accomplishment on 24 June each year. However, the road has not always been easy or pleasant, and the collective memory often recalls humiliations and resistance as well as hard-fought victories. Anxieties exist, and these are embodied in the collective memory. Quebec separatism is one response to that fear while another is Confederation, which allocates selective powers to provinces and, in a few cases, a special role to Quebec normally reserved for the federal government. One example is membership in La Francophonie, normally restricted to national governments. Another is immigration. Quebec has the power to control and manage immigration. Immigration, so necessary for Quebec to keep its population increasing, has resulted in a more diverse population where religious rights have become an issue (see Vignette 7.1). In June 2019, the Quebec government passed **Bill 21**, which restricts individuals from wearing religious symbols, such as hijabs, kippas, and turbans, in the public sector. This bill has sparked widespread debate over discrimination and **reasonable accommodation** of immigrants in Quebec.

The French language, Québécois culture, and a Québécois identity have generated a strong sense of belonging among the majority of Quebec citizens, forming the basis of ethnic pride, loyalty, and nationalism, which from time to time fuels the desire for an independent political state. Such feelings are particularly strong among the "old stock"—the descendants of some 10,000 settlers who migrated from France in the seventeenth and eighteenth centuries—but are less strong among anglophones and allophones. While the desire for separation has subsided, a political divorce is still on the minds of the few remaining hardcore separatists.

**THINK ABOUT IT**
Demography has political implications. One example is the number of seats in the federal House of Commons, which are determined largely by population size with minor adjustments—the **grandfather** and **senatorial** clauses—to accommodate historic factors.

## Vignette 7.1

### The Quiet Revolution and Natural Rate of Population Increase

Quebec's natural rate of population increase dropped dramatically following the Quiet Revolution. At that time, the Québécois began the transformation into a more secular society. No longer in the grip of the Roman Catholic Church, birth control measures became widespread, causing the birth rate to drop. For example, prior to 1960, Quebec had the highest birth rates in Canada, sometimes referred to as "the revenge of the cradles" (*la revanche des berceaux*). In 2018, the fertility rate of 1.59 was well below the replacement level of 2.1 (Girard, 2019). This demographic reality and a high immigration rate are creating a more diverse population, especially in Montreal.

For a more complete discussion of the historic origins of the concept of a political partnership, see "One Country, Two Visions" in Chapter 3, page 107.

**FIGURE 7.2 Language anxiety**

The maelstrom that erupted over Pastagate in 2013—when a language inspector told a Montreal Italian restaurant owner that words on the menu such as *botiglia*, *pasta*, and *antipasto* must have French translations—may seem trivial to those living outside of Quebec, but the since-resolved incident still reflects the sensitivity of the francophones to the anglicization of French in Quebec. Yet, this sensitivity is not new, and its roots go back to the British Conquest of New France in 1759 and to Lord Durham, who in 1838 recommended the linguistic assimilation of French-speaking subjects in its North American colony. With that language threat deeply embedded in the minds of the Québécois, the French language forms an indispensable defence against assimilation into English-speaking Canada and, for that matter, Anglo-America.

Source: Brian Gable/The Globe and Mail

For a brief account of John Ralston Saul's concept of Canada, see "Faultlines within Canada" in Chapter 1, page 7. For a broader historic discussion of two competing visions of Canada, see "Quebec's Place in Confederation" in Chapter 3, page 103, and "French/ English Language Imbalance" in Chapter 4, page 138.

Most Québécois place their first loyalty to Quebec but within Confederation.

Quebec's culture is largely derived from the historical experience of **francophones** living in North America for over 400 years and of their being part of Canada for more than 150 years. Clearly, Quebec's sense of place and identity is based on its struggle to survive within an English-speaking North America. The decision to join Confederation has had both benefits and costs. Confederation provides a safe place within North America, though relations between French- and English-speaking Quebecers have been strained from time to time. The resolution of these occasional disagreements has led to a type of federation built on compromise. This complex concept of compromise helps to defuse tensions between French- and English-speaking Quebecers. As a living, dynamic concept, "compromising" federalism continues to evolve and shape Quebec society.

"La Belle Province," while home to the largest francophone population outside of France, contains a minority composed of **anglophones**, whose mother tongue is English, and **allophones**, immigrants whose mother tongue is neither English nor French. These highly diverse minorities are concentrated in Montreal and Gatineau, across the Ottawa River from the nation's capital. The **Québécois** whose first language is French represent the dominant demographic force in the province, but their percentage of the total Canadian population continues to shrink (Vignette 7.2). The remaining Quebecers include Indigenous peoples, whose mother tongues include Cree, Inuktitut, and Innu-aimun. In northern Quebec, Cree, Inuit, and Innu (Naskapi) form the majority in most communities, where they tend to speak their native language, English, and French in that order. From time to time, social tensions surface between the French-speaking majority and the province's minority groups as the Québécois continue to assert their desire to be *"maîtres chez nous."*

## Quebec's Physical Geography

Quebec, the largest province in Canada, has a wide range of natural conditions and physiographic regions. Its climate varies from the mild continental climate in the St Lawrence Valley to the cold Arctic climate found in **Nunavik** (Inuit lands lying north of the fifty-fifth parallel). Four of Canada's physiographic regions extend over the province's territory—the Hudson Bay Lowlands, the Canadian Shield, the Appalachian Uplands (Photo 7.3), and the Great Lakes–St Lawrence Lowlands—and each has a different resource base and settlement pattern (Figure 6.4). The Canadian Shield extends over most of Quebec—close to 90 per cent—while the Appalachian Uplands and Great Lakes–St Lawrence Lowlands together form nearly 10 per cent. By far the smallest physiographic region is the Hudson Bay Lowlands, which constitutes less than 1 per cent of Quebec's land mass and where very few people live.

The heartland of Quebec is the St Lawrence Lowland. Formed from the Champlain Sea some 10,000 years ago, this physiographic region provides

PHOTO 7.1 On the historic Plains of Abraham, Quebec City hosts Canada's largest outdoor summer musical event, Festival d'été de Québec.

the best agricultural land in Quebec. Settlers from France began farming along the edge of the St Lawrence River some 400 years ago. New France was established within this region and, by means of the St Lawrence, spread into the interior of North America (Vignette 7.3). It remains the cultural and economic core of Quebec.

In "Information Society and Innovative Clusters," **Chapter 5**, page 161, Florida's theory is discussed within the broader context of the information/knowledge society.

## Contested Terrain 7.1

### *Maîtres Chez Nous*

Since the Quiet Revolution, the Quebec government has passed legislation to take control of the economy and, in doing so, strengthen the role of the Québécois. The creation of the Hydro-Québec monopoly was one such step while another was Bill 101, the Charter of the French Language. Bill 101, passed in 1977, limited the use of English in order to preserve the French language. Since then, the government has continued to revise and tighten the legislation designed to protect the French language. One example is the Office québécois de la langue française, whose role is to identify and eliminate commercial signs using English (Figure 7.2). Even so, Quebec nationalists want more restrictions on the use of English (Lemay, 2010). On the other hand, the business community fears that the language policy has already turned Quebec into a "hermit state," isolating Quebec but particularly Montreal from Canada and the rest of the world (Jarislowsky, 2012, p. A19; Aubin, 2013). Without a doubt, balancing the two perspectives, that is, protecting the French language without alienating business, represents a formidable challenge for the Quebec government. In the ideal world described by Richard Florida, talented people would move to Montreal and other urban centres in Quebec to stimulate the province's knowledge-based economy, but at the same time accommodate themselves to the French language and Quebec culture.

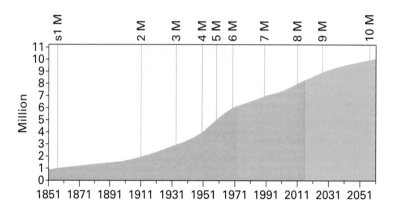

**FIGURE 7.3 Population of Quebec, 1851–2016, and projected population, 2021–2061**

In 2016, the Canadian census reported that the population of Quebec had reached 8.2 million and its population is projected to reach 10 million by 2061. From 2016 to 2061, the projected population growth is low, a consequence of two important demographic features: (1) the annual natural increase is expected to continue to decline; (2) the annual number of immigrants is likely to drop well below its peak of 56,000 in 2013 due to more restrictive government policies announced in 2019.

Source: Institut de la statistique du Quebec (2016: 10-12)

Aerial Archives/Alamy Stock Photo

**PHOTO 7.2** The Port of Montreal (2020) is a major container port. In 2018, nearly half of its container traffic came from the European Union. With the Comprehensive Economic and Trade Agreement (CETA) between Canada and the European Union in effect provisionally since September 2017 (awaiting full ratification by some European countries to the agreement), container traffic has been expected to increase significantly. Montreal has two geographical advantages over competing ports. First, it is close to major markets in Ontario and the US Midwest. Second, container traffic can reach Chicago and other cities on the Great Lakes by lower-cost lake transport. However, as container ships have increased in size, docking in Montreal's relatively shallow harbour has made this port less competitive with Atlantic ports, including Halifax.

## Vignette 7.2

### Demography Has Political Consequences

As Canada's population increases, the number of Canadians in each of the six regions has increased—but at different rates. In the twenty-first century, Quebec's rate of population is below the national average. Only Atlantic Canada has had lower rates. The political consequence for Quebec has been twofold: more seats but a lower proportion of the total seats in the House of Commons.[1] By comparing the number of seats in the House of Commons in 2000 and 2019, the degree of erosion of its political power is revealed. In 2000, Quebec had 75 seats that formed 24.9 per cent of the 301 seats in the House of Commons. By the 2019 federal election, Quebec had more three more seats for a total of 78 seats. Yet, its percentage of seats fell to 23.1 per cent of the 338 seats in the House of Commons.

## Vignette 7.3

### The St Lawrence River

The St Lawrence River provides a natural waterway into the interior of North America and, consequently, played a key role in the history of New France. After the construction of the St Lawrence Seaway in 1959, ocean ships could sail into the Great Lakes by making use of a series of locks, such as the eight locks on the Welland Canal that are managed by the St Lawrence Seaway Management Corporation. The St Lawrence Seaway is an essential part of North America's transportation system and links Quebec to North America's manufacturing belt. Cities along its shores from Sept-Îles to Montreal have benefited greatly from the waterway's role as a major shipping route. Montreal's favourable location on the St Lawrence (Photo 7.2 and Figure 7.4) gives it an economic advantage and fuels the city's growth.

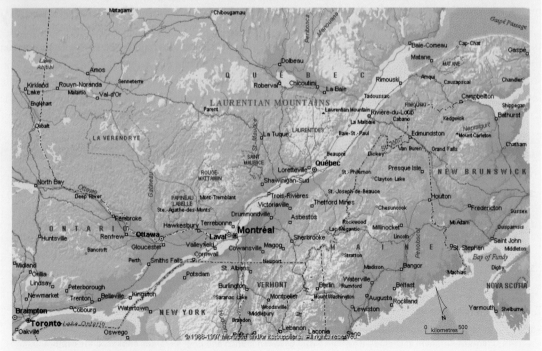

**FIGURE 7.4  The St Lawrence River**

Paul Hebert, Biodiversity Institute of Ontario. At: www.aquatic.uoguelph.ca/rivers/stlawmap.htm.

The Appalachian Uplands physiographic region is an extension of the Appalachian Mountains, which stretch northward from the state of Georgia. While this ancient geological feature reaches into Quebec and Atlantic Canada, its topography is much subdued and consists more of rugged hills and rolling plains. Most arable land in this region is in **Estrie**, where dairy farming prevails. Tourism has become an important source of income during summer on the Gaspé Peninsula. Mining and forestry are other economic activities in the region. With the exception of the Lake Champlain gap in the Appalachian Uplands, easy road access to the populous parts of New England is blocked by these rugged uplands. The Lake Champlain gap has therefore become a very important north–south transportation link between Montreal and points south in the US, especially New York City.

As the largest physiographic region in Quebec, the Canadian Shield is noted for its forest products and hydroelectric production—it has most of the hydroelectric sites in Canada because of a combination of heavy precipitation, large rivers, and significant changes in elevation. Beyond the **commercial forest** zone lie the lands of the Cree and Inuit, where the Cree must coexist with the massive La Grande hydro project. The Quebec government supports a hunting-and-trapping program, thus encouraging many Cree families to stay on the land. This program has important cultural and social values. In Arctic Quebec, a number of Inuit settlements are found along the coasts of Hudson Bay and Hudson Strait. In the Subarctic, near the

The geographic extent of Quebec's four climatic zones are shown in **Figure 2.5**, "Climatic zones of Canada," page 38.

Quebec–Labrador border, upward of 15,000 Innu live in nine communities.

With four climatic zones in Quebec, weather varies greatly. The four zones are Arctic, Subarctic, Atlantic, and Great Lakes–St Lawrence. The Subarctic climate zone extends over 60 per cent of Quebec, followed in extent by the Arctic, Great Lakes–St Lawrence, and Atlantic zones. The weather across Quebec falls within a predictable range for each climatic zone, but, like other regions of Canada, Quebec has had its share of extreme weather events, including the worst ice storm in Canadian history in 1998. More recently, the concern has become spring flooding. Heavy winter snowfall and warm spring temperatures combine to cause severe flooding, with 2017 and 2019 representing two of the worst flood years on record, and climate change expected to increase the risk of flooding in the future. In 2019, the Quebec government responded by identifying high-risk flood zones. The implication for those who own property in these zones is huge: it has reduced their property values, made home insurance either impossible or extremely costly, and restricted the rebuilding of flood-damaged houses (Harrold, 2019).

## Quebec's Historical Geography

Relative to some other parts of North America, the history of European settlement in Quebec is long, rich, and complicated by the period of British rule and then by the search for a place within Confederation (see Tables 7.1–7.3). Beneath the surface of

### TABLE 7.1   Timeline: Historical Milestones in New France

| Year | Geographic Significance |
|---|---|
| 1534 | Jacques Cartier sails into the Bay of Chaleur and claims the land for France. The following year, Cartier discovers the mouth of the St Lawrence River, which provides access to the interior of North America. |
| 1608 | Samuel de Champlain, described as the "Father of New France," founds a fur-trading post near the site of Quebec City. Champlain was instrumental in the development of the fur economy, which provided the initial economic basis for New France. |
| 1642 | Paul de Chomedey de Maisonneuve establishes Ville-Marie on Île de Montréal, which is strategically situated at the confluence of the Ottawa and St Lawrence rivers. Later, Ville-Marie was renamed Montreal. |
| 1701 | La Grande Paix de Montréal is proclaimed between New France and 40 First Nations surrounding the colony of New France. |
| 1759 | The struggle between France and England over North America sees the British defeat the French army on the Plains of Abraham at Quebec. The final battle between French and English forces ends with the capture of Montreal by the British. In 1763, the formal surrender of New France to England takes place with the Treaty of Paris. |

**TABLE 7.2 Timeline: Historical Milestones in the British Colony of Lower Canada**

| Year | Geographic Significance |
|---|---|
| 1763 | The Treaty of Paris awards New France to Great Britain. |
| 1774 | The British Parliament passes the Quebec Act, which recognizes that Quebec, as a British colony, has special rights, including use of the French language, the Catholic religion, and French civil law (see Figure 7.5). |
| 1791 | The British Parliament approves the Constitutional Act that creates two colonies in British North America called Upper Canada and Lower Canada. |
| 1841 | Based on the report of Lord Durham following the failed rebellions in Lower and Upper Canada of 1837 and 1838, the British Parliament passes the Act of Union that reunites the Canadas into a single colony and makes English the official language of the newly formed Province of Canada. |

**TABLE 7.3 Timeline: Historical Milestones for Quebec in Confederation**

| Year | Geographic Significance |
|---|---|
| 1867 | The Dominion of Canada is formed, the new state consisting of Quebec, Ontario, New Brunswick, and Nova Scotia. |
| 1898 | Ottawa extends Quebec's northern boundary to the Eastmain River, thus expanding Quebec's territory well beyond its core area of the St Lawrence Lowland into the Cree lands of James Bay in the Canadian Shield. |
| 1912 | Ottawa adds the Territory of Ungava to Quebec, thus extending Quebec to the Inuit lands of Nunavik. With the addition of these two northern areas in 1898 and 1912, Quebec's territory more than doubles. |
| 1927 | In settling a dispute between Canada and Newfoundland, Britain rejects Canada's claim that the boundary should be placed just inland from the shore. Instead, Britain declares that the boundary is to follow the Hudson Bay and Atlantic Ocean watersheds. Quebec does not recognize this boundary. |
| 1960 | The Quiet Revolution begins, transforming Quebec into a secular society with a prominent role for the provincial government in business and cultural matters. |

this search lies the deeply fractured French/English faultline. Quebec's historical geography can be divided into three periods: New France, British occupation, and Confederation.

## New France, 1608–1760

The introduction of North America to the French began in 1534 when Jacques Cartier sailed into the Bay of Chaleur and set foot on the shores of the Gaspé Peninsula. The first permanent French settlement in Quebec was established in 1608, when Samuel de Champlain founded a fur-trading post at the site of Quebec City, thus establishing a French colony in North America. Over three decades, on foot and by ship and canoe, Champlain explored the continent through what are now six Canadian provinces and five American states, and by doing so he created the territorial basis for the French Empire in North America. Although France eventually lost its North American colony, it left a cultural legacy in the form of the French language and the Catholic

**PHOTO 7.3** Estrie, formerly called the Eastern Townships, lies in the Appalachian Uplands physiographic region. Dairy farms are found in the rolling countryside, which is surrounded by wooded uplands. Hay is the principal crop and is used as feed for dairy cows.

Clara Parsons/Valan Photos

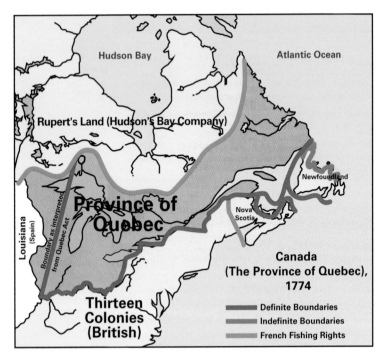

**FIGURE 7.5  Map of British North America, 1774**

The Quebec Act (1774) defined the lands of the Province of Quebec, which approximated the drainage basin of most of the St Lawrence River. What is now northern Quebec was part of Rupert's Land, a territory granted by the British Crown to the Hudson's Bay Company and defined by the watershed of the rivers flowing into Hudson Bay. At that time (1774), the Louisiana Territory (land west of the Mississippi River to the Rocky Mountains) was claimed by Spain.

Source: https://en.wikipedia.org/wiki/Constitutional_history_of_Canada

France to enjoy their good fortune. Others remained in the fur trade or settled in New France.

Geography played a part in New France's success both as a fur-trading empire and as an agricultural colony. The St Lawrence River provided a route to the interior, which gave the French explorers and fur traders an advantage over their English rivals, who had to contend with crossing the Appalachian Mountains or, in Canada after 1670, ply the trade further north through Hudson Bay. The famous French explorer, René-Robert Cavelier, Sieur de La Salle, reached the mouth of the Mississippi River at New Orleans in 1682. Early in the eighteenth century, French fur traders, led by Pierre Gaultier de Varennes, Sieur de La Vérendrye, established a series of fur-trading posts in Manitoba.

New France also established a successful agricultural society based on the seigneurial system. Once the land was cleared, the fertile soils in the St Lawrence Lowland provided a solid basis for essentially agricultural settlement. Farming took hold in New France, particularly following the efforts of Jean Talon (1626–94), the greatest administrator of New France.

### The Seigneurial System

When the first intendant of New France, Jean Talon, arrived in New France in 1665, he encountered a population of only 3,000 inhabitants, most of whom were men engaged in the fur trade. Talon had been instructed by Louis XIV to create a feudal agricultural society resembling that of rural France in the seventeenth century. Talon undertook three measures to achieve this goal. First, he recruited peasants from France. Second, he sent for young women—orphaned girls and daughters of poor families in France—to provide wives for the men of the colony. Third, he imposed the French feudal system of landownership, known as the seigneurial system. In the seigneurial system, huge tracts of land were granted to those favoured by the king, namely, the nobility, religious institutions of the Roman Catholic Church, military officers, and high-ranking government officials. The seigneur was obliged to swear allegiance to the king and to have his tenants cultivate the lands on his estate. In exchange for use of the land, the tenants owed certain obligations to their seigneur: paying

religion, and a French stamp on the landscape with its seigneurial landownership system.

During the seventeenth and eighteenth centuries, France had control over vast areas of North America. Its core, however, was the St Lawrence Valley, from which New France developed a vast fur-trading empire. The wealth from the fur trade was enormous and was the reason for France's interest in the New World. Almost every male French settler wanted to participate in the fur trade, which left only a few to clear the forest and till the land. Indeed, several canoes full of beaver pelts could make a man extremely wealthy compared with the meagre returns obtained from the back-breaking toil of clearing land and breaking the soil. Frenchmen who were *coureurs de bois* (fur traders; literally, "runners of the woods") often lived with Indigenous peoples. A few were extremely successful and returned to

yearly dues (*cens et rentes*) to their seigneur; working the seigneur's land, especially in regard to road maintenance (*corvée*); and paying rent for using the seigneur's grinding mill and bake ovens (*droit de banalité*).

By 1760, there were approximately 200 seigneuries. Seigneuries, which were usually 1 by 3 leagues (5 by 15 km) in size, were generally divided into river lots (*rangs*). These long, rectangular lots were well adapted to the St Lawrence Valley for several reasons, the most important of which was that each habitant had access to a river, either a tributary of the St Lawrence or the river itself. At that time, most people and goods were transported along the river system in New France. For that reason, river access was vital for each habitant family. The seigneurial system was abolished in 1854 by the legislature of the Province of Canada, but its long, narrow lots still mark the landscape.

## British Colony, 1760–1867

Following the defeat of the French, the British ruled Quebec for over 100 years. The British governor was installed at Quebec City along with a regiment of British troops, while the fur trade continued to flourish and the seigneurial system went unchanged. Most French Canadians were peasant farmers. After the Conquest of New France by the British, their life on the land remained much the same. Their social and economic lives revolved around the parish church and a landholding system centred on the seigneuries. Life in the towns and cities, however, changed radically due to a massive influx of British immigrants, the powerful political position of English Canadians, and their control of the commercial and industrial sectors of urban places. The saving grace for the Canadiens was their high fertility rate (*la revanche des berceaux*). By 1851, French Canadians accounted for only about half of the population of Montreal. From 1851 to 1951, the French Canadians increased their share of Montreal's population to form the majority. This growth was largely the result of an influx of Canadiens from rural Quebec, where land shortages forced many to seek work in Montreal, and from other urban areas, and to a lesser degree resulted from the slowing of immigrants from the British Isles.

Land hunger forced many French Canadians to migrate. By the middle of the nineteenth century, many had left the St Lawrence Lowland due to a land shortage. French Canadians migrated in three directions: to the Appalachian Uplands east and south of Montreal (the Eastern Townships, now known as Estrie), where they either purchased farms from English-speaking farmers or found jobs in textile mills; to the Canadian Shield, where they tried to exist on extremely marginal agricultural land; or to New England's industrial towns, where most were employed in textile factories. By the early twentieth century large numbers of French Canadians, perhaps as many as 1 million, had left Quebec for the United States, while only a small number settled in the Canadian West, which was calling out for homesteaders.

By the 1830s, political unrest was growing in both Upper and Lower Canada. A British governor appointed in England ruled each colony with the assistance of wealthy members of the community. This cozy arrangement not only concentrated power in the hands of a few but also led to blatant abuse by powerful elites. In Upper Canada, the political elite was known as the Family Compact; in Lower Canada it was the Château Clique. In 1837, rebellions broke out in each colony (Vignette 7.4). The British army crushed both rebellions.

Following the rebellions, the British government sent Lord Durham to British North America to seek a political solution. Durham recommended an elected rather than an appointed government, where power was dispersed among elected representatives rather than concentrated within an appointed elite. Durham also observed the French/English faultline, which he described as "two nations warring in the bosom of a single state." In his report, Durham recommended responsible (elected) government and the union of English-speaking people in Upper Canada with the French-speaking settlers of Lower Canada.[2] Lord Durham believed that assimilation of the French was desirable and possible, claiming that the French Canadians were "a people with no literature and no history" (Mills, 1988, p. 637). He recommended that English be the sole language of a new Province of Canada, and that a massive immigration of English-speaking settlers be launched

## Vignette 7.4

### The Rebellions of 1837–8

Louis-Joseph Papineau, a lawyer, seigneur, and politician, was the leader of the French-speaking majority in the Assembly of Lower Canada. Papineau had fought with the British forces against the invading American army at Chateauguay in 1812. A strong supporter of the Church and the seigneurial system, Papineau was a leading political figure of the Patriotes. In 1834, Papineau issued a list of grievances known as "The Ninety-Two Resolutions." At this time, the economy was depressed and tensions between the French-Canadian majority and the British minority were growing. Papineau sought to shift political power from the British authorities to the elected Assembly of Lower Canada. He planned to use his majority in the Assembly to pass legislation, including tax bills. The British government rejected his resolutions, and it was just a matter of time before an armed uprising broke out. When it did, the British reacted with force. Even with the strong support of rural areas, Papineau and his Patriotes were soundly defeated. Nearly 300 rebels were killed in six battles. Papineau fled to the United States, but in 1845 he was granted amnesty and returned to Quebec. Following a second uprising in Lower Canada in November 1838, the British captured hundreds of rebels and ultimately 12 men were sentenced and executed and another 58 were exiled to Australia (Bumsted, 2007, p. 169). A rebellion based on the same popular objections to elite rule also took place in Upper Canada in 1837, and it, too, was crushed. The British government sought to remedy the unrest in both of its colonies. It began this process with a fact-finding mission headed by Lord Durham. The result was the Act of Union in 1841.

to create an English majority in Lower Canada. In response to Durham's recommendations, the British Parliament passed the Act of Union in 1841, uniting the two colonies into the Province of Canada and creating a single elected assembly.

## From Confederation to the Quiet Revolution

Confederation, achieved in 1867, sought to unite two cultures—English and French—within a British parliamentary system. For Quebec, Confederation provided a political framework offering three benefits: an economic union with Ontario, Nova Scotia, and New Brunswick; a political environment where Roman Catholicism and, to a lesser degree, the French language were guaranteed protection by Ottawa; and provincial control over education and language. George-Étienne Cartier, one of the Fathers of Confederation and a French-Canadian leader, viewed these provincial powers as a way for Quebec to shape its own destiny within Confederation. Cartier

may have identified a fourth benefit—since Quebec and Ontario often had mutual economic interests, they could, by working together, influence federal policies and thereby shape the future of Canada.

Confederation also led to the expansion of the geographic size of Quebec (Figures 3.5 and 3.7). Since Confederation, Quebec's geographic size has increased greatly. It is now 1.5 million km². As Canada acquired more territory from the British government, Ottawa assigned to Quebec parts of Rupert's Land lying north of the St Lawrence drainage basin. In 1898, the Quebec government received the first block of Rupert's Land. The second was obtained in 1912.[3] Some of this land, however, was claimed by the British colony of Newfoundland. In its argument, Newfoundland demanded all of Quebec's territory that drained into the Atlantic Ocean. Though the British Privy Council awarded this land, known as Labrador, to Newfoundland in 1927 (Figure 3.7), to this day the Quebec government does not recognize the decision. As former Premier Jean Charest said in September 2008, "This is a traditional position that all governments have reiterated. There is a boundary line on which there is no agreement" (Robitaille, 2008).

Beyond the political benefits of Confederation, Canada provided the economic environment for the rapid growth of manufacturing in Quebec, but especially in Montreal. The key federal legislation was based on Prime Minister Macdonald's National Policy. In the early days, most manufacturing took place in Montreal and involved clothing and textiles. These firms were largely owned and operated by English-speaking Canadians. At Confederation, Montreal was the major metropolis and financial capital of Canada. Many of the country's largest companies and banks were headquartered in Montreal: the Canadian Pacific Railway, the Grand Trunk Railway, the Molson Bank, the Bank of Montreal, the Merchants' Bank, and the Bank of British North America. Montreal served as the primary port for trade with Britain and the United States.

## The Quiet Revolution

In 1960, the Quiet Revolution unleashed the forces of change that drove Quebec into a modern secular industrial society. Within that society, the state plays a key role. The election of the Liberal government of Jean Lesage marked a dramatic transformation in government, French-Canadian society, and the place of French within Quebec. His government initiated major political innovations that accelerated the process of social and economic change. In effect, the provincial government replaced the Catholic Church as the leader and protector of French culture and language in Quebec. The Quiet Revolution instilled a sense of pride and accomplishment among Quebecers. The main reforms of the Lesage government were hinged on state intervention in the Quebec economy through Crown corporations, and on the expansion of a French-speaking provincial civil service. The government's principal achievements were:

- nationalization of private electrical companies to form a public one, known as Hydro-Québec;
- modernization and secularization of the education system, making it accessible to all;

- investment of Quebec Pension Plan funds in Quebec firms, thereby stimulating the francophone business sector;
- establishment of Maisons du Quebec (quasi-embassies) in Paris, London, and New York, thus signalling to Ottawa that the Quebec government wanted to represent Quebec interests to the rest of the world.

With these accomplishments behind them, Quebecers felt confident about their future. Lesage's 1963 campaign slogan, *"Maîtres chez nous"* (Masters in our own house), became a reality. For federalists in Quebec, these achievements proved that a strong Quebec could function within Canada, but for separatists they were not enough. The rise of separatism in Quebec signalled that some Québécois felt only an independent Quebec could adequately represent French-Canadian interests. For them the slogan became *"Le Québec aux Québécois"* (Quebec for the Québécois). After two referendums, Quebecers have, for the time being, turned away from pursuing political separation and are focusing on gaining more economic and social powers from Ottawa. Then, too, Quebec nationalism, which is at the core of the separatist movement, has shifted somewhat from the goals and values of the older generation of francophones and has become more inclusive, i.e., embracing all French-speaking Quebecers, including immigrants (allophones) and bilingual anglophones. Even the federal government has referred to Quebec as a "nation" within Canada. Nonetheless, philosophical and jurisdictional disagreements are never far from the surface in the relationship between Quebec and Ottawa.

## Quebec Today

Quebec, a modern industrial society operating within a francophone environment, lies in Canada's heartland. While Quebec and Ontario have long served as a manufacturing core within Canada, both are striving to gain a secure foothold in the knowledge-based economy where technology is transforming traditional economic activities into a much more automated and digitized

**THINK ABOUT IT**

Why do Quebec governments, regardless of political affiliation, advocate a vision of Canada as a "partnership" between founding peoples?

For more on the Quiet Revolution, see **Chapter 3**, "Resurgence of Quebec Nationalism," page 109.

Discussion of "Quebec's Place in Confederation" in **Chapter 3**, page 103, includes more information on the historic twists and turns to Quebec's place within British North America and then within Confederation.

system. Until recently, the province has seen its place within Canada diminished mainly because its economic growth rate had fallen below the national average. In the late twentieth century, globalization of trade squeezed its manufacturing sector, resulting in the loss of many jobs. First, Quebec's clothing and textiles industry, which historically accounted for well over half of all Canadian production, felt the pinch early on as freer trade led to "the gradual elimination of import quotas and tariffs" (Finances Quebec, 2005). Second, Quebec was affected by two trade agreements. In 1995, the establishment of the World Trade Organization opened the floodgates to manufactured products from countries where labour costs were substantially lower. For Quebec's clothing and textiles industry, the loss of trade barriers meant the end of their dominant role within the Canadian market. The final blow came in 2001 when China joined the WTO and many thousands of jobs in Quebec's manufacturing sector

disappeared, only to resurface in China and other low-wage countries.

Yet, culture might trump the economy—or at least add to its vibrancy. Without a doubt, the francophone cultural world is one of Quebec's economic strengths. Following Richard Florida's thesis that creative people crave a vibrant arts community, Quebec's film industry has a worldwide reputation and its music community, ranging from popular to classical music, ranks highly within Canada and North America (Photo 7.4). Montreal provides the cultural and economic leadership so vital to the province's renaissance. After all, Montreal today, reflecting a bilingual and multicultural Canada, is a confident metropolis of close to 2 million people with an urban area population of over 4 million, shaped by the prominence of the French language, the forcefulness of its digitized businesses, and the unrelenting demand for skilled immigrants to drive its ever-evolving knowledge-based economy.

What does the future hold for Quebec? Can it reinvent itself as a knowledge-based economy? Its industrial structure helps to answer these questions, while the leading businesses provide another lens for understanding Quebec's present and future. Yet, the divide between urban and rural Quebec focuses on the recruitment of high-tech immigrants necessary to fuel a vibrant urban knowledge-based economy.

## Quebec's Economy

Quebec's economy ranks third in the country, comprising 23 per cent of the national GDP. While the St Lawrence River provides the advantage of low-cost water transportation to and from Europe, Quebec's economy has lagged behind Ontario, Western Canada, and British Columbia. Robert Hogue, senior economist with the Royal Bank of Canada, described Quebec's economy in 2016 as "in the slow lane" (Hogue, 2016, p. 7). But by 2019, Hogue recognized an end to Quebec's economic underperformance (Hogue, 2019). One sign of this resurgence was the drop in unemployment rates and the sharp increase in job openings in the technology sector. The shortage of skilled workers has

**PHOTO 7.4** Montreal has many fine facilities for the arts. The Maison Symphonique, situated in the Place-des-Arts cultural hub in the city's east downtown, is one such facility. The Maison Symphonique has many special features; most importantly, the music hall, with its exceptional acoustics, represents a feat of sound engineering (Dick-Agnew, 2011). Its urban access is outstanding as it is just metres from a subway line and ample underground parking exists for those travelling by car.

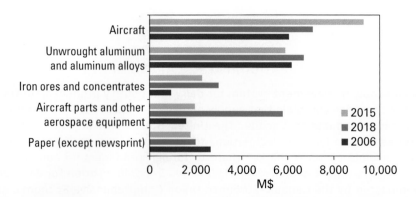

**FIGURE 7.6 Major export products from Quebec, 2006, 2015, and 2018 (millions of $)**

Aircraft and aircraft parts represented the leading export by value, making up 14 per cent of 2018 Quebec exports, which totalled $92.3 billion. The next largest exports by value were aluminum and iron ore. In 2018, the United States once again received the bulk (70 per cent) of Quebec's exports while China was the second-most important destination, at 6 per cent.

Source: Statistics Canada and Institut de la statistique du Québec (2019a).

prompted the Quebec government to increase the percentage of immigrants classified as in the economic sector and to reduce those from the refugee category. In this way, the Coalition Avenir Québec government reached its two goals: to reduce the number of immigrants by 20 per cent, but at the same time to satisfy the demand for more skilled workers (Sucar, 2019).

Quebec's exports account for a substantial share of Canada's high-tech exports in aerospace, biotechnology, information technologies, pharmaceuticals, and rail transportation (Figure 7.6). Equally important, the province has its share of high-tech start-up businesses, largely in Greater Montreal. Stingray Digital, for example, is now a global player in the digital music services field. But the real mark of this technology revolution lies in the field of artificial intelligence (AI).

## Industrial Structure

In 2019, Quebec had a population of more than 8.5 million, with 4.3 million workers who made up just under 23 per cent of Canada's labour force (Table 7.4). In the core region, the percentages of workers in the three sectors comprising Quebec's industrial structure are, as would be expected, very similar to those found in Ontario (see Table 6.1). In 2019, Quebec's primary sector accounted for just over 3 per cent of workers (mostly in agriculture), 18.2 per cent were in the secondary sector (mostly in manufacturing), and close to 80 per cent were in tertiary activities. International trade agreements—most notably, the new version of NAFTA—have benefited certain sectors of the economy, while others have not fared so well. Dairy farmers, some might say, were put at a disadvantage

## TABLE 7.4 Quebec Industrial Sectors by Number of Workers, 2005 and 2019

| Industrial Sector | Workers, 2005 | Workers, 2005 (%) | Workers, 2019 | Workers, 2019 (%) | Percentage Difference |
|---|---|---|---|---|---|
| **Primary** | 99,000 | 2.7 | 138,600 | 3.2 | 0.5 |
| **Secondary** | 827,000 | 22.2 | 788,000 | 18.2 | −4.0 |
| **Tertiary** | 2,791,000 | 75.1 | 3,454,600 | 79.6 | 4.5 |
| **Total** | 3,717,000 | 100.0 | 4,300,500 | 100.0 | |

Source: Adapted from Statistics Canada (2006, 2020a).

## Vignette 7.5

### Dairy Farming and International Trade Agreements

Canada has a supply management system for dairy and poultry producers. In trade nego-tiations, other countries complain that supply management prevents them from exporting dairy and poultry products to Canada. The United States saw access to the Canadian dairy market as a top priority in negotiations for the USMCA. To obtain trade agreements, Ottawa has surrendered some market share to foreign producers. In compensation, the federal Liberal government is delivering $1.75 billion in compensation for dairy producers negatively impacted by the Canada–European Union Comprehensive Economic and Trade Agreement (CETA) and the Comprehensive and Progressive Agreement for Trans-Pacific Partnership (CPTPP) (Harris, 2019). With approximately half of Canadian dairy farmers op-erating in Quebec, this compensation will ease the pain, but these trade agreements squeeze the profit margins on Canadian producers. Some may decide to continue, while others may find it unprofitable, given the stiff competition from foreign producers. With the USMCA now in force, dairy farmers will face stronger competition from US producers.

to obtain an agreement with the United States and Mexico (Vignette 7.5).

Quebec's economy has shifted more and more into an advanced economy where information, re-search, and service activities are widespread. At the same time, Quebec's tertiary sector has increased its share of the total labour force at the expense of the secondary (manufacturing) sector (Table 7.4). In ad-dition, as elsewhere, the application of technology to secondary activities has dampened the percent-ages from 2005 to 2019 by replacing workers with machines, including robotics.

The secondary sector, which consists of utilities, construction, and manufacturing, distinguishes the Quebec and Ontario industrial structures from those of the other geographic regions. As core regions, both Quebec and Ontario employ about 18 per cent of the total labour force in the secondary sector (Tables 6.1 and 7.4). Significantly, manufacturing is the leading activity (Statistics Canada, 2020a). In comparison, the four other geographic regions, the so-called hinterlands, have smaller secondary sec-tors with construction, not manufacturing, leading activity in that sector. In 2019, both British Colum-bia and Western Canada had around 16 per cent of their labour force in the secondary sector, while At-lantic Canada had 17.3 per cent and the Territorial North approximately 10 per cent.

### Knowledge-Based Economy

The next step in securing an advanced economy in Quebec goes beyond a few "spearhead" firms that employ robotic techniques. These firms are at the cutting edge of technology and, as such, are glob-al leaders in modern technology applied to manu-facturing. How other firms can gain a place in the global export business depends heavily on applying modern technology to the production process to create global product demand. The existing spear-head firms demonstrate that approach. The reality for Quebec is moving forward into the knowledge-based economy. Already, the province—but particularly Montreal—has moved forward in that direction. A number of firms have made a commercial success, while basic research continues to excel at its three universities and associated research units.

Montreal, like Toronto, has the advantage of a creative class that Florida argues is essential for an in-novative society so necessary for a knowledge-based economy. Unlike Toronto, however, Montreal may have difficulties in recruiting non-French speakers from the global pool of creative people. Both cities have witnessed the shift in the labour market, where the demand for highly trained tech workers has out-paced the supply. For Montreal, the number of highly skilled workers from the international labour pool who have a command of French narrows the selection process. Yet, relaxing the selection process runs up against the need to protect the French language. A solution to the recruitment of international talent so essential for the growth of Greater Montreal's high-tech and innovation sectors is not readily at hand.

Spearhead industries provide hope for the future. In fact, many economic gains in Quebec have come from the knowledge-based sector and its advanced manufacturing techniques that improve efficiency and reduce labour costs. Such high-tech firms require a global reach, something that a select number of Quebec companies have already achieved. Because Montreal has a critical mass of high-tech companies, several universities, and strong provincial support, it is the most important centre for the new economy in Canada. Leading components are found in aerospace, biotechnology, fibre optics, and computers (both hardware and software). Quebec also excels internationally in engineering/construction.

The knowledge economy is closely linked to research and development (R&D), a general term for activities in connection with corporate or governmental innovation. The investment costs are high and the prospects of success are not guaranteed. Except for large corporations, R&D is too risky. On the other hand, without R&D, the prospects for long-term success in the global market are diminished. The public sector has recognized this dilemma. Governments, both federal and provincial, have invested heavily in R&D at universities and public research institutes and also provide tax incentives for private research firms. Most funds come from the federal government, with minor support from provinces. In Quebec's case, its financial support to the tech industry is well above that in other provinces. For example, Ubisoft, a French-based company with its main office in Montreal, enjoys heavy subsidy from the Quebec government to help pay the salaries of its employees—up to 37.5 per cent (Serebrin, 2017). Beyond subsidies, the Quebec government often intervenes in the marketplace to support local firms. For example, the government strongly supported SNC-Lavalin's efforts to obtain a deferred prosecution agreement rather than face a criminal trial over past corruption charges. A deferred prosecution (or

**PHOTO 7.5** In 2007, Ubisoft, based in Montreal, designed and then released the popular video game series known as Assassin's Creed. This popular series generates the major source of revenue for Ubisoft.

remediation) agreement involves improved conduct, restitution for past practices, and upgraded internal controls to prevent future misconduct. In February 2019, Premier Legault asked Prime Minister Trudeau for "a speedy resolution to SNC-Lavalin's legal woes." In other words, have the company undergo a deferred prosecution agreement rather than a legal trial (Monpetit, 2019). Did these pleas result in a "sweetheart deal"? The company pleaded guilty, but it avoided losing the right to bid on federal contracts (*Globe and Mail*, 2019).

## Technological Spearheads

Each region has its technological spearheads. For Quebec, aerospace (Bombardier) and engineering (SNC-Lavalin) have long served as global spearheads. As Quebec enters the next decade, these spearheads remain intact, but Bombardier's aerospace and rail transportation are under different ownership. In 2020, Bombardier sold its interest in aircraft manufacturing to the aeronautic giant Airbus (*CBC News*, 2020). Airbus operates its Montreal facilities under Stelia Aéronautique, a subsidiary of Airbus. This shift in ownership may take Canada's aerospace industry to the next level, but under foreign ownership. At the moment, Canada has the world's fifth-largest aerospace industry, with most production located in Montreal.

REUTERS/Régis Duvignau

**PHOTO 7.6** As Bombardier moved to pay down its massive debt, it sold its remaining stake in the A220 program (formerly known as the C Series) to Airbus. As of 2019, Airbus owns a 75 per cent of the A220 program. The Quebec government owns 25 per cent.

As one of the largest aeronautics and space companies in the world, Airbus (2020) has positive plans, stating that "Canada will become one of five Airbus home countries in the world—eventually being on par with the UK, France, Germany, and Spain—meaning there is anticipated growth and opportunity in the aerospace industry for Canada." The short-term challenge lies in the collapse of the global air industry due to COVID-19. How long will it take for international air travel to regain its previous level? Or will it? In the meantime, Airbus is trapped in this global economic crisis.

In the following year, Bombardier disposed of its rail-building unit to French train giant Alstom SA, leaving the company with one activity: its private jet operation. In this case, the impact on Quebec is less profound because the headquarters of Bombardier Rail is based in Berlin, Germany, and Canadian production takes place mainly in Ontario. Nevertheless, Alstom SA (Lau, 2020) sent a positive message, suggesting that Montreal could become "the headquarters of Alstom of the Americas."

In early 2020, SNC-Lavalin emerged from its murky legal troubles virtually unscathed (see McArthur & Smith, 2012). In exchange for a guilty plea to illegal operations with the former Libyan government plus an agreement to pay $280 million in fines and comply with a probation order for three years,

SNC-Lavalin was declared by the court to be free to conduct business as usual. With the bad news behind it and a new vision in front of the company, prospects for a return to a strong presence in Canada and on the international scene look promising.

Hydro-Québec remains the cornerstone of Quebec's economy. With its vast hydroelectric facilities in place, low-cost electric power allows this public utility to dominate the energy market of Quebec and the northeastern United States, and to pay an annual dividend of over $2 billion to the province. While Hydro-Québec has benefited from its purchase of power from Churchill Falls in Labrador,[4] just what its role will be, if any, in the Muskrat Falls project remains unclear. But the province of Newfoundland and Labrador has its back against the wall because of the high cost of building the Muskrat Falls generation station. Hydro-Québec has deep pockets and the expertise to absorb this plant into its regional system and, at the same time, save Newfoundland and Labrador from falling into bankruptcy. Could Churchill Falls repeat itself?

## Corporate Headquarters

Corporate headquarters represent a significant economic signpost for Montreal. The loss of major corporate headquarters—aluminum-maker Alcan, hardware chain Rona, and aerospace giant Bombardier—has diminished Montreal's corporate image. All were taken over by foreign competitors and their corporate headquarters moved abroad. Offsetting these disappointments, tech firms such as Ubisoft, AI, Renorun, Lightspeed, and others have helped fill the void. Montreal remains the core of Quebec's economy, but its role as a centre of corporate power is based on local firms evolving into major ones. The Bombardier experience suggests that only a few Canadian firms survive in the fierce global competition.

## Bombardier

Bombardier, founded in 1942 in Valcourt, Quebec, by Joseph-Armand Bombardier, a mechanic, began as a manufacturer of snowmobiles (Ski-Doo) and later developed all-terrain vehicles and personal watercraft (Sea-Doo). Through acquisitions of existing firms, the company by the 1970s had expanded into train manufacturing and in the 1980s extended its corporate reach to include aircraft. By 2020, Bombardier had sold its interests to pay down its huge debts and the company retained its private jet business. Existing contracts are now the responsibility of the new owners. Airbus has taken over aerospace operations while Alstom SA is focusing on the rail transportation business, especially dealing with rapid urban transportation systems.

## SNC-Lavalin

SNC-Lavalin, one of the leading engineering and construction groups in the world, has its headquarters in Montreal as well as offices in over 50 countries. The company specializes in engineering assignments in four key sectors: oil and gas, mining and metallurgy, infrastructure, and hydro power. The company has undertaken both large and small assignments in each province and territory. In 2015, almost half of its $14.9 billion business took place in Canada while 24 per cent was in the Middle East/Africa, 20 per cent in Europe, and 7 per cent in Asia-Pacific (SNC-Lavalin, 2019). Federal contracts loom large in SNC-Lavalin's operation.

SNC-Lavalin is best known for its engineering projects in foreign countries. For instance, in August 2016 the company was awarded a contract worth $21.7 million to build mechanical and piping systems for a graphite mine in Mozambique (*Canadian Manufacturing*, 2016). More importantly, during Premier Li Keqiang's visit to Canada, SNC-Lavalin signed an agreement-in-principle for a new joint venture with China National Nuclear Corporation and Shanghai Electric Group to form a new company to develop, market, and build advanced-fuel CANDU® reactors (Marotte, 2016). This agreement furthers the 2014 understanding between SNC-Lavalin and China National Nuclear Corporation to collaborate on nuclear energy projects in China by applying the advanced-fuel CANDU reactor technique, thus reducing fuel costs for Chinese electrical utilities. In 2018, SNC-Lavalin signed a $12 million engineering service contract and a licensing agreement with China's Third Qinshan Nuclear

PHOTO 7.7 Hatch Ltd, along with its subcontractors, SNC-Lavalin and KGS Group, provided engineering services to Manitoba Hydro in the final design of the Keeyask Generating Station on the Nelson River. The project is a collaborative effort between Manitoba Hydro and four partner First Nations: Tataskweyak Cree Nation, War Lake First Nation, York Factory First Nation, and Fox Lake Cree Nation—known collectively as the Keeyask Hydropower Limited Partnership.

Power Company Limited (TQNPC) to upgrade Qinshan's CANDU reactors. However, discussions leading to much larger contracts are not expected until the Meng Wanzhou affair is over.

In the past, the company has landed spectacular contracts, such as a massive urban planning project in Algeria to build a new city to be called Hassi Messaoud near Algeria's largest oil field. This project did not proceed, indicating the risky nature of global operations. Another risk involves the challenges of securing contracts. Export-dependent firms run the risk of bending the rules, i.e., offering bribes to officials, to obtain contracts. The "Gaddafi disaster" ranks as one of the worst cases of bending the rules. Ben Aissa, a former SNC-Lavalin executive for the Middle East, asserted that kickbacks to the regime of Mu'ammer Gaddafi were necessary to obtain contracts in Libya. Be that as it may, in October 2014 a Swiss court formally declared Aissa guilty of foreign corruption, money laundering, and fraud, all related to activities in Libya (Hutchinson, 2015). Such firms as SNC-Lavalin and Bombardier always run a risk of being tainted by or drawn into corrupt practices when they operate in politically corrupt states. The cost can be high. SNC-Lavalin faced a criminal court trial in Canada based on the "Gaddafi disaster." The company was charged with fraud and corruption in connection with nearly $48 million in payments made to Libyan government officials between 2001 and 2011 (Cohen, 2015). As noted above, however, the company pleaded guilty, paid a $280 million fine, and can bid on federal government contracts.

## Quebec's Economic Anchor: Hydro-Québec

Unlike the two global-oriented private businesses considered technical spearheads, Hydro-Québec focuses its attention on the province and adjacent jurisdictions. With its monopoly in the electricity field, Hydro-Québec is well positioned to generate revenue for the province. In 2018, for instance, the company produced net revenues of $3.2 billion and paid a dividend of $2.4 billion to the province (2019). Nearly one-quarter of net revenues comes from the sale of electricity to the northeastern US. The prospect for future growth in the northeast is both promising and could be highly profitable, as it could push Hydro-Québec's share of total net profits and thus allow the transfer of more funds to the Quebec treasury. The reason for this geographic anomaly is based on the need for the northeast US to import most of its energy, resulting in extremely high prices for electricity. For example, electric prices for residential customers are more than four times higher in Boston than in Montreal (Hydro-Québec, 2019, p. 14). In an effort to capitalize on the northeast US market, Hydro-Québec has struck a long-term contract with Massachusetts to deliver electricity to its distribution companies, starting in 2022 (Figure 7.7). To facilitate this contract, Hydro-Québec is pushing ahead to connect power lines to the Maine border. From there, a US firm will build the remainder of the power lines to Lewiston, Maine (Hydro-Québec, 2020). However, strong opposition from environmental organizations may force the state to cancel the project (North American Megadam Resistance Alliance, 2020). Transmission lines to the northeast US will greatly increase Hydro-Québec's sales and profits. In 2018, sales to the US northeast accounted for 17 per cent of

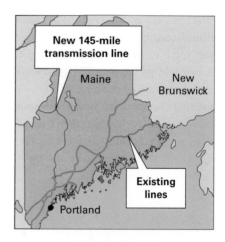

**FIGURE 7.7 Hydro-Québec's electric transmission route to the US northeast**

Source: North American Megadam Resistance Alliance (2020).

Hydro-Québec's total sales but 23 per cent of its net profit (Hydro-Québec, 2019, p. 39).

Within the Canadian market, Quebec is anxious to export more power to Ontario, but at present Ontario has more than enough power to satisfy its market, even though its power is much more expensive than Quebec power. From a political perspective, a Trans-Canada Energy Corridor might appeal to Quebec because it would allow its electric power to reach all parts of Canada, but since the appetite for oil pipelines in Quebec is very low, it is extremely unlikely that such a Canada corridor is politically feasible.

From its revenues, Hydro-Québec is able to conduct research to improve its performance at its research centre, IREQ (Institut de recherche d'Hydro-Québec). IREQ seeks ways to improve power system reliability and long-term operability, energy efficiency, ground transportation electrification, and emerging renewables, often in collaboration with universities, public research agencies, and industrial firms. This research centre consists of a broad range of scientists, technicians, engineers, and specialists. IREQ's activities are carried out in two facilities at Shawinigan and Varennes (just east of Montreal; Photo 7.8). Not surprisingly, robotics research plays a role in developing new technologies for inspecting and assessing production, transmission, and distribution facilities. IREQ has developed robots to inspect live transmission

Photo Hydro-Québec

© Photo Hydro-Québec

**PHOTO 7.8** IREQ's research facility at Varennes, just east of Montreal.

lines, de-ice ground wires and conductors, and inspect underwater structures at the many dams. Not so well known, researchers at IREQ are contributing to the development of all-electric and plug-in hybrid vehicles by developing high-performance lithium-ion batteries. In fact, Hydro-Québec holds 15 licences and 100 patents on battery materials, and companies using these materials include Sony, Merck, BASF, Phostech, PHET, and Solvionic (Hydro-Québec, 2016).

## The James Bay Project

This massive hydroelectric project, announced in 1971 by Premier Robert Bourassa, targeted three separate river basins (La Grande, Great Whale, and the Nottaway-Broadback-Eastmain-Rupert basins). The scope of the project was huge. It involves an area one-fifth the size of Quebec, but that area also serves as the homeland for the Cree. Construction of the first phase of the James Bay Project, La Grande, began in 1972 and was completed 13 years later at a cost of $13.7 billion (Bone, 2016, p. 174).

*Phase 1*: Located in the Hudson Bay drainage basin, the first phase of this massive construction undertaking began in 1972 with La Grande river basin. In order to increase the flow of water through the turbines, waters from three rivers (Eastmain, Opinaca, and Caniapiscau) were diverted into La Grande Rivière. The power is sent to southern markets in Quebec and the US via high-voltage transmission lines suspended from large steel towers. At that time, these "Crown" lands belonged to the province. The Cree and Inuit who inhabited these lands saw them as their homelands. Legal conflict was resolved at the negotiation table and the result was twofold. First, construction could proceed. Second, the 1975 James Bay and Northern Quebec Agreement (JBNQA) ensured the Cree and Inuit of certain benefits and land rights.

*Phase 2*: In 1985, the second phase, known as the Great Whale River Project, was announced. A combination of fierce opposition from the Quebec Cree and environmental organizations and the arrival of a natural gas pipeline to New England caused the government to cancel the Great Whale River

For discussion of the difficult relationship between Hydro-Québec and New-foundland and Labrador, see the **Chapter 10** section "Hydroelectricity: White Elephant or Megaproject of the Century?" on page 343.

segment of the James Bay Project. The arguments against Phase 2 were:

- From the Cree perspective, this hydroelectric project would create an industrial landscape where their traditional way of life would be threatened.
- From the perspective of the Sierra Club, the potential damage to the northern environment was unacceptable.
- From the perspective of US utility companies, the lower price for natural gas tipped the scales against signing a contract with Quebec.

*Phase 3*: In 2001, the Paix des Braves (Peace of the Braves) agreement allowed the third phase of the James Bay Project—involving diversion of waters from the Nottaway, Broadback, Eastmain, and Rupert river basins to La Grande Rivière—to proceed. In exchange for their permission, the Cree obtained economic benefits and guarantees of jobs in this $2 billion industrial project. The acceptance of such an agreement was an astonishing reversal for the Quebec Cree, who had bitterly opposed the project and who had mounted numerous national and international protests against further hydroelectric developments in their traditional lands. Some argue that the Cree now recognize that their participation in such economic developments is their only option. But feelings run high because efforts to protect the land for a hunting and trapping lifestyle have faltered. Paul Dixon, the Cree trapper representative, put it this way: "They [Quebec] promised the traditional way of life would continue undisturbed. Today, the whole territory has been slated for development" (Roslin, 2001, p. FP7).

By this time, however, most Cree had become settlement dwellers and their attachment to living on the land had weakened (Figure 7.8). Some, especially younger Cree, have chosen an urban lifestyle. For them, living on the land is no longer a viable option. Some say that the Cree leaders had to make a deal. Faced with a rapidly growing population, high unemployment rates, a critical shortage of public housing, and a desperate need for sewer and water systems, the Cree leaders had to seek an agreement with the Quebec provincial government.

Quebec wanted to develop the northern resources and the Cree needed revenue to operate their communities and to find work for their people. Under the terms of the Paix des Braves, the Cree are to receive $3.6 billion over 50 years (roughly $70 million a year), but these funds released Quebec from its obligations for economic and community development associated with the James Bay and Northern Quebec Agreement. Whether the Cree will benefit from this model of economic development remains to be seen. What is clear, however, is that similar agreements are taking place across the country, indicating that Indigenous peoples want to participate in economic development taking place on their traditional lands.

## The James Bay and Northern Quebec Agreement

The James Bay hydro project undertaken by Hydro-Québec was a watershed event for the evolution of Indigenous land claims in Canada. Such lands, until Supreme Court of Canada decisions in later years, were Crown lands under the authority of provincial governments. When construction began in 1972, the Cree asked the Inuit to join them in taking legal action to halt the construction until the Cree and Inuit land claims were addressed. The resulting compromise was the JBNQA. Under this agreement, both the federal and Quebec governments became responsible for providing the "treaty" benefits. As the first modern land claim agreement in Canada, this 1975 agreement provided land, cash, and self-administrative power over socio-cultural matters (education, health, and social services) to these two Indigenous groups. In exchange, the Cree and Inuit surrendered their claims to northern Quebec and allowed construction of Phase 1 (La Grande) to proceed.

## Quebec's Core

Quebec's population and economic activities are concentrated in the densely populated St Lawrence Lowland. Quebec's core, extending from Montreal to Quebec City, contains over 70 per cent of the province's population and over 80 per cent of its industrial output. Exports play a key role and most flow west to Ontario and south to the United States.

**THINK ABOUT IT**

Outside of northern Quebec, the legal status of lands occupied in the past by Indigenous peoples remained unchanged after the 1975 signing of the JBNQA, i.e., they were defined as Crown lands. Does this mean the Cree of northern Quebec were thus in an advantageous position vis-à-vis other First Nations? Indigenous title, which involves communal or group rights, was recognized in the 1997 ruling by the Supreme Court of Canada in *Delgamuukw v. British Columbia*.

**THINK ABOUT IT**

If you were the premier of Quebec, why would you prefer to supply New England with electricity rather than Ontario?

Transportation plays a key role because many firms rely on just-in-time deliveries. While rail and road transportation are essential elements in the just-in-time system that connects parts firms with manufacturers, the St Lawrence River provides an additional advantage to Quebec by affording easy access for bulk and container products to the interior of North America and its industrial heartland. High-voltage electric lines play a role, too, with power flowing to the northeast region of the United States and to Ontario and New Brunswick.

Quebec's hinterland lies to the north. It consists primarily of sparsely populated northern lands where the main economic pursuits involve forestry and mining. The relationship between the two regions is similar to the spatial divide between southern Ontario and northern Ontario. Both demonstrate a regional version of the core/periphery model. In the Quebec version the core's population is largely francophone while Indigenous peoples form a significant proportion of the North. The Arctic lands of Nunavik, for instance, are inhabited by Inuit, while further south, Quebec Cree live in eight communities in the region of Eeyou Istchee (Figure 7.8).

Within Quebec, five demographic features stand out. First, most population growth occurs in the larger cities found in the core. Second, most newcomers migrate to Montreal. Third, the majority of anglophones and allophones who reside in Quebec live in Montreal (Figure 7.9). Fourth, bilingualism is on the rise in Quebec, but particularly in Montreal. For that reason, the language faultline is most visible in this city and much of the work of the Office québécois de la langue française takes place in Montreal (Figure 7.2). Fifth, demography in Quebec's northern hinterland is sharply different from the core. Here, the majority of the population are Indigenous, mainly Cree and Inuit. Unlike the core, population growth is extremely high due to high fertility rates.

### Montreal: Heart of Bilingualism

Montreal, the metropolis of the province, serves as the industrial, commercial, and cultural focus of Quebec. More recently, Montreal has developed into a world-class technology centre specializing in artificial intelligence (AI). Yet the city is a paradox.

**FIGURE 7.8 Cree communities in Eeyou Istchee**

In a relatively short time (several decades), the Quebec Cree moved from the land to settlements. By 2016, virtually all of the 17,800 Cree resided in eight communities that comprise Eeyou Istchee, the Cree name for their homeland. The largest Cree community is Chisasibi, with nearly 5,000 inhabitants. The other communities are Eastmain, Mistissini, Nemaska, Waskaganish, Waswanipi, Wemindji, and Whapmagoostui.

Its complexity reveals a vibrant yet mixed linguistic population that provides the city with its unique character, as well as a language faultline. The sharp edge of earlier linguistic conflicts has not disappeared, but it has softened, especially among young Quebecers. One sign is the increase in those who are bilingual (now 55 per cent). As Jean-Pierre Corbeil

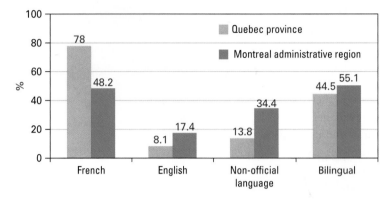

**FIGURE 7.9  Population by mother tongue, 2016: Quebec and Montreal**

The 2016 Canadian census revealed a large language gap between the province of Quebec and its largest city, Montreal. In the province as a whole 78 per cent of the residents spoke French as their mother tongue. In Montreal, only 48 per cent had French as their mother tongue, while just over 17 per cent declared English as their mother tongue. However, more and more Quebecers are bilingual, with Montreal leading the way with 55.1 per cent speaking both languages.

Source: Institut de la statistique du Québec (2019b, p. 14).

of Statistics Canada observed, the younger generation of Quebecers are more open to learning English than their elders and perceive it as an economic advantage. In short, "they don't perceive English as a threat" (Scott, 2017).

Montreal is the largest census metropolitan area in the province with an estimated 2020 population of 4.2 million (Table 7.5). Nearly half of Quebec's population lives in the Montreal CMA, which includes the cities of Laval and Longueuil as well as the municipalities of Beaconsfield, Baie-D'Urfé, Côte-Saint-Luc, Dollard-Des-Ormeaux, Dorval, Hampstead, Kirkland, L'Île-Dorval, Montréal-Est, Montréal-Ouest, Mont-Royal, Pointe-Claire, Sainte-Anne-de-Bellevue, Senneville, and Westmount. Like Toronto, Montreal has developed an effective combination of metro lines and surface bus transportation that provides

quick and inexpensive city transportation. Montreal is the growth engine for Quebec and also is the fourth-largest French-speaking city in the world. In that sense, Montreal is pulled into the global economic world where English dominates, but at the same time the province tries to protect the French language. Herein lies the challenge: the French language forms an indispensable defence against assimilation into the English-speaking world, but attracting immigrants who have the right combination of skills along with fluency in French has proven difficult.

Montreal is one of Canada's oldest cities. Historically rich but infrastructurally poor, the city (perhaps more than other Canadian cities) needs huge investment in its infrastructure. Like Canada's two other largest cities—Toronto and Vancouver—Montreal is defined by its access to water and beaches. Yet, these

**TABLE 7.5   Population of Census Metropolitan Areas in Quebec, 2001 and 2016**

| City | Population 2001 (000s) | Population 2016 (000s) | % Change 2001–16 |
|---|---|---|---|
| **Montreal** | 3,451.0 | 4,098.9 | 18.8 |
| **Quebec City** | 686.6 | 800.3 | 16.6 |
| **Gatineau** | 257.6 | 332.1 | 28.9 |
| **Sherbrooke** | 176.0 | 212.1 | 20.5 |
| **Saguenay** | 154.9 | 160.9 | 0.4 |
| **Trois-Rivières** | 137.5 | 156.0 | 13.5 |

Sources: Statistics Canada (2007, 2019a).

three cities have lost most of their beaches to industrial pollution. One sign of its plight took place in 2015 when Montreal discharged 5 billion litres of untreated sewage into the St Lawrence River over four days while repairs to the sewerage system were undertaken (Gerbel, 2015). Situated on an island, Montreal has a dozen bridges and overpasses that are well past their best years. Like other cities, the cost of improving its infrastructure is well beyond its means. Fortunately for Montreal, the federal government is responsible for two bridges crossing the St Lawrence River, the Jacques Cartier and Champlain bridges. In 2019, a modern Champlain bridge that connects the South Shore with the island of Montreal was opened. SNC-Lavalin designed the Réseau express métropolitain train that will extend rapid light rail transit from Montreal to the South Shore.

Following the Canada–US Free Trade Agreement in 1989 and, especially, the establishment of the rules-based World Trade Organization in 1995, Montreal's manufacturing sector had to respond to strong foreign competition. Labour-intensive manufacturing firms experienced great difficulty in competing with foreign firms that had substantially lower labour costs. Montreal's manufacturing firms made two major changes: labour-intensive plants substituted machinery for workers to increase productivity, and high-technology firms expanded their operations. By the late 1990s, Montreal's economy had become much more specialized in aerospace, computers, fibre optics, multilingual software, telecommunications, and other areas of industrial research and development. The provincial government has taken a leading role by providing subsidies for high-tech firms that relocate to Montreal and other Quebec cities. Universities, such as Université de Montréal and McGill University, serve as a critical link to the high-tech industry.

### Montreal and Toronto

At the time of Confederation, Montreal was the dominant city in Canada. In the 1970s, Toronto caught up to Montreal and gradually surpassed it. Beginning in the 1970s, especially with the election

Marc Bruxelle/iStockphoto

**PHOTO 7.9** The Samuel de Champlain Bridge, opened in 2019, will serve Montreal for years to come. This bridge consists of two traffic corridors with three lanes in each direction, a central corridor dedicated to the proposed Réseau express métropolitain train, and a multi-use path for cyclists and pedestrians.

| TABLE 7.6 Population Change: Montreal and Toronto, 1951–2020 (000s) | | | |
|---|---|---|---|
| Year | Montreal | Toronto | Difference |
| **1951** | 1,539 | 1,262 | 277 |
| **1961** | 2,216 | 1,919 | 297 |
| **1971** | 2,743 | 2,628 | 115 |
| **1981** | 2,828 | 2,999 | –171 |
| **1991** | 3,127 | 3,893 | –766 |
| **2001** | 3,426 | 4,683 | –1,257 |
| **2006** | 3,636 | 5,113 | –1,477 |
| **2011** | 3,824 | 5,583 | –1,759 |
| **2016** | 4,099 | 5,928 | –1,829 |
| **2020** | 4,221 | 6,197 | –1,976 |

Sources: Statistics Canada (2002, 2007, 2012, 2019a); Macrotrends (2020).

of the first PQ government in 1976, Montreal lost it place as the premier city in Canada. Sun Life's move from Montreal to Toronto in 1978 was a shift of symbolic importance. The principal reason for this shift in metropolitan power was the strong economic growth in southern Ontario powered by the Auto Pact and the resulting expansion of the automobile industry. A secondary factor was the economic and demographic fallout from the political unrest in Quebec and the very real possibility of Quebec separating from Canada. At that time, many anglophones and some corporations moved to Toronto. While the francophone business community and the provincial government kept the Montreal economy growing, by 1981 Toronto had a population of 3.0 million compared to Montreal's 2.8 million (Table 7.6). Since then, the momentum of Toronto's growth has caused the population gap to widen.

### Quebec City

Founded in 1608 by Samuel de Champlain, Quebec City is one of the oldest cities in North America. Quebec City, the historic capital of French Canada and the capital of modern-day Quebec, has the second-largest urban concentration in the province, totalling just over 800,000 people in 2016. Quebec City has a magnificent physical setting on high banks along the St Lawrence River with the rugged terrain of the Canadian Shield lying only a short distance to the north posing a sharp contrast to the gentle landscape of the St Lawrence Lowland. As the only walled city in North America and with buildings over 300 years old, the city has a vibrant tourist industry with many international visitors (Photo 7.10). In 1985, UNESCO selected Quebec City as a World Heritage Site.

The economic base of Quebec City revolves around three functions. First, it is an administrative centre. As the provincial seat of government, Quebec City employs a large number of civil servants. Université Laval, one of the largest universities in Canada, ranks highly among universities in North America. Second, Quebec City has a substantial manufacturing base that is benefiting from increased exports to the United States, largely because of a softer Canadian dollar. It also benefits from military contracts for shipbuilding. Third, the city is a world-class tourist centre. The Old World charm of Quebec City draws tourists from around the world, while special events such as its Winter Carnival are very popular. Then, too, Quebec City is only minutes away from excellent seasonal recreation areas—from skiing in the winter to water sports in the summer.

## Quebec's Northern Hinterland

Northern Quebec lies beyond the agricultural lands of Quebec, in a hinterland of boreal forest and tundra zones where permafrost is widespread. Defined

**PHOTO 7.10** A cruise ship moored at Quebec City, in the St Lawrence River.

Rolf Hicker Photography/Alamy Stock Photo

as Nord-du-Québec, this portion of Quebec has the smallest population with the lowest density. In 2018, its population was 45,558. Cree and Inuit comprised nearly 70 per cent of the total population (Institut de la statistique du Québec, 2020, p. 163).

Much further south, the rich farmland and industrial zone of the St Lawrence Valley presents a totally different industrial landscape. The northern hinterland, situated in the physiographic regions of the Canadian Shield and the Hudson Bay Lowland, remains the homeland of the Cree, Innu, and Inuit, where hunting and fishing play a prominent role in the Indigenous economy. The principal activity of the northern Quebec economy is hydroelectric generation, followed by forestry and mining. Forestry activities involve logging, sawmilling, and pulp and paper production. Its resource-based economy—hydroelectricity; nickel and iron ore; and lumber and paper products—depends on foreign markets. With commodity prices depressed, mines have either closed or cut back production. Forest companies face increased US tariffs related to the Buy America policy with the resulting decline in sales to US customers.

As an old resource hinterland, long-term prospects are not bright and employment is falling, partly due to market conditions and the automation taking place in the forest and mining industries. Surprisingly, the vast hydroelectric system that has placed its industrial stamp on the landscape requires few employees in its post-construction phase. Consequently, like northern Ontario, the resource-based economy is not generating jobs and the number of people residing in Quebec's North continues to drift south. On the other hand, the Inuit and Cree populations were increasing rapidly due to a high fertility rates, but, after 2016, those rates began to decline (Institut de la statistique du Québec, 2020, p. 163).

## New Political Realities

The Cree and Inuit represent the majority of the population in Nord-du-Québec. Both are seeking a new relationship with the province that provides more independence, but within Quebec. Such an arrangement does not exist—a semi-autonomous region within a province. What form that political relationship(s) will take is unclear. The attempt of the Inuit, as represented by Makivik, to gain a measure of autonomy along the lines of Nunavut remains a work in progress.

**Makivik Corporation** and **Kativik Regional Government** came into existence as a result of the James Bay and Northern Quebec Agreement. Makivik is the business arm that manages the Inuit compensation funds from the JBNQA and other revenues generated by their investments and companies. As well, Makivik represents the Inuit in political matters, such as negotiating the Nunavik Inuit Offshore Land Claim (resolved in 2008) and in seeking self-government. On the other hand, Kativik Regional Government delivers various public services to residents of Nunavik, including land-use planning, security, recreation and culture, and sanitation. In this sense, Nunavik already has a quasi-form of self-government. The advantage lies in managing their own affairs for nearly 50 years and gaining administrative experience. Yet the dream of a regional government remains unfulfilled. In 1983, Premier René Lévesque recognized this dream when he stated that an Inuit regional government within Quebec was possible. Such a government, controlled by the Inuit, would respond to their needs, desires, and aspirations. To achieve that goal, three formidable challenges had to be resolved. First, how can a regional government function within a province? This calls into question the division of powers between the province of Quebec and the soon-to-be-formed government of Nunavik. Matters are complicated by the involvement of the federal government; under the JBNQA, Canada subsidizes many of the services, including education and health, that it formerly delivered to the Inuit. Second, how can Nunavik (a non-ethnic government) treat all its residents equally and still promote Inuit culture? Lastly, how can less than 20,000 people living in 14 communities scattered over 500,000 km$^2$ govern themselves and also generate sufficient revenue to pay for their government?

The road to self-government is long and difficult. Somehow the structure, operations, powers, and design of this new form of government within a Canadian province can be achieved. The

## Vignette 7.6

### Run-of-the-River Hydroelectricity

As a mark of Inuit resilience and growing participation in the Nunavik economy, the Inuit-owned Pituvik Landholding Corporation, one of several non-profit landholding corporations created out of the JBNQA, is undertaking the construction of a run-of-the-river hydro project on the Inukjuak River. This $127 million project, with private-sector partner Innergex, a renewable resource firm, will supply electricity to the village of Inukjuak, population 1,800, and lead to the closure of the town's diesel-operated thermal plant (Willis, 2020). In a win-win situation, the release of greenhouse gases from the diesel plant will cease and the electric rates to residents will decrease.

process began with the JBNQA that created Indigenous organizations to administer and manage the funds associated with that Agreement (Vignette 7.6). The federal and provincial governments negotiated the details of an autonomous political region with Makivik. In 2011, a referendum was held on the proposed Inuit self-government proposal. The rank-and-file Inuit rejected the proposed political system, indicating that they could not see the advantage of this version of self-government over the existing governance conducted by the Kativik Regional Government (see Kativik Regional Government, 2009). Nearly 10 years later, Makivik signalled that it wanted to restart this journey by signing an agreement in 2019 with the federal government to begin negotiation with the people of Nunavik. Makivik's next step involves signing a similar agreement with the Quebec government (Rogers, 2019).

### Forest Industry

Forests cover nearly half of Quebec. In total, Quebec accounts for nearly 760,000 km² of forest, and most lies in the Canadian Shield. Most logging operations that produce softwood lumber and wood for pulp and paper mills are concentrated in the boreal forest found in the Canadian Shield.

Quebec has 22 per cent of Canada's productive forest lands. Quebec ranks first among Canada's geographic regions in terms of area of productive forest lands but it ranks second behind British Columbia in total volume of wood cut. Pulp and paper mills

form the heart of the province's forest production. Until recently, the demand for pulp and paper in the publishing world seemed to have no limits. Then came the digital age.

In the past, proximity to major US newspapers in Boston and New York represented a geographic advantage. By the start of the twenty-first century, signs of a decline were evident, and the well-being of many small towns that depended on pulp and paper mills was threatened. By 2020, demand for pulp and paper had dipped sharply, and many mills had closed. Additionally, in 2016 the US imposed duties on paper products. Quebec's secondary domestic market also went digital. In Canada, most newspapers have dual print and digital platforms. But the move to digital seems inevitable. One example is *La Presse* newspaper, which stopped its print operation for the Greater Montreal region in 2018 and now publishes exclusively in digital form (Labour Market Analysis Directorate, 2020). As more and more readers are turning to the Internet for their news rather than buying hard-copy newspapers and to e-readers for books, the pulp and paper industry has been in full retreat. Employment figures for the pulp and paper industry in Quebec reflect that decline. For example, in 1991 the high point of nearly 44,000 workers was reached, but by 2017 the number of employees had fallen to 21,000 (Natural Resources Canada, 2018). Forecasts to 2020 called for a 2.2 per cent decline in the size of the workforce, resulting in just under 20,000 forestry workers in the province (Labour Market Analysis Directorate, 2020).

## Vignette 7.7

### Indigenous Peoples Benefit from Resource Profit-Sharing Agreements

Indigenous peoples across Canada remain divided on participating in resource development projects. Those opposed are largely concerned about the potential environmental damage to the land and wildlife—both of which are key elements in their culture and economy. Those in favour see the benefits that flow from impact and benefit agreements as a positive element. As Stephen Buffalo, the president of the Indian Resource Council, put it, "From a First Nations standpoint, we're really trying to not be poor. Oil and gas, and energy, is one way to advance, and build our communities, and build houses and rec centres and hockey rinks" (Cryderman & McCarthy, 2016, p. B3). The Raglan nickel mine in Arctic Quebec illustrates this point. Makivik signed the Raglan Impact Benefit Agreement in 1995 with Falconbridge Ltd, thus allowing the Inuit to share in the profits. By 2015, this agreement had generated over $100 million for Nunavik residents (Rogers, 2015). Most benefits go to residents of Salluit and Kangiqsujjuaq (Photo 7.11), the two Inuit communities closest to the nickel mine at Raglan. Salluit receives the greatest share because it is closest to the mine and the port at Deception Bay. In 2014, after $14 million was shared among Salluit's 1,100 beneficiaries, each adult got $15,000 and every child received $3,500. With continued success under Glencore, an Anglo-Swiss resources multinational, payments to these communities continued into 2020.

## Mining Industry

Mining has always been important in northern Quebec. In 2018, the value of Quebec's metallic mineral production was $10 billion (Natural Resources Canada, 2019a). By value of output, gold production led the way, followed by iron ore.

Geology has favoured this part of the world. The Canadian Shield contains many mineral deposits. For Quebec, gold, iron, and nickel deposits provide much of its mineral wealth, and, unlike in the past, this wealth is shared with Indigenous communities (Vignette 7.7). The size of deposits ranges from small to large. For instance, the Labrador Trough contains large iron and nickel deposits. This unique geological structure extends for about 1,100 km southeast from Ungava Bay through both Quebec and Labrador. Further south, it turns southwest past the Wabush and Mont Wright areas to within 300 km of the St Lawrence River. Deposits of iron were first reported in 1895 by A.P. Low of the Geological Survey of Canada, the first geologist to investigate the region's mineral potential. At that time, however, these deposits had no commercial value because

more accessible mines could supply the needs of the iron and steel companies. After World War II, the United States was no longer self-sufficient in iron ore. Its steel mills called for more ore and that ore came from the Labrador Trough. Today, most iron ore production in Canada comes from this region, and in 2018 Quebec accounted for half of this production (Figure 7.10).

The Labrador Trough contains vast quantities of iron ore. Until the end of World War II, this iron

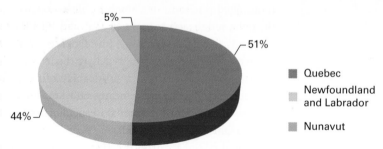

**FIGURE 7.10 Canadian mine production of iron ore, by province, 2018**

Note: Preliminary percentages. Production from Nunavut was not included for 2015.

Source: Natural Resources Canada (2019b).

Maarten Udema/Alamy Stock Photo

**PHOTO 7.11** The settlement of Kangiqsujjuaq in Arctic Quebec on Hudson Strait had a population in 2016 of 750, up from 696 in 2011.

ore did not have a commercial value because of its remote location. Two mining companies, Quebec Cartier Mining Company and the Iron Ore Company of Canada, undertook a massive development scheme to provide access to these rich deposits. By 1947, plans were laid for an open-pit mine in northern Quebec near the border with Labrador. In 1954 the Iron Ore Company established a town (Schefferville) for miners and their families, and later transmitted power from Churchill Falls to operate the mine and the town; between 1951 and 1954 the company also built a railway (the Quebec North Shore and Labrador Railway) to deliver the iron ore to the port at Sept-Îles on the north shore of the St Lawrence, a line extending nearly 600 km. From Sept-Îles the ore was transported to supply US steel mills in Ohio and Pennsylvania.

The demand for iron ore rose in the 1960s, resulting in the establishment of three more mining towns—Wabush and Labrador City in Labrador and Fermont, Quebec. At the same time, Quebec Cartier Mining Company built a

similar iron-mining operation by constructing the Cartier Railway from Port-Cartier on the St Lawrence River to the resource town of Gagnon. But by the 1980s world steel production had surpassed the demand, causing a severe slump in the demand for iron ore. To add to this economic problem, US steel plants were now less efficient than the new steel mills in Brazil, Canada, Korea, and Japan, and lower-cost iron mines had opened in Australia and Brazil. As lower-priced steel from these countries undercut the price of US steel, American steel companies had to reduce their output, close plants, and sell their shares in the two mining companies. The mining companies were forced to **restructure** their operations to reduce costs. The repercussions for workers were severe. The mining workforce was reduced and two mines, at Schefferville and Gagnon, were closed.

As the world business cycle improved in the twenty-first century, demand from iron and steel plants around the world, especially in China,

Mathieu Dupuis

**PHOTO 7.12** Mining operations at Malartic gold mine.

increased. In 2000 Rio Tinto, a British-Australian multinational, became the principal shareholder of the Iron Ore Company of Canada, and eight years later the Luxembourg-based ArcelorMittal purchased the Quebec Cartier Mining Company. The two companies increased their production accordingly. Rio Tinto's Iron Ore Company of Canada operates a pellet plant and mine at Labrador City and at Wabush Mines. The concentrated ore is shipped by rail to Sept-Îles for transshipment to world markets (Iron Ore Company of Canada, 2013). Arcelor-Mittal Mines Canada has two mines, Mont-Wright and Fire Lake, plus a pellet plant at Port-Cartier (ArcelorMittal, 2015).

Mine (and town) closures are not unusual events. Several northern Quebec communities are single-industry towns and rely on mining for their existence. Extraordinary measures are taken to survive. Residents of Malartic, for example, are relocating outside of town because one of the largest gold

deposits in North America exists under the town. As in other resource towns, times can be tough. In 2008, half of Malartic's workers were either on unemployment insurance or on welfare. But this $1 billion project, located in the famous Abitibi gold belt, breathed new life into the community by creating nearly 500 permanent jobs and some 800 construction jobs (Séguin, 2009). Since 2011, Malartic gold mine (Photo 7.12) has outpaced other mines to become one of the largest gold mines in Canada (Osisko, 2013).

As noted earlier, the cyclical nature of the mining industry, due to its dependence on world markets, poses a problem for resource communities. Global companies operate to make profits and have no commitment to local communities, so community prosperity and employment are tied to global demand. Low demand means layoffs and even the closure of mines and ore-processing mills. This boom-and-bust cycle is particularly hurtful to the narrowly based economies of resource hinterlands. The world demand for mineral products has gone through several cycles since World War II. For the last 10 years, commodity prices have edged downward and Quebec's iron-mining communities and their workers have suffered.

## Summary

Until 2020, Quebec's economy was in full swing. Unemployment was at a record low and industrial expansion in the high-tech sector was setting a hot pace. All of this came to an end when COVID-19 arrived. Quebec had more cases of the disease than any of the other five regions. In 2021 and beyond, this core region will depend heavily on the newly developed vaccines to pull out of this tailspin.

In spite of the hard blow from the novel coronavirus, language and culture remain the fundamental distinguishing features of Quebec. Placed in the historic context of cultural survival within an anglophone North America, the preservation of the French language and, therefore, the culture of this province remains Quebec's fundamental political goal.

Montreal is the focal point of language debates within Quebec. Even though the number of bilingual Quebecers is increasing, especially in Montreal, Quebec's francophone culture and French language remain strong. As the heartland of francophones in Canada and North America, Quebec has a special role to play. Cultural events like La Fête nationale du Quebec evoke a sense of ethnic nationalism and a love of the land and its people, which is popularly expressed as *"J'ai le goût du Québec."* Within this cultural context, the French language serves as a linchpin.

Is Quebec's position within Confederation weakening as its share of Canada's population declines? If so, the reason is simple: while Quebec's population has increased, other regions of Canada—Ontario, British Columbia, and Western Canada—have grown at a more rapid rate due to immigration. If this trend continues, Quebec's place in Canada could be seriously eroded. Yet two bright lights suggest a turnaround. First, Quebec's economy has regained its footing by recognizing the importance of the knowledge-based economy and thus extending beyond its traditional business pillars. Not only is the province devoting more public funds for scientific research initiatives than any of the other five regions, but Quebec is also encouraging talented Canadians and immigrants to join its technology economy. Its leading firms are spearheading research into advanced technology and applying that technology to their manufacturing processes. Already, Quebec has a few internationally established companies that can compete on the world stage; the challenge is to expand in this vital economic sector. Second, Hydro-Québec is flexing its economic muscle. With major hydroelectric dams producing low-cost electricity, this state-run corporation is well positioned to sell more power to the lucrative New England energy market. As well, Hydro-Québec stands as the dominant power corporation in Central and Atlantic Canada.

Quebec and Ontario have northern hinterlands. In both cases, Indigenous peoples form a significant portion of the population. Self-government is more advanced in Quebec's hinterland than in Ontario's. The explanation is founded on two factors. First, hydroelectric construction in northern Quebec transformed the Indigenous peoples from living on the land to become town dwellers. Second, the James Bay and Northern Quebec Agreement (1975) provided the legal conditions for the evolution towards self-government. While taking strikingly different approaches, the Cree and Inuit are well on their way to creating autonomous regional governments within Quebec.

## Challenge Questions

1. While the Quebec economy was revitalized in the last decade with a shift to knowledge-based firms, will the federal policy to support health-related businesses to manufacture much needed health products work in Quebec's favour?

2. The collapse of Bombardier has seen global companies purchase its air and rail components. Will these international giants provide a platform for growth for Quebec or will they shift production to other areas of the world?

3. Why is Montreal such a hub of technology in Canada?

4. Resource development has always been a prickly matter for Indigenous peoples. Have resource profit-sharing agreements, such as the Raglan Agreement, helped make such developments more acceptable to Indigenous peoples?

## Essay Questions

1. Montreal faces a quandary. On the one hand, the city wants to participate more fully in the global economy by attracting more members of the creative class who are so necessary for a successful advanced modern economy. On the other hand, the risk of relaxing French-language requirements for non-French-speaking immigrants could fly in the face of the province's language goal. How would you solve this quandary?

2. Since Confederation, Quebec's share of Canada's population has declined. Discuss the demographic factors causing this decline and comment on this trend continuing into the next decade.

JUNCTION
Smith-Dorrien/Spray

# 8 Western Canada

## Chapter Overview

The main themes in this chapter are:

- Western Canada in changing circumstances.
- Basic population and economic characteristics.
- Impact of low energy and commodity prices.
- The spread of technology throughout the economy.
- The shift in principal crops, from spring wheat to canola and pulses.
- Oil sands under pressure.

## Introduction

Western Canada, rich in natural resources, lies in the heart of North America. Consequently, geography dictates its need for access to tidewater to allow its exports to reach world markets. In the first decade of the twenty-first century, global demand for its resources, especially oil and potash, allowed Western Canada but particularly Alberta and Saskatchewan to experience record economic and population growth, thereby transforming the region into an economic engine for Canada. Yet the controversial issue of pipelines has added another layer to western alienation (Contest Terrain 1.1).

Western Canada faces changing circumstances. In the second decade, global demand for these resources slowed and their prices slumped. Alberta and Saskatchewan, while still two of the more prosperous provinces in Canada, faced troubling economic times. On top of that, anti-oil sands environmentalists vigorously opposed both the Trans Mountain pipeline expansion and an increase in oil sands production. Caught in the middle, Fort McMurray, the epicentre of Alberta's oil sands, was devastated by catastrophic wildfire in May 2016 and saw its growth cut short by a collapse in oil prices and a lack of fresh investments in expansion of the oil sands. On the other hand, Manitoba, lying outside of the oil bubble, continued its slow but steady growth. More trouble hit Western Canada's agriculture industry in 2018 when geopolitical crossfire between the United States and China over the arrest of Huawei executive Meng Wanzhou had unforeseen

← Lower Kananaskis Lake, pictured here, is part of a series of natural and constructed reservoirs in Alberta's Kananaskis and Bow valleys and is used for hydroelectricity, flood control, and water supplies.

consequences for Western Canada's agriculture industry: the Chinese government first banned canola and later meat products from Canada. In early 2020, the COVID-19 virus reached Western Canada, adding another negative impact to its economy. Despite these changing circumstances, Western Canada continues to grow, though at a slower rate.

## Western Canada within Canada

Western Canada ranks second in GDP behind Ontario and third in population size behind Ontario and Quebec (Figures 8.1 and 8.2). Its vast agricultural lands and energy deposits continue to provide the base for its remarkable economic and population growth. Western Canada, while still dependent on its resource economy, has created a powerful knowledge-based economy centred in its larger cities that deeply involves its universities.

Geography presents unique advantages and challenges to Western Canada. Enormous energy resources and fertile agricultural lands form the basis of its rapidly expanding economy and population. Challenges exist, too. The region's continental position makes transportation a central cost factor in accessing global markets. The controversial issue of pipelines carrying bitumen from the oil sands to tidewater has created a divide between the oil-rich provinces of Alberta and Saskatchewan and other provinces that are concerned about potential environmental impacts. Concerns about climate change drive much of the anti-pipeline rhetoric, but this perceived attack on the economies of Alberta and Saskatchewan has reignited western alienation. The effort to find a balance between reducing

**FIGURE 8.1 Western Canada**

The two highways, the Yellowhead and the Trans-Canada, follow the earlier rail routes of the CNR and CPR, respectively. The Trans Mountain expansion pipeline route now under construction closely follows the CPR line across British Columbia to tidewater at Burnaby.

Source: Reference map of the Prairie provinces, atlas.nrcan.gc.ca/data/english/maps/reference/provincesterritories/prairie_provinces/map.pdf. Natural Resources Canada, 2000. Reproduced with the permission of the Minister of Public Works and Government Services Canada, 2013.

carbon emissions and supporting the energy industry of Western Canada is a necessary but elusive political matter for Ottawa.

Western Canada faces another natural challenge: a dry continental climate. Normally, this climate provides sufficient precipitation for agriculture. In some years, however, annual precipitation falls well below the needed level of moisture and drought-like conditions appear, causing hardships for both farmers and ranchers. Climatologists refer to this aspect of a dry climate as a water deficit and evapotranspiration (Vignette 8.1). Innovative farming technology has greatly reduced the risk of crop failure, an example of the diffusion of knowledge-based innovations spreading to the agricultural sector. Concerns about climate change and global warming are real, but so far, precipitation patterns have not changed. Still, in a dry continental climate, water—especially drinking water—is limited. Major cities draw their water supplies from the North and South Saskatchewan rivers emanating from the Rocky Mountains, where the melting alpine glaciers, snowfall melt, and rain supply these rivers. As urban and industrial growth continues, demands for water are rising, creating a potential conflict between industrial and urban water demands. A major question relates to climate change and the melting of glaciers in the Rocky Mountains: when the glaciers are gone, will the reduced supply make prairie cities vulnerable to shortages of drinking water? The search for concrete solutions to these diverse demands for water remains in the future.

Reliance on the US market poses a third challenge. The problem is reliability. Even under NAFTA, access to Western Canada's largest market is constrained from time to time by US tariffs, particularly for cattle and softwood lumber. Attempts to diversify export markets, especially to Asia, have had mixed results. For oil-producing provinces, the threat of a US President blocking the Keystone XL oil pipeline project is real because President-elect Joe Biden made his position crystal clear: "I've been against Keystone from the beginning," Biden said in an interview with CNBC. "It is tarsands that we don't need—that in fact [are a] very, very high pollutant" (Jackson, 2020).

In addition, political disputes with China have made trade unreliable. Already, China's ban on Canadian meat products has made business particularly hard on ranchers, but not for farmers. The reason for the difference is that China can find other sources for meat but not for canola because Western Canada is the world's largest producer of canola. By purchasing canola from third parties, China is actually buying Canadian canola at a higher price.

As an exporting region, Western Canada trades mainly with the United States, Pacific Rim countries, and the European Union. Prices for its resource products follow a cyclical pattern. In the last decade, for example, high prices for oil and other commodities stimulated the economy, especially the economies of Alberta and Saskatchewan. Similarly, low prices for grains, livestock, and forest products have hampered these resource activities while high prices for canola and pulses have had the opposite effect. Recent trade restrictions by China and India have affected canola, meat, and pulse exports. Western Canada, then, depends on exporting its agriculture, energy, and other resources to global markets and a downturn in global trade can dampen Western Canada's economy. The **boom-and-bust cycle** associated with resource economies has a political wrinkle: China's targeting of Western Canadian exports for geopolitical reasons. As well, the COVID-19 pandemic has reduced world trade for 2020, but once a vaccine is available global trade and prices will hopefully rebound in the coming years.

## Western Canada's Population

By 2020, Western Canada's population reached 7 million (Statistics Canada, 2020b). In terms of the six geographic regions, Western Canada ranked third, with over 18 per cent of Canada's population. Its major cities contain most of its population, led by Calgary (1.4 million), Edmonton (1.3 million), and Winnipeg (nearly 800,000). Saskatoon and Regina add to this urban mix with an additional 540,000 residents.

Western Canada's sizable Indigenous population is a significant demographic and political element. By 2020, just over half a million Indigenous people lived in Western Canada, forming nearly 10 per cent of the population. Since the population growth of Indigenous peoples outpaces the rest of the population, their proportion of the total population seems assured of increasing. As well, this demographic fact

**THINK ABOUT IT**

By 2019, low global prices for oil had dampened Western Canada's economic performance. Oil prices fell dramatically but appear to have bottomed out by 2020. Is the author overly optimistic that the return of higher prices for oil can once again boost Western Canada's economy?

## Vignette 8.1

### Water Deficit and Evapotranspiration

Precipitation is both limited and highly variable on the Canadian Prairies. Some years result in drought conditions and crop failures. In those years, the Prairies have a "water deficit." This deficit is measured in terms of potential evapotranspiration, which is the amount of water vapour that can potentially be released from an area of the earth's surface through evaporation and transpiration (the loss of moisture through the leaves of plants). There is a water deficit if evapotranspiration is greater than the average annual precipitation. For example, most of the short grassland natural vegetation zone receives less than 400 mm annually, while its evapotranspiration exceeds 500 mm. The difference indicates a water deficit of over 100 mm. At that time, crops draw on the water reserves in the soil. When those underground reserves accumulated from past years are exhausted, crop failure occurs. The most vulnerable area for droughts lies in the short-grass vegetation zone known as Palliser's Triangle.

explains why First Nation reserves are able to increase their population size at the same time as many of the people move to cities, causing the urban Indigenous population to expand. Indigenous population growth adds another dimension to the need for concrete action involving reconciliation.

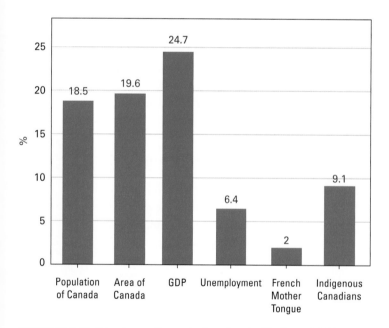

**FIGURE 8.2 Western Canada basic statistics, 2016**

Western Canada contains nearly 20 per cent of Canada's land mass and 19 per cent of its population. Its economic strength, as measured by its share of the national GDP, is almost 25 per cent. For comparison, Quebec has 19 per cent of Canada's GDP but accounts for 23 per cent of its population. Significantly, except for the Territorial North, Western Canada's population has the highest percentage of Indigenous Canadians.

Note: Percentages of population, area, and GDP are for Canada as a whole; unemployment, French home language, and Indigenous population percentages are for Western Canada.

Sources: Tables 1.1, 1.2, 5.6.

## Western Canada's Physical Geography

Western Canada has two major physiographic regions—the Interior Plains and the Canadian Shield—as well as small portions of two others—the Hudson Bay Lowlands and the Cordillera (Figure 2.1). The Rocky Mountains form a natural and political border between southern Alberta and British Columbia. Each physiographic region has a particular set of geological conditions, physical landscapes, and natural resources.

The tiny slice of the Cordillera, along the eastern flank of the Rocky Mountains in Alberta, provides logging and mining opportunities. Its spectacular mountain landscape attracts thousands of visitors each year. This region has two internationally acclaimed parks, Banff National Park (Photo 8.1) and Jasper National Park, which attract visitors from around the world. Calgarians are especially fortunate in having easy access to the Kananaskis Country Provincial Park, where a number of mountain recreational activities—camping, hiking, and skiing—are available.

In the Interior Plains are three physiographic regions that indicate the elevation of the land rising towards the Rocky Mountains: the Manitoba Lowland (250 m elevation); the Saskatchewan Plain (550 m);

and the Alberta Plateau (900 m). The topography of the Interior is well suited for agriculture. The surface varies from flat lands that were former glacial lake to rolling terrain formed by glacial deposits. The most favourable land for farming lies in the Fertile Belt, where the moisture conditions for crops are most favourable (Figure 8.4). In most years, the combination of evaporation from the land and water loss through transpiration from plants (known as evapotranspiration) is less than the precipitation occurring over the year (see Vignette 8.1). In the semi-arid climatic zone known as the Dry Belt, evapotranspiration more frequently exceeds the amount of annual precipitation than in the Fertile Belt. One indication of the dry conditions is the presence of desert-like sand dunes formed after the last ice age by aeolian winds. The Great Sand Hills represent the major sand dune area in the Dry Belt (Photo 8.1 and Figure 8.4). Not surprisingly, the Palliser Expedition in the mid-nineteenth century declared that this short-grass area was an extension of the Great America Desert and therefore was unsuited for agriculture.

The geology of the Interior Plains is composed of sedimentary rocks that contain valuable deposits of fossil fuels. By value, the four leading mineral resources are oil, gas, coal, and potash. Most petroleum production occurs in a geological structure known as the **Western Sedimentary Basin**, which underlies most of Alberta and portions of British Columbia, Saskatchewan, and Manitoba. While potash and coal mining take place deep in the earth's crust, some minerals are close to the surface, thus permitting open-pit mining. In southeast Saskatchewan, brown coal (lignite) is extracted through open-pit mining and then burned to produce thermal electricity. However, brown coal produces high levels of greenhouse gases. Accordingly, the Saskatchewan government has signalled that these mines will close by 2030, affecting about 1,300 workers. In its 2019 budget, Saskatchewan allocated an initial $10 million to assist in this transition (Taylor, 2019a).

In Alberta, coal used for producing electricity is also being phased out. On the other hand, the mining of coking coal continues and provides an important export product to Asian steel mills. The main concern about greenhouse gas emissions comes from the oil industry, especially the mining of bitumen in the oil sands, a huge petroleum reserve found in the **Athabasca tar sands. Extraction takes place** by both open-pit mining and sub-surface mining techniques that involve injecting steam deep underground to "liquefy" the **bitumen** and then pumping the slurry liquid to the surface.

The Canadian Shield, consisting mainly of bare rocks exposed at the surface, extends over one-third of northern Manitoba and Saskatchewan as well as a small part of Alberta. While logging takes place along the southern edge of the Canadian Shield, most economic activity is associated with mining and hydroelectricity. In northern Saskatchewan, uranium companies produce most of Canada's uranium from open-pit and underground mines. Manitoba's northern rivers, particularly the Nelson River, have huge dams and power stations.

A continental climate controls weather. Far from moderating ocean influences, this climate is characterized by cold, dry winters and hot, dry summers. The resulting range of temperatures is extreme—from lows of −30°C in January to +30°C in July. During the winter, Arctic air masses often dominate weather conditions in the Prairies, placing the region in an Arctic "deep freeze" (Figure 2.6). The hot, dry summer weather, on the other hand, results from the northward migration of hot, dry air masses from the Southwest US (Figure 2.7).

Annual precipitation, whether snow or rain, is among the lowest in all regions except the Territorial North (Figure 2.8). The region is dry for two main reasons. First, distance from the Pacific Ocean reduces the opportunity of moist Pacific air masses to reach Western Canada. Second, **orographic uplift** of these Pacific air masses over the Rocky Mountains causes them to lose most of their moisture, leaving little precipitation for Western Canada. In southern Alberta, strong winds that become warm and dry as they flow down a mountain slope are known as **chinooks**. On the other hand, the **Alberta clippers** with their strong, frigid winds produce true blizzard conditions, due to severe blowing and drifting snow.

Average annual precipitation is between 300 and 500 mm for much of the Prairies, with lower amounts common in Alberta and Saskatchewan. A most significant feature of precipitation in Western Canada is the irregularity of summer precipitation. Farmers prefer spring rain to help the crops and a dry fall to facilitate harvesting. Prolonged dry spells occur mainly in

The four physiographic regions found in Western Canada are discussed in the **Chapter 2** section "Physiographic Regions" on page 23.

Ron Erwin/All Canada Photos

**PHOTO 8.1** The Great Sand Hills of southwest Saskatchewan. Following the retreat of the last ice sheet some 10,000 years ago, the climate of southern Saskatchewan experienced arid to semi-arid conditions. During the arid period, the sand dunes expanded their spatial limits. The study of inland aquatic ecosystems suggests that before the arrival of settlers, droughts were more frequent and of greater magnitude. The Dust Bowl of the 1930s was the most impactful drought since settlers arrived in the late nineteenth century. Since then, a similar drought has not occurred and the Sand Hills remain in a relatively static state.

the Dry Belt. Natural Resources Canada (2010) has described the threat of drought in the Dry Belt:

> All regions of Canada can experience seasonal [summer] dry spells, but only in the Prairie provinces can precipitation cease for a month, surface water disappear for entire seasons, and drought persist for a decade or more.

The amount of precipitation tends to decrease across Alberta and Saskatchewan as both depend heavily on moisture from Pacific air masses. On average, Calgary receives 413 mm annually; Saskatoon's figure falls to 350 mm; Peace River 386 mm. Further east, precipitation increases, with Winnipeg recording an average annual amount of 514 mm. While Saskatoon depends heavily on precipitation from Pacific

air masses, southern Manitoba (including Winnipeg) receives heavy summer rainfall from the moist Gulf of Mexico air masses. As a result, southern Manitoba is rarely troubled by drought compared to the prairie lands in southern Saskatchewan and Alberta. The driest lands are found in the Dry Belt, also known as **Palliser's Triangle**,[1] where, on average, less than 350 mm fall each year. One exception is the Cypress Hills located in Palliser's Triangle. Average annual precipitation reaches 460 mm because of its high elevation causing orographic precipitation (Photo 8.2). **Evapotranspiration** provides one measure of water deficit/surplus by measuring transpiration and evaporation, thus providing an indication of dryness/drought (Vignette 8.1).

In Western Canada, the Prairies are the agricultural hub. Lying within the Interior Plains physiographic region, two natural vegetation zones

**PHOTO 8.2** The Cypress Hills, located along the Alberta–Saskatchewan border, tower above the wheat fields of Saskatchewan. At 600 m above the surrounding Interior Plains, the Cypress Hills stand out as a physiographic, climatic, and vegetation anomaly. As an isolated island of lodgepole pine and white spruce surrounded by the semi-arid Prairies, few thought that the pine beetle could reach this remote area. But that assumption was incorrect and efforts to stem the attack of this beetle on the pine forest of the Cypress Hills began in the summer of 2012. The infestations continue, and the causes are related to climate change and population dynamics. See Vignette 2.4, "Cypress Hills," for more on this unique area of Western Canada.

(parkland and grassland) and three **chernozemic** soil zones (black, dark brown, and brown) exist (Figure 8.3). The parkland is a transition zone between the boreal forest and the grassland natural vegetation zone (Photo 8.3). Within the grassland, the dry climate becomes more prevalent as the evaporation rate increases towards the American border. The result is a change in natural vegetation from tall grass to short grass. Beneath the two types of grasslands, chernozemic soils were formed; black chernozemic soils are associated with tall-grass natural vegetation and dark brown and brown soils with short-grass natural vegetation. Figure 8.3 illustrates the spatial expanse of these soils, while Figure 8.4 shows that the Fertile and Dry Belts closely parallel the location of these soil types.

## Climate Change and the Oil Sands

Climate change is slowly altering our weather. At the same time, the oil sands produce much of Canada's greenhouse emissions, and these emissions accelerate global warming, which in turn produces other changes to our climate. Alberta has one of the world's largest oil reserves. This oil is mixed with sand, hence the name Athabasca tar sands. Extracting the oil from the tar poses three major environmental challenges. First, the release of greenhouse gases to the atmosphere through the upgrading process is among the largest in Canada. Second, open-pit mining has created a scarred industrial landscape. Third, separating the oil from the bitumen requires large amounts of water drawn from the Athabasca

Barrett & MacKay/All Canada Photos

**PHOTO 8.3** Within the Fertile Belt, black and dark brown chernozemic soils have formed under tall-grass natural vegetation and provide farmers with one of the most fertile soils in Canada. In this photograph taken near Biggar just west of Saskatoon, three types of rotations systems are illustrated. The dark brown field represents **summer fallow** where chemicals are used to control weeds, known as chem fallow; the yellow field contains a spring wheat crop; and the green field consists of grassland used for pasture.

River. The resulting toxic waste is drained into huge tailing ponds adjacent to that river. Leakage into the Athabasca River from the tailing ponds poses a serious threat, but an even bigger threat is the inevitable release of treated waters from tailing ponds into the Athabasca River.

Alberta's oil sands industry produces 1.8 billion litres of toxic water each day. The issue facing the industry is what to do with this vast quantity of non-renewable water. Its solution is tailing ponds, but these are not without problems. For instance, since the toxic waters cannot be released into the local rivers and lakes, they must be stored in large ponds for an indefinite time. The amount of toxic water from processing bitumen to synthetic oil is increasing every day, thus forcing companies to either increase the size of existing tailing ponds or create new ones. Leakage from these ponds has a negative effect on the landscape, groundwater, and surface waters, including the Athabasca River. Indigenous communities downstream from the tar sands development, notably at Fort Chipewyan, have experienced health consequences, including unusually high rates of cancer.

Reclamation of tailing ponds remains an elusive and expensive problem. While the companies led by Suncor are searching for a solution, the oil companies have failed to find one. One solution calls for the release of "treated" water into the Athabasca River, but so far, government regulators have rejected such requests. Still, the reality is stark—the mines are going to close one day and all that water in the tailing ponds has to go somewhere. Rodney Guest, director of water enclosure in regional development for Suncor, argues that "if you want to do integrated water management and set yourself up for successful closure and reclamation, returning water [from the tailing ponds] is something that should have been enabled for the industry a long time ago" (French, 2020). By 2023, changes to Alberta and federal regulations may approve of such releases.

## Climate Change and Agriculture

Agriculture, both crop and livestock, depends on adequate water supplies. These supplies are sometimes short in the dry continental climate found in Western Canada. Two factors, one natural and the

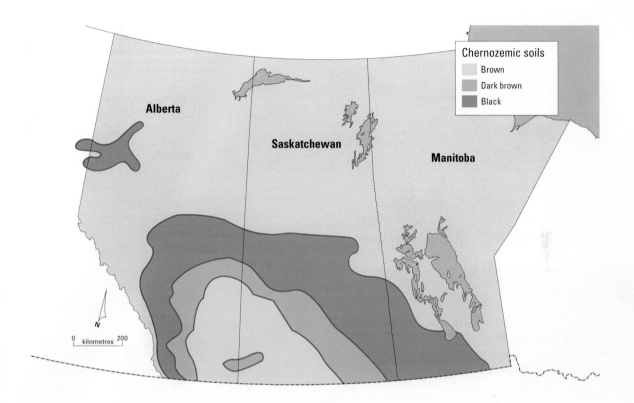

**FIGURE 8.3 Chernozemic soils in Western Canada**

Three types of chernozemic soils are found in the Canadian Prairies: black, dark brown, and brown. The differences in colour are due to the varying amount of humus in the soil, which, in turn, is a factor in the natural vegetation cover—short grass, tall grass, and parkland vegetation. The three types of natural vegetation reflect spatial differences in precipitation or, more precisely, in evapotranspiration. Much further north lies the Peace River Country, where its "degraded" black chernozemic soil was formed in a moister environment under an aspen forest where annual precipitation exceeds 500 mm. In comparison, annual average precipitation in the grassland zone is under 400 mm.

other human, are placing more and more pressure on the water resources of Western Canada. First, climate warming results in slightly higher average monthly temperatures and these higher temperatures are increasing the evapotranspiration rate. Second, as the population and industry of Western Canada grow, so does the demand for its scarce water supplies (Vignette 8.1).

Within Western Canada, the **Dry Belt**—Palliser's Triangle—is the most vulnerable area for drought (Figure 8.4). While average annual precipitation in the Dry Belt is the lowest in Western Canada—from place to place, precipitation varies from 300 to 400 mm per year—below-average precipitation results in so-called "dry years." A series of dry years in the 1930s resulted in the disastrous Dust Bowl, with the longest-lasting

drought conditions occurring in the Dry Belt, driving thousands of settlers off the land. The most recent dry spell extended from 1999 to 2002. By the summer of 2002, the cumulative effect of several dry years left reserves of soil moisture extremely low. With insufficient precipitation and low soil moisture, farmers in Saskatchewan, Manitoba, and Alberta saw their hay crops fail, leaving livestock without feed or water. From 2003 to 2019, annual precipitation has rebounded, creating a decade of "wet years." When arid conditions will return is unknown, but in a dry continental climate, a spell of adequate precipitation for 10 years or so is often followed by several years of below-average precipitation. From a historical perspective, map-makers in the late nineteenth century still labelled the Great Plains of the United States as the

**THINK ABOUT IT**

With much warmer ocean temperatures, Pacific air masses are more likely to contain sufficient moisture. Could this aspect of climate change increase precipitation for the Prairies?

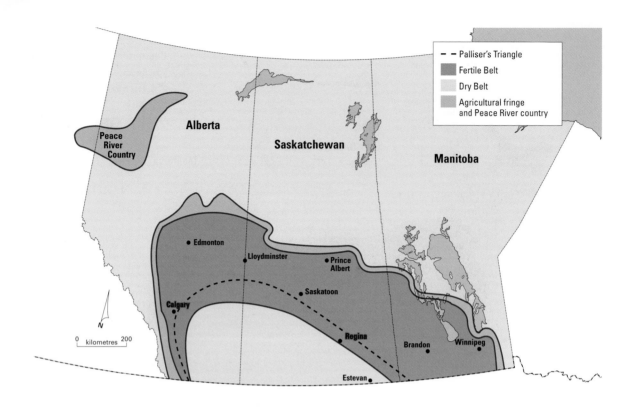

**FIGURE 8.4 Agricultural regions in Western Canada**

Farming in the Prairies can be divided into three areas: the Fertile Belt, the Dry Belt, and the Peace River Country. Each region has a distinct type of agriculture because of variations in physical geography. Key factors are limited moisture and the length of the growing season.

**Great American Desert.** American settlers following the Oregon Trail had no thoughts of stopping in the Great Plains but pushed across the Rocky Mountains to a more favourable climate for agriculture along the Pacific coast. The Palliser Expedition was charged with determining if the Canadian Prairies had the potential for agricultural settlement. Palliser's conclusion was mixed—short-grass lands (the Dry Belt) were not suitable for farming but long-grass lands (the Fertile Belt) could sustain the tilling and support agriculture (Spry, 1963). In 1858, another expedition, organized in Canada West (Ontario) and led by Henry Hind, confirmed that the long-grass area and parkland (the natural vegetation zone between the grasslands and the boreal forest) offered the best land for agricultural settlement.

With the ever-increasing drawing of water from the South and North Saskatchewan rivers for agricultural, industrial, and urban uses, what does the future hold? With the glaciers in the Rocky Mountains retreating, future supplies may be in jeopardy. Oddly, Manitoba faces the opposite problem—the annual threat of spring floods from the north-flowing Red River plus more annual precipitation than the rest of the Prairies (Winnipeg's annual precipitation is 521 mm while Saskatoon, on average, receives only 354 mm). Spring thaw comes earlier in North Dakota and, as the rising waters of the Red River reach Manitoba, river ice dams often form, causing the rising waters to overflow their banks into the extremely flat terrain of the Manitoba lowland. The Red River Floodway, completed in 1969, has kept floodwaters from reaching Winnipeg by diverting the northward-flowing river around the city, but other communities and farmland in the Red River Valley remain vulnerable. Here, spring and flooding are nearly synonymous. The extent of the April 2011 Red River flood is shown in Photo 2.14.

## Vignette 8.2

### Radioactive Waste from Abandoned Uranium Mines

Before the federal and provincial governments regulated uranium mining, radioactive wastes were often left at the abandoned mine site. Such is the case at Lake Athabasca where radioactive waste is slowly seeping into the lake and will eventually spread throughout the Mackenzie River system. For years, these dangerous wastes were recognized as a serious hazard to the environment but a decommissioning agreement between the federal and Saskatchewan governments was stalled over the sharing of the cost of cleanup. In fact, estimating cleanup costs was difficult and actual costs exceed the original estimate. In 2007, the federal and provincial governments announced an agreement to share equally the estimated cost of $24.6 million to deal with this waste. However, by 2018, the revised estimated cost reached $280 million as the cleanup work was much more extensive than originally anticipated (MacPherson, 2019). The Saskatchewan Research Council (SRC) is responsible for this multi-million-dollar reclamation project, which involves assessing and reclaiming the Gunnar Uranium Mine and Mill site, the Lorado Uranium Mill site, and 36 satellite mine sites in northern Saskatchewan. In 2020, reclamation work continued, but with no end to the cleanup in sight (SRC, 2012, 2016, 2020).

In **Chapter 2**, "Extreme Weather Events," page 45, the Red River Valley, spring floods, and the diversion of water around Winnipeg by the Red River Floodway are discussed.

## Western Canada's Historical Geography

Prior to the arrival of European colonists, Indigenous nations such as the Cree and Blackfoot lived in the lands now known as Western Canada and hunted buffalo and other game. Until they obtained horses, they hunted on foot. For thousands of years, the inhabitants of these lands employed various techniques to kill buffalo. One technique was the use of buffalo jumps, in which the bison were forced to stampede over a sudden and unexpected drop. The most famous buffalo jump is located in the foothills of the Rocky Mountains near Fort Macleod, Alberta. Known as the Head-Smashed-In Buffalo Jump, the site is a UNESCO World Heritage Site and home of the museum of Blackfoot culture.

Before Canada was formed in 1867, the fur trade played a role in Britain gaining political control over these lands. Beginning in 1670, the Hudson's Bay Company (HBC) obtained a royal charter from King Charles II that granted the company a monopoly over the region drained by all rivers and streams flowing into Hudson Bay. Canada's western interior was part of Rupert's Land. In 1821, when the company merged with its rival, the North West Company, the HBC acquired control over more land, known as the North-Western Territory (lands draining into the Arctic Ocean). In 1870, the British government ceded these lands to Canada, but with no mention of Indigenous peoples (Figure 3.5). The question of landownership was determined by the British government and later Canada. For First Nations, this question was resolved by treaties, but in the case of the Métis, their dream of a separate state ended at the Battle of Batoche in 1885.

How did this land transfer begin? In 1810, a small portion of land in Western Canada was first used by disposed Scottish Highlanders for agricultural purposes. At that time, Lord Selkirk, a Scots nobleman, acquired land in the Red River Valley from the Hudson's Bay Company with approval of local Indigenous tribes. The first Scottish settlers arrived in 1812 to form an agricultural settlement near Fort Garry, the principal HBC trading post in the region. This became known as the Red River Settlement. Selkirk's settlers, however, faced an unfamiliar and harsh environment and had great trouble establishing an agricultural colony. Over the years, many gave up and left for Upper Canada and the United States.

At the same time, many former officers and servants of the Hudson's Bay Company, along with

Michael Wheatley/All Canada Photos

**PHOTO 8.4** Head-Smashed-In Buffalo jump. Taking advantage of topography, this kill site provided ample bison meat and skins for Indigenous tribes in this area of southern Alberta. Some 10 kilometres before the cliff, the topography resembles a plain. The bison were encouraged by stone cairns and people waving blankets to move from the plain to the precipice where they fell to their deaths.

**THINK ABOUT IT**

The United States purchased Alaska from Russia in 1867 for $7.2 million while Great Britain paid the Hudson's Bay Company £300,000 or $1.2 million for regaining its rights to much of Canada. Who made the better deal?

their Indigenous wives and children, settled at Fort Garry. In addition to these English-speaking people were the French-speaking Métis who had worked for the North West Company. Because the Métis were Catholic and spoke French, they formed a separate cultural group within the settlement. After the consolidation of the Hudson's Bay Company and the North West Company, former North West Company employees were let go. Many of these workers were Métis, who then settled at Red River where they turned their attention to subsistence farming, freighting, and buffalo hunting.

During the negotiations with Britain over Confederation, the subject of the annexation of Rupert's Land into the Dominion of Canada arose, and provision was made in the British North America Act for its admission into Canada. In 1869, the Hudson's Bay Company signed the deed of transfer, surrendering to Great Britain its chartered territory for £300,000—with the notable exception of the lands surrounding

its posts and about 1,133,160 ha of farmland. In 1870, Great Britain transferred Rupert's Land to Canada.

## But What about the Original Inhabitants?

In the nineteenth century, Plains peoples and Métis formed the population of Western Canada. Both depended on the buffalo and the fur trade. In the last half of the century, commercial hunting of buffalo in the United States and Canada ended with the destruction of the great buffalo herds. With the virtual extinction of the buffalo, the Plains peoples (Sarcee, Blood, Peigan, Stoney, Plains Cree, Nakota, Lakota, Blackfoot, and Saulteaux) could no longer support themselves. The transfer of Hudson's Bay lands to Canada, coupled with Ottawa's plan to settle the arable lands of Western Canada, meant that the only option for Plains peoples was to sign treaties and live on reserves (Figure 3.11).[2] The Métis were also confronted by the impact of these historic changes on their way of life. Yet, because they had formed an organized settlement at Red River, the Métis were more able to resist Canada's desire to settle the Red River and the rest of the Prairies with farmers.

In 1867, the population at Red River was nearly 12,000, mostly Métis. The arrival of land surveyors and colonists led the Métis, under the leadership of Louis Riel, to mount the Red River Resistance in 1869. The Métis wanted to negotiate the terms of entry into Canada from a position of strength—that is, as a government with control over the Red River—and they obtained major concessions from Ottawa: guaranteed ownership of land, recognition of the French language, and permission to maintain Roman Catholic schools. In 1870, the fur-trading district of Assiniboia became the province of Manitoba. But their victory was hollow. First, Ottawa sent troops to exert Canada's control over the new province, forcing Riel and his followers to flee. Second, colonists began to pour into Manitoba, changing the demographic balance of power and overwhelming the Métis community.

Many Métis left the colony to search for a new place to live under their own governance in the Canadian West. Such a place was Batoche, just north of the site where Saskatoon now is situated. Within 15 years, however, settlers would again encroach on the Métis agricultural settlement, bringing with them Canadian governance as defined by Ottawa. In 1885, as before, the Métis, led by Louis Riel, started a resistance. This time, the Canadian militia defeated the Métis at the Battle of Batoche and Riel was captured, found guilty of treason, and hanged.

The experiences of First Nations groups during the early period of western colonization were somewhat different from those of the Métis. Groups such as the Blackfoot had roamed across the Canadian Prairies and the northern Great Plains of the United States long before the arrival of European colonists. These groups were semi-nomadic and hunted buffalo. By the 1870s, the buffalo had virtually disappeared from the Prairies, leaving the Plains peoples destitute. They had little choice but to sign treaties with the federal government. Between 1873 and 1876, all the First Nations groups (except for three Cree chiefs—Big Bear, Little Pine, and Lucky Man—and their followers) signed numbered treaties in exchange for reserves, cash gratuities, annual payments in perpetuity, the promise of educational and agricultural assistance, and the right to hunt and fish on Crown land until such land was required for other purposes. In 1882, impending starvation for his people also forced Big Bear to accept Treaty 6. Over the next few years, however, the Cree sought other concessions from the federal government. When these efforts failed, Cree warriors supported the doomed Métis resistance in 1885 by attacking several settlements, including Fort Pitt, the Hudson's Bay post on the North Saskatchewan River near the present-day Alberta–Saskatchewan border.[3]

Treaties with Ottawa offered First Nations peoples prospects for survival and supposedly time and federal support to find a place in a new economy, but the treaties also made them wards of the Crown. Confined to reserves, First Nations were isolated from the evolving Canadian society and became increasingly dependent on the federal government. Further north, the Woodland Cree and Dene (Chipewyan) tribes who lived in the boreal forest beyond fertile land were not as affected by the encroachment of western colonists. Although they, too, signed treaties, these northern peoples continued their migratory hunting and trapping lifestyle well into the next century. In 1930, the federal government transferred to the provinces the jurisdiction it had exercised over the Crown lands and natural resources of the region since its purchase from the Hudson's Bay Company in 1870. This transfer did not mention Indigenous rights, and nearly a century later the omission remains a bone of contention for Indigenous peoples. By the 1950s, life on the land had its hardships, ranging from food shortages to virtually no medical services for those still on the land. Consequently, many Indigenous peoples in the northern reaches of the Prairie provinces moved to settlements.

## Settlement of the Land

Colonization of the Prairies by Europeans required transportation infrastructure. In 1881, Ottawa announced generous terms: the Canadian Pacific Railway Company was awarded a charter, whereby the company received $25 million from the federal government, 1,000 km of existing railway lines in eastern Canada owned by the federal government, and over 10 million ha of prairie land in alternate square-mile sections on both sides of the railway to a maximum

The resistances of 1869–70 and 1885 are examined in **Chapter 3**; see pages 96 and 99.

Library and Archives Canada

**PHOTO 8.5** Louis Riel. The Métis search for a place within Confederation began with armed resistance in 1869–70 and 1885. Louis Riel was the political and spiritual leader of both rebellions. After the Métis insurgents lost the Battle of Batoche in 1885, Riel surrendered to the Canadian forces. He was tried and convicted of high treason, and on 16 November 1885 Riel was hanged as a traitor. He remains a hero to the Métis to this day.

depth of 39 km. The terms were successful—the CPR line was completed in 1885, with mostly foreign workers having overcome the difficult and dangerous labour involved in pushing the rail line across the Cordillera. As a result, the new Dominion achieved four important nation-forming goals:

- An east–west transportation link united Canada from coast to coast.
- The vast territory west of Rupert's Land was secured for Canada.
- With treaties in place, settlers could purchase farmland.

- The western grain economy, based on a rail transportation system to eastern ports and then by ship to Great Britain and other European countries, flourished.

The settling of Western Canada marks one of the world's great migrations and the transformation of the Prairies into an agricultural resource hub. At the same time, this transformation signalled the end of the hunting economy and placed diverse Indigenous peoples under a colonial system of assimilation in accordance with the Indian Act.

Under the Dominion Lands Act of 1872, settlers were promised "cheap" land in Manitoba—by building a house and cultivating some of the land, they could obtain 65 ha of land for only $10. Following 1872, an influx of prospective homesteaders began arriving, most coming from Ontario. However, until the Canadian Pacific Railway was completed across the Prairies, the region attracted few settlers. After 1885, settlers began to occupy lands in Saskatchewan and Alberta. The first wave came from Ontario, Great Britain, and the United States. The second wave came from Continental Europe.

By 1896, the federal government sought to increase immigration by promoting Western Canada in Great Britain and Europe as "the last agricultural frontier" in North America. The Canadian government initiated an aggressive campaign, administered by Minister of the Interior Clifford Sifton, to lure more settlers to the Canadian West. Thousands of posters, pamphlets, and advertisements were sent to and distributed in Europe and the United States to promote free homesteads and assisted passages. Prior to 1896, most immigrants came from the British Isles or the United States—these were "desirable" immigrants. Sifton's campaign, however, cast a wider net to areas of Central and Eastern Europe that were not English-speaking and therefore provided "less desirable" immigrants. This shift in strategy generated considerable controversy among some English-speaking Canadians who believed in the racial superiority of British people.

Nevertheless, Clifford Sifton's efforts paid off. After 1896, the majority of settlers—about 2 million—were Central or Eastern Europeans from Germany, Russia, and Ukraine. This large influx of primarily

See **Chapter 3,** "Sifton Widens the Net," page 101, for discussion of Sifton's immigration policy and of the plight of the pacifist Doukhobor sect.

non-English-speaking immigrants led to a quite different cultural makeup in Western Canada from that in Central Canada, where the French and English dominated. Within a remarkably short span of time, cultural and linguistic assimilation had forged a non-British but English-speaking society from the sons and daughters of these immigrants. Some, however, kept separate. For instance, Doukhobor settlers were Russian-speaking peasants whose adherence to communal living made adjustment and acceptance difficult if not impossible. By 1905, Alberta and Saskatchewan had sufficient populations to warrant provincial status. By the outbreak of World War I, almost all of the fertile lands of Western Canada were colonized.

The decision to build the CPR along a southern route (from Winnipeg to Regina to Calgary) had two repercussions for farms. First, the railway provided them with a means of getting their crop to market. Second, crop failure was high because one-quarter of the land opened to homesteaders was in the driest part of Western Canada known as Palliser's Triangle. Dissatisfaction with the monopoly held by the CPR prompted farmers to seek an alternative rail route to ship their grain to Europe. This northern rail line was known as the Hudson Bay Railway.

## Western Canada Today

Western Canada consists of the three Prairie provinces. Alberta, the economic giant of the three provinces, has 63 per cent of the population in Western Canada and accounts for 72 per cent of the region's GDP (Table 8.1). Each province has much natural wealth. Saskatchewan, for example, has most of the cropland and is the leading producer of potash and uranium. In addition to having the richest agricultural land in the

West, Manitoba produces vast amounts of hydroelectric power from the Nelson River. Even so, Alberta, the wealthiest province, holds the trump resource card—oil and gas. Indeed, Alberta's oil production in 2018 allowed Canada to rank as the fifth-largest producer in the world (*Natural Resources Canada*, 2019a). However, the recent fall in oil prices has stung. Both Alberta and Saskatchewan have witnessed a sharp drop in revenue from resource royalties and both suffered from low GDP growth and high unemployment rates over the past four years. By 2020, oil prices remained near record lows, suggesting that the best times for the oil sands are over.

## Industrial Structure

In 2020, Western Canada had a population of nearly 7 million, who made up 18 per cent of Canada's labour force. With a strong resource-based economy, the percentage of workers in the three categories comprising Western Canada's industrial structure is, as would be expected, very different from the employment structure in Ontario and Quebec. Western Canada's economy has shifted more into an advanced economy where information and research are widespread. In this sense, Western Canada is less vulnerable to the resource boom-and-bust cycle, but much lower oil prices have hurt. At the same time, the tertiary sector in Western Canada, while gaining the most workers, has lost some of its share of the total labour force (Table 8.2). In addition, the application of technology, especially in secondary activities, has dampened the percentage in this category from 2005 to 2019 by replacing workers with machines.

Given the importance of agriculture and natural resources, it is not surprising that employment

| TABLE 8.1 | Western Canada: Population and GDP, 2016 | | | | | |
|---|---|---|---|---|---|---|
| Province | Population | % of Western Canada | % of Canada | GDP ($ billions) | % of Western Canada | % of Canada |
| **Alberta** | 4,067,175 | 63.4 | 11.6 | 335.1 | 69.8 | 17.3 |
| **Saskatchewan** | 1,098,352 | 17.1 | 3.1 | 82.5 | 17.2 | 4.3 |
| **Manitoba** | 1,278,365 | 19.5 | 3.6 | 62.7 | 13.0 | 3.2 |
| **Western Canada** | 6,443,892 | 100.0 | 18.3 | 480.3 | 100.0 | 24.8 |
| **Canada** | 35,151,728 | | 100.0 | 1,934.6 | | 100.0 |

Sources: Adapted from Statistics Canada (2019a, 2019b).

| TABLE 8.2 | Western Canada Industrial Sectors by Number of Workers, 2005 and 2019 | | | | |
|---|---|---|---|---|---|
| Industrial Sector | Workers, 2005 | Workers, 2005 (%) | Workers, 2019 | Workers, 2019 (%) | Percentage Difference |
| Primary | 284,300 | 10.0 | 461,200 | 12.3 | +2.3 |
| Secondary | 468,600 | 16.5 | 601,700 | 16.0 | −0.5 |
| Tertiary | 2,095,300 | 73.5 | 2,687,100 | 71.7 | −1.8 |
| Total | 2,848,200 | 100.0 | 3,750,000 | 100.0 | |

Sources: Adapted from Statistics Canada (2006, 2020a).

by industrial sector in Western Canada reveals the relative prominence of primary activities. While Table 8.2 presents only a generalized picture of the western economy, the importance of the primary sector is undeniable. For instance, the percentage of people employed in this sector is more than six times that of the 1.9 per cent employed in the primary sector in Ontario, Canada's principal industrial core region. In fact, the percentage of Western Canadian workers in the primary sector increased from 10 per cent in 2005 to 12.3 per cent in 2019 (Table 8.2). The tertiary sector showed the greatest absolute growth with the addition of nearly 600,000 workers, although its percentage of the labour force dipped to 71.8 per cent. The oil sands and potash industries support a robust mining-oriented manufacturing sector in Edmonton, Calgary, and Saskatoon as well as in industrial centres in Ontario and Quebec. This expansion results in a strong construction industry and, together with the highly specialized manufacturing for that industry, accounts for the relatively stable performance of the secondary sector.

## Knowledge-Based Economy

The knowledge-based economy is closely linked to research and development (R&D). Governments, both federal and provincial, have invested heavily in R&D at universities and public research institutes as well as providing tax incentives for private research firms. While applied research takes place in a variety of fields, the focus is on agriculture, energy, and potash. The push for advancing technology into these sectors of the economy is largely generated by the need to export these products to foreign markets. The key is to apply modern technology to create economic advances. In the past, plant breeding

resulted in improvements in wheat and canola. Energy research looks into **carbon sequestration** in Alberta and Saskatchewan.

## Technological Spearheads

The spearheads of Western Canada, as might be expected, focus on primary-sector activities: agriculture, oil, and mining. Unexpectedly, however, the digital industry, so prominent in Toronto and Montreal, also has a foothold in the major cities of Western Canada. The reason is simple: the technological revolution is affecting all sectors of the economy by making them more efficient and, in the case of agriculture, more suitable for prairie weather conditions. Technology in agriculture has played and continues to play a critical role by ensuring greater yields, improving farming practices, and creating more efficient farm implements.

## Plant Breeding and Biotechnology

The first variety of spring wheat grown in the Prairies was known as Red Fife. Farmers from southern Ontario brought these seeds to Manitoba in the late nineteenth century. Unfortunately, the Prairies have a much shorter growing season than southern Ontario. Frost often damaged the Red Fife wheat crop, thus threatening agriculture in the Prairies. By 1910, this problem was resolved when federal plant breeders developed Marquis wheat, which has a shorter maturation period and therefore was more suitable for the West. Farmers quickly accepted Marquis wheat and harvests became more reliable and profitable.

Today, Western Canada is the global centre for biotechnology with the major research facilities located in Saskatoon, where research conducted by private seed developers, federal researchers, and university

**THINK ABOUT IT**

While Monsanto was legally correct to take the late Percy Schmeiser to court, did Monsanto step over a moral boundary?

plant breeders improves a wide variety of plants and seeds. Their combined efforts have increased yields, reduced plant diseases, and improved the quality of the final product.

In the 1970s, plant breeders at the University of Saskatchewan were able to alter rapeseed into a commercial product called canola. Since then, plant breeders have improved the quality of canola. The ultimate goal was achieved—a high-quality edible oilseed that would thrive on the Canadian Prairies. Canola oil has very little saturated fat—just 7 per cent, the lowest level of any vegetable oil. With consumers accepting canola oil, the area seeded to this crop grew substantially and soon exceeded spring wheat. The main reason for its popularity among farmers is its high price and the option to haul the seeds to local crushing plants, thus reducing transportation cost to tidewater and foreign markets.

One of the private seed developers, the global giant Monsanto, developed and patented a canola plant that is resistant to its Roundup herbicide (Monsanto, 2012). With these seeds, farmers are able to control weed competition and obtain high yields, but, besides the cost of the seed, farmers must sign a formal agreement with Monsanto that specifies that new seed must be purchased from the company every year. This is to prevent farmers from collecting seeds from last year's crop to save the cost of purchasing new seed. The company monitors the cropland to seek out such farmers and then take those farmers to court, arguing that seeds with its modified plant cells belong to Monsanto. The most famous case in Saskatchewan, *Monsanto Canada Inc. v. Schmeiser*, went to the Supreme Court of Canada. In 2004 the Court ruled in favour of Monsanto (Photo 8.6).

Saskatoon Star Phoenix–Richard Marjan/The Canadian Press

**PHOTO 8.6** Farmer Percy Schmeiser leaves a press conference after the Supreme Court of Canada, in the 2004 case of *Monsanto Canada Inc. v. Schmeiser*, ruled that Monsanto has the right to collect fees for canola seeds Schmeiser collected. The Court determined that Monsanto's patented invention of genetically modified plant cells applies to all seeds with those cell characteristics. To many ecologists and environmentalists, global companies like Monsanto and the modified crops they produce pose a serious threat to the environment.

## Technological Breakthrough: Horizontal Drilling in Oil Shale

Horizontal drilling, often called directional drilling, has revolutionized how oil and gas wells are drilled. Most importantly, horizontal drilling has greatly improved the capacity of the drilling system to reach previously inaccessible oil and gas deposits. While slanted drilling was first used in the 1930s, technical advances have pushed this type of drilling to the forefront. This form of drilling has several advantages. First, horizontal drilling will produce many times more oil and gas than a vertical well. A vertical well only penetrates a few feet of the oil or gas zone, but a well drilled horizontally may penetrate several thousand feet into this zone. Second, unproductive rock formations, such as the Bakken oil shale located primarily in southern Saskatchewan and North Dakota, have become productive due to horizontal drilling. But the story does not end here. Since the **Bakken Formation** has poor porosity, oil could not flow along these horizontal drill holes. The solution is hydraulic fracturing, which involves pumping fluid and rounded beads into it to break the shale and keep open the fissures thus created, which allows oil to flow. One downside to this technology is that the toxic fluid used in the process can enter the water table and underground aquifers, making the water unfit for drinking. Another environmental issue that has arisen with hydraulic fracturing or "fracking" is the instability it creates in the earth's crust, which is believed to lead to earthquakes, as has happened repeatedly in the state of Oklahoma.

## Technological Gamble: Carbon Capture and Storage

Carbon capture and storage (CCS) is a technology that can be used to help reduce the impact of greenhouse gas emissions by capturing $CO_2$ and storing it underground (Figure 8.5). This technology is pushing into uncharted territory where capital costs are high and the outcome uncertain. Like most technological gambles, the first-time construction process is a "learning one," as is the theoretical goal of capturing 90 per cent of the carbon contained in the fumes from burning coal. Valuable lessons are learned that might assure lower construction costs and a higher percentage of carbon capture in future plants. Alberta (with bitumen processing) and Saskatchewan (with lignite thermal coal burning) have large carbon emissions, and they have led the way in carbon capture and storage efforts. Both provinces and the federal government have provided funds to large coal and oil sands companies to develop carbon capture and storage technology.

### Quest Project

In Alberta, the Quest Project, a joint venture among Shell Canada (60 per cent), Chevron Canada Limited (20 per cent), and Marathon Canadian Oil Sands Holding Limited (20 per cent), came into commercial production in 2015 (Shell, 2015). It reduces carbon dioxide emissions from Shell's Scotford bitumen **upgrader** at Fort Saskatchewan (just east of Edmonton) by one-third. The upgrader converts oil sands bitumen into synthetic crude that can be refined into fuel and other products. By 2019, the Quest carbon capture and storage project north of Edmonton had four million tonnes of stored carbon dioxide.

### Saskatchewan Carbon Sequestration Project

Almost half of the electric power produced in Saskatchewan comes from lignite coal. Worse yet, 70 per cent of greenhouse emissions come from coal-fired thermal plants. Saskatchewan's carbon sequestration is designed to reduce those emissions. The cost of this facility was high, at $1.4 billion, but the goal to reduce greenhouse gas emissions by 90 per cent from this power plant certainly would be a huge step in the right direction. In 2014, SaskPower's coal-fired power plant carbon sequestration facility near Estevan, Saskatchewan, began operations, but a number of technical issues interrupted its operations. As a first-time construction effort, the plan fell short of expectations. The goal of capturing $800,000 each year was reached once, in 2016. In 2017, the figure was $507,000, and in the following year, $626,000 (Taylor, 2019b). According to Mike Monea of SaskPower (Wilt, 2016), "Nobody's ever put all this

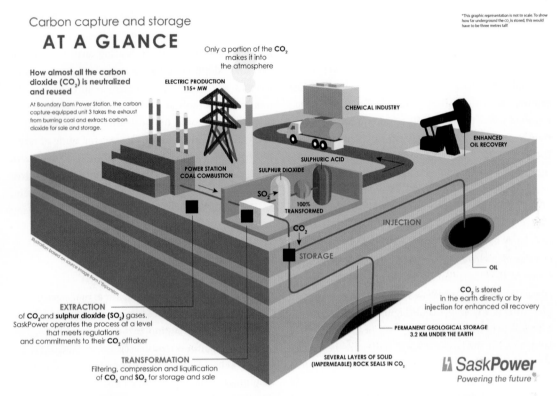

## Carbon capture and storage
# AT A GLANCE

*This graphic representation is not to scale. To show how far underground the $CO_2$ is stored, this would have to be three metres tall!

**How almost all the carbon dioxide ($CO_2$) is neutralized and reused**

At Boundary Dam Power Station, the carbon capture-equipped unit 3 takes the exhaust from burning coal and extracts carbon dioxide for sale and storage.

Only a portion of the $CO_2$ makes it into the atmosphere

ELECTRIC PRODUCTION 115+ MW

CHEMICAL INDUSTRY

ENHANCED OIL RECOVERY

POWER STATION COAL COMBUSTION

SULPHUR DIOXIDE

SULPHURIC ACID

$SO_2$

100% TRANSFORMED

$CO_2$

STORAGE

INJECTION

OIL

$CO_2$ is stored in the earth directly or by injection for enhanced oil recovery

**EXTRACTION**
of $CO_2$ and sulphur dioxide ($SO_2$) gases. SaskPower operates the process at a level that meets regulations and commitments to their $CO_2$ offtaker

PERMANENT GEOLOGICAL STORAGE 3.2 KM UNDER THE EARTH

SEVERAL LAYERS OF SOLID (IMPERMEABLE) ROCK SEALS IN $CO_2$

**TRANSFORMATION**
Filtering, compression and liquification of $CO_2$ and $SO_2$ for storage and sale

Illustration based on source image from L'Expansion

**SaskPower**
Powering the future®

**FIGURE 8.5 Carbon capture and storage at Boundary Dam Power Station**

Carbon capture involves trapping the carbon dioxide at the Boundary Dam Power Station and shipping the carbon dioxide gas by pipeline to the Weyburn-Midale oil field where the gas is pumped underground to enhance the extraction of oil.

Source: SaskPower.

equipment together before. Now [that] it has [been done], engineers are saying, 'We'd change this, or we wouldn't do this next time.'" While the cost is high, the sale of the carbon dioxide gas to the Weyburn-Midale field has more than compensated SaskPower for the operating cost of the carbon extraction process. As a result of injecting carbon dioxide into the oil basin, oil production increased.

## Western Canada's Economic Anchor: Agriculture

Agriculture was the economic spearhead that led to European settlement of the Prairies. While much has changed, it remains a key anchor of Western Canada's economy. In the twenty-first century, while still important, agriculture is no longer the principal engine of economic growth. Natural resource extraction, led by the oil and gas industry, has taken over that role. Still, agriculture is a sustainable resource, while oil and gas have a limited lifespan.

The critical trends in agriculture in Western Canada are:

- larger farms, fewer farmers, and older farmers;
- technology that allows for less fallow land and more cropland;
- adoption of advanced technology, i.e., biotechnology;
- depopulation of rural Western Canada and the demise of rural towns;
- growth of foreign markets for pulse and specialty crops.

## Larger Farms, Fewer Farmers, and Older Farmers

The irreversible trend of larger farms, fewer farmers, and older farmers continued into the twenty-first century. By 2016, Statistics Canada's *Census of Agriculture* reported fewer than 100,000 farms in Canada, down by 5.9 per cent from 2011 (Statistics Canada, 2017). Even more significant, the number of farm operations dropped below 200,000 for the first time, and the average farm size was over 1,000 acres (Statistics Canada, 2017). The total cropland, however, has increased slightly from 1971 to 2016 (Figure 8.6). While these figures apply to Canada, most farmland is found in Western Canada, where most farm operations take place. In terms of total Canadian field crop area, Western Canada accounts for 86 per cent with Saskatchewan alone providing nearly 47 per cent (Figure 8.7).

Saskatchewan, with nearly half of Canada's cropland, also has the largest average individual farm size, at nearly 1,800 acres. Since 1941, the number of farms has declined from 140,000 farms to 35,000 farms. As the number of farms declined, so did the number of farmers. The shift to larger farms increased the profitability of farms and operators. In turn, farmers could manage larger farms by increasing farm mechanization and adoption of technology. At the same time, farmers, particularly young farmers just entering the industry, took on heavy debt loads, making them particularly vulnerable to weakening demands, prices, and yields. Another critical factor is the aging of farmers: by 2016, nearly 55 per cent were over the age of 55. Fewer young people are opting for farming and/or have the capital to purchase farmland and equipment, so the question becomes: Who will farm the land 20 years from now?

## Agricultural Regions

Western Canada is blessed with a rich agricultural land base made up of rich chernozemic soils. Within the physiographic region of the Interior Plains, two distinct agricultural regions can be identified: (1) the **Fertile Belt** (black soil associated with parkland and long-grass natural vegetation; and (2) the **Dry Belt** (brown soils with short-grass natural vegetation).

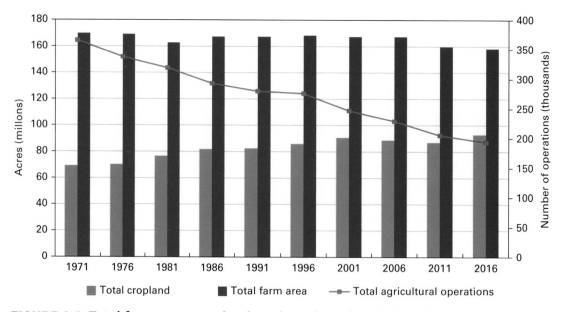

**FIGURE 8.6  Total farm area, cropland, and number of agricultural operations, Canada, 1971 to 2016**

The decline in agricultural operations (farms) indicates the effect of mechanization and the increase in larger farms, which allows efficient use of machinery. While this graph portrays Canada, the trend is found in all regions, including Western Canada.

Source: Statistics Canada (2018).

As well, the **agricultural fringe** and **Peace River Country** are on the northern edge of agriculture in the West with degraded black soils (Figure 8.3). These sub-regions have very different growing conditions from the two principal agricultural regions. The major factors controlling those conditions are the number of frost-free days and the soil moisture. The Fertile Belt provides the best environment for crop agriculture. The Dry Belt is a grain/livestock area. In the agricultural fringe and Peace River Country, the short growing season associated with threat of early frost in the late summer encourages farmers to grow feed grains and raise livestock.

### The Fertile Belt

The Fertile Belt extends from southern Manitoba to the foothills of the Rocky Mountains west of Edmonton (Figure 8.4). The higher levels of soil moisture, an adequate frost-free period, and rich soils make this belt ideal for a variety of crops and livestock. For over a hundred years, farmers planted grain seeds, especially spring wheat. By the twenty-first century, the acreage in grain had declined, while the planting of canola, pulse crops (peas and lentils; Photo 8.7), and specialty crops (buckwheat, canary seed, ginseng, herbs, spices, industrial hemp, mustard seed, safflower seed, and sunflower seed) had increased. This change was fuelled by global markets and by consistently low prices for wheat and higher prices for canola, pulse crops, and specialty crops.

### The Dry Belt

The Dry Belt contains both cattle ranches and large grain farms. It extends from the Saskatchewan–Manitoba boundary to the southern foothills of the Rockies and north nearly to Saskatoon (Figure 8.4). However, the driest area, or heart of the Dry Belt, occupies a much smaller area, stretching southward from the South Saskatchewan River to the US border. The arid nature of the Dry Belt is due to a combination of low annual precipitation and to longer, hotter summers resulting in high evapotranspiration rates. Within the Dry Belt, grain and hay are grown to supply winter feed for the cattle ranching that dominates in this area; chickpeas, which have a long tap root, represent a new crop. Cattle ranches are large because of the lower productivity of the

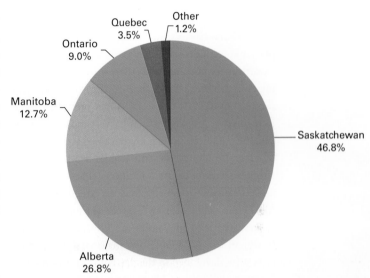

**FIGURE 8.7 Provincial distribution of total field crop area, 2016**

The dominance of Western Canada but especially Saskatchewan is revealed in this pie chart.

Source: Statistics Canada (2017).

dry land and the need for huge grazing areas to support a rotational grazing system.

The Dry Belt is often referred to as "Next Year Country," and dry summer weather often can lead to

**PHOTO 8.7** Canadian production of pulses is concentrated in Saskatchewan. A pulse is an edible seed harvested from the pod of a variety of annual leguminous plants. Pulses grown in Canada include dry beans, dry peas, lentils, and chickpeas. Production peaked in 2017 and then dropped sharply as its main customer, India, halted imports from Canada. Saskatchewan farmers grow 80 per cent of Canada's lentils (the three types of which are shown here). Lentils form a key ingredient in many curry dishes.

Justinc/Wikipedia

crop failure. However, farmers face a whole range of other natural hazards: summer frosts, hail, grasshoppers, and plant diseases such as stem rust. All of these hazards make farming much more difficult than farming in southern Ontario. In 2016, for example, early snowfall in the first week of October prevented some farmers from completing their harvest and those crops became classified as much lower valued feed grain.

Irrigation on these semi-arid lands has provided another solution to dry conditions (Photo 8.8). The most extensive irrigation systems are in southern Alberta. In fact, nearly two-thirds of the 750,000 ha of irrigated land in Canada are located in Alberta. In the 1950s and 1960s, two major irrigation projects were developed in the dry lands of Alberta and Saskatchewan: the St Mary River Irrigation District is based on the internal storage reservoirs of the St Mary and Waterton dams in southern Alberta, and Lake Diefenbaker serves as a massive reservoir on the South Saskatchewan River. Alberta irrigators have two advantages over their Saskatchewan counterparts. First and most important, southern Alberta has a longer growing season than Saskatchewan. Consequently, the selection of crops is wider, including corn, sugar beets, and other specialty crops that provide a high return per acre. Second, with most processing plants situated in southern Alberta, farmers have a shorter distance to market than do those in Saskatchewan.

**Peace River Country**

On the northern edge of agricultural lands, the Peace River Country is situated between 55°N and 57°N on the Alberta Plateau. This sub-region has relatively high elevations and its rivers have deeply cut into the landscape (Photo 8.9). Except for the area surrounding Grande Prairie, the growing season is much shorter than that found in the more southerly Fertile and Dry belts, but the longer length of daylight in the summer somewhat offsets that disadvantage. Grain, hay, and pasture dominate the land-use pattern, with livestock central to agricultural practices. Agricultural land is often surrounded by aspen forest.

## Canola: The Prairie Staple?

Grain production, particularly spring wheat, has been the prairie staple for over 100 years. Grains do well in dry conditions where other crops would fail. But two factors turned prairie farmers against spring wheat—low world prices and high rail transportation costs. Until 1995, the federal government subsidized grain exports. The cancellation of that subsidy, known as the Crow Rate (Kroeger, 2009), led grain farmers to seek alternative crops. From 1971 to 1995, the acreage seeded in spring wheat in Saskatchewan never fell below 10 million acres, but due to the loss of the Crow subsidy and higher prices for canola, farmers turned away from spring wheat (Saskatchewan Ministry of Agriculture, 2009, Tables 2.3, 2.9; Casséus, 2009).

Western Canada is the world's leading canola producer. After 1995, China began to import large quantities of canola, resulting in higher prices for Canadian canola. Soon canola was the leading crop in Western Canada, followed by spring wheat and lentils. By 2016, just over 11 million acres were planted in canola, while spring wheat occupied only

Russ Heinl/All Canada Photos

**PHOTO 8.8** In the dry lands of southern Alberta, water is king. Irrigation waters from the Oldman River reservoir allow some farmers to specialize in growing corn, sugar beets, potatoes, and other vegetables.

Mhalifu/Wikipedia

**PHOTO 8.9** The town of Peace River and nearby farms in the valley of the Peace River. Beyond the deeply entrenched river lies the Alberta Plateau, a sub-region of the Interior Plains. See "The Interior Plains" in Chapter 2, page 29, for more information.

6.7 million acres of cropland (Statistics Canada, 2017). Wheat had become a necessary secondary crop because it allowed the soil to replenish its nitrogen level after two or three years of growing canola. Farmers found this relationship profitable: two or three years of canola and then one year of wheat. More recently, farmers have turned to lentils over wheat because they more quickly add nitrogen to the soil. As shown in Table 8.3, canola is the new prairie staple (Photos 8.10 and 8.11). However, geopolitics changed the relationship between canola and spring wheat. In 2018, the dispute between Canada and China resulted in China cancelling its imports of Canadian canola by nearly 50 per cent. Oddly enough, Canadian exports increased in 2019 over the previous year because other countries—notably France and the United Arab Emirates (UAE)—increased imports of Canadian canola and then resold it to China (Dyer, 2019). Chinese demand for canola as a vegetable oil continues to grow, and the world price reached record highs in 2020. In Canada, canola prices in 2020 were up 30 per cent over the previous year, which left farmer Mary-Jane

Duncan-Eger, who grows canola near Regina, Saskatchewan, "super-mystified," but "pretty happy. As long as someone is buying it [at high prices], I don't care who" (Nickel & Gu, 2020).

Canola's popularity with prairie farmers lies in its profitability. Not only does canola command a higher price than wheat, but also farmers have the option to truck their crop to one of the many canola refineries. Yorkton has two canola refineries, but the largest canola crushing facility in North America is located just east of Saskatoon at the small town of Clavet. The Clavet facility was opened in 1996 and has undergone two expansions; with its current capacity the plant processes 1.5 million metric tonnes of canola each year. The Clavet plant and other canola crushing plants in Western Canada produce canola oil and specialty canola oils, as well as canola feed for livestock. The products are in high demand in North American and world markets. Global canola oil demand plus higher prices has prompted Canadian oilseed crushing firms to expand their production to meet export demands (Nickel & Gu, 2020).

**TABLE 8.3    Leading Crops by Millions of Acres, Western Canada, 2019**

| Province | Canola | Spring Wheat | Durum Wheat | Lentils |
|---|---|---|---|---|
| Manitoba | 3.3 | 2.8 | — | — |
| Saskatchewan | 21.0 | 8.7 | 4.1 | 3.4 |
| Alberta | 5.9 | 6.6 | 0.8 | 0.4 |
| Western Canada | 30.2 | 18.1 | 4.9 | 3.8 |

Source: Statistics Canada (2019c).

Fred and Myrna Budgeon

PHOTO 8.10 Weather is a constant challenge facing prairie farmers. Just when a farmer thinks a bumper crop is on the way, nature throws a curveball—or a snowball. In this case, the swathed canola field near Crossfield, Alberta, looked great in August 2012 (left) but along came strong winds and the canola was tangled into a mess (right), resulting in a drop in yields and profits.

© Robert Berdan

PHOTO 8.11 Canola has replaced spring wheat as the principal crop in Western Canada because it is more profitable. Still, spring wheat remains a popular crop for two reasons. First, spring wheat is used in most farmers' crop rotation scheme for canola. Second, wheat is a reliable crop in a dry climate. Canola is nitrogen deficient, meaning that the plant requires additional inputs of nitrogen fertilizers. For that reason, farmers are adding legume crops to their rotation scheme because legumes add more nitrogen to the soil than wheat.

For Western Canada's economy, the processing of canola represents an important value-added industry.

## Livestock Industry

The beef livestock industry is concentrated in southern Alberta. The main export market is the United States. In 2019, beef exports totalled $2.1 billion, with 70 per cent going to the United States, followed by Japan and China at 11 per cent and 5 per cent respectively (Statistics Canada, 2019d). The hog industry, on the other hand, is found mainly in Quebec, Ontario, and Manitoba. Hog exports reached $2.8 billion, with most production going to Japan (33 per cent), the United States (29 per cent) and China (18 per cent) (Statistics Canada, 2019d). In comparison with the previous year, China increased its purchases of both beef and pork. However, in June 2019 China banned imports of beef and pork from Canada, supposedly because of a feed additive found in pork products exported from Canada to China. But was this ban punishment for the arrest of Huawei executive Meng Wanzhou? On the other hand, maybe it was an honest health concern because five months later China lifted this ban after Canada provided a plausible explanation.

## Western Canada's Resource Base

Western Canada, with its vast resource base, is heavily dependent on its mining sector. Alberta's oil sands are at the top of the list (Figure 8.8) followed by the vast oil and potash reserves found in Saskatchewan. All depend on export markets. The required capital investments for additional production are huge. Until 2014, foreign investments drove the expansion of oil and potash. Since then, foreign investments have ground to a halt and those approved remain on the drawing board. The steep fall in commodity prices is the principal reason, but the oil sands are under increasing pressure from environmentalists, who are deeply concerned about its greenhouse emissions driving climate change. In 2019, the Nation Bank Financial Group (McClelland, 2019) predicted that oil and gas spending would remain low in the coming year while production was anticipated to rise by 6 per cent to 6 million barrels of oil equivalent a day compared to 2019. In the following year, the lockdown to prevent the spread of COVID-19 slowed both oil exploration and construction.

With such low commodity prices, the outlook for the resource base remains grim for the immediate future. With new investments stalled and prices below profit-making levels for new projects, the oil sands and potash are no longer the driving forces behind Alberta and Saskatchewan's economies. In the case of the oil sands, production has increased but the value of production and exports has dropped sharply because of low prices. Saskatchewan potash producers approached the problem of low prices by reducing output in an effort to allow global supply and demand to again push prices up. By 2020, this strategy had yet to solve the problem of low prices and most potash mines had either reduced production or temporarily closed their mining operations.

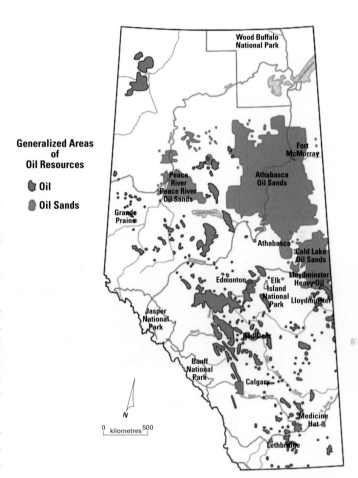

**FIGURE 8.8 Alberta's hydrocarbon resources: Oil sands and oil fields**

Alberta ranks third in the world in oil reserves. Alberta's total oil reserves are 170.8 billion barrels, of which crude bitumen reserves account for 169.3 billion barrels and conventional crude oil reserves for 1.5 billion barrels. Clearly, the oil sands formed the basis of former Prime Minister Stephen Harper's claim in 2006 that Canada was an emerging "energy superpower." Over a decade later, Prime Minister Justin Trudeau's vision is much less enthusiastic. In fact, lower oil prices mean that new projects are no longer viable and the full exploitation of the vast oil sands has been put to rest.

Source: Alberta (2007), from Energy Resources Conservation Board/Alberta Geological Survey.

## Low Prices for Oil

The slump in world oil prices hurt Alberta's and, to a lesser degree, Saskatchewan's economies. Oil prices have fallen sharply since 2014 and have remained low. Prices for Western Canada oil, known as Western Canadian Select, are even lower, falling well below West Texas Intermediate (WTI) prices. Land-locked Alberta oil companies hope that the twinning of the Trans Mountain pipeline to tidewater will boost oil revenues because tidewater prices are higher than WTI. Opposition to this pipeline lies in two areas: (1) the concern that it will allow the oil sands to increase production and thus add to greenhouse gas emissions; and (2) the fear of bitumen spills into rivers or harbours. Such spills are much more difficult to remove than **conventional oil** because of its tendency to sink rather than float on or near the water surface. In September 2019, the federally owned Trans Mountain Corp. issued "notice to proceed" directives to construction contractors, mobilizing the workforce it needs to expand the pipeline and Prime Minister Trudeau hoped the pipeline could be completed quickly (Curry & Walsh, 2019). Ten months later, the Supreme Court of Canada drove the final nail into the legal resistance by rejecting an appeal by BC First Nations that challenged federal approval of the Trans Mountain pipeline expansion project.

### Oil Sands Fields

The three oil sands fields are known as Athabasca (Fort McMurray), Peace River, and Cold Lake. With most oil sands deposits too deep for surface mining, an in-situ system is employed, which is similar to conventional oil production. Operations began with open-pit mining because of its low cost per unit of output; more recent operations have had to extract bitumen from much deeper deposits, necessitating the employment of the more expensive in-situ methods. The Cold Lake field, while the largest single oil sands deposit, is 400 m below the surface. In 1966, when Imperial Oil purchased the leases to this deposit, the technology to extract the oil was not in place. Imperial Oil's research unit devised new recovery technologies known as cyclic steam stimulation and gravity drainage (Figure 8.10).

Suncor Energy, the largest oil sands company, operates open-pit mines at Millennium and Steepbank and in-situ production at MacKay River and Firebag. The in-situ operations employ steam-assisted gravity drainage, where parallel pairs of horizontal wells are drilled: one for steam injection and one for oil recovery. The bitumen is then sent by pipeline to Suncor's upgrading facility at Fort McMurray. The other major open-pit mines are Syncrude Aurora and Mildred Lake.

### Pipelines, Promises, and Pollution

Alberta's oil sands projects symbolize all that is right and wrong with resource development. Vast profits drive the economy, create high-paying jobs, and generate a demand for Canadian manufactured products. In 2016, the Canadian Association of Petroleum Producers (CAPP) forecast 3.7 million barrels/day for 2030, up from 2017 production of 2.8 million barrels/day (Figure 8.11). Yet, these energy developments scar the landscape, pollute the waters, and emit carbon dioxide and other greenhouse gases into the atmosphere (Hodson, 2013). No longer are major oil sands projects assured of federal approval. Opposition is growing, oil prices are declining, and new investments in the oil sands are unlikely. Frontier's proposed $20.6 billion project was caught in this stormy climate and the company withdrew its application in 2020

### Contested Terrain 8.1

#### Drawers of Bitumen?

Canada and Canadians have long been considered **hewers of wood and drawers of water**. Alberta, for example, processes only 60 per cent of its crude bitumen production. To break away from this theme, more bitumen should be processed at home, thereby accomplishing three goals—more jobs in Alberta, a stronger manufacturing sector, and avoidance of shipping diluted bitumen (**dilbit**) that spells environmental disaster when unexpected but inevitable spills occur. Yet, from a business point of view, oil companies prefer to ship crude bitumen to existing refineries rather than build new plants in Alberta.

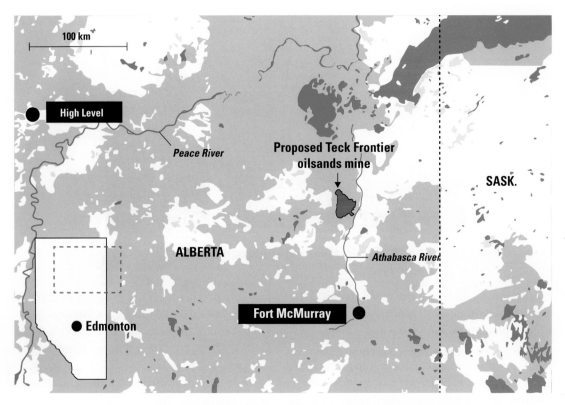

**FIGURE 8.9 Failed Frontier project at the northern edge of the oil sands**

Source: Rieger (2020).

(Figure 8.9). A disappointed Don Lindsay, the CEO of Teck Resources, wrote:

> Unfortunately, the growing debate around this issue [balancing the economic benefits of oil expansion with protecting the climate from increasing emissions of greenhouse gases] has placed Frontier and our company squarely at the nexus of much broader issues [global climate change] that need to be resolved [by Ottawa and Alberta]. In that context, it is now evident that there is no constructive path forward for the project. (Rieger, 2020)

Most pipelines must extend from Alberta to the United States to reach tidewater and higher prices. In the United States, political opposition to the expansion of the Alberta oil sands is strong and is reflected in the response to the Keystone II

project. As *New York Times* reporter Coral Davenport (2015) put it:

> The once-obscure Keystone project became a political symbol amid broader clashes over energy, climate change and the economy. The rejection of a single oil infrastructure project will have little impact on efforts to reduce greenhouse gas pollution, but the pipeline plan gained an outsize profile after environmental activists spent four years marching and rallying against it in front of the White House and across the country.

Pipelines represent a flashpoint between two opposing forces in Canadian society. Environmental groups are opposed to further development of the oil industry, especially the oil sands. On the other hand, Alberta wants to benefit from its oil resources. The challenge for Alberta is finding

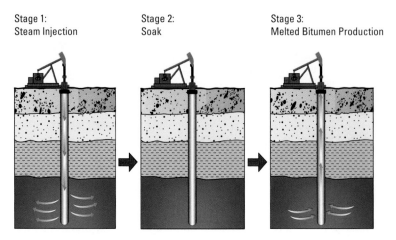

Stage 1:
Steam Injection

Stage 2:
Soak

Stage 3:
Melted Bitumen Production

**FIGURE 8.10 Cyclic steam stimulation (CSS)**

ways to get its oil to US and world markets. The Trans Mountain pipeline expansion from Alberta to BC represents the key element to reach tidewater and world markets. With the final legal challenge out of the way, construction began in 2020 with a planned completion date to tidewater at Burnaby within two years. Two other projects, the Keystone II and Line 3, would also allow more Alberta oil to reach refineries in the United States. The Canadian sections of two pipelines were completed by 2019, but construction in the United States has run into legal challenges. Keystone II would transport more Alberta oil to the Gulf coast refineries while Line 3, a replacement pipeline of an existing Enbridge pipeline, would increase the volume of oil shipped to Superior, Wisconsin,

and then by other pipelines to refineries in the US Midwest and eventually to Sarnia, Ontario.

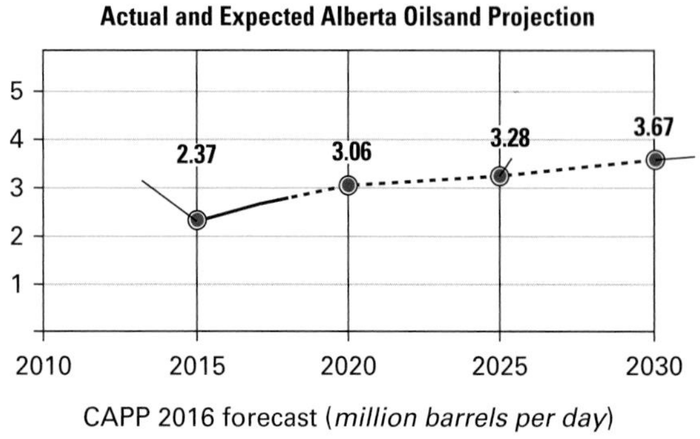

Other pipeline proposals failed to gain federal approval (Table 8.4). The ambitious Northern Gateway project, for instance, would have transported bitumen from Alberta's oil sands to Kitimat for shipment overseas. The rejection of this project had two components. First, in 2015, Prime Minister Justin Trudeau imposed a ban on oil tanker traffic on the north coast of British Columbia. Without ocean shipping, the pipeline project no longer worked. Second, in 2016, the Federal Court of Appeal ruled against the former federal government's approval of Enbridge's $7.9 billion Northern Gateway project because of the failure to properly consult First Nations. The Energy East pipeline ran into strong opposition in Quebec and, coupled with the decrease in oil prices, TransCanada cancelled its project that would have connected Hardisty, Alberta, and Saint John, New Brunswick (Figures 8.12 and 8.13). In 2020, as noted above, Teck Resources also withdrew its Frontier application.

Beyond the issue of high greenhouse gas emissions, the oil sands have taken a heavy toll on the local environment, including discharges into the Athabasca River. The Kurek report (Kurek et al., 2013) revealed that oil sands production is polluting air and water at greater rates and over a larger geographic area than previously thought. The findings of these researchers, published in the highly regarded *Proceedings of the National Academy of Sciences,*

**Actual and Expected Alberta Oilsand Projection**

2.37   3.06   3.28   3.67

2010    2015    2020    2025    2030

CAPP 2016 forecast (*million barrels per day*)

**FIGURE 8.11 Projected Alberta oil production to 2030**

Source: Bakx (2016).

| TABLE 8.4 | Recently Proposed Oil Pipelines to Tidewater | | | |
|---|---|---|---|---|
| Proponent and Pipeline | Point of Origin | Destination | National Energy Board Approval Status | Capacity (thousand bbl/d) |
| **Enbridge Northern Gateway*** | Bruderheim, Alberta | Kitimat, BC | Approved 2014 Rejected 2015 | 525 |
| **Canada Trans Mountain Expansion**** | Edmonton | Burnaby, BC | Approved 2016 Construction 2019 to 2022 | 590 |
| **TransCanada Energy East** | Hardisty, Alberta | Saint John, NB | Proposed 2016 Withdrawn 2018 | 1,100 |

* The Northern Gateway project was designed to deliver bitumen from the oil sands to world markets and thus gain access to higher prices and make Canadian oil less dependent on the US market. Enbridge planned two pipelines, one to transport diluted bitumen to Kitimat from the oil sands and the other one to bring **diluent** to the oil sands to add to bitumen, thus making it easier to flow in the pipeline. In June 2016, the Federal Court of Appeal ruled against the earlier federal approval of Enbridge's $7.9 billion Northern Gateway project because of Ottawa's failure to properly consult First Nations.

** Kinder Morgan proposed to twin its existing pipeline and use the new pipeline to bring more bitumen to its ocean vessel loading facility on Burrard Inlet. Fierce opposition to the project caused delays, leading Kinder Morgan to question the prospect of building this new pipeline. In 2018, the federal government purchased Kinder Morgan's interests for $4.5 billion in order to ensure completion of the project.

Sources: Adapted from Canadian Association of Petroleum Producers (2012a: 27); Proctor (2016); TransCanada (2016).

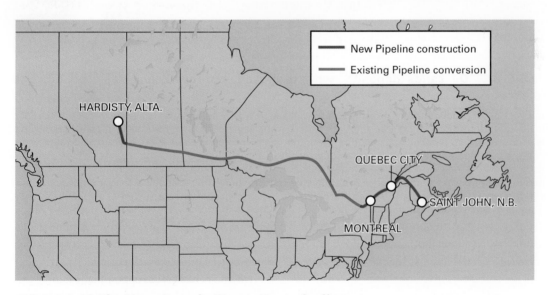

**FIGURE 8.12 The TransCanada Energy East pipeline**

In early 2016, TransCanada floated the idea of converting an existing gas line that extended from Alberta to Montreal and then constructing an oil pipeline from Montreal through Quebec City to the oil refinery near Saint John, New Brunswick. Public and political opposition from Quebec, as well as the sag in oil prices, forced the company to jettison its plan in October 2017.

Source: Bell (2016).

clearly refute industry's argument that pollution of the Athabasca River is caused largely by natural seepage rather than by their industrial operations, including seepage of toxic wastes from the huge tailing ponds near Fort McMurray.

Oil is now shipped primarily by rail. Yet the current method of moving oil to tidewater on both coasts by rail also has environmental and social implications. The Lac-Mégantic rail disaster of July 2013 in Quebec illustrates an extreme example. The braking system

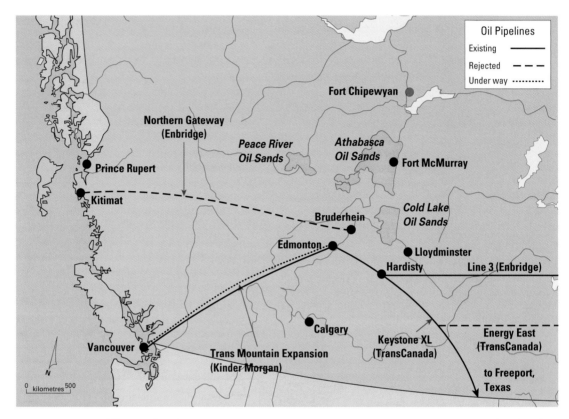

**FIGURE 8.13 Oil sands deposits, with proposed, approved, and rejected pipeline projects**

Construction of pipelines from Alberta to other areas in North America is designed to ensure that the oil will continue to flow in greater amounts than before. But political opposition to pipelines is strong. The Trans Mountain pipeline expansion is the most likely one to succeed. Keystone II and Line 3, while completed within Canada, ran into powerful opposition in the United States that seems to have derailed both projects. As well, two proposals failed outright. The Northern Gateway project was rejected by the Liberal government while the Energy East line was withdrawn by TransCanada after vigorous opposition from Quebec.

for the 74-car freight train carrying Bakken Formation crude oil failed and the train rolled downhill and unattended into the town of Lac-Mégantic, Quebec, where the tanker cars overturned and exploded, killing 47 people and destroying many buildings in the town centre.

## Mining in Western Canada

The mining industry has helped to diversify and enrich the economy of Western Canada. Like the oil and gas industry, mining depends on exports to foreign markets. The variety and value of mineral production in Western Canada are significant, with coal, gold, nickel, potash, and uranium leading the way. The

prospects for adding a major diamond mine in Saskatchewan look promising, thus broadening the array of commercial mineral developments.

Environmental groups oppose many mining projects because of their negative impacts. One target is the coal industry, while the other is the Alberta oil sands. Both alter the landscape and both add to climate change. The federal and provincial governments have called for the end of coal in the production of electricity. New federal regulations combined with much lower oil prices resulted in companies hesitating to invest in new oil sands projects.

Despite these environmental issues, mining still adds a great deal to the economy of Western Canada. In 2017, the value of mineral production, including coal, was $6.7 billion, down sharply from the high point three years before. The price decline was widespread as demand slipped badly, but oil, potash, and uranium prices took the brunt of the fall (Natural Resources Canada, 2019b). Alberta and Saskatchewan depend heavily on royalties from resource projects and these payments to the two provincial governments have also declined.

The geology of each province differs sufficiently to produce three distinct types of mining. Alberta contains rich bituminous coal reserves along the eastern slopes of the Rocky Mountains, while Saskatchewan has large lignite deposits. Both provinces use coal for thermal-electric power generation. Manitoba, on the other hand, produces its electricity from hydroelectric power stations. Only Alberta exports coal, mainly to Japanese and South Korean steel plants. Alberta metallurgical coal is mined in the East Kootenay and Peace River coalfields, then shipped by rail to BC ports for export to Asia.

Potash, uranium, and diamonds are the major mineral deposits in Saskatchewan, though only potash and uranium have producing mines. The **potash** deposit lies approximately 1 km below the surface of the earth, reaching its thickest extent around Saskatoon.

Canada (which, in effect, means Saskatchewan) is the world's largest producer and exporter of potash. Canadian Potash Exporters (Canpotex), based in Saskatoon, manages all Saskatchewan potash exports outside of North America. It is the world's largest exporter of potash, with its main customers being China, India, and Japan, as well as the US. The province has the largest and highest-quality deposit in the world, and with the closure in 2015 of the potash mine in New Brunswick, all of Canada's potash production—which is used to produce potassium-based fertilizers—comes from Saskatchewan (Vignette 8.3). World demand varies, but Canadian potash producers adjust production volume (Figure 8.14) to maintain price—at the expense of their workers, who are laid off. In 2018, for instance, production dropped sharply to a five-year low of 13.8 million tonnes. The depressed world market for potash shows no signs of improvement for Saskatchewan.

Uranium mining also takes place in Saskatchewan (Table 8.5). Production began in 1953 on the northern shores of Lake Athabasca near Uranium City. Since the late 1970s uranium mining has shifted south to the geological area of the Canadian Shield known as the Athabasca Basin. Currently, three mines are operating—Cigar Lake, McArthur River, and McClean Lake. The Rabbit Lake mine, the least profitable, was closed in 2015 because of the decline in world demand. A mill at Key Lake processes the ore into a uranium concentrate ($U_3O_8$) known as yellow cake. The product is either

## Vignette 8.3

### Potash: Saskatchewan's Underground Wealth

*Potash* is a general term for potassium salts. Potassium (K), a nutrient essential for plant growth, is derived from these salts. Roughly 95 per cent of world potash production goes into fertilizer, while the remainder is used in a wide variety of commercial and industrial products, ranging from soap to explosives.

In Saskatchewan, potassium salts are found in the Prairie Evaporite, which extends over much of southern Saskatchewan at varying depths. The potash mines near Saskatoon operate at just over 1,000 metres below the surface while the Belle Plain mine near Regina operates at the 1,600 m level. The deposit at each mine has a maximum thickness of 210 m. Since the Prairie Evaporite slopes downward towards the border with the United States, this potash formation reaches its greatest depth in Montana and North Dakota—depths that are not economical to mine. The more accessible potash deposits are found near Saskatoon, where six of the nine mines are located. In fact, Saskatoon claims to be the "Potash Capital of the World."

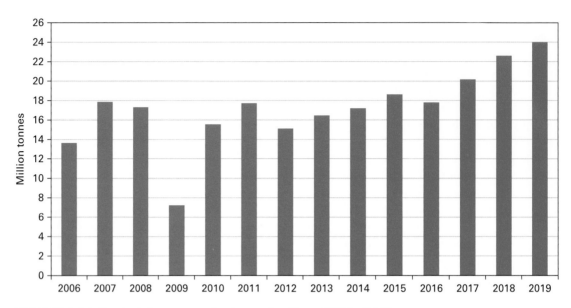

**FIGURE 8.14** **Saskatchewan potash production, 2006–2019**

While production has increased each year to 2019, annual prices suddenly declined 10 years ago from over US$900 per tonne in 2009 to US$300 in 2010. Since then, continued low prices have caused higher-cost mines to either reduce production or close temporarily. For example, the Colonsay mine reduced its output in 2016 and then was temporarily closed in 2019.

Sources: Natural Resources Canada (2019c, 2020).

exported to foreign countries, like China, or trucked to Ontario refineries at Blind River and Port Hope and to undisclosed refineries in the United States. Low prices continued into 2020, causing the uranium and potash companies to either slow or cease production. These companies hope that by lowering output, prices will again rise to previous levels.

Manitoba has two major mineral deposits—copper-zinc and nickel—both located in the Canadian Shield. Mining for copper and nickel in Manitoba is relatively expensive. As well, the high cost of shipping the processed product to distant markets adds to their economic disadvantage. Copper and zinc ore bodies are found near Flin Flon, a mining and smelter town in northern Manitoba that began production in 1930, shortly after a rail link to The Pas was completed in 1928. At one time, Flin Flon produced most of Canada's copper and zinc, but today it is an aging resource town with a declining population. Thompson, located some 740 km north of Winnipeg, is a nickel-mining town. In 1957, after a rail link to the Hudson Bay Railway was completed, the mine facility, smelter, and town were constructed. Unlike Flin Flon, Thompson was a specially designed resource town with a complete

array of urban amenities. The first nickel was produced in 1961. During the 1960s, Thompson's population soared to 20,000. Since then, the population of Thompson and of many other resource towns has dwindled: greater mechanization in the mining process results in a smaller labour force driven by declining nickel prices; and this, in turn, leads to a smaller service sector. In 1991, Thompson had a population of 14,977, but by 2016 it had fallen to 13,678. By the next census, this number could fall perhaps close to 10,000 as Vale, facing lower prices for nickel, plans to reduce its workforce (Froese, 2020).

## Forest Industry: Is a Revival in Sight?

The boreal forest stretches across the northern part of Western Canada and along the foothills on the eastern slopes of the Rocky Mountains. The bulk of the forested area lies in Alberta (Table 8.6). The forest industry depends on exports to the United States. As with other regions, Western Canada's forest industry hit the skids with the US housing crisis. Plants closed and little logging took place. Indigenous workers and businesses have been particularly

## TABLE 8.5 Uranium Mines and Mills in Northern Saskatchewan

| Facility | Licensee | Licence | Type |
|---|---|---|---|
| **Cigar Lake Mine\*** | Cameco Corporation | Operation | Licensed to mine up to an average of 8,200,000 kg of uranium per year |
| **Key Lake Mill** | Cameco Corporation | Operation | Licensed to mill up to an average of 7,200,000 kg of uranium per year |
| **McArthur River Mine** | Cameco Corporation | Operation | Licensed to mine up to an average of 7,200,000 kg of uranium per year |
| **McClean Lake Mill** | AREVA Resources Canada Inc. | Operation | Licensed to mine and mill up to 3,629,300 kg of uranium per year |
| Rabbit Lake Mine and Mill | Cameco Corporation | Maintenance | Ceased operations in 2016 |

\* Richest ore body in the world at nearly 16 per cent grade of $U_3O_8$. Most ore bodies are under 5 per cent grade.

Source: Canadian Nuclear Safety Commission (2017).

## TABLE 8.6 Forested Areas by Province, Western Canada

| Province | Area (ha) | % of Western Canada Forest |
|---|---|---|
| **Manitoba** | 18,968 | 28.4 |
| **Saskatchewan** | 20,043 | 30.0 |
| **Alberta** | 27,718 | 41.5 |
| **Western Canada** | 66,729 | 100.0 |
| **Percentage Canada** | | 21.5* |

\* Note: Canada's total forested area is 310,134 ha.

Source: Sawe (2017).

hard hit because they depend heavily on this industry for their livelihood. In an attempt to support pulp and paper mills, the federal government, under its Green Transformation Program, has provided financial assistance for investments in capital projects that improve environmental performance and economic efficiency. But the key to production depends on exports to the United States, with Canadian softwood lumber maintaining around 30 per cent of the US market prior to the ending of Softwood Lumber Agreement in October 2016. The US Lumber Coalition—the American lobby group—wants that figure lower. Judging by the intensity of the current situation and the protectionist American position during the Trump administration, Canadian softwood lumber producers can expect to pay anti-dumping duties averaging 2 per cent on exports of softwood lumber to the US for the foreseeable future.

## Western Canada's Urban Core

Urban centres in Western Canada continue to grow. From 2001 to 2016, the total population of the six census metropolitan areas of Lethbridge, Regina, Saskatoon, Winnipeg, Edmonton, and Calgary increased by 35 per cent, but three cities—Calgary, Edmonton, and Saskatoon—greatly exceeded this average. Calgary had a population increase of 46 per cent; Edmonton, 41 per cent; and Saskatoon, 31 per cent (Table 8.7). In 2016, these six cities accounted for 64 per cent of Western Canada's population of 6.4 million. This pattern of urban growth is expected to continue. Technology is driving the economies of all six cities. Regina, for instance, is attracting tech companies designed to facilitate autonomous farming (Melnychuk, 2020).

A second order of urban centres includes Airdrie, Red Deer, Grande Prairie, Medicine Hat, Wood Buffalo (Fort McMurray), Brandon, Prince Albert, Moose

For discussion of forestry exports to the US, see **Chapter 9**, "Dependency on the US Market," page 307.

PHOTO 8.12 Saskatoon, situated on the South Saskatchewan River, is Saskatchewan's largest city with a population of nearly 300,000 (2020). Known as the "Bridge City," Saskatoon has witnessed rapid population growth over the last 10 years, outpacing its southern rival, Regina. As with most Western Canada cities, Indigenous people have relocated to Saskatoon. Its Indigenous population is growing and totalled just over 31,000, comprising nearly 11 per cent of Saskatoon's residents in 2016.

Jaw, and Lloydminster (Table 8.8). From 2001 to 2016, the rate of urban growth varied considerably for the towns and smaller cities of Western Canada. This variation reflects differences in local economic growth and in the pace of consolidating populations into regional centres. From 2001 to 2016, Airdrie, a commuter town to Calgary, doubled its population (Table 8.8).

Within Western Canada, the Indigenous population continues to increase at a pace well beyond the natural increase of the population (Table 8.9). High fertility rates drive this population. From 2011 to 2016, the Indigenous population increased from 574,000 to 657,000 (Statistics Canada, 2013, 2019e), an increase of nearly 15 per cent. While First Nations reserves continued to grow, a substantial number of Indigenous people now live in urban centres (Peters & Anderson, 2013). Winnipeg has both the largest number and the highest percentage of Indigenous people. In 2016, nearly 93,000 Indigenous people lived in Winnipeg, making up 12.2 per cent of its total population (Statistics Canada, 2019e).

## Calgary–Edmonton Corridor

The Calgary–Edmonton Corridor has emerged as the most urbanized region in the Western Canada region and one of the densest in Canada. With major universities and colleges in its cities, it is a hub for the knowledge-based activities where high-tech industries thrive and cutting-edge research takes place. Over the past decade, this urban corridor has had a high rate of population growth, exceeding 25 per cent.

Anchored by Calgary and Edmonton, the 400-km corridor includes the cities of Airdrie and Red Deer and a host of smaller centres. Calgary has become one of Canada's key corporation headquarters, especially for the oil and gas industry. British Petroleum, Encana, Imperial Oil, Suncor Energy, Shell Canada, and Trans-Canada are headquartered in Calgary, as is Canadian Pacific Railway. With its proximity to Banff, the Rocky Mountains, and Kananaskis Country, Calgary offers easy access to mountain recreation. Edmonton, besides being the provincial capital, is a petrochemical industrial node. Known as the "Gateway to the North," Edmonton serves as a staging centre for the oil sands and for diamond mining in the Northwest Territories. Beyond Edmonton's strong resource sector, the city has turned into a hub for science and technology, much of which is focused on artificial intelligence research.

## Winnipeg: Core of Manitoba

While Manitoba missed out on the oil boom that propelled Alberta's economic and population growth, it does have hydroelectric power. As well, the province has a more diverse economy than Alberta and Saskatchewan. Winnipeg alone contains a wide range of industries, ranging from aerospace to agri-business and insurance.

Unlike the rest of Western Canada's cities, Winnipeg has a much longer history of colonization and settlement by Europeans. Winnipeg is located at the confluence of the Red River and the Assiniboine River—the location of Lord Selkirk's early nineteenth-century settlement for Scottish crofters that evolved into the Métis Red River Settlement (Vignette 8.4). As the "Gateway to the West," Winnipeg controlled the grain trade and

## Vignette 8.4

### Winnipeg and the Métis

As the birthplace of the Métis Nation and home of the largest Métis community in Canada, Winnipeg is unique among Canadian cities. Since the census began recording Indigenous people, Winnipeg has always had the largest number of Indigenous people of any city in Canada. Between 2006 and 2011, the number of Indigenous people increased from 68,380 to 92,810 (Winnipeg, 2016; Statistics Canada, 2019e). Most of this group are Métis, and they have deep historic roots in the Red River area, where, according to the 2016 census, they comprise nearly 56 per cent of the Indigenous population in Winnipeg (Statistics Canada, 2019e).

served as the wholesale hub for Western Canada until after World War II when the oil boom in Alberta stimulated urban growth in Calgary and Edmonton, causing Winnipeg's grip on commercial trade in Alberta to shrink. Even so, by 1951 Winnipeg remained the largest city in Western Canada, with a population of 357,000 compared to 177,000 for Edmonton and 142,000 for Calgary. Soon afterwards, the two Alberta cities passed Winnipeg.

#### TABLE 8.7  Census Metropolitan Areas in Western Canada, 2001–2016

| CMAs | Population 2001 | Population 2016 | % Change |
|---|---|---|---|
| Lethbridge | 87,388 | 117,394 | 34.3 |
| Regina | 192,800 | 236,481 | 22.7 |
| Saskatoon | 225,927 | 295,095 | 30.6 |
| Winnipeg | 676,594 | 778,489 | 15.1 |
| Edmonton | 937,845 | 1,321,426 | 40.9 |
| Calgary | 951,494 | 1,392,009 | 46.3 |
| Total | 3,072,048 | 4,140,894 | 34.8 |
| Western Canada | 5,073,323 | 6,443,892 | 27.0 |

Sources: Adapted from Statistics Canada (2007, 2019f).

#### TABLE 8.8  Population of Small Cities, Western Canada, 2001–2016

| Centre | Population 2001 | Population 2016 | % Change |
|---|---|---|---|
| Lloydminster | 20,988 | 34,583 | 64.8 |
| Moose Jaw | 33,519 | 35,053 | 4.6 |
| Prince Albert | 41,460 | 44,160 | 6.5 |
| Brandon | 46,273 | 58,003 | 25.4 |
| Grande Prairie | 36,983 | 61,166 | 65.4 |
| Airdrie | 20,382 | 61,581 | 202.1 |
| Wood Buffalo | 42,581 | 73,320 | 72.2 |
| Medicine Hat | 61,735 | 76,522 | 24.0 |
| Red Deer | 67,829 | 100,418 | 48.0 |

Further discussion of Indigenous demography is found in **Chapter 4**, "Indigenous Population," page 130.

Note: Except for Airdrie, all urban places in this table were classified by Statistics Canada as "census agglomerations." Airdrie falls under the category of a city within the Census Subdivision of Rocky View County.

Sources: Adapted from Statistics Canada (2007, 2012, 2016, 2019f).

**THINK ABOUT IT**

Do urban places offer a solution to the economic issues facing Indigenous peoples *and* cause social problems related to living in an urban situation? If so, what remedies are available?

**TABLE 8.9    Indigenous Population by Identity for Provinces in Western Canada**

| Province | Population 2001 | Population 2016 | % Change | % of 2016 Provincial Population |
|---|---|---|---|---|
| **Alberta** | 156,225 | 258,640 | 64.3 | 6.5 |
| **Manitoba** | 150,045 | 223,310 | 48.8 | 18.0 |
| **Saskatchewan** | 130,185 | 175,020 | 34.4 | 16.4 |
| **Western Canada** | 436,455 | 656,970 | 50.5 | 10.2 |
| **Canada** | 976,305 | 1,673,785 | 71.4* | |

* Ethnic mobility accounts for much of the population change in Canada while the change from 2001 to 2016 in Western Canada was due primarily to natural increase. Ethnic mobility was a major factor in Atlantic Canada, Quebec, and Ontario. For more on this subject see Table 4.10.

Source: Statistics Canada (2013, 2019e).

## Summary

Geography has dealt Western Canada a full hand of resources, but also two deuces—distance and climate. Locked in the heart of North America, exports are critical for its economy. At the same time, interior location generates a dry, continental climate with low precipitation, creating a degree of uncertainty for agriculture. With the arrival of settlers, Western Canada gained an agricultural economy. Since those early days, this economy has diversified, its population has become highly urbanized, and its resource sector continues to play an important role. The transition of an energy-based economy to a green economy remains far in the future. Even though the federal government has announced that it will invest profits from the Trans Mountain pipeline into "green" projects, just how these reinvested profits will wean Alberta and Saskatchewan off of fossil fuels is unclear.

Western Canada's population is clustered in its major cities. These urban centres are the driving force behind its economy. A significant percentage of this urban population belongs to Indigenous people engaged in the urban economy. Over 10 per cent of the populations of major cities in Western Canada were identified in the 2016 census as Indigenous. Winnipeg, for instance, has the highest percentage of Indigenous people, at just over 12 per cent in 2016. By the next census in 2021, the Indigenous urban footprint will be much larger.

Regional divisions have reached a new height with the controversy over climate change and more pipelines. The federal government faces a dilemma: it is committed to building the Trans Mountain pipeline but, at the same time, Ottawa is determined to lower Canada's greenhouse gases and fight global warming. How does it do both, or do the self-interests of Canada's regions, like the Gordian knot, pose an insoluble problem for the federal government?

## Challenge Questions

1. Weather plays a critical role in prairie agriculture. Besides a dry summer, what other weather events can reduce the size and quality of the harvest?
2. Discuss why the Trans Mountain expansion pipeline is supposed to result in higher prices for Alberta oil. In your answer, list the different global and regional pricing systems and explain how they affect price.
3. Many Indigenous people reside in Western Canada's major cities. Explain why this number is expected to increase in the years to come. Then explain why the population of Indigenous people living on reserves continues to grow.
4. Is Ottawa caught on the horns of a dilemma over the construction of the Trans Mountain pipeline and its goal of reducing greenhouse gas emissions?
5. Why is the reclamation of tailing ponds "the elephant in the room" for oil sands companies?

## Essay Questions

1. Geopolitics affects Western Canada exports. In 2018, a major importer, China, sharply curtailed imports of Canadian canola and meat products. What triggered China's decision and what was its impact on Western Canada?
2. The three Prairie provinces have different economies. Alberta and, to a lesser degree, Saskatchewan are heavily dependent on resource exports, especially oil. When prices are high, their economies soar, but when low prices hit, their economies suffer. Manitoba, for better or worse, avoids these economic swings. By examining the economies of each Prairie province, explain why this is the case.

# 9 British Columbia

## Chapter Overview

This chapter will focus on the following topics and issues:

- British Columbia's growing dominance within Canada.
- International trade as a fundamental economic element.
- Basic population and economic characteristics.
- The spread of technology through the economy.
- The possibility of natural gas as an economic anchor.
- The diminished role of forestry as an economic anchor in British Columbia.

## Introduction

At the crossroads between Asia and North America, international trade plays a fundamental role in the economy of British Columbia and that of Western Canada. In 2020, global trade has diminished due to COVID-19 and the rise of protectionism in the United States and other countries. Still, this Pacific province maintains its distinctive place and independent spirit on the western edge of Canada (Figure 9.1). The promise of its vast natural gas deposits satisfying the need for cleaner energy in Asian countries augers well for the future of the province and for the smog-affected cities of Asia. A major trade deal to send natural gas from BC to Asian markets would no doubt cement trade ties with that continent.

British Columbia's position in Canada represents a paradox. On the one hand, its orientation to Ottawa and Central Canada has never been easy. On the other hand, its natural inclination is for closer relations with the US Pacific Northwest and, more recently, with countries on the Pacific Rim. This paradox underscores British Columbia's often-strained relations with Ottawa, as reflected in the political concept of Cascadia and in BC opposition to oil pipelines from Alberta to the BC coast (Crowley, 2016). British Columbia, a rapidly growing region, has turned into a west coast powerhouse with Vancouver leading the way with its shipbuilding and filmmaking as economic spearheads. In the northern reaches of the province, natural gas production could replace the forest industry as the resource anchor and transform Kitimat into a major export port. But the giant venture depends on a stable market in Asia for LNG product.

← Lake O'Hara in Yoho National Park is only accessible to hikers and is famous for its spectacular alpine views.

Pierre Leclerc/Shutterstock

**FIGURE 9.1 British Columbia**

Vancouver's isolation from Central Canada and its close link to Washington, Oregon, and California are revealed in the following driving distances: Montreal, Ottawa, and Toronto are over 4,300 km east of Vancouver. Los Angeles is less than half the distance, at 1,735 km, while Bellingham, Washington, is just 85 km away, making it the most popular US shopping destination for Vancouverites. BC opposition to oil pipelines is stirring the national unity pot, creating a new dimension to the centralist faultline. Not surprisingly, BC has a closer association with the Pacific Northwest than with the rest of Canada. Academics refer to this sense of political place as Cascadia. Just how the closing of the Canada–US border will affect this close relationship probably depends on how long the closure lasts, how both countries have managed (or failed) to control the spread of COVID-19, and how soon newly discovered vaccines are widely distributed.

Source: Natural Resources Canada, 2007.

## British Columbia within Canada

Until 2020, British Columbia's economy was growing, based on its resource sector, its knowledge-based economy, and its geographically favourable location on the Pacific Rim. This combination has propelled BC into the Fourth Industrial Revolution, as described by Klaus Schwab (see Chapter 5). From that perspective, BC was well on its way to modernizing its economy by applying new technology to a variety of enterprises. Just how the COVID-19 pandemic and the ensuing lockdown of the economy will play out in the coming years is unknown. The question is not if this disease will stop the modernizing process but how it will reshape it.

This Pacific region, by persistently outpacing the national average for economic and population growth, is consolidating its position within Canada. At the time of entry into Confederation, BC was a minor player in the affairs of Canada. Today, BC is an economic and political force rivalling the two core regions of Ontario and Quebec, and with its anticipated natural gas developments the province could well pass Western Canada, which is so heavily reliant on oil sands projects. Greater Vancouver, as the third-largest city in Canada, symbolizes this remarkable pace of economic and population growth.

Geography has placed British Columbia at the western edge of Canada, far from the economic/political heart of the country. Often feeling forgotten by Ottawa, this geographic fact underscores the basis for tensions between BC and Central Canada. For most British Columbians, however, the dramatic interface between the sea and the mountains defines the province. The love affair with its Pacific coast dominates its sense of place. As former Premier Christy Clark said, "You can't understand British Columbians unless you can grasp the emotion that people feel about our coast. It's what makes us so different from Alberta and Ontario and other parts of the country" (Hunter, 2016).

From a physiographic perspective, the province is divided into two parts. The Cordillera accounts for the bulk of the area of the province, including the spectacular interface between the Pacific Ocean and the Coast Mountains. Lying beyond the Rocky Mountains, the Interior Plains occupies a small but energy-rich portion of its northeast corner. British Columbia has access to the Pacific Ocean except for its far north, where the **Alaska Panhandle** blocks access to the ocean.

For additional information on the Fourth Industrial Revolution and the Great Reset, see **Vignette 5.3**, "The Fourth Industrial Revolution," page 148.

**PHOTO 9.1** The City of Vancouver called for the widening of sidewalks to facilitate restaurants and pedestrians in densely populated areas. The sidewalks near Bayswater and Balaclava are shown here.

JIMMY JEONG/THE GLOBE AND MAIL

British Columbia is an emerging giant within Canada's economic system. This west coast region's economy is heavily based on its natural resources and the export of those resources and those produced in Western Canada, namely coal, grain, oil, and potash.

Four countries—the US, China, Japan, and South Korea—account for over 85 per cent of exports and imports moving through BC ports (Table 9.1). In 2019, the value of exports declined slightly from the all-time high of $46.5 billion in 2018 to $43.5 billion (BC Stats, 2020). Exports dropped 6.4 per cent in value, largely because of a decline of softwood lumber exports to the US market due to falling demand and additional US tariffs.

For more information on proposed pipelines from the Alberta oil sands, see the section "Pipelines, Promises, and Pollution" in **Chapter 8**, page 268.

British Columbia has diversified its foreign trade over the last 15 years. Prior to the global recession in 2009, the United States accounted for over 60 per cent of all exports, but now it is closer to 50 per cent. The economic crisis that began in late 2008 changed the very nature of BC's global exports. Now the question is, "How will trade restrictions resulting from COVID-19 reshape BC's exports in the coming years?"

The potential of natural gas shipments to Asia would only strengthen the growing ties to Asia. Pipelines may add more natural gas to its export list, but the idea of additional bitumen pipelines from the Alberta oil sands is a charged political issue. Ironically, the Trans Mountain pipeline has carried crude oil from Alberta to Greater Vancouver for over 60 years, and more recently it has transported bitumen from the oil sands, but concerns over the fear of a spill in the marine environment has spurred many environmentalists and Indigenous groups to protest the ongoing project. Regardless of the opposition, construction of this pipeline that began in 2020, if completed, offers a bright future for Alberta's oil sands.

British Columbia's scenic beauty supports a vibrant tourist industry, and its expanding knowledge-based industries, including the film and high-technology industries, help drive economic growth in new directions. Trade is crucial. Lumber, pulp, natural gas, and coal are the province's four main exports. Imports, especially from China, Japan, and South Korea, flow through Vancouver to markets across Canada. The expansion of CN and CP rail lines and the twinning of sections of the Trans-Canada Highway are facilitating access to the Port of Vancouver and exports to China and other Pacific Rim countries. While Prince Rupert remains in the shadow of Vancouver, new facilities at the Port of Prince Rupert signal its arrival as a major player in international shipping (Port of Prince Rupert, 2016). As well, Kitimat seems destined as a major liquid natural gas port for the huge natural gas deposits in northeast British Columbia. In 2016, Kitimat's chances to export bitumen from the Alberta oil sands were quashed by a federal moratorium on oil tankers using Dixon Entrance, Hecate Strait, and Queen Charlotte Sound.

The 2018 purchase of Kinder Morgan's Trans Mountain pipeline system by Ottawa seemingly guarantees the completion of the project. Yet, the possibility of spills from oil tankers in waters surrounding Vancouver is a real threat. Indigenous people who harvest food from these waters oppose this project, as do many environmentalists who link the pipeline expansion to an increase in greenhouse emissions from the oil sands.

## British Columbia's Population

British Columbia contains nearly 5 million people, comprising just over 13 per cent of Canada's population. Population size provides a measure of BC's importance within Confederation. Its population growth, which has consistently outperformed national increases, projects a promising future within Canada's six geographic regions (Figure 9.2).

Yet, BC's population distribution is uneven. This skewed characteristic takes on a core/hinterland pattern as most residents reside in the **Lower Mainland** and in Victoria and Kelowna. Population distribution, therefore, represents a critical economic and social divide. Along the BC northern coast and in much of the Interior, population densities are low and towns like Prince Rupert, Terrace, and Quesnel

**THINK ABOUT IT**
Oil spills are very difficult to remove from marine environments. Why is bitumen more difficult to clean up than oil?

**PHOTO 9.2** The seven-lane Pitt River Bridge just east of Vancouver was completed in 2009. As part of the Asia-Pacific Gateway and Corridor Initiative, this bridge serves to improve access to Vancouver along the north shore of the Fraser River, with easier and quicker flow for trucks carrying exports to ports in the Lower Mainland for shipment to Pacific Rim countries. Supported by both the provincial and federal governments, the Pitt River Bridge represents one phase of joint government efforts to create a super-highway corridor from Calgary to Vancouver.

have suffered population losses while the major urban centres continue to grow rapidly.

Greater Vancouver best illustrates this divide. The city, with its natural beauty, mild climate, and diverse population, is an ideal place for Richard Florida's "cultural class." Here, the performing arts, filmmaking, and the rest of the entertainment industry centred in Vancouver add to BC magic, making Vancouver one of the sixth most "livable" cities in the world (Jung, 2019). Unfortunately, Vancouver is one of the most expensive cities in which to establish roots because of high housing prices, caused in part by newcomers migrating to Greater Vancouver. With ever-increasing immigration, especially from China and Hong Kong, the Lower Mainland's population has become much more diverse than the rest of the province (Photo 9.3). In 2016, over half of its residents were classified by Statistics Canada (2017a) as belonging to visible minority groups, with Chinese forming the largest single group. Visible minorities in the rest of the province composed less that 10 per cent of that population. In fact, outside of Asia, Metro Vancouver has the largest portion of its residents with Asian backgrounds: 43 per cent of Metro Vancouver residents are of Asian heritage. The only major cities outside Asia that come close to Metro Vancouver for their portion of residents with Asian backgrounds are San Francisco (33 per cent Asian), London, England (21 per cent), Toronto (35 per cent), Calgary (23 per cent), and Sydney, Australia (19 per cent) (Todd, 2017).

Following the old adage that the larger the population, the more political clout a region has in Ottawa, BC influence in the affairs of state has increased. In part, this greater clout fuels political friction between BC and the federal government. The struggle for political power and respect is ongoing and underscores the centralist/decentralist faultline. From time to time, various signs of disenchantment with Ottawa emerge. To those living

Firework Productions Ltd

**PHOTO 9.3** Immigration plays a key role in the growth of Greater Vancouver. Chinese immigrants form the largest single group and the urban landscape of Greater Vancouver reflects this demographic fact in the form of Chinese-Canadian "ethnoburbs" as well as ethnic shopping centres and restaurants. One example of the vibrant Chinese community is the Vancouver Chinatown Night Market, pictured here, which is open on weekends throughout the summer. In 2020, however, the market was cancelled due to COVID-19; whether it reopens for 2021 and beyond remains to be seen.

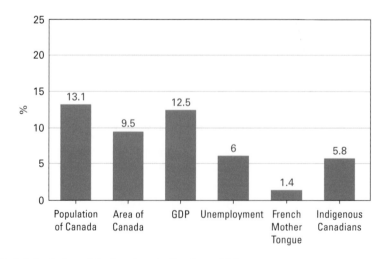

**FIGURE 9.2  British Columbia basic statistics, 2016**

BC's share of Canada's GDP and population continues to outpace the national average, but its small number of French-speaking Canadians is markedly different from some other regions in Canada. Percentages of population, area, and GDP are based on the national figure; unemployment while French home language, and Indigenous population percentages are reflected though a provincial lens.

in British Columbia, the province fits comfortably into the Pacific Northwest. In a sense, the Rocky Mountains are both a physical and political divide. The concept of **Cascadia**, consisting of Idaho, Oregon, Washington, and British Columbia, represents a populist expression of regionalism. Cascadia is a reflection both of regional ties that cross the international border and of a disconnect towards Ottawa and Central Canada.

## British Columbia's Physical Geography

The spectacular physical geography of British Columbia is perhaps the region's greatest natural asset. The variety of natural features is unprecedented (Figure 9.4). Then, too, British Columbia is famous for its mild west coast climate. The combination of two contrasting climates (west coast and interior) with mountainous terrain has resulted in a wide variety of natural environments or ecosystems. Three examples of natural diversity are rain forests along the coast, desert-like conditions in the Interior Plateau, and alpine tundra found at high elevations in many BC mountains. As well, its fjord-indented coastline provides many deep harbours

surrounded by the Coast Mountains. Burrard Inlet is one such fjord. Yet, the growth of ocean shipping activities, especially the proposed jump in the number of Suezmax supertankers carrying Alberta bitumen, increases the risk of a spill into Burrard Inlet (Figure 9.3).

The physical contrast between the wet BC coast and the dry Interior is largely due to the effect of the Coast Mountains on precipitation. Easterly flowing air masses laden with moisture from the Pacific Ocean are forced to rise sharply over this high mountain chain, and consequently most moisture falls as orographic precipitation on the western slopes while little precipitation reaches the eastern slopes.

The climate of the west coast is unique in Canada. Winters are extremely mild and freezing temperatures are uncommon. Summer temperatures, while warm, are rarely as high as temperatures common in the continental and dry climate of the Interior Plateau of British Columbia. Moderate temperatures, high rainfall, and mild but cloudy winters make the west coast of British Columbia an ideal place to live and a popular retirement centre for those Canadians wanting to escape long cold winters.

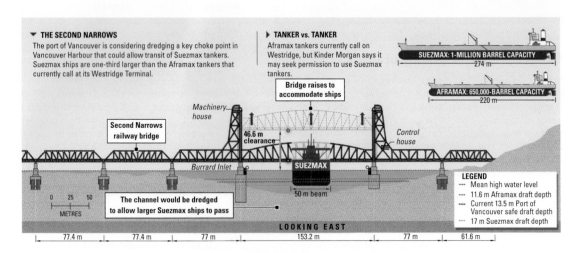

**FIGURE 9.3  The Second Narrows Bridge: Getting supertankers to port**

Burrard Inlet serves as the Greater Vancouver harbour. Its safe depth for tankers is 13.5 m. The Aframax tankers that now come to the federally owned oil terminal in Burnaby to load bitumen from the Alberta oil sands require 11.6 m draft depth. The original owners, Kinder Morgan, preferred the larger Suezmax supertanker, but its draft depth is considerably greater than 13.5 m and will require dredging at the Second Narrows Bridge.

Source: Illustration by John Sopinski and Michael Bird.

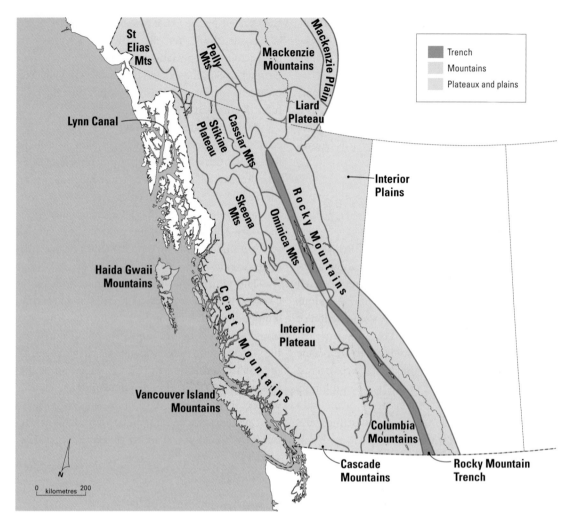

**FIGURE 9.4 Physiography of British Columbia**

British Columbia's complex topography is evident in the Cordillera, while the Interior Plains demonstrates a much less severe topography. With the grain of the land running north and south, BC's transportation system runs north and south much more easily than east and west. Imagine the difficulty of highway and railway construction across the Columbia Mountains. These mountains actually contain four mountain ranges, and each presented a problem for surveyors in finding a pass in order to construct the Canadian Pacific Railway. The north/south trending mountains included the Cariboo, Monashee, Selkirk, and Purcell mountains. Add the Rocky Mountains to the list and challenge of an east–west transportation system is revealed.

The Pacific Ocean has a powerful impact on BC's climate, resource base, and transportation system. Unlike in Atlantic Canada, the continental shelf in BC extends only a short distance from the coast. Within this narrow zone are many islands, the largest being Vancouver Island, followed by Haida Gwaii.[1] The riches of the sea include salmon, which return to the rivers, such as the Fraser and the Skeena, to complete their life cycle. Most of BC's natural wealth, however, is not in the sea but in the province's diversified physical geography, which provides valuable resources, particularly forests, natural gas, and hydroelectric power.

While BC is dominated by the Cordillera physiographic region, a small but valuable portion of

**PHOTO 9.4** Hell's Gate, located near Boston Bar, is confined by high canyon walls of the Coast Mountains that rise 1,000 m above the rapids. The Fraser River found a way through the Coast Mountains to the Pacific Ocean at Hell's Gate. Here, an Airtram carries tourists down to the visitors' centre by the river, and fishways enable salmon to head upstream to their spawning grounds. The Canadian Pacific Railway has its tracks on the lower reaches of the canyon while the Trans-Canada Highway is located in the upper reaches. In 1914, blasting through these mountains to improve the original route for the Canadian Pacific Railway caused a rockslide that blocked the salmon migration.

British Columbia extends into the Interior Plains physiographic region (Figure 2.1). Here, the geological structure is part of the petroleum-rich Western Sedimentary Basin. Significantly, a massive natural gas deposit was discovered in northeastern BC and is destined to form a resource anchor. In 2018, the federal government approved the LNG Canada project (Schmunk, 2018). This huge project could see a pipeline carrying natural gas from Dawson Creek in northeastern BC to a processing plant at Kitimat where the gas would be transformed into liquid gas suitable for ocean shipment to Asian customers. If all goes well, deliveries could begin as early as 2025.

Because of the rugged nature of the Cordillera, little arable land exists. Only about 2 per cent of the province's land is classified as arable. British Columbia's largest area of cropland lies outside of the Cordillera physiographic region in the Peace River Country. Within the Cordillera, most arable land is in the Fraser Valley, while a smaller amount can be found in the Interior, especially the Okanagan and Thompson valleys. This shortage of arable land poses a serious problem for British Columbia. With urban development spreading onto agricultural land, British Columbia lost some of its most productive farmland. From the end of World War II to the 1970s nearly 6,000 hectares of prime agricultural land were lost each year to urban and other uses. With only 5 per cent of BC's land mass classified as cropland, the provincial government responded to the serious erosion of its agricultural

**THINK ABOUT IT**

How have investors and speculators slipped around BC's Provincial Agricultural Land Commission to convert prime agricultural land into residential properties in BC's Fraser Valley? (See Tomlinson, 2016.)

## Vignette 9.1

### BC's Precipitation: Too Wet or Too Dry?

British Columbia is both dry and wet. It receives the greatest amount of precipitation along its Pacific coast. In simple terms, two precipitation areas exist in British Columbia—one in the Pacific climatic zone, where heavy precipitation occurs, reaching 3,000 mm of precipitation per year at Prince Rupert. Vancouver, on the other hand, receives just under 1,500 mm per year while Victoria gets only half that amount. In the Interior, precipitation figures are well below those of the Pacific coast. The figure for Kamloops, for example, is less than 300 mm per year while Kelowna's precipitation is around 350 mm per year.

land base by introducing BC's Land Commission Act in 1973. This Act formed the **Provincial Agricultural Land Commission**, which is charged with preserving agricultural land from urban encroachment and encouraging farm businesses (Provincial Agricultural Land Commission, 2014). With continuing pressure from urban land developers, this legislation remains under fire from market economy-oriented groups such as the Vancouver-based Fraser Institute, the central argument being that more "value" can be derived from non-agricultural use of the land (Katz, 2010).

### Climatic Zones

British Columbia has two climatic zones, the Pacific and the Cordillera. Because of the extremely high elevations in the Coast Mountains, few moist Pacific air masses reach the Interior Plateau. The spatial variation in precipitation is remarkable. Heavy orographic precipitation occurs along the western slopes of the Insular and Coast mountains, where 3,000 mm of precipitation fall annually in some locations (Vignette 9.1). In sharp contrast, the Interior Plateau receives less than 350 mm per year. In the Thompson Valley and Okanagan Valley of the Interior Plateau, hot, dry conditions result in an arid climate with sagebrush in the valleys and ponderosa pines on the valley slopes. Most rain falls in the winter. For those who live along the Pacific coast, the so-called **Pineapple Express**, which originates over the warm waters around Hawaii, brings

The three types of precipitation are described in **Chapter 2**, "Types of Precipitation," page 44.

torrential rains but also relatively warm weather in the winter months, while those inland receive heavy snowfalls.

## Challenges for the BC Coastal Landscape

British Columbia's coast, the interface between the ocean and the land, represents one of Canada's most dramatic landscapes. The challenge is to preserve this spectacular landscape for future generations. Its old-growth forests symbolize this unique ecosystem. Environmentalists made strong efforts to protect and preserve areas of this land of giant trees, but to little avail—until 1983, when social activists clashed with logging companies by chaining themselves to ancient Douglas fir trees to prevent the logging of old-growth forests in **Clayoquot Sound** on Vancouver Island. The search for a compromise was long and bitter because logging companies saw old-growth forests as prime logging areas. More than 30 years later, the creation of the **Great Bear Rainforest** (Figure 9.5) as a UNESCO **biosphere reserve** may have provided a solution where selective logging can take place; where core areas of the ancient forest can be preserved; and where the First Nations can find a place in both worlds—their traditional world and the Western market economy. As Dallas Smith, who represented the 26 First Nations in the establishment of conditions for any economic activity in the Great Bear Rainforest, has explained:

> Now it's necessary to take steps to ensure that our communities are able to share in

the economic success [resulting from sustainable logging], in the balance that we have achieved in the Great Bear. If that [meaning Third World conditions] is still the case 10 years from now, the Great Bear has failed. (Hunter, 2016)

Spills from shipping oil by pipelines, rail cars, and ships are inevitable. Cleaning up bituminous spills is particularly challenging, especially in a water environment. In 2010, an Enbridge pipeline in Michigan leaked bitumen into the Kalamazoo River with some sinking to the bottom of the river in oily globs. After two years, the cost of the cleanup totalled US$1.2 million (Hasemyer, 2016). On 21 June 2016, a much smaller oil spill occurred near Lloydminster, Saskatchewan. The Husky Oil pipeline ruptured and approximately 200,000 litres of heavy oil and diluents entered the North Saskatchewan River. Downstream, three communities (North Battleford, Prince Albert, and Melford) had their drinking water systems closed, but by mid-September the river water was again suitable for their water treatment plants. However, oil globs that sank to the bottom of the river remain and will take years to dissipate.

BC residents have every right to worry about the Trans Mountain pipeline that would cross their province to reach tidewater. While the risk of a leak or spill is low, they do happen. Everyone on the Pacific coast recalls the disastrous oil spill in 1989 from the tanker *Exxon Valdez*, caused by human error. The cleanup of the gooey mess on the marine landscape around Prince William Sound, Alaska, was next to impossible. For some BC residents, an oil pipeline carrying bitumen across BC to the coast represents an unacceptable risk. A spill from a tanker could foul the coastline for years to come, while a leak from the pipeline could pollute both land and rivers. From the perspective of the oil sands producers, access to tidewater is needed to obtain the Brent price for their product and thus increase their profits. Out of this pipeline squabble comes another challenge to national unity (see Contested Terrain 9.1).

The Trans Mountain expansion project has served as a lightning rod for those opposed to

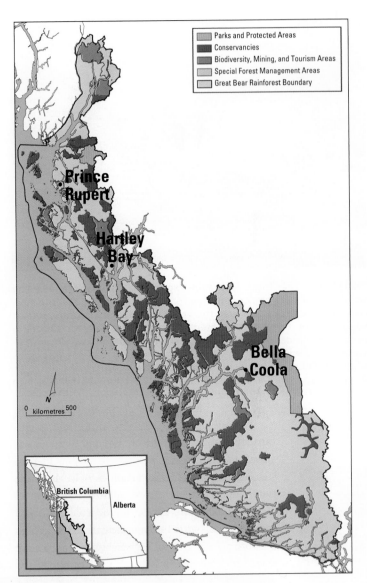

**FIGURE 9.5 Great Bear Rainforest Land Use Zones**

Source: BC Ministry of Forests, Lands and Natural Resource Operations (2016).

pipelines. Construction on the Trans Mountain pipeline expansion was delayed for over five years due to opposition to this project. During this time, Trans Mountain completed significant stakeholder engagements with communities, Indigenous groups, and landowners—this engagement is still ongoing. Construction finally began in 2019. The project consists of twinning the Trans Mountain pipeline's existing line from Strathcona County, Alberta (near Edmonton) to Burnaby, BC, increasing the storage

Trans Mountain

**PHOTO 9.5** The Trans Mountain expansion is moving ahead too slowly for Alberta and too quickly for BC. On 18 June 2019, the government of Canada approved the Trans Mountain expansion project. Following the October 2019 election, the TMX project developed a sense of political urgency. Accordingly, the federal government restated its commitment to complete the project "as soon as possible." In February 2020, the Trans Mountain Corporation Board of Directors approved a cost estimate of $12.6 billion to bring it into service by the end of 2022.

would deliver several "important benefits" to Canada, including "increased access to diverse markets for Canadian oil" and "considerable government revenues from the project" (Morgan, 2016). The pipeline expansion has incited fierce opposition, and even with the federal government having acquired ownership, this opposition will continue. Many fear a spill from one of the anticipated 400 oil tankers per year travelling through Vancouver's harbour. Twenty-one municipalities, including Vancouver, Burnaby, Port Moody, and Victoria, have vehemently opposed the expansion project, along with 17 First Nations, from the Squamish in BC to the Lummi Nation in the state of Washington.

## Waiting for the "Big One"?

A significant risk to the densely populated area of BC comes from nature itself—just off the coast of BC, the Pacific and North American tectonic plates overlap. The Pacific Ring of Fire of volcanic and earthquake activity encircles the Pacific basin, and Vancouver and Victoria lie within the Ring of Fire. Just south of Vancouver Island, the threat of the "Big One" comes from the smaller Juan de Fuca plate inching underneath the North American plate. As shown in Figure 9.8, the likelihood of earthquakes, and especially of a megathrust earthquake, is especially great in this region. While the "Big One" may not happen soon,

capacity at its terminal in Burnaby, and Aframax-size vessels to transport oil products to various markets (see Figures 9.6 and 9.7 and Photo 9.5). In May 2016, the National Energy Board approved the Kinder Morgan application, subject to 157 conditions that must be met, with the comment that the project

**THINK ABOUT IT**

Approval of the Trans Mountain expansion has benefits and costs. Among the costs are a risk of bitumen spill in Burrard Inlet. Still, the economic benefits are high, especially for Alberta oil sands producers and the province of Alberta. Is there a feasible way of keeping the pro- and anti-pipeline groups happy?

## Contested Terrain 9.1

### Piping Oil across British Columbia

Alberta is desperate to gain greater access for its oil to reach the Pacific coast. Without such access, the price for its oil will continue to fall well below global oil prices. On the other hand, BC sees the twinning of the Trans Mountain pipeline increasing the risk of an oil spill and damaging its environment. Underscoring this dispute is the province's perceived lack of support for its interests, which are often seen to be ignored in favour of so-called national interests. This perception runs deep in BC's history and can increase political tensions. The squabble between BC and Alberta over the proposed Trans Mountain expansion project crossing BC territory is a variation in this old political divide. With the federal government now pushing this project with renewed vigour following the 2019 election, just how will Victoria, encouraged by environmentalists and coastal First Nations, react? Whatever the outcome, the golden age for pipelines is over.

Rafal Gerszak for The Globe and Mail

**PHOTO 9.6** Tugboats escort the tanker *Aqualegend* to federal government's Westridge marine terminal in Burnaby, BC. *Aqualegend* is classed as an Aframax tanker, the largest type permitted to dock at Westridge terminal. Despite increasing opposition from city governments and environmental groups, among others, the federal government is pushing its plan to twin its Trans Mountain pipeline to increase bitumen shipments, and hopes also to increase the size of tankers used for transport.

the Vancouver/Victoria area is subjected to minor earthquakes on a regular basis. According to seismologist Alison Bird, who works for the Geological Survey of Canada in Victoria, every 14 months a period of around two weeks takes on a higher probability of an earthquake. During those two weeks, she will not park underground (Wagstaffe, 2016). However, the exact timing of the "Big One" could occur tomorrow or many decades from now. Regardless of when, seismologists are convinced that this megathrust earthquake will strike this heavily populated region (Wagstaffe, 2016). Not surprisingly, then, Canada's largest measured earthquake (magnitude 8.1) occurred in 1949 off the coast of the Haida Gwaii archipelago, and in August 2012 another major quake (magnitude 7.7) struck the same area. In 2019, three quakes measuring between 4.5 and 5.6

magnitude were recorded between Haida Gwaii and Vancouver Island (Figure 9.9).

## British Columbia's Historical Geography

Indigenous peoples lived along the Pacific coast of British Columbia for over 10,000 years before European explorers reached the northern Pacific coast in the mid-eighteenth century. The Spanish had already sailed northward from Mexico to California, but the Russians were the first to reach Alaska and establish fur-trading posts along its coast. In 1778, Captain James Cook established Britain's interest in this region by sailing into Vancouver Island's Nootka Sound (Photo 9.7), where he and his sailors found the Nootka village of Yuquot. The Nootka, now known as Nuu-chah-nulth, fished for salmon

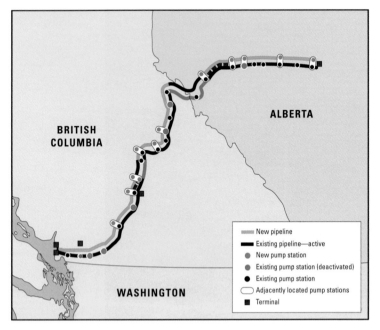

**FIGURE 9.6 Map of the proposed twinning of the Trans Mountain pipeline**

The federal government purchased the Trans Mountain pipeline from Kinder Morgan in 2018 for $4.4 billion. Ottawa formed the Trans Mountain Corporation, a Crown corporation, to undertake the project. Kinder Morgan sold its pipeline holdings because of the uncertainty of construction due to anticipated court challenges and protests. The company was concerned that further delays would increase the cost of the project. Regardless of the purchase of the project by Ottawa, opposition remains determined to stop the twinning of the Trans Mountain pipeline.

Source: Kinder Morgan (2015).

and hunted the sea otter. Upon landing, Cook engaged in trade for sea otter pelts, which opened up a profitable trade with China, although Cook did not live to see this trade flourish—he was killed in a skirmish with Indigenous people in the Hawaiian Islands on the return voyage. After the Royal Navy published Cook's record of his voyage, British and American traders came to the Pacific Northwest to seek the highly valued sea otters. Russian fur traders, based in Alaska, also harvested sea otters. Spain, which considered the lands Spanish territory, was disturbed by these interlopers and sent a fleet northward from Mexico in 1789. At Nootka Sound on the west coast of Vancouver Island, the Spanish seized several British merchant ships and built a small fort to support their claim. Times were changing in favour of the British. In 1792,

Captain George Vancouver of Britain's Royal Navy sailed around Vancouver Island. In the following year, Alexander Mackenzie of the North West Company travelled overland from Fort Chipewyan to just south of Prince George and then to the Pacific coast near Bella Coola, which is just over 400 km north of Vancouver. Under the Nootka Convention (1794), the Spanish surrendered their claim to the Pacific coast north of 42°N, leaving the British and Russians in control.

In the early nineteenth century, the North West Company established a series of fur-trading posts along the Columbia River. From 1805 to 1808, Simon Fraser, a fur trader and explorer, explored the Interior of British Columbia on behalf of the North West Company. He travelled by canoe from the Peace River to the mouth of the Fraser River. As elsewhere, the strategy of the North West Company was to develop a working relationship with local Indigenous groups based on bartering manufactured goods for furs. After 1821, when the North West Company merged with its rival, the Hudson's Bay Company, the HBC took charge of the Oregon Territory, which extended from the mouth of the Columbia River, at the present-day border between Oregon and Washington, to Russia's Alaska. In the late nineteenth century, a bitter dispute arose over the boundary of the Alaska Panhandle and access to Dawson City and the Klondike gold rush. The boundary dispute was settled in 1903 by a six-man tribunal, composed of American, Canadian, and British representatives. The settlement totally favoured the United States, suggesting that Canada's interests may have been sacrificed by Great Britain, which sought better relations with the United States.

In 1843, American settlers began to arrive on the coast from the eastern part of the United States. In the same year, the HBC relocated its main trading post from Fort Vancouver at the mouth of the Columbia River to Fort Victoria at the southern tip of Vancouver Island. The increasing number of American settlers who came west along the Oregon Trail represented a challenge to the authority of the Hudson's Bay Company. A few years later, the United States claimed the Pacific coast northward to Alaska, where Russian fur-trading posts existed. In 1846, Britain and the United States agreed to place the boundary

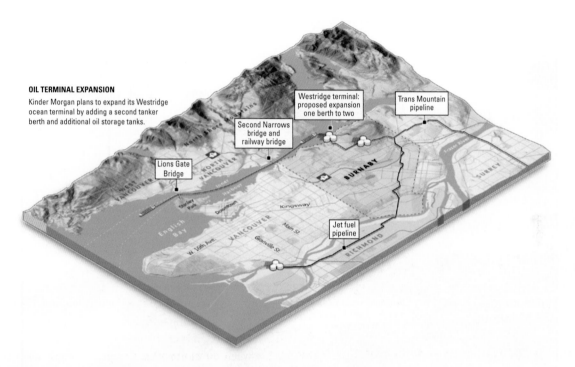

**OIL TERMINAL EXPANSION**

Kinder Morgan plans to expand its Westridge ocean terminal by adding a second tanker berth and additional oil storage tanks.

**FIGURE 9.7 Westridge oil terminal expansion, Burnaby, BC**

The federal government has inherited Kinder Morgan's planned expansion of its shipping capacity of bitumen that involves adding a second tanker berth and additional oil storage tanks at the Westridge terminal. Situated on Burnaby Mountain, local residents are concerned about the expansion plans. Kinder Morgan failed to assure them that the risks of an oil leak from its storage tanks are extremely low. Residents still remember the 2007 oil leak when a backhoe operator working on a sewage line accidentally ruptured the Trans Mountain pipeline, sending a large oil spill into Burrard Inlet.

Source: Sizing up BC's pipelines, *Globe and Mail*, 4 Aug. 2012. Illustration by John Sopinski and Michael Bird/The Globe and Mail. Sources: Port of Vancouver; Kinder Morgan; Enbridge; Google Maps; ESRI.

between the two nations at 49°N and then to follow the channel that separates Vancouver Island from the mainland of the United States (see Vignette 9.2). While the loss of the Oregon Territory in present-day Washington and Oregon was substantial, Britain was fortunate to hold onto the remaining lands administered by the Hudson's Bay Company. Britain recognized that its hold on these lands through the HBC was tenuous and could not withstand the political weight of the growing number of American settlers. Indeed, without the presence of the HBC and Britain's negotiating skills, Canada might well have lost its entire Pacific coastline.

The gold rush of 1858 brought about 25,000 prospectors from California to the Fraser River. The major finds were made in the BC Interior, where the town of Barkerville was built near Quesnel. By 1863, Barkerville had a population of about 10,000, making it the largest town in British Columbia. To ensure British sovereignty over territory north of 49°N, the British government established the mainland colony of British Columbia in 1858 under the authority of Sir James Douglas, who was also governor of Vancouver Island. Indigenous peoples were unable to stop this intrusion, although the Tsilhqot'in warriors made a powerful attempt that took the form of the Chilcotin War. In 1866, the two colonies were united. During Douglas's time as governor, land claims were settled on Vancouver Island, but not on the mainland (see Vignette 9.3) where the Chilcotin War of 1864 (Hopper, 2018) had erupted (see Figure 9.10).

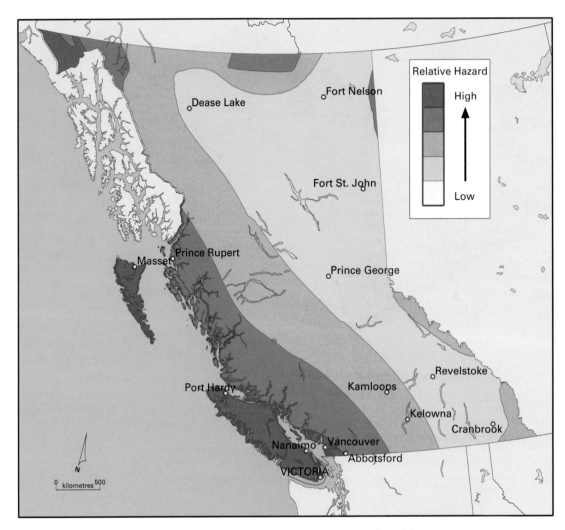

**FIGURE 9.8 Simplified seismic hazard map for British Columbia, 2015**

The probability of earthquakes declines from the coastal waters off BC to the Rocky Mountains. The critical zone falls along the coast of BC. As the massive North American plate edges slowly in a west/southwest direction at a rate of around 2 cm per year, it collides with the Pacific plate. In turn, the Pacific plate is moving in a northwest direction at a faster rate of around 10 cm per year. Such collisions result in earthquakes.

Source: Adapted with the permission of Natural Resources Canada.

**THINK ABOUT IT**

From studying **Figure 9.8**, would you conclude that the mountain chain found on Vancouver Island and on Haida Gwaii is geologically related and that a submerged portion of this mountain chain lies under the waters separating these two islands?

## Confederation

By the 1860s, the British government was actively encouraging its colonies in North America to unite into one country. Once the first four colonies were united in 1867, Ottawa adopted the British strategy to create a transcontinental nation. An important part of that strategy was to lure British Columbia into the "national fabric." The Canadian Pacific Railway was the first expression of this national policy.[2] In 1871, Prime Minister Macdonald promised that a railway to the Pacific Ocean would be built within 10 years after British Columbia joined Confederation. In Fort Victoria, however, some wanted to join the United States. By the middle of the nineteenth century, British Columbia had developed

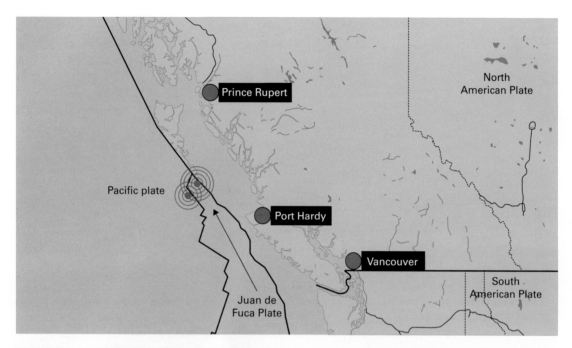

**FIGURE 9.9 Haida Gwaii earthquakes**

Three earthquakes took place south of Haida Gwaii in July 2019. The tectonic plates beneath the coastal waters of BC are actively moving. The two major plates, the Pacific and the North American plates, are moving towards each other at several centimetres per year. Consequently, tremors are common, and sometimes an outbreak of seismic activity takes place over a short period of time. The three 2019 quakes took place near the intersection of the Juan de Fuca and the Pacific plates. The small Juan de Fuca plate is subsiding beneath the North American plate.

Source: *CBC News* (2019, 5 July).

significant commercial ties with Americans along the Pacific coast. San Francisco was the closest metropolis and, with its railway to New York, offered the simplest and quickest route to London. In 1859, Oregon became a state and Washington was soon to follow. Commercial links with the United States were growing stronger. But the majority of people in Fort Victoria wanted to remain British. In 1871, the British Columbia government accepted the Prime Minister's offer and the province entered the new Dominion. Unfortunately, the slow progress in construction of the rail line caused friction and rekindled the movement to join the United States. While the Canadian government undertook surveys in the 1870s searching for the best route through the Cordillera, construction began in 1881 and on 7 November 1885 the "last spike" was driven at

Craigellachie, BC (Photo 9.8). Finally, the Canadian Pacific Railway stretched across the country, ending at Port Moody on Burrard Inlet. In 1887, the railway was extended 20 km westward to the small sawmill town of Vancouver.

Years later, in 1914, the Grand Trunk Pacific Railway, which connected with other rail lines to the east, was completed from Winnipeg to Prince Rupert, BC. All but the CPR were amalgamated in 1923 as a Crown corporation, Canadian National Railways, to give Canada two intercontinental railways.

## Post-Confederation Growth

At first, Confederation had little effect on British Columbia. The province was isolated from the rest

Library and Archives Canada/C-011201

**PHOTO 9.7** Captain James Cook's ships moored in Nootka Sound in 1778, as depicted in a watercolour by M.B. Messer. Four years earlier, the Spanish explorer Juan Hernandez sailed along the BC coast. However, there is speculation that Francis Drake, while on a secret mission to find a western entrance to the Northwest Passage, reached these waters in 1579 (Hume, 2000, p. B1).

## Vignette 9.2

### COVID-19 and the Arbitrary Nature of Boundary Lines

When nations establish boundaries between each other, surveyors are at the forefront, and not far behind are political leaders and government officials as well as geographers and geologists. But times can change, people can be affected by a border, and borders do change.

Canadians and Americans often speak of the forty-ninth parallel as *the* border, a logical line drawn on a map in the mid-nineteenth century, notwithstanding that much of Canada's population, most notably in Central Canada and Atlantic Canada, resides well below the forty-ninth parallel. Borders, wherever they exist, create anomalies and inconveniences for some people. When the COVID-19 pandemic reached North America and the Canada–US border was closed, golfers from Fort Fairfield, Maine, could no longer play a round at their course, the Aroostook Valley Country Club, because to get to the clubhouse they normally must drive across the border to Four Falls, New Brunswick. The golf course itself straddles the border, so on some holes you literally stand on the tee and hit it out of the country (Aroostook Valley Country Club, 2020; Mahoney, 2020).

A different and perhaps more significant pandemic-derived situation occurred on the other side of the continent south of Vancouver, some 5,500 km away from the Maine and New Brunswick golfers. When the forty-ninth parallel became the boundary line in Western Canada to Vancouver Island, it arbitrarily determined that about 30 km$^2$ at the southern tip of the Tsawwassen Peninsula would be part of Washington State although it has no road access to the United States. With the closed border resulting from COVID-19, this meant that the 1,300 residents of Point Roberts, Washington, effectively had nowhere to go, nor did their children, who, past elementary school, often attend school in BC. At the same time, Canadians from the Vancouver area with cottages at Point Roberts became unable to access their summer properties. One proposal is for Canada to purchase the tip of the peninsula from the US, and a purchase price floated by some proponents is $5 billion. Other solutions bandied about include Point Roberts declaring itself an independent fiefdom or becoming a US protectorate, like Puerto Rico and Guam (Quan, 2020). What do you think?

**THINK ABOUT IT**

The **Alaska boundary dispute** was settled in 1903 and the outcome clearly favoured the territorial claim of the United States. If Canada had the power to conduct its foreign affairs at that time, Ottawa would have insisted on setting the boundary along the Lynn Canal so as to gain access by water to the interior of northern BC and Yukon.

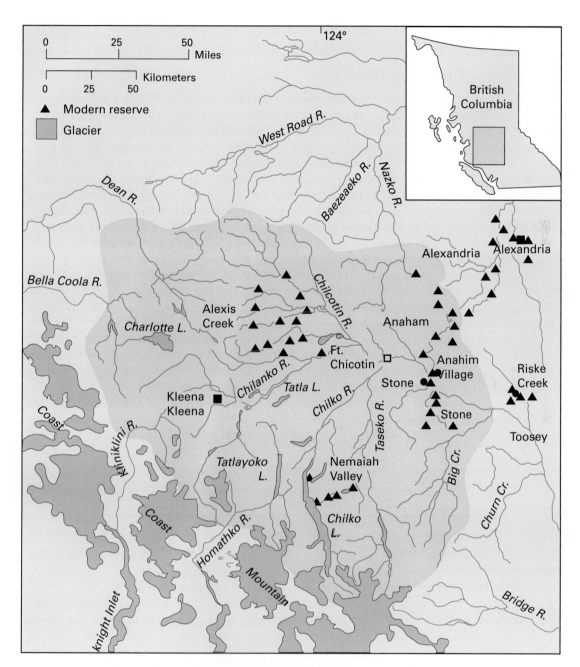

**FIGURE 9.10 The territory of the Tsilhqot'in peoples**

Source: *Handbook of North American Indians*, Vol. 6., Subarctic, ed. William C. Sturtevant, Smithsonian Institution 1981, Figure 1

of Canada, and goods still had to come by ship from San Francisco or London. When the Canadian Pacific Railway was completed in 1885, British Columbia truly became part of the Dominion, and BC's role as a gateway to the world began.

With the CPR line in place, Vancouver grew quickly and soon became the major centre on the west coast. By 1901, Vancouver had a population of 27,000 compared to Victoria's 24,000. As the terminus of the transcontinental railway, Vancouver became the transshipment point for goods produced in the Interior of BC and Western Canada. As coal, lumber, and grain were transported by rail from the Interior and the Canadian Prairies, the Port of

For further discussion of Indigenous rights and the modern treaty process, see **Chapter 3**, "Modern Treaties," page 91, and **Vignette 3.5**, "The Federal Government and Indigenous Peoples," page 84.

## Vignette 9.3

### Indigenous Title: Who Owns BC?

How much of BC belongs to First Nations? Up to 1993, only the 14 pre-Confederation Douglas treaties signed between 1850 and 1854 with the Coast Salish on Vancouver Island, as well as those bands belonging to Treaty 8 of 1899 in the northeast corner of the province, had acquired Indigenous title to a portion of their lands. For the rest, BC claimed that Indigenous title was extinguished upon BC entering Confederation. The 1973 Supreme Court of Canada ruling in the *Calder* case challenged BC's legal position of extinguishment. While the Supreme Court rejected the Nisga'a claim to Indigenous title, the justices' split decision opened the door for land claims. According to Frank Cassidy (1992, p. 11), this 1973 Supreme Court decision represented "a centrepiece in the historical development of the province of British Columbia." Yet, progress has been slow as only four final agreements had been reached by 2020 under the BC Treaty Process: the Tsawwassen First Nation (2009); the Maa-nulth Treaty (2011); and the Yale First Nation and the Tla'amin First Nation agreements (2016). The Final Agreement with the Nisga'a in 2000 took place outside of the BC Treaty Process. Yet another approach has emerged. As traditional urban lands are regained, real estate becomes a possible rental asset for First Nations. Dustin Rivers, a Squamish Nation councillor, expressed it this way (Smart, 2019): "For a lot of other First Nations across the country, natural resources is the one option they have for growing their economies. Whereas for us, the land has been completely impacted [by the city's growth] and so real estate is really the one thing we can get involved in that will make sense to generate revenue." See Photo 9.17 for a photograph of the tiny but highly valuable land in downtown Vancouver.

Vancouver spearheaded economic growth in the southwest part of the province. It was then possible to tap the vast natural resources of BC and ship them to world markets. By the twentieth century, Vancouver had become one of Canada's major ports. Unlike Montreal, Vancouver has an ice-free harbour, and as Canada's major Pacific port, Vancouver became the natural transportation link to Pacific nations. With the opening of the Panama Canal in 1914, British Columbia's resources were more accessible to the markets of the United Kingdom and Western Europe.

While BC's economy and population continued to grow in the 1920s, the Great Depression of the 1930s caused the province's economy to stall as exports declined. World War II called for full production in Canada, thereby pulling British Columbia's depressed resource economy out of the doldrums. Military production, including aircraft

manufacturing, greatly expanded BC's industrial output. As well, resource industries based on forestry and mining (especially coal and copper) were producing at full capacity.

When the war ended in 1945, BC's resource boom continued. With world demand for forest and mineral products remaining high, the provincial government focused its efforts on developing the resources of its hinterland, the Central Interior of British Columbia. The first step was to create a transportation system from Vancouver to Prince George, the major city in the Central Interior. The highway system was improved and extended from Prince George to Dawson Creek in 1952. But the completion of the Pacific Great Eastern Railway to Prince George in 1956 and then to Dawson Creek in 1958 opened the country, allowed for exports to foreign markets, and triggered economic growth, especially in the forest industry. With rail access to

Vancouver, forestry, as well as other resource industries, expanded rapidly, thereby leading to the integration of this hinterland into the BC and global industrial core.

Over the past two decades, BC's increasing economic strength, partly driven by the Asian economy, has outpaced that of all other regions in Canada. Trade is a dynamic force propelling British Columbia's economy, and as China and other Pacific Rim countries have led the world in economic growth, this growth has created new markets for Canadian products shipped through Vancouver. Trade opportunities are almost endless between British Columbia and the population of 3 billion people in the Pacific nations. Yet, BC continues to ship more raw materials than finished goods to these countries. In part, the failure to expand manufacturing in BC is related to much higher labour costs than in Asian countries. Another factor is the relatively small BC market that inhibits economies of scale that would lower cost of production.

## British Columbia Today

British Columbia is heading towards a greener and more technically advanced economy. The foundation of its economy rests on its resources and its advanced knowledge-based economy. Trade facilitates resource development and innovative firms. Most trade flows through the Port of Vancouver (Photos 9.8 and 9.9). In 2018, the value of exports climbed to a record $46.5 billion (Table 9.1).

The value of exports in 2019 reached $43.5 billion, with forest products and coal representing the top exports from BC, while Western Canada's exports of coal, grain, potash, and oil/bitumen add to the volume passing through BC ports. Imports consist of a variety of consumer goods, including automobiles and textiles, and they flow to all parts of Canada. The geopolitical significance of the United States in BC's trade pattern is clear—49 per cent of the value of exports flows to the United States. However, the remarkable decline from 2001 to 2019 in exports to the US, coupled with an increase to China, reveals an important trend. Softwood lumber is a major export to the US, but

PHOTO 9.8 Sir Donald Alexander Smith, a powerful banker and major financier of the Canadian Pacific Railway, drives the last spike at Craigellachie, just west of Eagle Pass in the Monashee Mountains, thus symbolizing completion of the CPR. The town of Revelstoke lies 20 km to the east of this famous pass. The divide of the Monashee Mountains separates the Columbia and Fraser drainage basins. Rogers Pass in the Selkirk Mountains lies further east. Rogers Pass, with its steep grade, high elevation, and frequency of avalanches, proved too difficult to maintain in later years. The answer was tunnels through the mountains—the Connaught Tunnel (1916) and the Mount Macdonald Tunnel (1988).

*Alexander Ross/Library and Archives Canada/C-003693.*

with the expiration of the Softwood Lumber Agreement in October 2016 the United States has signalled that it intends to impose tougher restrictions in the agreement. In 2019, the United States enacted new duties on Canadian softwood lumber, causing a sharp decrease in BC exports.

**Container** traffic represents the fastest-growing form of trade. Within the Pacific Rim, the flow of containers from China to BC ports continues to increase. BC has a decided advantage because its ports, especially Prince Rupert, provide the shortest North American sea links to China, Japan, and South Korea. According to the BC government, container traffic to all west coast ports was forecast to rise a staggering 300 per cent by 2020, thus reaching 9 million TEU (BC Ministry of Transportation, 2007). A measure of accuracy of that forecast comes from the 2018 data for Port of Vancouver, which recorded handling 3.3 million

**THINK ABOUT IT**

The Chinese population in British Columbia doubled from 4,200 in 1881 to 8,910 in 1891 (Roy, 1989, Table 1B). During this period, the building of the CPR railway drew many from China to British Columbia.

https://www.robertharding.com

**PHOTO 9.9** Vancouver's magnificent harbour has facilitated trade with Pacific Rim countries. The Burrard and Granville Street bridges cross False Creek, separating Kitsilano from downtown Vancouver. Just beyond the West End lies Stanley Park. Across the harbour, West and North Vancouver occupy the lower slopes of the North Shore Mountains.

**TABLE 9.1  Exports through British Columbia, 2001, 2006, 2009, 2015, and 2019**

| Country | 2001 (%) | 2006 (%) | 2009 (%) | 2015 (%) | 2019 (%) |
|---|---|---|---|---|---|
| US | 69.8 | 61.3 | 51.3 | 52.0 | 50.6 |
| China | 2.3 | 4.4 | 10.2 | 16.8 | 15.3 |
| Japan | 12.8 | 14.1 | 13.7 | 10.0 | 10.4 |
| South Korea | 2.2 | 4.1 | 6.6 | 5.1 | 6.1 |
| Other countries | 12.9 | 16.1 | 18.2 | 14.8 | 17.6 |
| Value in billions of dollars | 31.7 | 33.5 | 25.2 | 36.0 | 43.5 |

Sources: Adapted from BC Stats (2012, 2016, 2019a).

TEU of container cargo (TEU refers to containers measuring 20 feet) while the Port of Prince Rupert reached a record 1 million TEU, doubling its container traffic over the previous five years (*Vancouver Courier*, 2019).

## Industrial Structure

Is British Columbia turning into a core region? For over 50 years, developed nations have undergone a shift from primary and secondary industries

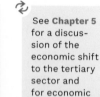

THE CANADIAN PRESS/Darryl Dyck

**PHOTO 9.10** CP's Port Metro in Vancouver, one of the busiest shipping hubs on the continent. The Port of Vancouver handled 144 million tonnes of cargo in 2019, down from the previous year's 147 million tonnes (Port of Vancouver, 2020). The **Asia–Pacific Gateway and Corridor** project is facilitating the flow of goods from Western Canada to the Pacific coast ports by upgrading highways and rail lines.

See **Chapter 5** for a discussion of the economic shift to the tertiary sector and for economic change in the twenty-first century.

to tertiary ones, where most innovative activities take place. This trend is taking place within British Columbia where about 80 per cent of the labour force is employed in the tertiary sector compared to less than 5 per cent in the primary sector (Table 9.2). Keep in mind that the advanced economy, driven by technological innovations, exists in all sectors. In the primary sector, for example, technical advances in oil and gas operations permit **horizontal drilling**, which, when combined with **hydraulic fracturing**, has unlocked natural gas deposits in northeast BC.

British Columbia, like other regions, has seen employment rise sharply, largely due to expansion of the knowledge-based industry. Technology firms, for instance, have exploded and much of that employment growth falls into tertiary sector. By 2019, tech workers outnumbered those in the mining, oil, gas, and forestry sectors and accounted for less than 5 per cent of the region's total workforce (Wilson, 2019). The twinning of the Trans Mountain pipeline may well boost the number of workers in construction and hence the primary sector for 2020 and 2021.

**TABLE 9.2**   British Columbia Industrial Sectors by Number of Workers, 2005 and 2019

| Economic Sector | Workers, 2005 | Workers, 2005 (%) | Workers, 2019 | Workers, 2019 (%) | % Difference |
|---|---|---|---|---|---|
| **Primary** | 76,200 | 3.6 | 115,500 | 4.4 | +0.8 |
| **Secondary** | 376,500 | 17.7 | 414,500 | 15.9 | –1.8 |
| **Tertiary** | 1,677,800 | 78.7 | 2,073,400 | 79.7 | +1.0 |
| **Total** | 2,130,500 | 100.0 | 2,603,400 | 100.0 | |

Sources: Statistics Canada (2006, 2020).

## Knowledge-Based Economy

Vancouver is quickly expanding into a major tech centre in North America. Microsoft, Sony Pictures, and Shopify have significantly impacted this west coast city. Microsoft has increased its presence and is now the largest corporate tenant in downtown Vancouver.

With such rapid growth in the tech business, the knowledge-based sector dominates Vancouver's contemporary economy with the emphasis on technology and innovation, plus an expansion of service industries that support such an economy. Following the concept of a creative class, these service industries include a vibrant entertainment and filmmaking sector coupled with outstanding arts and drama performances. In short, a Canadian version of a laid-back, "California" lifestyle, with hints of California's Silicon Valley, has taken root in Greater Vancouver. Firms like MacDonald, Dettwiler and Associates (MDA), with its RADARSAT invention, and Ballard Power Systems, with its fuel cell development, provide the innovative leadership. MDA is a world leader in the design and development of radar satellite missions and provides Canada with three observation satellites that record shipping activities over the Arctic Ocean, including the Northwest Passage. This system is known as RADARSAT Constellation Mission. Funded by the federal government, the three-satellite configuration tracks Canada's Arctic Ocean on a daily basis. In this way, RADARSAT Constellation Mission is defending Canada's Arctic sovereignty with a broad-area maritime surveillance system using the RADARSAT Constellation (Keyzer, 2016).

The evidence is clear—British Columbia's economy is changing and diversifying, but growth in the manufacturing sector remains elusive. In the past two decades, however, BC has experienced growth in high technology. As the front edge of the structural shift in the manufacturing industry across Canada, high-tech firms are playing a greater role in BC's economy and are providing jobs for highly skilled workers. High technology involves cutting-edge research in the manufacture of electronics, telecommunications equipment, and pharmaceuticals. BC has the fourth-largest high-tech workforce in

Canada.[3] According to Schrier and Hallin (2016), Ontario has the largest high-tech workforce, with 354,110 people, or 39 per cent of all Canadian high-tech workers, followed by Quebec (26 per cent), Western Canada (15 per cent), and BC (10 per cent).

The sharp edge of the advanced economy based on innovative industries lies in a variety of areas: fuel cell development by Ballard Power Systems; possible new technology applied to shipbuilding in BC, especially the polar-class icebreaker; and RADARSAT inventions by MacDonald, Dettwiler and Associates, Canada's principal space company. According to John MacDonald (2012), the co-founder of MacDonald, Dettwiler, "This cutting-edge project will create highly skilled jobs, and attract the world's best scientists, technicians and engineers to Canada's world-renowned space industry."

# Technological Spearheads

Each region has a distinct set of economic spearheads that reflect the major economic advances taking place in the region. In the case of BC, three economic high-growth industries—shipbuilding, filmmaking, and natural gas—are of special note.

## Seaspan Shipyard

Seaspan Shipyard in Vancouver (Photo 9.11) is one of Canada's major naval shipyards. It first gained national prominence in 2011 when it was awarded a federal contract under the National Shipbuilding Procurement Strategy valued at $8 billion for building 17 vessels, including a polar-class icebreaker (Chase & Marotte, 2011, p. A1). Shipbuilding takes time and the first coast guard vessel, the CCGS *Sir John Franklin*, was turned over to the Canadian Coast Guard in 2019. This vessel represents the first Offshore Fisheries Science vessel built under the National Shipbuilding Procurement Strategy. More success took place in 2020 when Seaspan was awarded a $2.4 billion contract for two supply ships (Orton, 2020).

The economic impact on Vancouver and the BC economy is huge. According to Jonathan Whitworth, CEO of Seaspan: "This is going to be a boom. It's not like building a (liquefied natural gas)

plant or a mine, where there are 1,500 jobs for about two years. This is work for decades. It's like winning the 2010 Olympics every two years" (Alldritt, 2012).

## Filmmaking

"Hollywood North" is a colloquialism used to describe film production industries north of its namesake in California. Toronto and Vancouver both see themselves as "Hollywood North," and indeed the Vancouver area has become a major film production centre (Photo 9.12). Filmmaking represents one aspect of the emerging and highly diversified urban knowledge economy, which

has also taken hold in Toronto and Montreal. In 2018, the Vancouver film industry generated $3.6 billion compared to Toronto at $2.9 billion (Orton, 2019).

## Advanced Drilling Techniques

Gas and oil deposits sometimes are found in horizontal strata in sedimentary basins. The Western Canadian Sedimentary Basin contains such deposits trapped in horizontal shale strata. The Bakken Shale Formation in southern Saskatchewan and northern North Dakota is one example; the Montney gas field in northeast BC and northwest Alberta is another. In each case, the oil or natural gas is trapped in a shale

PHOTO 9.11 Seaspan's Vancouver shipyard is located across the Burrard Inlet from downtown Vancouver and Stanley Park. Seaspan Shipyards is a leader in Canada's shipbuilding and ship repair industry and operates three shipyards in North Vancouver and Victoria. Seaspan is Canada's chosen non-combat shipbuilder under the National Shipbuilding Strategy (NSS), building state-of-the-art ships in Canada for the Canadian Coast Guard and Royal Canadian Navy. Through its NSS-related work, Seaspan Shipyards is creating jobs, generating economic benefits, and rebuilding Canada's shipbuilding and marine industries. By 2020, the federal government had awarded Seaspan $11 billion to build 19 vessels for the Canadian navy.

Darryl Dyck/for The Globe and Mail

**PHOTO 9.12** A stuntman dressed as Ryan Reynolds's Marvel Comics character Deadpool flips over a vehicle during filming on the Georgia Viaduct in Vancouver, 6 April 2015.

formation. Conventional drilling cannot access such deposits. The technological breakthrough in drilling techniques involves a combination of multi-stage hydraulic fracturing—commonly called **fracking**—and long-reach horizontal drilling able to access these "elephant" deposits. As a result, BC could become one of the world's largest natural gas producers. According to the National Energy Board (2015), Montney, Horn River, and the Liard Basin contain the three largest reserves of natural gas in Canada. Globally, these deposits are among the 10 largest shale gas deposits in the world (National Energy Board, 2015). Until recently, technology to extract such deposits did not exist, but recent advances in drilling technology, including multi-stage hydraulic fracturing, have allowed these natural deposits to be exploited. As shown in Figure 9.11, horizontal drilling allows the driller to reach the deposit. Once

the depth of the shale is determined, the driller inserts a "bit assembly" that allows the drill to turn horizontally.

## British Columbia's Fading Economic Anchor: Forestry

The forest has long been British Columbia's greatest natural asset. With just over 60 per cent of the province covered by forests, British Columbia contains about half of the nation's softwood timber and leads the nation in the export of forest products. With such a dominant position, this region is easily Canada's leading supplier of wood products. While BC remains at the front of Canada's forest producers, forestry no longer dominates the province's economy. Fifty years ago, forestry alone accounted for half of the provincial economy and for most of the employment. By 2018, the industry comprised only 2.9 per cent of BC's GDP and 2 per cent of employment (BC Stats, 2019c). This decline is due to the growth of other sectors of the economy and to the replacement of forest workers by machines. Another measure of the state of the forest industry is revealed by the annual value of exports. Since the global financial crisis of 2008, the value of forest exports has risen from $8 billion to nearly $15 billion in 2018, with the US and China accounting for 45 per cent and 28 per cent, respectively (BC Stats, 2020).

The forest industry is vital to many small communities in the Interior of BC. Among the challenges are wildfire devastation, high log costs, and low prices due to a slumping US market. By 2019, the supply of timber had slowed, partly because the harvest of damaged timber from the mountain pine beetle infestation had ended. In 2019, 22 interior mills either closed or curtailed operations, laying off thousands of workers. While exports of lumber, pulp, and logs to China have increased, this has not been enough to offset the reduction in sales to the US (Wood Resources International LLC, 2019).

## Natural Forest Regions

Climate and topography have divided British Columbia's vast coniferous **softwood forest** into two distinct regions: the rain forest along the coast and the boreal forest in the much drier Interior. Four sub-regions are found in the Interior: the Northern Forest, the Nechako Forest, the Fraser Plateau Forest, and the Columbia Forest (Figure 9.12). Within the rain forest, the mild, wet climate allows trees to grow to great heights for hundreds, even thousands, of years. Old-growth trees that are at least 250 years old are located along the Pacific coast, where fires are rare because of heavy precipitation throughout the year. The major species harvested are spruce and Douglas fir. In the Interior, the main species logged is the lodgepole pine. Since the climate in the Interior is much drier as well as colder in the winter and hotter in the summer than along the coast, the lodgepole pine and other trees are smaller and forest stands less dense. Trees have a shorter lifespan (120 to 140 years). While forest fires occur in all parts of BC, most occur in the dry, hot Interior. Climate change has seen severe winter temperatures

**FIGURE 9.11 Horizontal drilling**

Horizontal drilling takes place after vertical drilling has reached the horizontal shale strata. The next step requires the driller to alter the direction of the drilling to a horizontal one. At that point, fracking begins by pumping large quantities of pressurized, chemically treated water into the formation to fracture the rocks, allowing the natural gas to escape to the surface. Fracking has been outlawed in Nova Scotia and Quebec because this chemically treated water could enter aquifers and thus threaten the quality of well water (see Loki, 2015).

Source: Geology.com. http://geology.com/articles/horizontal-drilling/

become less frequent, allowing pine beetles to survive. Both wildfires and pine beetle infestations have reduced the size of the timber resource, causing both environmental and commercial problems.[+]

## Dependency on the US Market

Most softwood lumber is sold in the US market. However, US lumber producers lobby Washington to use political pressure to limit imports from Canada. Countervailing duties provide one political tool. In this way, the US producers can maintain market share and prices.

In order to protect US softwood lumber producers, the US government has kept softwood lumber outside of NAFTA and now the USMCA. Consequently, Washington can more easily reduce the volume of Canadian softwood lumber imports. Still, the dispute resolution panels in these agreements

**THINK ABOUT IT**
How do we explain why the Chinese government banned certain Canadian agricultural products in 2019 but sales of BC forest products increased?

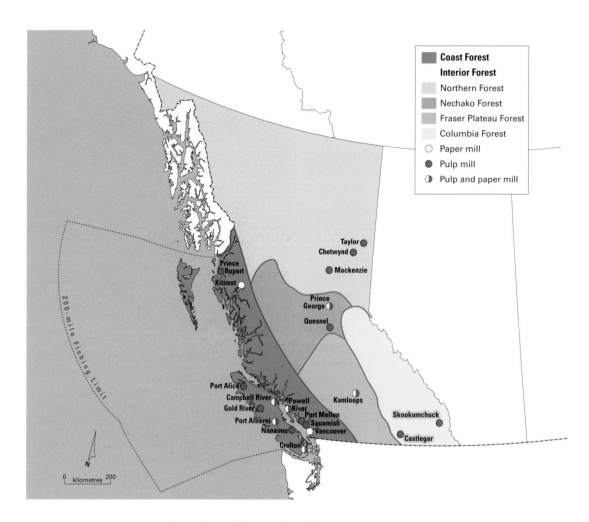

**FIGURE 9.12 Forest regions in British Columbia**

The Coast Rainforest is the most luxuriant coniferous forest in Canada. With its wet and mild marine temperatures and abundant rainfall, the Coast Rainforest is found almost entirely in mountainous terrain. The key species are Douglas fir, western red cedar, and western red hemlock. The northern area is characterized by significantly lower summer temperatures, which slows tree growth, while tree growth in the three southern areas face a shortage of moisture in the hot summer months.

**THINK ABOUT IT**

Canadians do not understand why softwood lumber did not fall under NAFTA and was excluded from the USMCA. What explanation can you offer? What remedies to this tilted playing field do you suggest?

have allowed Canada to appeal to those panels when the US Department of Commerce levies countervailing and anti-dumping duties on Canada softwood lumber.

Complicating matters for Washington, Canadian softwood lumber is highly valued by American construction firms and often its price is lower than the US softwood lumber. In 2015, Canadian softwood lumber made up about 30 per cent of the US market. In seeking a new softwood lumber agreement, the US negotiating position is strongly influenced by the US lumber lobby's demand that Canadian imports make up no more than 22 per cent of the US softwood lumber market. Not surprisingly, US importers of Canadian softwood lumber oppose such restriction because it leads to high lumber prices and eventually to higher home construction costs. Accordingly, the National Lumber and Building Materials Dealers Association (NLBMDA) continues to lobby Washington for a softwood lumber deal.

For BC, a drop in exports to the US has a drastic impact on the BC forestry industry and on many small forestry-dependent communities.

## The Future

The forest industry in British Columbia faces two major challenges. One is negotiations with the United States, and the other is climate change. In the short term, the biggest problem is reduced access to the US market. In 2020, a ruling from a World Trade Organization (WTO) panel declared that the US tariffs on Canadian softwood lumber must be withdrawn. However, since the US is blocking the WTO's dispute resolution system, a rollback in these tariffs may never take effect.[4]

In the long term, climate change may alter the natural vegetation of the BC Interior. Already climate change has seen slightly drier and warmer weather in the Interior, encouraging pine beetle infestations and more frequent summer wildfires.[5] The combination of political and natural factors has seen exports decline and sawmills close. This raises the question: what is the future for the forest industry? On the one hand, the future looks grim. On the other hand, could an industrial renaissance of the forest industry take place? Such a renaissance would see an emphasis on high-value products, skilled labour, and cutting-edge technology, plus an expansion of export to Asian markets.

## Mining, Energy, and Fisheries

The mineral wealth of British Columbia is found in both of the province's physiographic regions—the Cordillera and the Interior Plains. Each has a distinct geological structure and mineral and energy deposits. The Cordillera contains a wide variety of ore bodies ranging from diamonds to copper and gold, while the Interior Plains contains vast coal and petroleum deposits. In 2018, mineral production, led by coal and copper, totalled almost $10 billion (BC Stats, 2019b). While coal is king in mineral production, natural gas is soon expected to lead in terms of value of energy production. BC produced over $5 billion worth of coal in 2018 and $2.5 billion in copper (BC Stats, 2019b). Canada's commitment to reduce its greenhouse gases suggests that the future of BC's coal production may be affected. Coking coal exported to Asian steel mills may continue at its current level but thermal coal used for producing electricity is already under pressure and its mining operations are poised to close within 10 years.

## Natural Gas Exports: Dream or Reality?

Unlike the oil pipeline proposed to reach the Pacific coast, natural gas pipelines are viewed by the BC government and residents, including First Nations in BC, in a more favourable light. The main reason is that a leak in a natural gas pipeline or ship evaporates and thus has much less potential impact on the local environment than does a bitumen spill that soaks into the land or sinks to the bottom of lakes, rivers, or oceans (Contested Terrain 9.2). With the approval of the LNG Canada project in 2018, a proposed pipeline carrying natural gas from Dawson Creek to a proposed processing plant on the coast at Kitimat, where the gas would be liquefied for overseas export, seemed like a new reality for BC. At that time, gas prices were much higher than now. Construction for the LNG Canada project began in 2018 with most activity taking place in Kitimat. Assuming all would go well, the first exports of liquid gas would take

**PHOTO 9.13** Kitimat's proposed liquified gas plant

LNG Canada

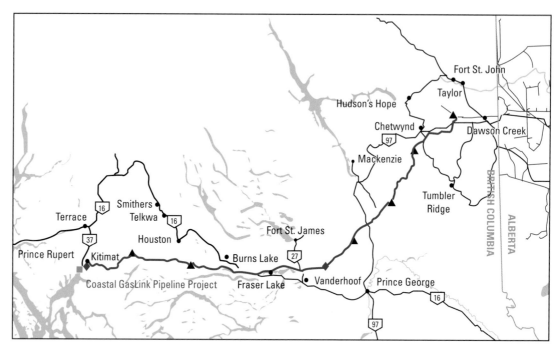

**FIGURE 9.13 Coastal GasLink Pipeline Project**

A pipeline would bring natural gas from the Montney gas fields near Dawson Creek to Kitimat, where LNG Canada proposed to build a liquefaction, storage, and loading terminal. When in operation, the plan is for the liquefied gas to be exported to Asian customers.

Source: Based on: http://lnginnorthernbc.ca/index.php/proposed-projects/lng-canada-gas-and-coastal-gaslink-pipeline/

## Contested Terrain 9.2

### LNG Canada

LNG Canada's proposal to build a gas pipeline from Dawson Creek to the Pacific coast was readily accepted (Figure 9.13). In complete contrast, the Trans Mountain pipeline expansion ran into stiff resistance from the province, First Nations, and environmentalists. The explanation lies in the debate over climate change: natural gas is less of a generator of greenhouse gases than oil and certainly coal. Then, too, natural gas from BC may replace coal-burning thermal plants in China and other Asian countries. On the other hand, the Trans Mountain expansion will allow the companies in the oil sands to expand their operations and, in doing so, add more greenhouse emissions into the atmosphere. Environmentalists perceive the oil sands as a threat to the earth and, as such, their opposition to this project has gained international status. Desperate to keep the project alive, the federal government purchased the entire holdings of Kinder Morgan in 2018. In sharp contrast, foreign ownership of LNG Canada has not stirred a reaction. Led by Royal Dutch Shell PLC of the Netherlands, the other partners are from Asia and represent the most likely markets for the liquefied natural gas: Petronas (Malaysia), PetroChina (China), Mistubishi (Japan), and Kogas (South Korea).

place in 2025 (Jang, 2019). Export of **liquefied natural gas** (LNG) to Asian countries constitutes a major export industry for British Columbia. In 2019, this promising reality involved two LNG projects but then a drop in gas prices turned the LNG gas scenario into a nightmare for LNG Kitimat. In 2019, the proposed Kitimat LNG project was a casualty of this price drop, causing Chevron to withdraw from the project. Now Kitimat has the prospect for only one LNG project and that depends on improved gas prices.

## Mining Industry

Both coal and copper remain important exports for British Columbia (Figure 9.14). BC coal production depends heavily on world demand for metallurgical coal used in steel mills, which fluctuates according to the global economic cycle. Concern over greenhouse emissions has resulted in Ottawa notifying provinces that thermal coal should be phased out by 2030. BC metallurgical coal production should not be affected. Copper, because it conducts electricity

well, finds a market in electric power systems, wiring of buildings and houses, and in the field of electronics. Boom-and-bust cycles are characteristic of the BC coal and copper industries. During resource booms, huge investments are made in new developments. Such was the case in the late 1970s when private and public funds went into the development of the vast Peace River coalfields near the Alberta border. Known as the Northeast Coal Project, production began in 1984 about the time demand for coal slumped. Struggling to hang on, the coal companies squeaked by until 2000 when the project collapsed. Prices then rose, reviving the BC coal industry.

Transportation costs are critical, and these have been minimized by unit trains and bulk-loading facilities. Unit trains consist of a large number of ore cars, sometimes over 100, pulled by one or more locomotives. The Roberts Bank terminal on the Strait of Georgia in Delta, BC, south of Vancouver, was designed as a large bulk-loading facility where coal in rail cars is dumped and then the coal is moved by conveyor belts to the ship's hold. These ships must be moored in deep

STR/AFP via Getty Images

**PHOTO 9.14** Huge liquefied natural gas tankers like this one at Tokyo are anticipated to be plying the waters near Kitimat in the coming years. If all goes to plan, by 2025 the first such LNG tanker could dock at Kitimat and then transport its cargo to any of several Asian ports, such as Tokyo, Hong Kong, or Mumbai.

Keith Douglas/Alamy Stock Photo

**PHOTO 9.15** Fairview Terminal at Prince Rupert.

water, which necessitated building a long causeway to reach the ships. Similar arrangements take place at Prince Rupert, where the port is a growing North American gateway with Asia (Photo 9.15).

## Mining and the Environment

The resource industry, by its very nature, alters the environment, often for the worse. In particular, mining operations pose a direct threat to the environment. While mining is an important economic activity, it produces toxic wastes. Tailing ponds are a common feature of mining operations where the waste products are stored. Alberta has oil sand tailing ponds. In all cases, such storage is like a time bomb because eventually one pond will spring a leak. Indeed, one of the worst catastrophes was the collapse of a massive tailing dam at Mount Polley copper/gold mine near the towns of Likely and Williams Lake (Photo 9.16). On 4 August 2014, 24 million m³ of toxic mine waste and contaminated water gushed from the tailing pond into nearby lakes and rivers, leaving behind debris that clogged salmon-bearing streams

(Meissner, 2016). Fortunately, no one was injured, but the landscape and streams were badly polluted. Five years after the spill, Imperial Metals, the owner of the tailing pond, has still not been charged. In fact, both the federal and provincial governments missed deadlines to proceed with charges. In the case of the federal government, the Fisheries Act had a five-year deadline, while the province has a three-year deadline under its Environmental Management Act and Mines Act. Both levels of government claimed they did not have sufficient evidence that the mining company was at fault (Meissner, 2019).

## Fishing Industry

British Columbia, like Atlantic Canada, has an important fishery. The BC fishery, as a renewable resource, ranks fourth in value of production among resource industries behind mining (including natural gas), forestry, and agriculture. Fish processing plants employ 25,000 full-time and part-time employees. More than 100 species of fish and marine animals are harvested from the Pacific Ocean, freshwater bodies,

The Canadian Press/Jonathan Hayward

**PHOTO 9.16** On 4 August 2014, the tailing dam burst at the Mount Polley mine, sending toxic contents downstream into Hazeltine Creek and Quesnel Lake near the town of Likely.

and aquaculture areas. Salmon is the most valuable species, followed by herring, shellfish, groundfish, and halibut. In 2017, the landed value from the sea reached $3.7 billion, with two-thirds associated with aquaculture (Fisheries and Oceans Canada, 2020).

Wild salmon catches vary from year to year. Salmon (chinook, sockeye, coho, pink, and chum) spend several years in the Pacific Ocean before returning to spawn in the Fraser and other rivers. The principal BC salmon-spawning rivers are the Fraser and the Skeena. In 2017, the harvest of wild salmon was 13.7 thousand tonnes (BC Seafood Industry, 2019; Fisheries and Oceans Canada, 2020). Such large annual fluctuations are common among the wild species. On the other hand, aquaculture productions remain steady.

Unfortunately, BC shares another similarity with Atlantic Canada—overexploitation of fish stocks, particularly the valuable salmon stocks. Pressure on the fish stocks, especially salmon, comes from four sources—Canadian commercial fishers,

American commercial fishers, the Aboriginal fishery, and the sports fishery. All want larger catches.

Management of the salmon fishery falls under the Pacific Salmon Treaty, which was renewed by Canada and the United States in 2019 and sets long-term goals for the sustainability of this resource. The Pacific Salmon Commission, formed by the governments of Canada and the US to implement the Pacific Salmon Treaty, does not regulate the salmon fisheries but provides regulatory advice and recommendations to the two countries. In Canada, Fisheries and Oceans Canada, in consultation with the Pacific Salmon Commission, has set annual quotas for salmon in Canadian waters.[6]

Salmon are migratory fish, so regulating salmon fishing is particularly challenging. Like other fish, they are common property until caught. This principle is based on the "rule of capture." Fishers therefore try to maximize their share of a harvest so no one else will take "their" fish. The problem is complicated further because the Canadian government

## FIGURE 9.14 **Mines in British Columbia**

Most coal mines lie along the eastern flank of the Rocky Mountains while the metal mines are located in the Interior. Mount Polley's open-pit copper mine, for example, is situated in the Interior Plateau near the town of Williams Lake. Its production was halted following the breach of its tailing pond, but within two years the mine was back to full production. Low copper prices caused the mine to close temporarily in 2019. The impact of the breach on the landscape is shown in Photo 9.16.

Source: Adapted from Mineral Resources Education Program of BC (2009).

For discussion of the "tragedy of the commons," see the section titled "Where Have All the Codfish Gone?" in **Chapter 10**, **page 333**.

cannot regulate the "Canadian" salmon stocks, i.e., those that spawn in Canadian rivers, because they migrate to American waters, where the American fishing fleet harvests them. The result is that the salmon stocks are threatened. This problem is commonly referred to as the "tragedy of the commons."

## Hydroelectric Power

Hydroelectric energy is a renewable energy source dependent on the hydrologic cycle of water, which involves evaporation, precipitation, and the flow of water due to gravity. British Columbia, with abundant water resources and a geography that provides many opportunities to produce low-cost energy, produces more hydroelectric power than all other provinces except Quebec. Major generating stations on the Peace River and Columbia River produce 80 per cent of BC Hydro power. The two power stations on

the Peace River are the massive W.A.C. Bennett Dam with its G.M. Shrum generating station (completed 1968) and the Peace Canyon Dam (completed 1980); a third station, Site C, is in the construction phase (Figure 9.15). In 2014, Victoria approved the project with a budget of $8.8 billion (Site C Clean Energy Project, 2014). As the third project on the Peace River, Site C will gain significant efficiencies by taking advantage of water already stored in the Williston Reservoir. This means it will generate approximately 35 per cent of the energy produced at W.A.C. Bennett Dam, with only 5 per cent of the reservoir area. Once built, Site C will produce enough electricity to power about 450,000 homes per year in B.C. In 2017, the estimated cost was updated to $10.7 billion (Morgan, 2017; Cox, 2019). Like the Muskrat Falls project in Labrador, the original estimate and the possible final cost of large-scale hydro projects could signal the end to such projects. As well, First Nations and environmental organizations are not happy because the project will flood 55 km$^2$ of river valley and affect wildlife that local Treaty 8 First Nations harvest.

The Columbia River has a combination of dams and generating stations. The 1964 Columbia River Treaty with the United States called for Canada to construct and store water at three dams, the Duncan (1967), Hugh Keenleyside (1968), and Mica (1973) dams, in exchange for electricity generated at the Grand Coulee generating station in Washington State. The Mica Dam, from the outset, was built with a generating station while the other two were only for water storage, although in 2002, immediately downstream from the Keenleyside dam, a new Arrow Lakes generating station was completed. The Mica, Arrow Lakes, and Revelstoke facilities, the latter completed in 1984 upriver on the Columbia, have produced most of the power on the BC side of the Columbia River.

Rio Tinto (formerly Alcan) owns and operates the Kemano hydroelectric plant, which was completed in 1954. The geographic area controlled by Rio Tinto extends far inland beyond the Coast Mountains to the Fraser/Nechako plateau. This large area of northwest British Columbia extends from Kitimat to Kemano on the coast and then to the Kenney Dam on the Nechako River southwest of Vanderhoof. A 75-km transmission line takes electrical power to Rio Tinto's Kitimat aluminum

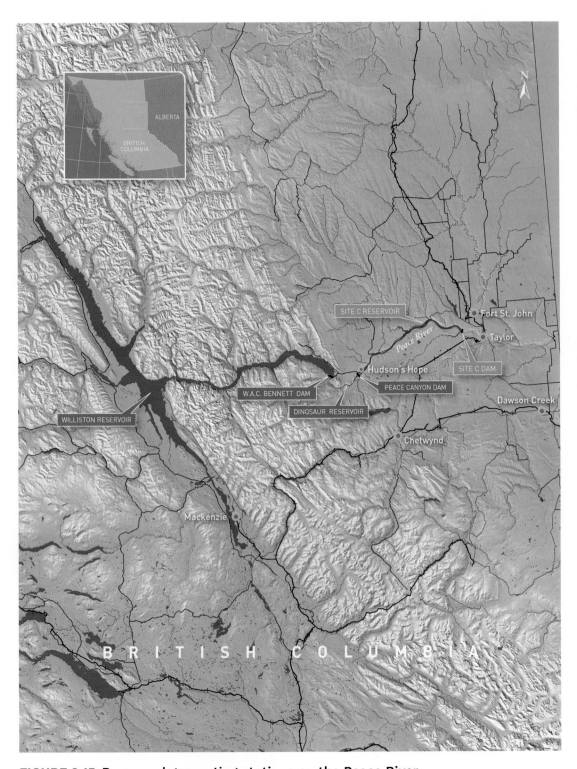

**FIGURE 9.15 Dams and generating stations on the Peace River**

Source: BC Hydro (2015a, 2015b).

**THINK ABOUT IT**

In 1951, Alcan began construction on the Kenney Dam across the Nechako River to create a huge reservoir. With the dam operational in 1954, these waters now flowed westward through a tunnel bored through the Coast Mountains to the Kemano generating station rather than eastward to the Fraser River. Why did Alcan have no legal cause to consult with the Cheslatta First Nation whose traditional lands were flooded?

smelter. Since its reservoir lies on the east side of the Coast Mountains, a 16-km tunnel drilled through the mountains connects Tahtsa Lake to the Kemano Powerhouse. Most power is consumed in the smelting of bauxite ore but the surplus energy is sold to BC Hydro.

These three giant industrial construction efforts—one on the Columbia River, another on the Peace River, and the third on the Nechako River—had enormous impacts on the economy and environment. They all involved the harnessing of waterpower from the province's rivers to generate low-cost electrical power, but they also flooded valuable farmland and First Nations lands and led to the loss of salmon spawning grounds. Such major engineering projects took place before environmental legislation became the law of the land and prior to the duty to consult First Nations being a requirement of resource projects. In today's world, such projects may have run into serious problems getting their environmental impact statements approved and receiving support from First Nations.

## British Columbia's Urban Core

The concentration of people in the Greater Vancouver area known as Metro Vancouver (Figure 9.16) dominates BC's urban core. From another geographic perspective, the four census metropolitan areas

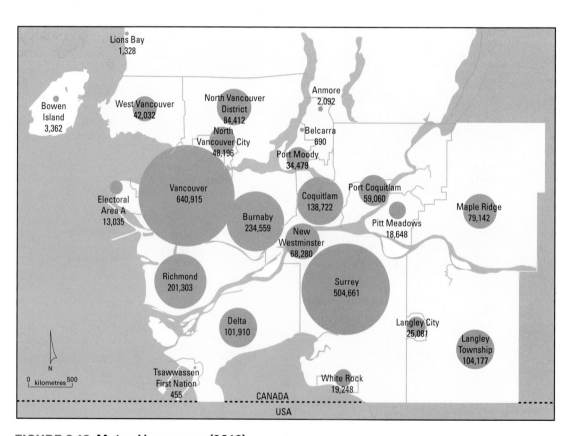

**FIGURE 9.16  Metro Vancouver (2016)**

Metro Vancouver consists of 21 municipalities and 11 First Nations, but only the Tsawwassen First Nation is a member of Metro Vancouver. Several First Nations are involved in real estate. For instance, the Squamish First Nation proposes to build an extensive urban zone beneath Burrard Bridge. For each municipality, Metro Vancouver delivers services such as drinking water, wastewater treatment, and solid waste management; monitors air quality; and is involved in planning, parks, affordable housing, and other issues of governance. Its boundaries correspond with the Vancouver census metropolitan area.

Source: Metro Vancouver (2015).

**THINK ABOUT IT**
Prince Rupert, while an expanding port, has seen its population decrease since 2001 (see **Table 9.4**). The answer lies in the downturn in both the fishing and forestry industries, causing workers to seek employment elsewhere.

of Vancouver, Abbotsford, Kelowna, and Victoria comprise 70 per cent of the population of British Columbia. They illustrate the powerful attraction of urban life. As well, they are the fastest-growing urban places in the province, with a combined population increase of just over 24 per cent from 2001 to 2016 (Table 9.3). By comparison, smaller urban centres grew by about 15 per cent over the same span of time and seven smaller centres actually saw their populations decline (Table 9.4). Their decline is related to the fading forest economy. Not surprisingly, fast-growing cities are associated with universities that provide an incubator for the advanced economy and add to Florida's concept of an "interesting" city. Eight universities, led by the University of British Columbia and Simon Fraser University, are located in the Metro Vancouver region. On Vancouver Island are the University of Victoria (Photo 9.18) and Vancouver Island University, in Nanaimo. Kelowna, Abbotsford, and Kamloops also house major universities. Only Prince George, with the University of Northern British Columbia, does not fit into this pattern.

## Greater Vancouver

With one of the most spectacular physical settings in the world, Vancouver, located on the shores of Burrard Inlet, is framed by the snow-capped peaks of the North Shore Mountains. The Lions Gate Bridge passes over Burrard Inlet, thereby linking Vancouver with the North Shore and its main urban centres of West Vancouver and North Vancouver. From West Vancouver, the Sea-to-Sky Highway leads to the Whistler ski resort. To the west is the island-studded Strait of Georgia, while the Fraser River and its deltaic islands (flat, low islands composed of silt and clay near the mouth of the river) mark Vancouver's southern edge. Vancouver has a mild, marine climate, with a California-like dry, warm summer. Winter, however, with its overcast skies and rainy weather, is less appealing to some people.

As one of the great ports on the Pacific coast of North America and the largest in Canada, Vancouver's economic strength stems partly from its role as a trade centre. With most of the world's population located along the Pacific Rim, the Port of Vancouver

David Wei/Alamy Stock Photo

**PHOTO 9.17** As a form of economic development, the Squamish Nation is proposing to build 3,000 units of housing on the site of a former village at the south end of the Burrard Street Bridge.

handles over $65 billion worth of trade goods annually (Port of Vancouver, 2020).

Vancouver's rich and vibrant culture provides a suitable base for attracting the "creative class" members of the information society, with places like Granville Island (Vignette 9.4) as one element in the broad cultural world that appeals to "creative" people. But all is not well in Vancouver's housing market, which has priced many out of the market. In fact, a survey by Demographia declared

PHOTO 9.18 Campus of the University of Victoria with the Pacific Ocean in the background.

**TABLE 9.3** Census Metropolitan Areas in British Columbia, 2001–2016

| Centre | Population 2001 | Population 2016 | Percentage Change |
|---|---|---|---|
| **Abbotsford** | 147,370 | 180,518 | 22.5 |
| **Kelowna** | 147,739 | 194,882 | 32.0 |
| **Victoria** | 311,902 | 367,770 | 17.9 |
| **Vancouver** | 1,986,965 | 2,463,431 | 24.0 |
| **Total** | 2,593,976 | 3,206,602 | 23.6 |
| **British Columbia** | 3,907,738 | 4,648,055 | 19.0 |

Sources: Adapted from Statistics Canada (2007, 2017b).

PHOTO 9.19 Wine country in the Okanagan provides a tourist attraction. Cyclists can take the 650-km Kettle Valley Rail Trail that crosses 18 restored railway trestles and passes through two tunnels as it winds along Myra Canyon. Food and wine are available at numerous wine markets along the trail (Bisby, 2019).

**TABLE 9.4 Urban Centres in British Columbia, 2001–2016**

| Centre | Population 2001 | Population 2016 | Percentage Change |
|---|---|---|---|
| Kitimat | 10,285 | 6,394 | –37.8 |
| Dawson Creek | 10,754 | 12,178 | 13.2 |
| Prince Rupert | 15,302 | 12,687 | –17.1 |
| Terrace | 19,980 | 15,723 | –21.3 |
| Powell River | 16,604 | 16,783 | 0.1 |
| Squamish | 14,435 | 17,479 | 21.1 |
| Salmon Arm | 15,388 | 17,904 | 16.4 |
| Williams Lake | 19,768 | 18,277 | –7.5 |
| Quesnel | 24,426 | 23,146 | –10.0 |
| Cranbrook | 24,275 | 26,083 | –3.1 |
| Port Alberni | 25,299 | 25,112 | 0 |
| Fort St John | 23,007 | 28,396 | 9.3 |
| Parksville | 24,285 | 28,922 | 9.2 |
| Campbell River | 35,036 | 37,861 | 4.1 |
| Penticton | 41,564 | 43,432 | 4.2 |
| Duncan | 38,613 | 44,451 | 6.6 |
| Courtenay | 45,205 | 54,157 | 8.9 |
| Vernon | 51,530 | 61,334 | 7.5 |
| Prince George | 85,035 | 86,622 | 2.1 |
| Chilliwack | 74,003 | 101,512 | 9.3 |
| Nanaimo | 85,664 | 104,936 | 7.8 |
| Kamloops | 86,951 | 103,811 | 4.4 |
| Total | 787,409 | 905,507 | 15.0 |
| British Columbia | 3,907,738 | 4,639,748 | 18.7 |

Source: Adapted from Statistics Canada (2007, 2017b).

## Vignette 9.4

### Granville Island

Granville Island is the site of a well-known public market in the heart of downtown Vancouver. Situated in False Creek and lying beneath Granville Bridge, the island has turned into a key gathering spot for both locals and tourists. For many years, Granville Island was a sawmilling centre as logs could be towed through False Creek. In the 1970s, everything changed—sawmilling was out and an upscale residential and specialized commercial area was in. Besides Granville Island Public Market, other enterprises have widened its appeal—artists' studios and shops, a wide variety of restaurants, and features like the Kids Market, Maritime Market, and Coast Salish Houseposts, a joint endeavour between the Emily Carr College and First Nations. Granville Island is unique to Vancouver and has added another dimension to the wide-ranging cultural attractions in the Greater Vancouver area.

Al Harvey/Slide Farm

**PHOTO 9.20** Aerial view of Granville Island.

that Vancouver is the third-least-affordable city in the world, just behind Hong Kong and Sydney, Australia. Demographia found that the average family dwelling costs nearly 11 times more than the average household income, making it virtually impossible for those families to purchase a house (Schmunk, 2016). One effort to reduce the hot housing market was a 15 per cent tax on residential properties sold to foreign nationals and foreign-controlled corporations. Another was to assess owners of vacant houses and condos a 1 per cent tax based on the value of their housing units (*CBC News*, 2016). In addition, an unexpected proposal came from the Squamish Nation to build rental housing units under the Burrard Bridge on its Indigenous land. If this real estate project takes place, two positive outcomes are more rental units for Vancouverites and more rental income for this First Nation.

## Summary

The dramatic interface between the sea and the mountains defines British Columbia. The physical barrier represented by the mountains of the Cordillera historically isolated BC from the rest of Canada and, at the same time, has drawn its society more closely to the adjacent American states. In its early days, BC's economy was based on the forest industry and the export of natural resources. By the twenty-first century a new economy had emerged with an emphasis on technology and innovation and an expansion of service industries that support such an economy. At the same time, a shift in the resource economy has emerged along with a resurgence of Indigenous-run businesses. While the forestry industry has fallen on hard times, the promise of natural gas development and exports also seems to be floundering over a surplus of gas and a decline in gas prices. Resistance to the construction of the Trans Mountain pipeline expansion continues to haunt this now federal-owned project. One consequence has sharpened the economic disparity between Coastal BC, with its growing knowledge-based economy, and the Interior, which depends on the struggling resource sector.

Overall, however, BC's share of Canada's economy and population, driven by its urban core, is expected to expand in the years to come. Such growth can only enhance its political power in Ottawa. As one of six regions, BC's economic and population growth remains well above the national rates. Yet, its export-oriented economy may suffer a setback with the failure of the LNG plant at Kitimat to proceed. Then, too, the dampening of world trade caused by COVID-19 has serious consequences for its export-based economy. Still, once it is past the gridlocked international economy, BC's future looks bright.

## Challenge Questions

1. The Cordillera has long marked a key physical separation of BC from the rest of Canada. These **grooves of geography** have encouraged north/south interactions with the United States, as defined by the transborder regional concept of Cascadia. Did the construction of the CPR overcome this physical barrier in the nineteenth century?

2. Reconciliation takes many forms. Control of traditional land represents one form. Designation of the Great Bear Rainforest as a UNESCO biosphere reserve may herald a path for solutions to environmental issues and lead to sustainable development involving a host of Coastal First Nations, while real estate developments are providing another path for First Nations with urban lands. Discuss.

3. After examining the rising costs of Site C and the experience of Muskrat Falls in Labrador, do you believe large-scale hydro projects no longer make economic sense?

4. Why did Chevron abandon its leadership and investment in the LNG project?

## Essay Questions

1. While housing prices in Greater Vancouver are at record highs, many want to own a house because it represents a form of investment in the long run. Yet, given the predictions of climate change on ocean levels, why might someone not purchase a house on one of the deltaic islands located at the mouth of the Fraser River?

2. Indigenous place names reflect the changing political landscape. Besides Haida Gwaii (formerly the Queen Charlotte Islands), what other historic place names have been renamed to indicate Indigenous presence in British Columbia? What more can and should be done to further Indigenous reconciliation in BC?

# 10 Atlantic Canada

## Chapter Overview

Important issues and topics examined in this chapter include:

- Atlantic Canada's physical and historical geography.
- Population, urban centres, and economic affairs.
- Opportunity gained: the shellfish industry; opportunity lost: the Muskrat Falls hydro project.
- Low energy and mineral prices.
- Spearheads: lobster exports, shipbuilding, and software businesses.

## Introduction

For many centuries, the vast expanse of the Atlantic Ocean has shaped every aspect of Atlantic Canada. This undeniable connection to the sea has marked the region and its people. History, plus the geographic fact that this region lies far from the places of economic and political power in Central Canada, defines Atlantic Canada and separates it from the other regions. As an older part of Canada, its prime resources, whether coal, northern cod, or timber, have been consumed and what remains is only a shadow of its original state. Adding to the challenges, the region's fractured geography limits economic growth, leads to high unemployment levels, and encourages out-migration. While geography did endow Atlantic Canada with vast offshore oil reserves, oil prices collapsed in 2014, greatly diminishing their value. Not surprisingly, then, Atlantic Canada remains the weak sister of Canada's regions. Nevertheless, sparks of economic rejuvenation are emerging in its major cities, especially Halifax, Moncton, and St John's.

While the task of revitalizing Atlantic Canada's economy remains a work in progress, four trends suggest a more positive future:

- the population growth in urban centres continues;
- the knowledge-based economy is expanding;
- key industrial sectors are on more solid ground;
- before the COVID-19 pandemic struck in 2020, tourism had been growing.

← The small fishing village of Cape St Charles, Labrador, Canada. Although Newfoundland and Labrador's economy has become increasingly tied to the oil and gas industry, fisheries remain an important part of the province's economic and cultural identity.

## Atlantic Canada within Canada

Stretching along the country's eastern coast, Atlantic Canada consists of two parts: the Maritimes (Nova Scotia, Prince Edward Island, and New Brunswick) and Newfoundland and Labrador[1] (Figure 10.1). Separated from the mainland by Cabot Strait, the island of Newfoundland stands alone in the Atlantic Ocean while the Labrador Peninsula abuts Quebec. Still, in spite of its fractured geography, Atlantic Canada retains its rich and enduring sense of place that has grown out of the region's history, its early British and French settlements, and its close ties to the North Atlantic.

The Atlantic Ocean has dominated this region from the early days of the fishery to the "Golden Age of Wooden Ships and Iron Men" and through two world wars, to the economic dream of an Atlantic Gateway to Europe. In recent times, offshore petroleum developments have had positive impacts while the collapse of the northern cod fishery served a deadly blow to isolated coastal communities known as outports. Outports like Little Bay Islands (Photo 10.1) represent the past, while the future lies in urban centres, led by Halifax, St John's, and Moncton. The transition to the unfolding economy of the twenty-first century is based on the technological revolution driving the knowledge-based economy.

The fractured geography of Atlantic Canada reveals a shrinking economy in Newfoundland and Labrador and a growing one in the Maritimes. Within Atlantic Canada, urban centres are leading the way into the future. The largest city, Halifax, with a population of just under half a million, is adapting to a new knowledge-based economy. The employment of modern technology in the design and building of world-class naval warships typifies how this new technical world penetrates a wide spectrum of Halifax's economy. Other large cities, such as St John's, Moncton, Saint John, and Charlottetown, are following this same path by introducing technology into their local economies.

As the region in Canada first exploited and then settled by Europeans, Atlantic Canada has experienced both growth and decline over the years. Atlantic Canada has become, in the regional version of the core/periphery model, a slow-growing region. Past exploitation of its renewable resources, especially cod and timber resources, has diminished its

In **Chapter 1**, "Canada's Geographic Regions," page 5, the rationale for Canada's six geographic regions, including Atlantic Canada, is elaborated.

Photo by John Harries

**PHOTO 10.1** The sharp interface between land and sea demonstrates why the inland fishery and outports comprised a way of life at the height of the cod fishery. With the decline of cod stocks, outports became a dying breed. In 2019, Little Bay Islands joined hundreds of other abandoned outports along the coast of Newfoundland. With only 20 homes in this once thriving island community that lived and breathed by cod, the decision by its residents to accept a relocation offer by the provincial government was both understandable and inevitable. For more on this subject, see Vignette 10.3 and "Where Have All the Codfish Gone?" later in this chapter.

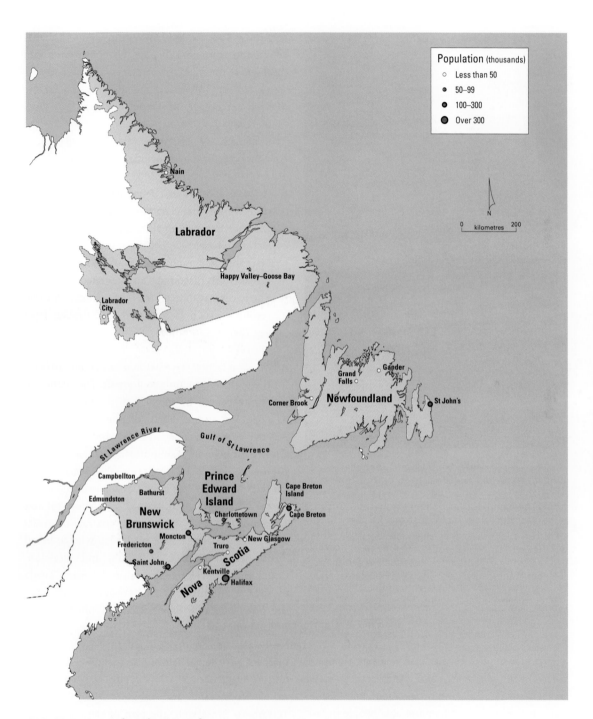

**FIGURE 10.1 Atlantic Canada**

Atlantic Canada contains four provinces, Nova Scotia, New Brunswick, Newfoundland and Labrador, and Prince Edward Island. Atlantic Canada has the smallest population and the weakest economy—except for the Territorial North—of Canada's six regions. Geography endowed the sea with rich fish stocks, mineral wealth, and petroleum deposits, but not with an abundance of fertile soils. While oil made Newfoundland and Labrador a "have" province when oil prices were high, the low prices now have pushed this province back into "have-not" territory. Added to that economic downturn, the disastrously expensive Muskrat Falls hydro project may sink that province below the fiscal water level. New Brunswick, Nova Scotia, and Prince Edward Island remain classified as "have-not" provinces and they each receive equalization payments from the federal government (Canada, Department of Finance, 2015). The largest city is Halifax, with an urban population of just under 420,000, followed by St John's at 212,000.

PHOTO 10.2 Halifax's harbour dominates its landscape. When the British colonized Halifax in 1749, they were attracted by its magnificent harbour. The high hill overlooking the harbour offered a perfect location for a fortress to defend the new town and its naval base. Named the Halifax Citadel (upper left), this fortress is an impressive star-shaped masonry structure complete with defensive ditch, earthen ramparts, musketry gallery, powder magazine, garrison cells, guard room, barracks, and school room. The Citadel is now a National Historic Site.

resource base. Atlantic Canada's troubles are epitomized by the subpar economic performance relative to the rest of Canada and by the seemingly unstoppable out-migration of its more able people to faster-growing regions of Canada.

One measure of Atlantic Canada's overall economic performance is reflected in its per capita gross domestic product figures and its level of unemployment. Except for the Territorial North, Atlantic Canada's GDP per capita is the lowest in Canada and its unemployment rate the highest (Figure 10.2 and Table 10.1). Within Atlantic Canada, Newfoundland and Labrador has consistently had the highest unemployment rate, while New Brunswick, with its Acadian population, has by far the highest percentage of French-speaking residents (Table 10.1).

The primary reasons for Atlantic Canada's weak economic performance include the following:

- A small and dispersed population limits prospects for internal economic growth.
- Distance from national markets stifles its manufacturing base.
- Fractured geography and four distinct political jurisdictions discourage an integrated economy.
- The natural resource base is restricted and some resources, such as cod, coal, and timber, have lost their importance.

All of these factors have made it extremely difficult for the region's economy to flourish. The economic lockdown caused by the COVID-19 pandemic adds to a gloomy future. Furthermore, over the years Atlantic Canada has become heavily dependent on Ottawa for economic support through equalization payments and social programs. Prospects turned for the better when Atlantic Canada received a second chance with the discovery of offshore oil and gas deposits, a huge shipbuilding contract from Ottawa, and the appearance of the knowledge-based businesses in Halifax, St John's, and Moncton. Could these developments cause Atlantic Canada to shed its moniker as a "have-not" region? On the downside, the expectations of Muskrat Falls in Labrador have floundered, and the prospects for its power reaching the lucrative New England markets have faded. Nova Scotia, however, is obtaining electricity at a lower rate than customers in Newfoundland and Labrador (see Contested Terrain 10.1). As well, the plan of the Energy East pipeline delivering bitumen to the Irving refinery near Saint John, New Brunswick, failed. A shipment of Alberta oil by tanker ship from Vancouver to Saint John via the Panama Canal was successful in July 2020, but it is uncertain if this sea route will become a regular feature. In 2020, as in other regions, the coronavirus pandemic froze the economy and unemployment soared. What the post-COVID-19 future will bring is unknown, but Atlantic Canada will have to make major adjustments.

## An Ongoing Demographic Problem?

Since Confederation, Atlantic Canada's population has increased at a rate well below the national average. From 2001 to 2016, Atlantic Canada's population increased by 3.9 per cent, well below the national increase of 14.8 per cent. The anemic annual growth is predicted to continue into the future (Chaundry, 2012, p. 95). However, efforts to encourage immigrants to select cities in Atlantic Canada may make a difference. Internal differences in population growth also persist. From 1996 to 2016, for example, the region's population increased in the Maritimes but decreased in Newfoundland and Labrador (Table 10.5).

By 2016, Atlantic Canada, with 2.4 million people, comprised 6.6 per cent of Canada's population (Statistics Canada, 2020a). Its population size ranks fifth out of the six Canadian regions, thus providing a rough measure of its importance within Canada. But back in 1871, Atlantic Canada's share of the nation population was 20 per cent (Figure 1.3). Since then, its fragmented geography has made economic growth difficult and kept population increases low.

Regional population distribution falls into six clusters around the principal cities—Halifax, St John's, Saint John, Moncton, Fredericton, and Charlottetown. Accounting for nearly 1.1 million people, these six urban centres comprise approximately half of Atlantic Canada's population.

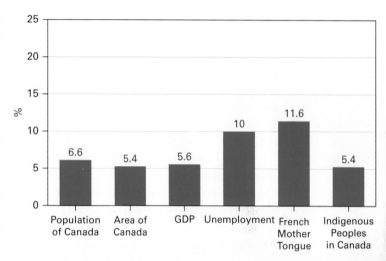

**FIGURE 10.2 Atlantic Canada basic statistics, 2016**

One measure of Atlantic Canada's weak economic performance is revealed by the following figures: the region has 6.6 per cent of Canada's population but produces only 5.1 per cent of the country's GDP.

Percentages of population, area, and GDP are for Canada as a whole; unemployment, French home language, and Indigenous population percentages are for Atlantic Canada.

Sources: Tables 1.1, 1.2, 5.6.

## Atlantic Canada's Physical Geography

Atlantic Canada's physical geography emphasizes the fragmented nature of this geographic region of Canada and the sharp physical division between the Maritimes and Newfoundland and Labrador. Underscoring this basic divide are its two physiographic regions: the Appalachian Uplands and the Canadian Shield. The Appalachian Uplands are located in the Maritimes and the island of Newfoundland, while the Canadian Shield lies in Labrador. In terms of geologic time, the Appalachian Uplands are the worn-down remnants of an ancient mountain chain. Formed in the Paleozoic era, the Appalachian Mountains

| TABLE 10.1 | Basic Statistics for Atlantic Canada by Province, 2016 | | | |
|---|---|---|---|---|
| Province | Population (000s) | % French-Speaking | % of National GDP | Unemployment Rate (%) |
| **Prince Edward Island** | 143 | 3.3 | 0.1 | 10.7 |
| **Newfoundland and Labrador** | 518 | 0.5 | 1.5 | 13.4 |
| **New Brunswick** | 747 | 31.8 | 1.6 | 9.5 |
| **Nova Scotia** | 924 | 3.2 | 1.9 | 8.3 |
| **Atlantic Canada** | 2,332 | 11.6 | 5.1 | 10.0 |
| **Canada** | 35,152 | 22.5 | 100.0 | 7.0 |

Sources: Statistics Canada (2017a, 2019a, 2019b, 2019c).

have been subjected to erosional forces for some 500 million years. As Photo 2.8 illustrates, streams have cut deeply into the Cape Breton Highlands of the Appalachian Uplands, resulting in rugged, hilly terrain. In Labrador, the most prominent feature of this portion of the Canadian Shield is the uplifted and glaciated Torngat Mountains (Photo 10.3). Unlike the rest of the Canadian Shield, the Labrador portion was subjected to a mountain-building process (**orogeny**) in which the rocks were folded and faulted some 750 million years ago. More recently in geologic time, these mountains were covered with glaciers, which, as the glaciers slowly moved down slope, carved the mountain-features and eventually reached the sea, where they created a fjorded coastline (see Photo 2.2).

The weather of Atlantic Canada is quite varied because of the frequent meeting of continental air masses with marine air masses. The flow of continental air

masses from the northwest brings warm weather in the summer and cold weather in the winter. Yet, with no part of Atlantic Canada more than 200 km from the Atlantic Ocean or Gulf of St Lawrence, moderate, marine-type weather predominates. The result is generally unsettled weather. Still, Atlantic Canada, especially Labrador, has a strongly continental aspect to its climate and, coupled with the cold Labrador Current, takes on a more Arctic-like climate. Storms are not uncommon, especially in the fall when hurricanes reach the Maritimes. Usually tropical storms lose their punch by the time they reach Nova Scotia, but sometimes this is not the case. For example, 2019's Hurricane Dorian was downgraded to a Category 2 storm, but Hurricane Juan, which made landfall on 29 September 2003, brought its full fury.

The clash of cold Arctic air with warmer, humid air from the south results in winter storms. In

Alexandra Koblenko/All Canada Photos

**PHOTO 10.3** The Torngat Mountains, a national park reserve since 2005, stretch along the fjorded coast of northern Labrador. One such fjord is Ramah Bay (with an iceberg floating in its waters). The mountains were recently, in geologic time, subjected to alpine glaciation, resulting in extremely sharp features, including arêtes, cirques, and horns. These mountains, including Mount Caubvik (also known as Mont D'Iberville), straddle the Quebec/Labrador boundary. They attain heights of 1,652 m (5,420 ft) above sea level and are located near the sixtieth parallel. For both reasons—high elevation and high latitude—the Torngat Mountains lie beyond the tree line.

summer, occasional incursions of hot, humid air from the Gulf of Mexico occur, but the dominant weather is cool, cloudy, and rainy. In the winter, influxes of moist Atlantic air produce relatively mild snowy weather except in Labrador (and to a lesser extent in the New Brunswick interior), where it can become extremely cold for extended periods.

Annual precipitation is abundant throughout Atlantic Canada, averaging around 100 cm in the Maritimes and 140 cm in Newfoundland, but this gradually diminishes further north in Labrador. Much precipitation comes from **nor'easters**—strong winds off the ocean from the northeast—that draw their moisture from the Atlantic Ocean. Atlantic Canada, especially the Maritimes and the island of Newfoundland, has foggy weather. Thick, cool fog forms in the chilled air above the Labrador Current when it mixes with warm, moisture-laden air from the Gulf of Mexico. With onshore winds these banks of fog move far inland, but the coastal communities experience the greatest number of foggy days. Both St John's and Halifax, for instance, experience considerable foggy and misty weather (Vignette 10.1).

## Vignette 10.1

### Weather in St John's

While occupying a more southerly location than Victoria, British Columbia, St John's has a cooler climate, partly because of its very cold offshore waters (Table 2.2). Even so, St John's, like Victoria, is an ice-free port. However, unlike Victoria, a winter ice pack lies offshore, and spring-time icebergs are not uncommon off the coast. Melting of sea ice begins in spring, retreating northward along the land-fast ice attached to the Labrador coast.

Generally speaking, weather is characterized by fog, overcast skies, and frequent storms and rain. Fog is common from April to September. Throughout the year, a salty smell is in the air. While most of the year has mild temperatures, strong northwest winds result in heavy winter snowfalls. Also, St John's does not escape the wrath of tropical storms—such as Hurricanes Igor (2010) and Leslie (2012)—that leave behind a path of destruction that includes toppled trees, torn power lines, and roofs ripped from buildings (Photo 10.4). But, in 2020, St John's did escape the fury of Hurricane Laura that savaged the east coast of the United States.

Jutting into the Atlantic Ocean, St John's feels the full brunt of strong winds from the North Atlantic. As David Phillips (1993, p. 155), a climatologist and the spokesperson for Environment Canada's Meteorological Service, explains, "Of all major Canadian cities, St John's is the foggiest, snowiest, wettest, windiest, and cloudiest."

CTV News

**PHOTO 10.4** In March 2017, St. John's suffered from hurricane-like winds. Here, a group of women hold on to a lamppost in the downtown area.

With such varied weather conditions, Atlantic Canada has three climatic zones—Atlantic, Subarctic, and Arctic zones. The great north–south extent of this region is one reason. For example, the distance from the southern tip of Nova Scotia (44°N) to the northern extremity of Newfoundland and Labrador (60°N) is over 2,000 km. Then, too, Atlantic Canada is the meeting place of Arctic and tropical air masses and ocean currents, resulting in wet, cool, and foggy weather. In addition, close proximity to the Atlantic Ocean exerts a moderating effect on the region's climate.

North of 55 degrees latitude is the Arctic zone in northern Labrador, in the Torngat Mountains and then along its coast. An Arctic storm track funnels extremely cold and stormy weather along the Labrador coast while the **Labrador Current** (Figure 10.3) brings icebergs from Greenland to the Labrador and Newfoundland coastlines and its cold waters contribute to the formation of land-fast ice along the Labrador coast and the northern coastline of Newfoundland. Beyond the land-fast ice in the open sea, the Labrador Current carries ice floes and icebergs as far south as the Grand Bank. By July, Labrador waters are ice-free.

The Arctic zone is associated with tundra vegetation as the summers are too cool for tree growth. The Subarctic climate zone exists over the interior of Labrador. The interior of Labrador experiences much warmer summer temperatures than its forested coastal areas. The Atlantic zone includes the Maritimes and the island of Newfoundland. For most of the year, this more southerly area is influenced by warm, moist air masses that originate in the tropical waters of the Caribbean Sea and the Gulf of Mexico. Only in the winter months does the Arctic storm track dominate weather conditions. The coastal areas of the Maritimes and Newfoundland can be affected by tropical storms in the late summer and fall.

The main air masses affecting the region originate in the interior of North America and from the Gulf of Mexico and the North Atlantic Ocean. Consequently, summers are usually cool and wet, while winters are short and mild but often associated with heavy snow and rainfall. Most precipitation falls in the winter, and temperature differences between inland and coastal locations are striking. Temperatures are usually several degrees warmer in the winter near the coast than at inland locations. During the summer, the reverse is true, with coastal areas usually several degrees cooler.

Along the narrow coastal zone of Atlantic Canada, the climate is strongly influenced by the Atlantic Ocean. The summer temperatures of coastal settlements along the shores of Newfoundland are markedly cooled by the cold water of the Labrador Current. Another effect of the sea occurs in the spring and summer—fog and mist result when the warm waters of the northeast-flowing **Gulf Stream**, which originates in the Gulf of Mexico, mix with the cold, southerly flowing Labrador Current. In the winter, the clash of warm and cold air masses sometimes results in severe winter storms characterized by heavy snowfall (Conrad, 2009, pp. 36–7).

## Environmental Challenges/ Disasters

Atlantic Canada has faced several environmental challenges with disastrous consequences. One was the hazardous waste site on Cape Breton Island known as the Sydney Tar Ponds, where pollutants from the coke ovens of a Sydney steel mill had been dumped for many years. Fortunately, remedial measures that began back in 1998 have turned this ecological disaster into a livable area known as Open Hearth Park. This park consists of a 39-hectare green area that features several sports fields, walking trails, art installations, a playground, and panels chronicling the steel plant's troubled history. This reclamation project was completed in 2012. Controversy remains, however, because the toxic wastes from the former Sidney steel plant were not removed but buried about 2 metres below the ground. The buried toxic wastes leave one question unanswered: will this toxic sludge remain stable or will it seep into the local environment? A federal government assessment of 2014 (Canada, 2014) concluded that the sludge had been contained reasonably well, and the site continues to show no signs of leakage, noting:

> The Project has successfully reduced or contained contaminant levels and largely

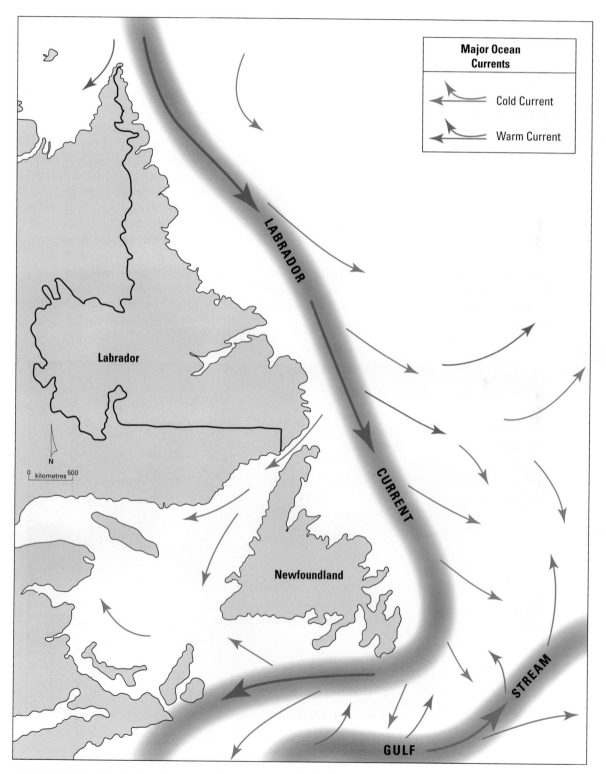

**FIGURE 10.3** **The Labrador Current and the Gulf Stream**

Source: Macpherson (1997). Modified by Duleepa Wijayawardhana, 1998. Reprinted by permission of Gary E. McManus and Clifford H. Wood, *Atlas of Newfoundland and Labrador* (St John's: Breakwater Books, 1991), Plate 5.2.

## Vignette 10.2

### The Annapolis Valley

The Annapolis Valley is a low-lying area in Nova Scotia. At its western and eastern edges the land is at sea level, but it rises to about 35 m in the centre. The area is surrounded by a rugged, rocky upland that reaches heights of 200 m and more. The fertile sandy soils of the Annapolis Lowlands originate from marine deposits that settled there about 13,000 years ago. After glacial ice retreated from the area, seawaters flooded the land, depositing marine sediments that consisted of minute sand and clay particles. Isostatic rebound then caused the land to lift and slowly these lowlands emerged from the sea. In the seventeenth century, the favourable soil of the Annapolis Valley attracted early French settlers, the Acadians, who built dikes to protect parts of this low-lying farmland from the high tides of the Bay of Fundy and Minas Basin. Today, the Annapolis Valley's stone-free, well-drained soils and its gently rolling landforms provide the best agricultural lands in Nova Scotia. In Photo 10.5, at high tide, waters from the Minas Basin (seen in the background) extend into the low, wet land in the foreground. Land use is changing with vineyards replacing apple orchards. Local wineries now are common in the Annapolis Valley.

Barrett & MacKay/All Canada Photos

**PHOTO 10.5** Nova Scotia's Annapolis Valley, just north of Wolfville near Cape Blomidon. In the foreground is a small apple orchard, for which the Annapolis Valley is famous; in the middle is a tidal stream; in the background are the waters of the Minas Basin. As in other apple-growing areas in Canada, vineyards are replacing fruit trees.

eliminated contaminant migration from the sites. It has ensured the sites are ready to be used safely by the community.

Two other environmental concerns are hydroelectric projects and their effect on traditional lands and possible mercury poisoning of fish and wildlife, and the collapse of the cod fishery.

## Muskrat Falls

Across Canada, hydro projects have involved the flooding of Indigenous lands and the subsequent decay of submerged vegetation that produces methylmercury. In turn, methylmercury can work its way through the food chain and lead to high levels of mercury in fish and other forms of wildlife. The James Bay hydro developments resulted in high levels of mercury in the reservoirs, much to the anguish of the Quebec Cree. This lesson is well documented in scientific literature and etched in Indigenous memories; the Labrador consumers of wildlife have not forgotten, nor have they forgotten their past experience with the Churchill Falls Hydro project.

History should be a good teacher. But David Massell (2016) casts doubt on this idea with his historical account of the Muskrat Falls project. The colonial attitude of the government officials of the day did not consider the need for Inuit and Innu to be part of the conversation when the Churchill Falls hydro project was undertaken in 1971–4. At that time, legal rights to Indigenous lands were only on the verge of becoming recognized by Canadian governments. By the time of the Voisey's Bay nickel project and the proposed Muskrat Falls project on the Lower Churchill River, the Inuit and Innu had the courts on their side. More than that, the New Dawn Agreement of 2008 between the Innu Nation and the Newfoundland and Labrador government contained compensation to the Innu (worth about $100 million over 30 years) for the flooding of hunting grounds that occurred when the Churchill Falls hydroelectric project was built in the early 1970s.

Yet, with the construction of the Muskrat Falls hydro project, conflict arose again. Protests by Labrador Indigenous activists and land defenders caught the attention of Premier Dwight Ball. In October of

2016, when they occupied the site and blocked access to workers, demanding both the clearing of all vegetation and removal of soil before the first phase of reservoir flooding could begin (Bailey, 2016). Their fear was that fish would absorb methylmercury, exposing both the Innu and Inuit to the dangers of Minamata disease or methylmercury poisoning. However, in spite of the plea from Nunatsiavut Government President Johannes Lampe, the reservoir was filled before wetland capping was completed (Brake, 2019).

## Where Have All the Codfish Gone?

The habitat of the northern cod ranges from Georges Bank and the Bay of Fundy in the south to the Grand Banks and inshore of Newfoundland and Labrador to southern Baffin Bay, located between the southwest coast of Greenland and Baffin Island. Yet, these huge stocks collapsed under the onslaught of the international industrial fishing industry, which employed more advanced fishing technology and a strategy of processing the cod on factory ships. The demise of the northern cod stocks represents a classic example of the **tragedy of the commons** (Hardin, 1968) where public control of the resource, in this case by Fisheries and Oceans Canada, was unable to exert its

**PHOTO 10.6** As with all hydroelectric projects, one negative impact is the creation of high levels of methylmercury in the reservoir. Levels of this poison peak about three years after a dam's reservoir is first flooded, but elevated methylmercury levels can persist for decades.

THE CANADIAN PRESS/Andrew Vaughan

power beyond Canada's maritime border. Not only did the cod stocks lose their way but so did the inshore fishers. In turn, coastal communities, such as Great Harbour Deep, were abandoned. In the case of Little Bay Islands, located on Newfoundland's Northern Peninsula, people had fished for cod for centuries. In 2019, its remaining residents accepted the provincial government offer of a cash settlement to leave the community.

Robert Clapp (1998, p. 129) examined the issue of overexploitation of the northern cod and attributed its collapse to technological advances that permit larger and larger catches until the resource is exhausted. Clapp offers the resource cycle in an unregulated environment as an explanation for ecological crises; in other words, what begins as a rich resource leads to overexploitation and the collapse of the resource.

The cause of overexploitation of the northern cod is well known. Much is due to the use of bottom draggers by the Canadian and foreign fishing fleets.

The attraction of this form of fishing is its cost efficiency, but scraping the seafloor for fish is environmentally disastrous. Fleets of trawlers create enormous waste because "non-commercial" fish—i.e., species of fish not being specifically sought, called the bycatch—are simply discarded. In addition, the trawlers destroy fragile ocean-floor ecosystems, including reefs and breeding habitat. As fishing technology advanced, catches of cod jumped from 400,000 metric tonnes per year to nearly 1 million metric tonnes in the 1950s. By the 1960s, the annual catch reached a peak of almost 2 million metric tonnes. European and Soviet trawlers accounted for most of this catch.

Ironically, the local inshore fishers did not employ such highly sophisticated technology but rather employed a simple hook-and-line system, as well as gillnets and cod traps (Photo 10.7). Yet, even though the coastal fishers did not have the capacity to overfish, they suffered the most as their way of life and their communities disappeared.

JOHN EASTCOTT AND YVA MOMATIUK/National Geographic

**PHOTO 10.7** In the past, the inshore fishery involved more than making an economic return. It was a way of life for those living in outports.

With the cod stocks failing, the Canadian government announced in 1992 a moratorium on cod fishing in the waters of Atlantic Canada. By then, the foreign fishing vessels had left because their chances of catching sufficient cod had diminished. Thirty years later, inshore fishers observed signs of a recovery, but federal fisheries officials were not convinced and recommended a continuation of the "controlled catch." This decision meant that only a few fishers had a sustainable livelihood (Fisheries and Oceans Canada, 2015). Cod stocks still remain precariously low, but the pressure to raise the allowable catch is strong. However, George Rose, a fishery scientist, has warned that increasing the allowable catch of northern cod will hamper cod recovery (Adey, 2019; Rose & Walters, 2019), arguing that "the more we take now, the slower that rebuilding is going to be, and we're going to keep our stock below its maximum reproductive potential for a much longer period of time." Yet the dilemma is not easily resolved because while a total moratorium is the best biological solution, fishers and recreational fishers want the size of the catch to increase.

## Atlantic Canada's Historical Geography

Atlantic Canada was the first part of North America to be discovered by Europeans. They made contact with the Indigenous peoples who lived in various parts of Atlantic Canada. Most were Algonquian-speaking groups such as Mi'kmaq, while Inuit occupied the Arctic coast of Labrador.

In 1497, John Cabot reached the rocky shores of Atlantic Canada (the exact location, Cape Bonavista, Newfoundland, or Cape Breton Island, Nova Scotia, is in dispute). Yet, Newfoundland and Labrador, the first stretch of North America's Atlantic coastline explored by Europeans, was one of the last areas to be widely settled, although in 1610 the newly formed Newfoundland Company sent Englishman John Guy to start a colony in Newfoundland at Cupids in Conception Bay, which became the second-oldest English colony in North America, after Jamestown in Virginia. The Cupids colony struggled as an agricultural and fishing adjunct to the growing English fishery, but some early settlers appear to have

remained (Gilbert, 2020). In sharp contrast, French colonies found root in the early seventeenth century in the Maritimes, where the land and climate were more favourable for agriculture.

In England, Cabot's report of the abundance of **groundfish**—cod, grey sole, flounder, redfish, and turbot—in the waters off Newfoundland lured European fishers—chiefly English, French, and Basque—to make the perilous voyage across the Atlantic to these rich fishing grounds, though some, especially the Basques, possibly had been fishing these waters at an earlier date. In any event, the Newfoundland coast quickly became a popular area for European fishers and landings on shore were made for drying the fish and establishing temporary habitation during the fishing season. This pattern of migratory fishing dominated the Newfoundland fishery until political circumstances changed in Europe and North America.

During this time, the French presence in the Newfoundland fishery was particularly strong, and Plaisance on the Avalon Peninsula's southwest coast was its largest settlement. With the defeat of the French in 1760, two events shaped the settlement of Newfoundland. First, French access was limited to what was called the French Shore, after 1783 stretching from Cape St John on the north coast around the Northern Peninsula and along the west coast of the island to Cape Ray in the far southwest, and permanent French settlement was restricted to the islands of Saint-Pierre and Miquelon. These French fishing rights did not end until 1904. Today, descendants of early French settlers reside in several communities along Newfoundland's southwest coast. Second, the emergence of a strong resident fishery marked the foundation of a Newfoundland society. English Protestant and Irish Catholic families settled along the Newfoundland coast, each locating in distinct places, and by the 1750s over 7,000 permanent residents, mostly English, lived in hundreds of small fishing communities along the Newfoundland coast.

At the dawn of the eighteenth century, British possessions in Atlantic Canada contained few people and were little more than names on a map. On the ground, the French colony of l'Acadie and their allies, the Mi'kmaq, were the most numerous inhabitants of the Maritimes, while French and English settlers occupied coastal settlements in Newfoundland with the **Beothuk** still occupying the interior of Newfoundland.

Over the first half of the eighteenth century, war between the two European colonial powers in North America—England and France—was almost continuous. During that time, the French forged an alliance with the Mi'kmaq and Maliseet, drawing them into the conflict with the English and their Iroquois allies. Under the terms of the 1713 Treaty of Utrecht, France surrendered Acadia to the British. However, many French-speaking settlers, the Acadians, remained in this newly won British territory, which was renamed Nova Scotia. During the previous century, the Acadians had established a strong presence in the Maritimes with settlements and forts. Most Acadians lived in the Annapolis Valley, near the Bay of Fundy coast, tilling the soil; others farmed on Île Saint-Jean (Prince Edward Island). Until the mid-1700s, Britain made little effort to colonize these lands, leaving the Acadians alone in this British-held territory (see Figure 10.4).

**FIGURE 10.4 Atlantic Canada in 1750**

European settlement in Atlantic Canada was concentrated in the Maritimes. In 1605, a handful of French settlers established the first permanent European settlement in North America north of Florida, at **Port Royal** on the Bay of Fundy coast of present-day Nova Scotia. During the seventeenth century and part of the eighteenth century, French settlers spread into the Annapolis Valley (Vignette 10.2) and other lowlands in the Maritimes. By 1750, French-speaking Acadians numbered over 12,000. These French settlements, united by culture, language, and a common economy, became known as Acadia. In the coming decade, the British deported Acadians to various English colonies in North America and back to Europe and arranged for New Englanders to settle on these lands instead.

Source: Emanuel Bowen, A new & accurate map of the islands of Newfoundland, Cape Breton, St. John and Anticosta (London: William Innys et al., 1747). BAnQ, G 3400 1750 B6.

The Mi'kmaq remained close to the Acadians, but as the British power took hold they became strangers in their own land. Between 1725 and 1779, the Mi'kmaq signed a series of peace and friendship treaties with Great Britain, but events turned against the Mi'kmaq and Acadians with the founding of Halifax in 1749. The British efforts to remove the French presence took the form of British and German settlers arriving in Nova Scotia and the expulsion of the Acadians in 1755 from Nova Scotia, and in 1758 from Île Royale (Cape Breton Island) and Île Saint-Jean. This tragic event was known as the **Grand Dérangement**. During this time, relations between the British and the Mi'kmaq, who were former allies of the Acadians, deteriorated. British rangers were unleashed to harass the Mi'kmaq, to destroy their villages, and to drive them far beyond the British settlements. With the final defeat of the French forces, France signed the Treaty of Paris in 1763, ceding all French territories in North America to the British except for the islands of Saint-Pierre and Miquelon near the southern coast of Newfoundland.

The next event to influence the evolution of the Maritimes was the American Revolution. Following victory by the American colonies, approximately 40,000 Loyalists made their way to Nova Scotia and New Brunswick, where they occupied the fertile lands of the recently departed Acadians and the prime hunting lands and fishing areas of the Mi'kmaq. With its superb harbour for ships of the British navy, Halifax became known as the "Warden of the North." Over the next 100 years, more and more British settlers came to the Maritimes. Nova Scotia alone received 55,000 Scots, Irish, English, and Welsh. Most Scots went to Cape Breton and the Northumberland shore. The driving forces pushing them from the British Isles were the **Scottish Highland clearances** and the **Irish famine**, which resulted in large influxes of migrants with Celtic cultural roots. These immigrants helped to define the dominantly Scottish character of Cape Breton and the Irish character of Saint John. The cultural impact of these Celtic peoples still resonates, and people of Scottish descent are still the largest ethnic group in Nova Scotia ("New Scotland").

## Head Start, Slow Start

In the early nineteenth century, the harvesting of Atlantic Canada's natural wealth increased. This frontier hinterland of the British Empire exploited its rich natural resources—the cod off the Newfoundland coast and the virgin forests in the Maritimes—and became heavily involved in transatlantic trade of these resources. Furthermore, the availability of timber and the region's favourable seaside location provided the ideal conditions for shipbuilding. By 1840, Nova Scotia and New Brunswick entered the "Golden Age of Sail," becoming the leading shipbuilding centres in the British Empire.

After the American Civil War, New England industrialized, leading to greater trade between the Maritimes and New England. In addition, Britain's move to free trade in 1849 meant the loss of Atlantic Canada's protected markets for its **primary products**, resulting in even greater interest by Maritime firms in the American market. Just before Confederation, the end of the Reciprocity Treaty cut off access to the Maritimes' natural trading partner, New England, resulting in the deterioration of the Maritimes' economic position.

## The Maritimes Join Confederation—Reluctantly

The provinces of Atlantic Canada joined Canada at different times and for different reasons. Nova Scotia and New Brunswick entered at the time of Confederation; Prince Edward Island followed in 1873 (Figure 10.5); Newfoundland rejected the proposal and did not come on board until 1949.

With Central Canada now the main market for Maritime goods, distance became an enemy. To offset the disadvantage of geography, Ottawa's answer was the Intercolonial Railway (completed in 1876) that linked the Maritimes with Central Canada. The Intercolonial was operated and subsidized by the federal government: freight rates were kept low to promote trade, and Ottawa paid the annual deficits. Even so, manufacturing in the Maritimes declined. One exception was the production of steel rails as the completion of the CPR to the Pacific coast led to increasing railway construction and to a need

For more details on Loyalist migrations to Canada, see "The Loyalists" in **Chapter 3**, page 104.

**FIGURE 10.5  The Maritime Provinces: First to enter Confederation**

New Brunswick and Nova Scotia joined the Province of Canada (Quebec and Ontario) to form the Dominion of Canada in 1867; Prince Edward Island entered Confederation six years later.

Source: *Atlas of Canada* reference map—Maritime Provinces, atlas.nrcan.gc.ca/data/english/maps/reference/provinceterritories/maritimes/map.pdf. Natural Resources Canada, 2000. Reproduced with the permission of the Minister of Public Works and Government Services Canada, 2013.

for steel in the early twentieth century. By taking advantage of Cape Breton's coalfields and iron ore from Bell Island, Newfoundland, the steel industry[2] in Sydney prospered, accelerating Nova Scotia's economic growth well above the national average. However, in 1919, the Maritime economy suffered a deadly blow when federal subsidies for freight rates were eliminated. Immediate access to the national market became more difficult and, with the loss of sales, many firms had to lay off workers, while others were forced to shut down. Even before these troubled times, the Maritimes economy was unable to absorb its entire workforce, leading many to migrate to the industrial towns of New England and Central Canada. From then on, out-migration became a fact of life in the Maritimes.

## Newfoundland Joins Confederation

Newfoundland's boundary was finalized in 1927—except Quebec has never formally recognized much of the Labrador Peninsula having been awarded at that time to Newfoundland by the British Judicial Committee of the Privy Council. The political process of Newfoundland joining Canada had two steps. First, a rejection took place in 1869 when voters brought to power an anti-Confederation government, despite other Newfoundland political leaders voicing interest and attending the Quebec Conference in 1864 (Hiller, 1997); second, some 80 years later, an acceptance was barely won in a referendum. In the first referendum of 1948, Newfoundlanders faced three choices: continuance of the Commission of Government for five years, joining Canada, and a return to responsible government (i.e., quasi-independence within a fast-fading British Empire). Responsible government took 44.5 per cent of the vote, followed by joining Canada at 41.1 per cent. In the second referendum, Commission of Government was dropped off the ballot and voters faced two choices, with a slim majority, 52.3 per cent, voting for joining Canada over an independent Newfoundland. The province officially added "and Labrador" to its name in 2001.

## Atlantic Canada Today

The sea has shaped Atlantic Canada. As a result, Atlantic Canada contains a natural beauty and captivating cultural roots that continue to foster an enviable quality of life for Atlantic Canadians. Yet, the economy of Atlantic Canada remains the weakest of the regions in southern Canada. Within Atlantic Canada, Newfoundland and Labrador (Figure 10.6), after riding the oil boom for more than a decade, has fallen on hard times again. The heavy debt from the Muskrat Falls hydroelectric project is adding to hard times. The lockdown imposed by COVID-19 has devastated the tourist industry and dampened growth in the rest of the economy.

Across the region, major projects have closed, such as the potash mine in New Brunswick, or slowed production, as with the iron ore mines in Labrador. The prospect for strong economic growth remains elusive until oil and ore prices rebound to former levels. In addition, the loss of jobs in the Alberta oil sands has brought to an end the Big Commute of oilfield workers from Newfoundland to Alberta (CBC News, 2009; Roberts, 2016a). On the bright side, tourism (until the global pandemic) and shellfish exports have benefited from a low Canadian dollar, while federally funded shipbuilding remains a key pillar.

But opportunities do exist. The first opportunity was the discovery and exploitation of offshore oil and gas deposits, which began the process of rejuvenating Newfoundland and Labrador's economy. Geography dictated that, because large oil deposits are located 200–300 km east of Newfoundland beneath the seafloor of the Grand Banks, Newfoundland and Labrador received the economic stimulus and royalties. From 2008 to 2014, offshore royalties exceeded $2 billion annually and formed over one-third of the province's revenues. With the sharp fall of oil prices in 2015, offshore royalties declined to under $1 billion. With oil prices falling to record lows in 2020, the province faces continued declining offshore royalties. Offshore oil projects, such as Husky Energy's West White Rose, are in trouble because of low oil prices. Husky Energy is unable to complete its half-finished West White Rose project and has asked the province for a buy-in to financially support the project (Global News, 2020). Given Newfoundland and Labrador's grim financial situation, the answer was no.

Nova Scotia's promise of a similar oil bonanza failed and only minor deposits of natural gas have been exploited near Sable Island. With gas production now having been shut down, Nova Scotia seems unlikely to enjoy an energy windfall.

The second opportunity—again, centred on Newfoundland and Labrador—stems from the huge nickel deposit at Voisey's Bay, Labrador, and the **hydrometallurgy** processing of nickel concentrate into nickel at the Long Harbour facility near St John's. The Long Harbour plant started production in July 2014, and represents a value-added component rarely associated with resource development in Atlantic Canada.

See "The Territorial Evolution of Canada" in **Chapter 3**, page 73.

**THINK ABOUT IT**

Since the debt load from the construction of the Muskrat Falls project could plunge the government of Newfoundland and Labrador into insolvency, would national unity be served if the federal government purchased the Muskrat Falls dam as it did the Trans Mountain pipeline project in Western Canada and BC?

**FIGURE 10.6 Newfoundland and Labrador**

When Newfoundland entered Confederation in 1949, Canada gained a territory, population, and the remaining part of Britain's North American empire. While an integral part of Atlantic Canada, Newfoundland and Labrador occupies a different space, economy, and culture from the Maritimes.

Source: *Atlas of Canada* reference map—Newfoundland and Labrador, atlas.nrcan.gc.ca/data/english/maps/reference/provincesterritories/newfoundland/map.pdf. Natural Resources Canada, 2002. Reproduced with the permission of the Minister of Public Works and Government Services Canada, 2013.

A third opportunity had been linked to Canada's largest oil refinery, an ocean location, and the proposed Energy East pipeline. The failure of this pipeline to move to the construction stage ended this opportunity. The Irving refinery near Saint John was designated as the end point of the proposed pipeline. On the shore of the Bay of Fundy, the Irving refinery could have processed bitumen from Alberta for consumption in Atlantic Canada and world markets. In 2020, Alberta oil arrived in Saint John by ship from Vancouver, but whether the sea round becomes a regular feature remains uncertain.

## Equalization Payments

Atlantic Canada has long benefited from equalization payments. While the calculations are complex, the funds come from the federal government out of its general tax revenues. Only recently did Newfoundland and Labrador break from the pattern of dependency as a consequence of its offshore oil royalties. Lower oil prices may force the province back into the "have-not" category of provinces receiving equalization payments.

In 2020–1, Atlantic Canada received just over $4.8 billion in equalization payments (Department of Finance Canada, 2017). Unless some spectacular event takes place of the magnitude of the discovery of vast offshore oil deposits, the Maritimes is destined to remain dependent on equalization payments.

## Industrial Structure

Atlantic Canada's primary resources are fish, forests, minerals, and petroleum. These resources remain essential building blocks, but the region's economic future lies in its tertiary sector, especially high-technology industries. One example is the software company Verafin, which is located in St John's. Its success lies in its popular financial crime management software that is employed across North America. Verafin's success confirms that you can locate to Atlantic Canada rather than Central Canada—you just need a unique approach to a problem (in this case, preventing Internet crimes). A link to a university is essential, as software employees are in high demand. Verafin, for example, has hired a large number of Memorial University's computer science graduates over the past few years.

Employment statistics provide a picture of the basic economic structure of Atlantic Canada. In 2019, employment in primary activities accounted for 7.6 per cent of the labour force; secondary employment constituted 17.3 per cent; and tertiary employment was 75.1 per cent (Table 10.2). Like other regions, Atlantic Canada has experienced the same trends with percentage decreases in the primary and secondary sectors and an increase in the tertiary sector. But unlike other regions, the total number of workers has increased only slightly, indicating a stagnant economy (Table 10.2). Another indicator of the weak economy is the high rate of unemployment—in 2016, Atlantic Canada's unemployment rate was 10 per cent compared to the national average of 6 per cent (Table 10.1). By late 2020, the impact of COVID-19 had hit Atlantic Canada hard, with a rise in unemployment to an average of 14 per cent (Statistics Canada, 2020b)—despite the fact that the region had fared comparatively well in dealing with the novel coronavirus and had established an Atlantic Canada "bubble" that allowed relatively unencumbered travel and commerce within the region. Newfoundland and

For more on equalization payments, see **Chapter 5**, "Equalization Payments," page 166.

| TABLE 10.2 | Atlantic Canada Industrial Sectors by Number of Workers, 2005 and 2019 | | | | |
|---|---|---|---|---|---|
| Economic Sector | Workers, 2005 | Workers, 2005 (%) | Workers, 2019 | Workers, 2019 (%) | % Difference |
| Primary | 62,500 | 5.8 | 91,400 | 7.6 | 1.8 |
| Secondary | 171,700 | 16.0 | 207,200 | 17.3 | 1.3 |
| Tertiary | 841,600 | 78.2 | 900,200 | 75.1 | –3.1 |
| Total | 1,075,800 | 100.0 | 1,198,800 | 100.0 | |

Sources: Statistics Canada (2006, 2020b).

Labrador, with an unemployment rate close to 20 per cent, suffered the most from the lockdown caused by the virus.

## Technological Spearheads

Atlantic Canada has its economic spearheads. These spearheads represent a major economic thrust for the region and also illustrate the region's unique character as it adds the knowledge-based sector to its resource economy. The federal government has always provided an economic spearhead. A recent example sees Nova Scotia undertaking a major role in Ottawa's National Shipbuilding Strategy, which seeks to modernize the Royal Canadian Navy to meet the demands of the twenty-first century.

Atlantic Canada provides a parallel to Western Canada, where the blending of advanced knowledge-based firms with a strong resource sector is well underway. What must be recognized is that the so-called knowledge economy is radiating its advanced technology to all other sectors. In this sense, Atlantic Canada is transforming, especially in the major urban centres. On the other hand, rural Atlantic Canada is shrinking, both in terms of its share of the regional economy and the population. The most extreme cases involve the abandonment of outport communities on the island of Newfoundland.

## Shipbuilding at Halifax

Under its National Shipbuilding Strategy, the federal government elected to refurbish the Royal Canadian Navy in 2010. Most importantly for the shipbuilding companies, the federal government has committed funds to selected shipyards for the next 30 years and, with maintenance contracts, possibly for the rest of the twenty-first century. Irving's Halifax Shipyard was selected as one of the two contractors. Halifax Shipways is building the Royal Canadian Navy's future fleet, beginning with Arctic offshore patrol vessels, followed by 15 warships. On the Pacific coast, North Vancouver's Seaspan is responsible for building coast guard ships, including oceanographic vessels.

Irving Shipbuilding received a $25 billion federal contract to build 21 combat ships for the navy over 30 years. To undertake this massive project, Irving built the largest shipyard in North America (Photo 10.8). Most importantly, this

shaun/iStockphoto

**PHOTO 10.8** The Halifax Shipyard facility is the largest single building for constructing ships in North America. Selected by Ottawa to build the Royal Canadian Navy's future combat fleet, the shipyard's future is secure.

federal contract is triggering a series of complementary economic activities designed to create a world-class shipbuilding industry in Halifax. Already, Irving has issued over 200 contracts to Canadian companies worth over $1 billion (Irving, 2016). Further in the future, maintenance of these ships would cost billions. Having built the ships, the Irving shipyard will have an inside track on maintenance contracts that would extend over another 30–50 years. In 2019, Canada announced a $500 million contract to Irving to carry out maintenance work on its combat frigates (Al-Hakim, 2019). Yet, this massive defence spending is both costly and slow-moving. For example, "cutting steel" required Irving to look for expertise outside of Canada, and it turned to Odense Maritime Technology, a Danish engineering and naval architectural firm (Doucette, 2013). Cutting steel for the eight Arctic and offshore patrol ships (AOP-SA) began in 2015 with a delivery date of 2018. However, HMCS *Harry DeWolf*, the first AOPS built at the Halifax shipyard, was finally delivered to the Royal Canadian Navy at the end of July 2020 and then, in mid-October, it returned to dock during a training mission when its freshwater generator and communications systems failed—and then it was discovered that some cooling pumps also had failed (Berthiaume, 2020). Building and maintaining a $400 million Arctic patrol ship clearly is an onerous undertaking.

There is a downside to relying on federal support for navy contracts. The danger lies in the reliability of such funding. Canadian shipyards cannot survive without federal government contracts. Similar to the boom-bust cycle affecting the mineral industry, shipyards go from hard times to good times as Ottawa struggles to decide how to spend its finite resources. Like all Canadian shipyards, Halifax Shipyard Limited underwent a dramatic slowdown in the new construction and refit business during the late 1990s and throughout the 2000s due to a reduction in federal government funding for construction of warships, icebreakers, ferries, and scientific vessels. Past economic downturns have caused Ottawa to curtail its defence spending. Could such a scenario happen in the future?

## Hydroelectricity: White Elephant or Megaproject of the Century?

In 2011, the proposed Muskrat Falls hydroelectric project on the Lower Churchill River was portrayed as the megaproject of the century. Finally, Newfoundland and Labrador would rightfully benefit from low-cost hydroelectric power and, at the same time, break the geographic advantage held by the Quebec transmission route (Figure 10.7). But construction delays and cost overruns mounted, turning this undertaking into what Premier Dwight Ball called "the greatest fiscal mistake in Newfoundland and Labrador's history" (McKenzie-Sutter, 2019). With the project completed in 2019 at a cost of $12.6 billion, the project has placed the province in financial jeopardy. Only additional financial support from Ottawa will save the taxpayers of Newfoundland and Labrador from shouldering this heavy burden.

In 2011, the dream of turning a natural site for hydro power into a reality looked promising. The challenge was twofold: the cost of construction in a remote area was unpredictable and transmitting the generated power to distant markets by underwater cables was unproven. So what was the lure of this venture? The proposal involves two power stations, at Gull Island and Muskrat Falls on the Churchill River. Together, these stations would produce 3,074 megawatts (MW) of electricity (Churchill Falls power station, which achieved full production in 1971, produces 5,425 MW). Like Churchill Falls, the market for the generated electricity lies far from the power plants. The logical transmission line to these markets runs through Quebec. However, the Newfoundland and Labrador government opted for an Atlantic Canada electrical power system that would allow for exports to New England. This ambitious political decision involved an unproven transmission route and subsea cables, one under the Strait of Belle Isle from Labrador to Newfoundland and the other beneath the Cabot Strait between Newfoundland and Nova Scotia. From Nova Scotia, the power would move through high-voltage transmission lines to New Brunswick and then to New England.

**THINK ABOUT IT**
Canada has always struggled with spending its finite resources on its military. As a member of NATO, Canada has always fallen short in military spending compared to other members. Our performance reveals a low priority on the military compared to a much higher priority for domestic needs.

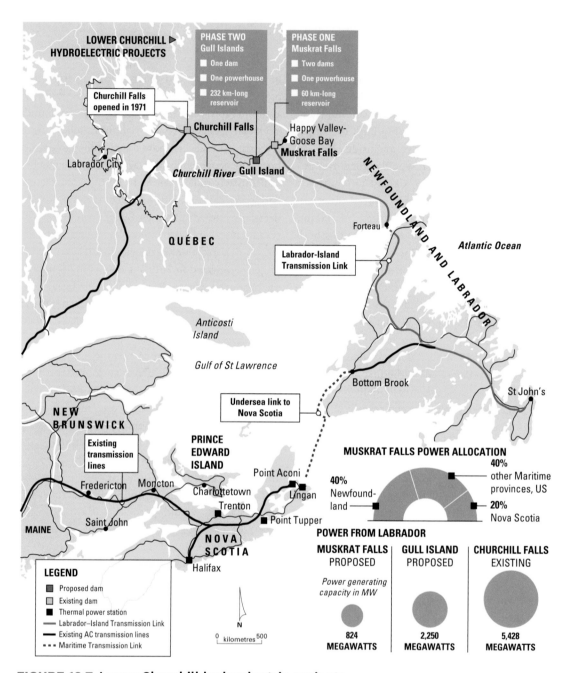

**FIGURE 10.7 Lower Churchill hydroelectric projects**

The dream of hydropower propelling Newfoundland and Labrador into a clean energy future collapsed under the weight of the huge cost overrun in the construction of the Muskrat Falls dam and powerhouse. Instead, Newfoundlanders face the burden of paying for the debt through taxation and high electric rates. Not surprisingly, the proposed second phase, Gulf Island, has been shelved. The Maritime Link that connects Newfoundland to Nova Scotia began operating in 2017 (Emera, 2020).

Adapted from McCarthy (2011).

Work on the Muskrat Falls project began in 2012, with an estimated cost at $6.2 billion that included the cost of building the Muskrat Falls hydro project, power transmission from Labrador across the island of Newfoundland, and the Maritime Link to carry power from Newfoundland to

Nova Scotia and to the United States. Four years later, the cost estimate had ballooned to over $12 billion and Stan Marshall, the newly appointed CEO of Nalcor Energy, the provincial energy corporation, stated that what he now had to oversee was a "boondoggle." As he said, "It was a gamble and it's gone against us" (Roberts, 2016b). Among the problems, according Marshall, have been: a lack of Nalcor experience and that of its principal—Italian—contractor on such a large project in a cold environment; a project too large for the energy needs of the province; lower demand and falling energy prices; and a gross underestimate of cost to begin with (a problem shared by many megaprojects) (Roberts, 2016b).

But that's not all. Part of the deal is that the undersea cable between Newfoundland and Nova Scotia is provided by Emera Inc., a publicly traded Nova Scotia energy transmission firm that is the sole owner of Nova Scotia Power. This Maritime Link, at a cost of $1.6 billion to Emera, was completed in 2017 while the Muskrat Falls project came online in 2020 at a cost of nearly $13 billion. Emera is guaranteed 20 per cent of the Muskrat Falls power generation for the next 40 years—all for 20 per cent of the original estimate of $7.4 billion (see Contested Terrain 10.1). By 2016, the cost of cancelling the project had become prohibitive. And added to Nalcor's woes, local protests in October 2016, which could end up costing hundreds of millions of dollars, delayed the partial flooding of the reservoir at Muskrat Falls, a necessity to protect the infrastructure before winter (Bailey, 2016; Roberts, 2016b).

## Atlantic Canada's Traditional Economic Anchor: The Fishing Industry

Nature has given Atlantic Canada a vast continental shelf that provides an excellent physical environment for fish: the warm ocean currents from the Gulf Stream and the cold Labrador Current create ideal conditions for fish reproduction and growth. The continental shelf extends almost 400 km offshore (Figure 10.8). In some places, where the continental shelf is raised, the water is relatively shallow. Such areas are known as banks. The largest banks are the Grand Banks off Newfoundland's east coast and Georges Bank off the south coast of Nova Scotia (Vignette 10.3). Climate change is warming the waters of the North Atlantic. The impact on the fish biomass varies. The northern cod prefers cold waters, while shellfish thrive in warmer water.

Although each province relies on the fishery, striking differences exist between Newfoundland/Labrador and the Maritime provinces. One difference is fishing grounds. Newfoundlanders, traditionally, have fished in the waters of the Grand Banks, in the inshore fishery around the island of Newfoundland, and along the shore of Labrador. On the other hand, fishers from the Maritimes ply more southern waters around Georges Bank and smaller banks just offshore of Prince Edward Island and Nova Scotia. Fishing for the highly valued lobster (Figure 10.9) takes place in shallow waters, with the most productive area found near Yarmouth, Nova Scotia.[3]

## Contested Terrain 10.1

### The 20-for-20 Agreement

The agreement between Emera and Nalcor, the NL Crown corporation that developed Muskrat Falls, has been called the "20-for-20" agreement, whereby Nova Scotia Power gets 20 per cent of the power and contributes 20 per cent of the project's cost. The saving grace for Nova Scotia is that Emera agreed to contribute 20 per cent of the original estimated cost of $7.4 billion and not the true cost that ballooned to $12.7 billion by 2019. Accordingly, Nova Scotia will get 20 per cent of the energy provided by Muskrat Falls but pay only 12.1 per cent of the total costs (Le Blanc, 2020).

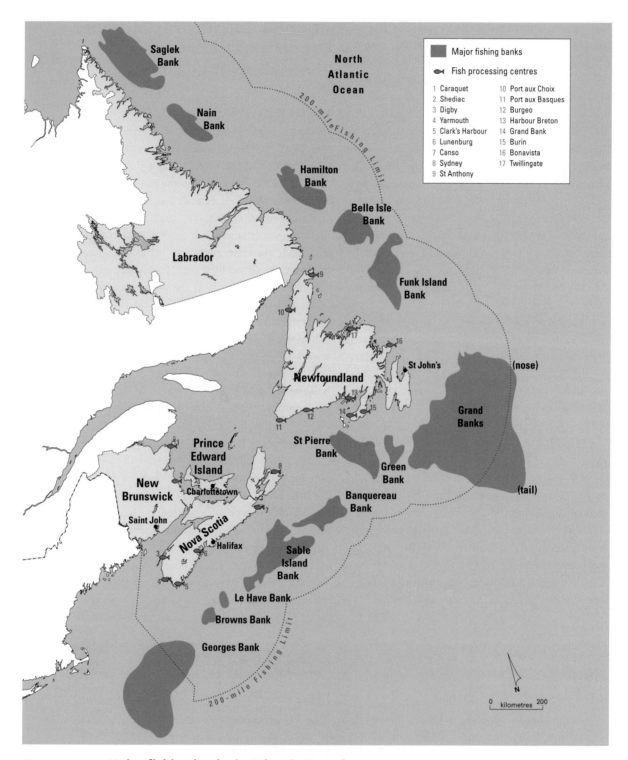

**FIGURE 10.8 Major fishing banks in Atlantic Canada**

The Atlantic coast fishery operates within a vast continental shelf that extends some 400 km eastward into the Atlantic Ocean, southward to Georges Bank, and north to Saglek Bank. Within these waters are at least a dozen areas of shallow water known as "banks." The Grand Banks of Newfoundland is the most famous fishing ground while Georges Bank contains the widest variety of fish stocks. Scallops, for instance, are harvested in beds on Georges Bank and Browns Bank. The lobster fishery lies much closer to land and consists of a dozen inshore areas that are highly regulated. These areas extend from the Gulf of St Lawrence, down the Scotian Shelf, and into the Bay of Fundy.

A second difference is found in the nature and value of the catch. While the value of the Atlantic fisheries reached a record high of $3.4 billion in 2017 (Fisheries and Oceans Canada, 2019a), shellfish, led by lobster, crab, and shrimp, made up nearly 90 per cent of the total value (Table 10.3). Geography plays a role, too. With the collapse of the cod fishery, ground fish has been replaced by shellfish as the number one fish stock. Shellfish accounted for 90 per cent of the value of Atlantic

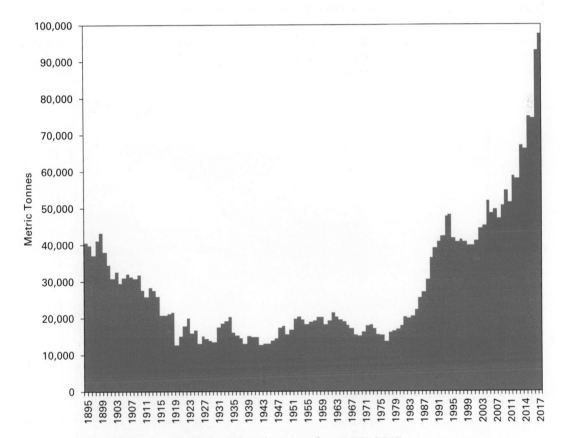

**FIGURE 10.9 Lobster landings in Atlantic Canada, 1895–2017**

Lobster is by far the most valued species, accounting for just under half of the catch by value in Atlantic Canada. Lobster landings reached a historic high in 2017 at 97,452 metric tonnes and higher prices combined to push the value of this catch to $942 million.

Source: Fisheries and Oceans Canada (2019a).

**TABLE 10.3  Value of Commercial Fish Landings, by Province, 2017 ($ millions)**

| Species | NS | NB | PE | QC | NL | Total |
|---|---|---|---|---|---|---|
| Groundfish | 91.1 | 1.7 | 0.7 | 15.9 | 117.9 | 227.3 |
| Pelagic fish | 62.7 | 17.6 | 9.3 | 3.7 | 17.0 | 110.4 |
| Shellfish | 1,255.5 | 376.7 | 264.6 | 368.4 | 631.1 | 3,045.8 |
| Others | >0.1 | 0.6 | 0.0 | 0.0 | 15.0 | 15.7 |
| Totals | 1,409.4 | 385.9 | 274.6 | 388.0 | 781.0 | 3,399.1 |

Note: Totals may not add up due to rounding.

Source: Adapted from Fisheries and Oceans Canada (2019a).

## Vignette 10.3

### Georges Bank

As part of the Atlantic continental shelf, Georges Bank (Figure 10.10) is a large shallow-water area extending over nearly 40,000 km². Water depth usually ranges from 50 to 80 m, but in some areas the water is 10 m or less. Georges Bank is one of the most biologically productive regions in the world's oceans because of the tidal mixing that occurs in its shallow waters. This brings to the surface a continuous supply of regenerated nutrients from the ocean sediments. These nutrients support vast quantities of minute sea life called plankton. In turn, large stocks of marine life, including cod, flounder, haddock, lobster, and scallops, feed on plankton.

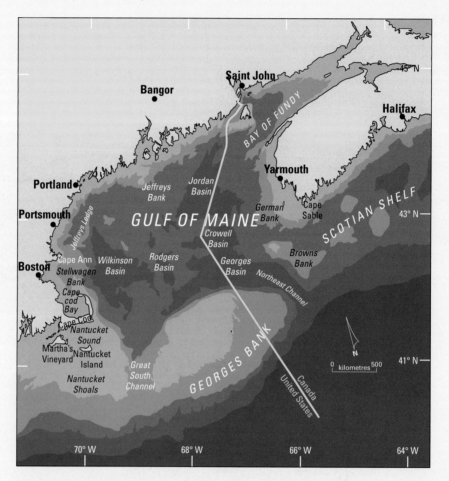

**FIGURE 10.10 Georges Bank: The Canada–US boundary**

In the nineteenth century, both American and Canadian fishing vessels plied the waters of Georges Bank for groundfish and shellfish. After World War II, Canada claimed the northern half of Georges Bank but the United States claimed the entire area. In 1984, the World Court established the boundary for the disputed territory, with the US receiving control over two-thirds of the area. Canada obtained the rights to the northeast corner, which is particularly rich in shellfish, including lobsters and scallops.

Source: http://celebrating200years.noaa.gov/magazine/globec/map_gulfofmaine_650.jpg

Canada's landed fish in 2017. The spatial pattern varies, with lobster accounting for the most valuable fish harvested by Maritimers, while Newfoundlanders focus on queen crab and shrimp. Cod fell to less than 15 per cent of the value of the catch in Newfoundland and Labrador (Fisheries and Oceans Canada, 2019a). Still, the allowable catch of cod has increased over the last five years as Fisheries and Oceans Canada estimates that the cod stocks are increasing.

Climate change has warmed the waters around the Maritimes, where lobster prefer temperatures between 10 and 16 degrees Celsius. The result is an increase in the lobster biomass. Added to the increase in the abundance of lobster, fishers are trapping more lobsters at a time when prices have increased. In 2019, prices ranged from $7 to $13 per pound, depending on the time of year—up by more than triple from the 2003 prices (Ryan, 2019). Those good times ended in 2020 when the price dropped to $8 per pound because the COVID-19 outbreak in China ended those important exports.

Geopolitics has come into the picture, too. China has banned US lobster imports and has turned to Atlantic Canada to fill this gap. The lobster industry forms a key element in the recent surge in exports to China. Since 2013, lobster exports to China have grown rapidly (Doucette, 2019). China forms a pillar in the Nova Scotia government's economic strategy, where it ranks second to the US in Nova Scotia imports. Unfortunately, in January 2020, when COVID-19 struck China it stopped importing lobster. Nova Scotia's lobster industry remains depressed with lower prices and exports. The hope is that exports to China will return.

Seafood export is an expanding industry in Nova Scotia and less so in other provinces of Atlantic Canada. Yet, the opportunity exists. As noted above, until the COVID-19 pandemic, fresh lobster was exported to China in growing numbers (Photo 10.9), thus providing a boost to Maritime fishers. At the same time, Chinese companies are entering the Nova Scotia fish business. For example, in 2014 the Chinese firm Zoneco (better known in China as Zhangzidao) purchased Capital Seafoods in Eastern Passage (Withers, 2016). By 2013, Nova Scotia firms were exporting fresh

**PHOTO 10.9** Live lobster was in high demand in Chinese restaurants before the outbreak of COVID-19. The hope is that the rapidly growing Chinese middle class will return to high-end restaurants that specialize in the preparation of live lobster.

AP Photo/Andy Wong

lobster by air to China, which involves placing them in wet newspapers in styrofoam coolers in Halifax, then loading the coolers on a cargo plane for an 18-hour flight to Shanghai (Ong & Mulvany, 2015). Chinese demand was driven by Atlantic Canada's competitive price and high quality of lobster, and more recently it had been driven by China's ban on US lobster imports. Unfortunately, the trade issues between Canada and China have cooled lobster exports. At its height, Nova Scotia's exports to China reached nearly $1 billion in 2019, roughly 18 times more than a decade ago, with $728 million of this total represented by seafood products, primarily live lobster exports (Bundale, 2020). Yet with the outbreak of COVID-19, first in China and then globally, and ongoing diplomatic tensions with China, those heady days are over for now.

Newfoundland fishers no longer rely on cod but on crab and shrimp. In fact, cod landings are a minuscule fraction of past catches (Figure 10.11). In 2018, cod landings were only 16,300 metric tonnes; in contrast, over 245,000 metric tonnes were landed in 1990, shortly before the closure of the fishery. In 2018, Newfoundland reported that the total value of the fisheries catch was just over

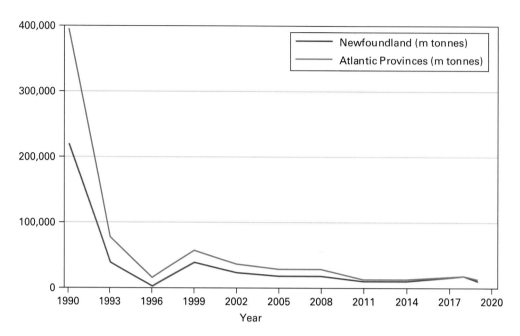

**FIGURE 10.11 Cod landings for Newfoundland/Labrador and Atlantic Canada, 1990–2018 (metric tonnes live weight)**

Source: Based on data from Fisheries and Oceans Canada (2019b).

**PHOTO 10.10** Captain Gary Denny of the Pictou Landing First Nation is one of the beneficiaries of the 1999 Supreme Court of Canada ruling that acknowledged the treaty right of Mi'kmaw fishers to make a moderate livelihood from the commercial fishery. Gary and his crew are busy throughout the year. In May and June, they set lobster traps near Cheticamp. Starting in July, the crew fish for snow crab in the Gulf of St Lawrence and by fall they return to Pictou Landing to fish herring and rock crab. When those seasons close in November, Denny heads to Nova Scotia's South Shore to crew on a boat in the winter lobster fishery. In 2015, Fisheries and Oceans Canada estimated that about 365 land-based workers and 1,310 fishers participate in the Indigenous commercial fishery in Atlantic Canada (Beswick, 2015).

$700 million, with less than 2 per cent of that attributed to cod; queen crab and shrimp accounted for 37 and 36 per cent, respectively (Fisheries and Oceans Canada, 2019b).

In addition, fewer fishing licences are allotted for crab compared to the old days when Newfoundlanders focused on cod. As a result, the fishery is concentrated in fewer and fewer hands and that fact has led to the demise of many coastal fishing villages. Another change in the fisheries is that the Mi'kmaw fishers are active in lobster fishing in the Maritimes (Photo 10.10). Their involvement stems from the Supreme Court of Canada's landmark 1999 *Marshall* decision that opened the door for a share of the commercial fishery, but over the years this involvement has not been without conflict because non-Indigenous fishers object to the Mi'kmaq being allowed to conduct their own lobster fishery. Indeed, it can be argued that the non-Indigenous lobster fishers protest having to share "the commons" at all. Most recently, in October 2020 a Mi'kmaw lobster pound in southwest Nova Scotia was destroyed by fire and a vehicle was torched outside an Indigenous lobster facility (Tunney, 2020). However, the tide is changing. In a transformative move, Halifax-based Clearwater Seafoods sold the company for about $1 billion to a partnership between Premium Brands of British Columbia and a coalition of Mi'kmaw First Nations, a move that "is basically catapulting the First Nations of Canada to a major player in the global seafood industry" (McKinley, 2020). Clearwater holds Canadian harvest licences for a variety of species including lobsters, scallops, crabs, and clams—all of which will be available to Indigenous fishers. The Mi'kmaw coalition will have a 50 per cent share of Clearwater (Withers, 2020). As Membertou Chief Terry Paul expressed it: "We're a player now. In order to be in business, you first have to play the game. You have to play to win, and we won" (Withers, 2020).

## Atlantic Canada's Resource Wealth

For over a decade, Atlantic Canada put its stock in energy and mineral development. The leading sectors of the resource economy are petroleum, mining, fishing, forestry, and agriculture. In 2017, oil production, valued at $7.7 billion, led the way, followed by mining at $4.2 billion, fish landings at $3 billion, forest exports at $2.6 billion, and farm receipts at $1.8 billion (Table 10.4). Following the slump in the global economy in 2014, prices for oil and iron dropped. Of course, the global economy could move back into a scenario of high prices for oil and iron, but for now the demand and prices are stuck in the low end of the boom-and-bust cycle. Within Atlantic Canada, Newfoundland and Labrador dominate the resource economy.

## Petroleum Industry: The Leading Edge

Offshore oil production provides the leading edge for resource development in Atlantic Canada, but this production is found only in Newfoundland and Labrador. Natural gas, by comparison, is a weak sister and generates far less revenue. The hoped-for gas deposits off Nova Scotia have failed to materialize and both projects—the Deep Panuke Offshore Gas Development and the Sable Offshore Energy Project (SOEP)—ceased production, in 2018 and 2019 respectively (Figure 10.12). The gas production went mainly to New England via a series of pipelines (Statistics Canada, 2016).

Oil deposits, consisting of a **light sweet crude**, are situated in sedimentary basins near the Grand Banks. Within the Jeanne d'Arc Basin, oil and natural gas deposits have been discovered and four oil projects—Hibernia, Hebron, Terra Nova, and White Rose—are now operating. In 2017, production totalled 13.3million $m^3$, which amounted to 15 per cent of Canada's output (Canadian Association of Petroleum Producers, 2018). These four oil projects, unlike those in Alberta, receive the much higher Brent price for their oil. Even so, the province is no longer enjoying record levels of royalties because of low global oil prices. Low prices are driving the province back into "have-not" status.

Hibernia (Vignette 10.4) uses a fixed platform, as does Hebron, while the Terra Nova and White Rose oil fields employ floating production storage and offloading (FPSO) vessels. Oil is offloaded from the FPSOs onto a shuttle tanker. Workers are taken to the offshore sites by helicopter on an in-and-out

| TABLE 10.4 Value of Resources, 2017 ($ millions) | | | | | |
|---|---|---|---|---|---|
| Resource | NL | NB | NS | PE | Atlantic Canada |
| **Petroleum** | 7,703 | 0 | >1 | 0 | 7,703 |
| **Minerals** | 3,513 | 397 | 248 | 5 | 4,163 |
| **Fisheries** | 781 | 546 | 1,409 | 275 | 3,011 |
| **Forest exports** | 128 | 1,825 | 616 | 28 | 2,597 |
| **Farm cash receipts** | 139 | 614 | 565 | 506 | 1,824 |
| **Total** | 12,264 | 3,382 | 2,838 | 814 | 19,686 |

Sources: Natural Resources Canada (2018, 2019); Canadian Association of Petroleum Producers (2018); Fisheries and Oceans Canada (2019b); Statistics Canada (2019d).

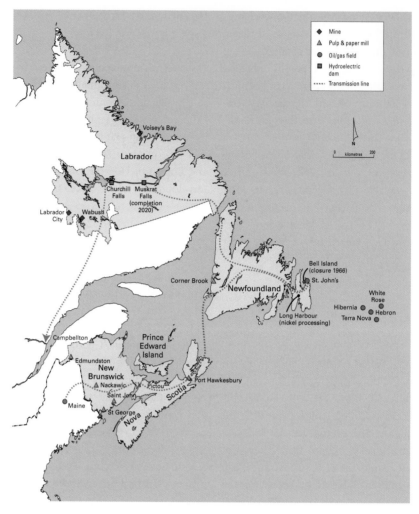

**FIGURE 10.12  Natural resources in Atlantic Canada**

basis, and in 2009 a helicopter taking workers to a White Rose FPSO and to Hibernia went down at sea, killing 17 with only one survivor. This was not the first disaster related to oil drilling off the Newfoundland coast. In February 1982, the *Ocean Ranger*, a semi-submersible mobile drilling vessel conducting exploratory drilling in the Hibernia field, sank during a North Atlantic storm packing 190 km/h winds with waves topping 20 m. All 84 workers aboard the vessel were lost (Collier, 2016; CBC Digital Archives, 2020).

Today, the Hibernia drilling site has an annual output of about 30 million barrels and adds greatly to Newfoundland's energy output and provincial royalties. Prices fluctuate, causing an unreliable source of royalties for the government. The low point was in 2019 when the price hit a low of US$20/barrel, while the highest price was over $120/barrel in 2012. The price of Brent crude oil in July 2020 was just over $40 per barrel.

Megaprojects boost regional development, but they also present problems. One is the tendency to underestimate the cost of the project, and the other is related to a boom–bust cycle. The boom occurs during construction when a large labour force is employed, and the bust takes place when the project is completed and requires few workers. More precisely, megaprojects are capital-intensive undertakings. Second, megaprojects in resource hinterlands lose much of their spinoff effects to industrial areas. As a consequence, economic benefits related to the manufacture of

**PHOTO 10.11** Neil's Harbour is a small fishing village on the northern tip of Cape Breton. The protected harbour is ideal for mooring small fishing boats.

## Vignette 10.4

### The Hibernia Platform

The Hibernia oil project is located 315 km east of St John's, Newfoundland, on the Grand Banks. To tap the estimated 615 million barrels of oil from the Hibernia deposit, an innovative offshore stationary platform was needed. About 4,000 workers built a specially designed offshore oil platform that can withstand the pounding storms of the North Atlantic and crushing blows from huge icebergs. The massive concrete and steel construction sits on the ocean floor, with 16 "teeth" in its exterior wall designed to absorb the impact of icebergs.

The 111-m-high Hibernia platform, which includes oil-storage units, weighs over 650,000 tonnes, and is the largest gravity-base structure of its kind in the world. In the summer of 1997, the platform was placed on the ocean floor just above the oil deposits. The depth of the water at this point is about 80 m, leaving the oil platform approximately 30 m above the ocean surface. This structure is designed as a platform for the oil derricks, and houses pumping equipment and living quarters for about 185 offshore workers, as well as a storage facility for the crude oil. The rig extracts oil from the Avalon reservoir (2.4 km under the seabed) and from the Hibernia reservoir (3.7 km deep). The crude oil is then pumped from the Hibernia storage tanks to an underwater pumping station and then through loading hoses to three 900,000-barrel supertankers for shipment to foreign refineries.

Source: Adapted from Cox (1994).

THE CANADIAN PRESS/Jonathan Hayward

**PHOTO 10.12** The Hibernia platform has a massive concrete base that supports its drilling and production-facilities as well as the workers' accommodations. Since the platform, with a topside length of 98 m and width of 34 m, was positioned on the ocean floor in 1997, the province has joined the ranks of other oil-producing provinces. The government of Newfoundland and Labrador at first received half of the royalties generated by these offshore developments. With a new agreement with Ottawa, in 2006 the province received all of the oil revenues. By 2009, oil revenues had made Newfoundland and Labrador a "have" province. With the sharp drop in oil prices in 2015 and continuing to 2020, oil revenues dropped by half, causing the provincial budget to slip into the red.

the essential parts for building a megaproject go outside the hinterland, as does the processing of the resource once the project is up and running. Interventions by the government of Newfoundland and Labrador to address this classic problem have had mixed results. The biggest success story comes not from the petroleum industry but from the agreement with the developers of the Voisey's Bay nickel mine whereby the government of Newfoundland and Labrador obtained a commitment from the company, Vale,[4] to process the ore at Long Harbour in Placentia Bay. In 2013, operations to process the ore began, adding much more to the economy than mining.

# The Mining Sector: Boom-and-Bust Performer

Atlantic Canada is endowed with world-class mineral deposits. The Canadian Shield in Labrador has rich deposits of iron ore and nickel (Figure 10.12). In 2011, with high commodity prices, the value of mineral production in Atlantic Canada reached a record $6.8 billion. By 2017, however, lower commodity prices saw this figure drop to $4.2 billion (Table 10.4). Since 2014, prices on the two leading minerals, nickel and iron, fell by over 50 per cent (Natural Resources Canada, 2015). As well, the lead-zinc mine near Bathurst, New Brunswick, ceased production in 2015. More bad news fell on the mining industry when, in 2016, the Potash Corporation announced the temporary closure of its mine near Sussex, New Brunswick, because of weak demand and low prices. Potash production ceased in 2016, but in 2019 New Brunswick's Department of Transportation ordered road salt that will keep the mine open for a few years. However, prospects for a return to potash production are not in sight (CBC News, 2019).

## Nickel Mining and Processing

Discovered in 1993, the Voisey's Bay nickel deposit lies along the coast of Labrador approximately 350 km north of Happy Valley–Goose Bay. In 1996, Inco Ltd acquired the rights to the Voisey's Bay property and then sold it nearly a decade later to Vale, the giant Brazilian-owned mining company. Vale began its production in 2005. At its Ovoid site, mining operations employ an open-pit system. The more expensive underground mining will take place at two other deposits—the Western Extension and Eastern Deeps. Since the Ovoid deposit lies close to the surface and is only a short distance from open water, the Voisey's Bay mine is one of the lowest-cost nickel mines in the world. It consists of 32 million tonnes of relatively rich ore bodies—2.8 per cent nickel and 1.7 per cent copper.

A concentrator reduces the ore into three parts: nickel, copper, and waste ore. The copper concentrate is sent to Europe while the nickel concentrate goes to Long Harbour on Newfoundland's Avalon Peninsula for final refining. This processing at the mine site and at Long Harbour represents the much desired "value-added" that all resource-based provinces seek but rarely obtain.

## Resource Development and Indigenous Land Claims: Voisey's Bay

The Voisey's Bay mining development sparked a renewed interest in comprehensive land claim settlements.[5] At the time the proposed development was taking form in 2003, neither Indigenous group in Labrador had reached such an agreement. Consequently, Inco (now Vale) negotiated impact and benefit agreements (IBAs) with the Labrador Inuit and Innu, thus allowing the project to proceed before comprehensive agreements were reached. For the Inuit and Innu, the IBAs included employment opportunities, provided the Indigenous workers had a basic command of English necessary for the workplace and at least a high school education. Unfortunately, relatively few qualified.

The next order of business was to settle land claims. By 2005, the Labrador Inuit and the federal government signed the comprehensive land claim agreement that created the Inuit government of Nunatsiavut. In 2011, the New Dawn Agreement between the Innu Nation of Labrador and the province established the parameters—in regard to claim area and compensation—for an eventual agreement with Ottawa. No final agreement has been reached for the approximately 2,400 members of the Innu Nation who live in Sheshatshiu and Natuashish. Such an agreement is complicated by the overlapping claim of the NunatuKavut Community Council (formerly known as the Labrador Métis Association), which has approximately 6,000 members and is comprised of those of mixed Inuit and European settler heritage.

## Forest Industry: A Weak Sister

Beyond the sea, Atlantic Canada's most important renewable resource, historically, has been its forests. The rugged Appalachian Uplands in Atlantic Canada encompass 22.9 million ha of forest. The forest industry, both logging and pulp and paper processing, is concentrated in New Brunswick. Logging is both an important employer and an income generator for woodlot owners. Unlike in the rest of Canada, where forest land is usually Crown land, the proportion of private timberlands to Crown lands in the Maritimes is extremely high. Private timberlands make up 92 per cent of the commercial forest in Prince Edward Island, 70 per cent in Nova Scotia, and 50 per cent in New Brunswick. In Newfoundland and

Labrador, like the rest of Canada, private ownership makes up only 2 per cent of the forested area. On average, the rate of logging on private lands is very high, sometimes exceeding the annual allowable cut estimated by the province. The high rate of logging often takes place on farms where timber sales are an important source of income.

Yet, the best days for this industry are long gone. In fact, the forest industry in Atlantic Canada (and across Canada's boreal forest) is contracting due to diminishing demand and low prices in the US. Other factors contributing to the weak state of the forest industry are declining demand for newsprint due to a slumping newspaper industry; rising electricity costs in Atlantic Canada, which constitute a large portion of operating costs in pulp and paper; and the expiration of the Canada–US lumber agreement in 2016. The weak nature of

the forest industry is revealed by the drop in the value of forest products from $4 billion in 2001 to just over $2.5 billion in 2014 (Table 10.4). The downward cycle, as elsewhere in Canada, is linked to exports to the United States. All forest operations have suffered: logging, sawmilling, and pulp and paper plants. Pulp and paper mills have been hit hard, with numerous mills closing in recent years—in New Brunswick, at Bathurst, Dalhousie, Newcastle, South Nelson, and Saint John; in Nova Scotia, at Port Hawkesbury, Liverpool, and Hantsport; and in Newfoundland, at Stephenville and Grand Falls. Then, too, pulp and paper mills are no longer getting a free ride by disposing of their toxic effluence in water bodies. In fact, they face increasing scrutiny from provincial environmental agencies (Photo 10.13).

In addition, an Indigenous right to timberlands has brought another player into the forest industry.

THE CANADIAN PRESS/Andrew Vaughan

**PHOTO 10.13** Local fishing boats pass the Northern Pulp mill near Pictou, Nova Scotia, in protest against the mill's plan to dump millions of litres of effluent daily into the Northumberland Strait. In the past, such pollution was accepted as the cost of development, but not now. After closing the mill, Northern Pulp has had second thoughts and, in April 2020, the company proposed to build a modern effluent treatment facility (*Pictou Advocate*, 2020).

In 2005, the Supreme Court of Canada ruled that the Mi'kmaq of Nova Scotia and New Brunswick have the right to participate in commercial logging activities but that they must have permits from their respective provinces. The two provincial governments purchased timberlands from Irving Forest Corporation and then allocated logging permits to the Mi'kmaw loggers. Since then, logging has continued to provide some economic support for Mi'kmaw communities.

## Agriculture: Limited in Size

Agriculture is limited by the physical geography in Atlantic Canada. Arable land constitutes less than 5 per cent of the Maritimes. Arable land is scarcer in Newfoundland and Labrador, making up less than 0.1 per cent of its territory. This province has the least amount of farmland—just over 6,000 ha.

Though limited in size, agricultural production significantly contributes to the economy of Atlantic Canada. In 2017, the value of agricultural production in the region was about $1.8 billion (Table 10.4). New Brunswick, Nova Scotia, and Prince Edward Island provide 98 per cent of this figure. Specialty crops, especially potatoes and apples, account for much of this value.

Atlantic Canada has nearly 400,000 ha in cropland and pasture. Almost all of this farmland is concentrated in three main agricultural areas—Prince Edward Island, the Saint John River Valley in New Brunswick, and the Annapolis Valley in Nova Scotia. Potatoes and tree fruit are important cash crops, though vineyards are gaining ground in the Annapolis Valley. In all three agricultural areas, dairy cattle graze on pasture. The dairy industry in Atlantic Canada has benefited from the orderly marketing of fluid milk products through marketing boards.

Prince Edward Island is the leading agricultural area in Atlantic Canada (Photo 10.14). It has almost half of the arable land in the region. Most of Prince Edward Island's 155,000 ha of farmland are devoted to potatoes, hay, and pasture, with the principal cash crop being potatoes. Since the 1980s, most potato growers have had contracts with the island's major potato-processing plants—Irving's processing plant near Summerside and

**PHOTO 10.14** The rich, red soils of Prince Edward Island are famous for growing potatoes, which are the primary cash crop in the province. Prince Edward Island is Canada's leading potato province, responsible for almost one-third of Canadian production. Its potatoes are grown for three specific markets: seed, table potatoes, and processing. Seed potatoes are sold to commercial potato growers and home gardeners to produce next year's crop; table potatoes go to the retail and food service sectors; and processing potatoes are manufactured into french fries, potato chips, and other processed potato products.

Barrett & MacKay/All Canada Photos

McCain's plant at Borden–Carleton now dominate the potato industry on the island. The second major agricultural area, the Saint John River Valley, is in New Brunswick. Its 120,000 ha of arable land make up about one-third of Atlantic Canada's farmland. The Saint John River Valley has the best farmland in New Brunswick. Nova Scotia has nearly one-quarter of Atlantic Canada's farmland, with 105,000 ha. Nova Scotia's famous Annapolis Valley, the region's third agricultural area, is the site of fruit orchards and market gardens. The valley's close proximity to Halifax, the major urban market in Atlantic Canada, has encouraged vegetable gardening. In both New Brunswick and Nova Scotia, potatoes are a major cash crop. Almost all potato farmers in these two provinces seed their potatoes under contract to McCain Foods, a multinational food-processing corporation based in New Brunswick. The company has benefited from NAFTA after the removal of tariffs on its food products, especially french fries and potato chips, for export to the United States, and will continue to do so under the new USMCA.

## Atlantic Canada's Population

Atlantic Canada's population is slowly growing, but this growth is so slow that the region lags well behind the national rate of population increase. As revealed by Statistics Canada, from 2001 to 2016 Atlantic Canada's population increased by only 2.1 per cent, far behind Canada's figure of 17.2 per cent (Table 10.5). Much of the explanation lies in the region's inability to attract immigrants, who represent the main driving force of Canada's population increase, while an added factor is the relocation of its residents to other parts of Canada where the economy is increasing much more rapidly.

Within Atlantic Canada, three trends are apparent. First, Newfoundland and Labrador has experienced population decline, while the Maritime provinces have seen modest growth (Figure 1.3 and Table 10.5). From 1996 to 2016, the Newfoundland and Labrador population declined by just over 32,000. On the other hand, the Maritimes, led by PEI, performed much better than Newfoundland and Labrador over this 20-year period.

### TABLE 10.5    Population Change in Atlantic Canada, 1996–2016

| Province | 1996 | 2006 | 2011 | 2016 | Change 1996–2016 | % Change 1996–2016 |
|---|---|---|---|---|---|---|
| **PE** | 134,557 | 135,851 | 140,204 | 142,907 | 8,350 | +6.2 |
| **NL** | 551,792 | 505,469 | 514,536 | 519,716 | −32,076 | −5.8 |
| **NB** | 738,133 | 729,997 | 751,171 | 747,101 | 8,968 | +1.2 |
| **NS** | 909,282 | 913,462 | 921,727 | 923,598 | 14,316 | +1.6 |
| **Atlantic Canada** | 2,333,764 | 2,284,779 | 2,327,638 | 2,333,322 | −442 | −0.1 |

Sources: Statistics Canada (2002a, 2007, 2012, 2017b).

## Vignette 10.5

### The Passing of the Big Commute

The attraction of the **Big Commute** from Newfoundland to the Alberta oil sands was steady, high-paying jobs. Many thousands of Newfoundland trades workers have regularly commuted to Alberta to work for salaries that started above $100,000 a year, not including overtime. Oil sands companies paid for their air travel from St John's to Fort McMurray, and once there they were fed and housed at company expense (*CBC News*, 2007, 2009; Storey, 2009). It is believed that they brought back hundreds of millions of dollars for Newfoundland and Labrador, a hidden economic boost for a recently anointed "have" province and a monetary infusion that kept some communities viable—and at the same time dependent on the fortunes of an industry practically at the other end of the country.

The hidden costs—to families, to social structure, to individual lives and values—are perhaps even more difficult to discern. Commuting across the country has entailed working 14 days on site, flying for 16 hours, and spending six days at home. The alternative was living hand-to-mouth in Newfoundland (Quinn, 2012).

But all good things end eventually. In the case of long-distance commuting from St John's to Fort McMurray, the end began with the economic downturn in the oil industry in 2014. In that year, as many as 30,000 Newfoundland workers were regularly moving through the St John's airport per week, en route to jobs in the oil patch and in Canada's North by company charter flights. With the continued downturn in the fortunes of the oil sands, commuting to Fort McMurray is no longer an option for Newfoundlanders.

The second trend reveals that the most population increase took place in Atlantic Canada's major cities, making these urban nodes more and more dominant. In fact, this urbanization pattern exists across Canada, and it shows no sign of changing. Atlantic Canada has four large cities: Halifax, St John's, Moncton, and Saint John (Table 10.6). Their share of their respective provincial population ranges from 44 per cent for Halifax and 40 per cent for St John's to 19 per cent for Moncton and 17 per cent for Saint John.

Most of rural Atlantic Canada is found in its smaller cities, often those with a population under 50,000. Significantly, the population growth of these smaller cities is much lower. From 2001 to 2016, this pattern of smaller growth in the centres with a population under 50,000 is confirmed by 10 of 11 of these cities having a population increase below 6 per cent (Table 10.7). Labrador City saw its population dropped by nearly 7 per cent over this 15-year period. Low prices for iron ore resulted in layoffs, and most workers left for other places. Urban centres losing population over this 15-year period were led by Campbellton, NB, whose population declined by 16 per cent (Table 10.7). With

the closure of businesses, few jobs are available and young people are leaving to seek work in other parts of the province, especially Moncton. Cape Breton, a former coal mining and steel centre, experienced a population decline of 7.1 per cent over the 2001–16 period.

In sum, Atlantic Canada remains the least urbanized region of Canada with just over half of its population living in urban centres. In comparison with other southern regions, the difference is both striking and an indicator of how much more urban growth (or rural decline) in Canada's regions is likely. At the top end of the scale, Ontario and British Columbia have close to 90 per cent of total population classified as urban. As well, Atlantic Canada has none of Canada's largest cities: Halifax (Vignette 10.6) ranks twelfth in population. Equally significant, Atlantic Canada's fractured geography prevents Halifax from serving as the primary city for the region. Instead, Halifax serves as the urban focal point for the Maritimes, while St John's fills a similar role for Newfoundland and Labrador. Halifax's advantage is its deep, ice-free harbour, its role as a naval base, and its relatively large population/

**TABLE 10.6  Census Metropolitan Areas in Atlantic Canada, 2001–2016**

| Centre | Population 2001 | Population 2016 | % Change |
|---|---|---|---|
| Saint John, NB | 122,678 | 126,202 | 2.9 |
| Moncton, NB | 118,678 | 144,810 | 22.0 |
| St John's, NL | 172,918 | 205,955 | 19.1 |
| Halifax, NS | 359,183 | 403,390 | 12.3 |
| Total | 773,457 | 880,357 | 13.8 |
| Atlantic Canada | 2,285,729 | 2,333,322 | 2.1 |
| Canada | 30,007,094 | 35,151,728 | 17.2 |

Source: Adapted from Statistics Canada (2002b, 2007, 2017b).

**TABLE 10.7    Urban Centres in Atlantic Canada, 2001–2016**

| Urban Centre | Population 2001 | Population 2016 | % Change |
|---|---|---|---|
| Labrador City, NL | 7,744 | 7,220 | –6.8 |
| Gander, NL | 9,651 | 13,234 | 37.1 |
| Bay Roberts, NL | 10,531 | 11,083 | 5.2 |
| Grand Falls–Windsor, NL | 13,340 | 14,171 | 6.2 |
| Campbellton, NB | 18,820 | 15,746 | –16.3 |
| Summerside, PE | 14,654 | 16,587 | 13.2 |
| Edmundston, NB | 22,173 | 23,524 | 5.9 |
| Kentville, NS | 25,172 | 26,222 | 4.2 |
| Miramichi, NB | 18,508 | 27,523 | 48.7 |
| Corner Brook, NL | 26,153 | 31,917 | 22.0 |
| Bathurst, NB | 32,523 | 31,110 | –3.0 |
| New Glasgow, NS | 36,735 | 34,487 | –4.3 |
| Truro, NS | 44,276 | 45,753 | 3.3 |
| Charlottetown, PE | 57,234 | 69,325 | 21.1 |
| Fredericton, NB | 81,346 | 101,760 | 25.1 |
| Cape Breton, NS | 109,330 | 98,722 | –9.7 |

Sources: Statistics Canada (2002b, 2017b).

Canaport LNG

**PHOTO 10.15** The strategic location of the Canaport LNG facility, Canada's only operational LNG terminal, is ideal for access to the huge New England energy market. Liquefied natural gas arrives from overseas, mainly the Middle East. Here, the liquefied gas is stored in containers at –162ºC, then is regasified and sent by pipeline to New England markets.

See **Chapter 4**, "Urban Population," page 123, for further understanding of Atlantic Canada's lagging urbanization.

market. Halifax serves as a major container port and shipbuilding centre. The Confederation Bridge, of course, serves to bind PEI to New Brunswick and Nova Scotia (Photo 10.17). On the other hand, St John's today is focused on offshore oil, the fishing industry, and government services, and is a centre for Arctic marine research and resupply. The only other CMAs in the Atlantic region are Moncton and Saint John, New Brunswick. Within the Maritimes, Saint John is ideally situated as an energy hub. Moncton is a "gateway" to both Nova Scotia and PEI, and with a large francophone population is a "gateway," too, to the Acadian French area of northern New Brunswick.

## Vignette 10.6

### Halifax

Halifax, the capital of Nova Scotia and the largest city in Atlantic Canada, was founded in 1749. By 2020, Halifax had a population of approximately 413,000, well over its 2016 figure of 403,390. As in the past, its strategic location allows Halifax to play a major role on the Atlantic coast as a naval centre, an international port, and a key element in the Atlantic Gateway concept. Along the east coast of North America, its deep, ice-free harbour is ideally suited for huge post-Panamax ships. Yet, because of its relative distance from the major markets in North America and its reliance on transferring goods between ships, trains, and trucks, Halifax cannot provide lower transportation costs than New York. The economic strength of Halifax rests on its defence and port functions, its service function for smaller cities and towns in Nova Scotia, and its role as a provincial administrative centre. Halifax also has a small manufacturing base and a growing service sector, as well as a small but growing high-technology industry. In 2013, the federal government awarded a 30-year shipbuilding contract to Irving Shipbuilding, which has stimulated the economy of Halifax and secured its continued population growth.

**PHOTO 10.16** The Halifax skyline hugs its harbour.

Barrett & MacKay/All Canada Photos

Barrett & MacKay/All Canada Photos

**PHOTO 10.17** The Confederation Bridge reduces Atlantic Canada's fractured geography by connecting Prince Edward Island with New Brunswick. As an integral part of the Trans-Canada Highway system, at 12.9 km it is the longest bridge over ice-covered waters in the world. After the bridge's opening in 1997, the economic impact on Prince Edward Island has been significant in four areas: increased tourism; a real estate boom; expanded potato production and potato-based processed foods; and greater export of time-sensitive and high-priced seafood. These economic gains help to account for the province's increased population. For instance, from 1996 to 2016, PEI's population increased at a faster rate (6.2 per cent) than that of the other provinces in Atlantic Canada (Table 10.5).

## Summary

Atlantic Canada, on the eastern rim of Canada, remains a slow-growing region. Low commodity prices, high unemployment, and strong out-migration are common to all four provinces. Yet, Atlantic Canada, but particularly the Maritimes, has a second chance. Its major cities, led by Halifax, exhibit strong growth. Unfortunately, Newfoundland and Labrador faces a much harder reality marked by a steady population decline and the Muskrat Falls debacle. Low oil prices also may result in the closure of the Come-by-Chance oil refinery.

Within Atlantic Canada, Newfoundland and Labrador remains dependent on its natural resources, pushed along by its fisheries, offshore petroleum resources, and rich Labrador nickel deposits. Huge cost overruns for the construction of the Muskrat Falls hydroelectric project threaten to sink its economy, forcing a possible federal bailout. Its declining population and high unemployment rate seem destined to continue into the next decade. On the other hand, the Maritime provinces, while still among the "have-nots," are moving forward. Economic rejuvenation has appeared in the few major cities, while a surge in lobster exports has breathed new life into the fisheries. The vulnerable nature of exports was brought home in 2020 when sales to China suddenly evaporated with the arrival of a global pandemic. How long this might last and what longer-term impacts the COVID-19 scourge might bring are yet to be known.

What does the future for Atlantic Canada hold? Is Atlantic Canada destined to remain a slow-growing region? Outside the urban centres, the economic situation seems hopeless unless global prices for its commodities rise sharply. Within the core/periphery construct, Atlantic Canada fits the model of a declining region, and past efforts to break out of that mould have so far failed.

The resource sector, including oil, is struggling because of low global prices. Fisheries, the traditional economic anchor, appeared to make a comeback based on exports to China. Unexpectedly, this market dried up. Just what the rebooting of a post-pandemic Atlantic Canada will look like is unclear, but Atlantic Canada seems destined to remain a slow-growing member of Canada's six regions.

## Challenge Questions

1. Offshore oil and iron/nickel mining have provided Newfoundland and Labrador with an opportunity to break its downward economic spiral, but what global events caused these developments to fail to fulfill this goal?
2. Why does the flooding of a reservoir cause a sharp increase in methylmercury?
3. Since the 1999 *Marshall* decision, Indigenous fishers have gained a foothold in a profitable commercial fishing industry. Why is the purchase of Clearwater Seafoods so critical to gaining more fishing licences and access to offshore fishing?
4. Why are the major cities of Atlantic Canada enjoying population growth while rural areas are losing population or seeing very slow growth?

## Essay Questions

1. At first, the prospects for Newfoundland and Labrador experiencing an economic turnaround looked bright with the announcement of the construction of two hydroelectric dams on the Lower Churchill River. In April 2016, the new CEO of Nalcor Energy, the provincial energy corporation, called Muskrat Falls a "boondoggle" that would push the provincial government deep into debt and force a sharp rise in prices for electricity. What happened between the original announcement and the end of the construction of this huge project?
2. Halifax is benefiting from a federally funded navy shipbuilding project. Secure for now, could the economic shutdown of Canada's economy due to COVID-19 force the federal government to slow or, worse yet, cancel further shipbuilding contracts?

# 11 The Territorial North

## Chapter Overview

Topics and issues examined in this chapter include the following:

- The evolving concept of the Territorial North.
- The dualistic nature of the region's population and economy.
- Governance, the birth of Nunavut, and the impact of modern land claim agreements.
- Climate change, the Northwest Passage, and Arctic sovereignty.
- Megaprojects.

## Introduction

More and more, the Territorial North is transforming, albeit slowly, into a place where Indigenous governance holds sway and where Arctic conditions no longer dominate the physical landscape. Resource development remains a key element, but how it can better involve northerners and their governments remains a puzzle. The solution may be buried in acts of reconciliation, and those acts may take much of the twenty-first century.

The Territorial North is distinct from other geographic regions. Located in the highest latitudes of Canada, far beyond the economic heartland of Canada, this sparsely populated land remains a paradox, where Indigenous governance is emerging while its resource-based economy is faltering. Indeed, its oil and gas sector present two challenges. First, this sector is suffering from low global prices. Second, Arctic oil and gas no longer have the blessing of the federal government. Unlike other regions, its economic base is extremely narrow and heavily dependent on financial support from Ottawa. In this decade of the twenty-first century, COVID-19 dominates events in the North, especially its impact on four key issues:

1. the evolving place of Indigenous peoples;
2. the rapid pace of climate change;
3. Arctic sovereignty; and
4. resource development.

When exploring these topics, what does the future hold for the Territorial North and its Indigenous peoples?

← Bylot Island, Nunavut, is uninhabited by humans, but Inuit hunters have travelled there for centuries due to its seal, fish, and whale populations.

Cavan Images/Alamy Stock Photo

## The Territorial North within Canada and the World

The Territorial North has the largest geographic area of the six regions of Canada, but it contains the smallest population and has the weakest economy. Its geographic extent stretches over 3.9 million km², roughly 70 per cent in the Arctic and 30 per cent in the Subarctic. The Arctic Ocean provides additional space for the Territorial North. In the past, the Arctic Ocean was a frozen body of water for most of the year. In the twenty-first century, the Arctic Ocean has seen more open water in the late summer than ever before, transforming the Northwest Passage into a more active international waterway and throwing into question Canadian control of this body of water.

### FIGURE 11.1 The Territorial North

The Territorial North consists of three territories. Their borders are fixed, although the marine boundary between Yukon and Alaska remains unsettled. As well, the seabed beneath the international waters of the Arctic Ocean has yet to be determined. At the moment, three countries—Russia, Denmark, and Canada—all claim the seabed beneath the North Pole.

Source: *Atlas of Canada*, 2006, The Territories, atlas.nrcan.gc.ca/site/english/maps/reference/provincesterritories/northern_territories. Reproduced with the permission of the Minister of Public Works and Government Services Canada, 2013.

The Territorial North is caught in the vice of climate change. Unlike in the past, the physical geography of this region is no longer stable. Instead, climate change presents a natural force that is altering the physical face of the North and forcing governments to address the consequences for the inhabitants of the North. Already the thawing of permafrost is causing havoc, while open water is becoming more and more common, making commercial shipping across the Northwest Passage a more regular event. As a result, Canada faces increasing pressure to accept this sea route as an international body of water rather than one under its control.

The Indigenous population in the Territorial North continues to increase, from 51.7 per cent of the total population in 2001 to 52.5 per cent in 2016. This trend is based on high fertility rates for the Indigenous population and the decline in southerners coming to the territories for resource and public service jobs. Yet, this region has a shortage of skilled workers in the Indigenous workforce and therefore senior positions in the resource and public sectors are still held by southerners. While the official unemployment rate for 2016 was 11 per cent, those falling into the category of underemployed in the Indigenous workforce likely push this rate well above 20 per cent (see Figure 11.2). Many people, particularly in small communities, operate in an informal economy where non-commercial hunting and fishing play a significant role.

## The Way Forward to a More Sustainable North

The emergence of post-colonial Indigenous governance began in the last century with the federal acceptance of Indigenous title to traditional land and the resulting emergence of comprehensive land claim negotiations. The modern treaty era began in 1973 after the Supreme Court of Canada decision (*Calder et al. v. Attorney General of British Columbia*) recognized Indigenous rights for the first time. This decision led to the development of the federal Comprehensive Land Claims Policy. Concurrently, but stemming from Quebec court decisions, the James Bay and Northern Quebec Agreement was concluded

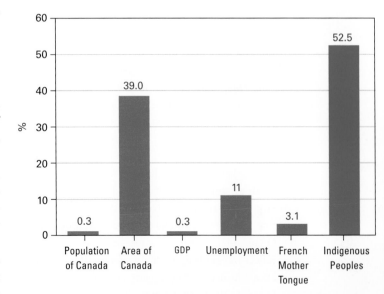

**FIGURE 11.2 The Territorial North basic statistics, 2016**

Note: Percentages of population, area, and GDP are based on Canada; unemployment, French home language, and Indigenous population percentages are based on the Territorial North.

Sources: Tables 1.1, 1.2, 11.1.

in 1975. Professor Chris Southcott (2018, p. 3) summarizes this as the start of the way forward:

> During the 1970s, southern Canada changed its perception of resource development in the Canadian North. At the beginning of the decade, most observers outside of the Yukon and Northwest Territories, as well as many within the territories, saw resource development as something that was going to be of great benefit to the North (Rea, 1968). This changed in the 1970s when the voices of the Indigenous peoples of the region first started to be heard. The Berger Inquiry of that decade was probably the best known instance of people outside the region being able to hear what Indigenous communities thought about resource development in their region (Berger, 1977).

The first modern land claim agreement (LAC) took place in 1984 when the Inuvialuit achieved control over their land and economy. However, this agreement did not include local self-government—that dimension of LACs was added in the 2005 Tlicho LAC. Within the Tlicho (Dogrib) First Nation, the impact benefit agreement (IBA) signed with the diamond company Diavik provided specific employment benefits. For most employed northerners, the public sector, but especially the three territorial governments, represents the major employer.

Governance represents a first step towards an Indigenous style of economy and control over their society (Vignette 11.1). The creation of Nunavut, a quasi-Inuit government, flowed out of the Inuit LAC and pushed the level of Indigenous governance from local to territorial. However, Ottawa rejected an ethnic governance for Nunavut and insisted on one that included all residents. Does such a demand by Ottawa demonstrate an imposed solution, or does it reflect the existing guidelines for territorial governance within Canada (Vignette 11.1)? Lackenbauer and Légaré (2018, p. 285) regard Nunavut as a "litmus test of the evolving process of Confederation-building." In other words, does political space at the territorial level rule out a purely ethnic form of governance? Still, the concept of nested federalism in the Arctic strikes a fresh chord in the ongoing evolution of Indigenous governance (Wilson et al., 2020). But why the Arctic and not the Subarctic? The answer lies in the homogeneity of the Inuit culture and the dominance of its Inuit population. Equally important, the Arctic was spared the imposed forms of Indigenous governance flowing from the Indian Act.

The way forward is both complicated and uncertain. However, northern governance may offer a path towards a sustainable economy by recasting resource development in a more progressive form.

Going beyond IBAs, such a form might involve partnerships between Indigenous organizations and territorial governments and resource companies. Through such working arrangements, profits from the development would be shared more widely.

## Population

Few people live in the Territorial North. In fact, the town of Lethbridge, Alberta, has a larger population than the three territories comprising the Territorial North. With just under 114,000 residents, the Territorial North has by far the smallest population of the six geographic regions and is therefore the least heard by Ottawa. While its tiny populations make it one of the world's most sparsely populated areas, the majority of people live and work in the three urban centres of Whitehorse, Yellowknife, and Iqaluit. The attraction of these three capital cities lies in employment opportunities generated by their territorial governments.

Unlike the other geographic regions, Indigenous peoples form a slight majority of the population in the Territorial North (Table 1.1). At the time of Confederation, the Indigenous population was declining, an ongoing result of the impact of European diseases. However, in the twentieth century their numbers rebounded sharply, largely due to improved access to health care and store foods (Bone, 2019).

The North is divided into three territories—Yukon, Northwest Territories, and Nunavut. Within each territory, the percentage of Indigenous peoples varies from a decided majority in Nunavut, to a

**THINK ABOUT IT**

Can you make a case that Nunavut is really a hybrid version of an ethnic territory?

**THINK ABOUT IT**

The Arctic seabed claim by Canada, if granted by UNCLOS, would represent a major extension of Canada's territory. But should it fall under federal jurisdiction or should the responsibility for its governance be assigned to the three territorial governments?

## Vignette 11.1

### Territorial Expansion: Rupert's Land, the Arctic Islands, and the Arctic Seabed

The Territorial North fell under Canadian jurisdiction in three stages. Until the last stage, Indigenous peoples were not involved in this decision-making process. First, the transfer of Rupert's Land to Canada by Britain took place in 1870. Second, Great Britain transferred the Arctic Islands to Canada in 1880. Third, in 1985, Canada declared a 200-mile economic zone that extended its control over the Arctic Ocean. In addition, in the same year Canada announced its Arctic Waters Pollution Prevention Act. Still, the last remaining territory that may become part of Canada consists of a portion of the seabed of the Arctic Ocean, which now lies in international waters. Canada submitted its claim to the United Nations Convention on the Law of the Sea (UNCLOS) in 2019 (Natural Resources Canada, 2019a).

balance in the Northwest Territories, to a minority in Yukon. The predominance of Indigenous peoples reflects several demographic factors. First, Indigenous peoples were born and raised in the North. Few leave the region. Second, Indigenous peoples, but particularly the Inuit, have a high rate of natural increase, thus fuelling their numbers and increasing the northern population. Third, relatively few southern Canadians have chosen to live in the Territorial North, especially Nunavut (Table 11.1). The explanation for the limited number of southerners relocating to the North lies in the relatively few economic opportunities. Most who do move to the North are temporary migrants that often return south within five to 10 years.

Several demographic factors stand out for the Territorial North. One is the heavy concentration of population in the territorial capitals (Figure 11.3).

**THINK ABOUT IT**

While Inuit population growth rate is the main element causing the number of people in the Territorial North to increase, the 2016 census reported that the number of Inuit residing in southern Canada has also reached an all-time high.

**TABLE 11.1  Total Population and Indigenous Population, Territorial North, 2016**

| Territory | Total Population | Indigenous Population | % Indigenous Population |
|---|---|---|---|
| Yukon | 35,874 | 8,195 | 22.8 |
| Northwest Territories | 41,786 | 20,860 | 50.0 |
| Nunavut | 35,944 | 30,550 | 85.0 |
| Territorial North | 113,604 | 59,605 | 52.5 |

Source: Adapted from Statistics Canada (2018).

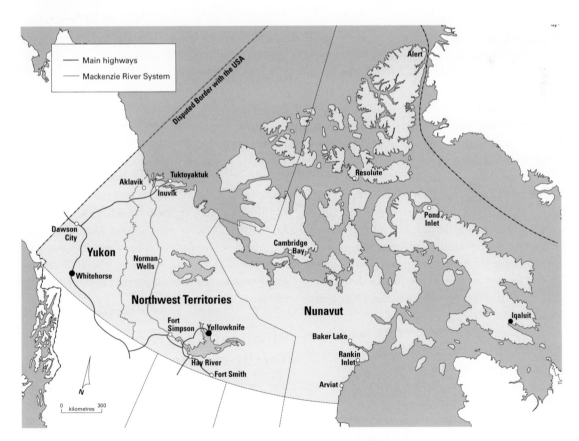

**FIGURE 11.3  Major urban centres in the Territorial North**

The major cities are the territorial capitals: Whitehorse, Yellowknife, and Iqaluit. With most government jobs found in these cities, they have a strong economic base compared to other northern centres. As a result, these three cities are expected to see their populations increase in the coming years, while the reverse is likely to happen in many of the smaller centres.

**TABLE 11.2    Population of the Three Capitals**

| Capital | Population 2006 | Population 2016 | Percentage Change | Percentage of Territory Population, 2006 | Percentage of Territory Population, 2016 |
|---|---|---|---|---|---|
| Iqaluit | 4,796 | 7,590 | 57.3 | 16.3 | 20.9 |
| Yellowknife | 18,700 | 19,569 | 10.4 | 45.1 | 45.2 |
| Whitehorse | 22,898 | 28,225 | 24.3 | 75.4 | 77.0 |

Sources: Statistics Canada (2012, 2016); Nunavut Bureau of Statistics (2016); NWT Bureau of Statistics (2016); Yukon Bureau of Statistics (2016).

**TABLE 11.3    Components of Population Growth for the Territories, 2016**

| Demographic Event | Canada | Yukon | NWT | Nunavut | Territorial North |
|---|---|---|---|---|---|
| Births per 1,000 persons | 10.6 | 11.6 | 14.4 | 24.3 | 17.0 |
| Deaths per 1,000 persons | 7.4 | 5.7 | 5.3 | 4.9 | 5.3 |
| Natural rate of increase (%) | 0.3 | 0.6 | 0.9 | 1.9 | 1.2 |
| Net interprovincial migrants | | 206 | −911 | 117 | −588 |

Source: Adapted from Statistics Canada (2020a).

Whitehorse provides the strongest example, with 77 per cent of Yukon's total population residing in this capital city in 2016 (Table 11.2). A second factor is that the North's population is increasing at a rapid rate. From 2001 to 2016, the population of the Territorial North increased by 27 per cent. This population growth is due exclusively to a high rate of natural increase. Most of this increase comes from the Indigenous population, especially the Inuit. Nunavut, for example, exhibits the highest rate of natural increase of the three territories, while Yukon reflects a strong in-migration, largely due to job opportunities. Not surprisingly, isolated mineral projects, ranging from diamond to iron mines, no longer result in resource towns but rely heavily on air commuting for their labour force, with the vast majority coming from southern locations.

The population of the Territorial North is also affected by interprovincial movement. In-migration to the North normally occurs when economic expansion creates jobs, thus drawing workers and their families from southern Canada. When economic contraction takes place, these same workers and their families often return to southern Canada. As Table 11.3 indicates, the outflow from the Northwest Territories reflects a sluggish economic situation, while the inflow in Yukon marks a small upswing in its economy. Another feature is the increase in mobility of the Indigenous population. While the numbers remain small, more and more Indigenous migrants have moved to southern cities in search of jobs and urban amenities, such as post-secondary education, training, and specialized medical care. For instance, until the twenty-first century, virtually all Inuit lived in the Arctic. In 2016, 27 per cent resided outside of Nunangat (the Arctic), including 1,280 in Ottawa and 1,110 in Edmonton (Statistics Canada, 2019). The geographic pattern of this drift to the south reflects the location of these major cities and the four Inuit regional homelands. Edmonton, for instance, houses mainly Inuit from the western Arctic, while Ottawa draws from Nunavik and Nunavut. If this trend continues, the 2021 census might well record over 30 per cent of Inuit residing outside of Nunangat.

## Physical Geography of the Territorial North

The Territorial North is undergoing an amazing physical transformation. How far this warming will reach remains uncertain. For example, will the Arctic return to temperatures common in a warmer geological period known as The Last Interglacial (LIG) that took place 130,000 to 116,000 years ago? At that time, all forms of ice had melted, leaving the Arctic Ocean an open sea (Guarino et al., 2020).

The discussion in **Chapter 4**, "Population Density," page 120, provides insight into the issue of the limited capacity of the Arctic to support people.

vadimgouida/iStockphoto

**PHOTO 11.1** The South Nahanni is one of the world's great wild rivers. Located in the boreal wilderness of Nahanni National Park Reserve in the southwest part of the Northwest Territories, this untamed river is seen surging through the steep-walled First Canyon. Downstream, its waters rush past hot springs, plunge over a waterfall twice the height of Niagara, and cut through canyons more than 1 km deep.

When this transformation will occur remains equally puzzling—could it occur in this century or the next? When this transformation is complete, the physical processes shaping the landscapes will have changed to those found in more temperate climates. Stream erosion, for example, will play a dominating role while frost shattering will not be substantial.

The initial impact of a warmer climate involves the melting of all types of ice: **sea ice**, ground ice (permafrost), and glaciers. One dramatic example took place in August 2020 when the Milne Ice Shelf, located at the edge of Ellesmere Island in northern Nunavut, was the latest victim of global warming. Most of this huge ice shelf broke loose from the land and collapsed into the sea. At the same time, biological impacts are taking place, but at a much slower pace. Plants and animals are extending their presence into higher and higher latitudes. Eventually, the Arctic zone could disappear, perhaps as early as the next century.

In this decade, however, the physical geography of the Territorial North retains much of its characteristic cold environment. Permafrost, while retreating, remains a factor. The bottom line is that while warming is taking place, cold still persists throughout most of the year and affects human activities. The cold environment includes permafrost (Figure 2.9) and long winters with sub-zero temperatures. The region's main climate zones, the Arctic and the Subarctic (Figure 2.5), are shifting in their geographic extent as the Subarctic slowly stretches northward while the geographic extent of the Arctic shrinks.[1] In the classic Arctic climate, summer is limited to a few warm days interspersed with colder weather, including freezing temperatures and snow flurries. The Subarctic climate has a longer summer that lasts at least one month. During the short but warm summer, the daily maximum temperature often exceeds 20°C and sometimes reaches 30°C.

Arctic air masses still dominate the weather patterns in the Territorial North. They remain characterized by dry, cold weather and originate over the ice-covered Arctic Ocean, moving southward in the winter. However, as the ice cover diminishes, the character of Arctic air masses is changing.

In the past, the frozen Arctic Ocean kept summer temperatures cool even though the sun remains above the horizon for most of the summer. These cool summer temperatures, which Köppen defined as an average mean of less than 10°C in the warmest month, prevent normal tree growth. For that reason, the Arctic climate region has tundra vegetation, which includes lichens, mosses, grasses, and low shrubs. However, the natural vegetation is responding to warmer and longer summers, causing the tree line to slowly shift northwards. In the very cold Arctic Archipelago, much of the ground is bare, exposing the surface material. As there is little precipitation in the Arctic Archipelago (often less than 20 cm per year), this area is sometimes described as a "polar desert."

The Arctic climate does extend into lower latitudes in two areas: along the coasts of Hudson Bay and the Labrador Sea. These cold bodies of water chill the summer air along the adjacent coasts. In this way, the Arctic climate extends along the coasts

**PHOTO 11.2** The Yukon River Valley at Dawson City. For Indigenous peoples as well as for fur traders and prospectors, this long and winding river has been an important transportation route in the history of the Territorial North.

of Ontario, Quebec, and Labrador well below 60°N, sometimes extending as far south as 55°N. In the face of a warming climate, these Arctic intrusions below the sixtieth parallel may disappear sometime in the twenty-first century.

The geology of the Territorial North provides much of its wealth. For example, the sedimentary basins of the Interior Plains and Arctic Lands contain large deposits of oil and natural gas. Even the sedimentary strata beneath the Arctic Ocean just beyond Canada's current jurisdiction hold vast energy deposits. But will these deposits be left in the ground or developed? The answer to that question depends on two factors: the demand for oil and gas in the second half of the twenty-first century and whether a political decision is made not to develop these resources in order to slow emissions of greenhouse gases. So far, Canada's answer seems to favour the "leave it in the ground" approach. Evidence of this direction came in 2016 when Canada placed a five-year moratorium on Arctic offshore oil and gas exploration. In 2022, this moratorium will be reviewed and might be extended for another five or even 10 years.

The Cordillera and Canadian Shield of the Territorial North have already yielded some of their mineral wealth to prospectors and geologists. These minerals include diamonds, gold, lead, uranium, and zinc. Since its discovery in 1962, an extremely high-grade iron deposit on Baffin Island has attracted mining companies. The Mary River Project, underway since 2015, originally called for mining the ore, shipping to port by rail, and then to markets in Europe by ship, but sharply falling iron ore prices have put some of these plans on hold and even threaten the firm with bankruptcy. This economic uncertainty raises the question, "Are mega resource projects unable to support the economy of the Territorial North?"

## Environmental Challenge: Climate Change

The Territorial North is facing a major environmental challenge—the warming of its land and waters. As the ice retreats from the Arctic Ocean, the forces of climate change are transforming the Arctic, tightening the links between this seemingly remote region and the rest of the world in matters of ocean shipping and resource development, leaving questions of sustainable development and the pursuit of peace for future considerations. However, the vast petroleum deposits under the Arctic Ocean now appear to have lost much of their attraction for two reasons: the threat of their commercial development to the Arctic waters and the shift away from fossil fuels to renewable forms of energy.

Climate change is more rapid in the Arctic than the rest of the world. Temperature increases in the Arctic are much higher than in the provinces because of the **albedo effect**, whereby greater solar warming of the land and water occurs because of the reduction of ice and snow cover. The Arctic Ocean is particularly vulnerable to this change. In the late summer of 2020, Arctic Ocean sea ice extended over 3.7 million km², signalling the second-lowest in the 42-year continuous satellite record (Ramsayer, 2020). According to Stroeve and Notz, the Arctic Ocean might be free of summer ice by the mid-twenty-first century, but the actual

## Contested Terrain 11.1

### Less Ice, More Whales

Climate change affects the Inuit way of life, which is dependent on shore ice for hunting seals and other sea mammals. Thinner ice than normal endangers hunters travelling on snowmobiles, while less ice than normal reduces the time available for fishing and hunting marine mammals. Yet, the warming of Arctic waters as a consequence of climate change is causing a variety of whales found in the North Atlantic Ocean to spend more time in the Arctic Ocean, possibly providing a secure marine food source for the Inuit.

timing is a function of natural climate variability and anthropogenic warming caused by increased atmospheric $CO_2$ concentrations (Stroeve & Notz, 2018; Thackeray & Hall, 2019).

As discussed in Chapter 2, climate change includes the increase over time of the earth's average surface temperature. Several factors are involved in greater temperature increases occurring in the Arctic, such as heat transfer from lower latitudes to higher ones, but the primary factor is the albedo effect. Light from the sun takes the form of short-wave radiation while energy emitted from the earth's surface takes the form of long-wave radiation. Long-wave radiation is more readily absorbed by the atmosphere and thus warms the atmosphere whereas short-wave radiation escapes into outer space without warming the atmosphere. The Arctic, historically, has had a high albedo because of its cover of snow and ice, which means most solar energy is reflected back into outer space without warming the atmosphere. However, as ice and snow cover decreases in the Arctic, its albedo will shift from high to low, meaning that the solar energy reaching the Arctic will be more effective in warming the atmosphere and thus raising temperatures well above their long-term averages (Figure 11.4).

The impact of climate change in the Arctic is expected to have both positive and negative impacts on the wildlife and northern peoples. By the end of the twenty-first century, climate change may result in an ice-free Arctic Ocean each summer, thus allowing for unimpeded ocean transportation across the Northwest Passage, including shipments of petroleum and mineral deposits in the Arctic. The vast copper and zinc deposits located inland at Izok and High Lake in Nunavut are a case in point. Land transport, with the melting of permafrost, will be another matter. Wildlife will be affected. Already scientists have noted negative impacts on polar bears but a positive effect on seal populations. The huge migrating caribou herds that have their calving grounds in the Arctic could be affected.

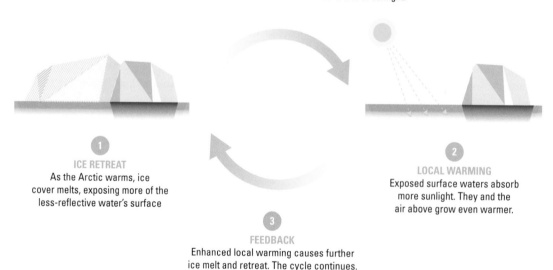

**Sea Ice Albedo Feedback Cycle**
A major factor in the rapid warming of icy places like the Arctic is sea ice albedo feedback, a cycle that makes warming more severe where ice is lost. A surface's "albedo" is how reflective it is of sunlight.

**1 ICE RETREAT**
As the Arctic warms, ice cover melts, exposing more of the less-reflective water's surface

**2 LOCAL WARMING**
Exposed surface waters absorb more sunlight. They and the air above grow even warmer.

**3 FEEDBACK**
Enhanced local warming causes further ice melt and retreat. The cycle continues.

**FIGURE 11.4  Sea ice albedo feedback cycle**

In the past, ice covered the Arctic Ocean, and in doing so reflected much of the incoming solar energy. As the ice cover diminished in extent, warming of the ocean waters increased. According to the UCLA Center for Climate Science, the Arctic Ocean could be, like Hudson Bay, "functionally ice free" in the summer by 2044 and no later than 2067.

Source: © 2019 UCLA Center for Climte Science.

The reduction of the size of calving grounds would have a negative impact on preferred space for reproduction. The Dene and Inuit communities that rely on these herds for much of their country food may have to purchase more of their food from local stores. On the other hand, more open and warmer seas would permit a return of large numbers of bowhead whales and other marine species to Arctic waters, allowing greater harvests by the Inuit.

## Historical Geography of the Territorial North

### European Contact

At the times of initial contact with Europeans, seven Inuit groups and seven Indigenous groups belonging to the Athapaskan language family (also known as Dene) occupied the Territorial North. The Inuit stretched across the Arctic: the Mackenzie Delta Inuit lived in the west; further east were the Copper Inuit, Netsilik Inuit, Iglulik Inuit, Baffinland Inuit, Caribou Inuit, and Sadlermiut Inuit. Inuit also lived in northern Quebec and Labrador. By the early twentieth century, two groups (most of the Mackenzie Delta Inuit and all of the Sadlermiut Inuit) would succumb to diseases that European whalers brought to the Arctic. The Indigenous tribes that resided in what is today the territorial Subarctic were the Kutchin, Hare, Tutchone, Dogrib, Tahltan, Slavey, and Chipewyan. More recently, these groups are known in the aggregate as the Dene. These Indigenous peoples had developed hunting techniques well adapted to two cold but different environments. Cultural traits, such as the ethic of sharing, developed from this dependency on the land and sea for food.[2]

### Early European Exploration

Though the Vikings were the first to make contact with northern Indigenous peoples around 1000, little is known of those encounters. At that time, the Arctic Ocean had much less ice cover because of a warmer climate. Five centuries later, the Arctic had become much colder. In 1576, Martin Frobisher, in searching for a Northwest Passage to the Far East, reached Baffin Island.[3] Unfortunately for Frobisher, his expedition took place at the height of the Little Ice Age, and his ships met with heavy ice conditions in Davis Strait (which separates Baffin Island from Greenland).

Over the next three centuries, the search for a Northwest Passage through Arctic waters led to misadventure for various European explorers, including John Franklin, whose famous last expedition ended in disaster with all hands lost (Vignette 11.2). However, cultural exchange between Europeans and the original inhabitants of these lands remained limited until the nineteenth century, when the trade in fur pelts and whaling peaked in North America.

### Whaling and the Fur Trade

Whaling began in the late sixteenth century in the waters off Baffin Island, with whalers from the Basque Country of Spain and France among the first to exploit this resource. During those early years, whalers had little opportunity or desire to make contact with the Inuit living along the Arctic coast. The Inuit probably felt the same, particularly those who had heard stories of the nasty encounter with Frobisher's men. During early summer, whaling ships set sail from British, Dutch, and German ports for Baffin Bay, where they hunted whales for several months—for the fat to be rendered into lamp oil and for baleen or so-called "whalebone" from the jaws of right, bowhead, and gray whales used in the manufacture of such items as umbrellas, buggy whips, and corsets. By September, all ships would return home. In the early nineteenth century, the expeditions of John Ross (1817) and William Parry (1819) sailed farther north and west into Lancaster Sound. Their search for the Northwest Passage had limited success but opened virgin whaling grounds for whalers. These new grounds were of great interest as improved whaling technology had reduced the whale population in the eastern Arctic. In fact, the period from 1820 to 1840 is regarded as the peak of whaling activity in this area. At that time, up to 100 vessels were whaling in Davis Strait and Baffin Bay.

As whaling ships went further to find better whaling grounds, it became impossible to return to their home ports within one season. By the 1850s, the practice of "wintering over" (that is, allowing

**THINK ABOUT IT**

Photo 3.2, page 65, illustrates a skirmish between Frobisher's men and the Baffin Island Inuit. Such hostilities were not unusual. In the late nineteenth century, for example, the Labrador Inuit and settlers still had bloody encounters. Do such encounters in the form of vigorous protests still occur in Labrador along the Indigenous/non-Indigenous faultline?

The Little Ice Age is discussed in **Vignette 2.12**, "Fluctuations in World Temperatures," page 46.

## Vignette 11.2

### The Northwest Passage and the Franklin Search

In 1845, Sir John Franklin headed a British naval expedition to search for the elusive Northwest Passage through the Arctic waters of North America. This British naval expedition set out at the end of the Little Ice Age, meaning that ice conditions would have been much more challenging than those occurring today. Franklin and his crew never returned. Their disappearance in the Canadian Arctic set off one of the world's greatest rescue operations, which involved upward of a dozen search parties and was conducted on land and by sea and stretched over a decade. The British Admiralty organized the first search party in 1848. Lady Franklin sent the last expedition to look for her husband in 1857. These expeditions accomplished three things: (1) they found evidence confirming the loss of Franklin's ships (the *Erebus* and *Terror*) and the death of their crews; (2) one rescue ship under the command of Robert McClure almost completed the Northwest Passage; and (3) the massive rescue effort resulted in a greater knowledge and mapping of the numerous islands and various routes to the north and west of Baffin Island in the Arctic Ocean. The exact sequence of events that led to the Franklin disaster is not known. However, archaeological work, conducted in the early 1980s on the remains of members of the expedition, revealed that lead poisoning, possibly caused by the tin cans in the ships' food supplies, may have contributed to the tragic demise of the Franklin expedition. In 2010, Parks Canada began a serious underwater search for the two ships. At the end of the summer of 2016, both ships, the HMS *Erebus* (2014) and the HMS *Terror* (2016), had been located about 100 km apart—the *Terror* in Terror Bay offshore of King William Island and to the south the *Erebus* on the bottom of Queen Maud Gulf near O'Reilly Island just off the coast of the Adelaide Peninsula. Survivors made a desperate decision—to march south to the Back River and to follow that river to a Hudson's Bay Company fur-trading outpost. No one made it to the Back River. Ongoing archaeological work at the sites of the two shipwrecks came to an indefinite halt in 2020 due to the COVID-19 pandemic.

ships to freeze in sea ice along the coast) was adopted by English, Scottish, and American whalers. This allowed whalers to get an early start in the spring, providing for a long whaling season before the return trip home at the onset of the next winter. Wintering over took place along the indented coastlines of Baffin Island, Hudson Bay, and the northern shores of Quebec and Yukon. Permanent shore stations were established at Kekerton and Blacklead Island in Cumberland Sound, at Cape Fullerton in Hudson Bay, and at Herschel Island in the Beaufort Sea. Life aboard whaling ships was dirty, rough, and dangerous, and many sailors died when their ships were caught in the ice and crushed.

The Inuit sought trade with the whalers to obtain useful goods, including knives, needles, and rifles, which made domestic life and hunting easier.

While this relationship brought some advantages for the Inuit, there were also negative social and health aspects, including the rise in alcoholism and the spread of European diseases (Vignette 11.3). Just as the twentieth century began, demand for products made from whales—whalebone corsets, lamp oil—decreased sharply, ending the whale trade. This unexpected end represented the loss of Inuit access to highly valued trade goods. Somehow, they had to find other means of obtaining these goods.

In the early twentieth century, European fashion had turned to Arctic fox pelts, which caused the Hudson's Bay Company to establish trading posts in the Arctic. This provided a replacement for whaling and associated trade. The fur trade had already been successfully operating in the Subarctic for some time—a relationship between European traders and

## Vignette 11.3

### European Diseases

Whalers, fur traders, and missionaries introduced new diseases to the Arctic. As the Inuit had little immunity to measles, smallpox, and other communicable diseases such as tuberculosis, many of them died. In the late nineteenth century, the Sadlermiut and the Mackenzie Delta Inuit were exposed to these diseases. According to Dickason (2002, p. 363), in 1902 the last group of Sadlermiut, numbering 68, died of disease and starvation on Southampton Island, "a consequence of dislocations that ultimately derived from whaling activities." The Mackenzie Delta Inuit, whose numbers were as high as 2,000, almost suffered the same fate but managed to survive. Herschel Island, lying just off the Yukon coast, was an important wintering station for American whaling ships. Whalers often traded their manufactured goods with the local Mackenzie Delta Inuit, who became involved with the commercial whaling operations. Through contact with the whalers, European diseases, such as smallpox, took their toll. By 1910, only about 100 Mackenzie Delta Inuit were left. Gradually, Inupiat Inuit from nearby Alaska and white trappers who settled in the Mackenzie Delta area intermarried with the local Mackenzie Delta Inuit, which secured the survival of these people. Today, their descendants are called Inuvialuit. At the end of World War I, the worldwide flu epidemic reached Canada and by the 1920s had spread along the Mackenzie River, infecting Dene tribes; many people died, just as had occurred in 1918–19 along the northern Labrador coast, where the flu decimated local Inuit populations with the highest **mortality rates** in the world (Budgell, 2018).

the Subarctic Indigenous peoples was established through the trade of fur pelts, especially beaver. Soon the Inuit were deeply involved in the fur trade. The working relationship between the Hudson's Bay Company and the Inuit was based on barter: white fox pelts could be traded for goods.

Throughout the nineteenth and twentieth centuries, European fur companies controlled the fur economy. Fur-trading posts dotted the northern landscape. Indigenous peoples integrated trade goods into their traditional way of life—including their hunting techniques and their migration patterns—and were therefore heavily dependent on trade. In fact, when game was scarce, Indigenous groups relied on the fur trader for food. Unfortunately, in the Territorial North, game became scarce around fur-trading posts from overexploitation.

The problems of a growing dependency on European goods and a changing way of life for northern Indigenous peoples were compounded by the arrival of Western colonists in the late nineteenth century. Indigenous people were subjected to Western ideas and rules propagated by missionaries

and police, who now lived at the trading posts. Worse yet, on behalf of the Canadian government, both Anglican and Catholic missionaries took young Indigenous children from their families and placed them in church-run residential schools, where they were taught in either English or French. In this failed assimilation project, most children learned to read and write in English or French, but they were inadequately prepared for northern life. As they lost the opportunity to learn from their parents about how to live on the land, they became trapped between the two very different worlds of their Indigenous communities and the larger Canadian society. Under these circumstances, they lost their Indigenous language, beliefs, and cultural customs.

Fur traders opposed many of these imposed Western cultural adaptations because they needed Indigenous people on the land to trap. Nevertheless, the influence of the churches, the power of the state, and the number of non-Indigenous residents in the North increased in the twentieth century, placing Indigenous cultures under siege and crippling their land-based economy.

## From the Land to Indigenous Settlements

Following World War II, Inuit communities were relocated to coastal settlements by the federal government. Relocation continues to be a controversial subject in northern history. Williamson (1974), Elias (1995), Marcus (1995), and Rowley (1996) provide different perspectives. In the eyes of the federal government, leaving Indigenous peoples in what was seen to be a failing hunting/trapping economy was not an option. Living off the land was sometimes a challenge, but the shortage of cash/credit from trapping to purchase goods at the trading post was critical. One option might have been to subsidize the hunting/trapping economy by providing the necessary cash to Indigenous families as well as more time to adjust to relocation, as is now done in northern Quebec where Cree hunters and trappers are paid for living on the land and acquiring country food for themselves and others. When relocation to settlements became the order of the day, few people had a full command of English (or French in Quebec), which would become so necessary for participating in the affairs of settlement life. Still, the apparent political urgency caused Ottawa to push for relocation, and these settlements and the newcomers were both ill-prepared. Hunters and their families had their lives turned upside down.

After 70 years of settlement life, Inuit have now established themselves as urban dwellers with strong attachments to the land. Settlement has seen a transformation of Inuit life, with most employment found in government. Nunavut, however, still falls short of living conditions in the rest of the country. Narrowing this gap remains a national challenge as the economic capacity of Nunavut falls far short of addressing it. Nunavut has had a rapid increase in population growth. Since the first census in 1921, the number of Inuit has increased from 3,269 to 65,000. Virtually everyone resides in communities, both small and large. Iqaluit, the capital city, is by far the largest urban centre with a population of nearly 8,000 in 2016 with prospects of reaching 10,000 by the next census.

Access to store food and medical services has resulted in a population boom. Today, the Indigenous population forms a clear majority in the Territorial North, especially in Nunavut. On the other hand, the increased population has not matched the availability of public housing and jobs, resulting in overcrowding and chronic **underemployment**. As well, Indigenous communities face deep-rooted social dysfunctions, resulting in extremely high suicide rates among young people (Contenta, 2015). The causes are various: some are traced back to cultural dislocation and devaluation while others are related to the social stress found in small Indigenous communities. A key factor, especially among young people, is the cultural shock of living within a dominant nation-state. Pressures to accept the ways and language of the nation-state are relentless though sometimes subtle. Such an oppressive political situation of internal colonialism was termed the "Fourth World" in the 1970s by Canadian First Nation scholar and leader George Manuel (Manuel & Posluns, 1974; see Bone, 2016, p. 12). Past actions—whether social engineering or the environmental impacts of megaprojects—can reverberate for generations to come. High suicide rates are one measure of this cultural shock. In 2018, the suicide rate in Nunavut was 76 per 100,000 persons, while in the rest of Canada it was 11 (Nunavut Bureau of Statistics, 2019).

Another, more tangible factor contributing to social dysfunction is the fact that Indigenous communities have no solid economic base, resulting in heavy dependency on government for the impoverished and few opportunities for young people. The two principal sources of income are wages and various forms of government payments, including social assistance. The major employer is the government. As well, lower-income households, especially the elderly, rely on the sharing of country food by those who can afford to hunt and fish. Another alarming trend reported by Chan (2006) is that the increase in the consumption of store food rich in carbohydrates, particularly by younger generations, has already caused obesity and diabetes.

Perhaps the most positive outcome of settlement life is the emergence of Indigenous political leaders. This new generation of leaders has had a hand in transforming the Indigenous economy and Indigenous society through successful negotiations for comprehensive land claim agreements, for the

Comprehensive land claim agreements are discussed in **Chapter 3** under the heading "Modern Treaties," page 91.

**THINK ABOUT IT**

Canada, Russia, and Denmark all claim the North Pole as part of their extended continental shelves and hence under their jurisdiction. The resolution of these overlapping claims poses a major political challenge for the twenty-first century. Why would these countries want control of an immeasurably small compass point known as the North Pole?

Alexndra Koblenko/All Canada Photos

**PHOTO 11.3** Pangnirtung is a small but fast-growing hamlet on the coast of Baffin Island. Like most Inuit communities, its natural increase far outstrips that of other Canadian urban centres. From 2006 to 2016, Pangnirtung's population grew from 1,325 to 1,481, an increase of 12 per cent (Statistics Canada, 2017). Most significant, 40 per cent of its population was under the age of 15. Such an age structure is common in developing countries. Unlike many Arctic communities, Pangnirtung has a strong fishing industry based on turbot (Greenland halibut). Besides involving fishers, the community-owned Pangnirtung Fisheries Ltd employs local workers to process the fish. Demand is strong, with exports of turbot to China increasing each year.

first effectively Indigenous territory within Canada (Nunavut), and for their international involvement in the Arctic Council.

## From Forgotten to Strategic Region

Until after World War II, the government never paid much attention to the Territorial North. It was not considered a "priority" region and thus received minimum attention. With the exception of the Klondike gold rush in Yukon at the end of the nineteenth century, the North's economy was left in the hands of the nomadic Dene and Inuit who hunted and trapped, moving seasonally with the wild animals, such as the caribou. Ottawa had adopted a laissez-faire policy to minimize federal expenditures,

leaving the fur traders and missionaries to deal with the food and health needs of a hunting society.

With the outbreak of World War II, the Territorial North became a strategic region. Military investments in military bases, highways, landing fields, and radar stations were undertaken by Canada and the United States. The Territorial North served as a buffer zone between North America and the Soviet Union for over 50 years, ending with the collapse of the Soviet Union in 1991.[4] Yet, when the international threat subsided, the federal government lost interest in the region again. For Coates et al. (2008, p. 1), "Arctic sovereignty seems to be the zombie— the dead issue that refuses to stay dead—of Canadian public affairs. You think it's settled, killed and buried, and then every decade or so it rises from the grave and totters into view again."

For discussion of the program to build patrol ships for the Arctic, see the section "Shipbuilding at Halifax" in **Chapter 10**, page 342.

## Arctic Sovereignty and the Northwest Passage

In the twenty-first century, Arctic sovereignty gained a sense of national urgency. This urgency has several elements. First, climate change means more open water in the Arctic Ocean, making trans-Arctic shipping a reality. The first signs of the Northwest Passage turning into a commercial ocean route came in 2013 when the *Nordic Orion* sailed from Vancouver through the Northwest Passage with a cargo of coal for a Finnish destination. In the following year, the MV *Nunavik* delivered nickel ore from a mine in Arctic Quebec to China by sailing through the Northwest Passage.

Canada must exert control over these waters and seabed or forfeit its claim. Four methods are employed to maintain surveillance. Patrolling this vast region by aircraft based in southern Canada provides one method; the Canadian Rangers, "Indigenous foot soldiers," offer a second method. More recently, RADARSAT satellite surveillance has introduced an innovative means that provides more accurate and fuller coverage of the entire area. Coming soon, a fourth method—surface patrol ships, perhaps based at Cambridge Bay and Resolute—will supplement the first three surveillance systems.

The international community recognizes Canada's ownership of the islands in the Arctic Ocean. (There is one exception, however. Hans Island, a 1.3-km² "rock," lies between Greenland and Ellesmere Island [see Photo 11.4].) The ownership of the waters surrounding these Arctic islands does not have the same international understanding. Some countries, including the United States, consider the

**PHOTO 11.4** The barren Hans Island lies in Nares Strait midway between Greenland and Canada. While the ocean border between the two countries is settled, Hans Island remains a sovereignty puzzle because it lies within the territorial waters of both Canada and Denmark (Greenland). The logical decision would be to divide the island into two parts, one Danish and the other Canadian, but so far this diplomatic decision has not been reached. Rather, on the infrequent occasions that Danish or Canadian troops have set foot on the island, they have left a bottle of liquor with a note saying either "Welcome to the Danish Island" or "Welcome to Canada" (Luedi, 2019).

Northwest Passage to be international waters. Over the years, Canada has sought to legalize its sovereignty over the Arctic. In 1907, Canada first announced the "sector principle," which divided the Arctic Ocean among those countries with territory adjacent to the Arctic Ocean (Figure 11.5). More recently, Canada has looked to environmental legislation as a means of exercising its sovereignty over Arctic waters. In the age of supertankers, container vessels, and cruise ships, the threat of toxic spills is more likely than ever before.[5] The Arctic Council provides a diplomatic means to maintain Canada's sovereignty, and direct negotiations with Russia provide another avenue.

## The Territorial North Today

The Territorial North remains far from Canada's ecumene. Its major resources depend on the global market. People reside in settlements, towns, or cities. Rural communities and farms, as found in southern Canada, do not exist. Another surprising fact is that mining sites are no longer associated with resource towns. Industry has opted for air commuting. This long-distance system sees southern workers flown to the mine site where they work for a week or so; then they are returned to the pickup point, often their hometown (Quenneville, 2014; NWT Bureau of Statistics, 2014). The three diamond mines provide examples. Each is located in a remote area but the companies house their workers in camps and fly them to and from Yellowknife and Edmonton rather than build a permanent community where the workers' families would live.

Within the North, another difference is apparent—Arctic urban centres are very small and isolated from one another (Figure 11.6). From Statistics Canada's perspective, these settlements do not qualify as **urban areas** because their populations are less than 1,000. In 2016, for example, approximately three-quarters of these centres had populations under 1,000 and more than 40 per cent of the Territorial North's population lived in three cities: Whitehorse (26,898), Yellowknife (19,234), and Iqaluit (6,254). By 2020, the urban pattern remained the same, though the populations of the three largest centres had increased. Most significantly, these three centres accounted for 48 per cent of the Territorial

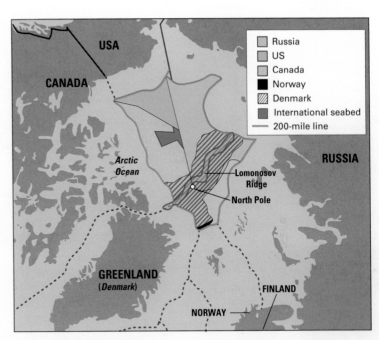

**FIGURE 11.5 The Arctic Basin and national borders**

Now that four of the five countries (excluding the United States) have made their initial claims to the Arctic seabed, the remaining issue is to resolve the overlapping claims. The elephant in the room is the 2014 claim by Denmark that extends into areas claimed by Canada and Russia. Applications to claim parts of the "international zone" of the Arctic seabed are restricted to five countries: Canada, Denmark (Greenland), Russia, the United States, and Norway, the first three of which are seeking to claim the North Pole. However, one small portion of this seabed lies 2,500 or more metres underwater and it remains an international area.

Source: Milne (2016).

North's population. Equally significant, Iqaluit experienced the greatest rate of increase from 2006 to 2016 and this trend continued into 2020.

## Industrial Structure

As a northern frontier, the Territorial North's economy depends heavily on private investment to develop its natural resources and on transfer payments to pay for its public sector.[6] In sum, the Territorial North is a high-cost area for economic development, social programs, and geopolitical challenges. With a limited tax base, the three governments of the Territorial North must depend on Ottawa. All of this translates into a simple fact: Canadians in other parts of the country are called on to invest in the country's last frontier for decades to come.

**FIGURE 11.6  Inuit Nunangat**

This map shows the four Inuit regions of Canada. Three regions—Inuvialuit in the NWT, Nunavik in Quebec, and Nunatsiavut in Newfoundland and Labrador—have attained some degree of autonomy within long-established political jurisdictions, but only the territory of Nunavut is a stand-alone political entity within Canada.

Source: Aboriginal Affairs and Northern Development, Inuit Relations Secretariat, Inuit Nunanga Map, 15 Oct. 2010. at: 222.aadnc-aandc.gc.ca/eng/1100100014250/1100100014254

Canadians should take solace from the territorial version of equalization payments called Territorial Formula Financing—transfer payments and the cost of sovereignty, including those Arctic patrol vessels under construction at Irving's Halifax Shipyard, are essential to nation-building.

In terms of employment, the primary sector in the Territorial North accounts for a much larger proportion of the workforce than it does in other geographic regions. For example, in 2019, approximately 5 per cent of the workers were in the primary sector compared to less than 2 per cent in Ontario. The reverse is true for secondary employment, with Ontario having 17.8 per cent of its workforce in this sector compared to only 10 per cent in the Territorial North. Both the Territorial North (85 per cent) and

Ontario (80 per cent) have a large tertiary or service sector (Table 11.4). However, the two tertiary sectors are different in that public employment accounts for a higher proportion of tertiary workers in the Territorial North than in Ontario, where the private

**TABLE 11.4   Employment by Industrial Sector, Territorial North, 2019**

| Economic Sector | North Workers (%)* | Ontario Workers (%) | Percentage Difference |
|---|---|---|---|
| **Primary** | 4.7 | 1.9 | 2.8 |
| **Secondary** | 10.0 | 17.8 | –7.8 |
| **Tertiary** | 85.3 | 80.3 | 5.0 |
| **Total** | 100.0 | 100.0 | |

*Author's estimates for Territorial North.

Sources: Table 6.1; Statistics Canada (2020b).

sector—especially the financial and technology sectors—has a strong presence. Not only is the high proportion of workers in the public sector a significant factor in the economy, it is also an indicator of the future. Indigenous governance is on the move: as more Indigenous students gain qualifications, the number of public Indigenous employees will increase. Coupled with reconciliation efforts, the future direction of governance in the three territories involves different versions of Indigenous governance.

## Changing Governance

In 2020, the Territorial North consists of three territorial governments: Yukon, the Northwest Territories, and Nunavut. Territorial governments have fewer powers than provincial governments, and in this sense they are political hinterlands. Ottawa's policy of devolving powers to the territories is old hat. What is on the agenda is a more powerful form of Indigenous governance. Change is now happening in two directions. First, the federal government continues to empower territories. For example, it has transferred its power over natural resources and the substantial amount of tax revenue from companies extracting natural resources to Yukon and the Northwest Territories (Vignette 11.4). Next in line is Nunavut.

Second, self-government for Indigenous peoples has emerged from comprehensive land claim agreements. This process began in the first decade of the twenty-first century because the original mandate from Ottawa excluded consideration of

local self-governance. Since then, a number of First Nations have local self-government that affects its members. On the other hand, the Nunavut agreement of 1999 was an enormous step forward, but Nunavut was formed not as an Inuit government but as a public one.

While efforts to address the issue of Indigenous title to Crown land is not new, the 1974 Supreme Court ruling in the *Calder* case opened the door. Since that ruling, the federal government has accepted that Indigenous peoples have a claim to lands not covered by treaties. Most of these lands are found in the Territorial North. Ottawa devised a system of negotiations known as comprehensive land claims. These claims are modern treaties and require negotiations between the Indigenous claimant group, Canada, and the relevant territory. Until 2005, such negotiations did not deal with self-government.

## The Territory of Nunavut

In 1992, Indigenous governance took a huge leap forward with the creation of a territorial-level government called Nunavut. In that year, a referendum saw residents favour the splitting of the Northwest Territories roughly along the lines of the Arctic (Inuit-occupied lands) and Subarctic (Dene/Métis-occupied lands). Nunavut thereby was carved out of the eastern half of the previous Northwest Territories. In 1993, a land settlement agreement between Canada and the Inuit of the eastern Arctic included a commitment by the federal government to create a new territory. This commitment allowed for a

**THINK ABOUT IT**

What is the difference between an ethnic government and a public one?

---

## Vignette 11.4

### Resource-Sharing with the Northwest Territories, 2015

In 2014, the federal government and the government of the Northwest Territories (GNWT) concluded a resource-sharing arrangement whereby half of the revenues generated by resource developments would flow to the GNWT. In turn, the GNWT shares up to 25 per cent of its portion of resource revenues with participating Indigenous governments. This new revenue is in addition to any amounts Indigenous governments previously received under land claim and self-government agreements. In the Territorial North, resource revenue-sharing arrangements are negotiated within the context of the comprehensive land claims process.

six-year transition period to give the Inuit time to form the government, recruit civil servants, and select a capital city. By means of a plebiscite, Iqaluit was selected as the capital of the new territory. Following an election in February 1999, the 19 members of the Nunavut Assembly took office on 1 April 1999. Unlike First Nations, the Inuit created a public form of government, meaning that every resident—Indigenous and non-Indigenous—has the same political rights.

The creation of a separate territory for the Inuit brought hopes for a brighter future. Through an Inuit government, a sustainable economy was thought to be achievable within 20 years. The Bathurst Mandate (Nunavut, 1999) gave voice to that hope, but the cruel reality told a different story. As Légaré (2008, p. 367) writes:

> For now, though, the urgent socio-economic plight of Nunavut does not bode well for the future. The vision of a viable Nunavut society by the year 2020, as expressed through the Bathurst Mandate, seems to be, at least for now, an illusion.

## Indigenous Economy

While Indigenous people have participated in both the informal and wage economies for centuries, the contemporary Indigenous economy is a response to the intrusion of the market economy into the North. The informal economy provides much of the country food so desired by Indigenous northerners. However, with few exceptions, such as trapping, the informal economy falls into the category of subsistence and therefore does not generate cash or provide tax revenue. The three territorial governments receive a small portion of their revenue from royalties produced by mining operations. In the case of Nunavut, Nunavut Tunngavik Inc. collects a 12 per cent royalty from mining operations on lands under its jurisdiction. Royalties from mining operations on lands not included in the Nunavut land claims agreement will come from the Nunavut government when an agreement on royalties is concluded with the federal government.

Geographically speaking, the land-based hunting and trapping part of this mixed or informal economy is most prevalent in small, isolated communities. The reverse is true in larger communities, especially the capital cities of each territory where public employment prevails. Mining operations, such as the Mary River iron mine, lean heavily on flying workers to the mine site from communities within Nunavut and beyond. As noted above, the era of resource towns is over, meaning that in-migration from the south is very limited. Not surprisingly, Indigenous workers are drawn to employment opportunities on the public side of the tertiary sector (Table 11.4). Jobs in mining projects are limited and IBA provisions account for most Indigenous workers in the mining sector.

In the opening commentary for *Indigenous Peoples and Resource Development* (Bone & Anderson, 2017), the authors argue that sustainable development is the preferred route to an advanced Indigenous economy. Royalties could be considered one element of a growing economy, but renewable resources form the basis of such an economy. One example presented in this chapter is the success of locally owned fisheries companies on Baffin Island. Another involves control of commercial enterprise. Such control results from comprehensive land claim agreements that have provided capital for investment in business enterprises. Climate change plays a role, too. Arctic tourism has become an important element of the northern economy. In 2016, the largest cruise ship to pass through the Northwest Passage, the *Crystal Serenity*, arrived on 29 August (Photo 11.5). To take advantage of the visit, the annual Nunavut Arts Festival was held to coincide with the ship's arrival, and Nunavut artisans found that the wealthy tourists purchased many of their art pieces. The warming climate has opened the Northwest Passage and allowed Arctic cruise ships to reach small Arctic communities for a few weeks each summer. Every summer in recent years, about 10 cruise ships carrying a total of about 2,600 passengers have sailed through all or part of the Northwest Passage. For example, at the three shore visits at Cambridge Bay in 2016 from the *Crystal Serenity*, cruise passengers spent an estimated $200,000, an amount of no small significance for individuals and communities (George, 2016). With sophisticated marketing directed towards these visits and by working closely with the cruise lines, as happened with Crystal Cruise Lines, more can be expected in this realm. The arrival of COVID-19 in 2020 put an end to cruise ships in the Arctic, at least for the foreseeable future. Only time will tell if this type of Arctic tourism will reappear in this decade.

## Economic Spearheads

It may seem odd to speak of "economic spearheads" for a resource frontier, but the dual economy of the Territorial North is reflected in certain unique qualities, tied to the people and the land, that spur the economy in Indigenous communities (Bone & Anderson, 2017). An early spearhead, the fruits of which are still manifest and have been reflected in the recent opportunities presented by Arctic cruise ships, was the encouragement and marketing of Inuit soapstone carving by Canadian artist and writer James Houston in the late 1940s and 1950s. In 1957 Houston introduced printmaking to Inuit artists at Cape Dorset (Barz & Roed, 2008), and for many years now the works of Nunavut artists have been highly valued in Canadian and international markets.

Capital provided by comprehensive land claim agreements has also allowed Inuit organizations to invest in the market economy. These corporations use cash settlements from the agreements to support local business and to establish new business entities. For example, the Inuvialuit Regional Corporation (IRC), the business arm of their agreement, invests funds in such enterprises as shipping, air transport and travel, energy services, catering, and bonds and stocks. The success is reflected in the fact that the IRC makes an annual payment of over $500 each to 5,000 Inuvialuit members over the age of 18 (Inuvialuit Regional Corporation, 2020). This annual payment varies only slightly from year to year because it is based on 15 per cent of the income generated by the IRC for the preceding 10-year period; in 2020 the individual payments were for $740. Similar payments are made to Inuit members belonging to other land claim agreements.

Global trade has allowed fishers from Baffin Island to market their product in China. Chinese restaurants demand fresh fish. The Inuit-owned and Iqaluit-based Baffin Fisheries Coalition, one of several Baffin Island fisheries companies, harvests turbot and northern shrimp from Baffin Bay. The company is owned by five hunter and trapper

Chris Corday/CBC

**PHOTO 11.5** In August 2016, the *Crystal Serenity*, a 280-m-long luxury cruise liner, became the largest commercial cruise ship to sail through the Northwest Passage. The *Crystal Serenity*, with 1,000 passengers and a crew of 600, stopped at Ulukhaktok (formerly Holman Island), Cambridge Bay, and Pond Inlet. Vicki Aitaok, cruise ship co-ordinator for Cambridge Bay, was responsible for five cruise ship visits over a tight two-week window in late August. The hamlet typically welcomes 100 passengers from small cruises for an afternoon visit. But with the *Crystal Serenity*'s stop, 150 passengers arrived at a time by zodiac "so as to not overwhelm the community" (Brown, 2016).

associations (HTAs): Amarok HTA (Iqaluit), Pangnirtung HTA (Pangnirtung), Mayukalik HTA (Kimmirut), Mittimatalik HTA (Pond Inlet), and Namautaq HTA (Clyde River). The company owns and operates the 64-m Arctic shrimp trawler, the *Sivulliq*, and has two factory-freezer, fixed-gear vessels and two large factory-freezer multi-species trawlers (Baffin Fisheries, 2016). Similarly, the operations of the community-owned Pangnirtung Fisheries are expanding because of high demand from Chinese buyers—a similar pattern as has occurred with Nova Scotia lobster. The path to a sustainable fisheries economy, like the boost to Arctic tourism from global warming, owes its success to the turbot reaching higher latitudes because of the warming of the waters of Baffin Bay (Bone, 2016, p. 293).

## Comprehensive Land Claim Agreements

Though the JBNQA (1975) represents the first modern treaty, it preceded the federal negotiating system for treaties known as comprehensive agreements. The

Baffin Fisheries

**PHOTO 11.6** Five hunter and trapper associations based in communities on Baffin Island own this Inuit company, Baffin Fisheries Coalition. Its ship, the *MV Sivullik*, lying off the coast of Baffin Island, is the largest shrimp harvester in the North.

## Contested Terrain 11.2

### Climate Change and Arctic Tourism

Cruise lines that arrange tours to small Arctic communities profit greatly from the high-end tourists who seek such exotic "adventure"—though some on the *Crystal Serenity*'s 2016 trip across the Arctic reportedly were surprised by the lack of ice—and local residents in the very few communities where these ships stop stand to profit from the influx of wealthy visitors. Many others, however, do not benefit, and the threat to the environment is real from an oil spill, or worse, a cruise ship sinking. As the larger cruise liners sail through the Northwest Passage, will a point be reached beyond which local people will find the flood of tourists for a few short weeks unacceptable? With the appearance of COVID-19 in 2020, Arctic cruises halted their operations, making moot this question of over-saturation of communities. However, if Arctic cruises again reach Inuit communities, this question will have to be addressed.

For further discussion of land claims, see **Chapter 3**, "Modern Treaties," page 91.

JBNQA was the result of a court-imposed negotiation over the construction of the first hydroelectric dam and reservoirs associated with the James Bay Project.

Comprehensive land claim agreements (Table 11.5) are designed to satisfy Indigenous land claims based on the long-time use of the land for hunting, fishing, and trapping. In Canada, Indigenous land claims are settled by treaty: the Indigenous group surrenders its claim to all the land in exchange for title to a smaller amount of land, a cash settlement, and, in most instances, usufructuary right to hunt and fish over a larger territory owned by the Crown. In simple terms, land claims are an attempt by Indigenous peoples and the federal government to resolve the issue of Indigenous rights.[7] Each agreement is very similar to the 1984 Inuvialuit Final Agreement (IFA). One common feature repeated in more recent agreements is that dual institutions allow one foot in the

**TABLE 11.5   Comprehensive Land Claim Agreements in the Territorial North**

| Indigenous Group | Date of Agreement | Cash Value | Land (km²) |
|---|---|---|---|
| Inuvialuit | 1984 | $45 million (1977$) | 90,650 |
| Gwich'in | 1992 | $75 million (1990$) | 22,378 |
| Sahtu/Métis | 1993 | $75 million (1990$)* | 41,000 |
| Inuit (Nunavut) | 1993 | $580 million (1989$) | 350,000 |
| Yukon First Nations | 1993 | $243 million (1989$) | 41,440 |
| Dogrib (Tlicho) | 2003 | $152 million (1997$) | 39,000 |
| Déline (Sahtu/Métis) | 2014 | Self-government* | |
| Norman Wells (Sahtu/Métis) | 2019 | Self-government* | |

* The Sahtu Dene and Métis Comprehensive Land Claim Agreement was signed in 1993, paving a way for Sahtu communities like Déline, Norman Wells, Colville Lake, Fort Good Hope, and Tulita to pursue self-government agreements. Déline achieved self-governance in 2014 while Norman Wells signed an agreement-in-principle in 2019.

Sources: Canada (1985, pp. 6, 31; 1991, p. 3; 1993a, p.3; 1993b, pp. 81, 215; 2004); Indigenous and Northern Affairs Canada (2015, 2016).

marketplace and the other in the traditional world. In the case of the IFA, the economic sector is the Inuvialuit Regional Corporation, which manages and invests the cash settlement received as part of the agreement through other separate corporations, such as the Inuvialuit Development Corporation. The second sector, the Inuvialuit Game Council, is responsible for environmental issues that affect their hunting economy. These two distinct structures were the Inuvialuit's attempt to straddle two worlds: their old world based on harvesting game and a new world as part of the Canadian and global economies. The IFA was silent on one important element so necessary for Indigenous peoples—self-government—although an agreement-in-principle for self-government was signed in 2015 by the federal and NWT governments and by the long-time chair of the Inuvialuit Regional Corporation, Nellie Cournoyea. In 2006, self-government became part of comprehensive land claim agreements.

## Country Food

Food security is a critical issue for Indigenous people living in small communities. While store-bought food dominates the table of many Indigenous families, country food holds a special place. Those who do not have a wage income rely more heavily on country food. While country food embodies a connection to the spirituality of the past and remains a key element of Indigenous culture and practices, store food dominates the table of most people. While Indigenous cultural identities vary across the Territorial North, certain core elements maintain their distinctness. These core elements include a strong attachment to the land, to country food, and to the ethic of sharing. Country food is food obtained from the land, a preferred source of meat and fish. As equivalent store-bought foods are expensive, most Indigenous northerners keep their food costs low by consuming country food. While it is true that there are substantial costs expended in harvesting country food, to some degree this cost is offset by the pleasure and spiritual rewards of being on the land and participating in hunting and fishing. Sharing also remains an important component in the harvesting and distribution of country food among family members, relatives, and close friends.

Over the years, interest in trapping has diminished because of low prices for furs and a reduction in demand for fur. Fur is not in fashion, partly because of the effective lobbying by animal rights groups. The value of fur production in the Northwest Territories, for instance, has slipped below $1 million annually—the 2016–17 figure was just over $900,000 (NWT Bureau of Statistics, 2019a). This is considerably below the figure of $6.1 million in 1987–8 (NWT Bureau of Statistics, 1990). Trapping is not an easy occupation. Besides the physical challenge, price fluctuations can mean a good harvest can lose much of its value. The future for this industry is not promising.

Figure 3.12, "Modern treaties," page 92, shows the geographic extent of modern land claim agreements in the Territorial North.

## Frontier Development in the Territorial North

Until Prime Minister John Diefenbaker's "Northern Vision" in the late 1950s, Ottawa paid little attention to the Territorial North. With his Roads to Resources program, Ottawa began to invest in highway construction with the goal of encouraging resource developments. But the Territorial North is so vast and so sparsely populated, the case for spending large sums on road-building is difficult to make—the cost of highway construction is extremely expensive, which accounts for the paucity of highways in the Territorial North. One reason for the high cost is the presence of permafrost; another is the distance between places, which translates into extra expenses to assemble road-building equipment and materials.

The Territorial North has few highways. Nunavut has none that connect to the national highway system. The most prominent highways in the North are Yukon's Alaska Highway and Dempster Highway and several in the Northwest Territories, including the Mackenzie Highway, Yellowknife Highway, Fort Smith Highway, and Liard Trail. **Winter roads** greatly extend the road system, making the trucking of heavy equipment, building supplies, and other goods possible in the winter. In late 2012, the completion of the Deh Cho Bridge (Photo 11.7) greatly reduced the cost of trucking goods to Yellowknife and other centres along the Mackenzie River served by road. CN operates on a single track to Hay River, Northwest Territories, where it connects with the river barge system on the Mackenzie River.

In assessing the cost of transportation, the value of the mineral is taken into account. For example, copper, lead, nickel, and zinc are low-grade ores (much of the ore has no commercial value). Even after the first-stage separation of some of the waste material from the valuable mineral, the enriched ore still remains a bulky product, with significant waste material remaining that can be removed only through smelting. Shipping such a low-value commodity is very expensive. Ideally, such ore is transported to a smelter by ship (Vignette 11.5). Railways

agefotostock/Alamy Stock Photo

**PHOTO 11.7** The Deh Cho Bridge crosses the Mackenzie River near Fort Providence. The bridge replaced the ferry system in the summer and the ice road in the winter.

## Vignette 11.5

### Sea Transportation on the Arctic Ocean

Arctic transportation takes advantage of nature. In late summer when the shore ice melts along the western Arctic, a narrow stretch of water opens between the shore and the polar pack ice. Small ships take advantage of this open water to bring supplies to communities located along the coast of the Beaufort Sea. Most of these supplies are transported by barge northward along the Mackenzie River. In the eastern Arctic, after the shore ice has retreated, ocean-going ships bring fresh supplies to Arctic communities. The Arctic pack ice covers most of the Arctic Ocean in the winter. Here, only specially reinforced ships and icebreakers can traverse the ice-covered waters. How thick is the ice? One-year ice is about 1 m thick while older ice can reach 5 m thick. Such voyages by icebreakers in older ice are not common. In August 1994, two icebreakers, the American *Polar Sea* and the Canadian *Louis S. St Laurent*, ploughed through thick ice on a scientific voyage to the North Pole. Canada has commissioned a new icebreaker, CCGS *John G. Diefenbaker*, costing just over $1 billion. The construction job for this icebreaker was awarded to Vancouver's Seaspan Shipyard with a delivery date of 2022.

are the second-most effective transportation carrier for low-grade ore. The critical nature of transportation for such mines is clear in the example of the lead-zinc deposit at Pine Point in the Northwest Territories. Discovered in 1898 by prospectors heading overland to the Klondike gold rush, the Pine Point deposit was not developed until 1965, when a railway was extended to the mine site. With a means of transporting the ore to a smelter, the company, Cominco, could send massive amounts of ore by rail to its smelter at Trail in British Columbia. The mine closed in 1983, leaving Pine Point a ghost town.

The Northern Vision of the 1950s regarded resource towns as part and parcel of a means of settling the North—Pine Point, for example. The flaw in this vision soon became apparent as the sustainability of such towns based on non-renewable resources was limited. In fact, the life expectancy of resource towns tends to be short because when the mine closes, no economic support remains for the community. Some companies have avoided this problem by turning to **air commuting**, which may be an effective way to obtain skilled southern workers for remote resource projects but does have drawbacks for the North. Southern-based air commuting systems hurt the North's economy because: (1) workers spend their wages in their home communities in southern Canada, thereby stimulating

provincial, not territorial, economies; and (2) workers who reside in a province but work in the territories pay personal income tax to provincial rather than to territorial governments, thereby depriving territorial governments of valuable personal income tax. For Indigenous communities, air commuting is advantageous because it provides access to high-paying jobs in the mining industry and, at the same time, allows workers' families to remain in their Indigenous communities. Known as "cultural commuting," the fly-in and fly-out work schedule has another attraction by allowing workers time to hunt and fish on their week(s) off.

## Megaprojects

Resource megaprojects provide a connection to the global economy and an economic link for the territorial economies. Yet, the inherent instability of this economic system—due to the volatility of commodity prices—has serious consequences for the success or failure of these huge resource projects, and similar consequences for Indigenous peoples who became integrated into this volatile economic system.

On a resource frontier like Canada's North, megaprojects rely on external factors such as capital, mining expertise, and southern labour through fly-in/fly-out systems for their workers. Indigenous workers and businesses do participate, but only on the margins. It is paradoxical to think of megaprojects as an anchor because of their reliance on commodity prices and their short lifespans, but this is the reality for the Territorial North. In the mid-twentieth century, the region entered a new phase of resource development characterized by megaprojects controlled by multinational companies. **Megaprojects** have three critical features:

- huge capital investment, often exceeding $5 billion;
- long construction period, usually over five years to complete;
- profitability affected by the commodity price cycle.

Megaprojects have integrated the Territorial North's economy into the global economy, thereby firmly locking the North into a resource hinterland role in the world economic system. These huge undertakings are vulnerable to construction cost overruns and deteriorating commodity price fluctuations associated with the downside of the global boom-and-bust cycle (Flyvbjerg, 2014). Cost overruns are often attributed to an underestimation of the costs and time required to complete a megaproject in the challenging physical setting of the North.

The recent megaprojects in the Territorial North involved diamond mines and the massive Mary River iron ore project, owned by Luxembourg-based ArcelorMittal and Baffinland Iron Mines, which began production in 2015. As well, an even more ambitious project announced in 2012 (Jordan, 2012) remains on the drawing board, the Izok Corridor proposal of the Chinese state-owned MMG Ltd (formerly Minmetals Corporation), which calls for five underground and open-pit mines producing lead, zinc, and copper (Weber, 2012, p. B1). Since 2014, commodity prices for these minerals dropped sharply, pushing the Izok Corridor project well outside the magic circle of viability.

Gold mining at the Discovery mine came to an end in 1969, causing the economy of the Northwest Territories to slip into troubled waters. The discovery of diamonds in the Northwest Territories in the mid-1980s brought new hope (MacLachlan, 1996).

Yet, the time from discovery to production was over 10 years. By 1998, diamond mining at Ekati mine had rejuvenated the economy of the Northwest Territories. By 2014, two other mines, Diavik and Snap Lake, were operating and, along with Ekati, were supplying the world with around 15 per cent of the annual production of diamonds. Unexpectedly, in 2015, De Beers announced the closing of Snap Lake due to high levels of water seeping into the underground mining operations. Efforts to control the water problem proved expensive, causing the mine to lose money each year (see Quenneville, 2015a, 2015b). By 2016, another De Beers mine, Gahcho Kué, came into production.

Miners are flown to the mine sites while bulky supplies, such as the annual supply of diesel fuel, are trucked along ice roads to the remote mines, thus keeping transportation costs relatively low. All of these diamond mines are located in the Slave Geological Province that straddles the border between the Northwest Territories and Nunavut.

Proponents of resource development describe megaprojects as the economic engine of northern development, though others challenge this assumption, claiming that they offer few benefits to the region and, more particularly, to the Indigenous communities (Bone, 2016, pp. 133–5). These large-scale ventures are designed for the export market. By injecting massive capital investment into the construction of giant engineering projects, megaprojects create a short-term economic boom. However, most construction expenses are incurred outside hinterlands because the manufactured equipment and supplies are produced not in hinterlands but in core industrial areas. This reduces the benefits of megaprojects to the hinterland economy and virtually eliminates any opportunity for economic diversification. As well, since all megaprojects in the Territorial North are based on non-renewable resources, these developments last for a limited time. At the end of a project, the local economy suffers a collapse. The impact of mine closures has affected each of the three territories. Four examples are the lead/zinc mine at Faro, Yukon (1998); the gold mine Discovery near Yellowknife (1969) and the Snap Lake diamond mine (2015), both in the Northwest Territories; and the Jericho diamond mine (2014) in Nunavut.

In spite of these shortcomings, megaprojects offer the only route to large-scale mining operations. Such projects are not sustainable, but they do inject much-needed capital and create short-term prosperity—a boom during construction. Megaprojects in resource hinterlands are high-risk ventures to both the operator and the region. The region is vulnerable to the boom-and-bust cycle and the inevitable closure of the mine. From this, there is no escape. On the other hand, multinational companies can reduce their risks in three ways. First, they can create a consortium of companies and thereby spread the investment risk among several firms. Second, they can arrange for long-term sales of the product at a fixed price before proceeding with construction. Third, they can obtain government assistance, which often takes the form of low-interest loans, cash subsidies, and tax concessions.

Four megaprojects are discussed in the following sections: the Mackenzie Gas Project; the Norman Wells Oil Expansion and Pipeline Project; the NWT Diamonds Project; and the Mary River Project. Not all proposals are successful. For example, the Mackenzie Valley Pipeline Project of the 1970s looked like a game-changer for the Northwest Territories, but the project stumbled during its inquiry and ended in the dustbin. The same fate met the Mackenzie Gas Project.

## The Mackenzie Gas Project, 2000

Near the mouth of the Mackenzie River, large deposits of natural gas exist. The three natural gas fields in the Mackenzie Delta are Taglu, Parsons Lake, and Niglintgak. In 2000, Imperial Oil proposed the Mackenzie Gas Project, which would see a 1,220-km pipeline system along the Mackenzie Valley, linking northern natural gas sources to southern US markets. In 2003 the pipeline was estimated to cost $5 billion, but by 2007 Imperial Oil reassessed the cost of the pipeline, the gas fields, and the gas-gathering system at $16.2 billion (CBC News, 2007).

With more gas deposits discovered due to the fracturing technique that releases gas from shale deposits, North America is now awash in natural gas, driving its price to new lows. The Mackenzie Gas

Project, like the Mackenzie Valley Pipeline Project, failed the commercial test and Imperial Oil was forced to shelve it.

## The Norman Wells Oil Field, 1920–2020

The Norman Wells oil field was discovered in 1920. Until the pipeline to southern Canada was built, production was limited to providing for local communities and mining sites along the Mackenzie River and briefly, during World War II, as the central component of the Canol Project. In 1982, Esso Resources Canada (Imperial Oil) obtained federal permission to build a pipeline and ship the oil to Canadian and US markets (Figure 11.7). Prior to the pipeline, annual output was less than 180,000 m$^3$. With the completion of the pipeline in 1985 and the expansion of oil production by a factor of 10, the Norman Wells oil field became a major player in the Territorial North. From 2008 to 2016, however, production from the Norman Wells field decreased from nearly 1.4 million m$^3$ to just under 600,000 m$^3$ (NWT Bureau of Statistics, 2015, p. 21). In 2016, slope instability near Fort Simpson threatened a leak into the Mackenzie River. Consequently, the pipeline was shut down and Imperial Oil halted oil production. By 2019, the pipeline problem was repaired and oil production resumed, but at a lower level. As a result, the role of Norman Wells in the northern resource economy is but a shadow of its former self and closure is likely in the coming decade.

## NWT Diamonds

Canada is now the third-largest producer of diamonds in the world, behind Botswana and Russia, and accounts for 15 per cent of the world supply, thanks in large part to the three operating diamond mines in the Northwest Territories—Ekati, Diavik, and Gahcho Kué.

How did this remarkable and unexpected discovery come about? Until 1991, geologists believed that the Canadian Shield was not a geological structure where diamonds could be formed. Two prospectors, Charles Fipke and Stewart Blusson, proved them wrong and turned conventional thinking on

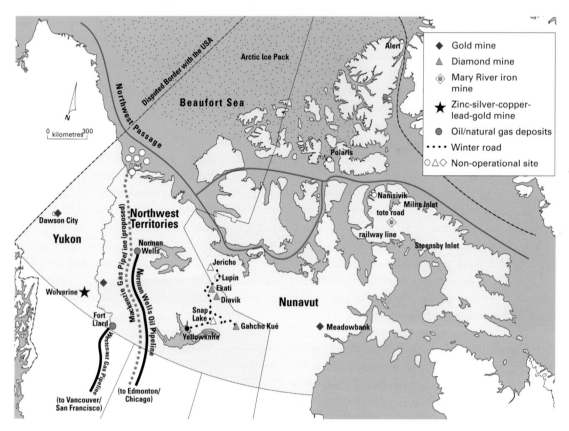

**FIGURE 11.7 Resource development in the Territorial North**

The mineral wealth of the Territorial North lies mainly in the Northwest Territories. Diamonds, gold, natural gas, and oil drive this territory's resource economy. In contrast, the resource economies of Yukon and Nunavut are much smaller. Petroleum exploration in the Beaufort Sea is complicated by the border dispute between Canada and the United States. The US claims a narrow strip of the Canadian section of the Beaufort Sea—an area of 21,436 km². Mines often have a short lifespan. Jericho, Polaris, Snap Lake, and Nanisivik are abandoned mines. Also, major new developments, such as the Mary River Project in Nunavut, are at the whim of commodity prices. When iron ore prices fell, the Mary River plans for a railway to an all-season port at Steensby Inlet were set aside.

its head when they discovered diamond-bearing **kimberlite** near Lac de Gras in the Northwest Territories. The output figures are dazzling—Northwest Territories diamond production went from zero in 1997 to a high of $2.1 billion in 2011. By 2019, the value of diamond production had climbed back to $2 billion due in part to the opening in 2016 of De Beers's Gahcho Kué mine, the largest diamond mine in Canada.

Not only is diamond mining the leading resource sector in the Northwest Territories, its production came on stream just as gold mining was ending. With the closing of the Giant gold mine at Yellowknife (Vignette 11.6), the last gold was mined in 2004 but closing down operations lasted until

2005. Already Diavik mine has gone to the more expensive underground mining, causing its output to slow. Unless new discoveries take place, Diavik mine will close in 2023 and Ekati in 2030. With non-renewable resource projects as an economic base, the Northwest Territories' economy could fall into a **staples trap**, that is, economic collapse when the staple runs out because the region has been unable to diversify its narrow resource-based economy.

## The Mary River Project

Nunavut is now the site one of the major iron mines in the world. This enormous deposit of high-grade iron ore was first recorded by Murray

## Vignette 11.6

### Toxic Time Bombs: The Hidden Cost of Mining

Mining brings jobs and wealth to the North but it also leaves behind toxic wastes. The short lifespan of most mines—less than 20 years—results in a geography of toxic time bombs. But why don't companies accept the social responsibility for cleaning up their mess? The answer is that they wish to skirt the high cost of cleanup. New and more stringent regulations have corrected this situation—except in cases of bankruptcy, which are not uncommon in the mining industry. For example, gold mining near Yellowknife has ended but hidden costs remain. The refining of gold at the Giant gold mine at Yellowknife left residues of arsenic. Now closed, this mining operation has left behind 237,000 tonnes of arsenic trioxide, a by-product of gold refining. Since the last mining company (Royal Oak Mines) declared bankruptcy, the cost of the cleanup, estimated at a quarter of a billion dollars, is left to the federal government—and that means the Canadian taxpayer (Bone, 2016, p. 187; Danylchuk, 2007).

Watts in 1962. At the time, Watts was conducting airborne reconnaissance prospecting across central and northern Baffin Island. Back in 1962, mining companies were not interested in deposits located in remote areas of the Arctic, and so this extremely large and rich deposit remained untouched for many years. Rising demand and prices for iron ore altered the dynamics of its profitability. With China's industrialization taking hold, its iron and steel industries needed more and more coal and iron—two of China's major imports. As a result, the price of iron ore soared during the first decade of the twenty-first century, reaching a peak in 2011. During that time, interest in the Mary River deposit turned from a dream into a commercial reality. In 2013, the Nunavut Impact Review Board accepted the environmental and social reports prepared by the company, Baffinland. At the same time, the company concluded its impact benefit agreement with the Baffin Island Inuit, thus clarifying their responsibilities to deliver specific benefits to the Inuit.

Such projects are risky. Construction often takes multiple years. For Baffinland, construction took five years to reach production stage. By then, the price of iron ore had fallen from a high in January 2011 of $180/metric tonne to $50/metric tonne in January 2015. The impact on the Mary River Project was severe. The original plan to build a railway to Steensby Inlet and then construct port facilities was cancelled and the company opted for a less expensive road route to Milne Inlet—costing some $4 billion less (Jordan, 2013). Shipment of ore from Milne Inlet began in August 2015 (Photo 11.8). The company's proposal to expand the mine's shipping schedule out of Milne Inlet during the winter months, which may have adversely affected marine life, was initially rejected in April 2015 by the Nunavut Planning Commission. Similarly, in 2019 Baffinland proposed to significantly increase the volume of coal shipped by using rail to transport it to ore-carrying vessels, but this proposal is before the Nunavut Impact Review Board (Photo 11.9), where it will undergo an environmental assessment. The issue goes to the heart of resource development: employment is welcomed but negative impacts on the environment and wildlife are not accepted. The company's trump card is that its proposal will ensure the mining operation will continue. If not, the mine could close—at least until the price of iron ore goes up.

Prior to the 1993 Nunavut land claim agreement, the Inuit had little control over megaprojects. Since then, the Inuit gained a measure of control through the Nunavut Impact Review Board. In 2019, when Baffinland Iron Mines proposed a $900 million railway expansion, the proposal pitted economic gains against environmental concerns (Bell, 2019). This

Baffinland Iron Mines

**PHOTO 11.8** The bulk carrier *Federal Tiber* departs from Baffinland's Milne Inlet port with a full load of iron ore bound for Nordenham, Germany.

proposal became so contentious that the final day of public hearings ended badly, leaving many confused and frustrated (Photo 11.9). Baffinland argued that its proposed Milne Inlet railway and the expansion of production to 12 million tonnes of iron ore each year are essential for the project to survive in these days of low iron ore prices.

## Megaprojects: Economic Saviour or Achilles Heel?

The colonial visions of a northern frontier coloured geographers' interpretations of the Territorial North and its peoples for much of the twentieth century. In the twenty-first century, the emergence of Indigenous self-government combined with reconciliation efforts could lead the way to a new version of governance in the North. While the details remain cloudy, the prospects of a solution that reflects negotiated solutions rather than ones imposed by Ottawa are encouraging.

The frontier premise was based on the belief that "great wealth was just waiting to be discovered by outsiders." The Klondike gold rush (1897–8) provides a classic example when prospectors from the south flooded to the Yukon to pan for gold along the Klondike River and its tributaries. In the process, the existing Indigenous economy was disrupted, and few Indigenous people benefited from the gold rush. A contemporary version of this image consists of large multinational corporations with their vast capital and advanced technology undertaking megaprojects—mining for gold, diamonds, lead, and zinc, and drilling for oil and gas. In the political world of the twenty-first century, Indigenous peoples have a stronger case to participate in resource development, often through impact benefit agreements.

Megaprojects are international instruments of resource development and have made important contributions to the northern economy. Table 11.6 shows the value of production for minerals and petroleum for the year 2018. Often, these projects and the resources extracted are touted in the press as "the engines of economic growth." Certainly, megaprojects give the regional economy a boost, but is that boost enough to lead to regional diversification in the Territorial North?

Companies developing resources in the Territorial North are faced with challenges such as

**TABLE 11.6** Mineral and Petroleum Production in the Territorial North, 2018 ($ millions)

| Mineral Product | Yukon | NWT | Nunavut | Territorial North |
|---|---|---|---|---|
| **Metals** | 211 | 0 | 1,164 | 1,375 |
| **Non-metals** | 6 | 2,111 | 0 | 2,117 |
| **Petroleum\*** | 0 | 100 | 0 | 100 |
| **Total** | 217 | 2,211 | 1,164 | 3,592 |

\*Value of oil and gas production is an estimate.

Sources: Adapted from Natural Resources Canada (2019b); NWT Bureau of Statistics (2019b).

overcoming physical barriers unique to the region and coping with downturns in world prices. Megaprojects in the Territorial North are based on non-renewable resources and therefore do not allow for sustainable growth. Another problem is the impact on the environment, an issue of particular concern to Indigenous peoples. The Mary River project is troubled by such concerns, and these concerns have divided the population (Photo 11.9).

These challenges are compounded by the long time between construction and operation, which means the company faces considerable risk. Capital investment is high, construction is long, and returns are slow. When successful, these corporations reap large profits. But success is an elusive feature. Failures do occur. The Snap Lake diamond mine failed to make a profit after seven years. In 2015, after investing $2.2 billion on mine construction and operation expenses, the mine was closed (Reuters, 2016).

Megaprojects, financed by global funds, have created a narrow oil and mining economy dependent on global markets and prices. As a result, the North experiences boom-and-bust cycles. These cycles are compounded by the non-renewable nature of the resources. The most recent commodity cycle is at a low point, causing a contraction in the North's resource economy and an increase in out-migration. Clearly, the resource economy failed in two ways. First, it failed to provide a solid basis for the northern economy. Second, it failed to protect the environment. Indigenous northerners often oppose resource projects because of their limited benefits and damage to wildlife.

Most benefits to northerners flow from IBAs between the developer and the local Indigenous organization. On the downside, northerners, particularly Indigenous peoples, often see resource development as a threat to their way of life. Even with IBAS, the economic impact is often short-lived because mining operations have a limited lifespan. Nevertheless, IBAs have been signed with nearly a dozen companies with mining operations. These agreements include the Tlicho government, the Lutselk'e Dene First Nation, the hamlet of Kugluktuk, the Kitikmeot Inuit Association, the Kivalliq Inuit Association, and the Quikiqtani Inuit Association. One expression of Indigenous opposition to resource projects came in 2016 when the Canadian government, after consultations with Indigenous

**PHOTO 11.9** Nunavut Impact Review Board hearing on Mary River mine proposal. Balancing the concern about the environment and wildlife with the Mary River mine and railway is complicated. The following commentary was reported in the *Nunatsiaq News* (Anselmi, 2019): "The Nunavut Impact Review Board brought its final hearing on Baffinland's proposed expansion of the Mary River mine to an abrupt halt on Nov. 6, the fifth day of the hearing, because the board needs time to consider a motion from Aluki Kotierk, the president of Nunavut Tunngavik Inc., to adjourn the hearing for eight to 12 months. Kotierk said many questions are still unanswered and not enough time has been provided to properly review information."

groups, declared a five-year moratorium on Arctic offshore oil and gas exploration.

In almost all cases, the resource is shipped abroad, where it is transformed into a higher-value product. As well, the spinoff effects of resource construction often leak to southern Canada because the economic structure in the Territorial North is so small and because most workers at mines reside outside of the region (Quenneville, 2014; NWT Bureau of Statistics, 2014; Skura, 2016). Consequently, diversification of the North's economy is much slower than in more developed regions. From this perspective, resource development based on non-renewable products fails to diversify the northern economy and represents an Achilles heel rather than an economic saviour. If non-renewable resource development fails to diversify the northern economy, then perhaps Watkins (1977) was correct when he foresaw that the North was doomed to slip into a staples trap.

## Summary

We have examined four key topics crucial to the Territorial North:

- the evolving place of Indigenous peoples;
- the rapid pace of climate change;
- Arctic sovereignty; and
- resource development.

Given these topics, what does the future hold for the Territorial North and its Indigenous peoples in a warmer climate? The answer will unfold in the twenty-first century as the struggle between two visions—a resource frontier and an Indigenous homeland—comes to a conclusion. However, the elephant in the room is COVID-19. How badly will this disease affect the peoples of the Territorial North and their economy?

Megaprojects represent the economic engine in a resource frontier, but as we have seen, this engine often sputters and fails to meet the concept of economic sustainability. Indigenous governance takes a different stance, where the focus of resource development is on sustainability and the well-being of its residents. While these two visions are not exclusive to each other, finding middle ground is not easy. One economic path for Indigenous peoples goes well beyond the traditional harvesting of the land and sea into commercial but sustainable enterprises. Another path calls for educated Indigenous workers filling administrative and professional jobs in both public and private institutions. Indigenous businesses have already begun to find a place within the evolving northern economy.

Nunavut has the best chance to evolve into an Indigenous government because it has demography and geography on its side. Nunavut's population growth is driven by the high Inuit fertility rates and by the reluctance of non-Inuit people to make their home in the Arctic. Equally important, Inuit culture and language continue to dominate the lives and livelihoods of Nunavut residents. On the other hand, how much room exists for Nunavut to step outside of the existing governance model found in the rest of Canada? From the perspective of the federal government, and in the spirit of reconciliation, Canada has no choice but to back the people of Nunavut and the Indigenous communities in Yukon and the Northwest Territories as they search for a place in an uncertain future.

## Challenge Questions

1. Comprehensive land claim agreements have two elements: one is focused on business and the other on the environment. While these two elements have helped Indigenous peoples gain a measure of control, in what ways are they at cross-purposes?

2. Why would the British naval expedition led by Sir John Franklin stand a better chance of navigating the Northwest Passage today than in 1845?

3. How has climate change improved the lot of Inuit commercial fishers?

4.  Megaprojects are the driving force behind the economy of the Territorial North. What is it about these projects that could lead to a staples trap rather than the diversification of the territorial economy?

5.  The largest megaproject, the Mary River iron ore project on Baffin Island, is close to bankruptcy because of the falling price for iron ore. Given that global price instability is a cyclical phenomenon, does this mean that resource projects provide unreliable economic benefits to the people and various governments in the Territorial North?

## Essay Questions

1.  As of the end of October 2020, Nunavut had had no confirmed cases of COVID-19. For Nunavut, its success in avoiding COVID-19 resulted from the Nunavut government imposing travel restrictions for those coming from southern Canada and insisting that all visitors self-quarantine for two weeks. All changed suddenly in November when the virus somehow gained a footing in several communities around Hudson Bay (see Figure 12.2). The virus, once established, can quickly spread, taking a devastating toll on residents in isolated communities, so that by 1 December 2020 Nunavut had recorded 181 cases, compared to a combined 62 cases in the other two territories. Still, Nunavut remained able to cope. In southern Canada and the United States the situation is much bleaker. In the United States, for instance, a new confirmed case was added to that country's horrible tally every second of every day and total deaths had reached 270,000 by the beginning of December, with well over a thousand dying each day and hospitals overrun with new patients. What are the reasons for this huge discrepancy between Nunavut and the United States?

2.  Arctic sovereignty involves several political hot spots. One is the Northwest Passage. Why is Canada's claim weakened as the polar ice cap melts?

3.  Why is nested federalism more likely to take place in the Arctic than in the Subarctic of the Territorial North?

4.  Arctic cruises have increased dramatically in the last two decades. Before the novel coronavirus pandemic that struck in 2020, the Northwest Passage alone attracted around 10 to 12 cruise ships each summer, bringing nearly 2,500 passengers to visit Arctic communities. In August 2016, the scale of cruise ships plying the Northwest Passage reached a record level, with the passage of the *Crystal Serenity* representing a quantum leap in regard to tourism. If we can get past the COVID-19 economic shutdown, could this form of tourism lead to a sustainable industry for Arctic communities?

# 12

# Canada: A Country of Regions within a Global Economy

## Introduction

"Canada is big—preposterously so," wrote geographer Kenneth Hare (1968, p. 31). This geographic fact remains a constant, but it has also led to a country of regions. Over time, each region has developed a sense of regional consciousness, with each having its own political agenda and economic objectives that sometimes collide with those of the federal government and other regions. In turn, these six regions embody the complex nature of Canada, expose threats to national unity, and reveal the dominant position of Central Canada. As well, economic and social inequalities within Canadian society sometimes erupt into national crises. Yet, in spite of these frictions, Canada's six regions have stood the test of time within the framework of a federal system of governance, again demonstrating that Canada is a country of regions, and a country in which compromise provides a key solution to regional and national disagreements. One such contentious issue is systemic racism. Exposing it represents a first step; finding lasting solutions is a more difficult final step. As Assembly of First Nations National Chief Perry Bellegarde stated:

> History has not always been fair to First Nations peoples, but we are living in a special time when we are making ourselves heard as never before. We have the opportunity to look at the truths of our collective history and to raise up

Indigenous leaders who also contributed greatly to the growth and development of Canada. We need to tell our stories and have our stories live alongside those of our brothers and sisters. (Curry, 2020)

Regionalism is a dynamic phenomenon. Canada's regional geography is no exception. Over time, the character and identity of the country and its regions have evolved. By the twenty-first century, Canada's social character and identity were totally different from how they were at the time of Confederation in 1867. While the forces behind this process of change are complex and interrelated, immigration has played a central role in Canada's transformation by keeping Canada's population increasing and enriching the diversity of its citizens. In addition, the voice of Indigenous peoples, long silenced, now echoes across Canada. The Truth and Reconciliation Commission of Canada (Sinclair, 2015) signals a new beginning, while the tragic story of Chanie Wenjack represents the worst of the past colonial period (Figure 12.1).

In 2020, Canada was turned upside down as the COVID-19 pandemic derailed its economy, challenged its health system, and followed a regional pattern, with Central Canada taking the brunt of the infections (Figure 12.2). How the economic, political, and social impacts of this virus will play out remains unknown, but for

---

← A wind farm harvests wind energy in southern Alberta. Canada's economy relies heavily on natural resource extraction, but climate change and climate policy can be expected to alter how these sectors work in the future.

**FIGURE 12.1 Gord Downie's *The Secret Path* and the death of Chanie Wenjack**

The late Gord Downie, Tragically Hip frontman and songwriter, hoped that his graphic novel, *Secret Path*, with art by Jeff Lemire, and Downie's album of the same name would help to inform others of the dark side of Canada's residential schools. Downie sang about Chanie, a young boy who, in October 1966, fled from the Cecilia Jeffrey Indian Residential School in Kenora and tried to walk to his home at Ogoki Post on the Marten Falls Reserve some 500 km north of Thunder Bay. His body was found along the railway tracks leading to Thunder Bay.

Source: Still from the animated version of *Secret Path*, art by Jeff Lemire.

now, Canada's leaders are searching for solutions (Vignette 12.1).

In spite of the pandemic, Canada continues to move into a knowledge-based economy based on the digital revolution where the emphasis is on automation, digitalization, and robotics. In fact, COVID-19 has accelerated the shift to online commerce and education. Working and studying at home has become the norm. Toronto, Montreal, and Vancouver are driving much of this knowledge-based rebooting of the Canadian economy, but smaller urban centres are not far behind. At the same time, Canada's dependence on its resource economy has diminished and the prospects for the oil and gas sector look particularly bleak. With low prices for oil, development of the vast deposits of oils sands has stalled. At the same time, the prospect for Arctic oil and gas development now seems unlikely. Beyond fossil fuels, other natural resources, such as forests, are also in decline. Once the dominant feature of British Columbia, the forest industry now plays a much smaller and diminished role than in the past.

Canada's economy, while full of challenges and uncertainty, has not shaken off its reputation as a combination of a resource and manufacturing economy supported by trade. That said, low commodity prices and federal climate initiatives such as the carbon tax have cooled the energy sector while growing demand for high-tech continues to propel Canada's economy. Canadians do not lack inventiveness but securing a technological base within Canada in a fiercely competitive world is not easy.

Carbon Engineering, based in BC, may well lead the world in reducing the amount of carbon dioxide in the atmosphere when a full-scale plant is built in Texas (Photo 12.1). Carbon Engineering, for which Bill Gates was an early investor, is past the experimental or R&D phase and is now commercializing, including engineering the world's largest Direct Air Capture

**FIGURE 12.2 COVID-19 in Canada**

As this map displays, the number of COVID-19 cases and deaths has varied across Canada's six regions. Bearing in mind that the map represents a snapshot of a moment in time, Central Canada—but particularly Quebec—had experienced the largest number of people infected by COVID-19 since the beginning of the pandemic, as well as the highest number of deaths. As of 1 December 2020, Quebec, with 22 per cent of Canada's population, had accounted for 37.5 per cent of the country's cases and over 58 per cent of the COVID deaths. The explanation for this spatial pattern is largely related to the population size of each region, but in the case of Quebec, the earlier spring school holidays in that province took place before COVID-19 had spread widely in Canada, and the large number of snowbirds, students, and tourists who left for warmer climates and then returned home from highly infected countries, such as France and the United States, spread the virus within Quebec earlier, but particularly in Montreal. Notably, too, at the beginning of the first wave, treatment protocols were not as effective in limiting the number of deaths.

Note: Cases/deaths are indicated for each province/territory.

Source: Glacier Media (2020).

(DAC) plant, capable of removing one million tons of CO$_2$ per year from the atmosphere.

In this concluding chapter, six critical topics are addressed: Canada's regional character; national unity; regional divides among its six regions; reconciliation; urban Canada; and income inequality. The last topic, the reshaping of Canada due to COVID-19, remains in its early stages but its impact has dominated events since early 2020.

## Vignette 12.1

### The Arrival of COVID-19

The unexpected happened in 2020—the arrival of a pandemic disease known as COVID-19 caused a global shutdown. Canada was no exception. While we can only speculate on the long-term effect of this disease on Canada and its regions, the evidence so far indicates a traumatic impact. While a recovery is certain, what form it will take is unknown. Will online learning, distance education, and telemedicine become more central in the lives of Canadians? Will restaurants and bars in some regions of the country once again be safe meeting places and watering holes? Will economies become more regional in focus, or will they reach out even more globally through the Internet? Regardless, we can expect the spatial structure of Canada with its regions to survive. The relationships between these six regions will no doubt shift somewhat but the key factors are unlikely to change, with the two core regions, Ontario and Quebec, continuing to dominate economic and political affairs, Western Canada and British Columbia challenging this dominance, Atlantic Canada remaining the weak sister, and the Territorial North remaining outside of these main corridors of power.

**PHOTO 12.1** Canadian technology goes well beyond software companies and reaches into efforts to mitigate $CO_2$ emissions and thus slow the rate of climate change. One step in that direction was taken by Carbon Engineering, which has successfully developed a pilot plant in BC that removes $CO_2$ from the atmosphere. Plans to build a full-scale plant in Texas, funded by development company 1Point5, are underway. If successful, Carbon Engineering could ease the climate emergency.

Carbon Engineering Ltd

# Regional Character and Structure

Canada's character—you might even say what makes it interesting—consists of its regional variations and the ensuing political struggle to balance regional interests with national ones. While these struggles come and go, they represent faultlines in Canadian unity. In the last decade, Indigenous issues, the oil sands expansion, and climate change formed the major faultlines.

## Oil Sands Expansion and Global Warming

The link between oil sands expansion and global warming has caused serious rifts within Canada and sparked the rebirth of western alienation. In fact, oil sands developments have ignited an ongoing and bitter battle with environmental organizations and Indigenous groups related to the construction of the Trans Mountain pipeline expansion. The reason is simple: if completed, the volume of exports would increase, thus allowing oil sands companies to expand their production but with an environmental cost of increasing greenhouse gas emissions.

Oil, pipelines, and tidewater offer a glimpse into regional necessities for land-locked provinces. At the same time, the federal Liberal government pursues policies, such as a carbon tax, designed to reduce greenhouse emissions and passed legislation that ensures major projects do not have a negative impact on "human health, the environment, and local communities." This bill, known as C-69, is rightly or wrongly perceived in much of Western Canada as anti-pipeline legislation and, by inference, the beginning of the end for oil sands production. Canadian unity is further damaged by provinces, but particularly BC and Quebec, that oppose Alberta's energy goals. More specifically, BC is opposed to the Trans Mountain pipeline, while Quebec has rejected oil pipelines crossing its territory, thus ruling out the now-cancelled Energy East pipeline to Saint John, New Brunswick.

The 2019 federal election put the pipeline dilemma in the spotlight. The depth of western opposition was revealed in the ballot box, with no Liberal candidates winning a seat in Alberta or Saskatchewan. While the issues in the 2019 election were complex, they boil down to Ottawa trying to walk a tightrope between supporting its international commitment to reduce greenhouse gas emissions and, at the same time, encouraging oil production by purchasing the Trans Mountain pipeline project. Yet, mounting pressure to "leave fossil fuels in the ground" has placed a dark cloud over the oil sands. Oil sands companies, seeing the writing on the wall, have curtailed new ventures, with Teck Resources withdrawing its application in 2020 for its Frontier mine that would have been the largest oil sands project in Alberta.

## Regional Energy Divides

Canada's six geographic regions—Ontario, Quebec, Western Canada, British Columbia, Atlantic Canada, and the Territorial North—continue to have flare-ups when conflicting interests widen the cracks between Ottawa and regions, especially when such policy intrudes on provincial jurisdiction. For instance, while the Liberal government's efforts to meet the Paris Accord reduction in greenhouse gas emissions are laudable, the cost to national unity has been high. The reason is that the burden of such a policy falls unevenly among the six geographic regions. Western Canadians see this policy as threatening their petroleum industry, while the Territorial North can no longer bank on the explorations of the vast energy reserves in the Beaufort Sea and other parts of the Arctic Ocean seabed.

The uneven distribution of energy resources goes well beyond fossil fuels. Quebec, British Columbia, Manitoba, and Labrador are blessed with ideal physical conditions to produce low-cost hydroelectric power. Quebec, in particular, has an additional advantage of its proximity to the US Northeast, where electricity rates are among the highest in North America. As well, the purchase of power from Churchill Falls by Hydro-Québec has proven very profitable. While a sore point in Newfoundland and Labrador, the two provinces may have turned the corner and are now exploring ways to work together on hydroelectric projects and transmission to markets (Vignette 12.2). Just what will

## Vignette 12.2

### A New Beginning: Quebec and Atlantic Canada

After years of bitter relations between Quebec and Newfoundland and Labrador over the Churchill Falls agreement, the premier of Quebec, François Legault, met with his counterpart, Liberal premier Dwight Ball of Newfoundland and Labrador, in January 2020 to chart a new future just prior to a meeting of the Council of Atlantic Premiers, to which Legault was invited (Cowan, 2020). At the top of their agenda was clean energy collaboration. Ball and Legault had met on several occasions over the previous year, and although Ball has now stepped aside, the new Liberal government in Newfoundland and Labrador can be expected to continue to keep open the channels of communication. While no specific agreements were reached between Quebec and Atlantic Canada, the ice has been broken to explore ways to develop, transmit, and exchange hydroelectricity.

result from such discussions remains for the future, but the prospect of Hydro-Québec playing a role in Atlantic Canada could result in several positive developments, including lower electrical rates and increasing power exports to the United States.

## Federal Energy Policy

Ottawa is caught on the horns of a dilemma: how to reduce greenhouse gases and maintain a strong energy industry. In 2018, Ottawa introduced a carbon tax that each province and territory was expected to apply to its residents, but four provinces—Alberta, Saskatchewan, Ontario, and New Brunswick—opposed this measure. The unexpected consequence is a major breach between Western Canada and the Liberal federal government that continues to simmer, largely because Alberta and Saskatchewan are most affected by this federal legislation.

Yet, the transition to a smaller carbon footprint is inevitable during this century. Such a time frame allows for adjustments as the energy sector slows and workers shift to other occupations. The oil sands are a prime example: it has been suggested that much of the oil sands will remain in the ground by the turn of the next century.

## Indigenous Reconciliation

From the removal of a statue of Canada's first prime minister, Sir John A. Macdonald, from the front of Victoria's City Hall to the Truth and Reconciliation Commission headed by Justice (now Senator) Murray Sinclair, reconciliation efforts are underway. That said, the road to reconciliation is not an easy one, partly because federal actions towards Indigenous peoples and their resulting plight created a negative image that was accepted by Canadian society as a reality. This negative image remains embedded in Canadian society. In spite of such setbacks, Canadian society and its governments are in a position to settle outstanding land claims and support Indigenous governance. One way forward is resolving who forms Indigenous governments: the elected or hereditary members of an Indigenous community (Contested Terrain 12.1).

## Urban Canada and the Advanced Economy

Within each of Canada's regions, the large urban centres provide the driving force for change and innovation. The share of Canada's population and its advanced economy are expanding in metropolises, particularly Toronto, Montreal, and Vancouver. These three cities are closely linked to the advanced global economy and attract skilled workers from around the world. They flourish because they attract the global creative class, making them more able to focus on urban sustainability and more livable with one exception: the high cost of housing. One urban expression of the creative class takes the form of innovative clusters, the most famous of which is Silicon Valley in California. Not only are cities competing

## Contested Terrain 12.1

### Governance and Reconciliation

Indigenous governance is both complicated and incomplete, making some reconciliation efforts difficult. Take, for example, the conflict between the elected and hereditary governments of the Wet'suwet'en Nation in northern British Columbia, where a treaty has yet to be signed with the Crown. On one hand, Na'moks, a spokesman for the Wet'suwet'en hereditary chiefs, said during a news conference in Smithers, BC, in 2020 that the Coastal GasLink pipeline had no authority to proceed without consent from the five hereditary clan chiefs. On the other hand, Coastal GasLink has signed agreements to proceed with the elected First Nation councils along the 670-km pipeline route from northeastern BC to an LNG terminal in Kitimat. Who has the authority to represent the members of the Wet'suwet'en Nation? The solution, if there is one, best comes from within the Wet'suwet'en Nation.

for creative people and innovative clusters, but they have recognized the need for a quality of urban life that demands a fresh vision of the design and function. So critical is quality of life to Canada's future that Alan Wallace (2016), the former director of planning and development for Saskatoon, stated that urban Canada stands on the "threshold of pivotal change" where cities are not just growing bigger but more sustainable. In this vein, in 2008, then Vancouver Mayor Gregor Robertson put his city on a path to become "the greenest city in the world by 2020." In 2020, the Vancouver's green action plan highlighted 10 goals, which included climate and renewables, green buildings, green transportation, zero waste, access to nature, clean water, local food, clean air, green economy, and a lighter footprint (City of Vancouver, 2020). Of these goals, the city has reached seven and has exceeded the goal related to urban transportation with major advances in cycling routes and transit networks.

While the larger cities are reinventing themselves into more attractive places to live through gentrification of old industrial areas and environment-friendly innovations such as green roofing, smaller cities can learn from their experience and avoid their mistakes in urban design and planning. As Wallace (2016) points out, cities like Saskatoon, "London, St Catharines, Halifax, Oshawa, Victoria, Windsor, Regina, and Sherbrooke, to name a few, all have populations under half a million. These cities are growing but hopefully not just bigger." Traffic congestion and satellite towns are common features of urban Canada, but these mid-sized cities can rejig their future by making three critical choices between:

- automobile traffic or rapid transit;
- suburban expansion or development of the downtown core;
- investment in roads and freeways or promotion of education and research.

## The Future

Canada exists as a country of regions within the global economy. In a country so large and diverse, regional tensions are inevitable. In the next decades, the country needs to encourage the digital revolution, build cultural and economic bridges between its regions, provide more powers and revenue to its cities, and deal with the COVID-19 pandemic. In so doing, the economy and national unity can be strengthened.

The coming decade faces opportunities and many challenges. One challenge, even when vaccines become widely available, is how to adjust to COVID-19 (and whatever public health crises may await us in the future), which has ricocheted into all corners of Canadian society. Another is how to decouple from globalization and thereby ensure supplies of medical products. A third revolves around Canada's trading relations with China, which have been compromised by the Meng Wanzhou affair. Finally, the massive investment by the federal and Ontario governments into the Oakville automobile

Ken Davies/Masterfile

**PHOTO 12.2** Toronto, Canada's largest city, has positioned itself as a global hub in digital technology and urban design. As the headquarters for most Canadian firms, Toronto is seen on the world stage as reliable and stable. Its universities play an important role in its innovative economy, while a steady flow of immigrants supports communities within Toronto known as **ethnoburbs** (Li, 2009). On the downside, homelesness is a growing issue as income inequality widens in the city.

plant in late 2020 and the promise of more for the GM plant in Oshawa will rejuvenate Ontario's economy and transform Oakville into the major North American centre for electric car production, signalling not only the rebirth of Ontario's automobile industry but also the political importance to Ottawa of this core region.[1]

Navigating through climate change and energy issues continues to haunt Ottawa and its regions. So far, the federal government has not found the right balance to address climate change and the gaping policy divide regarding energy between Ottawa and Western Canada. As Ottawa moves more aggressively on its climate policy in the coming years, will it throw a wet blanket over the oil and gas industry or will it throw Western Canada a lifeline to a fossil-free economy? Unity, however frail or fractured it sometimes appears, is the linchpin holding the nation and its six regions together. In the coming decade, there is one certainty: Canada will remain a country of six geographic regions and will continue to experience regional tensions in its search for an advanced economy within a greener Canada and a changing global world.

## Challenge Questions

1. The climate crisis is real. Looking at greenhouse emissions across the country, why are Quebec's emissions so much lower than those in Alberta?

2. Wet'suwet'en Nation is struggling with the critical issue of pipeline construction across its traditional territory, sparking a division between elected band governments and hereditary ones. Explain why a solution to this division best comes from within the We'suwet'en Nation, rather than from the outside, such as by the Supreme Court of Canada.

3. Is Quebec's Bill 21—which bans public workers and those seeking certain public services from wearing religious symbols—out of step with religious freedom guaranteed under the Canadian Charter of Rights and Freedoms, or, like Quebec's language laws, is it best understood as protecting the secular identity of Québécois?

## Essay Questions

1. "Canada is big—preposterously so," wrote geographer Kenneth Hare in 1968. Even more important than size, why is the concept of regional consciousness crucial for understanding the nature of Canada, and how have Indigenous issues helped alter that regional consciousness?

2. Canada faces several challenges moving into the next decade. One is low commodity prices that have crippled Canada's resource economy, while another is trade with China, which has slowed because of the Meng Wanzhou affair. Discuss one of these two challenges and its varying impact on Canada's six regions.

# Glossary

**age dependency ratio** The ratio of the economically dependent sector of the population to the productive sector, arbitrarily defined as the ratio of the elderly (those 65 years and over) plus the young (those under 15 years) to the population of working age (those 15 to 64 years); the old-age dependency ratio is similar to the age dependency ratio except that it focuses only on those over 64.

**agricultural fringe** Agriculture at its physical limits. Along the southern edge of the boreal forest and in the Peace River Country, farmers have cleared the land, but the short growing season prevents most crops from maturing, and consequently many farmers turned instead to cattle.

**air commuting** Travel to a work site in a remote area, such as a mine, by aircraft owned or hired by the company. Employees remain at the work site for a week or longer, working long shifts (often 12 hours per day), then have a week or two at home. The company pays for the air transportation and for food and lodging at the work site. Until the 1970s, resource towns housed workers and their families.

**air drainage** The movement of colder, heavier air to lower elevations, leaving warmer, lighter air in the higher elevations.

**air pollution** Any chemical, physical, or biological agent that modifies the natural characteristics of the atmosphere.

**Alaska boundary dispute** Territorial dispute between Canada and the US to establish the boundary between Alaska and Yukon and British Columbia. In 1903 an international tribunal (three Americans, two Canadians, and one British member) decided in favour of the United States, with the two Canadian members dissenting.

**Alaska Panhandle** A strip of the Pacific coast north of 54° 40'N latitude that was awarded to the United States in 1903 and that prevented access to the Pacific Ocean for Yukon and northwest BC.

**albedo effect** Proportion of solar radiation reflected from the earth's surface back into the atmosphere.

**Alberta clipper** A low pressure system that begins when warm, moist winds from the Pacific Ocean come into contact with the Rocky Mountains and then the winds form a chinook in southern Alberta; winter storms occur over the Canadian Prairies when it becomes entangled with the cold Arctic air masses. Eventually, the storm reaches Ontario and Quebec. Also, "Alberta Clipper" is the name of a natural gas pipeline that runs from Alberta to the US Midwest.

**Allophones** A term used by Statistics Canada to identify those whose mother tongue is not English, French, or one of the Aboriginal languages.

**alpine permafrost** Permanently frozen ground found at high elevations.

**Anglophones** Those whose mother tongue is English.

**Arctic Circle** An imaginary line that signifies the northward limit of the sun's rays at the time of the winter solstice (21 December). At a latitude of 66° 32'N, the sun does not rise above the horizon for one day of the year (the winter solstice). Except for a short period of twilight, darkness prevails for 24 hours. At the summer solstice (21 June), the sun's rays do not fall below the horizon, providing constant daylight for 24 hours.

**Arctic ice pack** Floating sea ice in the Arctic Ocean that has consolidated into an ice pack, with an extent of over 10 million km². New sea ice (less than one year in age) is often about 1 m thick; old sea ice can reach 5 m in thickness. Ice ridges are formed, reaching 20 m in thickness. Global warming is reducing the geographic extent and thickness of the Arctic ice pack, with the possibility of the ice pack disappearing by 2100.

**arêtes** Narrow serrated ridges found in glaciated mountains. Arêtes form when two opposing cirques erode a mountain ridge.

**artificial intelligence (AI)** The branch of computer sciences that emphasizes the development of "intelligent" machines, thinking and working like humans.

**Asia-Pacific Gateway and Corridor** A system of transportation infrastructure, including British Columbia's Lower Mainland and Prince Rupert ports, road, and rail connections, that reaches across Western Canada and into the economic heartlands of North America, including major airports and border crossings.

**Assembly of First Nations (AFN)** National advocacy organization for status Indians, i.e., the more than 630 First Nations in Canada.

**Athabasca tar sands** The largest reservoir of crude bitumen in the world and the largest of three major oil sands deposits in Alberta; also known as the oil sands.

**Bakken Formation** A geological structure containing large quantities of oil trapped in shale. It lies in Williston Basin in southern Saskatchewan and Manitoba and extends into North Dakota, Montana, and South Dakota.

**Beothuk** Before the arrival of fishing boats from Europe, the Beothuk, who probably spoke an Algonkian language, hunted and fished on the island of Newfoundland. Relations with fishers and settlers often resulted in conflicts, which confined the Beothuk to the inland portion of the island. With access to coastal resources cut off and under attack by settlers, the Beothuk struggled to survive in the resource-poor interior. In 1829, the last of the Beothuk died.

**Big Bear (Mistahimaskwa)** The last of the great chiefs prior to widespread European settlement of the Prairies, who had a vision to unite the Plains Cree to stand together against the impending wave of settlers and to find a way to sustain their culture.

**Big Commute** Air travel by Newfoundland trades workers to and from the Alberta oil sands, on a cycle such as 20 days in Alberta and eight days back home in Newfoundland; ended when oil prices collapsed.

**Bill 9** An Act to increase Quebec's socio-economic prosperity and adequately meet labour market needs through successful immigrant integration, enacted in 2019.

**Bill 21** Quebec legislation in 2019 requiring teachers, police officers, judges, and many others in authority not to wear religious items like crucifixes, hijabs, kippas, and turbans while performing their duties.

**biosphere reserve** Designation by the United Nations of lands and waters that in turn are protected by provincial or state legislation. Such UNESCO reserves contain core areas where no resource development is permitted; buffer zones where limited resource extraction is permitted; and transition zones where resource development takes place in a sustainable manner.

**bitumen** A tar-like mixture of sand and oil.

**Black Lives Matter** A social movement by the African-American community against police violence towards Black people in the United States; now active in some Canadian urban centres such as Toronto, the movement gained widespread support in 2020 following several unjust police killings of Blacks in the US.

**boom-and-bust cycle** A rapid increase in economic activities in a resource-oriented economy, often based on the value of a single commodity, quickly followed by a downturn when the commodity price(s) falls due to a drop in world demand, which is usually associated with a contraction in the business cycle.

**Brent oil price** A major trading classification of sweet light crude oil that serves as a major benchmark price for purchases of oil worldwide; named for a North Sea oil field, the Brent price in recent years has been slightly higher than the continental North American West Texas Intermediate price. *See oil prices.*

**business cycle** A series of irregular fluctuations in the pace of economic activity in the world market (capitalist) economy. These fluctuations consist of four phases: "contraction" (a slowdown in the pace of economic activity); "trough" (the lowest level of economic activity); "expansion" (a sharp increase in the pace of economic activity); and "peak" (the maximum level of economic activity).

*Calder* **case** Supreme Court of Canada ruling in 1973 that Indigenous peoples have some undefined collective rights, based on historic occupation, possession, and use of traditional territories, known as "Indian title" (now called "Indigenous [or Aboriginal] title"). These rights are not property rights, which involve the full weight of ownership.

**Canada–US Free Trade Agreement (FTA)** Trade agreement between Canada and the United States enacted in 1989.

**carbon sequestration** Carbon capture and storage technology involving the capture of $CO_2$ and other greenhouse gas (GHG) emissions from fossil-fuel power stations or other large carbon emitters and storage of the $CO_2$ in deep, stable geological formations.

**Cascadia** The name proposed for an independent sovereign state advocated by a grassroots movement in the Pacific Northwest, which would include British Columbia, Washington, Oregon, and Idaho.

**census metropolitan area** An urban area with a population of at least 100,000, with at least 50,000 people residing in the core, together with adjacent smaller urban centres and even rural areas that have a high degree of economic and social integration with the larger urban area.

**Château Clique** The political elite of Lower Canada, composed of an alliance of officials and merchants who had considerable political influence with the British-appointed governor; similar to the Family Compact in Upper Canada.

**chernozemic** A soil order identified by a well-drained soil that is often dark brown to black in colour; associated with the grassland and parkland natural vegetation types and located in the Prairies climatic zone.

**chinook** A dry, warm, downslope wind in the lee of the Rocky Mountains in Alberta. Also called a rain shadow wind because it has dropped most of its moisture on windward slopes.

**cirques** Large, shallow depressions found in mountains at the head of glacial valleys that are caused by the plucking action of alpine glaciers.

**Clayoquot Sound** Located on the west coast of Vancouver Island, Clayoquot Sound in 1993 became the centre of environmental protests against logging in old-growth rain forests.

**climate** An average condition of weather in a particular area over a very long period of time.

**climate change** Since the mid-twentieth century, increased levels of carbon dioxide in the atmosphere caused by the use of fossil fuels, which have led to a rapid increase in global temperatures and thus to changing climates.

**climatic zone** A geographic area where similar types of weather occur.

**commercial forest** Forest lands able to grow commercial coniferous (softwoods), deciduous (hardwoods), and mixed woods timber within an acceptable time frame.

**comprehensive land claim agreement** Agreement based on territory claimed by an Indigenous group that was never ceded or surrendered by treaty. Such agreements extinguish the Indigenous claim to vast areas in exchange for a relatively small amount of land, capital, and the organizational structure to manage their lands and capital.

**container** A sealed steel "box" of standardized dimensions (measured in 20-foot equivalent units or "TEU") for transporting cargo by ship, rail, and truck.

**continental air masses** Homogeneous bodies of air that have taken on moisture and temperature characteristics of the land mass of their origin. Continental air masses are normally dry and cold in the winter and dry and hot in the summer.

**continental effect** Land masses heat up and cool more quickly than oceans.

**continentalism** Policies, like the Free Trade Agreement, that promote Canadian trade and economic ties with the United States.

**continuous permafrost** Extensive areas of permanently frozen ground in the Arctic, where at least 80 per cent of the ground is permanently frozen.

**convectional precipitation** An upward movement of moist air that causes the air to cool, resulting in condensation and then precipitation.

**conventional oil and gas** Deposits that can be recovered through natural flow or pumping to the surface.

**core** An abstract area or real place where economic power, population, and wealth are concentrated; sometimes described as an industrial core, heartland, or metropolitan centre.

**core/periphery model** A theoretical concept based on a dual spatial structure of the capitalist world and a mutually beneficial relationship between its two parts, which are known as the core and the periphery. While both parts are dependent on each other, the core (industrial heartland) dominates the economic relationship with its periphery (resource hinterland) and thereby benefits more from this relationship. The core/periphery model can be applied at several geographical levels: international, national, and regional.

**country food** Food, primarily game, such as caribou, fish, and sea mammals, obtained by Indigenous people from the land and sea. Although First Nations, Inuit, and Métis now live in settlements, they fish and hunt for cultural and economic reasons.

**COVID-19 pandemic** Global epidemic declared in March 2020 by the World Health Organization to be a pandemic of a highly contagious (primarily respiratory) disease caused by a novel coronavirus; this new disease was first identified in Wuhan, China, in late 2019 and by the end of the third week of November 2020 there were more than 59.4 million confirmed cases worldwide with 1.4 million deaths—the US alone had had about 13 million cases and over 265,000 deaths; Canada, in contrast, had experienced over 330,000 cases and 11,455 deaths.

**creative class** Culture workers, from artists to computer programmers, who, Richard Florida argues, are the key to a flourishing and progressive city and who are attracted to urban centres rich in diversity and culture.

**crude birth rate** The number of births per 1,000 people in a given year.

**crude death rate** The number of deaths per 1,000 people in a given year.

**culture** The sum of attitudes, habits, knowledge, and values shared by members of a society and passed on to their children.

**culture areas** Regions within which the population has a common set of attitudes, economic and social practices, and values.

**demographic transition theory** The historical shift of birth and death rates from high to low levels in a population. The decline in mortality precedes the decline in fertility, resulting in a rapid population growth during the transition period.

**demography** The scientific study of human populations, including their size, composition, distribution, density, growth, and related socio-economic characteristics.

**denudation** The process of breaking down and removing loose material found at the surface of the earth. In this way, erosion and weathering lead to a reduction of elevation and relief in landforms.

**deposition** The deposit of material on the earth's surface by various processes such as ice, water, and wind.

**dilbit** Bitumen diluted with a diluent.

**diluent** A hydrocarbon substance used to dilute crude bitumen so that it can be transported by pipeline.

**discontinuous permafrost** Permanently frozen ground mixed with unfrozen ground in the Subarctic. At its northern boundary about 80 per cent of the ground is permanently frozen, while at its southern boundary about 30 per cent of the ground is permanently frozen.

**dispute settlement mechanism** Binding arbitration to resolve trade disputes, as built into the FTA, NAFTA, and USMCA.

**drainage basin** Land sloping towards the sea; an area drained by rivers and their tributaries into a large body of water: in Canada, the four major drainage basins are the Pacific, Arctic, Hudson Bay, and Atlantic basins; a small portion of southern Saskatchewan and Alberta drains to the Gulf of Mexico. Rivers and lakes are also described as having basins, that is, the catchment areas from which all waters flow to a particular larger water body, such as the Red River Basin and the Lake Ontario Basin.

**drumlins** Low, elliptical hills created by the deposit of glacial till, believed to be from subglacial megafloods, and shaped by the movement of the ice sheet; also called whalebacks or hogbacks.

**Dry Belt** An agricultural area in the semi-arid parts of Alberta and Saskatchewan, primarily devoted to grain farms and cattle ranches, where crop failures due to drought are more common. *See* Palliser's Triangle.

**Eastern Townships** An area of Quebec in the Appalachian Uplands lying south and east of the St Lawrence Lowland and near the US border. The region is now referred to as Estrie.

**economies of scale** A reduction in unit costs of production resulting from an increase in output.

**ecumene** The portion of the land that is settled.

**energy poverty** In the classical definition, developing countries where access to energy is limited; in the case of Ontario, the high cost of energy that reduces low-income families' access to energy.

**erosion** The displacement of loose material by geomorphic processes such as wind, water, and ice by downward movement in response to gravity.

**eskers** Long, sinuous mounds of sand and gravel deposited on the bottom of a stream flowing under a glacier; eskers appear on the land surface after the glacier has retreated.

**Estrie** An administrative region that overlaps most of the area formerly called the Eastern Townships.

**ethnic group** People who have a shared awareness of a common identity/ancestry and who identify themselves with a particular culture.

**ethnic mobility** Switching one's ethnic identity from one census to the next, as has occurred among the Indigenous population as Indigenous identity is no longer seen as disadvantageous but as a source of pride, or in some instances, personally advantageous.

**ethnic origin** A Statistics Canada definition, which refers to the ethnic or cultural origins of the respondent's ancestors. An ancestor is someone from whom a person is descended and is usually more distant than a grandparent.

**ethnoburbs** Suburban residential and business areas with a significant ethnic character composed of new Canadians.

**ethnocentricity** The viewpoint that one's ethnic group is central and superior, providing a standard against which all other groups are judged.

**evapotranspiration** Part of the water cycle: the sum of evaporation of water from the soil and water bodies to the air and the transpiration of water from plants and its subsequent loss as vapour.

**Family Compact** A group of officials who dominated senior bureaucratic positions, the executive and legislative councils, and the judiciary in Upper Canada.

**faulting** The breaking of the earth's crust as a result of its differential movement; often associated with earthquakes.

**fault line** A crack or break in the earth's crust. A complex fault line is known as a fault zone; major fault lines exist between two tectonic plates.

**faultlines** Application of a geological phenomenon to the economic, social, and political cracks that divide regions and people.

**Fertile Belt** Area of long-grass and parkland natural vegetation in Western Canada associated with black and dark-brown chernozemic soils. It supports a mixed farming area where crop failures due to drought are less common.

**fertility rate** The number of live births per 1,000 women aged 15 to 44 in a given year; also known as the general fertility rate. The fertility rate is much more indicative of changes in fertility behaviour than is the crude birth rate because it is based on those women of child-bearing age rather than the general population.

**First Nations people** By Statistics Canada definition, those Indigenous persons who report a single response of "North American Indian" to the Indigenous identity census question.

**5G wireless technology** The fifth generation of mobile networks; beyond speed improvement, 5G will allow networks to link with many devices, such as the Internet of Things (IoT) (e.g., self-driving vehicles, robotic surgery, and infrastructure monitoring).

**folding** The bending of the earth's crust.

**fracking** A technique involving the injection of water and unidentified chemicals underground at very high pressure to create fractures in the underlying shale rock formations, thus releasing the oil or gas for extraction; hydraulic fracturing.

**francophones** Those whose mother tongue is French.

**French Canadians** Canadians with roots to Quebec and who likely still speak French.

**Frog Lake Massacre** As part of the Cree uprising during the 1885 Northwest Resistance, a band of Cree warriors from Big Bear's band led by Wandering Spirit raided the Hudson's Bay Company store at Frog Lake in search of food. During this raid, nine settlers, including the Indian agent and two Catholic priests, were killed.

**frontal precipitation** Condensation and then precipitation that occur when a warm air mass is forced to rise over a colder air mass.

**glacial erosion** The scraping and plucking action of moving ice on the surface of the land.

**glacial spillways** Deep and wide valleys formed by the flow of massive amounts of water originating from a melting ice sheet or from water escaping from glacial lakes.

**glacial striations** Scratches or grooves in the bedrock caused by rocks embedded in the bottom of a moving ice sheet or glacier.

**glacial troughs** U-shaped valleys carved by alpine glaciers.

**global circulation system** The movement of ocean currents and wind systems that redistribute energy around the world.

**globalization** An economic/political/social process driven by international trade and investment, as well as by migration and the spread of Western popular culture, that leads to a single world market and wide-ranging impacts on the environment, cultures, political systems, and economic development.

**global warming** An increase in global temperature due to the greenhouse effect caused by increased levels of carbon dioxide, chlorofluorocarbons, and other pollutants in the atmosphere; the main contributor is the burning of fossil fuels.

**Grand Dérangement** In 1755, the British demanded that the Acadians take an oath of allegiance to Britain. They refused and their expulsion began. Between 1755 and 1763, approximately 10,000 Acadians were deported.

**grandfather clause** Guarantees each province has no fewer seats than it had in 1985.

**Great American Desert** The treeless Great Plains as described by American explorers in the nineteenth century; in fact, this region has a semi-arid climate and a grasslands vegetation cover.

**Great Bear Rainforest** Temperate rain forest along British Columbia's central and north coast, an area of 6.4 million hectares with 85 per cent of the old-growth forest designated in 2016 as protected from logging by the BC government.

**greenhouse effect** The absorption of long-wave radiation from the earth's surface by the atmosphere.

**greenhouse gases** Water vapour, carbon dioxide, and other gases that make up less than 1 per cent of the earth's atmosphere but are essential to maintaining the temperature of the earth.

**grooves of geography** Physiographic structure, such as plains and mountains, that facilitates or impedes movement between adjacent regions.

**gross domestic product (GDP)** An estimate of the total value of all materials, foodstuffs, goods, and services produced by a country or province in a particular year.

**groundfish** Fish that live on or near the bottom of the sea. The most valuable groundfish are cod, halibut, and sole.

**Gulf Stream** A warm ocean current paralleling the North American coast that flows from the Gulf of Mexico and Caribbean towards Newfoundland.

**habitants** French peasants who settled the land in New France under a form of feudal agriculture known as the seigneurial system.

**"hard" and "soft" countries** Portrayal by John Ralston Saul of countries as "hard" and "soft" in terms of their relationships with minority groups. Hard nations with homogeneous populations tend to treat minorities harshly. Soft nations have more diverse populations and as a result of a history of interaction among different cultural groups, the value of harmonious relations has taken root.

**heartland** A geographic area in which a nation's industry, population, and political power are concentrated; also known as a core.

**hewers of wood and drawers of water** Biblical phrase applied by sociologists and others to the labouring classes of capitalism doing the most menial, low-paid work necessary for the operation of capitalist society. Within the context of the core/periphery model, this term refers to periphery regions where primary production prevails; core areas, on the other hand, focus on the processing of those raw products. Its application to a country's economy refers to the export of raw materials rather than of finished goods.

**hinterland** A geographic area based on resource development that supplies the heartland with many of its primary products; also known as a periphery.

**hollowing-out** The relocation of manufacturing plants from one country to another, which leaves the economy of the original country much weakened.

**Holocene epoch** The current geological division of the Geological Time Chart. It began some 11,000 years ago and is associated with the warm climate following the last ice age.

**homeland** A land or region where a relatively homogeneous people and their ancestors have been born and raised, and thus have developed a strong attachment to that place; a sense of place.

**homesteader** A settler who obtained land. In Western Canada, quarter sections of 160 acres were available as homesteads under the federal government's plan known as the Dominion Lands Act where a settler paid a $10 fee for a quarter section with the requirements that a habitable residence be built within three years and that the land be cleared for farming and a portion of cleared land be under cultivation.

**horizontal drilling** Recently developed technology used in drilling for oil and gas, as opposed to vertical oil and gas drilling, which has existed for a long time.

**hydraulic fracturing** A method used to fracture rock formations in order to allow oil or natural gas to flow from impervious geological strata; fracking.

**hydrometallurgy** A process that produces nickel, copper, and cobalt directly from ore, thus avoiding the smelting process and eliminating environmentally unfriendly sulphur dioxide and dust emissions.

**ice age** A geological period of severe cold accompanied by the formation of continental ice sheets. The most recent ice age, the Pleistocene, began some 2 million years ago and ended with the beginning of the Holocene epoch some 11,000 years ago.

**igneous rocks** Rock formed when the earth's surface first cooled or when magma or lava that has reached the earth's surface cools.

**Indian Act** Canadian legislation first enacted in 1876, bringing together in one statute earlier pre-Confederation laws. The Indian Act continues, with amendments, to define the relationship between Ottawa and registered status Indians.

**Indigenous ancestry** According to Statistics Canada, those who report an Aboriginal identity as well as those who report being Aboriginal to the ethnic origin question, which focuses on the ethnic or cultural origins of a person's ancestors.

**Indigenous identity** According to Statistics Canada, those persons identifying with at least one Aboriginal group, that is, North American Indian, Métis, or Inuit, and/or those who report being a treaty Indian or a registered Indian, as defined by the Indian Act, and/or those who report they are members of an Indian band or First Nation.

**Indigenous peoples** All Canadians whose ancestors lived in Canada before the arrival of Europeans; includes status and non-status Indians, Métis, and Inuit.

**Indigenous rights** The practices, customs, and traditions that Indigenous peoples practised prior to contact with or large-scale settlement by Europeans. One Indigenous right, the right to hunt and fish on Crown lands, has legal status and is protected by the Canadian Constitution. Given the diversity among Indigenous peoples, Indigenous rights vary from group to group. Indigenous people whose chiefs signed treaty agreements on behalf of their tribes also have treaty rights.

**Indigenous settlements** Small Indigenous centres, often found on reserves or in remote, northern locations.

**Indigenous title** A legal term that recognizes an Indigenous interest in traditionally occupied land.

**industrial structure** The sectors of a national, regional, or local economy—primary (e.g., resource extraction and harvesting), secondary (e.g., manufacturing, construction), and tertiary (services)—and the extent to which the whole economy is driven by each of these sectors.

**informal economy** The non-commercial segment of an economy, such as hunting, fishing, and berry-gathering for subsistence, as well as those economic activities, for cash, barter, or in-kind payment, that never find their way into government statistics or taxation schemes.

**Inuit** People descended from the Thule, who migrated into Canada's Arctic from Alaska about 1,000 years ago. The Inuit do not fall under the Indian Act, but are identified as an Aboriginal people under the Constitution Act, 1982.

**Irish famine** The great famine in Ireland that took place between 1845 and 1852 when the principal crop and source of food, the potato, was devastated by blight, causing widespread crop failures. Many Irish immigrated to Atlantic Canada, especially to Saint John, New Brunswick.

**isostatic rebound** The gradual uplifting of the earth's crust following the retreat of an ice sheet that, because of its weight, depressed the earth's crust. Also known as postglacial uplift.

**James Bay and Northern Quebec Agreement** (JBNQA) A 1975 agreement between the Cree and Inuit of northern Quebec and the federal and Quebec governments that allowed the James Bay Project to proceed and provided the Indigenous peoples with specific rights and benefits.

**just-in-time** A system of manufacturing in which component parts are delivered from suppliers at the time required by the manufacturer, so that manufacturers do not bear the cost burden of building and maintaining large inventories.

**Kativik Regional Government** Administrative organization for Inuit in Nunavik formed in 1978 after the James Bay and Northern Quebec Agreement and given the responsibility to deliver public services to its residents and to provide technical assistance to the 14 Inuit communities with Nunavik.

**kimberlite** Intrusions of igneous rocks in the earth's crust that take a funnel-like shape. Diamonds are sometimes found in these rocks.

**knowledge-based economy** Sector of post-industrial economy based on the use of inventions and scientific knowledge to produce new products and/or services, often in engineering, management, and computer technology fields.

**Labrador Current** Cold ocean current flowing south in the North Atlantic from Greenland and Labrador.

**Lake Agassiz** Largest glacial lake in North America that covered much of Manitoba, northwestern Ontario, and eastern Saskatchewan.

**latitude** A measure of distance north or south, in degrees and minutes, along imaginary lines that encircle the globe parallel to the equator.

**light sweet crude** The most highly valued crude oil, which because of its low level of sulphur has a pleasant smell and, more importantly, requires little processing to become gasoline, kerosene, and diesel fuel.

**liquefied natural gas** (LNG) A liquid form of natural gas chilled to −162°C. The cooling process, called liquefaction, reduces the volume to one six-hundredth of its original volume.

**longitude** The distance east or west from the prime meridian at Greenwich, England, an imaginary line that runs through both the North and South poles, as measured in degrees and minutes.

**Lower Mainland** A local term describing Vancouver and the surrounding area extending from the North Shore Mountains to the border with the United States and eastward to include the Fraser Valley.

**Loyalists** Colonists who supported the British during the American Revolution. About 40,000 American colonists who were loyal to Britain resettled in Canada, especially in Nova Scotia and Quebec.

**Makivik Corporation** A non-profit organization owned by the Inuit of Nunavik and created in 1978 pursuant to the JBNQA. Its central mandate is to receive and manage the funds derived from the JBNQA.

**Manifest Destiny** The belief and subsequent political actions in nineteenth-century America that the United States, by divine right, should expand to the Pacific coast; in the view of some, this expansion was to include all of North America, thus incorporating Canada. The term was coined by journalist John L. O'Sullivan in 1845, in the context of the annexation of Texas and the Oregon Territory.

**Manitoba Act of 1870** Legislative Act of Parliament that created Canada's fifth province. Also known as the "postage stamp" province, its initial territory only encompassed the Red River Colony.

**manufacturing belt** A contiguous industrial zone in North America noted for its manufacturing and heavy industry. In Canada, this belt extends from Windsor to Quebec City, stretching across the Great Lakes and St Lawrence Lowlands.

**marine air masses** Large homogeneous bodies of air with moisture and temperature characteristics similar to the ocean where they originated. Marine air masses normally are moist and relatively mild in both winter and summer.

**megaprojects** Large-scale construction projects, often related to resource extraction, that exceed $1 billion and take more than two years to complete.

**metamorphic rocks** Rocks formed from igneous and sedimentary rocks by means of heat and pressure.

**Métis** People of mixed biological and cultural heritage, usually either French–First Nations peoples or English– or Scottish–First Nations peoples.

**Metrolinx** A Crown corporation responsible for regional transportation in the Greater Toronto Area and the Golden Triangle

**modernization** A progressive transition from a traditional society to a modern one; underlying theme in Rostow's Stages of Economic Growth theory.

**mortality rate** The number of deaths per 1,000 people in a given year; also called crude death rate.

**muskeg** A wet, marshy area found in areas of poor drainage, such as the Hudson Bay Lowlands. Muskeg contains peat deposits.

**Nalcor Energy Corporation** An energy Crown corporation created by the Newfoundland and Labrador government in 2007.

**nation** A group of people sharing a sense of community based on any or all of several characteristics, including language, ethnicity, religion, a common history; a geographically bounded territory with a central government, laws, regulations, and shared norms.

**National Energy Program (NEP)** A bold policy of the federal Liberal government in 1980 to keep Canadian oil prices lower than the rapidly rising world oil prices, provide manufacturers in Ontario and Quebec with low-priced western oil, foster oil exploration in the Arctic, and increase federal government revenues from oil sales. The NEP ended in 1985 after a Progressive Conservative government replaced the Liberals in power.

**National Policy** A policy of high tariffs instituted in 1879 by the federal government of John A. Macdonald to insulate Canada's infant manufacturing industries from foreign competition and thus create a national industrial base.

**non-status Indians** Those of Amerindian ancestry who are not registered as Indians under the Indian Act.

**nor'easters** Strong winds off the North Atlantic from the northeast that bring stormy weather.

**North American Free Trade Agreement (NAFTA)** Trade agreement among Canada, the United States, and Mexico that came into effect in January 1994, forming the world's largest free trade area.

**northern frontier** View of Canada's North as a place of resource wealth to be exploited.

**Northwest Passage** Sea route(s) through the Arctic Ocean connecting the Atlantic and Pacific Oceans that can be traversed only in the summer.

**Nunavik** Homeland of the Inuit of northern Quebec, with a semi-autonomous political unit known as the Kativik Regional Government.

**oil prices** Either of two pricing systems for oil in North America. Tidewater cities use the Brent crude oil price while inland cities use the West Texas Intermediate (WTI) price.

**Oregon Territory** Territory in the Pacific Northwest, the possession of which was disputed between the US and Great Britain. The Oregon Treaty of 1846 between the United States and Great Britain determined the boundary at the forty-ninth parallel but with Vancouver Island remaining within British North America.

**orogeny** Mountain-building, a geologic process that takes place as a result of plate tectonics (movement of huge pieces of the earth's crust). The result is distinctive structural change to the earth's crust where mountains are formed.

**orographic precipitation** Rain or snow created when air is forced up the side of a mountain, thereby cooling the air and causing condensation followed by precipitation.

**orographic uplift** Air forced to rise and cool over mountains. If the cooling is sufficient, water vapour condenses into clouds and rain or snow occurs.

**outsourcing** Arrangement by a firm to obtain some parts or services from other firms.

**Paleo-Indians** Considered by archaeologists the first people of North America because they shared a common hunting culture, which was characterized by its uniquely designed fluted-point stone spearhead.

**Palliser's Triangle** Area of short-grass natural vegetation in southern Alberta and Saskatchewan named after Captain John Palliser, who led the British North American Exploring Expedition (the Palliser Expedition) of 1857–9, formed by the Royal Geographical Society and the British government to explore the Canadian Prairies and determine the possibilities for agricultural settlement.

**pass system** Regulation introduced following the Northwest Resistance of 1885 requiring Indians on reserves in the West to obtain permission from the local Indian agent before leaving their reserve; later this was extended to all reserves and remained government policy until the 1940s.

**patterned ground** The natural arrangement of stones and pebbles in polygonal shapes found in the Arctic where continuous permafrost is subjected to frost-shattering as the principal erosion process.

**Peace River Country** Aspen parkland region at the northern edge of agriculture in northwest Alberta and northeast British Columbia.

**peneplain** A more or less level land surface caused by the wearing down of ancient mountains; represents an advanced stage of erosion.

**periphery** The weakly developed area surrounding an industrial core; also known as a hinterland.

**permafrost** Permanently frozen ground.

**physiographic region** A large geographic area characterized by a single landform; for example, the Interior Plains.

**physiography** A study of landforms, their underlying geology, and the processes that shape these landforms; geomorphology.

**Pineapple Express** A strong and persistent flow of warm air from the southwest associated with heavy rainfall that originates in the waters adjacent to the Hawaiian Islands.

**pingos** Hills or mounds that maintain an ice core and that are found in areas of permafrost.

**plate tectonics** The study of movement in the seven large pieces or "plates" of the Earth's outermost layer, the lithosphere, as well as in smaller remnant plates, such as the Juan de Fuca plate south and west of Vancouver Island.

**Pleistocene epoch** A minor division of the Geological Time Chart beginning nearly 2 million years ago and associated with several (likely, four) glacial advances interrupted by the retreat of these advances when comparatively warmer climate prevailed. The last advance, called the Wisconsin, ended about 11,000 years ago.

**pluralistic society** A society where small groups within the larger society are permitted to maintain their unique cultural identities; multiculturalism.

**population density** The total number of people in a geographic area divided by the land area; population per unit of land area.

**population distribution** The dispersal of a population within a geographic area.

**population growth** The rate at which a population is increasing or decreasing in a given period due to natural increase and net migration; often expressed as a percentage of the original or base population.

**population increase** The total population increase resulting from the interaction of births, deaths, and migration in a population in a given period of time.

**population optimum** The situation in which a population can maintain the maximum number of individuals and a high standard of living for all members of the population.

**Port Royal** The settlement founded in the summer of 1605 on the north shore of the Annapolis Basin near the mouth of the Annapolis River by a French colonizing expedition led by Pierre du Gua de Monts and Samuel de Champlain.

**postglacial uplift** The gradual rising of the earth's crust following the retreat of an ice sheet that, because of its weight, depressed the earth's crust. Also known as isostatic rebound.

**potash** A general term for potassium salts. The most important potassium salt is sylvite (potassium chloride). Potassium (K) is a nutrient essential for plant growth.

**potlatch** Ceremonial feast of Northwest Coast First Nations involving lavish gift-giving by the host. The potlatch, as well as the sun dance, was banned by 1884 changes to the Indian Act as being contrary to European values and was finally reinstated by amendments to the Act in 1951.

**Poundmaker (Pitikwahanapiwiyin)** An outstanding political leader of the Plains Cree who played a key role in setting the terms for Treaty 6; imprisoned, along with Big Bear, following the Northwest Resistance of 1885 despite his efforts as a peacemaker, and died shortly after his release.

**primary products** Goods derived from agriculture, fishing, logging, mining, and trapping; products of nature with no or little processing.

**primary sector** Economic sector involving the direct extraction/production of natural resources that includes agriculture, fishing, logging, mining, oil and gas, and trapping.

**Provincial Agricultural Land Commission** An independent British Columbia agency responsible for administering the province's land-use zone in favour of agriculture.

**Provisional Government** Government formed in 1869 by the Métis, under the leadership of Louis Riel, in order to negotiate the terms to permit the Red River Colony to join Canada as a province.

**quaternary sector** Knowledge-based economic activities that provide high-technology information services, such as computing, information and communication technologies, and research and development.

**Québécois** A term that has evolved from referring to French-speaking residents of Quebec to meaning all residents of Quebec.

**Quiet Revolution** A period in Quebec during the Liberal government of Jean Lesage (1960–6) characterized by social, economic, and educational reforms and by the rebirth of pride and self-confidence among the French-speaking members of Quebec society, which led to a resurgence of francophone ethnic nationalism.

**rain shadow effect** A dry area on the lee side of mountains where air masses descend, causing them to become warmer and drier.

**rate of natural increase** The surplus (or deficit) of births over deaths in a population per 1,000 people in a given time period.

**reasonable accommodation** The accommodation by government, within limits, of the needs and desires of those groups within society—e.g., ethnic minorities, disabled people, religious groups, immigrants—who are disadvantaged by their identity. In Quebec, the Bouchard-Taylor Commission of 2008, in the context of an increasingly secular Quebec society, reported on this problem to mixed reviews, because it opted for seeking to accommodate religious minorities.

**recent immigrants** Statistics Canada term that refers to landed immigrants who arrived in Canada within five years prior to a given census.

**Red River migration** British-instituted migration organized by the Hudson's Bay Company whereby perhaps as many as 1,000 settlers from Fort Garry travelled by horse-drawn wagons to Fort Vancouver in 1841 to shore up the British claim to the Oregon Territory.

**region** An area of the earth's surface defined by its distinctive human and/or natural characteristics. Boundaries between regions often are transition zones where the main characteristics of one region merge into those of a neighbouring region. Geographers use the concept of regions to study parts of the world.

**regional consciousness** Identification with a place or region, including the strong feeling of belonging to that space and the willingness to advocate for regional interests.

**regional geography** The study of the geography of regions and the interplay between physical and human geography, which results in an understanding of human society, its physical geographical underpinnings, and a sense of place.

**regional identity** Persons' association with a place or region and their sense of belonging to a collectivity.

**regionalism** The division of countries or areas of the earth into different natural/political/cultural parts.

**regional service centres** Urban places where economic functions are provided to residents living within the surrounding area.

**relief** A measure of elevation of the land relative to sea level, which is designated as zero; a relief map indicates elevation and/or topographic features, such as a mountain range, by different colours.

**reserve** Under the Indian Act, lands "held by her Majesty for the use and benefit of the bands for which they were set apart; and subject to this Act and to the terms of any treaty or surrender."

**residential schools** Boarding schools for Indigenous children and youth funded by the federal government and run by various churches from the 1880s to 1996 that effectively sought to acculturate Canada's First Peoples by taking away their cultural, language, and spiritual belief systems and replacing these with Euro-Canadian systems.

**residual uplift** The final stages of isostatic rebound.

**resource frontier** The perception of the Territorial North as a place of great mineral wealth that awaits development by outsiders.

**resource town** An urban place where a single economic activity focused on resource extraction (e.g., mining, logging, oil drilling) dominates the local economy; single-industry town. Also, a company town built near an isolated mine site to house the mine workers and their families.

**restrained rebound** The first stage of isostatic rebound.

**restructure** To make economic adjustments deemed necessary by fierce competition, whereby companies reduce costs by reducing the number of workers at their plants.

**Robinson treaties** Two 1850 treaties signed between the Crown (Canada West) and the Ojibwa First Nations of Lake Superior and the Ojibwa Indians of Lake Huron. Under the terms of both agreements, the Crown secured an area of 52,400 square miles mostly in central and northern Ontario. For the first time, reserves were part of the agreement. The Crown paid the Ojibwa peoples a lump sum as well as an annual payment in perpetuity.

**Scottish Highland clearances** Forced displacements of poor tenant farmers in the Scottish Highlands during the eighteenth and nineteenth centuries. Migration ensued, and in 1812 Scottish settlers arrived at Fort Garry to found Lord Selkirk's experimental colony. Most of the Scottish crofters who came to what would become Canada, perhaps 100,000, settled in Nova Scotia. The clearances were part of a process of change of estate land use from small farm leases to large-scale sheep herding.

**scrip** Under the Manitoba Act of 1870, certificates issued by Ottawa to the Métis to settle their land claims and to allow them to obtain land. This scrip was issued to individuals and was redeemable in Dominion lands in Manitoba.

**sea ice** Ice formed from ocean water. Types of sea ice include: (1) "fast ice" frozen along coasts and that extends out from land; (2) "pack ice," which is floating, consolidated sea ice detached from land; (3) the "ice floe," a floating chunk of sea ice that is less than 10 km (six miles) in diameter; and (4) the "ice field," a chunk of sea ice more than 10 km (six miles) in diameter.

**Sea-to-Sky Highway** Highway that winds through the spectacular Coast Mountains, linking communities from West Vancouver to Whistler. Since rock slides occur frequently, the highway was widened and straightened to reduce the chances of rock slides and to improve safety and reliability for the 2010 Winter Olympic Games.

**secondary sector** The sector of the economy involved in processing and transforming raw materials into finished goods; the manufacturing sector of an economy.

**sedimentary basins** Structural depressions in sedimentary rock caused by a bending of sedimentary strata into huge bowl-like shapes. Petroleum may accumulate in sedimentary basins.

**sedimentary rocks** Rocks formed from the layered accumulation in sequence of sediment deposited in the bottom of an ocean.

**seigneurs** Members of the French elite—high-ranking officials, military officers, the nascent aristocracy—who were awarded land in New France by the French king. A seigneur was an estate owner who had peasants (habitants) to work his land.

**senatorial clause** Guarantees that no province has fewer seats in the House of Commons than it has in the Senate.

**sense of place** The special and often intense feelings that people have for the area where they live.

**settler state** A country settled, governed, and dominated by (chiefly European) immigrants, such as Canada, the United States, Australia, and New Zealand, often with the original inhabitants having been pushed to the margins of society.

**smog** The most visible form of air pollution, caused when heat and sunlight react with various pollutants emitted by industry, vehicle exhaust, pesticides, and oil-based home products.

**"soft" countries.** *See* "hard" and "soft" countries.

**softwood forest** The predominant forest in Canada. Softwood forests consist mainly of coniferous trees, characterized by needle-like foliage.

**sovereignty-association** A concept designed by the Parti Québécois under the Lévesque government and employed in the 1980 referendum. This was based on the vision of Canada as consisting of two "equal" peoples. Sovereignty-association called for Quebec sovereignty within a partnership with Canada based on an economic association.

**specific land claims** Claims made by treaty Indians to rectify shortcomings in the original treaty agreement with a band or that seek to redress failure on the part of the federal government to meet the terms of the treaty. Many of these have involved the unilateral alienation of reserve land by the government.

**sporadic permafrost** Pockets of permanently frozen ground mixed with large areas of unfrozen ground. Sporadic permafrost ranges from a trace of permanently frozen ground to an area having up to 30 per cent of its ground permanently frozen.

**staples thesis** Harold Innis's idea that the history of Canada, especially its regional economic and institutional development, was linked to the discovery, exploitation, and export of particular staple resources in Canada's vast frontier.

**staples trap** The economic and social consequences on a region and its population following the exhaustion of its resources; the opposite outcome of the positive outcome of economic diversification anticipated in the staples thesis of Canadian political economist and historian Harold Innis, who linked the discovery, exploitation, and export of particular staple resources in Canada's vast frontier to Canadian regional development.

**status (registered) Indians** Indigenous peoples who are registered as Indians under the Indian Act.

**strata** Layers of sedimentary rock.

**subsidence** A downward movement of the ground. Subsidence occurs in areas of permafrost when large blocks of ice within the ground melt, causing the material above to sink or collapse.

**summer fallow** The farming practice of leaving land idle for a year or more to accumulate sufficient soil moisture to produce a crop or to restore soil fertility; summer fallowing is being replaced by continuous cropping.

**super cycle** Extended periods of high global growth driven by the emergence of large, new economies that are undergoing the early stages of industrialization. The concept is based on two premises: (1) that demand will tend to outstrip supply and thus keep prices high; and (2) that in a global economic downturn, demand from industrializing countries will keep price declines to a minimum.

**terraces** Old sea beaches left after the sea has receded; old flood plains created when streams or rivers cut downward to form new and lower flood plains. The old flood plain (now a terrace) is found along the sides of the stream or river.

**terra nullius** The doctrine according to which European countries claimed legal right to ownership of the land occupied by First Nations peoples and Inuit because the land was not cultivated and lacked permanent settlements.

**tertiary/quaternary sector** The economic sector engaged in services such as retailing, wholesaling, education, and financial and professional services; the quaternary sector, for which at present statistical data are not compiled, involves the collection, processing, and manipulation of information.

**thermal expansion** The increasing volume of ocean waters as water warmth increases.

**till** Unsorted glacial deposits.

**topography** The shape of the surface of the land; contour maps, using isolines (contour lines), are one representation of topography and/or topographic features, with each line on the map representing the same elevation above sea level.

**tragedy of the commons** The destruction of renewable resources that are not privately owned, such as fisheries and forests.

**Trans-Pacific Partnership** Twelve countries (Canada, United States, Mexico, Australia, New Zealand, Peru, Chile, Singapore, Vietnam, Malaysia, Japan, and Brunei) that negotiated a free trade agreement. The agreement was effectively voided before ratification following the 2016 US presidential election when President-elect Trump reiterated his campaign promise to reject the TPP.

**treaty Indians** Indigenous people who are descendants of First Nations peoples who signed a numbered treaty and who benefit from the rights described in the treaty. All treaty Indians are status Indians, but not all status Indians are treaty Indians.

**treaty rights** Specific rights that apply only to the First Nation(s) that signed the treaty in question. While no two treaties are identical, the list of rights always included land (reserves). These rights are protected in the Constitution Act.

**Turing test** "Can machines think?" The question posed by British mathematician and computer scientist Alan Turing in 1950.

**Tyrrell Sea** Prehistoric Hudson Bay as the Laurentide Ice Sheet receded. Its extent was considerably greater than that of present-day Hudson Bay because the land had been depressed by the weight of the ice sheet.

**underemployment** Generally, workers who are employed, but not in the desired capacity, whether in terms of compensation, hours, or level of education, skill, and experience. In this text, "underemployment" refers to persons in small communities where the very few jobs are already filled and, because these potential workers are aware that no job opportunities exist, they do not seek jobs elsewhere.

**unemployment** Lack of paid work, but this term and statistics based on it measure only those who are seeking paid employment.

**upgrader** A processing plant that breaks large hydrocarbon molecules (such as bitumen) into smaller ones by increasing the hydrogen-to-carbon ratio. The product is supplied to refineries, which will process it into gasoline, jet fuel, diesel, propane, and butane.

**urban areas** Communities with economic and social functions that differentiate them from rural places; the common practice of defining urban population is by a specified size that assumes the presence of urban economic and social functions. Statistics Canada considers all places with a combination of a population of 1,000 or more and a population density of at least 400 per km² to be urban areas. People living in urban areas make up the urban population. People living outside of urban areas are considered rural residents and, by definition, constitute the rural population.

**weathering** The decomposition of rock and particles in situ.

**western alienation** Feeling on the part of those in Western Canada and BC—derived from past government actions and a natural periphery response to the core—that they have little influence on federal policy and that Central Canada controls the government in Ottawa.

**Western Canadian Select** One of several global oil-pricing systems; this one prices heavy crude oil from the Western Canadian Sedimentary Basin, including bitumen from the Athabasca tar sands.

**Western Sedimentary Basin** Within the geological structure of the Interior Plains, normally flat sedimentary strata that are bent into a basin-like shape. These basins often contain petroleum deposits.

**winter roads** Temporary ice roads over muskeg, lakes, and rivers built during the winter to provide ground transportation for freight and travel to remote northern communities and work sites.

# Websites

## CHAPTER 1

www.youtube.com/watch?v=NuZ6wWESCVg
Laurence C. Smith imagines the effect of climate change on the world of 2050. This YouTube video is based on his book *The World in 2050: Four Forces Shaping Civilization's Northern Future*.

http://news.nationalpost.com/news/canada/the-giant-flaw-in-canadian-maps-you-never-noticed-mapmakers-keep-pretending-we-own-the-north-pole
In 1907, Senator Pascal Poirier argued that Canada should claim lands and seas to the North Pole based on the sector theory. Accordingly, the 141 west longitude extends from Yukon to the North Pole. However, this boundary is not recognized in the international community. Instead, the Exclusive Economic Zone forms the outermost sea boundary to a maximum of 200 nautical miles.

geography.about.com/od/politicalgeography/a/coreperiphery.htm
The origins and transformation of the core/periphery theory are presented here.

## CHAPTER 2

www.youtube.com/watch?v=6ZAuRpK4tkc
NASA illustrates the loss of the polar ice cap over time.

https://www.earthquakescanada.nrcan.gc.ca/historic-historique/events/19490822-en.php
Details on the 1949 earthquake off Haida Gwaii.

http://news.nationalpost.com/full-comment/canada-russias-toxic-waste-dump
Russia uses Baffin Bay as dumping ground for toxic materials from its space program.

www.cbc.ca/news/technology/polar-bear-populations-can-be-monitored-by-satellite-1.2710341
Satellite technology counts polar bears.

http://news.nationalpost.com/news/canada/the-beast-is-alive-how-the-fire-that-tried-to-destroy-fort-mcmurray-is-still-burning-near-the-albertasaskatchewan-border
Columnist Tristin Hopper reports on "The Beast" wildfire going underground.

www.theglobeandmail.com/news/british-columbia/tug-sinking-shows-oil-spill-response-resources-inadequate-transport-minister/article32694781/
Oil spill in BC waters demonstrates both the risk of oil spills and the lack of preparedness by federal marine operations.

## CHAPTER 3

https://atlas.gc.ca/ette/en/index.html
Maps that illustrate the territorial evolution of Canada and an animated version of Canada's territorial development are found here.

faculty.marianopolis.edu/c.belanger/quebechistory/events/quiet.htm
An account of the Quiet Revolution in Quebec.

https://www.cbc.ca/archives/topic/separation-anxiety-the-1995-quebec-referendum
CBC Digital Archives provides a close look at "separation anxiety" in Canada associated with the 1995 referendum.

www.mhs.mb.ca/docs/pageant/13/selkirksettlement1.shtml
The Manitoba Historical Society has documented Lord Selkirk's land grant of 1811.

http://en.wikipedia.org/wiki/Haldimand_Proclamation
The Haldimand Proclamation.

www.llbc.leg.bc.ca/public/PubDocs/bcdocs/322107/north_east_coal_facts.pdf
Boom and bust: the Northeast Coal Project.

## CHAPTER 4

www.cbc.ca/history/EPISCONTENTSE1EP14CH3PA3LE.html
CBC provides an account of the internment of Japanese Canadians living in BC.

www.youtube.com/watch?v=yGd764YU9yc
Gord Downie's *The Secret Path*, the animated version of the graphic novel by Downie and artist Jeff Lemire, which aired on CBC television on 23 October 2016, the fiftieth anniversary of 12-year-old Chanie Wenjack's death. The young Indigenous boy fled from a residential school in Kenora and died of exposure along the CN rail line as he sought to walk hundreds of kilometres to his home at Ogoki Post on the Marten Falls Reserve. The video includes opening and closing sequences of Downie visiting Chanie's sisters on the reserve in northern Ontario, where Downie went right after completing his final tour with the Tragically Hip.

www.theglobeandmail.com/opinion/why-black-canadians-are-facing-us-style-problems/article30939514/
Columnist Doug Saunders describes the nature of discrimination faced by Black Canadians.

www.idlenomore.ca
Official website of the grassroots Indigenous movement that emerged in late 2012.

https://www150.statcan.gc.ca/t1/tbl1/en/tv.action?pid=1710000901
Statistics Canada's population estimates are provided quarterly.

www.theglobeandmail.com/news/toronto/the-quest-to-understand-kensington-market-torontos-weird-little-island/article32302041/
Does Toronto's Kensington Market fit Florida's image of a culturally diverse city?

www.youtube.com/watch?v=HJooje7taXU
Short video on effort to improve education for a First Nation in northern Ontario.

## CHAPTER 5

https://www.youtube.com/watch?v=lbB_iVmpnGM
Bank of Canada sees rough waters ahead for Canada's economy.

www.theglobeandmail.com/report-on-business/give-fuel-cells-a-chance-says-toyota-canada-president-larry-hutchinson/article32587525/
Discussion of the wave of the future: technology and electric cars lead to sharply reduced greenhouse gas emissions.

www.theglobeandmail.com/opinion/on-energy-pm-needs-to-lead-with-his-head-not-heart/article31727993/
Columnist Lawrence Martin offers his ideas on the controversial topic of pipelines.

## CHAPTER 6

https://www.cbc.ca/news/canada/kitchener-waterloo/university-waterloo-engineering-building-robohub-talos-1.4882589
The University of Waterloo opens "Robohub" in its engineering building.

www.statcan.gc.ca/kits-trousses/projet-cyber-project/manufact2-eng.htm
Students can test the premise: Ontario and Quebec were the Canadian leaders in manufacturing at the time of Confederation and they maintained that dominance into the twenti-eth-first century.

## CHAPTER 7

https://www.theglobeandmail.com/featured-reports/article-how-canadas-dairy-farmers-are-preparing-for-a-new-more-competitive/
How Canada's dairy farmers are preparing to compete in future trade.

www.greatlakes-seaway.com/en/
Official site of the Great Lakes–St Lawrence Seaway system.

https://www.canadiangeographic.ca/article/celebrating-60-years-st-lawrence-seaway
History of the St Lawrence Seaway plus archival photographs and a tour of the seaway.

## CHAPTER 8

https://www.cer-rec.gc.ca/nrg/ntgrtd/mrkt/snpsht/2020/01-05cndrtrngcfpp-eng.html
A look at Canada's plan to move away from coal-fired power plants.

www.youtube.com/watch?v=j6zBun7zZs0
Can carbon capture work?

www.saskmining.ca/commodity_info/Commodities/1/potash.html
The history of potash mining in Saskatchewan.

www.youtube.com/watch?v=0WPnZv5TdYE
Pipeline technology.

## CHAPTER 9

https://globalnews.ca/video/7134587/trans-mountain-pipeline-project-clears-another-hurdle/
Trans Mountain pipeline approved by Supreme Court of Canada.

https://dailyhive.com/vancouver/vancouver-post-amazon-hq2
Vancouver is set to become Amazon's unofficial HQ2.

https://globalnews.ca/news/6085491/bc-foreign-buyers-tax-lawsuit-tossed/
A Supreme Court judge dismisses a class action lawsuit claiming foreign buyers tax is unconstitutional.

www.youtube.com/watch?v=eBirhxxA5R0
BC launches $100 million tech fund.

## CHAPTER 10

https://www.thechronicleherald.ca/business/regional-business/husky-energy-suspends-west-white-rose-project-in-newfoundland-428002/
In 2020, Husky Energy suspends West White Rose Project in Newfoundland.

https://www.theglobeandmail.com/canada/article-economic-storm-brews-over-newfoundland-and-labrador/
Newfoundland and Labrador's economic outlook.

www.offshore-technology.com/projects/hibernia/
Hibernia, Jeanne d'Arc Basin, and its technology.

## CHAPTER 11

https://nunatsiaq.com/stories/article/canada-submits-its-arctic-ocean-claim-to-the-united-nations/
Canada submits its claim to the Arctic seabed.

https://www.washingtonpost.com/travel/2020/08/31/indigenous-communities-are-educating-tourists-high-arctic-one-cruise-voyage-time/
How Indigenous communities are educating Arctic tourists.

www.arctic-council.org/index.php/en/
Formation and mandate of the Arctic Council, as well as Canada's role in the Arctic Council.

www.statsnwt.ca/
The Bureau of Statistics of the Northwest Territories provides not only a wide variety of statistical data but also links to Yukon and Nunavut statistical data.

## CHAPTER 12

https://www.statcan.gc.ca/eng/covid19
Data on the impact of the COVID-19 pandemic on Canada.

https://www.canada.ca/en/environment-climate-change/news/2019/06/canadas-plan-for-climate-change-and-clean-growth.html
Canada's plan for climate change and clean growth.

# Notes

## CHAPTER 1

1. Geography, like other social sciences, has evolved over time. In fact, a central theme in Johnston and Sidaway's *Geography and Geographers* (2016) is that this evolution shows little sign of diminishing. Why is that? One reason is that the paradigms come and go with shifts in global societal concerns. Another reason is that geographers have become more specialized, which has resulted in more types of geography, i.e., medical, recreation, and urban geographies are but a few of the types of human geography practised by today's geographers. Regional geography, once the core of the discipline, is now on the margins of human geography. Its future depends on reformulating itself. Critical thinking plays a role in such a transformation. This text is an attempt at such reformulation.

2. Yet, by their very nature, theories must simplify the real world. In doing so, when applied to actual regions, they often lose touch with the complexity and variety of economic, political, and social forces at play. Added to this shortcoming, economic theories are based on past events, which means that, as the world changes, they must either be adjusted to fit the new economic circumstances or be replaced by more robust hypotheses.

## CHAPTER 2

1. Canadians have various visions of themselves, their region, and their country. For the most part, these visions are rooted in the physical nature and historical experiences that have affected Canada and its regions. For example, people see Canada as a northern country because of its location in North America and because of its climates, which are often noted for long, cold winters. Louis-Edmond Hamelin's concept of nordicity exemplifies the impact of "northernness" from a geographer's perspective. Hamelin (1979) provides a measure of "northernness" according to five geographic zones—Extreme North, Far North, Middle North, Near North, and Ecumene (southern Canada). Songwriters, too, have been intrigued by Canada's northern nature, and well-known writers, from Jack London and Robert Service to Margaret Atwood, Pierre Berton, and Farley Mowat, have written about the North and, in doing so, have etched out another parameter of Canadian identity.

2. The Champlain Sea covered Anticosti Island and the northern tip of the island of Newfoundland. For the purposes of this text, the eastern extent of this physiographic region ends just east of Quebec City.

3. The distance between latitudes is almost constant at 111 km. On the other hand, the distance between longitudes varies from 111 km to nearly zero because of the spherical shape of the earth, which causes longitude lines to become closer and closer towards the North Pole and South Pole. The distance between the equator (0°) and 1°N is approximately 111 km and between 89°N and the North Pole (90°N) is nearly zero.

4. The mean annual temperature of a location on the earth's surface is a measure of the energy balance at that point. Solar energy is the source of heat for the earth, and this energy is returned to the atmosphere in a variety of ways. Therefore, a global energy balance exists. However, there are regional energy surpluses and deficits in different parts of the world. For example, the Arctic has an energy deficit, while the tropics have a surplus. These energy differences drive the global atmospheric and oceanic circulation systems. When the mean annual temperature is below zero Celsius, it indicates that an energy deficit exists.

## CHAPTER 3

1. Under the terms of the British North America Act, the Dominion of Canada was composed of four provinces (Ontario, Quebec, New Brunswick, and Nova Scotia). Modelled after the British parliamentary and monarchical system of government, the newly formed country had a Parliament made up of three elements: the head of government (a governor general who represented the monarch), an upper house (the Senate), and a lower house (the House of Commons). This Act was modified several times to accommodate Canada's evolving political needs and its gradual movement to independent nationhood. The patriation of Canada's Constitution in 1982 removed the last vestige of Canada's political dependence on the United Kingdom, although Canada still recognizes the British monarch as its symbolic head.

   After the defeat of the French by the British in 1763, Pontiac, the Odawa chief in the Ohio Valley, led a successful uprising against the British. By capturing the forts in the Ohio Territory, he exposed Britain's precarious hold on this region, which the British had just obtained from the French. However, Pontiac and his followers could not hold these forts against the British because, with French forces driven back to France, Pontiac had no source of ammunition and muskets. He concluded that his best move would be to make peace with Britain. The British came to the same conclusion, though for other reasons. Without the help of Pontiac and the other chiefs in this region, Britain would lose control over these lands. Britain therefore had to form an alliance with them. With that objective in mind, George III announced an important concession to these Indigenous peoples in the Royal Proclamation of 1763, namely, that the King recognized them as valued allies and that the land they used to hunt and trap was "Indian land" within the British Empire. In 1783, the American revolt against Great Britain ended with an American victory, which opened the lands west of the Appalachian Mountains to settlement by New Englanders and, at the same time, ended the dream of a vast "Indian land" within the British Empire.

2. The Manitoba Act of 1870 recognized the legal status of farms and other lands occupied by the Métis as "fee simple" private property. The lands allotted to the Métis were distributed after 1875, but much

of the scrip land was sold and then occupied by non-Métis. For more on this subject, see Tough (1996, ch. 6). Flanagan (1991) argues that the federal government of the day, while often slow in settling the Métis claims, did not act in bad faith. Taking the opposite position, Sprague (1988) claims that the Métis were victims of a deliberate conspiracy by the federal government to prevent a Métis land base in Manitoba. Milne (1995) provides a summary of this controversy. The 2013 Supreme Court of Canada ruling stated that the federal government, over 140 years earlier, "acted with persistent inattention and failed to act diligently" in regard to the land grant provision of the Manitoba Act of 1870, and emphasized that "repeated mistakes and inaction . . . persisted for more than a decade" (CBC News, 2013b).

3. The original Magna Carta goes far back in history to 1215, when King John of England was forced to sign a charter known as the Magna Carta. In this charter, he promised to consult regularly with the country's nobles before collecting new taxes, and to stop interfering in affairs of the Church.

4. While the French language was not recognized by the Quebec Act, 1774, the governor made use of the French language in conducting his business with local officials. For example, the judges appointed by the governor had to know both languages in order to facilitate the business of the court. In short, while English was the official language of British North America, the British colony of Quebec functioned in both the French and English languages.

5. Riel is considered both a Father of Confederation and a traitor to the country. Born in the Red River Colony in 1844, Louis Riel studied for the priesthood at the Collège de Montréal. The founder of Manitoba and the central figure in both the Red River Resistance (1869–70) and the Northwest Resistance (1885), he was captured shortly after the Battle of Batoche, where the Métis forces were defeated. After a trial in Regina, the jury found Riel guilty of treason but recommended clemency. Appeals were made to Manitoba's Court of Queen's Bench and to the Judicial Committee of the Privy Council. Both appeals were dismissed. A final appeal went to the federal cabinet, but the government of John A. Macdonald wanted Riel executed. Riel was hanged in Regina on 16 November 1885. His body was interred in the cemetery at the Cathedral of St Boniface in Manitoba.

6. Riel's execution has had a lasting effect on Canada. In Quebec, French Canadians felt betrayed by the Conservative government and federalism: Canada's French-speaking population believed they could not count on the federal government to look after French-Canadian interests. It was also a blow against a francophone presence in the West. In Ontario, Riel's death satisfied the anti-Catholic and anti-French majority. In the West, Riel's hanging resulted in the marginalization of both the Métis and Indigenous groups, especially those who participated in the uprising.

## CHAPTER 4

1. The debate between tolerance and intolerance is one of the great debates of our times. Canada, like many other countries, is a pluralistic, multicultural nation. For Canada, reconciliation represents an attempt to view the history of the country through the traditional lens of settlers and the "other" via the experience of Indigenous peoples. This debate can move forward only by respecting the norm of tolerance. That does not mean that everything must be tolerated—a civilized society has no choice but to condemn practices that cause harm to others and injure citizens or undermine the fabric of peaceful coexistence. But it means the basic rule must be tolerance. Preserving that tolerance is grounded in respect for the innate human dignity of each person. It compels us to cultivate and sustain inclusive institutions and attitudes. And it demands an unwavering commitment to the rule of law.

2. "Race," unlike ethnicity, is based on physical characteristics. Racial types are frequently assigned a set of social characteristics, which is known as "stereotyping." Sociologists define "race" as the socially constructed classification of persons into categories on the basis of real or imagined physical characteristics such as skin colour. Others consider "race" a means of creating major divisions of humankind on the basis of distinct physical characteristics.

3. French and English, as the official languages, represent the traditional duality of Canadian society. With the establishment of the Province of Canada in 1841, the relationship flowered into a partnership, with English-speaking Canada West and French-speaking Canada East sharing political power. In 1867, the British North America Act (section 133) established that both French and English "may be used by any Person in the Debates of the Houses of Parliament of Canada and of the Houses of the Legislature of Quebec," as well as in federal courts, but it was not until the Official Languages Act of 1969 that French truly began to be entrenched in the institutions of Canadian society. The assignment of education to the provinces in the BNA Act (section 93) and the stipulation that Roman Catholic (i.e., francophone) schools had equal standing with Protestant (i.e., anglophone) schools ensured that French would retain a dominant position in Quebec, at least for the time being.

4. In 1974, the Quebec Liberal government passed Bill 22 (Loisur la langue officielle), which made French the language of government and the workplace. In 1977, the Parti Québécois government introduced a much stronger language measure in the form of Bill 101 (Charte de la langue française). This legislation eliminated English as one of the official languages of Quebec and required the children of all newcomers to Quebec to be educated in French. Four years later, Bill 178 required all commercial signs to use only French. The French language has made modest gains outside of Quebec. In 1969, New Brunswick passed an Official Languages Act, which gave equal status, rights, and privileges to English and French, and the federal Parliament passed the Official Languages Act, which declared the equal status of English and French in Parliament and in the Canadian public service.

## CHAPTER 5

1. Trade disputes remain troublesome. In April 2009, for example, the United States rekindled the softwood lumber dispute by imposing a 10 per cent tariff on lumber from four provinces that, according to Washington, exported more to the US than the 2006 lumber agreement specified. The Free Trade Agreement, which was replaced by the North American Free Trade Agreement, really means freer trade rather than free trade. As we have seen, four trade agreements—the Auto Pact (1965; nullified in 2001), the FTA (1989), NAFTA (1994), and the USMCA (2020)—have led to a realignment of the Canadian economy so that it is more thoroughly integrated with the North

American economy. These trade agreements have seen more and more manufactured goods exported to the US, thus breaking the old pattern of exporting primarily low-value unprocessed or semi-processed resources, and the volume of exports to the US has grown dramatically. In spite of these trade agreements, however, Washington is prepared to defend US business interests by imposing trade barriers, as has been the case with duties on softwood lumber and grain, to restrict the natural flow of certain Canadian goods into the US. The purpose of these duties is twofold: (1) to protect US farmers and forest companies in the short run by imposing duties on targeted Canadian exports, and (2) to force Canada to accept a long-term agreement that will limit its grain and lumber exports. Most recently, on 16 August 2020, the US imposed a 10 per cent tariff on Canadian aluminum imports but then withdrew the tariff a month later just as Canada was about to impose retaliatory measures; however, Washington promised to revisit the issue after the November 2020 presidential election (Harris & Panetta, 2020). Historically, the main US target has been Canadian softwood lumber.

## CHAPTER 6

1. In 1970, mercury was discovered in the fish near the Grassy Narrows Reserve, which is about 500 km downstream from the pulp mill. Levels of methyl mercury in the aquatic food chain were 10 to 50 times higher than those in the surrounding waterways (Shkilnyk, 1985, p. 189). These levels were similar to those found in the fish of Minamata Bay, Japan. Over 100 residents of this Japanese village died from mercury poisoning in the 1960s, and over 1,000 people suffered irreversible neurological damage. Because they depend on fish and game, the Ojibwa at the Grassy Narrows Reserve ate fish on a daily basis and many complained of mercury-related illnesses. Unlike the Minamata incident no one died in the immediate aftermath, but the economic, social, health impacts on the Ojibwa have been an industrial tragedy of immense proportions. As we now know, this problem for Grassy Narrows has continued.

2. Robotics have moved from simple to more complex work situations. These advances have played a key role in keeping Canadian assembly plants competitive in two ways. First, robotics technology has kept the cost of labour low by supplementing traditional workers' tasks with robotic ones. Over time, the role of robotics in assembly plants has expanded from welding to a variety of operations, including laser applications, palletizing, press loading, and the assembly line. Second, robotic "workers," programmed on the floor of the assembly line by a human worker, are extremely accurate, thus reducing flaws in assembly process.

3. The 2014 sale to Saudi Arabia of light armoured vehicles valued at $15 billion was questioned by human rights advocates because of Saudi Arabia's dire human rights record.

## CHAPTER 7

1. For the 2019 federal election, the House of Commons had 336 seats. Reapportionment takes place every 10 years based on population figures from the census. The last reapportionment, based on the 2016 census, added 30 new seats to the Commons: Ontario (15), BC (6), Alberta (6), and Quebec (3).

2. By responsible government, Lord Durham meant a "political system in which the Executive is directly and immediately responsi-

ble to the Legislature, in which the ministers are members of the Legislature, chosen from the party which includes the majority of the elected representatives of the people" (Lucas, 1912, I, p. 138).

3. In 1912, Quebec gained northern territories inhabited by the Inuit and Cree. Ottawa ceded these lands to Quebec with the understanding that the Quebec government would be responsible for settling land claims with the Indigenous peoples in these territories. At the time of the 1995 referendum, the Cree in northern Quebec, in response to the separatist claim to territorial independence, declared that they have the right to secede from Quebec. They argued that if Quebec has the right to secede from Canada, then the Cree have the right to secede from Quebec. From a geopolitical perspective, the partitioning of Canada or Quebec makes sense only to those supporting ethnic nationalism.

4. The case of Churchill Falls is an interesting one. The divide between the Atlantic Ocean and Hudson Bay drainage basins marks the Labrador–Quebec boundary. For historical reasons, the Quebec government does not formally recognize this boundary, but it does treat the area as part of Newfoundland and Labrador. Newfoundland and Labrador, through its provincial corporation Nalcor Energy, owns the large Churchill Falls hydroelectric project, but virtually all of this power is purchased by Hydro-Québec at well below market value by the terms of a contract originally signed in 1969. Hydro-Québec then transmits it across Quebec to markets in the Great Lakes–St Lawrence Lowlands and the United States. A 25-year renewal clause—at an even lower rate—kicked in on 1 September 2016 after the Quebec Court of Appeal rejected Newfoundland and Labrador's claim that the terms of the original contract were unfair, and the Quebec Superior Court ruled a week later that Hydro-Québec has the right to purchase all but two small blocks of Churchill Falls power (Boone, 2016).

## CHAPTER 8

1. In the mid-nineteenth century, the British government faced the question as to how much of Rupert's Land was suitable for new settlement. The area under consideration was the grasslands found in what is now the Prairies. One thought was that the grasslands were an extension of the Great American Desert. In 1857, the Palliser Expedition set out from England to assess the potential of Western Canada for settlement. Well documented by Spry (1963), this expedition spanned three years (1857–60). In his report to the British government, John Palliser identified two natural zones in the Canadian Prairies. The first zone was described as a sub-humid area of tall grasses, while the second, located further south, was described as a semi-arid area with short-grass vegetation. Palliser considered the area of tall grasses to be suitable for agricultural settlement. He named this area the Fertile Belt. In Manitoba this belt is south of the Canadian Shield and stretches to the border with the United States. Palliser believed that the semi-arid zone, located in southern Alberta and Saskatchewan, was a northern extension of the Great American Desert. His belief was reinforced by the Great Sand Hills (Photo 8.1). According to Palliser, these semi-arid lands were unsuitable for agricultural settlement. The area described by Captain Palliser became known as Palliser's Triangle—its area overlaps with, but is slightly larger than, the agriculture zone known as the Dry Belt (see Figure 8.4). Homesteaders called these lands "heartbreak territory"

and most abandoned their attempts at farming because of the frequency of drought-induced crop failures. David Jones's *Empire of Dust* (1987) captures the settling and abandonment of homesteads in the 1930s while Arthur Kroeger's *Hard Passage* (2007) is a personal recollection of the struggle of the author's family to homestead in Palliser's Triangle and their eventual defeat.

2. The sudden need to adjust to British rule from the 1870s on caused shock waves among the Indigenous peoples on the Prairies. The building of the Canadian Pacific Railway announced the coming of settlers and marked the demise of the great buffalo herds. Two novels illustrate the powerful impact of agricultural settlement on the Indigenous peoples, while the Métis revolts paint another picture of the clash between the old and the new. Rudy Wiebe's *The Temptations of Big Bear* (1973) focuses on the Cree; Guy Vanderhaegh's *The Englishman's Boy* (1996) looks at the Cypress Hills Massacre; George Stanley's classic *The Birth of Western Canada: A History of the Riel Rebellions* (1992) is a valuable account of the Métis in a changing world.

3. Big Bear (Mistahimaskwa) is best known for his refusal to sign Treaty 6 in 1876 and for his band's involvement in violent conflicts associated with the 1885 North-West Rebellion. The last clashes between the Cree and the early settlers took place at Frog Lake, Fort Battleford, Fort Pitt, and Cut Knife Hill. With the arrival of the Canadian militia from eastern Canada, the Cree were defeated.

## CHAPTER 9

1. In December 2009 the British Columbia government, as part of a reconciliation agreement with the Haida, officially renamed the Queen Charlotte Islands as Haida Gwaii, which in Haida means "islands of the people." Since the 1980s the archipelago of more than 150 islands had commonly been referred to both as Haida Gwaii and as the Queen Charlottes (*CBC News*, 2009).

2. Besides the issue of luring British Columbia into Confederation, there were other political reasons for constructing a transcontinental railway. First, there was the urgent need to exert political control over the newly acquired but sparsely settled lands in Western Canada. As in British Columbia, the perceived threat to this territory was from the United States. Second, there was the need to create a larger market for manufactured goods produced by the firms in southern Ontario and Quebec.

3. The provincial government created the Technical University of British Columbia in 1997 and this virtual university began to provide online courses in 2000. The objective is to prepare students for the high-tech industry. The university offers certificate programs in electronic commerce and software development. High-technology companies are encouraged to locate offices and research laboratories near its Surrey campus. Students undertake internships and co-operative work sessions with high-technology firms. Its theoretical basis lies in the concept of high-tech clusters around a university. In 2002, the BC government placed the Technical University under the aegis of Simon Fraser University and it was renamed SFU Surrey.

4. Problems over free and fair trade have been particularly frequent in the forest industry. American lumber production, which operates mainly in the Pacific Northwest and Georgia, can produce a maximum of 15 billion board feet per year. Canadian lumber production nearly doubles the American figure. In fact, lumber production from British Columbia is roughly equal to that of the entire United States. The main difference is that US-produced lumber serves its domestic market, while most Canadian-produced lumber is exported to the United States, Japan, and other foreign customers. Trade disputes over lumber exports can therefore significantly affect BC's forest industry.

5. Climate change has altered the environment for the boreal forest. These changes are revealed in two natural elements. First, in the past, cold winters kept the pine beetle under control. In recent years, however, this pest has have spread and multiplied as a result of milder winters. Temperatures of at least $-38°C$ for four days or longer are required to kill off pine beetle infestation. If cold winters return, then the pine beetles will be controlled. On the other hand, if milder winters are a feature of climate change, then there will be no stopping the pine beetle from spreading across Canada's boreal forest. Second, the current warmer and drier climate results in a greater frequency and intensity of wildfires. As BC's climate warms further, wildfires will become more and more of a threat to human settlements in the boreal forest as well as to the very existence of this massive vegetative zone.

6. In 2000, Ottawa tried to alleviate the pressure on salmon stocks by reducing the fleet of 4,500 fishing vessels by about one-third. However, this announcement sparked a strong reaction and little was accomplished. At the same time, Ottawa allowed Indigenous fishers, who have treaty rights to harvest fish for subsistence purposes, a share of the commercial stock. In 1999 Ottawa successfully negotiated a new Pacific Salmon Treaty with the United States, which was renewed in 2009 and again in 2019 for another 10 years (Pacific Salmon Commission, 2019). Ottawa is able to exert some management of fish stocks in the Pacific Ocean because of its 200-mile fishing zone and because of its role in the Pacific Salmon Commission. Salmon fishing on the Pacific coast is regulated, based on the Pacific Salmon Treaty, which determines the size of the catch taken by each nation.

## CHAPTER 10

1. On 30 April 1999, the Newfoundland House of Assembly gave unanimous consent to a constitutional amendment that would officially change the name of the province to Newfoundland and Labrador. An amendment to the Canadian Constitution was proclaimed on 6 December 2001 formalizing the name change.

2. For over 100 years, coal and iron mining provided the basis for the Nova Scotia iron and steel industry. The iron and steel industry in Cape Breton Island near Sydney, Nova Scotia, was for a long time the heavy industrial heartland of Atlantic Canada. During that time, Sydney was the principal city on Cape Breton Island and the second-largest city in Nova Scotia. Sydney's fate was closely tied to its major industrial firm, the Sydney steel mill, and to Nova Scotia coal mines. The mill and mines prospered in the early part of the twentieth century, and both the town of Sydney and steel production expanded, with much steel exported as rails for the construction of railways in Western Canada. Two dark sides to this iron and steel complex existed. One was the loss of life in the coal mines. While the pay was good, danger went with the job, and for some the cost was their lives. In 1956 and again in 1958, the Springhill mine near the head of the Bay of Fundy was the site of two underground explosions that killed nearly 100 miners. In 1992, the Westray mine in Pictou County, Nova Scotia, was the site of another mine disaster that took 26 lives. The second dark side was the environmental deg-

radation caused by seepage of toxic fluids from the steel mill, which resulted in the Sydney Tar Ponds.

A major turning point occurred after World War II when demand for steel dropped and the size of the labour force was reduced. This process of deindustrialization, while delayed by federal and provincial subsidies, eventually saw the steel mill closed. By 2001, the dream of a heavy industrial base in Nova Scotia was gone. Without the steel and coal industry, Sydney and Cape Breton fell on hard times.

3. The lobster is found in the waters of Atlantic Canada. A nocturnal creature that hides under rocks or in crevices most of the day, the lobster is generally found in waters less than 50 m in depth. The largest populations are found on Georges Bank, around Nova Scotia, and in the southern Gulf of St Lawrence. The most productive grounds are near Yarmouth on the southern tip of Nova Scotia. Traps are set on the seabed either individually or in groups of up to eight on a line. The traps are hauled to the fishing vessel by powered winches, emptied, re-baited, and lowered again. The catch is transported live to harbour where it is often kept in seawater-permeated wooden crates for later sale.

4. In 2006 the Brazilian mining company CVRD (now named Vale) purchased the Canadian nickel-mining company Inco, including its Sudbury operations and the Voisey's Bay mine site, for approximately $17 billion. Its Canadian-based subsidiary, originally Vale Inco, is now named Vale Canada Limited.

5. On 26 May 2004 the Labrador Inuit voted 76 per cent in support of the agreement, with an 86.5 per cent voter turnout. The provincial and federal governments passed legislation in 2004 and 2005, respectively, giving legal effect to the Labrador Inuit Land Claims Agreement Act. This agreement contains the provision that the Labrador Inuit will receive 25 per cent of the revenue from mining and petroleum production on their settlement land, as well as 5 per cent of provincial royalties from the Voisey's Bay project. The federal environmental review panel examining the possible environmental and social impacts of the mine proposal at Voisey's Bay expressed concern about the disposal of the 15,000 tonnes of mine tailings to be produced each day. The mining company proposed to deposit the toxic tailings in a pond and prevent this from draining into surrounding streams and rivers by building two dams. While federal and provincial environmental officials are satisfied with the company's solution to the tailings problem, local people, especially the Inuit and Innu, are skeptical and worried about the effects of these toxins on the wildlife they depend on for food. In 2002, the Labrador Innu signed a Memorandum of Agreement in regard to Voisey's Bay that gives them 5 per cent of provincial revenues from the project and the assurance that a final land claim agreement will include a chapter on Voisey's Bay that would detail any further compensation and environmental protections. In 2011 the Innu Nation ratified the New Dawn Agreement with the province, an agreement that is expected to form the basis of a final agreement that also involves the federal government.

## CHAPTER 11

1. There is a third climatic zone in the Territorial North—the Cordillera. However, the Cordillera climate, often described as a mountain climate, is affected by elevation (as elevation increases, temperature drops). North of 60°N, the Cordillera climate is also affected by latitude so that boreal natural vegetation is found at lower elevations and tundra natural vegetation at high elevations.

2. The Inuit employed the kayak and harpoon to hunt seals, whales, and other marine mammals, which enabled them to occupy the Arctic coast from Yukon to Labrador. The First Nations hunted and fished in the northern coniferous forest, where the birchbark canoe, the bow and arrow, and snowshoes enabled them to hunt in summer and winter. The Dene tribes relied heavily on big game like the caribou, the Chipewyans often following the caribou to their calving grounds in the northern barrens of the Arctic. Both the Inuit and the Dene moved across the land in a seasonal rhythm, following the migratory patterns of animals. Operating in small and highly mobile groups, these hunting societies depended on game for their survival.

3. Sometime around the year 1000 the Vikings made contact with the ancestors of the Inuit, the Thule (c. 1000 to 1600 CE). The Thule originated in Alaska where they hunted bowhead whales and other large sea mammals. They quickly spread their whaling technology across the Arctic, travelling in skin boats and dogsleds. With the onset of the Little Ice Age in the fifteenth century, climate conditions affected the distribution of animals and the Thule who depended on them. An increased amount of sea ice blocked the large whales from their former feeding grounds, resulting in the collapse of the Thule whale hunt. With the loss of their main source of food, the Thule had to rely more on locally available foods, usually some combination of seal, caribou, and fish. By the eighteenth century, the Thule culture had disappeared and had been replaced by the Inuit hunting culture. In 1576, the Frobisher voyage to Baffin Island may have been the last European encounter with a group of Thule, some on land, others in their kayaks. Relations quickly soured. During a skirmish between Frobisher's men and the Inuit, five of his men were lost, three of the Inuit were captured, and Frobisher was hit by an arrow. The Inuit and one kayak were taken back to England, as often was done in the early years of European exploration, as proof of Frobisher's discovery. All three of the captives soon succumbed to European illness.

4. For the Americans, Canada's North provided a secure transportation link to the European theatre of war and, in 1942, to Alaska. The air routes consisted of the Northwest Staging Route and Project Crimson. Each consisted of a series of northern landing strips that would enable American and Canadian warplanes to refuel and then continue their journey to either Europe or Alaska. In the Northeast, Project Crimson involved constructing landing fields at strategic intervals to allow Canadian and American planes to fly from Montreal to Frobisher Bay (now Iqaluit) and then to Greenland, Iceland, and, finally, England. In Canada's Northwest, American aircraft came to Edmonton and then flew along the Northwest Staging Route to Fairbanks, Alaska, where their major military base was located. The Alaska Highway, built at the same time, provided road access to the various landing fields and to Alaska. The US Army command had decided that the oil needed by the American armed forces in Alaska must be made secure by increasing oil production at Norman Wells in the NWT and sending it by pipeline across several mountain ranges to Whitehorse and then northward to the military facilities at Fairbanks. Known as the Canol Project, the oil pipeline was completed in 1944, but with the disappearance of the Japanese threat it was closed within a year.

After World War II, the geopolitical importance of northern Canada changed. The North's new strategic role was to warn of a surprise Soviet air attack. The defence against such an attack was a series of radar stations that would detect Soviet bombers and allow sufficient response time for American fighter planes and (later) American missiles to destroy the Soviet bombers. In the 1950s, 22 radar stations, called the Distant Early Warning (DEW) Line, were constructed in the Territorial North along 70°N. Before the end of the Cold War, these radar stations were abandoned and replaced with more sophisticated methods of detecting incoming Soviet planes or missiles. With the collapse of the Soviet Union, Ottawa withdrew its military establishment at Inuvik, did not proceed with its plans for a military base at Nanisivik, and downsized its operation at Alert.

5. The ownership of Arctic waters between the islands in Canada's archipelago remains unclear. Although this route has only recently been used for commercial purposes, a number of "unknown" countries have sent nuclear submarines under the ice cover, and the Americans in the past made several trips through the Northwest Passage on the surface without asking Canada's permission: in 1969, an American tanker, the SS *Manhattan*, to test the route's viability for shipping oil from Alaska's Prudhoe Bay; in 1970, the *Manhattan* again; in 1985, the US Coast Guard icebreaker *Polar Sea*. The political fallout over what was considered the most direct challenge to Canada's sovereignty in the Arctic led to the signing of the Arctic Co-operation Agreement in 1988 by Prime Minister Brian Mulroney and US President Ronald Reagan. The document states that the US is to refrain from sending icebreakers through the Northwest Passage without Canada's consent; in turn, Canada will always give consent. The issue of whether the waters are international or internal was left unresolved.

The seabed of the Arctic Ocean lies beyond the boundaries of the five Arctic countries. Each Arctic country is making a claim for a portion of the seabed to the United Nations. In 2014, the Danish government extended its claim to include the North Pole and areas formerly claimed by Canada and Russia. The 200-nautical-mile (370-km) line indicates the extent of each country's economic area. The reaction of Russia has been muted so far but Ottawa sent its scientists back into the field. Canada was expected to make its claim in 2014, but the Danish submission forced Ottawa to take a second look or lose much of the seabed and the North Pole. The Canadian government finally filed its submission with UNCLOS in May 2019.

6. With a small tax base, large transfer payments from Ottawa to the three territorial governments play a determining role in their budgets. Given the late start in the process of economic and social development, the Territorial North has a great deal of catching up in terms of infrastructure and in terms of equipping its Indigenous population with the skills and tools to compete in the market economy. From this perspective, transfer payments, as large as they are, are insufficient to narrow the gap between the North and the South.

Most workers are employed by one of three governments: federal, territorial, or local. Local governments are settlement councils, band councils, and other organizations funded by a higher level of government. The reason the tertiary sector is so large in the Territorial North is that geography demands such an investment of people and capital to ensure the delivery of public services. Territorial governments must spend more money per resident than do provincial governments to provide basic services, such as education and nursing services. Much of the cost differential is attributed to overcoming distance in the Territorial North and hiring staff for small communities. However, the social importance of the public service sector goes beyond the number of employees. The wide geographic distribution of public jobs across the North is a major social benefit to those in small communities. As a result, employment opportunities, while concentrated in the three capital cities, exist in every community. In small, remote communities, where few jobs exist and where potential workers have given up searching for jobs, underemployment rates are often as high as 60 per cent. The territorial governments' ability to implement affirmative action hiring practices runs up against the low levels of educational attainment among the Indigenous population.

7. In 1974, the first comprehensive land claim submission came from the Dene/Métis, who claimed most of the Mackenzie Basin north of 60°N. This land was called Denendeh. While this was a bold attempt similar to that later pursued in the creation of Nunavut, chiefs and elders from the Great Slave Lake area refused to approve it, primarily because it contained no reference to self-government and it called for the surrender of Aboriginal rights.

As the first land claim agreement achieved under the federal system, the Inuvialuit Final Agreement served as a model for subsequent ones. Since 1984, as shown in Table 11.6, seven more comprehensive agreements have been reached or extended. Self-government was not covered in the first agreements. The Nunavut (1993) and Tlicho (2003) final agreements did spell out the specific nature and unique structures of self-government for the Inuit and the Dogrib. In 2015, the Déline Self-Government Agreement (FSGA) provided the earlier Sahtu Dene and Métis Comprehensive Land Claim Agreement (1993) with the power of governance.

The Yukon First Nations agreement, signed in 1993, was different in that it only established the basic elements of final agreements for each of the 14 Yukon First Nations, leaving the negotiations for a final agreement to each Yukon First Nation. Known as the Umbrella Final Agreement, this 1993 arrangement provided the basic framework within which each of the 14 Yukon First Nations (Carcross/Tagish; Champagne and Aishihik; Tr'ondek Hwech'in; Kluane; Kwanlin Dun; Liard; Little Salmon/Carmacks; Nacho Nyak Dun; Ross River Dena; Selkirk; Ta'an Kwäch'än Council; Teslin Tlingit Council; Vuntut Gwitchin; and White River) could conclude a final claim settlement agreement. White River, Ross River Dena, and Liard never did complete final agreements and remain under the jurisdiction of the Indian Act (Indigenous and Northern Affairs Canada, 2010). The other 11 First Nations achieved final agreements between 1995 and 2006.

## CHAPTER 12

1. As the principal core region of Canada, Ontario has the most seats in the House of Commons. The political implications dictate that Ottawa must pay attention to Ontario and its automobile industry. In addition, electric cars fit nicely into Ottawa's plans for a green Canada and the reduction of carbon emissions into the atmosphere.

# Bibliography

**CHAPTER 1**

*Atlas of Canada*. (2009, 25 Feb.). Official languages, 1996. atlas.nrcan. gc.ca/site/english/maps/peopleandsociety/lang/officiallanguages/1

Coates, K. (2015). *Sharing the wealth: How resource revenue agreements can honour treaties, improve communities and facilitate Canadian development*. Aboriginal Canada and the Natural Resource Economy Series 6. Ottawa: Macdonald-Laurier Institute. http://www.macdonaldlaurier.ca/files/pdf/MLIresource revenuesharingweb.pdf

Friedmann, J. (1966). *Regional development policy: A case study of Venezuela*. MIT Press.

Immigration, Refugees and Citizenship Canada. (2020, 30 Oct.). 2020 Annual report to Parliament on immigration. https://www.canada.ca/en/immigration-refugees-citizenship/corporate/publications-manuals/annual-report-parliament-immigration-2020.html

Johnston, R.J., & Sidaway, J.D. (2016). *Geography & geographers: Anglo-American human geography since 1945* (7th edn.). Routledge.

Ontario. (2020, 29 Apr.). Resource revenue sharing. https://www.ontario.ca/page/resource-revenue-sharing

Samuelson, P. (1976). *Economics*. McGraw-Hill.

Saul, J.R. (1997). *Reflections of a Siamese twin: Canada at the end of the twentieth century*. Viking.

Scott, A.J. (Ed.). (2001). *Global city-regions: Trends, theory, policy*. Oxford University Press.

_____. (2019). City-regions reconsidered. *Environment and Planning A: Economy and Space*, 51(3), 554–80.

Simpson, J. (1993). *Faultlines: Struggling for a Canadian vision*. HarperCollins.

Statistics Canada. (1871). 1871 census (Canada). *Library and Archives of Canada*. http://www.bac-lac.gc.ca/eng/census/1871/Pages/about-census.aspx

_____. (2016, 16 Mar.). Estimates of population, Canada, provinces and territories. *CANSIM Table* 051-0005. http://www5.statcan.gc.ca/cansim/a26?lang=eng&id=510005

_____. (2017, 6 Feb.). Population and dwelling counts, for Canada, provinces and territories, 2016 and 2011 censuses—100% data. http://www12.statcan.gc.ca/census-recensement/2016/dp-pd/hlt-fst/pd-pl/Table.cfm?Lang=Eng&T=101&S=50&O=A

_____. (2018, 8 June). Canadian international merchandise trade: Annual review, 2017. *The Daily*, Table 3. https://www150.statcan.gc.ca/n1/daily-quotidien/180606/dq180606c-eng.htm

_____. (2019a). *Table 36-10-0402-01, Gross domestic product (GDP) at basic prices, by industry, provinces and territories (x 1,000,000)*.

_____. (2019b, 3 Apr.). English, French and official language minority in Canada. https://www12.statcan.gc.ca/census-recensement/2016/as-sa/98-200-x/2016011/98-200-x2016011-eng.cfm

_____. (2019c). Aboriginal peoples highlight tables, 2016 census. *Data products*. https://www12.statcan.gc.ca/census-recensement/2016/dp-pd/hlt-fst/abo-aut/Table.cfm?Lang=Eng&S=99&O=A&RPP=25

Wright, T. (2019, 16 June). Poll suggests majority of Canadians favour limiting immigration levels. *CBC News*. https://www.cbc.ca/news/politics/canadians-favour-limiting-immigration-1.5177814

**CHAPTER 2**

Bonsal, B.R., Aider, R., Gachon, P. & Lapp, S. (2013). An assessment of Canadian prairie drought: Past, present, and future, *Climate Dynamics*, 41, 501–16. doi:10.1007/s00382-012-1422-0

Christopherson, R.W. (1998). *Geosystems: An introduction to physical geography* (3rd edn). Prentice-Hall.

Clarke, G.K.C., Jarosch, A.H., Anslow, F.S., Radić, V., & Menounos, B. (2015). Projected deglaciation of Western Canada in the twenty-first century. *Nature Geoscience*. doi:10.1038/ngeo2407

Conrad, C.T. (2009). *Severe and hazardous weather in Canada: The geography of extreme events*. Oxford University Press.

Cutforth, H.W., Akinremi, O.O., & McGinn, S.M. (2000). Seasonal and spatial patterns of rainfall trends on the Canadian Prairies. *Journal of Climate*, 14, 2177–82.

Dearden, P., & Mitchell, B. (2012). *Environmental change and challenge: A Canadian perspective* (4th edn). Oxford University Press.

de Loë, R. (2000). Floodplain management in Canada: Overview and prospects. *Canadian Geographer*, 44(4), 354–68.

Englander, J. 2012. *High tide on Main Street: Rising sea level and the coming coastal crisis*. The Science Bookshelf.

European Space Agency. (2015, 20 July). Cool summer boosts Arctic ice. http://www.esa.int/Our_Activities/Observing_the_Earth/CryoSat/Cool_summer_boosts_Arctic_ice

French, H.M., & Slaymaker, O. (Eds). (1993). *Canada's cold environments*. McGill-Queen's University Press.

French, J. (2020, 1 Feb.). Companies could be allowed to release treated tailing pond water into Athabasca River by 2023. https://edmonton journal.com/news/local-news/companies-could-be-allowed-to-release-treated-tailings-pond-water-into-athabasca-river-by-2023

Friedlingstein, P., Jones, M.W., O'Sullivan, M., Andrew, R.M., Hauck, J., Peters, G.P., Peters, W., Pongratz, J., Sitch, S., Le Quéré, C., Bakker, D.C.E., Canadell, J.G., Ciais, P., Jackson, R.B., Anthoni, P., Barbero, L., Bastos, A., Bastrikov, V., Becker, M., Bopp, L., et al. (2019). Global carbon budget 2019. *Earth System Science Data*, 11, 1783–838. https://essd.copernicus.org/articles/11/1783/2019/

Global News. (2015). Mount Polley mine. http://globalnews.ca/tag/mount-polley-mine/

Hamelin, L.-E. (1979). *Canadian nordicity: It's your North, too* (William Barr, Trans.). Harvest House.

Hannah, L., Roehrdanz, P.R., Bahadur, K., Fraser, E.D.G., Donatti, C.I., Saenz, L., Wright, T.M., Hijman, R.J., Mulligan, M., Berg, A., & van Soesbergen, A. (2020, 12 Feb.). The environmental consequences of climate-driven agricultural frontiers. *PLOS ONE*. https://doi.org/10.1371/journal.pone.0228305

Hare, F.K., & Thomas, M.K. (1974). *Climate Canada*. Wiley.

Hunter, J. (2020, 9 Feb.). Who's in charge of keeping B.C. dry as sea levels rise? Globe and Mail. https://www.theglobeandmail.com/canada/british-columbia/article-whos-in-charge-of-keeping-bc-dry-as-sea-levels-rise-with-no/

Kokelj, S., Tunnicliffe, J.F., Lacelle, D., Lantz, T.C., & Fraser, R.H. (2015). Retrogressive thaw slumps: From slope process to the landscape sensitivity of northwestern Canada. *GeoQuébec 2015 Conference*. https://www.researchgate.net/publication/283307961_Retrogressive_thaw_slumps_From_slope_process_to_the_landscape_sensitivity_of_northwestern_Canada

Kurek, J., Kirk, J.L., Muir, D.C.G., Wang, X., Evans, M.S., & Smol, J.P. (2013). Legacy of a half century of Athabasca oil sands development recorded by lake ecosystems. *Proceedings, National Academy of Sciences,* 110(5), 1761–6.

Laycock, A.H. (1987). The amount of Canadian water and its distribution. In M.C. Healey & R.R. Wallace (Eds), *Canadian Arctic resources* (13–42). Department of Fisheries and Oceans.

McClearn, M. (2018, 5 Mar.). Rising seas and climate change: Everything you need to know. *Globe and Mail.* https://www.theglobeandmail.com/canada/article-sea-change-primer/

Menounos, B., Osborn, G., Clague, J.J., & Luckman, B.B.. (2009). Latest Pleistocene and Holocene glacier gluctuations in Western Canada. *Quaternary Science Review,* 28, 2049–74.

Mount Polley Independent Expert Engineering Investigation and Review Panel. (2015, Jan.). Report on Mount Polley tailings storage facility breach. https://www.mountpolleyreviewpanel.ca/sites/default/files/report/ReportonMountPolleyTailingsStorageFacilityBreach.pdf

Natural Resources Canada. (2020, 6 Oct.). Energy and greenhouse gas emissions (GHGs). https://www.nrcan.gc.ca/science-data/data-analysis/energy-data-analysis/energy-facts/energy-and-greenhouse-gas-emissions-ghgs/20063

Orland, K. (2018, 16 Jan.). Oilsands ponds full of 340 billion gallons of toxic sludge spur fears of environmental catastrophe. *Financial Post.* https://financialpost.com/commodities/energy/340-billion-gallons-of-sludge-spur-environmental-fears-in-canada

Prairie Climate Centre. (2019). Climate change: The basics. *Climate Atlas of Canada.* https://climateatlas.ca/climate-change-basics

Ramsayer, K. (2020, 21 Sept.). Arctic sea ice minimum at second lowest on record. https://www.nasa.gov/feature/goddard/2020/2020-arctic-sea-ice-minimum-at-second-lowest-on-record

Rasid, H., Haider, W., & Hunt, L. (2000). Post-flood assessment of emergency evacuation policies in the Red River Basin, southern Manitoba. *Canadian Geographer,* 44(4), 369–86.

Slocombe, D.S., & Dearden, P. (2009). Protected areas and ecosystem-based management. In P. Dearden & R. Rollins (Eds), *Parks and protected areas in Canada: Planning and management* (3rd edn) (342–70). Oxford University Press.

Smith, L.C. (2011). *The world in 2050: Four forces shaping civilization's northern future.* Plume.

Warren, F.J., & Lemmen, D.S. (Eds). (2014). *Canada in a changing climate: Sector perspectives on impacts and adaptations.* Natural Resources Canada. http://www.nrcan.gc.ca/sites/www.nrcan.gc.ca/files/earthsciences/pdf/assess/2014/pdf/Full-Report_Eng.pdf

Weber, B. (2015, 10 Dec.). Timelapse video shows lake falling off a cliff in Northwest Territories, creating a large temporary waterfall. *National Post.* http://news.nationalpost.com/news/canada/timelapse-video-shows-lake-falling-off-a-cliff-in-northwest-territories-creating-a-large-temporary-waterfall

Zhang, X., Vincent, L.A., Hogg, W.D., & Niitsoo, A. (2000). Temperature and precipitation trends in Canada during the 20th century. *Atmosphere-Ocean,* 38(3), 395–429. doi:10.1080/07055900.2000.9649654

**CHAPTER 3**

Ardelean, C.F., Becerra-Valdivia, L., Pedersen, M.W., Schwenninger, J.-L., Oviatt, C.G., Macías-Quintereo, J.I., Arroyo-Cabrales, J., Sikora, M., Ocampo-Diaz, Y.Z.E., Rubio-Cisneros, I.I., Watling, J.G., de Medeiros, V.B., De Oliveira, P.E., Barba-Pingarón, L., Ortiz-Butrón, A., Blancas-Vázquez, J., Rivera-González, I., Solis-Rosales, C., Rodríguez-Ceja, M., Gandy, D.A., et al. (2020). Evidence of human occupation in Mexico around the Last Glacial Maximum. *Nature,* 584, 87–92. https://www.nature.com/articles/s41586-020-2509-0

Berton, P. (1970). *The National Dream.* McClelland and Stewart.

_____. (1972). *The Last Spike.* McClelland and Stewart.

Bone, R. (2016). *The Canadian North: Issues and challenges* (5th edn). Oxford University Press.

Brownlie, R.J. (2003). *A fatherly eye: Indian agents, government power, and Aboriginal resistance in Ontario, 1918–1939.* Oxford University Press.

Bumsted, J.M. (2007). *A history of the Canadian peoples* (3rd edn). Oxford University Press.

Canada. (1882). *Census of Canada 1880–81,* vol. 1. MacLean, Rogers & Company.

_____. (1892). *Census of Canada 1890–91,* vol. 1.

Cardinal, H. (1969). *The unjust society: The tragedy of Canada's Indians.* Hurtig.

Carter, S. (2004). "We must farm to enable us to live": The Plains Cree and agriculture to 1900. In R.B. Morrison & C. Roderick Wilson (Eds), *Native peoples: The Canadian experience* (320–40). Oxford University Press.

*CBC News.* (2006, 22 Nov.). Quebecers form a nation within Canada. https://www.cbc.ca/news/canada/quebecers-form-a-nation-within-canada-pm-1.624141

_____. (2011, 29 Apr.). Quebec Inuit vote against self-government plan. www.cbc.ca/news/canada/north/story/2011/04/29/nunavik-government-referendum.html

_____. (2013a, 18 Feb.). At least 3,000 died in residential schools, research shows. www.cbc.ca/news/canada/story/2013/02/18/residential-schools-student-deaths.html

_____. (2013b, 8 Mar.) Métis celebrate historic Supreme Court land ruling. www.cbc.ca/news/politics.story/2013/03/08/pol-metis-supreme-court-land-dispute.html

Dickason, O.P., with D.T. McNab. (2009). *Canada's First Nations: A history of founding peoples from earliest times* (4th edn). Oxford University Press.

_____ & Newbigging, W. (2019). *Indigenous peoples within Canada: A concise history* (4th edn). Oxford University Press.

Dyck, N. (1985). *Indigenous peoples and the nation-state.* ISER Books.

First Nations University of Canada. (2020). About us. https://www.fnuniv.ca/about-us/

Flanagan, T. (1991). *Métis lands in Manitoba.* University of Calgary Press.

*Globe and Mail.* (1995, 31 Oct.). "No—by a Whisker."

Haig, T. (2019). Ottawa signs historic agreement with Métis in three provinces. *Radio Canada International.* https://www.rcinet.ca/en/2019/06/28/ottawa-signs-historic-agreement-with-metis-in-three-provinces/

Halligan, J.J., et al. (2016, 13 May). Pre-Clovis occupation 14,550 years ago at the Page-Ladson site, Florida, and the peopling of the Americas. *Science Advances,* 2(5), e1600375. doi:10.1126/sciadv.1600375

Hirst, K. (2019, 11 Apr.). Some of the earliest colonists to America followed the Pacific Rim. *ThoughtCo.* www.thoughtco.com/pacific-coast-migration-model-prehistoric-highway-172063

Innis, H. (1923). *A history of the Canadian Pacific Railway.* McClelland and Stewart. http://www.gutenberg.ca/ebooks/innis-historyofthecpr/innis-historyofthecpr-00-h.html

Kerr, D., & Holdsworth, D.W. (Eds). (1990). *Historical atlas of Canada, volume III: Addressing the twentieth century 1891–1961.* University of Toronto Press.

Kulchyski, P. (2013). *Aboriginal rights are not human rights: In defence of Indigenous struggles.* Arbeiter Ring Publishing.

Laxer, J. (2012). *Tecumseh and Brock: The War of 1812.* Anansi.

Lewis, M., & Brocklehurst, S.-J. (2009). *Aboriginal mining guide.* Canadian Centre for Community Renewal. http://www.sdsg.org/wp-content/uploads/2011/06/AboriginalMiningGuide_online_complete_0.pdf

Library and Archives of Canada. (2012, 1 Mar.). Métis scrip records. www.collectionscanada.gc.ca/metis-scrip/005005-3100-e.html

Lower, J.A. (1983). *Western Canada: An outline history.* Douglas & McIntyre.

McVey, W.W., & Kalbach, W.E. (1995). *Canadian population.* Nelson Canada.

Manuel, G. (1974). *The fourth world: An Indian reality.* Collier/Macmillan.

Miller, J.R. (2000). *Skyscrapers hide the heavens: A history of Indian–White relations in Canada* (3rd edn). University of Toronto Press.

Milloy, J.S. (1999). *A national crime: The Canadian government and the residential school system.* University of Manitoba Press.

Milne, B. (1995). The historiography of Métis land dispersal. *Manitoba History,* 30, 30–41.

Moffat, B. (2002). Geographic antecedents of discontent: Power and Western Canadian regions 1870 to 1935. *Prairie Perspectives*, 5, 202–28.

Morrison, W. (2003). Forging the national dream. https://www.youtube.com/watch?v=DRuwCrQ7Qkw

Nadasdy, P. (1999). The politics of TEK: Power and the Introduction of Knowledge. *Arctic Anthropology*, 36(1/2), 1–18.

Nepinak, D. (2014, 11 Apr.). New First Nations Education Act an "illusion of control." *CBC News*. http://www.cbc.ca/news/aboriginal/new-first-nations-education-act-an-illusion-of-control-1.2607178

Pedersen, M.W., et al. (2016, 10 Aug.). Postglacial viability and colonization in North America's ice-free corridor. *Nature*. doi:10.1038/nature19085

Porter, J. (2013, 13 Feb.). First Nations must "learn from" De Beers deal. *CBC News*. http://www.cbc.ca/news/canada/thunder-bay/first-nations-must-learn-from-de-beers-deal-1.1327592

Ranere, A.J., Piperno, D.R., Holst, I., Dickau, R., & Iriarte, J. (2009, 31 Mar.). The cultural and chronological context of early Holocene maize and squash domestication in the Central Balsas River Valley, Mexico. *Proceedings, National Academy of Sciences*, 106(13), 5014–18. https://www.pnas.org/content/106/13/5014

Romaniuc, A. (2000). Aboriginal population of Canada: Growth dynamics under conditions of encounter of civilisations. *Canadian Journal of Native Studies*, 20, 95–137.

Route Champlain. (2017). Cahiague, a Huron-Wendat village. https://routechamplain.ca/en/listings/cahiague-village-huron-wendat/

Sifton, C. (1922). The immigrants Canada wants. *Maclean's*, 35(7), 16.

Sinclair, M. (2015). *Honouring the truth, reconciling for the future. Summary of the final report of the Truth and Reconciliation Commission of Canada*. http://www.trc.ca/assets/pdf/Honouring_the_Truth_Reconciling_for_the_Future_July_23_2015.pdf

Sprague, D.N. (1988). *Canada and Métis, 1869–1885*. Wilfrid Laurier University Press.

Statistics Canada. (2003). *Historical statistics of Canada*. Statistics Canada Catalogue no. 11-516-XIE. www.statcan.ca/english/freepub/11-516-XIE/sectiona/sectiona.htm

_____. (2017, 25 Oct.). Aboriginal peoples in Canada: Key results from the 2016 census. *The Daily*. https://www150.statcan.gc.ca/n1/daily-quotidien/171025/dq171025a-eng.htm

Taylor, C. (1993). *Reconciling the solitudes*. McGill-Queen's University Press.

Thomas, D.H. (1999). *Exploring ancient Native America: An archaeological guide*. Routledge.

Tough, F. (1996). *As their natural resources fail: Native peoples and the economic history of northern Manitoba, 1870–1930*. University of British Columbia Press.

Tracie, C.J. (1996). *Toil and peaceful life: Doukhobor village settlement in Saskatchewan, 1899–1918*. Canadian Plains Research Centre, University of Regina.

Universities Canada. (2020). Facts and stats. https://www.univcan.ca/universities/facts-and-stats/

White, G. (2006). Cultures in collision: Traditional knowledge and Euro-Canadian governance processes in northern land-claim boards. *Arctic*, 59(4), 401–14.

Willow, A.J. (2014). The new politics of environmental degradation: Un/expected landscapes of disempowerment and vulnerability. *Journal of Political Ecology*, 21, 237–57.

Wilson, G.N. (2008). Nested federalism in Arctic Québec: A comparative perspective. *Canadian Journal of Political Science*, 41(1), 71–92.

_____. (2017). Nunavik and the multiple dimensions of Inuit governance. *American Review of Canadian Studies*, 47(2), 148–61.

**CHAPTER 4**

Agrell, S. (2011, 28 Mar.). Discussion: What is holding Canadian cities back? *Globe and Mail*. https://www.theglobeandmail.com/news/toronto/discussion-whats-holding-canadian-cities-back/article535503/

Bélanger, A., & Gilbert, S. (2006, Sept.). The fertility of immigrant women and their Canadian-born daughters. *Report on the Demographic Situation in Canada 2002*. Statistics Canada Catalogue no. 91-209-XPE. www.statcan.gc.ca/pub/91-209-x/91-209-x2002000-eng.pdf

Bernier, J. (1991). Social cohesion and conflicts in Quebec. In G.M. Robinson (Ed.), *A social geography of Canada*. Dundurn Press.

Blatchford, A. (2018, 17 July). Physicians urge Ottawa to pay another $21B over decade for seniors health care. *CBC News*. https://www.cbc.ca/news/politics/senior-health-care-federal-1.4749684

Bohnert, N., Chagnon, J., & Dion, P. (2014, 17 Oct.). Population projections for Canada (2013 to 2063). Statistics Canada Catalogue no. 91-529-X. http://www.statcan.gc.ca/pub/91-520-x/91-520-x2014001-eng.htm

Bone, R.M. (2016). *The Canadian North: Issues and challenges* (5th edn). Oxford University Press.

_____. (2020). Indigenous population size: Changes since contact. *Canadian Journal of Native Studies*, 39(2), forthcoming.

Canada. (1884). *Census of Canada, 1880–1881*. Department of Agriculture.

Caron-Malenfant, É., Coulombe, S., Guimond, E., Grondin, C., & Lebel, A. (2014). La mobilité ethnique des autochtones du Canada entre les recensements de 2001 et 2006. *Population*, 69(1), 29–53. doi:10.3917/popu.1401.0029

Citizenship and Immigration Canada. (2011, 27 Oct.). *Annual report to Parliament on immigration 2011*. www.cic.gc.ca/english/resources/publications/annual-report-2011/section2.asp#part2_1

_____. (2016, Apr.). New report reveals popular destination provinces for new immigrants to Canada. *CIC Newsletter*. http://www.cicnews.com/2016/04/report-reveals-popular-destination-provinces-immigrants-canada-047644.html#z6J8QI0vxvzpBIZb.99

Cole, D. (2020). *The skin we're in: A year of Black resistance and power*. Doubleday.

Denevan, W.M. (1992). The pristine myth: The landscape of the Americas in 1492. *Annals, Association of American Geographers*, 82(3), 369–85.

Dickason, O.P., with McNab, D.T. (2009). *Canada's First Nations: A history of founding peoples from earliest times* (4th edn). Oxford University Press.

Dimock, M. (2019, 17 Jan.). Defining generations: Where Millennials end and Generation Z begins. *FactTank*. https://www.pewresearch.org/fact-tank/2019/01/17/where-millennials-end-and-generation-z-begins/

Emrich, R. (2019, 17 Oct.). We need more programs like the global talent stream to boost Canadian tech sector. *Globe and Mail*. https://www.theglobeandmail.com/business/commentary/article-we-need-more-programs-like-the-global-talent-stream-to-boost-canadian/

Foot, D., with Stoffman, D. (1996). *Boom, bust and echo: How to profit from the coming demographic shift*. Macfarlane, Walter & Ross.

Gilbert, A. (2001). Le français au Canada, entre droits et géographie. *Canadian Geographer*, 45(1), 175–9.

Human Resources and Development Canada, Employment and Social Development. (2015, 18 Mar. Canadians in context—Aging population. *Indicators of Well-being in Canada*. http://www4.hrsdc.gc.ca/.3ndic.1t.4r@-eng.jsp?iid=33

McGrath, J.M. (2016, 23 Sept.). How the waters of Grassy Narrows were poisoned. *TVO*, http://tvo.org/article/current-affairs/shared-values/how-the-waters-of-grassy-narrows-were-poisoned

McLachlin, B., Rt. Hon., P.C. (2015, 29 May). Reconciling unity and diversity in the modern era: Tolerance and intolerance. Remarks made at the Aga Khan Museum, Toronto. *Globe and Mail*. https://www.theglobeandmail.com/news/national/unity-diversity-and-cultural-genocide-chief-justice-mclachlins-complete-text/article24698710/

McVey, W.W., & Kalbach, W.E. (1995). *Canadian population*. Nelson Canada.

Mooney, J. (1928). *The Aboriginal population of America north of Mexico*. Smithsonian Miscellaneous Collections. Smithsonian Institution.

National Inquiry into Missing and Murdered Indigenous Women and Girls. (2018). *Reclaiming power and place: The final report of the National Inquiry into Missing and Murdered Indigenous Women and Girls*. https://www.mmiwg-ffada.ca/final-report/

Redfin. (2019, 11 Mar.). Redfin ranks the best Canadian cities for public transit in 2019. Cision. https://www.newswire.ca/news-releases/

redfin-ranks-the-best-canadian-cities-for-public-transit-in-2019-897916453.html

Royal Commission on Bilingualism and Biculturalism. (1970). *Report. Book IV: Cultural contributions of the other ethnic groups.* Queen's Printer.

Shkilnyk, A.M. (1985). *A poison stronger than love: The destruction of an Ojibwa community.* Yale University Press.

Sinclair, M., Chair. (2015). *Honouring the truth, reconciling for the future: Summary of the final report of the Truth and Reconciliation Commission of Canada.* http://www.trc.ca/websites/trcinstitution/index.php?p=890

Smith, L.C. (2010). *The world in 2050: Four forces shaping civilization's northern future.* Dutton.

Statistics Canada. (1997). *Mortality—Summary list of causes, 1995.* Catalogue no. 84-209-XPB. Minister of Industry.

_____. (2002). *Census of Canada 2001—Census geography. Highlights and analysis: Canada's 2001 population.* www12.statcan.ca/English/census01/

_____. (2003a, 28 Feb.). Components of population growth. www.statcan.ca/English/Pgdb/demo33a.htm

_____. (2003b, 21 Jan.). *Census of Canada 2001—Aboriginal peoples of Canada: A demographic profile.* Analysis series 96F0030XIE2001007. www12.statcan.ca/english/census01/products/analytic/companion/abor/contents.cfm

_____. (2005, 25 Jan.). Population by religion, by province and territory (2001 census). http://www.statcan.gc.ca/tables-tableaux/sum-som/l01/cst01/demo30a-eng.htm

_____. (2006). *Annual demographic statistics 2005.* Catalogue no. 91-213-XIB. www.statcan.ca/english/freepub/91-213-XIB/0000591-213-XIB.pdf

_____. (2007a). Births and birth rate, by province and territory. www40.statcan.ca/l01/cst01/demo04b.htm

_____. (2007b). Deaths and death rate, by province and territory. www40.statcan.ca/l01/cst01/demo07bhtm

_____. (2007c). Portrait of the Canadian population in 2006: Subprovincial population dynamics: Canada's population becoming more urban. www12.statcan.ca/english/census06/analysis/popdwell/Subprov1.cfm

_____. (2009a). Ethnocultural portrait of Canada: Ethnic origins, 2006 counts, for Canada, provinces and territories. www12.statcan.ca/english/census06/data/highlights/ethnic/pages/Page.cfm?Lang=E&Geo=PR&Code=01&Data=Count&Table=2&StartRec=1&Sort=3&Display=All&CSDFilter=5000

_____. (2009b). *Canadian demographics at a glance: Population growth in Canada.* www.statcan.gc.ca/pub/91-003-x/2007001/figures/4129879-eng.htm

_____. (2011). *2011 census of population.* Statistics Canada Catalogue no. 98-314-XCB2011043. http://www12.statcan.gc.ca/census-recensement/2011/dp-pd/tbt-tt/Rp-eng.cfm?TABID=2&LANG=E&APATH=3&DETAIL=0&DIM=0&FL=A&FREE=0&GC=0&GK=0&GRP=1&PID=103395&PRID=0&PTYPE=101955&S=0&SHOWALL=0&SUB=0&Temporal=2011&THEME=90&VID=0&VNAMEE=&VNAMEF=

_____. (2012a, 11 Apr.). Population and dwelling counts for Canada, provinces and territories, 2011 and 2006 censuses. www12.statcan.gc.ca/census-recensement/2011/dp-pd/hlt-fst/pd-pl/Table-Tableau.cfm?LANG=Eng&T=101&S=50&O=A

_____. (2012b, 30 May). The Canadian population in 2011: Population counts and growth. www12.statcan.gc.ca/census-recensement/2011/as-sa/98-310-x/2011001/fig/fig2-eng.cfm

_____. (2013a, 24 Jan.). Population and growth rate of metropolitan and non-metropolitan Canada, 2006 and 2011. www12.statcan.gc.ca/census-recensement/2011/as-sa/98-310-x/2011001/tbl/tbl2-eng.cfm

_____. (2013b, 7 May). Number and distribution of population reporting an Aboriginal identity and percentage of Aboriginal people in the population, Canada, provinces and territories, 2011. *Aboriginal peoples in Canada: First Nations people, Métis and Inuit.* National Household

Survey document 99-011-x. Table 2. http://www12.statcan.gc.ca/nhs-enm/2011/as-sa/99-011-x/2011001/tbl/tbl02-eng.cfm

_____. (2014a, 12 June). Dependency ratio (2011 census and administrative data), by age group for July 1st, Canada, provinces, territories, health regions (2013 boundaries) and peer groups." http://www5.statcan.gc.ca/cansim/pick-choisir?lang=eng&p2=33&id=1095336, p. 24

_____. (2014b, 4 Mar.). National Household Survey, ethnic origin. Catalogue no. 99-010-X2011028. http://www12.statcan.gc.ca/nhs-enm/2011/dp-pd/dt-td/Rp-eng.cfm?LANG=E&APATH=3&DETAIL=0&DIM=0&FL=A&FREE=0&GC=0&GID=0&GK=0&GRP=0&PID=105396&PRID=0&PTYPE=105277&S=0&SHOWALL=0&SUB=0&Temporal=2013&THEME=95&VID=0&VNAMEE=&VNAMEF=

_____. (2015a, 19 Mar.). Birth and total fertility rate, by province and territory. http://www.statcan.gc.ca/tables-tableaux/sum-som/l01/cst01/hlth85b-eng.htm

_____. (2015b, 23 Jan.). Visual census—Language, Canada. Tables 4.1 and 4.2. Catalogue no. 98-315-XWE. http://www12.statcan.gc.ca/census-recensement/2011/dp-pd/vc-rv/index.cfm?LANG=ENG&VIEW=D&TOPIC_ID=4&GEOCODE=01&CFORMAT=jpg#fd4_1

_____. (2015c, 27 Nov.). Dependency ratio. http://www.statcan.gc.ca/pub/82-229-x/2009001/demo/dep-eng.htm

_____. (2016a, 16 Mar.). Estimates of population, Canada, provinces and territories. CANSIM Table 051-0005. http://www5.statcan.gc.ca/cansim/a26?lang=eng&id=510005

_____. (2016b, 10 Feb.). Population of census metropolitan areas. http://www.statcan.gc.ca/tables-tableaux/sum-som/l01/cst01/demo05a-eng.htm

_____. (2016c, 7 Jan.). Religion (108), immigrant status and period of immigration (11), age groups (10) and sex (3) for the population in private households of Canada, provinces, territories, census metropolitan areas and census agglomerations, 2011 National Household Survey. Catalogue no. 99-010-X2011032. http://www12.statcan.gc.ca/nhs-enm/2011/dp-pd/dt-td/Rp-eng.cfm?TABID=2&LANG=E&APATH=3&DETAIL=0&DIM=0&FL=A&FREE=0&GC=0&GK=0&GRP=0&PID=105399&PRID=0&PTYPE=105277&S=0&SHOWALL=0&SUB=0&Temporal=2013&THEME=95&VID=0&VNAMEE=&VNAMEF=

_____. (2016d, 4 Oct.). Components of population growth, Canada, provinces and territories, annual (persons). CANSIM Table 051-0004. http://www5.statcan.gc.ca/cansim/a21

_____. (2016e, 21 Sept.). *Focus on geography series, 2011 census.* Census subdivision of Timmins, CY—Ontario. https://www12.statcan.gc.ca/census-recensement/2011/as-sa/fogs-spg/Facts-csd-eng.cfm?LANG=Eng&GK=CSD&GC=3556027

_____. (2017). Distribution of foreign-born population, by region of birth, Canada, 1871 to 2036. https://www.statcan.gc.ca/eng/dai/btd/othervisuals/other009

_____. (2017b, 25 Oct.). Ethnic and cultural origins of Canadians: Portrait of a rich heritage. https://www12.statcan.gc.ca/census-recensement/2016/as-sa/98-200-x/2016016/98-200-x2016016-eng.cfm

_____. (2019a, 30 Sept.). Annual demographic estimates: Canada, provinces and territories, 2019. Table 1.2, Annual population estimates and factors of demographic growth—Canada. https://www150.statcan.gc.ca/n1/pub/91-215-x/91-215-x2019001-eng.htm

_____. (2019b). Aboriginal peoples highlight tables, 2016 census. https://www12.statcan.gc.ca/census-recensement/2016/dp-pd/hlt-fst/abo-aut/Table.cfm?Lang=Eng&T=101&S=99&O=A

_____. (2019c, 30 Oct.). National cannabis survey, third quarter 2019. https://www150.statcan.gc.ca/n1/daily-quotidien/191030/dq191030a-eng.htm

_____. (2019d, 28 Mar.). Population and demographic factors of growth by census metropolitan area, Canada. https://www150.statcan.gc.ca/n1/pub/91-214-x/2019001/section01-eng.htm

_____. (2020a, 10 Mar.). Crude birth rate, age-specific fertility rates and total fertility rate (live births). Table 13-10-0418-01. https://www150.statcan.gc.ca/t1/tbl1/en/tv.action?pid=1310041801. doi:https://doi.org/10.25318/1310041801-eng

_____. (2020b, 10 Mar.). Deaths and mortality rates, by age group. Table 13-10-0710-01. https://www150.statcan.gc.ca/t1/tbl1/en/tv.action?pid=1310071001. doi:https://doi.org/10.25318/1310071001-eng

_____. (2020c). Estimates of the components of international migration, quarterly. Table 17-10-0040-01. https://www150.statcan.gc.ca/t1/tbl1/en/cv.action?pid=1710004001#timeframe.doi:https://doi.org/10.25318/1710004001-eng

_____. (2020d, 29 Oct.). Canada's total fertility rate hits a record low. *The Daily*. https://www150.statcan.gc.ca/n1/daily-quotidien/200929/dq200929e-eng.htm

_____. (2020e, 2 Nov.). Statistics on Indigenous peoples: Key indicators. https://www.statcan.gc.ca/eng/subjects-start/indigenous_peoples

Taylor, C. (1994). *Multiculturalism: Examining the politics of recognition.* Princeton University Press.

Trewartha, G.T., Robinson, A.H., & Hammond, E.H. (1967). *Elements of geography* (5th edn). McGraw-Hill.

Walks, R.A., & Bourne, L.S. (2006). Ghettos in Canada's cities? Racial segregation, ethnic enclaves and poverty concentration in Canadian urban areas. *Canadian Geographer, 50*(3), 273–97.

## CHAPTER 5

Atkin, D. (2000, 15 Nov.). In a hot-wired world, everything's personal. *National Post*, C1, C6–C7.

Bell, D. (1976). *The coming of the post-industrial society.* Basic Books.

Britton, J.N.H. (Ed.). (1996). *Canada and the global economy: The geography of structural and technological change.* McGill-Queen's University Press.

Brooks, S. (2012). *Canadian democracy* (7th edn). Oxford University Press.

Burney, D., & Hampson, F.O. (2012, 20 Jan.). The last thing we need is another foreign policy review. *Globe and Mail*, A13.

*Canadian Press.* (2016, 30 June). Enbridge's Northern Gateway pipeline approval overturned by Federal Court. http://www.bnn.ca/enbridge-s-northern-gateway-pipeline-approval-overturned-by-federal-court-1.518578

Cleary, S., & Grant, J.A. (Conference Co-Chairs). (2019, 14–15 June). *Green finance: New directions in sustainable finance research and policy.* Queen's University.

Cooper, S. (2020, 28 Aug.). Canada's top doctor "optimistic" after Canada–China vaccine partnership collapses. *Global News*. https://globalnews.ca/news/7303586/canadas-top-doctor-optimistic-after-canada-china-vaccine-partnership-collapses/

Courchene, T.J., with Telmer, C.R. (1998). *From heartland to North American region state: The social, fiscal and federal evolution of Ontario.* Monograph Series on Public Policy, Centre for Public Management. Faculty of Management, University of Toronto.

Department of Finance Canada. (2015, 30 Oct.). Federal support to provinces and territories. http://www.fin.gc.ca/fedprov/mtp-eng.asp

_____. (2019). Major transfer payments for 2019–20 . Letters to provinces and territories. https://www.fin.gc.ca/fedprov/2018-12-09/manitoba-eng.asp

Drucker, P. (1969). *The age of discontinuity.* Heinemann.

Duffin, E. (2020, 22 Jan.). Unemployment rate in Canada in 2019 by provinces. *Statista*. https://www.statista.com/statistics/442316/canada-unemployment-rate-by-provinces/#statisticContainer

Evans, P. (2016, 16 May). Canadian housing market hits $508,097 average price in April as sales rise to record. *CBC News*. http://www.cbc.ca/news/business/crea-housing-april-1.3583942

Feehan, J. (2014). Canada's equalization formula: Peering inside the black box . . . and beyond. *SSP Research Papers, 7*(24). School of Public Policy, University of Calgary. http://policyschool.ucalgary.ca/sites/default/files/research/feehan-equalization.pdf

Florida, R. (2002a). The economic geography of talent. *Annals, Association of American Geographers, 92*, 743–55.

_____. (2002b). *The rise of the creative class: And how it's transforming work, leisure, community and everyday life.* Basic Books.

_____. (2005). *Cities and the creative class.* Routledge.

_____. (2008). *Who's your city? How the creative economy is making where to live the most important decision of your life.* Basic Books.

_____. (2012). *The rise of the creative class—Revisited.* Basic Books.

_____ & Jackson, S. (2010). Sonic city: The evolving economic geography of the music industry. *Journal of Planning, Education and Research, 29*(3), 310–21.

_____, Mellander, C., & Stolarick, K. (2010). Talent, technology, and tolerance in Canadian regional development. *Canadian Geographer, 54*(3), 277–304.

Ford, M. (2015). *Rise of the robots: Technology and the threat of a jobless future.* Basic Books.

Green, D.A., Riddell, W.C., & St-Hilaire, F. (2017, 23 Feb.). *Income inequality in Canada.* Institute for Research on Public Policy.

Harris, K., & Panetta, A. (2020, 15 Sept.). U.S. calls of tariffs on Canadian aluminum—for now. *CBC News*. https://www.cbc.ca/news/politics/aluminum-tariffs-trade-trump-trudeau-1.5724391

Harvey, D. (1989). *The urban experience.* Johns Hopkins University Press.

Heap, A. (2005, 31 Mar.). China—The engine of a commodities super cycle. *Citigroup*. www.fallstreet.com/Commodities_China_Engine0331.pdf

Hodgson, G. (2016, 14 Jan.). Change of course needed to revive Canada's manufacturing. Conference Board of Canada. http://www.conferenceboard.ca/press/speech_oped/15-01-16/change_of_course_needed_to_revive_canadian_manufacturing.aspx

Hogue, R. (2019, 25 Apr.). Focus on Canada's housing market. *RBC Economic Research*. http://www.rbc.com/economics/economic-reports/pdf/canadian-housing/housing-millennials-apr2019.pdf

Hracs, B.J., Grant, J.L., Haggett, J., & Morton, J. (2011). Tale of two scenes: Civic capital and retaining musical talent in Toronto and Halifax. *Canadian Geographer, 55*(3), 365–82.

Innis, H. (1930). *The fur trade in Canada: An introduction to Canadian economic history.* Yale University Press.

Jamzer, S. (2020, 19 Mar.). How auto parts manufacturers could help during the COVID-19 crisis. *CBC News*. https://www.cbc.ca/news/canada/windsor/volpe-apma-medical-1.5501729

Keenan, G. (2015, 13 Feb.). Made in Mexico: An emerging auto giant powers past Canada. *Globe and Mail*. http://www.theglobeandmail.com/report-on-business/international-business/latin-american-business/mexico-feature/article22987307/

La Caixa. (2015, 22 June). Has the commodity supercycle come to an end?" *La Caixa Economic Research Department*. http://www.fxstreet.com/analysis/economic-monthly-report/2015/06/22/

Li, M. (2018, 27 July). World oil 2018–2050: World energy annual report (Part 2). *Seeking Alpha*. https://seekingalpha.com/article/4191075-world-oil-2018minus-2050-world-energy-annual-report-part-2

McGregor, J. (2016, 25 Nov.). U.S. lumber coalition files petition, restarting Canada–U.S. softwood lumber hostilities. *CBC News*. http://www.cbc.ca/news/politics/softwood-lumber-canada-united-states-filing-friday-1.3868117

McKenna, B. (2016, 11 Jan.). Business hiring, speeding plans at lowest since 2009: Bank of Canada. *Globe and Mail*. http://www.theglobeandmail.com/report-on-business/economy/businesses-outside-oil-patch-now-feeling-sting-of-commodity-price-rout-boc/article28105709/

McVey, W.W., & Kalbach, W.E. (1995). *Canadian population*. Nelson Canada.

Mann, C.L. (2016, 1 June). Policymakers: Act now to break out of the low-growth trap and deliver on our promises." *OECD Ecoscope*. https://oecdecoscope.wordpress.com/2016/06/01/policymakers-act-now-to-break-out-of-the-low-growth-trap-and-deliver-on-our-promises/

Milner, B. (2016, 26 Aug.). How to diversify an economy: Four lessons for Canada. *Globe and Mail*, B8.

OECD. (2019). Inequality. http://www.oecd.org/social/inequality.htm

OICA (International Organization of Motor Vehicle Manufacturers). (2020a). 2019 production statistics. http://www.oica.net/category/production-statistics/2019-statistics/

_____. (2020b). 2020 (to June) Production statistics. http://www.oica.net/2020-statistics/

Parkinson, D. (2020, 23 Mar.). Unemployment claims reach nearly one million as businesses battered by pandemic. *Globe and Mail*. https://www.theglobeandmail.com/business/article-unemployment-claims-reach-nearly-one-million-as-businesses-battered-by/?utm_medium=Newsletter&utm_source=Breaking%20News&utm_type=text&utm_content=BreakingNews&utm_campaign=2020-3-24_15&cu_id=gkSs6Fa9lWraYpqWEBHPzn587nrKyU6E

Patterson, M., Hazel, M., & Saunders, D. (2019, 16 Apr.). Annual review of the labour market, 2018. https://www150.statcan.gc.ca/n1/pub/75-004-m/75-004-m2019002-eng.htm

Proctor, J. (2020, 28 Sept.). Meng Wanzhou appears in court to argue U.S. misled Canada on extradition case. *CBC News*. https://www.cbc.ca/news/canada/british-columbia/meng-wanzhou-huawei-evidence-1.5739876

Rostow, W.W. (1960). *The stages of economic growth: A non-communist manifesto*. Cambridge University Press.

Sachs, J.D. (2015). *The end of poverty: Economic possibilities for our times*. Penguin Books.

Schwab, K. (2016). *The fourth industrial revolution*. World Economic Forum.

_____. (2020, 3 June). It's time for a massive reset of capitalism. *Globe and Mail*. https://www.theglobeandmail.com/opinion/article-its-time-for-a-massive-reset-of-capitalism/

Statista. (2019). U.S., Canada and Mexico vehicle production 2018. https://www.statista.com/statistics/204240/us-and-canada-and-mexico-vehicle-production/

Statistics Canada. (2006, 10 Feb.). Labour force survey. *The Daily*. http://www.statcan.ca/Daily/English/060210/d060210a.htm

_____. (2009, 16 Jan.). Chart 21.1 (data) unemployment rate. www41.statcan.gc.ca/2008/2621/grafx/htm/ceb2621_000_1-eng.htm#table

_____. (2010, 29 Jan.). Labour force, employed and unemployed, numbers and rates, by province. http://www.statcan.gc.ca/tables-tableaux/sum-som/l01/cst01/labor07b-eng.htm

_____. (2011, 7 Apr.). Canada's international merchandise trade: Annual review. *The Daily*, Table 1. www.statcan.gc.ca/daily-quotidien/110407/t110407b1-eng.htm

_____. (2012a, 6 July). Labour force survey estimates (LFS), by North American Industrial Classification System (NAICS), sex and age group, unadjusted for seasonability, May 1977 to June 2012. CANSIM Table 282–007. www5.statcan.gc.ca/cansim/a26?lang=eng&retrLang=eng&id=2820007&pattern=282-0001..282-0042&tabMode=dataTable&srchLan=-1&p1=-1&p2=-1

_____. (2015, 28 Jan.). Annual average unemployment rate, Canada and provinces 1976–2014. http://www.stats.gov.nl.ca/statistics/Labour/PDF/UnempRate.pdf

_____. (2016a, 4 Nov.). Labour force characteristics, seasonally adjusted, by province (monthly). http://www.statcan.gc.ca/tables-tableaux/sum-som/l01/cst01/lfss01a-eng.htm

_____. (2016b, 8 Jan.). Distribution of employed people, by industry, by province. http://www.statcan.gc.ca/tables-tableaux/sum-som/l01/cst01/labor21a-eng.htm

_____. (2016c, 6 Apr.). Annual merchandise trade: Canada's top 10 principal trading partners, seasonally adjusted, current dollars. Table 3. http://www.statcan.gc.ca/daily-quotidien/160406/t003a-eng.htm

_____. (2019, 31 May). Employment and unemployment rate, annual, population centres and rural areas. Table 14-10-0106-01. https://www150.statcan.gc.ca/t1/tbl1/en/tv.action?pid=1410010601&pickMembers%5B0%5D=1.10&pickMembers%5B1%5D=4.1&pickMembers%5B2%5D=5.1

_____. (2020a, 16 Mar.). Gross domestic product (GDP) at basic prices, by industry, monthly (x 1,000,000). Table 36-10-0434-01. https://www150.statcan.gc.ca/t1/tbl1/en/cv.action?pid=3610043401#timeframe. doi:https://doi.org/10.25318/3610043401-eng

_____. (2020b, 17 Mar.). Employment and unemployment rate, annual, population centres and rural areas. Table 14-10-0106-01. https://www150.statcan.gc.ca/t1/tbl1/en/tv.action?pid=1410010601

_____. (2020c, 18 Mar.). Canadian international merchandise trade database. https://www5.statcan.gc.ca/cimt-cicm/home-accueil?lang=eng

_____. (2020d, 4 Aug.). Labour force survey, August 2020. https://www150.statcan.gc.ca/n1/daily-quotidien/200904/dq200904a-eng.htm

_____. (2020e). Labour force characteristics by industry, annual (x 1,000). Table 14-10-0023-01. https://doi.org/10.25318/1410002301-eng

Trading Economics. (2016). Canada GDP annual growth rate: 1962–2016. http://www.tradingeconomics.com/canada/gdp-growth-annual

US Energy Information Administration (USEIA). (2019, 22 May). Spot prices in crude oil.

Wherry, A. (2016, 20 Jan.). Trudeau touts Canada's diversity and resourcefulness in Davos. *CBC News*. http://www.cbc.ca/news/politics/trudeau-davos-future-look-economy-harper-1.3412182

Yalnizyan, A. (2010). *The rise of Canada's richest 1%*. Canadian Centre for Policy Alternatives.

## CHAPTER 6

Alexander, D. (2017, 21 June). Royal Bank to cut 450 jobs, mostly at head office, in banking's shifting landscape. *Financial Post*. https://business.financialpost.com/news/fp-street/royal-bank-to-cut-450-jobs-in-head-office-revamp

Arcand, A., Wiebe, R., McIntyre, J., & Bougas, C. (2015, 14 May). Hamilton's economy continues its recovery in 2015. *Conference Board of Canada*. http://www.conferenceboard.ca/press/newsrelease/15-0514/hamilton_s_economy_continues_its_recovery_in_2015.aspx

Atkins, E. (2020, 5 Nov.). GM to reopen Oshawa assembly plant; as many as 2,300 workers to be employed. *Globe and Mail*. https://www.theglobeandmail.com/business/article-gm-to-reopen-oshawa-assembly-plant-will-spend-13-billion-to-retool/

Berman, D. (2016a, 7 Sept.). In-branch tellers bear the brunt of RBC cost cuts. *Globe and Mail*. http://www.theglobeandmail.com/report-on-business/streetwise/in-branch-tellers-bear-the-brunt-of-rbc-cost-cuts/article31751181/

_____. (2016b, 28 Sept.). Laurentian Bank to shut down dozens of branches, cut 300 jobs. *Globe and Mail*. http://www.theglobeandmail.com/report-on-business/laurentian-bank-to-shut-down-dozens-of-branches-cut-300-jobs/article32110758/

_____ & Kiladze, T. (2016, 22 July). Shaking up Scotiabank: Brian Porter's vision for a bank of the future. *Globe and Mail*. http://www.theglobeandmail.com/report-on-business/shaking-up-scotiabank-brian-porters-vision-for-a-bank-of-the-future/article31085736/

Bernard, A. (2015, 27 Nov.). Recent trends in Canadian automotive industries. *Statistics Canada*. https://www150.statcan.gc.ca/n1/pub/11-626-x/11-626-x2013026-eng.htm

*Brantford Expositor.* (2020, 26 Oct.). Tensions high at site of Caledonia land dispute. https://www.brantfordexpositor.ca/news/local-news/tensions-increase-at-site-of-caledonia-land-dispute

Canadian Auto Workers Union. (2012, Apr.). *Re-thinking Canada's auto industry: A policy vision to escape the race to the bottom.* https://d3n8a8pro7vhmx.cloudfront.net/caw/pages/29/attachments/original/1335189435/554AutoPolicyDocumentweb.pdf?1335189435

*CBC News.* (2006, 1 Nov.). Caledonia land claim: Historical timeline. www.cbc.ca/news/background/caledonia-landclaim/historical-timeline.html

_____. (2019, 2 Jan.). 2019: Waterloo region tech leaders predict change on new year horizon. https://www.cbc.ca/news/canada/kitchener-waterloo/waterloo-region-tech-sector-predictions-1.4963521

_____. (2020, 10 Aug.). Demonstrators calling for meeting with federal ministers over Caledonia development. https://www.cbc.ca/news/canada/hamilton/caledonia-demonstrators-trudeau-1.5680937

CBRE Canada. (2019). Canadian cities need bigger, better tech clusters to complete globally. https://www.cbre.ca/en/about/media-center/canadian-cities-need-bigger-better-tech-clusters-to-compete-globally

Cole, T. (2009, 28 Aug.). Hamilton's dead. Or is it? *Globe and Mail.* http://www.theglobeandmail.com/report-on-business/rob-magazine/hamiltons-dead-or-is-it/article1264739/

Cuddy, J. (2015). *From laggard to leader (almost). Commentary 5.* Northern Policy Institute, Thunder Bay. http://www.northernpolicy.ca/upload/documents/publications/commentaries/paper-from-laggard-to-leader--almost--no.pdf

Darling, G. (2007). *Land claims and the Six Nations in Caledonia, Ontario.* Centre for Constitutional Studies. www.law.ualberta.ca/centres/ccs/Current-Constitutional-Issues/Land-Claims-and-the-Six-Nations-in-Caledonia-Ontario.php

Dickason, O.P., with McNab, D.T. (2009). *Canada's First Nations: A history of founding peoples from earliest times* (4th edn). Oxford University Press.

Dicken, Peter. (1992). *Global shift: The internationalization of economic activity* (2nd edn). Guilford Press.

Di Matteo, L. (2006, 6 Sept.). Breakaway country. *National Post*, FP19.

Drummond, D., & Burleton, D. (2008). Time for a vision of Ontario's economy. http://www.td.com/document/PDF/economics/special/td-economics-special-db0908-ont.pdf

*Economist, The.* (2015, 9 Apr.). Canada's car industry: The road to nowhere. economist.com/news/business-and-finance/21648065-canadian-government-no-longer-propping-up-carmakers-dead-not-forgotten

Florida, R. (2002). *The rise of the creative class: And how it's transforming work, leisure, community and everyday life.* Basic Books.

_____. (2012). *The rise of the creative class—Revisited.* Basic Books.

_____ & Jackson, S. (2010). Sonic city: The evolving economic geography of the music industry. *Journal of Planning, Education and Research*, 29(3), 310–21.

_____, Mellander, C., & Stolarick, K. (2010). Talent, technology, and tolerance in Canadian regional development. *Canadian Geographer*, 54(3), 277–304.

Gee, M. (2019, 17 June). The Raptors' victory parade was more than a celebration—It was a glimpse of today's Canada. *Globe and Mail.* https://www.theglobeandmail.com/canada/toronto/article-the-raptors-finals-run-and-celebration-parade-has-shown-what-a/

*Global News.* (2020, 8 Oct.). Ottawa, Ontario rolling out half a billion dollars for Ford's electric vehicle overhaul. https://globalnews.ca/news/7385543/electric-vehicles-ford-oakville-investment-federal-ontario-governments/

Green, K.P., Jackson, T., & Herzog, I. (2016, 6 July). High electricity prices putting rural Ontario in energy poverty. *Fraser Forum.* https://www.fraserinstitute.org/blogs/high-electricity-prices-putting-rural-ontario-in-energy-poverty

Hracs, B.J., Grant, J.L., Haggett, J., & Morton, J. (2011). Tale of two scenes: Civic capital and retaining musical talent in Toronto and Halifax. *Canadian Geographer*, 55(3), 365–82.

Immigration Canada. (2019). Moving2Canada. https://moving2canada.com/ontario-tech-stream/

Indigenous and Northern Affairs Canada (INAC). (2009). Chronology of events at Caledonia. www.ainc-inac.gc.ca/ai/mr/is/eac-eng.asp

Industry Canada. (2015a, 21 July). Motor vehicle manufacturing (NAICS 3361): Employment. https://www.ic.gc.ca/app/scr/sbms/sbb/cis/employment.html?code=3361&lang=eng

_____. (2015b, 7 July). Motor vehicle parts manufacturing (NAICS 3363): Employment. https://www.ic.gc.ca/app/scr/sbms/sbb/cis/employment.html?code=3363&lang=eng

_____. (2019, 10 Jan.). Canadian automotive industry. https://www.ic.gc.ca/eic/site/auto-auto.nsf/eng/am00767.html

International Great Lakes Study. (2012, Mar.). *Final report to the International Joint Commission: Lake Superior regulation: Addressing uncertainty in upper Great Lakes water levels.* www.ijc.org/iuglsreport/wp-content/report-pdfs/Lake_Superior_Regulation_Full_Report.pdf

Ipperwash Inquiry (Ont.) & Linden, S.B.. (2007). *Report of the Ipperwash Inquiry.* Ministry of the Attorney General, Queen's Printer for Ontario.

Keenan, G. (2015, 13 Feb.). "Made in Mexico: An emerging auto giant powers past Canada. *Globe and Mail.* http://www.theglobeandmail.com/report-on-business/international-business/latin-american-business/mexico-feature/article22987307/

Klasing, A. (2016, 30 Aug.). Why is Canada denying its Indigenous peoples clean water? *Globe and Mail.* http://www.theglobeandmail.com/opinion/why-is-canada-denying-its-indigenous-peoples-clean-water/article31599791/

Leslie, K. (2014, 11 July). Ottawa urged to settle Six Nations land claim in Caledonia. *CTV News.* http://ctvnews.ca/politics/ottawa-urged-to-settle-six-nations-land-claim-in-caledonia-1.1909627

McNeil, M. (2019, 17 Sept.). New $30-million steel processing facility opens at Stelco in Hamilton. *Hamilton Spectator.* https://www.thespec.com/news/hamilton-region/2019/09/17/new-30-million-steel-processing-facility-opens-at-stelco-in-hamilton.html

Mehta, D. (2016, 14 Apr.). Ottawa, Ontario First Nation sign settlement over Camp Ipperwash. *Globe and Mail.* http://www.theglobeandmail.com/new/politics/ottawa-ontario-first-nation-sign-settlement-over-camp-ipperwash/article29640093/

Moazzami, B. (2003). Forecasting northern Ontario's Aboriginal population. *Canadian Journal for Native Studies*, 23(1), 83–90.

Moro, T. (2016, 13 Jan.). Native claims on Caledonia housing land heat up. *Hamilton Spectator.* www.thespec.com/news-story/6230665-native-claims-on-caledonia-housing-land-heat-up/

*National Post.* (2007, 1 June). Ipperwash report. A14.

Natural Resources Canada. (2019a, 31 May). Canada mineral production. https://www.nrcan.gc.ca/maps-tools-and-publications/publications/minerals-and-mining-publications/canadian-mineral-production/17722#s6

_____. (2019b). *Forest fact book: 2018–2019.* http://publications.gc.ca/collections/collection_2019/rncan-nrcan/Fo1-17-2019-eng.pdf

_____. (2020). Canadian mineral production. https://www.nrcan.gc.ca/sites/www.nrcan.gc.ca/files/pdf/Canadian_mineral_production_e_access.pdf

OICA (International Organization of Motor Vehicle Manufacturers). (2020). Production statistics. http://www.oica.net/category/production-statistics/2019-statistics/

Ontario Forest. (2019, 20 June). Forestry. https://www.investinontario.com/forestry#largest-markets

Ontario Ministry of Agriculture. (2016, 6 Jan.). Statistical summary of Ontario agriculture. http://www.omafra.gov.on.ca/english/stats/agriculture_summary.htm#first

Ontario Ministry of Finance. (2015). Ontario real GDP per capita. *Ontario's long-term report on the economy: Chapter 2: Long-term Ontario economic projection*, Chart 2.11. http://www.fin.gov.on.ca/en/economy/ltr/2014/ch.2.html#ch2_c10

_____. (2020). Ontario trade fact sheet. https://www.sourcefromontario.com/tradefactsheet/en/page/tradefactsheet_ontario.php

Osberg, L. (2018). *The age of increasing inequality: The astonishing rise of Canada's 1%.* Lorimer.

Patrick, R. (2017). Indigenizing source water protection. In R.M. Bone & R.B. Anderson (Eds), *Indigenous peoples and resource development in Canada.* Captus Press.

Royal Bank of Canada. (2019, June). Provincial outlook. http://www.rbc.com/economics/economic-reports/pdf/provincial-forecasts/provtbl.pdf

Shecter, B. (2015, 30 Mar.). Bank of Montreal tests new smaller branches without physical tellers. *Financial Post.* http://business.financialpost.com/news/fp-street/bank-of-montreal-tests-new-smaller-branches-without-physical-tellers

Shkilnyk, A.M. 1985. *A poison stronger than love: The destruction of an Ojibwa community.* Yale University Press.

Siekierska, A. (2016, 14 Nov.). Signs in Toronto urge white people to join "alt-right". *Toronto Star.* https://www.thestar.com/news/gta/2016/11/14/signs-in-toronto-urge-white-people-to-join-alt-right.html

Spurr, B., Keenan, E., Oved, M.O., Poisson, J., Jimenez, M. & Rider, D. (2017, 5 May). Not in service. *Toronto Star.* https://projects.thestar.com/bombardier-ttc/

Statistics Canada. (2006). Canadian statistics: Distribution of employed people, by industry, by province. www40.statcan.ca/101/cst01/labor21c.htm

_____. (2007a). Population urban and rural, by province and territory: 1851 to 2001. www40.statcan.ca/l01/cst01/demo62g.htm

_____. (2007b). Population and dwelling counts, for census metropolitan areas and census agglomerations, 2006 and 2001 censuses—100% data. www12.statcan.ca/english/census06/data/popdwell/Table.cfm?T=201&S=3&O=D&RPP=150

_____. (2012, 11 Apr.). Population and dwelling counts, for census metropolitan areas and census agglomerations, 2011 and 2006 censuses. www12.statcan.gc.ca/census-recensement/2011/dp-pd/hlt-fst/pd-pl/Table-Tableau.cfm?LANG=Eng&T=201&S=3&O=D&RPP=150

_____. (2017a, 6 Feb.). Population and dwelling counts highlight tables, 2016 census.

_____. (2017b). Algoma, DIS [census division], Cochrane, DIS [census division], Kenora, DIS [census division], and Thunder Bay, DIS [census division]: Census profile. 2016 census. Statistics Canada Catalogue no. 98-316-X2016001. https://www12.statcan.gc.ca/census-recensement/2016/dp-pd/prof/index.cfm?Lang=E

_____. (2019a, 28 Mar.). Population and demographic factors of growth by census metropolitan area, Canada. https://www150.statcan.gc.ca/n1/pub/91-214-x/2019001/section01-eng.htm

_____. (2019b). Thunder Bay, (CMA). Focus on Geography Series, 2016 census. https://www12.statcan.gc.ca/census-recensement/2016/as-sa/fogs-spg/Facts-CMA-Eng.cfm?TOPIC=9&LANG=Eng&GK=CMA&GC=595

_____. (2020a). Labour force characteristics by industry, annual (x 1,000). Table 14-10-0023-01. https://doi.org/10.25318/1410002301-eng

_____. (2020b, 13 Nov.). Principal statistics for the motor vehicle and motor vehicle parts manufacturing industries on an annual basis. Table 16-10-0117-02. https://www150.statcan.gc.ca/t1/tbl1/en/tv.action?pid=1610011702

Thomson, C. (2020, 3 Oct.). OPP arrest 25th person over Caledonia housing site dispute. *CTV News.* https://kitchener.ctvnews.ca/opp-arrest-25th-person-over-caledonia-housing-site-dispute-1.5131701

Toronto Housing Market Analysis 2019. (2019). Appendix 1. https://www.toronto.ca/legdocs/mmis/2019/ph/bgrd/backgroundfile-124480.pdf

Windmill Developments. (2015, 30 Mar.). *Zibi: Domtar lands redevelopment.* http://www.windmilldevelopments.com/wp-content/uploads/2015/05/Zibi_ExecutiveSummary_Final.pdf

Wine Country Ontario. (n.d.). All about icewine. http://winecountryontario.ca/wine-101/story-icewine

## CHAPTER 7

Airbus. (2020). Airbus in Canada. https://www.airbus.com/company/worldwide-presence/canada.html

ArcelorMittal. (2015, Aug.). Transforming tomorrow. http://corporate.arcelormittal.com/who-we-are/interactive-map#/N_America/canada/mount_wright_mining_complex

Aubin, H. (2013, 19 Feb.). Henry Aubin: Taxes, Bill 101 drive people away. *Montreal Gazette.* www.montrealgazette.com/news/Henry+Aubin+Taxes+Bill+drive+people+away/7981947/story.html#ixzz2Mn1IOTOD

Bombardier. (2019). The C Series aircraft flies to greater success. https://www.bombardier.com/en/media/articles/The-C-Series-Aircraft-Flies-To-Greater-Success.html

Bone, R.M. (2016). *The Canadian North: Issues and Challenges* (5th edn). Oxford University Press.

Boone, M. (2016, 1 Sept.). From bad to worse: Churchill contract renewal means even less revenue for N.L. *CBC News.* http://www.cbc.ca/news/canada/newfoundland-labrador/upper-churchill-contract-renewal-means-less-money-for-newfoundland-1.3451376

Bumsted, J.M. (2007). *A History of the Canadian Peoples* (3rd edn). Oxford University Press.

*Canadian Manufacturing.* (2016, 25 Aug.). SNC-Lavalin wins $21.7 million mine construction contract in Mozambique. http://www.canadianmanufacturing.com/procurement/snc-lavalin-wins-21-7m-mine-construction-contract-in-mozambique-174578/

Carmichael, K. (2019, 9 Aug.). Why Quebec's economy is enjoying its "best boom" ever—despite the fall of Bombardier and SNC. *Financial Post.* https://financialpost.com/news/economy/why-quebecs-economy-is-enjoying-its-best-boom-ever-despite-the-fall-of-bombardier-and-snc

*CBC News.* (2020, 13 Feb.). Bombardier exits the commercial plane business, sells remaining A220 stake to Airbus. https://www.cbc.ca/news/business/bombardier-financial-results-airbus-c-series-1.5462182

Cohen, G.J. (2015, 19 Feb.). RCMP lays corruption charges against SNC-Lavalin. *Canadian Lawyer.* https://www.canadianlawyermag.com/news/general/rcmp-lays-corruption-charges-against-snc-lavalin/273054

Conference Board of Canada. (2020). *Provincial Outlook Long-Term Economic Forecast: 2020.* https://www.conferenceboard.ca/temp/86f26434-393a-43cc-9486-e1d4840b5344/10593_PO-LT_2020.pdf

Cryderman, K., & McCarthy, S. (2016, 23 Sept.). Anti-pipeline accord could deepen divide in Indigenous communities. *Globe and Mail,* B3.

Dick-Agnew, D. (2011, 26 Sept.). A new home for the Montreal Symphony Orchestra. *Azure.* http://www.azuremagazine.com/article/a-new-home-for-the-montreal-symphony-orchestra/

Finances Quebec. (2005). Québec's clothing and textile industries: The difficult path ahead. *Economic Fiscal and Budget Studies,* 1(4). http://www.finances.gouv.qc.ca/documents/EEFB/en/eefb_vol1_no4a.pdf

Gerbel, T. (2015, 29 Sept.). Montreal to dump 8 billion litres of sewage into St. Lawrence River. *CBC News.* http://www.cbc.ca/news/canada/montreal/st-lawrence-river-sewage-bonaventure-mill-interceptor-1.3248937

Girard, C. (2019). Les naissances au Québec et dans les régions en 2018. *Données sociodémographiques en bref,* 23(3). Institut de la statistique du Québec. http://www.stat.gouv.qc.ca/statistiques/conditions-vie-societe/bulletins/sociodemo-vol23-no3.pdf#page=3

*Globe and Mail*. (2019, 18 Dec.). SNC-Lavalin got what it wanted. https://www.theglobeandmail.com/opinion/editorials/article-snc-lavalin-got-what-it-wanted-its-still-a-win-for-the-rule-of-law/

Harris, K. (2019, 16 Aug.). Bibeau unveils $1.75B in compensation for dairy farmers harmed by trade deals. *CBC News*. https://www.cbc.ca/news/politics/bibeau-trade-deal-1.5249405

Harrold, M. (2019, 5 July). Tempers flare over Quebec's new flood zone maps. *CTV News*. https://montreal.ctvnews.ca/tempers-flare-over-quebec-s-new-flood-zone-maps-1.4495101

Hogue, R. (2016, June). *Provincial outlook*. RBC Economics. http://www.rbc.com/economics/economic-reports/pdf/provincial-forecasts/provfcst-jun2016.pdf

_____. (2019, June). Quebec—A new economic powerhouse? *Provincial outlook*. RBC Economics. http://www.rbc.com/economics/economic-reports/pdf/provincial-forecasts/que.pdf

Hutchinson, B. (2015, 18 Mar.). Inside the clandestine world of SNC-Lavalin's fallen star, Riadh Ben Aissa. *Financial Post*. http://business.financialpost.com/legal-post/inside-the-clandestine-world-of-snc-lavalins-fallen-star-riadh-ben-aissa

Hydro-Québec. (2016). Technological innovations. http://www.hydroquebec.com/innovation/en/innovations.html

_____. (2019). *Annual report 2018*. http://www.hydroquebec.com/data/documents-donnees/pdf/annual-report.pdf

_____. (2020). Appalaches-Maine interconnection. https://www.hydroquebec.com/projects/appalaches-maine-interconnection/

Institut de la statistique du Québec. (2019a, 23 May). Valeur des exportations internationales par produits, Québec et Canada, 2017 et 2018. http://www.stat.gouv.qc.ca/statistiques/economie/commerce-exterieur/exp_prod.htm

_____. (2019b, Apr.). Québec handy numbers. http://www.stat.gouv.qc.ca/quebec-chiffre-main/pdf/qcm2019_an.pdf

_____. (2020). *Le bilan démographique du Québec 2019*. https://www.stat.gouv.qc.ca/statistiques/population-demographie/bilan2019.pdf

Iron Ore Company of Canada. 2013. "The company." http://www.ironore.ca/en/the-company_1/

Jarislowsky, S. (2012, 28 Sept.). The French myth isolates Quebec." *Globe and Mail*, A19.

Kativik Regional Government. 2009. *Proposed Timeline for the Creation of the Nunavik Regional Government*. www.nunavikgovernment.ca/en/documents/NRG_Timeline_En_Oct_09.pdf

Labour Market Analysis Directorate, Service Canada, Quebec. (2020). Québec sectoral profile 2018–2020: Paper manufacturing. At: https://www.jobbank.gc.ca/content_pieces-eng.do?cid=11268

Laforest A. (2020, 5 Feb.). Le gouvernement Legault a atteint ses cibles de réduction en immigration en 2019. *Actualité politique*. https://www.journaldequebec.com/2020/02/05/le-gouvernement-legault-atteint-ses-cibles-en-reduction-de-limmigration-1

Lau, R. (2020, 17 Feb.). Alstom SA to acquire Bombardier Transportation for US$8.2 billion. *CTV News*. https://montreal.ctvnews.ca/alstom-sa-to-acquire-bombardier-transportation-for-us-8-2-billion-1.4814919

Lemay, M. (2010, 30 Apr.). Francophones have reason to be paranoid. *Montreal Gazette*. www.vigile.net/Francophones-have-reason-to-be

Lucas, C.P. (1912). *Lord Durham's report of the affairs of British North America* (Vol. 1). Clarendon Press.

McArthur, G., & Smith, G. (2012, 27 Sept.). SNC-Lavalin's Gadhafi disaster: The inside story. *Globe and Mail*. www.theglobeandmail.com/report-on-business/rob-magazine/snc-lavalins-gadhafi-disaster-the-inside-story/article4570115/?page=all

Macrotrends. (2020). Montreal, Canada metro area population 1950–2020. https://www.macrotrends.net/cities/20384/montreal/population

Marotte, B. (2016, 22 Sept.). SNC-Lavalin strikes deal to build nuclear reactor in China. *Globe and Mail*. http://www.theglobeandmail.com/report-on-business/industry-news/energy-and-resources/snc-lavalin-strikes-deal-to-build-nuclear-reactors-in-china/article32000350/

Mills, D. (1988). Durham report. In James H. Marsh (Ed.), *The Canadian Encyclopedia* (2nd edn, pp. 637–8). Hurtig.

Monpetit, J. (2019, 14 Feb.). Why Quebec sees SNC-Lavalin as an asset, not a liability. *CBC News*. https://www.cbc.ca/news/canada/montreal/snc-lavalin-quebec-prosecution-1.5018472

Natural Resources Canada. (2018, 26 Sept.). Forest industry employment (Quebec). https://cfs.nrcan.gc.ca/statsprofile/employment/qc

_____. (2019a, 31 May). Canadian mineral production. https://www.nrcan.gc.ca/maps-tools-and-publications/publications/minerals-and-mining-publications/canadian-mineral-production/17722

_____. (2019b, 9 Aug.). Iron ore facts. https://www.nrcan.gc.ca/iron-ore-facts/20517

North American Megadam Resistance Alliance. (2020, 28 Oct.). Maine: NECEC-CMP corridor. http://northeastmegadamresistance.org/cmp-corridor-maine/

Osisko. (2013). Canadian Malartic at a glance. www.osisko.com/mines-and-projects/canadian-malartic/canadian-malartic-in-brief/

Port of Montreal. (2020). Historical, cumulative and detailed statistics. http://www.port-montreal.com/PMStats/html/frontend/statistics.jsp?lang=en&context=about

Robitaille, A. (2008, 29 Apr.). Charest mise sur le Nord. *Le Devoir*. http://www.ledevoir.com/politique/quebec/208131/charest-mise-sur-le-nord

Rogers, S. (2015, 11 Dec.). The Raglan agreement at 20: How it's shaped Nunavik's mining industry. *Nunatsiaq Online*. http://www.nunatsiaqonline.ca/stories/article/65674the_raglan_agreement_at_20_how_its_shaped_nunaviks_mining_industry/

_____. (2019, 20 June). Nunavik Inuit sign deal with Ottawa to launch self-government negotiations. *Nunatsiaq News*. https://nunatsiaq.com/stories/article/nunavik-inuit-sign-deal-with-ottawa-to-launch-self-government-negotiations/

Roslin, A. (2001, 10 Nov.). Cree deal a model or betrayal? *National Post*, FP7.

Scott, M. (2017, 2 Aug.). Census 2016: English is making gains in Quebec. At: https://montrealgazette.com/news/local-news/census-2016-bilingualism-hits-all-time-high-in-quebec-across-canada

Séguin, R. (2009, 14 July). Tiny Quebec town is sitting on a gold mine. *Globe and Mail*. www.theglobeandmail.com/news/national/tiny-quebec-town-is-sitting-on-a-gold-mine/article1217078

Serebrin, J. (2017, 6 Sept.). Finance minister defends subsidies as Ubisoft expands to Saguenay. *Montreal Gazette*. https://montrealgazette.com/business/local-business/ubisoft-expands-to-saguenay-projects-1000-jobs-over-10-years

SNC-Lavalin. (2019). *Engineering & beyond: 2018 annual report*. https://www.snclavalin.com/~/media/Files/S/SNC-Lavalin/investor-briefcase/en/2019/annual-report-2018-en.pdf

Statistics Canada. (2002). *2001 Census of Population*. Statistics Canada Catalogue nos. 97F0007XCB2001004 and 97F0007XCB2001010 (Quebec—Québec, Code 24).

_____. (2006). Distribution of employed people, by industry, by province. www40.statcan.ca/101/cst01/labor21c.htm

_____. (2007). Population and dwelling counts, for census metropolitan areas and census agglomerations, 2006 and 2001 censuses—100% data. www12.statcan.ca/english/census06/data/popdwell/Table.cfm?T=201&S=3&O=D&RPP=150

_____. (2009, 30 Sept.). Population of Canada, provinces and territories in the last 50 years. Table 1. https://www12.statcan.gc.ca/census-recensement/2006/as-sa/97-550/table/t1-eng.cfm

_____. (2012, 11 May). Population and dwelling counts, for Quebec, by census metropolitan areas and census agglomerations,

2011 and 2006 census. www12.statcan.gc.ca/census-recensement/2011/dp-pd/hlt-fst/pd-pl/Table-Tableau.cfm?LANG=Eng&T=202&PR=24&S=0&O=D&RPP=50

_____. (2019a, 20 Feb.). Population and dwelling counts highlight tables, 2016 census. https://www12.statcan.gc.ca/census-recensement/2016/dp-pd/hlt-fst/pd-pl/Table.cfm?Lang=Eng&T=201&S=3&O=D

_____. (2019b, 30 July). Unemployment rate. Labour force characteristics by province, territory and economic region, annual. Table 14-10-0090-10. https://www150.statcan.gc.ca/t1/tbl1/en/tv.action?pid=1410009001.

_____. (2020a). Labour force characteristics by industry, annual (x 1,000). Table 14-10-0023-01. https://doi.org/10.25318/1410002301-eng

_____. (2020b). Population estimates on July 1st, by age and sex. Table 17-10-0005-01. https://www150.statcan.gc.ca/t1/tbl1/en/tv.action?pid=1710005001

Sucar, D. (2019, 16 Aug.). CAQ kept its promise to reduce immigration: study. *Montreal Gazette.* https://montrealgazette.com/news/caq-kept-its-promise-to-reduce-immigration-study

Willis, A. (2020, 8 Nov.). Inuit-owned Pituvik partners with Innergex to build hydroelectric plant in northern Quebec. *Globe and Mail.* https://www.theglobeandmail.com/business/article-inuit-owned-pituvik-partners-with-innergex-to-build-hydroelectric/

**CHAPTER 8**

Alberta. (2007). Oil reserves. www.energy.gov.ab.ca/docs/oil/pdfs/AB_OilReserves.pdf

Bakx, K. (2016, 23 June). Oilpatch lowers expectations for future growth. *CBC News.* http://www.cbc.ca/news/business/capp-oilsands-2016-forecast-1.3648752

Bell, J. (2016, 26 Jan.). Energy East pipeline: What you need to know. *CBC News.* https://www.cbc.ca/news/business/energy-east-pipeline-explained-1.3420595

Canadian Nuclear Safety Commission. (2017, 27 Jan.). Northern Saskatchewan. nuclearsafety.gc.ca/eng/resources/nuclear-facilities/index.cfm

Casséus, L. (2009). Canola: A Canadian success story. *Canadian agriculture at a glance.* Statistics Canada Catalogue no. 96-325-X.

Curry, B., & Walsh, M. (2019, 23 Oct.). Trudeau wants Trans Mountain pipeline completed as "quickly as possible." *Globe and Mail.* https://www.theglobeandmail.com/politics/article-tax-cuts-will-be-first-order-of-business-trudeau-says-after-re/

Davenport, C. (2015, 6 Nov.). Citing climate change, Obama rejects Construction of Keystone XL oil pipeline. *New York Times.* http://www.nytimes.com/2015/11/07/us/obama-expected-to-reject-construction-of-keystone-xl-oil-pipeline.html?_r=0

Dyer, E. (2019, 31 Aug.). Even as Beijing shuns Canada's canola, Canadian wheat sales to China soar. *CBC News.* https://www.cbc.ca/news/politics/wheat-canola-china-canada-trade-1.5263313

French, J. (2020, 1 Feb.). Companies could be allowed to release treated tailings pond water into Athasbasca River by 2023. *Edmonton Journal.* https://edmontonjournal.com/news/local-news/companies-could-be-allowed-to-release-treated-tailings-pond-water-into-athabasca-river-by-2023

Froese, I. (2020, 17 June). Thompson bracing for job losses after northern Manitoba mine owner admits to bleeding $300K a day. *CBC News.* https://www.cbc.ca/news/canada/manitoba/thompson-job-losses-vale-bleeding-money-1.5616489

Hodson, P.V. (2013). History of environmental contamination by oil Sands extraction. *Proceedings of the National Academy of Sciences,* 110(5), 1569–70. doi:10.1073/pnas.1221660110

Jackson, H. (2020, 1 Nov.). Canada's support for Keystone XL "unwavering" regardless of U.S. election: O'Regan. *Global News.* https://globalnews.ca/news/7434680/keystone-pipeline-joe-biden-oregan/

Jones, D.C. (1987). *Empire of dust: Settling and abandoning the prairie dry belt.* University of Alberta Press.

Kroeger, A. (2007). *Hard passage: A Mennonite family's long journey from Russia to Canada.* University of Alberta Press.

_____. (2009). *Retiring the Crow Rate: A narrative of political management.* University of Alberta Press.

Kurek, J., Kirk, J.L., Muir, D.C.G., Wang, X., Evans, M.S., & Smol, J.P. (2013). Legacy of a half century of Athabasca oil sands development recorded by lake ecosystems. *Proceedings of the National Academy of Sciences,* 110(5), 1761–6.

McClelland, C. (2019, 21 Oct.). Oil producers' spending for next year to remain flat amid cash crunch, political uncertainty. *Financial Post.* https://business.financialpost.com/commodities/energy/oil-producers-spending-for-next-year-to-remain-flat-amid-cash-crunch-political-uncertainty

MacPherson, A. (2019, 4 June). There is life after remediation: Gunnar mine reclamation forging ahead despite legal battle. *Saskatoon Star-Phoenix.* https://thestarphoenix.com/news/local-news/gunnar-mine-reclamation-forging-ahead-despite-legal-battle-over-cost

Melnychuk, M. (2020, 12 Nov.). Agricultural tech company putting Canadian headquarters outside Regina. *Regina Leader Post.* https://leaderpost.com/news/local-news/agricultural-tech-company-putting-canadian-headquarters-outside-regina

Monsanto Canada. (2012, 7 Oct.). Monsanto Canada unveils DEKALB® canola seed processing plant in Lethbridge, Alberta. *Monsanto in the News.* www.monsanto.ca/newsviews/Pages/NR-2012-07-10.aspx

Natural Resources Canada. (2010, 20 Aug.). *Canada in a Changing Climate, Prairies.* www.nrcan.gc.ca/earth-sciences/climate-change/community-adaptation/642

_____. (2019a, 9 Aug.). Crude oil facts. https://www.nrcan.gc.ca/crude-oil-facts/20064

_____. (2019b, May). Canadian mineral production. https://www.nrcan.gc.ca/maps-tools-and-publications/publications/minerals-and-mining-publications/canadian-mineral-production/17722

_____. (2019c, 27 Nov.). Potash facts. https://www.nrcan.gc.ca/science-data/science-research/earth-sciences/earth-sciences-resources/earth-sciences-federal-programs/potash-facts/20521

_____. (2020, 28 Feb.). Annual statistics of mineral production. https://sead.nrcan-rncan.gc.ca/prod-prod/ann-ann-eng

Nickel, R., & Gu, H. (2020, 10 Aug.). Demand for Canadian canola soars as shippers find roundabout way to reach China. *Global News.* https://globalnews.ca/news/7262233/canadian-canola-prices-shipping-china/

Peters, E.J., & Anderson, C. (Eds). (2013). *Indigenous in the City: Contemporary Identities and Cultural Innovations.* University of British Columbia Press.

Rieger, S. (2020, 23 Feb.). Teck withdraws application for $20B Frontier oilsands. *CBC News.* https://www.cbc.ca/news/canada/calgary/teck-frontier-1.5473370

Saskatchewan Ministry of Agriculture. (2009). Crop statistics. www.agriculture.gov.sk.ca/agriculture_statistics/HBv5_P2.asp

Saskatchewan Research Council (SRC). (2012). Project CLEANS (Cleanup of Abandoned Northern Sites). www.src.sk.ca/About/Featured-Projects/Pages/Project-CLEANS.aspx

_____. (2016). Project CLEANS. http://www.src.sk.ca/about/featured-projects/pages/project-cleans.aspx

_____. (2020, 30 Mar.). Project CLEANS 2020 Work Season Update. https://www.src.sk.ca/news/project-cleans-2020-work-season-update

Sawe, B.E. (2017). Forest land by Canadian province and territory. *World Atlas*. https://www.worldatlas.com/articles/forest-land-by-canadian-province-and-territory.html

Shell Canada. (2015, 6 Nov.). Shell launches Quest Carbon Capture and Storage Project. http://www.shell.ca/en/aboutshell/media-centre/news-and-media-releases/2015/oil-sands/shell-launches-quest-carbon-capture-and-storage-project.html

Spry, I.M. (1963). *The Palliser Expedition: An account of John Palliser's British North American Expedition 1857–1860*. Macmillan.

Stanley, G.F.G. (1936). *The birth of Western Canada: A history of the Riel rebellions*. Reprint 1992. University of Toronto Press.

Statistics Canada. (2006). Canadian statistics: Distribution of employed people, by industry, by province. www40.statcan.ca/101/cst01/labour21c.htm

_____. (2007). Population and dwelling counts, for Canada, provinces and territories, 2006 and 2001 censuses—100% data. www12.statcan.ca/english/cnesus06/data/popdwell/Table.cfm?T=101

_____. (2012). Population and dwelling counts, 2011 census. www5.statcan.gc.ca/bsolc/olc-cel/olc-cel?catno=98-310-XWE2011002&lang=eng

_____. (2013, 7 May). Number and distribution of population reporting an Aboriginal identity and percentage of Aboriginal people in the population, Canada, provinces and territories, 2011. *Aboriginal peoples in Canada: First Nations people, Métis and Inuit*. National Household Survey document 99-011-x. Table 2. http://www12.statcan.gc.ca/nhs-enm/2011/as-sa/99-011-x/2011001/tbl/tbl02-eng.cfm

_____. (2016, 21 Sept.). Census subdivision of Airdrie, CY—Alberta. *Focus on Geography Series, 2011 census*. https://www12.statcan.gc.ca/census-recensement/2011/as-sa/fogs-spg/Facts-csd-eng.cfm?LANG=Eng&GK=CSD&GC=4806021

_____. (2017, 10 May). Saskatchewan remains the breadbasket of Canada. *Census of Agriculture*. 95-640-X. https://www150.statcan.gc.ca/n1/pub/95-640-x/2016001/article/14807-eng.htm

_____. (2018, 23 Mar.). A portrait of a 21st century agricultural operation. Census of Agriculture. 95-640X. https://www150.statcan.gc.ca/n1/pub/95-640-x/2016001/article/14811-eng.htm.

_____. (2019a, 20 Feb.). Population and dwelling count highlight tables, 2016 census. https://www12.statcan.gc.ca/census-recensement/2016/dp-pd/hlt-fst/pd-pl/Table.cfm?Lang=Eng&T=101&S=50&O=A

_____. (2019b, 27 Sept.). Gross domestic product (GDP) at basic prices by industry, provinces and territories (x 1,000,000). Table 36-10-0402-01. https://www150.statcan.gc.ca/t1/tbl1/en/tv.action?pid=3610040201. https://doi.org/10.25318/3610040201-eng

_____. (2019c, 1 Sept.). Estimated areas, yield, production, average farm price and total farm value of principal field crops. Table 32-10-0359-01. https://www150.statcan.gc.ca/t1/tbl1/en/cv.action?pid=3210035901

_____. (2019d, 7 Aug.). Red meat exports by country—year to date cumulative. dhttp://www.agr.gc.ca/eng/industry-markets-and-trade/canadian-agri-food-sector-intelligence/red-meat-and-livestock/red-meat-and-livestock-market-information/exports/red-meat-exports-by-country/?id=1419965032803

_____. (2019e, 17 June). Aboriginal identity (9), age (20), registered or treaty Indian status (3) and sex (3) for the population in private households of Canada, provinces and territories, census metropolitan areas and census agglomerations, 2016 census—25% sample sata. Data tables, 2016 census. https://www12.statcan.gc.ca/census-recensement/2016/dp-pd/dt-td/Rp-eng.cfm?TABID=2&LANG=E&APATH=3&DETAIL=0&DIM=0&FL=A&FREE=0&GC=0&GK=0&GRP=1&PID=110588&PRID=10&PTYPE=109445&S=0&SHOWALL=0&SUB=0&Temporal=2017&THEME=122&VID=0&VNAMEE=&VNAMEF=

_____. (2019f, 20 Feb.). Population and dwelling counts, for Canada, provinces and territories, census metropolitan areas and census agglomerations, 2016 and 2011 censuses—100% data. https://www12.statcan.gc.ca/census-recensement/2016/dp-pd/hlt-fst/pd-pl/Table.cfm?Lang=Eng&T=201&S=3&O=D

_____. (2020a). Labour force characteristics by industry, annual (x 1,000). Table 14-10-0023-01. https://doi.org/10.25318/1410002301-eng

_____. (2020b, 8 Nov.). Population estimates, quarterly. Table 17-10-0009-01. https://www150.statcan.gc.ca/t1/tbl1/en/tv.action?pid=1710000901

Taylor, S. (2019a, 23 Oct.). Saskatchewan government's fall agenda includes cash for coal workers, growth plan. *Globe and Mail*. https://www.theglobeandmail.com/politics/article-saskatchewan-governments-fall-agenda-includes-cash-for-coal-workers/

_____. (2019b, 7 May). Sask. carbon capture facility likely to fall short of annual target: CEO. *CBC News*. https://www.cbc.ca/news/canada/saskatchewan/sask-carbon-capture-short-of-target-ceo-says-1.5126409

TransCanada. (2016). Energy East pipeline project. At: http://www.transcanada.com/energy-east-pipeline.html

Vanderhaeghe, G. (1996). *The Englishman's boy*. McClelland & Stewart.

Wiebe, R. (1973). *The temptations of Big Bear*. McClelland & Stewart.

Wilt, J. (2016, 9 Feb.). After three decades in Canada, is carbon capture technology doomed? *Alberta Oil*. http://www.albertaoilmagazine.com/2016/02/is-carbon-capture-technology-doomed/

Winnipeg, City of. (2016). Aboriginal persons highlights. *Economic and demographic information*. http://winnipeg.ca/cao/pdfs/2011Aboriginal_Persons_Highlights_National_Household_Survey.pdf

**CHAPTER 9**

Alldritt, B. (2012, 25 Apr.). This is going to be a boom: Seaspan CEO. www.nsnews.com/story.html?id=6514682

Aroostook Valley Country Club. (2020). Aroostook Valley. http://www.avcc.ca/home.htm

BC Hydro. (2015a). Peace Region. https://www.bchydro.com/energy-in-bc/our_system/generation/our_facilities/peace.html

_____. (2015b). Columbia Region. https://www.bchydro.com/energy-in-bc/our_system/generation/our_facilities/columbia.html

BC Ministry of Forests, Lands and Natural Resource Operations. (2016, 20 Oct.). Great Bear Rainforest land use zones. https://www.for.gov.bc.ca/tasb/slrp/lrmp/nanaimo/CLUDI/GBR/Orders/GBR_LandUseZones_20161020.pdf

BC Ministry of Transportation. (2007). Pacific Gateway. www.th.gov.bc.ca/PacificGateway/index.htm

BC Seafood Industry. (2019). 2017 year in review. https://www2.gov.bc.ca/assets/gov/farming-natural-resources-and-industry/agriculture-and-seafood/statistics/industry-and-sector-profiles/year-in-review/bcseafood_yearinreview_2017.pdf

BC Stats. (2012, Aug.). Annual data for BC Exports with selected destinations and commodity details. www.bcstats.gov.bc.ca/StatisticsBySubject/ExportsImports/Data.aspx

_____. (2016). BC exports: Data tables. http://www.bcstats.gov.bc.ca/StatisticsBySubject/ExportsImports.aspx

_____. (2019a, 2 May). Annual B.C. exports. https://www2.gov.bc.ca/gov/content/data/statistics/business-industry-trade/trade/trade-data

_____. (2019b). Production. https://www2.gov.bc.ca/gov/content/industry/mineral-exploration-mining/further-information/statistics/production

_____. (2019c, Nov.). B.C. economic accounts & gross domestic product. https://www2.gov.bc.ca/gov/content/data/statistics/economy/bc-economic-accounts-gdp

_____. (2020, 5 Aug.). Annual B.C. origin exports. https://www2.gov.bc.ca/assets/gov/data/statistics/business-industry-trade/trade/exp_annual_bc_exports.pdf

Bisby, A. (2019, 5 July). A five-day tour of the Okanagan's best food, wine and bike trails. *Globe and Mail*. https://www.theglobeandmail.com/life/travel/article-a-five-day-tour-of-the-okanagans-best-food-wine-and-bike-trails/

Cassidy, F. (1992). Aboriginal land claims in British Columbia: A regional perspective. In K. Coates (Ed.), *Aboriginal land claims* (10–43). Copp Clark.

*CBC News*. (2009, 11 Dec.). Queen Charlotte Islands renamed Haida Gwaii in historic deal. www.cbc.ca/canada/british-columbia/story/2009/12/11/bc-queen-charlotte-islands-renamed-haida-gwaii.html

_____. (2016, 16 Nov.). City of Vancouver approves empty homes tax. http://www.cbc.ca/news/canada/british-columbia/city-of-vancouver-approves-empty-homes-tax-1.3853542

_____. (2019, 5 July). 3 earthquakes detected within minutes off B.C. coast. https://www.cbc.ca/news/canada/british-columbia/earthquakes-bc

Chase, S., & Marotte, B. (2011, 20 Oct.). Halifax, Vancouver win $33-billion in shipbuilding sweepstakes. *Globe and Mail*, A1.

Cox, S. (2019, 1 Feb.). BC Hydro awarded $90 million in Site C dam contracts without asking for bids, documents reveal. *The Narwhal*. https://thenarwhal.ca/bc-hydro-awarded-90-million-in-site-c-dam-contracts-without-asking-for-bids-documents-reveal/

Crowley, B.L. (2016, 29 Jan.). For eco-warriors: No amount of tinkering will make pipelines acceptable. Macdonald-Laurier Institute. http://www.macdonaldlaurier.ca/for-eco-warriors-no-amount-of-tinkering-will-make-pipelines-acceptable-brian-lee-crowley-in-the-citizen/#

Fisheries and Oceans Canada. (2020, 31 Jan.). Sea fisheries landings. https://www.dfo-mpo.gc.ca/stats/commercial/sea-maritimes-eng.htm

Hasemyer, D. (2016, 20 July). Enbridge's Kalamazoo spill saga ends in $177 million settlement. *Inside Climate News*. https://insideclimatenews.org/news/20072016/enbridge-saga-end-department-justice-fine-epa-kalamazoo-river-michigan-dilbit-spill

Hopper, T. (2018, 27 Mar.). What really happened in the Chilcotin War, the 1864 conflict that just prompted an exoneration from Trudeau. *National Post*. https://nationalpost.com/news/canada/what-really-happened-in-the-chilcotin-war-the-1864-conflict-that-just-prompted-an-exoneration-from-trudeau

Hume, S. (2000, 5 Aug.). Did Francis Drake discover B.C.? *National Post*, B1–B2.

Hunter, J. (2016, 1 Feb.). Key players in Great Bear Rainforest deal find common ground. *Globe and Mail*. http://www.theglobeandmail.com/news/british-columbia/key-players-in-great-bear-rainforest-deal-find-common-ground/article28475126/

Jang, B. (2019, 16 Nov.). Inside Canada's next boom town as a B.C. village transforms. *Globe and Mail*. Report on Business, B1, B2.

Jung, A. (2019, 4 Sept.). Vancouver is the sixth most liveable city in the world, new report says. *CTV News*. https://bc.ctvnews.ca/vancouver-is-the-sixth-most-liveable-city-in-the-world-new-report-says-1.4578255

Katz, D. (2010, 6 Jan.). The Agricultural Land Reserve doesn't work—so let's get rid of it. *BC Business Online*. www.bcbusinessonline.ca/bcb/business-sense/2010/01/06/alr-tear-down-wall

Keyzer, W. (2016, 17 June). MDA to deliver a broad-area maritime surveillance system using the RADARSAT Constellation Mission. http://mdacorporation.com/news/pr/pr2016061702.html

Kinder Morgan. (2015). Trans Mountain: Maps. http://www.transmountain.com

Loki, R. (2015, 28 Apr.). 8 dangerous side effects of fracking that the industry doesn't want you to hear about. *AlterNet*. http://www.alternet.org/environment/8-dangerous-side-effects-fracking-industry-doesnt-want-you-hear-about

MacDonald, J. (2012, 24 Apr.). Cuts threaten Canada's satellite eye on the Arctic. *Vancouver Sun*. http://democracyastray.blogspot.ca/2012/04/cuts-threaten-canadas-satellite-eye-on.html

Mahoney, L. (2020, 18 July). Americans banned from Aroostook Valley Country Club by Canadian government. *Bangor Daily News*. https://bangordailynews.com/2020/07/18/sports/americans-banned-from-aroostook-valley-country-club-by-canadian-government/

Metro Vancouver. (2015). About us. http://www.metrovancouver.org/about/Pages/default.aspx

Meissner, D. (2015, 18 Jan.). B.C. megathrust earthquake could rupture like a zipper, expert says. *CBC News*. http://www.cbc.ca/news/canada/british-columbia/b-c-megathrust-earthquake-could-rupture-like-a-zipper-expert-says-1.2917261

——. (2016, 4 Aug.). Mount Polley mine disaster hits 2-year mark, fallout still causes divisions. *CBC News*. http://www.cbc.ca/news/canada/british-columbia/mount-polley-anniversary-1.3706850

——. (2019, 4 Aug.). Mount Polley mine disaster 5 years later; emotions, accountability unresolved. *CBC News*. https://www.cbc.ca/news/canada/british-columbia/mount-polley-mine-disaster-5-years-later-emotions-accountability-unresolved-1.5236160

Mineral Resources Education Program of BC. (2009). www.bcminerals.ca/files/bc_mine_information.php

Ministry of Forests, Lands and Natural Resource Operations. (2011, Mar.). *The forest industry snapshot: A selection of monthly economic statistics.* www.for.gov.bc.ca/ftp/het/external/!publish/web/snapshot/201103.pdf

Morgan, G. (2016, 19 May). NEB approves Kinder Morgan's Trans Mountain pipeline expansion with 157 conditions. *Financial Post*. http://business.financialpost.com/news/energy/national-energy-board-recommends-approval-of-kinder-morgans-trans-mountain-pipeline-expansion?__lsa=a3a3-f506

_____. (2017, 11 Dec.). B.C. to proceed with controversial Site C dam, cost soars to $10.7 billion. *Financial Post*. https://business.financialpost.com/commodities/energy/b-c-to-proceed-with-controversial-site-c-dam-cost-soars-to-10-7-billion

National Energy Board. (2015, 16 Oct.). Frequently asked questions: An assessment of the unconventional petroleum resources in the Montney Formation, west-central Alberta and east-central British Columbia. https://www.neb-one.gc.ca/nrg/sttstc/ntrlgs/rprt/ltmtptntlmntnyfrmtn2013/ltmtptntlmntnyfrmtn2013fq-eng.html

Natural Resources Canada. (2015, 12 Apr.). Simplified seismic hazard map for Canada, the provinces and territories. http://www.earthquakescanada.nrcan.gc.ca/hazard-alea/simphaz-en.php

Orton, T. (2019, 3 Apr.). B.C. takes Hollywood North title as production hits $3.6b in 2018. *Business Vancouver*. https://www.vancouverisawesome.com/2019/04/03/hollywood-north-bc-3-billion-production/

_____. (2020, 15 June). Seaspan's Vancouver Shipyards land $2.4b contract for navy vessels. *BIV*. https://biv.com/article/2020/06/seaspans-vancouver-shipyards-land-24b-contract-navy-vessels

Pacific Salmon Commission. (2019). The Pacific Salmon Treaty. https://www.psc.org/publications/pacific-salmon-treaty/

Port of Prince Rupert. (2016). Cargo performance proves port's resilience in shifting economic conditions. http://www.rupertport.com/news/releases/2015-performance-volumes

Port of Vancouver. (2020). Statistics overview. https://www.portvancouver.com/about-us/statistics/

Provincial Agricultural Land Commission. (2014). About the ALC. http://www.alc.gov.bc.ca/commission/alc/content/about-the-alc

Quan, D. (2020, 18 Oct.). Is it time for Canada to buy this little piece of America? *Toronto Star*, 1, 6–7.

Roy, P.E. (1989). *White man's province*. University of British Columbia Press.

Schmunk, R. (2016, 27 Jan.). Vancouver's housing market is world's 3rd most-unaffordable: Study. *Huffington Post*. http://www.huffingtonpost.ca/2016/01/26/vancouver-housing-unaffordable-study_n_9081516.html

_____. (2018, 2 Oct.). $40B LNG project in northern B.C. gets go ahead. *CBC News*. https://www.cbc.ca/news/canada/british-columbia/kitimat-lng-canada-1.4845831

_____ & Hallin, L. (2016, June). Profile of the British Columbia technology sector 2015. BC Stats. http://www.bcstats.gov.bc.ca/Publications/RecentReleases.aspx

Seaspan. (2015, 24 June). Seaspan's Vancouver Shipyards celebrates start of construction of first NSPS vessel. http://www.seaspan.com/seaspans-vancouver-shipyards-celebrates-start-of-construction-on-first-nsps-vessel

Site C Clean Energy Project. (2014, 16 Dec.). Site C to provide more than 100 years of affordable, reliable, clean power. https://www.sitecproject.com/site-c-to-provide-more-than-100-years-of-affordable-reliable-clean-power

Smart, A. (2019, 5 May). Major housing development planned on Indigenous land in the heart of Vancouver. *CKPG Today*. https://ckpgtoday.ca/2019/05/05/major-housing-development-planned-on-indigenous-land-in-heart-of-vancouver/

Statistics Canada. (2006). Distribution of employed people by industry, by province, 2005. www40.statcan.ca/l01/cst01/labor21c.htm

_____. (2007). Population and dwelling counts, for census metropolitan areas and census agglomerations, 2006 and 2001 censuses—100% data. www12.statcan.ca/english/census06/data/popdwell/Table.cfm?T=201&S=3&O=D&RPP=150

_____. (2017a, 29 Nov.). Greater Vancouver, RD [census division], British Columbia and British Columbia [province] (table). Census profile. 2016 census. Statistics Canada Catalogue no. 98-316-X2016001. https://www12.statcan.gc.ca/census-recensement/2016/dp-pd/prof/index.cfm?Lang=E

_____. (2017b, 6 Feb.). Population and dwelling counts highlight tables, 2016 census. https://www12.statcan.gc.ca/census-recensement/2016/dp-pd/hlt-fst/pd-pl/index-eng.cfm

_____. (2020). Labour force characteristics by industry, annual (x 1,000). Table 14-10-0023-01. https://doi.org/10.25318/1410002301-eng

Todd, D. (2017, 28 Mar.). Vancouver is the most "Asian" city outside Asia. What are the ramifications? *Vancouver Sun*. http://vancouversun.com/life/vancouver-is-most-asian-city-outside-asia-what-are-the-ramifications

Tomlinson, K. (2016, 20 Nov.). On B.C.'s farmland, mega-mansions and speculators reap the rewards of lucrative tax breaks. *Globe and Mail*. http://www.theglobeandmail.com/news/investigations/farmland-and-real-estate-in-british-columbia/article32923810/

*Vancouver Courier*. (2019, 14 May). Prince Rupert to add second container terminal, quadruple capacity. https://www.vancourier.com/prince-rupert-to-add-second-container-terminal-quadruple-capacity-1.23822494

Wagstaffe, J. (2016, 28 Mar.). Why the risk of the "Big One" in B.C. is heightened every 14 months. *CBC News*. http://www.cbc.ca/news/canada/british-columbia/earthquakes-bc-slow-slip-1.3794192

Wilson, K. (2019, 28 Feb.). These tech companies are the industry's top empoyers in B.C. *Georgia Straight*. https://www.straight.com/tech/1206886/these-tech-companies-are-industrys-top-employers-bc

Wood Resources International LLC. (2019, 2 July). China increases Canadian, Russian pulp and log imports amid US trade tensions. https://www.canadianbiomassmagazine.ca/china-increases-canadian-russian-pulp-and-log-imports-amid-us-trade-tensions/

## CHAPTER 10

Adey, J. (2019, 13 July). Scientist says DFO may be overestimating N.L. cod stocks by 35 per cent. *CBC News*. https://www.cbc.ca/news/canada/newfoundland-labrador/northern-cod-stocks-1.5208150

Al-Hakim, A. (2019, 15 Aug.). Federal government awards Irving Shipbuilding Inc. $500M contract to maintain navy fleet. *Global News*. https://globalnews.ca/news/5768860/federal-government-irving-shipbuilding-500m-contract/

Bailey, S. (2016, 25 Oct.). N.L. premier to meet with Aboriginal leaders over Muskrat Falls protests. *CTV News*. http://www.ctvnews.ca/canada/n-l-premier-to-meet-with-aboriginal-leaders-over-muskrat-falls-protests-1.3130434

Berthiaume, L. (2020, 22 Oct.). Navy investigating unexplained breakdown on brand-new Arctic patrol vessel. *CTV News*. https://www.ctvnews.ca/canada/navy-investigating-unexplained-breakdown-on-brand-new-arctic-patrol-vessel-1.5156408

Beswick, A. (2015, 27 Jan.). Week-end focus: Marshall decision still ripples through Native fishery. *Chronicle Herald* (Halifax). http://thechronicleherald.ca/novascotia/1265170-weekend-focus-marshall-decision-still-ripples-through-native-fishery

Brake, J. (2019, 23 July). Inuit ask premier to halt imminent flooding of Muskrat Falls. *Aboriginal Peoples Television Network*. https://aptnnews.ca/2019/07/23/inuit-ask-premier-to-halt-imminent-flooding-of-muskrat-falls/

Bundale, B. (2020, 5 Feb.). Exclusive: N.S. exports to China hit nearly $1 billion, but 2020 trade hampered by coronavirus. *Chronicle Herald* (Halifax). https://www.thechronicleherald.ca/business/local-business/exclusive-ns-exports-to-china-hit-nearly-1-billion-but-2020-trade-hampered-by-coronavirus-407393/

Canada. (2014, 28 July). *Final evaluation of the Sydney Tar Ponds and coke ovens remediation project (final report)*. http://www.safecleanup.com/fnl_rprt.pdf

Canadian Association of Petroleum Producers. (2018). Value of producers sales eastcoast offshore. https://www.capp.ca/publications-and-statistics/statistics/statistical-handbook.

CBC Digital Archives. (2020). The Ocean Ranger disaster. https://www.cbc.ca/archives/topic/the-ocean-ranger-disaster

*CBC News*. (2007, 29 Oct.). Long commute, huge rewards. www.cbc.ca/canada/newfoundland-labrador/story/2007/10/29/big-commute.html

_____. (2009, 29 Oct.). The Big Commute. www.cbc.ca/nl/features/bigcommute/

_____. (2016, 27 Oct.). Battle over Muskrat Falls: What you need to know. http://www.cbc.ca/news/indigenous/muskrat-falls-what-you-need-to-know-1.3822898

_____. (2019, 5 May). Road salt deal secures future of Sussex NB mine for 2 years, creates 16 jobs. https://www.cbc.ca/news/canada/new-brunswick/sussex-jobs-potash-mine-road-salt-1.5124297

Chaundry, D. (2012, Oct.). *Meeting the skills challenge: Five key labour market issues facing Atlantic Canada*. Report of Atlantic Provinces Economic Council. www.apec-econ.ca/files/pubs/%7BBA615AD5-336A-4448-980F-A121DD036733%7D.pdf?title=Meeting%20the%20Skills%20Challenge%3A%20Five%20Key%20Labour%20Market%20Issues%20Facing%20Atlantic%20Canada&publicationtype=Research%20Reports

Clapp, R.A. (1998). The resource cycle in forestry and fishing. *Canadian Geographer*, 42(2), 129–44.

Collier, K. (2016, Oct.). The loss of the *Ocean Ranger*, 15 February 1982. *Newfoundland and Labrador Heritage*. https://www.heritage.nf.ca/articles/economy/ocean-ranger.php

Conrad, C.T. (2009). *Severe and hazardous weather in Canada: The geography of extreme events*. Oxford University Press.

Cox, K. (1994, 12 Nov.). How Hibernia will cast off. *Globe and Mail*, D8.

Department of Finance Canada. (2017). Major federal transfers. https://www.canada.ca/en/department-finance/programs/federal-transfers/major-federal-transfers.html

Doucette, K. (2013, 7 Mar.). $288-million deal will kick-start design of Arctic patrol ships, Ottawa announces. *National Post.* news.nationalpost.com/2013/03/07/288-million-deal-will-kick-start-design-of-arctic-patrol-ships-ottawa-announces/

_____. (2019, 12 Nov.). Nova Scotia premier defends trade mission to China as two Canadians remain detained. *Globe and Mail.* https://www.theglobeandmail.com/canada/article-nova-scotia-premier-defends-trade-mission-to-china-as-two-canadians/

Emera. (2020) Maritime Link infrastructure. https://www.emeranl.com/maritime-link/maritime-link-infrastructure

Fisheries and Oceans Canada. (2015). *2014 4X5Yb Atlantic cod stock status update.* DFO Can. Sci. Advis. Sec. Sci. Resp. 2015/010.

_____. (2016, 6 Oct.). Seafisheries landings. http://www.dfo-mpo.gc.ca/stats/commercial/sea-maritimes-eng.htm

_____. (2019a, 31 Jan.). 2017 Atlantic Coast Commercial Landings, by Region. https://www.dfo-mpo.gc.ca/stats/commercial/land-debarq/sea-maritimes/s2017aq-eng.htm

_____. (2019b). Seafisheries landed quantity by region, 2018. https://www.dfo-mpo.gc.ca/stats/commercial/land-debarq/sea-maritimes/s2018aq-eng.htm

Gilbert, W. (2020). ". . . the fishing room and meddow gardens and meddow ground": Landownership at the Cupids Cove Plantation, 1610–2010. *Newfoundland and Labrador Studies, 35*(1), 77–102.

*Global News.* (2020, 14 Sept.). Newfoundland and Labrador can't afford buy-in for Husky-led oil project: Premier. https://globalnews.ca/news/7334508/newfoundland-and-labrador-cant-afford-buy-in-for-husky-led-oil-project-premier/

Hardin, G. (1968). The tragedy of the commons. *Science, 162,* 1243–8.

Hiller, J.K. (1997). The debate: Confederation rejected, 1864–1869. *Newfoundland and Canada: 1864–1949.* www.heritage.nf.ca/law/debate.html

Irving Shipbuilding. (2016). Canadian impact. http://shipsforcanada.ca/canadian-impact/#CA

Le Blanc, R.D. (2020, 5 Mar.). *Misguided project.* Commission of Inquiry Respecting the Muskeg Falls Project (Vol. 1). https://www.muskratfallsinquiry.ca/files/Volume-1-Executive-Summary-Key-Findings-and-Recommendations-FINAL.pdf

McKenzie-Sutter. (2019, 4 July). N.L. premier defends decision to carry on with Muskrat Falls megaproject. *CTV News.* https://www.ctvnews.ca/canada/n-l-premier-defends-decision-to-carry-on-with-muskrat-falls-megaproject-1.4494465

McKinley, S. (2020, 29 Nov.). Clearwater deal inspires Mi'kmaq pride. *Toronto Star,* A3.

McLellan, D.A. (2014, 17 Jan.). Opinion: Why building new refineries in Canada is uneconomic and undesirable. *Financial Post.* http://business.financialpost.com/news/energy/opinion-why-building-new-refineries-in-canada-is-uneconomic-and-undesirable?__lsa=a3a3-f506

Macpherson, J. (1997). Cold ocean. *Newfoundland and Labrador Heritage.* www.heritage.nf.ca/environment/ocean.html#amherst

Massell, D. (2016, 21 Sept.). History lingers at Muskrat Falls. *Niche.* http://niche-canada.org/2016/09/21/history-lingers-at-muskrat-falls/

Natural Resources Canada. (2015, 16 Aug.). Preliminary estimate of the mineral production of Canada, by province, 2014. http://sead.nrcan.gc.ca/prod-prod/2014p-eng.aspx

_____. (2018, 26 Sept.). Statistical data. https://cfs.nrcan.gc.ca/statsprofile/overview/ns

_____. (2019, 31 May). Annual statistics of mineral production. http://sead.nrcan.gc.ca/prod-prod/ann-ann-eng.aspx?FileT=2017&Lang=en

Ong, Y., & Mulvany, L. (2015, 4 Aug.). Lobster prices, exports skyrocket as China's hunger for the lucky Canadian crustacean soars. *Bloomberg News.* http://business.financialpost.com/news/economy/lobster-prices-exports-skyrocket-as-chinas-hunger-for-the-lucky-canadian-crustacean-soars

Phillips, D. (1993). *The day Niagara Falls ran dry!* Canadian Geographic and Key Porter Books.

*Pictou Advocate.* (2020, 9 Apr.). Northern Pulp prepared to invest in modernizing mill and revitalizing Nova Scotia's forest sector. https://pictouadvocate.com/2020/04/09/northern-pulp-prepared-to-invest-in-modernizing-mill-and-revitalizing-nova-scotias-forestry-sector/

Quinn, G. (2012, 1 Aug.). Long-distance commutes the normal life for many Canadians. *Financial Post.* business.financialpost.com/2012/08/01/long-distance-commutes-the-new-normal-for-many-canadians/

Roberts, T. (2016a, 16 Feb.). Bursting of Alberta's oil bubble on display at St. John's airport. *CBC News.* http://www.cbc.ca/news/canada/newfoundland-labrador/airport-st-johns-alberta-downturn-1.3443452

_____. (2016b, 24 June). It's official: Muskrat Falls a boondoggle, says Stan Marshall. *CBC News.* http://www.cbc.ca/news/canada/newfoundland-labrador/stan-marshall-muskrat-falls-update-1.3649540

Rose, G.A., & Walters, C.J. (2019, Nov.). The state of Canada's iconic northern cod: A second opinion. *Fisheries Research, 219.* https://www.sciencedirect.com/science/article/abs/pii/S0165783619301614

Ryan, H. (2019, 10 June). The lobster trap. *Toronto Star.* https://projects.thestar.com/climate-change-canada/nova-scotia/

Statistics Canada. (2002a). *Census of Canada 2001—Census geography. Highlights and analysis: Canada's 2001 population.* www12.statcan.ca/English/census01

_____. (2002b, 16 July). Population and dwelling counts, 2001 census. Catalogue no. 93F0050XCB2001013.

_____. (2006). Canadian statistics: Distribution of employed people, by industry, by province. www40.statcan.ca/l01/cst01/labor21c.htm

_____. (2007). Population and dwelling counts, for census metropolitan areas and census agglomerations, 2006 and 2001 censuses—100% data. www12.statcan.ca/english/census06/data/popdwell/Table.cfm?T=201&S=3&O=D&RPP=150

_____. (2012, 24 Jan.). Population and dwelling counts, for Canada, provinces and territories, 2011 and 2006 censuses. www12.statcan.gc.ca/census-recensement/2011/dp-pd/hlt-fst/pd-pl/index-eng.cfm

_____. (2016). Sales of natural gas, monthly. CANSIM (database), Table 129-0003. http://www5.statcan.gc.ca/cansim/a26?lang=eng&retrLang=eng&id=1290003&&pattern=&stByVal=1&p1=1&p2=-1&tabMode=dataTable&csid=

_____. (2017a, 31 Aug.). Census in brief: English, French and official language minorities in Canada. https://www12.statcan.gc.ca/census-recensement/2016/as-sa/98-200-x/2016011/98-200-x2016011-eng.cfm

_____. (2017b). Population and dwelling count highlight tables, 2016 census. https://www12.statcan.gc.ca/census-recensement/2016/dp-pd/hlt-fst/pd-pl/index-eng.cfm

_____. (2019a, 6 Nov.). Employment and unemployment rate, annual, population centres and rural areas. Table 14-10-0106-01. https://www150.statcan.gc.ca/t1/tbl1/en/tv.action?pid=1410010601

_____. (2019b, 6 Nov.). Gross domestic product (GDP) at basic prices, by industry, provinces and territories (x 1,000,000). Table 36-10-0402-01. https://www150.statcan.gc.ca/t1/tbl1/en/tv.action?pid=3610040201

_____. (2019c, 20 Feb.). Population and dwelling counts, for Canada, provinces and territories, 2016 and 2011 censuses—100% data. https://www12.statcan.gc.ca/census-recensement/2016/dp-pd/hlt-fst/pd-pl/Table.cfm?Lang=Eng&T=101&S=50&O=A

_____. (2019d, 13 Nov.). Farm cash receipts, annual (x 1,000). Table 32-10-0045-01. https://doi.org/10.25318/3210004501-eng.

_____. (2020a, 16 July). Population estimates, quarterly. Table 17-10-0009-01. https://www150.statcan.gc.ca/t1/tbl1/en/tv.action?pid=1710000901; https://doi.org/10.25318/1710000901-eng.

_____. (2020b). Labour force characteristics by industry, annual (x 1,000). Table 14-10-0023-01. https://doi.org/10.25318/1410002301-eng

Storey, K. (2009, 20 Oct.). Help wanted: Demographics, labor supply and economic change in Newfoundland and Labrador. *Challenged by Demography: A NORA Conference on the Demographic Challenges of the North Atlantic Region*, Alta, Norway.

Tunney, C. (2020, 19 Oct.). Minister says Mi'kmaw fishermen being "let down" by police in wake of weekend blaze. *CBC News*. https://www.cbc.ca/news/politics/emergency-debate-lobster-fishery-dispute-ministers-1.5767602

Withers, P. (2016, 18 May). Nova Scotia exports continue to be buoyed by lobster sales to China. *CBC News*. http://www.cbc.ca/news/canada/nova-scotia/lobster-sales-china-buoy-ns-exports-1.3586699

_____. (2020, 9 Nov.). First Nations partner with BC company in $1B purchase of Clearwater Seafoods. *CBC News*. https://www.cbc.ca/news/canada/nova-scotia/mi-kmaq-purchase-clearwater-seafoods-1.5796028

**CHAPTER 11**

Anselmi, E. (2019, 7 Nov.). Inuit organizations raise caribou concerns at Baffinland hearing. *Nunatsiaq News*. https://nunatsiaq.com/stories/article/inuit-organizations-raise-caribou-concerns-at-baffinland-hearing/

Baffin Fisheries. (2016, 3 Aug.). Baffin Fisheries on track to harvest 100% of quota with Inuit-owned vessels in 2016. http://www.baffinfisheries.ca/media/

Barz, S.B., & Roed, B. (2008). Inuit printmaking. *The Canadian Encyclopedia*. http://www.thecanadianencyclopedia.ca/en/article/inuit-printmaking/

Bell, J. (2019, 14 Nov.). Mary River: If financial viability is a factor, then prove it. *Nunatsiaq News*. https://nunatsiaq.com/stories/article/mary-river-if-financial-viability-is-a-factor-then-prove-it/

Berger, T.R. (1977). *Northern frontier, northern homeland: The report of the Mackenzie Valley Pipeline Inquiry* (2 vols). Minister of Supply and Services.

Bone, R.M. (2016). *The Canadian North: Issues and challenges* (5th edn). Oxford University Press.

_____ & Anderson, R.B. (Eds) (2017). *Indigenous peoples and resource development*. Captus Press.

_____. (2019). Indigenous population size: Changes since contact. *Canadian Journal of Native Studies*, 39(2), 1–13.

Brown, C. (2016, 29 Aug.). Massive cruise ship brings new era of Arctic tourism to Cambridge Bay. *CBC News*. http://www.cbc.ca/news/canada/north/massive-cruise-ship-brings-new-era-of-arctic-tourism-to-cambridge-bay-1.3739491

Budgell, A. (2018). *We all expected to die: Spanish influenza in Labrador, 1918–1919*. ISER Books.

Chapter:Canada. (1985). *The western Arctic claim: The Inuvialuit Final Agreement*. Department of Indian Affairs and Northern Development.

_____. (1991). Comprehensive land claim agreement initialled with Gwich'in of the Mackenzie Delta in the Northwest Territories. Communiqué 1-9171. Department of Indian Affairs and Northern Development.

_____. (1993a). Formal signing of Tungavik Federation of Nunavut Final Agreement. Communiqué 1–9324. Department of Indian Affairs and Northern Development.

_____. (1993b). *Umbrella Final Agreement between the Government of Canada, Council for Yukon Indians and the Government of the Yukon*. Department of Indian Affairs and Northern Development.

_____. (2004). Agreements. Department of Indian and Northern Affairs. www.ainc-inac.gc.ca/pr/agr/index_e.html#Comprehensive%20Claims%20Agreements

*CBC News*. (2007, 12 Mar.). Mackenzie gas line still "leading case" despite bloating $16.2B cost outlook. www.cbc.ca/cp/business/070312/b031292A.html#skip300x250

Chan, L.H.M. (2006). Food safety and food security in the Canadian Arctic. *Meridian* (Publication of the Canadian Polar Commission), 1–3.

Coates, K. Lackenbauer, P.W., Morrison, W., & Poelzer, G. (2008). *Arctic front: Defending Canada in the Far North*. Thomas Allen.

Contenta, S. (2015, 4 Apr.). Nunavut's youth suicide epidemic—"Who is next? How do we stop this?" *Toronto Star*. https://www.thestar.com/news/insight/2015/04/04/nunavuts-youth-suicide-epidemic-who-is-next-how-do-we-stop-this.html

Danylchuk, J. (2007, 18 Dec.). Giant, glittering and tarnished. *Up Here*. www.uphere.ca/node/175

Dickason, O.P. (2002). *Canada's First Nations: A history of founding peoples from earliest times* (3rd edn). Oxford University Press.

Elias, P.D. (1995). *Northern Aboriginal communities: Economies and development*. Captus Press.

Flyvbjerg, B. (2014). What you should know about megaprojects and why: An overview. *Project Management Journal*, 45(2), 6–19.

George, J. (2016, 30 Aug.). Western Nunavut's Crystal Serenity encounter runs smoothly. *Nunatsiaq Online*. http://www.nunatsiaqonline.ca/stories/article/65674no_problems_mar_huge_cruise_ship_visit_in_western_nunavut/

Guarino, M.-V., Sime, L.C., Schröeder, D., Malmierca-Vallet, I., Rosenblum, E., Ringer, M., Ridley, J., Feltham, D., Bitz, C., Steig, E.J., Wolff, E., Stroeve, J., & Sellar, A. Sea-ice-free Arctic during the Last Interglacial supports fast future loss. *Nature Climate Change*, 10 (2020), 928–32. https://doi.org/10.1038/s41558-020-0865-2

Indigenous and Northern Affairs Canada (INAC). (2010, 15 Oct.). The history of land claims and self-government in the Yukon. www.aadnc-aandc.gc.ca/eng/1100100028417/1100100028418

_____. (2015). Backgrounder—Déline Final Self-Government Agreement. https://www.aadnc-aandc.gc.ca/eng/1387314654000/1387314707746

_____. (2016). General briefing note on Canada's self-government and comprehensive land claims policies and the status of negotiations. https://www.aadnc-aandc.gc.ca/eng/1373385502190/1373385561540

Inuvialuit Regional Corporation. (2020, 21 Apr.). 2020 distribution of nearly 3.5M to be paid to Inuvialuit beneficiaries May 1. https://www.irc.inuvialuit.com/sites/default/files/IRC2020DistributionPayment.pdf

Jordan, P. (2012, 5 Sept.). Nunavut mining rush attracts China's MMG. *Globe and Mail*, B3.

_____. (2013, 11 Jan.). Baffinland Iron Mines sharply scales back Mary River Project. *Globe and Mail*. www.theglobeandmail.com/globe-investor/baffinland-iron-mines-sharply-scales-back-mary-river-project/article7227358/

Lackenbauer, P.W., & Légaré, A. (2018). A more accurate face on Canada to the world: The creation of Nunavut. In D. Heidt (Ed.), *Reconsidering Confederation*. University of Calgary Press.

Légaré, A. (2008). Canada's experiment with Aboriginal self-determination in Nunavut: From vision to illusion. *International Journal on Minority and Group Rights*, 15, 335–67.

Luedi, J. (2019, 28 May). Hans Island—Property of Canada or Denmark? *World Atlas*. http://www.worldatlas.com/articles/hans-island-boundary-dispute-canada-denmark-territorial-conflict.html

MacLachlan, Letha. 1996. *NWT Diamonds Project: Report of the Environmental Assessment Panel*. Ottawa: Canadian Environmental Assessment Agency.

Manuel, G., & Posluns, M. (1974). *The Fourth World: An Indian reality*. Collier-Macmillan Canada.

Marcus, A.R. (1995). *Relocating Eden: The image and politics of Inuit exile in the Canadian Arctic*. University Press of New England.

Milne, R. (2016, 12 Sept.). Denmark rejects Russia call for swift talks on Arctic rights. *Financial Times*. https://www.ft.com/content/d1810bd4-77e5-11e6-97ae-647294649b28

Natural Resources Canada. (2019a, 12 July). Extending our outer limits: Canada's 2019 Arctic Ocean continental shelf submission to the United Nations. https://www.nrcan.gc.ca/simply-science/extending-our-outer-limits-canadas-2019-arctic-ocean-continental-shelf-submission-united-nations/22165

_____. (2019b). Annual statistics of mineral production. At: https://sead.nrcan-rncan.gc.ca/prod-prod/ann-ann-eng.aspx

NWT Bureau of Statistics. (1990). Fur production and value. *Statistical Quarterly*, 12.

_____. (2014, Dec.). *2014 NWT survey of mining employees*. http://www.iti.gov.nt.ca/sites/www.iti.gov.nt.ca/files/2014_nwt_survey_of_mining_employees_overall_report.pdf

_____. (2015). Fuel production. *Northwest Territories—2014 . . . by thenumbers*. http://www.statsnwt.ca/publications/bythenos/2014NWT%20by%20the%20nos.pdf

_____. (2019a). Value of pelts. https://www.statsnwt.ca/publications/statistics-quarterly/index.php

_____. (2019b, Mar.). *Statistics Quarterly*. https://www.statsnwt.ca/publications/statistics-quarterly/index.php

Nunavut. (1999). *The Bathurst Mandate Pinasuaqtavut: What we've set out to do*. Legislative Assembly.

Nunavut Bureau of Statistics. (2016). Nunavut population estimates, 2015. http://www.stats.gov.nu.ca/en/home.aspx

_____. (2019). Nunavut suicides by regions: 1999 to 2018. http://www.stats.gov.nu.ca/en/home.aspx

Quenneville, G. (2014). Fly-in, fly-out and fed-up. *Up Here Business*. http://upherebusiness.ca/post/97075639467

_____. (2015a, 13 Mar.). Snap Lake mine could close if dissolved solid limit not raised: De Beers. *CBC News*. http://www.cbc.ca/news/canada/north/snap-lake-mine-could-close-if-dissolved-solid-limit-not-raised-de-beers-1.2993214

_____. (2015b, 7 Dec.). N.W.T. braces for economic sting of Snap Lake mine shut down. *CBC News*. http://www.cbc.ca/news/canada/north/snap-lake-shutdown-layoffs-1.3353295

Ramsayer, K. (2020, 15 Sept.). 2020 Arctic sea ice minimum at second lowest on record. NASA. https://climate.nasa.gov/news/3023/2020-arctic-sea-ice-minimum-at-second-lowest-on-record/

Rea, K.J. (1968). *The political economy of the Canadian North: An interpretation of the course of development in the Northern Territories of Canada to the early 1960s*. University of Toronto Press.

Reuters. (2016, 23 July). De Beers puts Canadian Snap Lake diamond mine up for sale. http://www.rcinet.ca/eye-on-the-arctic/category/general/general-politics/

Rowley, G.W. (1996). *Cold comfort: My love affair with the Arctic*. McGill-Queen's University Press.

Skura, E. (2016, 12 Oct.). Baffinland not meeting Inuit employment goals at Mary River: QIA. *CBC News*. http://www.cbc.ca/news/canada/north/baffinland-qia-mary-river-review-1.3800652

Southcott, C. (2018). Introduction: Dealing with resource development in Canada's North. *The Northern Review*, 47, 3–8.

Statistics Canada. (2012, 11 Apr.). Population and dwelling counts, for Canada, provinces and territories and population centres. www12.statcan.gc.ca/census-recensement/2011/dp-pd/hlt-fst/pd-pl/Tables-Tableaux.cfm?LANG=Eng&T=800

_____. (2016, 16 Mar.). Estimates of population, Canada, provinces and territories. cansim table 051-0005. http://www5.statcan.gc.ca/cansim/a26?lang=eng&id=510005

_____. (2017). Census profile, 2016 census: Pangnirtung (table). Statistics Canada Catalogue no. 98-316-X2016001. https://www12.statcan.gc.ca/census-recensement/2016/dp-pd/prof/index.cfm?Lang=E

_____. (2018, 18 July). Aboriginal population profiles, 2016 census. https://www12.statcan.gc.ca/census-recensement/2016/dp-pd/abpopprof/index.cfm?Lang=E

_____. (2019, 18 July). *Focus on geography series, 2016 census: Census metropolitan areas*. Statistics Canada Catalogue no. 98-404-X2016001. https://www12.statcan.gc.ca/census-recensement/2016/as-sa/fogs-spg/Facts-cma-eng.cfm?LANG=Eng&GK=CMA&GC=835&TOPIC=9

_____. (2020a, 18 Nov.). Estimates of the components of demographic growth, annual. Table 17-10-0008-01. https://doi.org/10.25318/1710000801-eng

_____. (2020b). Labour force characteristics by industry, annual (x 1,000). Table 14-10-0023-01. https://doi.org/10.25318/1410002301-eng

Stroeve, J., & Notz, D. (2018). Changing state of Arctic sea ice across all seasons. *Environmental Research Letters*, 13(10). https://iopscience.iop.org/article/10.1088/1748-9326/aade56

Thackeray, C.W., & Hall, A. (2019). An emergent constraint on future Arctic sea-ice albedo feedback. *Nature. Climate Change*, 9, 972–8. https://doi.org/10.1038/s41558-019-0619-1

UCLA Center for Climate Science. (2019). Sea ice albedo feedback cycle. www.ioes.ucla.edu/climate

Watkins, M. (1977). The staple theory revisited. *Journal of Canadian Studies*, 12(5), 83–95.

Weber, B. (2012, 28 Dec.). Ottawa set to eye China's Nunavut mine plan. *Globe and Mail*, B1.

Williamson, R.G. (1974). *Eskimo underground: Socio-cultural change in the Canadian central Arctic*. Occasional Papers II. Almqvist &Wiksell.

Wilson, G.N., Alcantara, C., & Rodon, T. (2020). *Nested federalism and Inuit governance in the Canadian Arctic*. University of British Columbia Press.

Yukon Bureau of Statistics. (2016). *Yukon statistical review, 2015*. http://www.eco.gov.yk.ca/stats/pdf/Annual_Review_2015.pdf

## CHAPTER 12

City of Vancouver. (2020). *2020 Action plan: Greenest city*. https://vancouver.ca/files/cov/Greenest-city-action-plan.pdf

Cowan, P. (2020, 13 Jan.). Quebec premier promises co-operation with N.L. during first visit to province. *CBC News*. https://www.cbc.ca/news/canada/newfoundland-labrador/francois-legault-dwight-ball-meeting-energy-1.5424975

Curry, Bill. (2020, 30 Aug.). Statue debate reignites after protesters topple Montreal's John A. Macdonald monument. *Globe and Mail*. https://www.theglobeandmail.com/politics/article-statue-debate-re-ignites-after-protesters-topple-montreals-macdonald/

Glacier Media. (2020, 22 Nov.). Interactive amp: Today's COVID-19 cases in Canada. https://biv.com/article/2020/11/interactive-map-todays-covid-19-cases-canada

Hare, F. (1968). Canada. In John Warkentin (Ed.), *Canada: A geographical interpretation*. Methuen.

Li, Wei. (2009). *Ethnoburb: The new ethnic community in urban America*. University of Hawaii

Sinclair, M., Chair. (2015). *Honouring the truth, reconciling for the future: Summary of the final report of the Truth and Reconciliation Commission of Canada*. http://www.trc.ca/websites/trcinstitution/index.php?p=890

Wallace, A. (2016, 22 Oct.). Alan Wallace: Saskatoon's next mayor must move minds. *StarPhoenix (Saskatoon)*. http://thestarphoenix.com/news/local-news/alan-wallace-saskatoons-next-mayor-must-move-minds

# Index

Note: Page numbers in italics indicate figures or captions.